Learning Disabilities and Brain Function

A Neuropsychological Approach

Second Edition

To Biddy
with affection and without permission

William H. Gaddes

Learning Disabilities and Brain Function

A Neuropsychological Approach,
Second Edition

With a Foreword by Helmer R. Myklebust

With 52 Figures

Springer-Verlag
New York   Berlin   Heidelberg   Tokyo

William H. Gaddes
Department of Psychology
University of Victoria
Victoria, British Columbia
Canada V8W 2Y2

Graphic design on cover by William D. West

Library of Congress Cataloging in Publication Data
Gaddes, William H.
    Learning disabilities and brain function.
    Bibliography: p.
    Includes index.
    1. Learning disabilities.   2. Learning—Physiological
aspects.   3. Neuropsychology.   I. Title.
RJ496.L4G33 1985   618.92′89   84-22167

Typeset by Bi-Comp, Incorporated, York, Pennsylvania.
Printed and bound by R.R. Donnelley & Sons Company, Harrisonburg,
Virginia.
Printed in the United States of America.

9 8 7 6 5 4 3 2 1

ISBN 0-387-96065-1 Springer-Verlag New York Berlin Heidelberg Tokyo
ISBN 3-540-96065-1 Springer-Verlag Berlin Heidelberg New York Tokyo

Prelude

And now, I said, let me show in a figure how far our nature is enlightened or unenlightened: Behold! Human beings living in an underground den, which has a mouth open towards the light and reaching all along the den; here they have been from their childhood, and have their legs and necks chained so that they cannot move, and can only see before them; being prevented by the chains from turning round their heads. Above and behind them a fire is blazing at a distance, and between the fire and the prisoners there is a raised way; and you will see, if you look, a low wall built along the way, like the screen which marionette players have in front of them, over which they show the puppets. . . .

Like ourselves, I replied; and they see only their own shadows, or the shadows of one another, which the fire throws on the opposite wall of the cave.

Plato, *The Republic*, Book VII

Modern psychology takes completely for granted that behavior and neural function are perfectly correlated, that one is completely caused by the other. . . . One cannot logically be a determinist in physics and chemistry and biology, and a mystic in psychology.

D. O. Hebb (1949)

Foreword

Reading this volume, chapter by chapter, I had a feeling of exuberance and exhiliration. It is both a privilege and a challenge to write a foreword for this second edition of *Learning Disabilities and Brain Function*. The scope and quality of the scientific and clinical insights expressed are unusual. It is difficult to do justice to the book within the constraints of a foreword. I can only reflect its significance to instructors, scientists, and clinicians in education, psychology, psychiatry, pediatrics, speech pathology and neurology.

In the early chapters are discussions of brain function as it relates to learning and learning disabilities, with many implications for better understanding of the neurology of behavior. These chapters are followed by an articulate consideration of neuropsychological disorders, definition, identification and diagnosis of the cognitive dysfunctions that underlie learning disabilities. There is an analysis of the role of perception, as well as of the significance of impared sensory and motor-cognitive processes. The concluding chapters comprise a clear, erudite, yet practical discourse on the spectrum of language disorders, including the spoken, read, and written forms. Dr. Gaddes provides a constructive review of what it means when children have aphasia, of how this language disorder has implications for other types of learning. He elucidates and evaluates the status of our knowledge relative to childhood dyslexia and dysgraphia. This analysis holds promise for clarification of the issues that have been disconcerting, especially to educators and psychologists.

Dr. Gaddes adheres to the scientific evidence but in so doing he reveals the various ways in which carefully programmed remediation can benefit many children throughout the school years. I found this emphasis especially noteworthy for special educators and for regular teachers as well. Because of his wide experience as an educator and neuropsychologist, Dr. Gaddes does not simply present scientific evidence and overlook the pressing problems confronting those who are responsible for evaluating and teaching children who have learning disabilities. He presents evidence with a frame of reference, a point of view, that recognizes the urgency of being able to remediate and alleviate the total complex of circumstances that surround children, educationally and socially. He urges that all who are involved share knowledge so that these children can be better understood, their well-being fostered more effectively, and the confusions that commonly are associated with them be relieved. And if we professionals do not interact and share knowledge, the result will be less, not better services for the children we serve.

In studying this volume one cannot but be mindful of the ways that the learning-disability concept has prevailed upon other fields which focus on children. As manifested by this volume, this concept has significantly influenced education. It has enhanced and fostered special education, as can be observed in any school. Less obvious is the fact and the manner in which it has penetrated general education. There is a movement toward greater awareness of individual differences and needs, of how patterns of learning differ, verbally and nonverbally. Moreover, learning itself as a manifestation of cognitive behavior, and its role in the acquisition of meaning has taken on new significance. This volume, through its interdisciplinary contributions, broadens this salient new emphasis in our schools and in society.

Perhaps we can see an even greater impact of the learning-disability concept in the fields of psychology, psychiatry and neurology. Neuropsychology now is one of the prominent branches of psychology. But the construct that cognitive dysfunctions result in disturbed learning processes has been recognized by other specialties in psychology. The division of clinical child psychology has presented monographs that are important contributions. Pediatric and school psychology are both heavily involved in meeting the needs of children with psychoneurological cognitive disturbances. Psychologists working in these specialty areas will find that this volume has many observations and suggestions that bear directly on the ways children with learning disabilities can be evaluated and helped through programs designed specifically for the dysfunctions defined through careful, systematic, objective analysis of the impositions on learning.

This volume, the theme of which is cognitive functions as they relate to the neurology of learning, is relevant and purposeful also in other respects. As the science of learning disabilities develops, it might be that its most consequential influence will be in cognitive psychology. The concept of learning disabilities itself is based primarily on constructs evolved by cognitive psychologists during the past several decades. Many scientists agree that the most fundamental behavioral manifestation of a learning disability is the dysfunction of otherwise normal cognitive processes. Throughout this volume an underlying theme is that this construct must not be overlooked. Rather, the emphasis is that this basic character of learning disabilities be recognized as the true meaning of the problems confronted by many children; a neurocognitive deficit is a severe imposition on both academic learning and social adjustment.

The learning-disability concept also has been relevant to developments in the fields of pediatric neurology and child psychiatry. Not many years ago there was little awareness of the childhood aphasias, the childhood dyslexias and dysgraphias; these and other neurogenic involvements now are appraised and treated routinely. Although these language disorders often are subtle symptomatically, pediatric neurologists and child psychiatrists are aware that these neuropsychological conditions must be identified before children who have these learning disabilities can profit from available programs. These specialists play a vital role in diagnosis and program planning, medically and educationally. It is gratifying that scientists in neurology, psychiatry and psychology are evolving what is essentially a new field of endeavor, referred to as behavioral neurology. The learning-disability concept has been an important frame of reference for these developments. Year by year the ways in which even minor brain dysfunctions result in constraints on learning and behavior are demonstrated. This volume makes a significant contribution in this regard as we pursue greater and greater recognition of the meaning of behavior, both normal and abnormal. Finally, it seems purposeful to reflect briefly on how the science of learning disabilities relates to the concept of *mind*. That a learning disability impedes development and use of the mind must be stated and emphasized. Although rarely mentioned, this is the most imperative of all of the implications of this disorder. Investigation of the nature of learning disabilities has made a meaningful contribution to further definition, to further elucidation, of the concept of mind. Deficiencies in perception, in memory, in verbal and nonverbal symbolic representational learning, that is, in cognition, provide rich opportunities for us to gain insights into the brain-behavior relationships that comprise the construct we refer to as mind. These implications are a predominant concern of this book. As such, this volume can be used effectively by students in neuropsychology, and by those specializing in other branches of child psychology, in pediatric neurology, in child psychiatry and in special education. Practitioners in these and other fields will find it to be a practical guide in their day-to-day responsibilities. In fact, all of us who are concerned about learning, with the urgent consequences of what it means to have impositions on the development of the minds of a large number of children, should study it carefully.

Helmer R. Myklebust
Northwestern University

Foreword to the First Edition

Some may say that this book is long overdue; others, including myself, will state that the book appears at just the right time. The latter is likely more true, for it is doubtful that many in the professions would, until now, link issues of learning disabilities with those of neurophysiological dysfunction in the manner in which ultimately must be the case. As a matter of fact, there are those who deny the relationship completely. Lee Wiederholt (1974)[1] in his short, but excellent, review of the historical perspectives of learning disabilities, traces the early interest in this problem to the work of Gall (1802), and to his successors Broca (1861), Jackson (1864), Bastian (1869), and a few others. Each of these men would, at the time of this writing, be considered to have interests in the field of neurology, although at the time of their investigations, neurology per se was but a gleam in the eye of the anatomical beholder.

A relative detour then took place. Cerebral palsy, in the decades of the 1940s and 1950s, caught the attention of researchers through the work of Winthrop Morgan Phelps (orthopedist) and George Deaver (phyciatrist) and one or two other medically oriented individuals. This was related to the writing of W. J. Little (1810–1894). It was, however, Kurt Goldstein, Heinz Werner, both eminent German scientists, and Alfred A. Strauss, a distinguished German neuropsychiatrist, who, as refugees of Hitlerian Germany, emigrated to the United States and stimulated several psychologists to further investigate the issues of psychological dysfunction in children with identifiable neurological dysfunction. At this point, interest in the problem of psychological dysfunction essentially moved from the field of neurology to that of clinical psychology, and for nearly two decades, all but a few of the investigators who were working in this area ignored the neurological foundations of the problem. Exceptions to this statement were Newell Kephart and myself, both psychologists working closely with Werner and Strauss. Ruth Melchior Patterson, Bluma Weiner, Charlotte Philleo, and, to a lesser extent, the late Thorlief Hegge, all members of the psychological research group of the Wayne County (Michigan) Training School, kept alive the basic research direction of Werner and Strauss (1935–1955). Arthur Benton (Iowa) approached the problem from the point of view of the motor components of neurophysio-

---

[1] With the exception of Wiederholt (1974), and Cruickshank et al., (1957/1965), no other dates included in parentheses here are listed as references. They are included in the Foreword solely as benchmarks in the brief historical sketch included herein.

logical dysfunction. The unusual perceptual psychopathology observed by these researchers in the performance of exogeneous types of mentally retarded children were later determined to be identical to those of the athetoid and spastic types of children and youth with cerebral palsy (Cruickshank, Bice, Wallen, & Lynch, 1957/1965), by Shaw (1955) with some epileptic children, and with other clinical groups of children with neurological problems studied by the group of students working under me at Syracuse University between 1950 and 1965. Kirk's famous efforts with the Illinois Test of Psycholinguistic Abilities (1960) again focused the perceptual problems of some children on the malfunction of the neurological system, and his work, along with that of myself, Joseph Wepman (1960), and Mildred McGinnis (1963), again brought the issue full circle to the early efforts and interests of the 1800s of Gall, Broca, Bouillaud (1825), Wernicke (1881), Marie (1902), and Head (1926).

In 1980, if the education of these children is to be carried out within an appropriate milieu, it will be done so by teachers, psychologists, pediatricians, and parents who are thoroughly familiar with the interrelationships between neurological dysfunction and perceptual processing deficits. This is the theme of this book. Neurological dysfunction leads to perceptual processing deficits which, in turn, result in a variety and complexity of learning disabilities.

In more than 175 years, between the first published work of Gall in the area of phrenology and the publication of the current book by William Gaddes, there has been a waxing and waning of interest in this significant problem of childhood growth and development. The problem has been characterized by ignorance and ignoring, by attitudes of *laissez faire,* and by a manifestation of permissiveness in child rearing. Only lately, through the research that began appearing about 1950, has this problem been closely related by some to the work of the early "neurologists," and to a problem embedded in unique characteristics of perceptual processing deficits and pathology.

William Gaddes has written an important and very timely book. It puts forth a number of changes in educational and child management that will be required of all in teacher education and subsequently by those educators who are at the firing line with children and youth. *Learning and perception are neurological.* Herein is the basis for the preparation of a new type of educator—the neuroeducator. The neurophysiological structure and intactness of the human organism are fundamental to learning and adjustment. The late Alexander Luria pointed this out, but too few people recognized the truth of what he said so well. Instead, a great gulf existed. Educators did not really see or understand the importance of neurons to spelling, for example. Motor activities involved in handwriting were not viewed by the average educator as being intimately related to neurophysiological growth and development, except in the most gross manner. Clumsiness in the gymnasium, poor coordination in running, or inability to target in baseball were seldom seen to have any relationship to reading, number concepts, or writing.

For years, some of us have been stressing the interrelationship of figure–ground pathology, dissociation, failure to sequence, inability to obtain closure, disabilities of intersensory organization, forced responsiveness to stimuli extraneous to the task, and a myriad of other manifestations of perceptual processing deficit as fundamental aspects of perceptual pathology—each alone and more often in multiples as related to learning and to learning disabilities. Dr. Gaddes understands these interrelationships, too, and he has prepared here a book so fundamental as to insure that it will have an impact on the future of education, not only for those with learning disabilities, but for all children and youth.

There are those who will not accept this book. Among them are those who advocate the education of the ''whole child'' without recognizing that the whole child is a complex neurological structure. There will be those with pet recipes for teaching reading or arithmetic, yet who fail to understand that the concepts of sets, borrowing, and subtracting, memory involved in multiplication and division, and the capacity to make fine discriminations in the orthographic forms required in reading, each and all have a neurological base. There are those who reject the school entirely as a source of education and learning. Another group of educators who will reject this book are those who advocate, along with Patrick Dennis, permissiveness. They are those who fail to see structure as an effective tool of learning—structure encompassed in the neurophysiological system of the organism. This book is going to require an effort on the part of these groups of people to reorient themselves to education per se and to become familiar with the basic elements out of which learning is made possible.

This book contains within its covers elements that are basic to the learning of all children. Until educators incorporate them thoroughly into their understanding of the total educational process, the needs of children will not be adequately served. The emphasis in this book is not on how to teach arithmetic, reading, or spelling, but on the basic neurological ingredients that make such learning possible. It is the considered opinion of the undersigned that this is one of the most fundamental books to have appeared in the lengthening list of those concerned with the field of both general and special education. It is a keystone in the professional library and in the growing literature on learning disabilities.

William M. Cruickshank, Ph.D.
University of Michigan
Ann Arbor, 1980

Preface

The response to the first edition of this book during the past five years by psychologists, educators, parents, and a reassuring number of medical personnel, has been generally encouraging, and in some cases enthusiastic. However, in presenting complex theoretical material to a mixed professional readership, there is always the risk of misinterpretation by some because of their differences in education and training. While the book contains descriptions of basic research (usually micro-investigations), applied research (usually macro-investigations), and many clinical diagnostic procedures, the professional with little or no background in neuropsychology is encouraged to continue to improve his or her theoretical knowledge and to seek competent clinical supervision.

This edition contains up-dated research studies and new technical topics that have appeared in the last five years. Brain scanning techniques, generally unknown in 1979, are included, and clinical techniques like dichotic listening are described in much more theoretical and clinical detail to avoid their possible abuse. Some new case studies have been added.

The author of any technical book owes a great debt to many people. The researchers and writers on whom I have drawn are listed in the References. Among my university colleagues I am indebted to Drs. Keith Hastings (Mathematics), Derek Styles (Genetics), Lorne Rosenblood (Statistics), and Clare Porac for her discussions of handedness. Readers of various chapters in the first draft of the revision were Drs. Dan Bachor, Roger Graves, Lloyd Ollila, Don Read, Anthony Risser, Otfried Spreen, Esther Strauss and Louis Sutker, all of whom made valuable suggestions. Dr. C.K. Leong, of the University of Saskatchewan, provided advice on sequencing, and Dr. Thomas Tillemans, of Acadia University, supplied numerous European references to help reduce the North American emphasis in the presentation.

Helpful translations of foreign-language reviews of the first edition have been done competently by Drs. Janet Bavelas (Spanish), Charlotte Girard (French), Giusseppe Multari (Italian), and Otfried Spreen for the numerous German reviews. In fact, the especially positive response in German-speaking countries has led to a translated edition that is currently in production (Springer-Verlag).

Dr. A.G. Richards, Chief Nuclear Physician, Royal Jubilee Hospital, has been generous in providing consultation time and copies of research papers regarding the different tomographic methods of brain scanning. Anthony Risser has supplied detailed expositions of the NMR scanner,

xii

and Kevin O'Brien assisted very ably with one of the clinical cases. William D. West has replaced the simple sketches of the first edition with a fine collection of drawings that are both didactic and artistic.

I am particularly pleased that Dr. H.R. Mykelbust agreed to write the Foreword to this edition. I continue to owe a debt of long-standing to Dr. William M. Cruickshank, who encouraged me over a period of five years to continue with the writing of the original book. In many ways I have looked to him and Helmer Mykelbust as my two major mentors in the field of learning disabilities.

Because of the additions and revisions in this edition, it should be better suited to use as a textbook than was the first edition. It is hoped that its use in upper undergraduate and graduate training classes in both school psychology and special education will provide useful knowledge and skills that will improve the validity of diagnostic procedures and lead to better remedial measures with learning impaired children and adults.

Because of the exemplary way in which the whole staff of Springer-Verlag has managed the production of both editions, I express my gratitude for their help.

And finally, my thanks to my wife, Biddy, who did the final proof-reading of the entire book in page-proof form. As always, any errors or weaknesses in the book can be attributed only to myself.

William H. Gaddes
October, 1984

Preface to the First Edition

The number of psychologists actively interested in brain–behavior relationships has been increasing rapidly during the past two decades, but only since the mid-1960s have papers appeared in any number to link these relationships to special education and problems of classroom learning; there have been only a handful of books on the subject since the early 1970s. Even yet, very few neuropsychologists have attempted to communicate the fascinating subject matter of their researches to clinical psychologists, school psychologists, and teachers, even though at the present time it provides great promise in revealing systematic knowledge concerning the processes by which children and adults acquire academic skills. This is surprising in that many neurologists and some educators, usually those such as Montessori and Binet with medical training, have recognized the importance of neurological knowledge for education for more than 70 years. In 1872 Hughlings Jackson, the eminent British neurologist, gave the Hunterian Oration at Oxford University in which he said, "In a physiological inquiry into education we must widen our field of investigation beyond the popular conception of mind. Much harm has resulted from an artificially abrupt separation betwixt mind and body" (Jackson, 1958, p. 265). Very few people, however, even after more than 100 years, have taken him seriously; this book is designed to accept his challenge.

Although neuropsychology is a respectable science in its own right and has much to offer special education, until very recently there has been general opposition to its admission into the realm of education. Even today, many educators, with little or no knowledge of this discipline, will insist defensively that teaching a learning-disabled child is an "educational" and not a "medical" problem. Of course it is, but it can profit from medical input.

No doubt the disagreement among physicians, psychologists, and educators stems from the basic fact that a multidisciplinary applied science is very difficult, even hazardous, to develop and practice. Almost no one is knowledgeable in the theories and practices of all three disciplines. Even so, a neuroscientific view of perceptual and learning disorders has gradually gained moderate acceptance among many educators and enthusiastic endorsement by some.

During the 1970s, increasing numbers of conferences and workshops on neuroscience and education have been available to teachers, and educational journals are printing more and more related papers (e.g., "The Neural Bases of Language and Reading"). In 1975, the first international conference on the neuropsychology of learning disorders was held in Kørsor, Denmark (Knights & Bakker, 1976), and in 1978 the annual Yearbook of the Society for the Study of Education devoted its entire content to *Education and the Brain* (Chall & Mirsky, 1978). This interest has been a radical reversal in attitude from the period prior to 1965, when such an interest was out of fashion. Some psychologists (e.g., Skinner, 1938, p. 423) and most educators (e.g., Englemann, 1967; Gallagher, 1957, 1966; Reger, 1965) advised against a rapprochement between neurology and psychology, thinking it too difficult and impractical.

When this book was first planned, I was advised by many to abandon it. Many psychologists warned, "It will be too simple for neuropsychologists and too difficult for teachers." Others suggested I write two books, one on neuropsychology and one on remedial education, but good books already existed in those two areas, though they were not being read by both groups. I was convinced that diagnosticians needed to know what teachers did, and teachers needed some degree of knowledge of the school psychologist's skills and responsibilities. No one had ever produced a book directed at these two populations, and it seemed to me that professional training in education and psychology could profit from such an approach. I was fully aware of the hazards of such an undertaking when, 15 years ago, I wrote, "In attempting to advise teachers of brain-injured children, one is caught between the two dangers of oversimplification, and hence distortion, and over-elaboration, and hence confusion" (Gaddes, 1966b). Nevertheless, I persisted with the book, encouraged by the results of presenting a neuropsychological approach to professionally mixed audiences for the past 15 years. Teachers have been enthusiastic to learn more about brain functions when these are expressed in simple language and are shown to have particular relevance for their problems in the classroom. School psychologists, for the most part, have been favorably impressed to learn more neuropsychology and what it can offer for clinical assessment. Medical doctors have welcomed an opportunity to integrate their professional skills with those of the educational system in dealing with children with special needs.

In planning the book, many decisions had to be made about what to include and what to omit. The neurological fundamentals, presented mainly in Chapters 3 and 4, are described in simple and concise terms. A layman with no formal training in neurology and neurophysiology should be able to read these chapters with no problems. A glossary is provided to explain the technical terms, although most explanations are in nontechnical language, particularly those of new ideas when they first appear. Basic concepts in neuropsychology are frequently repeated to assist the reader in a normally complex subject matter.

Where the neurology is presented at an introductory level, the neuropsychology is repeatedly documented with research findings and is presented on a level suitable for graduate students in both psychology and education. The writing, as before, avoids jargon and technical obscurities, in order to encourage a broad readership. Physicians, parents, teachers, psychologists, and anyone interested in the problems of learning should find much of interest in the book, but those who prefer elitist, erudite books on special and narrow topics may be offended by its breadth.

The discussion of remedial education is related to the neuropsychology but, like the discussions of neurology, it is less developed in depth. Students are encouraged to read books on neurology written by neurologists, and books on remedial education written by educators. However, it is hoped that, whereas neuropsychology is the major emphasis, there is enough reference to neurology and special education to provide an integrated picture in theory and practice.

WILLIAM H. GADDES
June, 1980

Contents

1 Neurology and Behavior: Some Professional Problems

Models [of human behavior] which leave out man's physical organism are bound to be inadequate for the task of making behavior intelligible.
Edwin R. Guthrie (1950)

. . . I prefer to think of man's humanity as vested in his bodily structure and function, not least, in the activities of his brain.
Oliver L. Zangwill (1976)

This book is expressly written for educational diagnosticians, clinical psychologists, school psychologists, and remedial teachers who are committed to develop for their learning impaired students prescriptions based on a broad spectrum of relevant diagnostic knowledge. This knowledge should include, in addition to the social history of the student, a record of academic achievement, a psychological assessment of cognitive strengths, and, in those cases of known brain damage or suspected central nervous system dysfunction, a neurological examination. In summary, the in-depth study of the neurologically impaired learning disabled student should include a synthesis of educational, psychological, social, and neurological data. Such an approach is ambitious and requires educational diagnosticians to learn some basic neurology and neuroanatomy and a useful body of neuropsychology, in addition to their expertise in professional education and psychology.

Many teachers, educators, school psychologists, and others may reply, "Why should an educator bother to learn about the brain and nervous system when behavior modification is more relevant and more useful? Is neuropsychology really relevant to good teaching? Does neuropsychological knowledge make a person a better teacher?" These are all important questions and need to be recognized and examined before one decides to embrace neuropsychology as an educational aid. The whole question relates to one's theoretical concept of child behavior and whether a within-child model or a behavioral model is preferred. It seems evident that these

1

two models reflect the age-old conflict in psychology between accepting objective or subjective data. The iconoclasm of John B. Watson in the early 1920s gave way to a more tolerant admission, by some, of the perceptual variables so brilliantly demonstrated by the gestalt psychologists. By the 1940s two camps were fairly well established in which theorists tended to identify either with the behaviorists or the field-theoretical (gestalt) researchers. During the 1950s perceptual and phenomenological forces, as proposed by Carl Rogers and others, gained considerable recognition and respectability, but these within-subject variables were exclusively psychological.

It was not until the early 1960s that the rising interest in the rapidly increasing study of neuropsychology provided an added dimension to the concept of the within-child model. As well as perceptual and dynamic forces operating within the child, neurology and neuropsychology were providing new knowledge about neurophysiological correlates of behavior, many of which could be identified physically. Where the hypothetical constructs of dynamic personality theory were completely speculative, the findings of neurophysiology were largely observable, and the discoveries emerging from neuropsychology were in many cases demonstrable. This meant that the speculative component that dominated dynamic psychology was much reduced and hence implied scientific progress in the study of human behavior.

Many psychologists welcomed the objectivity of neurophysiological measures and were impressed with the new opportunity to validate neuropsychological methods of measuring behavior (Reitan, 1955b). Several new journals appeared in neuropsychology in the early 1960s, Kirk coined the term "learning disabilities" in 1963, and planners of conferences in special education began to invite neurologists and neuropsychologists to tell them about their research activities. Teachers began to see a new avenue of help, and some may have embraced the new neurological model prematurely, with more enthusiasm than knowledge. No doubt some harm was done by those who labeled children as "brain injured" or "minimally brain damaged," to mention just two of the 2000 terms that appeared about this time (Spreen, 1976, p. 450). Whereas some professionals may have used this knowledge unwisely, what it did was to provide a more complete account of the child. The within-child variables were now both psychological (inferred) and neurological (in some cases directly observed and sometimes inferred). The environmental forces were still identifiable, which meant that the child now could be observed more accurately physically, psychologically, and socially. It soon became evident that the neuropsychological data that could be obtained were invaluable in providing a fuller understanding of the child with a chronic perceptual deficit, a perceptual–motor dysfunction, or some types of chronic and severe learning problems (Gaddes, 1968).

Is the Medical Model a Help or a Threat?

Many educators who are opposed to using neuropsychological knowledge frequently provide warnings that are more typical of political stereotyping of an adversary than of a knowledgeable evaluation. Any theoretical model of behavior must be assessed critically in terms of its objective values and weaknesses; otherwise it may be accepted or maligned by an observer more in terms of its emotional compatibility or dissonance with his or her perceptual and cognitive satisfactions.

Let us look at some of the frequent objections to and the alleged weaknesses of the neuropsychological model of learning disabilities. Most of these do not stand up to close, logical scrutiny.

1. It stresses disease. Many behavioral psychologists and educators have warned against the "medical model." It stresses disease and pathology, they will tell you, and it ignores the potential for change that is inherent in dynamic theories of personality and current learning theories. It is true that in the past some medical doctors, with little or no training in psychology and education, and reinforced with the concept of the correlation between pathological, physical conditions and deficit behavioral syndromes, have advised parents of mentally impaired children of the hopelessness of their child's condition. This is related to the next two points.

2. It stresses chronicity.

3. Hence, it is unduly pessimistic. The reader will recognize that all three of these "objections" are not inherent in the theoretical model, but are abuses of it by inept professional workers. Many able pediatricians are aware of these practical weaknesses and stress the importance of psychosocial factors. One pediatrician has warned that looking for "soft neurological signs" may even "distract [the physician] from looking at environmental factors" (Schmitt, 1975).

4. It encourages drug therapy and minimizes the value of psychoeducational intervention. It is true that some extreme proponents of drug treatment tell us that "these drugs can produce immediate psychological growth" and such a child showing these dramatic changes "thus refutes Skinner and Pavlov" (Wender, 1976). Pihl (1975) has told us that "the physical model begets physical intervention" and Schmitt (1975) has echoed this view. Again the reader will recognize this as a poor use of a model and not an inherent weakness in its theory. The neuropsychological view of human behavior does not encourage promiscuous drug therapy; use or abuse depends on the knowledge and skill of the attending physician. I know of one residential treatment

center using a neuropsychological diagnostic approach to learning disabled children where all children on admission are removed from medication unless a carefully researched medical reason can be provided for its prescription.

5. Neurological knowledge is incomplete. This is true, but that is no reason to refuse to use what we do know about brain–behavior relationships. "We can take for granted that any theory of behavior at present must be inadequate and incomplete. But it is never enough to say, because we have not yet found out how to reduce behavior to the control of the brain, that no one in the future will be able to do so" (Hebb, 1949, p. xiii).

6. Some known brain-damaged children are free of learning disabilities, and most learning disabled children have no conclusive evidence of brain damage or dysfunction. These statements are true, and their seeming contradictions may be explained as we get into the discussions of neurology and neuropsychology later in the book.

7. Labeling a child as "brain-damaged" or "MBD" (minimal brain dysfunction) is damaging to the child, frightening to the parents, and confusing to the school. True, but this is unnecessary and ill advised. Again, it is not recommended by the neuropsychological approach, but such labeling may be done unwittingly by inexperienced or poorly trained professional personnel dealing with the case.

8. Giving a child an organic label permits the school to shift the responsibility for evaluation to the physician (Schmitt, 1975) and to neglect the child, at least partially. True, but labeling should not be a substitute for a solution.

9. A search for organic factors may blind the diagnostician to the presence and importance of psychosocial etiological forces. If this happens it is more likely to result from the limited skill of the clinician than from a weakness in the theoretical model. A team approach to the study of the child, which at least includes the teacher, the parent, and the neuropsychologist, should guard against a distorted view of the child.

10. Much research comparing behavioral and neurological variables is oversimplified. True, "studies in which groups of children labeled as children with learning disorders, hyperactives, MBD cases, etc. are compared with controls . . . suggest behavioral and neurological 'homogeneity' within such groups and simple one-to-one relationships between neurological factors on the one hand and behavioral and learning problems on the other" (Kalverboer, 1976). Again, however, the presence of poorly designed research in any area is a weakness not of that area of knowledge but of the people investigating it.

Let us now look at the promising advantages of and the basic reasons for a neuropsychological diagnostic approach to human behavior and learning disabilities in particular.

1. Neuropsychology is a well-established science in its own right; it began with the research of the neurophysiologists during the nineteenth century and grew with the added impetus of the two world wars in the twentieth century. This large body of knowledge, which is increasing rapidly, is relevant to all human behavior, and educators should be aware of it if they are to have a maximal understanding of any learning disabled child.

2. All behavior is mediated by the brain and central nervous system, and to understand a child's disturbed behavior an investigator is better prepared if supplied with neuropsychological information about that child. The reader will recognize that in the past this statement has not enjoyed complete agreement from everyone. Behavioristic psychologists in particular have recommended an "empty organism" approach, in which an accurate measure of stimulus and response is all that is needed. In 1938 Skinner proposed a completely dualistic position.

> There are two independent subject matters (behavior and the nervous system) which must have their own techniques and methods and yield their own respective data. . . . I am asserting, then, not only that a science of behavior is independent of neurology but that it must be established as a separate discipline whether or not a rapprochement with neurology is ever attempted. [B. F. Skinner, 1938]

Although this statement was very clear and proved strongly influential with thousands of psychologists all over the world, Skinner did recognize the value of knowing about a brain lesion in a case of aphasia (B. F. Skinner, 1938, p. 424). If we were to paraphrase Skinner in this regard, we might conclude that neuropsychological knowledge was redundant or irrelevant in the understanding and treatment of normal behavior, where the physiological systems of the person were normal and healthy both structurally and functionally, *but was required for understanding and treating impaired behavior* resulting from a lesion or lesions in the brain and central nervous system. And we concur basically with this view. However, neuropsychological studies of *normal* brain function are already adding significantly to the understanding of learning strategies of *all* academic learners with or without evidence of neurological dysfunction.

Skinner's support for an exclusively behavioristic view of normal behavior in the 1930s and 1940s was a powerful voice. An equally powerful voice, objecting to this restrictive view, proposed a neuropsychological theory of behavior for understanding not only deficit behavior but also normal behavior. Hebb (1949), in his classic book, recognized Skinner's influential support of a positivistic view of behavior, but he wrote, "The present book is written in profound disagreement with such a program for psychology" (Hebb, 1949, p. xiv). Although he supported a neuropsychological view of behavior, he made it clear that psychology is not physiology: "The problem of understanding behavior is the problem of understanding the total action of the nervous system, and *vice versa*" (p. xiv), and "this does not make the psychologist a physiologist, for precisely the same reason that the physiologist need not become a cytologist or biochemist, though he is intimately concerned with the information that cytology and biochemistry provide" (p. xv).

More recently the same view has been made relative to education (Pollack, 1976): "Undoubtedly, learning itself is a psychological process and should not be reduced to physiology. Yet to ignore the role of brain structure and function as fundamental to learning theory is to build an abstraction devoid of essential mainsprings." Moreover, it is not just the recognition of neurological data that is useful but its application in deciding on an appropriate treatment program. Diagnostic understanding of the status of the child's brain and nervous system, coupled with skilled remedial teaching, has shown, in numerous cases, marked mental improvement never before expected in bilaterally brain-damaged children. Maria Montessori, a medical doctor, was one of the first to use this medical–pedagogical approach and, as a result, electrified the worlds of both education and medicine at the turn of the century with her success in teaching mentally retarded children (Montessori, 1964). With our recent improved knowledge of neuropsychology and its relation to remediation, many severely impaired children who might have been abandoned 20 years ago to the back ward of a mental hospital are now being successfully trained, many to be relatively self-sufficient in a sheltered workshop or special environment. Others, less severely impaired, are being educated and trained, sometimes in highly skilled trades or crafts.

3. Neuropsychological data are essential to a diagnostic understanding of a child with a perceptual, cognitive, or motor deficit. Those educators who consider neuropsychology irrelevant to teaching are likely stressing symptoms and neglecting causes. Although they might freely advise *against* neurology and *for* behavior modification, it is highly likely they would avoid choosing a family doctor only interested in symptoms. The medical student is typically taught to recognize a pattern of symptoms as a particular disease condition. Once having recognized the disease from its symptoms, a doctor knows the probable cause or causes gained from medical research and the large body of empirically supported related knowledge and *treats* the *cause*. In other words, he

or she[1] possesses knowledge, beyond the actual symptoms, that is theoretically related to the basic cause, and this knowledge enables provision of a better and quicker treatment. An analogy that I have previously used (Gaddes, 1969a) may help to relate this to learning. A person may be a successful automobile driver with little or no mechanical knowledge, but *only as long as the car is free of mechanical damage or dysfunction.* A professional auto racer in the Indianapolis 500 race is required to understand his car mechanically. "While he is driving, he is primarily using his knowledge and experience of driving, with his mechanical knowledge as a valuable supplement. Should anything go wrong, this mechanical knowledge enables him to think diagnostically and make quick decisions, which in turn make him a better driver" (Gaddes, 1969a). Similarly, the neuropsychologically trained teacher is better equipped to recognize learning deficits in an orderly way, and the school psychologist, to make more detailed and helpful diagnoses. While it is not likely to alter the artistic qualities of the teacher's teaching strategies, the resulting increased knowledge and improved understanding of the child should lead to a better choice of valid forms of remediation.

The astute reader may have detected a procedural difference between the problems facing the educational diagnostician and those confronting the physician. A physician is dealing with a changing physical condition the etiology of which may be understood. Most disease conditions, such as infections, react in a homeostatic pattern; that is, the infection gradually decreases with treatment, and the body regains its normal levels of equilibrium. However, some physical problems faced by the physician are static. Orthopedic problems, such as broken legs that result in different leg lengths, require physiotherapy and remedial shoes to correct them. Such remedies are not cures but attempts to deal with a chronic state of physical abnormality. In these cases there is no disease condition, but a deficit in organic structure and function.

Children with traumatic brain damage or underdeveloped brain structure (agenesis), like those with orthopedic problems, possess an ongoing and permanent structural deficit in their brains that may alter their normal sensory, cognitive, or motor responses. A knowledge of brain–behavior relationships will help the school or clinical psychologist to alert the teacher to the nature of these changes.

---

[1] Throughout this book, specific social roles that may be assumed by either sex (e.g., teacher, doctor, parent) will be referred to by the pronouns "he or she." However, particular syndromes or specific forms of behavior (e.g., the epileptic patient, the elementary school student, the learning disabled child) will be described as a hypothetical person, and may be frequently referred to by the pronoun "he" in its generic sense, to indicate a person of either sex. This practice avoids a tedious repetition of "he or she" and promotes greater clarity of meaning and economy of sentence structure.

4. Because a neuropsychological examination of the child provides a systematic description of his or her behavioral and cognitive strengths and weaknesses and so provides information regarding the *nature* of the learning disability, it helps to realize that all learning disabled children are different; they are not a homogeneous population and should not be treated alike (Myklebust, 1967a). A battery of neuropsychological tests can provide detailed information about the various characteristics of a child's learning disorder whether or not there is evidence of brain damage or dysfunction.

5. The neuropsychological approach to learning disabilities should not supplant other successful theories or methods but should be used along with them. In fact, a thorough understanding of organically impaired learning disordered children and adults needs the best aspects of a behavioral, a psychosocial, a cognitive, and a neuropsychological approach. Neuropsychology should never be used exclusively in educational diagnosis, but along with other models of behavior to enrich them. Exact knowledge of human behavior is still so minimal that no one who wishes to learn about it can afford to exclude any segment of reliable knowledge related to it. If clinical psychologists or educational diagnosticians choose to blind themselves arbitrarily to major segments of knowledge about human behavior, their understanding and hence their diagnoses and prescribed treatments will be sadly limited and in some cases so wrong as to be useless or even dangerous.

6. Competent in-depth neuropsychological study of the child can relieve parental anxieties and doubts and provide additional help to the school.

7. A neuropsychological approach to understanding perception, cognition, and motor behavior has been actively supported by a large number of eminent researchers and scholars. Hebb has told us that "modern psychology takes completely for granted that behavior and neural function are perfectly correlated, that one is completely caused by the other" (Hebb, 1949). A. R. Luria, the distinguished Russian neuropsychologist, has not only examined sensorimotor and cognitive functions in detail in brain-damaged patients but has produced brilliant insights in the teaching of spoken language, reading, writing, spelling, and arithmetic (Luria, 1966, 1970, 1973). Myklebust, one of the most prolific writers in the area of learning disabilities, has clearly stated his approach: "It is our presumption that learning disabilities as defined here are the result of minor disturbances of brain function" (Myklebust, 1967a). Cruickshank (1979), an equally prolific and influential writer in special education, conceives of learning disabilities as "the result of perceptual processing deficits which, in turn, are or may be the result of a (diagnosed or inferred) neurophysiological dysfunction." Although an appeal to authorities does not validate a theory, it

is encouraging to know that a number of highly competent scholars have tested the neuropsychological approach for a period of more than 40 years and have found it both promising and fruitful. Until knowledge is complete in any area, no more can be expected of any theory.

Degrees of Brain Damage

In the previous discussions, references have been made to brain-damaged children and, although at one point it was stated that this was not a homogeneous population, few attempts had been made to examine the various categories of brain damage and cerebral dysfunction. That attempt will now be made.

The essential concept professed here is that all human subjects represent varying degrees of cerebral function from exceptional through normal to severely impaired. Some people presumably possess brains and nervous systems that are perfect in structure and healthy and optimal in function. Others unfortunately inherit imperfect brains with genetic defects, or they may suffer traumatic injury, pre- or postnatally, to their previously normal brains. Still others may be free of pathology but may have inherited a brain structure and function with a weak aptitude for processing written language or spatial or numerical stimuli. Because of the massive complexity of cerebral neural structure, the infinite possibilities of loci of damage, and the almost limitless continuum of intensity and extent of damage, the nature of cognitive impairment resulting from central nervous system dysfunction or genetic uniqueness is incalculable. This means that no two brain-injured children are similar, and any group research with these children includes a heterogeneous population. For this reason many comparisons of "brain-injured" and "normal" children have been unreliable, frequently insignificant, and essentially meaningless. To avoid this weakness it is necessary to identify different groups of children with basic similarities, e.g., the same range of intensity of dysfunction or the same lesion locus.

In our own laboratory we have selected the first of these criteria for gross classification and the second for subclasses within those groupings. Other clinics will develop their own classification systems, but the following system is basically similar to most clinical groupings.

Clinical Classifications (Table 1.1)

1. Brain-damaged, with "hard signs"
2. Borderline dysfunction (MBD) with "soft signs"
3. Learning disabled with no positive neurological signs

4. Normal

5. Psychiatric

Brain-Damaged Subjects

For a subject to be included in this class there must be conclusive medical or clinical evidence of tissue damage and resulting behavioral deviation. Brain surgery, postmortem study, and a variety of medical tests enable the surgeon to report the nature, extent, and intensity of the tissue damage. Other sources of unequivocal signs of central nervous system damage include "strokes" (cerebral bleeding), hemiplegia (paralysis on one side of the body, e.g., left arm and left leg), brain tumor (detected by X-ray techniques), or penetrating head injury. Severe and localized dysrhythmias revealed on the electroencephalogram (EEG) may indicate the presence of actual damaged or scar tissue, or an area of the brain where electrochemical functions are abnormal. The last named may result in intermittent epileptic seizures.

In severe bilateral brain damage the person may be unable to walk, handle things, move about, or talk normally. In cases of brain damage that is highly localized and outside the cerebral speech and sensorimotor areas, mental impairment may be minimal or nonexistent. *Some brain-damaged people are intellectually superior.*

Borderline Dysfunction or MBD

During the past 20 years, the diagnostic term "minimal brain dysfunction," or MBD, has become common in medical and clinical psychological practice. This has referred to the child with no conclusive neurological signs on medical examination, or very minimal indications, and the presence of "soft signs." It has been a confusing label to most teachers because it appeared in the late 1940s from medical studies as "minimal brain damage" in children with learning and behavior problems and the concept, both medically and psychologically, has been changing as more precise neuropsychological knowledge has emerged.

This has been frustrating for educators and probably has led to one elementary school principal sending the following letter to parents of the children in his school:

> At ____ Elementary School we realize that there are about 1% of the children who will have unusual difficulty in learning to master the basic skills, but we don't accept that any of these children are "brain-injured" or "minimally brain-damaged." Such labels are of no use to the child, and in any case the "experts" cannot agree on their meaning. At ____

Table 1.1. Neuropsychological Clinical Classifications

Brain-Damaged	MBD	Learning Disability with No Positive Neurological Signs	Normal	Psychiatric
Hard Signs	Soft Signs	Specific Learning Disability	No Learning Problems	Emotional Disturbance
Conclusive signs of brain tissue damage or dysfunction Examples: brain tumor, bleeding, penetrating injury, EEG, grade iii[a]	Developmental delay, language retardation, motor clumsiness, perceptual deficits, right–left problems, hyperactivity, poor body image, poor hand–eye coordination,	Cause may be: a. Genetic deficit, b. Subtle brain dysfunction not detectable on standardized neurological examination c. anatomical variations in brain development Examples: reading or arithmetic deficit	No conclusive neurological or behavioral signs	Learning disability is secondary to inattention, anxiety, or other correlate of emotional disturbance; it may have an organic cause or may result from a biochemical dysfunction
Hemiplegia (half-paralysis) Hemiparesis (half-partial paralysis)	EEG, Grade i or ii[a]			

[a] EEG, electroencephalogram: grades i, ii, and iii indicate minimal, moderate, and severe pathology, respectively (see Chap. 3).

School we will concentrate on remedial teaching methods to help these
children.

This is a commendably positive attitude but it still reflects little qualitative understanding of the children and a certain antipathy to the so-called
experts. To help this situation, teachers need some clarification on this
category of children, which along with the next group who have no positive neurological signs make up the largest group of learning disabled
students.

This section contains a symptomatic description of MBD children that
is designed to help the teacher. In the Clinical Addendum at the end of
Chapter 3 appears a discussion of the problems of definition faced by the
clinical research psychologist.

It may help the teacher to remember that:

1. His or her responsibility is to be aware of the child's cognitive and
   behavioral strengths and weaknesses and to design an appropriate remediation program regardless of the clinical category in which the
   child may be placed by the psychologist.

2. The type of child clinically categorized as MBD reflects a pattern of
   behavior on a continuum ranging from (a) brain-damaged (documented
   medically) to (b) MBD (many "soft neurological signs" and no "hard"
   or strongly conclusive ones) to (c) learning disabled, with no neurological signs, either "hard" or "soft," to (d) normal (no learning problems, except those that can be resolved by completely motivational
   management).

3. A list of the most common soft signs includes:
   a. Signs that reflect a developmental delay: speech and language retar-
      dation, motor clumsiness, perceptual deficits (e.g., visual rotations,
      reversals, or inversions; auditory phonetic imperception; poor fin-
      ger localization), poor right–left orientation, meaningless and hy-
      peractive motor activity, and being aware of only one hand being
      touched when, in fact, both have been simultaneously stimulated.
      The teacher will recognize that these behaviors are common among
      children up to about age 8, but if they persist in large numbers
      beyond that age, it may be useful to refer the child for neurological
      and neuropsychological examination.
   b. Inability to copy simple geometric forms, "sloppy" writing and
      copying, faulty hand–eye coordination. The teacher will recognize
      that boys, until about the age of 9 or 10, are usually inferior to girls
      the same age in writing and drawing, and these differences are
      generally believed to result from a different pattern of neural matu-
      ration in boys.

4. Frequently the presence of a number of soft signs coexists with hyperactivity and a severe learning disability, but this is not always true.

Consequently, we cannot conclude that soft signs indicate either hyperactivity or a learning disability. Any experienced teacher can think of some learning disabled children who are quiet and amenable to direction and some physically clumsy children who are competent students.

5. While the physician or psychological researcher may continue to use the MBD label because it is useful for categorizing a particular clinical group of children, the teacher is better advised to avoid the label and to deal only with the child's learning problems. The school psychologist's interpretation of the possible limiting effects of the soft signs should be useful for the teacher in providing a more detailed understanding of the child's skills and potential.

Learning Disabled with No Positive Neurological Signs

This group of children is particularly interesting because its members are usually of above average global intelligence and free of perceptual and motor deficits but frequently suffer from a developmental language disability. This is the child with a "specific learning disability" or a "congenital learning problem." The causes are not understood but may be the result of genetic deficits, particular biochemical imbalances, or a localized brain dysfunction so obscure as to be undetected on a standard neurological examination.

Normal

Normal children are free of neurological deficits for the most part and show normal learning skills.

Psychiatric

Children whose learning disabilities are psychiatric in origin usually manifest no perceptual, cognitive, or motor deficits nor any conclusive neurological signs. Their learning problems are believed to result from inattention, emotional disturbance, cultural deprivation, parental rejection, or environmental deficiency.

Three Levels of Neuropsychological Investigation

1. The first and most scientifically valid level of neuropsychological investigation includes a direct observation of the learner's brain by the neurosurgeon during brain surgery, by the pathologist at autopsy, or

by the medical researcher using technically complex medical tests (e.g., angiography, a brain scan, a Wada amytal test, etc.). These data are correlated with the assessment scores of the psychologist, the educational records of the teacher, and the social history of the parents or the family. This level of investigation permits the most accurate method of observing the brain–behavior relationships of a particular student because it correlates two independent sets of data (neurological and behavioral), and these data can be correlated objectively. For example, a massive left-hemisphere stroke will result in serious language impairment (aphasia) in most adults and some degree of language problems in school-age children.

2. While level 1 is scientifically the most desirable observational approach, the majority of academic achievers are never subjected to brain surgery or advanced neurological investigating techniques, and for these reasons nothing is known directly about the details of the structure or function of their brains. Whereas in level 1 there were two sources of objective observations, in level 2 there is only one. All that the educational diagnostician knows for sure is the behavioral data reported by the teacher, parent, and/or school psychologist. Any ideas about brain function in these cases are speculations usually made by the medical specialist or the experienced neuropsychologist. While the diagnostician in this approach must speculate about possible cerebral function or dysfunction from observable behavioral signs, this is an acceptable method of diagnosis by neurologists and neurosurgeons who call it "presumptive diagnosis" (Penfield, 1977, p. 46). But to attempt this type of neurological prediction requires advanced training and experience in clinical neurology or neuropsychology. By law only a medical practitioner can make definitive statements publicly about brain function. This means that the clinical neuropsychologist, who may have opinions about the cerebral dysfunction of a particular patient, will communicate these predictions privately to the medical doctor or to the court that has requested this opinion. In the latter case, the neuropsychologist may have to make a statement such as, "This patient has shown a number of behavioral signs similar to medically documented cases with known right-hemisphere lesions." In clinical reports to school personnel or parents regarding a learning disabled child, the school psychologist should never make statements about the child's brain function or dysfunction, but only about observed cognitive, perceptual–motor, or behavioral deficits. Level 2 only allows reliable statements about behavior and speculation about brain function.

3. Level 3 includes what is frequently called erroneously "neuropsychological screening" by some school psychologists. As we shall see, it is actually "psychoeducational assessment" or screening. Because of

the recent invasion of school psychology by neuropsychology, very few university special educators are qualified to teach developmental neuropsychology (Moss, 1979) and hence most teacher trainees still receive little or no exposure to it. Their information must be gleaned from popular writers, from one- or two-day workshops, or from professional educational journals that sometimes present material that is confusing, vague, or in some cases actually misleading. As a result of their sketchy knowledge, some educational diagnosticians feel free to make statements about brain function using a few tests (e.g., a Wechsler, a Bender–Gestalt, a Frostig, and maybe two or three subtests from the Halstead–Reitan Battery), and this type of practice has led to legitimate criticism (Coles, 1978). "If some school psychologists or teachers with little or no training in clinical neuropsychology are willing to make diagnostic statements about a child's brain, using an incomplete battery of tests, most of which were never intended as discriminators of abnormal brain function, then they are inviting a vigorous and justified attack such as Coles's" (Gaddes, 1981a, p. 33). Not only are test batteries frequently too brief and inappropriate, but the investigator may confuse "neuropsychological assessment" with "psychoeducational assessment." As we have seen in level 1, "the behavioral relationship is empirically validated (i.e., based on 'hard data') and in the direction of *brain-to-behavior*" (Gaddes, 1981b, p. 326), while in level 2, which includes closed head injuries (e.g., hemorrhages, infections, tumors, concussion, etc.), or a number of "soft" neurological signs, or a developmental learning problem (e.g., dyslexia) with no neurological signs on a standard neurological examination, the direction of presumptive diagnosis is from *behavior-to-brain*. In level 3, the diagnostician with little training in neuropsychology is better advised to accept the test and interview findings as a *psychoeducational* problem because that, in fact, is what it is. The use of a few neuropsychological tests can enrich the behavioral data, but their use does not necessarily make the report a "neuropsychological assessment." Legitimate statements can be made regarding cognitive and behavioral strengths and weaknesses and learning strategies, but no public statements should be made about neurological functions because of the lack of a comprehensive test battery and the meager training and experience of the diagnostician.

This is not to imply that the diagnostician should not indulge in private speculations about the *possible* brain functions or dysfunctions of the child or adult being examined. Such speculations are to be encouraged because this is how one learns the complex processes involved in neuropsychological diagnosis. School psychologists who wish to add neuropsychological knowledge and clinical procedures to their present repertoire of professional skills will need to find some experienced person to monitor and direct their attempts in neuropsychological diagnosis. This may be done formally during a sabbatical study year or informally in an ongoing professional relationship in one's place of employment. Once the school psychologist has reached a level of competence, then he or she can move from level 3 to 1 and 2, but as long as the chief responsibility is to provide definitive information for diagnosis and remediation in a school setting, it is best to keep it as a psychoeducational exercise (i.e., level 3).

Some Professional Problems

The introduction of new ideas and practices in any applied professional field is likely to produce some professional difficulties. Some of these are discussed in the following sections.

Communication

Neurology and neuropsychology possess their own medical concepts and language; some might say "jargon." For example, a report on a 7-year-old girl by a neuropsychologist in a medical center might tell us that "her sensory-perceptual tests suggest right-sided involvement," which can mean that her tactile recognition of letters and forms with her right hand is inferior to that of her left hand. Or, "there is evidence for involvement of right-sided motor function," which is jargon for "her right hand is slower and weaker in responding." Or, "there remained evidence of motor involvement of the right upper extremity," which when translated into plain language tells us that she is relatively slower in tapping with her right hand.

To avoid discouraging educators and others from reading about neuropsychology, we will avoid this type of language in this book, and technical terms, when they have to be used, will be explained.

Even so, neuropsychology is a complex subject matter, and trying to explain it in simple language risks the possibility of distortion or serious omissions. Every school psychologist who plans to include neuropsychological findings in a report to teachers and parents must learn to deal with this problem. Successful report writing requires a sound knowledge of neuropsychology and learning theory, understanding test results from a comprehensive battery, (ideally) some first-hand classroom teaching experience, and a creative imagination to put all this information together into a meaningful description from which can come a successful remedial program.

Translating Theory to Practice

To understand and treat organically impaired learning disabled (LD) children and adults includes at least four steps: (1) a thorough neurological examination and clinical report from the neurologist; (2) a complete neuropsychological examination and report of the subject's (S's) perceptual–motor and cognitive/behavioral strengths and weaknesses; (3) a comprehensive report of S's academic strengths and weaknesses and an analysis of the nature of the learning problem; and (4) a remedial prescription constructed on the basis of all the information in (1), (2), and (3).

Many neuropsychologists produce a fine synthesis of (1), (2), and (3), but they fail to produce (4), probably because of an ignorance of the methods of special education. They sometimes rationalize this professional lack by claiming that they are not teachers but clinical psychologists, and therefore they feel no responsibility to develop educational programs. Others may claim that because the learner possesses a chronic and hence an incurable brain lesion, that no remedial program exists that can correct the problem. Others have claimed that there is no demonstrated relevance between biological factors and the choice of teaching strategies. This book proposes a thesis in direct contradiction to the negativism of the above points of view. While there is no comprehensive and systematic theory yet constructed relating biology and learning, there is a large body of useful teaching techniques for LD students that have grown out of a knowledge of cognitive deficits associated with specific types of cerebral dysfunctions, and the reader will find them described throughout this book. As well as the present writer, several others have produced evidence to support the use of neurological knowledge in preparing programs of educational intervention (Adams, 1978; Hartlage & Reynolds, 1981; Hartlage & Hartlage, 1977; Hynd & Obrzut, 1981).

A knowledge of an LD student's cerebral areas of dysfunction and their related cognitive deficits can suggest remedial methods that might not otherwise have been considered. For example, when a child has difficulty learning the alphabet because of a left-hemisphere dysfunction, he may be taught by singing (see the case of Pearson Morsby in Chapter 9). Such an approach makes use of the knowledge of cerebral asymmetry and supports the belief that the researcher provided with detailed and relevant knowledge is more likely to hit on original and useful solutions. Pasteur told us more than a century ago, "In the fields of observation, chance favors the prepared mind" (quoted by Geschwind, 1982).

Is Neuropsychology Relevant to Education?

While we have already stated that neuropsychological tests tell us about neurological status and that this knowledge is an aid to preparing remedial intervention strategies, many psychologists and educational diagnosticians, with little or no knowledge of the neuropsychological literature and testing procedures, find this idea difficult to accept. How do these behavioral tests tell us about brain function, and how is this knowledge related to educational practice? The scientifically skeptical reader cannot be expected to accept these claims on faith; they must be empirically demonstrated.

To examine the validity of using neuropsychological knowledge in understanding and treating learning problems, it is necessary to recognize the four steps already listed above. Let us look for supporting evidence of each of these.

First, "How valid are neuropsychological tests in revealing the locus and nature of brain dysfunctions?" During the 1950s several pioneer researchers addressed this question (e.g., Reitan, 1955b; Teuber, 1959; Teuber & Mishkin, 1954). During the 1940s Halstead had produced the first battery of tests specifically designed to investigate behavioral deficits in human Ss following brain damage (Halstead, 1947). From an original group of 27 tests, Halstead selected 13 that seemed to show themselves clinically to be most sensitive to the effects of traumatic brain damage. Reitan tested the validity of 10 of these tests (Reitan, 1955b) by administering them to 50 medically documented brain-damaged Ss and 50 matched normal controls. He found that the brain-damaged Ss scored significantly lower than the controls on 8 of these tests. From these he calculated a composite Impairment Index that showed a high level of predictive validity in discriminating patients with various types of cerebral dysfunctions. He later (Reitan, 1959) published a detailed list of test signs with their levels of statistical accuracy in predicting the loci of localized lesions and the probable nature of cerebral dysfunction. He was able to verify the accuracy of his tests by predicting lesion sites from test results prior to brain surgery and comparing these predictions to the actual status of the patient's brain as reported by the neurosurgeon after craniotomy. Correlational studies of highly localized brain lesions and related behavioral deficits in adults have produced a large body of information. Studies of children are more difficult because of the normal changes with growth and development. In cases of diffuse cerebral dysfunctions, behavioral correlations are not as clearly defined or as reliable, but while these tests do not tell us everything that we need to know about brain function, they do usually provide enough predictive information in most cases that they need to be taken seriously. In Chapter 4 the reader will see that Reitan's "hit rates" in diagnosis were unusually high. Many other clinical neuropsychologists in medical settings have also acquired this type of predictive expertise.

The second stage relates the neuropsychological test results and the educational strengths and weaknesses of a particular subject. Where the first group of tests tells us details about S's visual, auditory, and tactile perception; motor speed and accuracy; sensorimotor integration and sequencing abilities; memory, reasoning, and verbal processing, the educational achievement tests give us detailed information about S's academic learning problems. If a phonetic imperception is detected in the neuropsychological testing, it may partially explain S's failure in spelling. There is an extensive literature in this area of investigation (Bakker, 1972, 1979; Doehring, Backman, & Waters, 1983; U. Kirk, 1983b; Leong, 1975, 1976, 1980; Malatesha & Aaron, 1982; Obrzut, 1981; Pirozzolo, 1979; Rourke, 1975, 1976a, 1976b, 1978a, 1978b; Senf, 1969; Tallal, 1976; Warrington, 1970).

The third and last stage relates all three previous levels to the final one, the production of a remedial prescription. For example, a left temporal dysfunction with phonetic auditory imperception, with a pattern of dysphonetic spelling errors (Boder, 1971), will likely indicate an emphasis on a visual–motor approach to teaching spelling. We will refer to this integrated diagnostic remedial approach throughout the book.

Batteries of neuropsychological tests have grown out of studying brain function, and for this reason they tend to be more comprehensive behaviorally. Diagnostic test batteries developed by non-neurologically trained school psychologists usually contain behavioral gaps. They often omit tests of tactile perception, visual or auditory sequencing, simultaneous bilateral stimulation, and other measures of lateral asymmetry. Because of this they are less complete. Clinicians who have worked with comprehensive neuropsychological test batteries and have related their findings carefully to cognitive function and learning strategies are likely to lose their initial skepticism about the usefulness of these tests. Even so, like any instrument that provides only partial information, their usefulness can be recognized, but their validity in each case should be questioned and assessed.

Territoriality and Special Education

The psychology of belief has always fascinated philosophers and psychologists. Most investigators agree that what people believe rests on both rational content and emotional satisfaction. And if a proposal is emotionally repugnant or threatening, they may choose not to accept it, regardless of its obvious rational appeal. This can account for the great variability in religious and political beliefs and the delusional thinking of the psychotic patient when emotional disturbance displaces rational perception.

In a much less extreme situation, the special educator who has been happy with an empty organism model of behavior and behavior modification techniques for treatment may choose to resist the acceptance of a model of behavior that includes biological factors and a complex new diagnostic armament. If some educators have no interest in studying neurology, learning a new model of behavior, and acquiring a large collection of new diagnostic skills, they can choose not to go that route. After all, a purely behavioral approach has served them well, and they can find many writers to reinforce their wish to retain their territory of behaviorism and to avoid invading the realm of medicine. No doubt, this common urge to identify with one theory and not another can account for the resistance by some educators and psychologists to neuropsychology.

Is Educational Neuropsychology Too Time Consuming?

Neuropsychological testing of one subject can take between 5 and 6 hours, and with consultations with medical personnel and others it will take much more time. How can this be practical for a school psychologist? First, this level of diagnostic study is only needed for a minority of academic underachievers. Most are allocated to a remedial program by an *administrative* decision with little or no formal testing. However, there are two classes of students for whom neuropsychological information is useful: (1) any child who is obviously neurologically impaired (e.g., a hemiplegic or epileptic child) and who is not responding successfully to the available school programs, and (2) a child with no evidence of neurological impairment who, after several administrative referrals to the school's available remedial programs, is still not able to learn.

Examples of the second type are numerous. Frequently, bright children who are poor readers, spellers, and/or arithmetic calculators may be referred for visual and auditory tests, physical examinations, and studies of nutrition. Although the test results are usually negative, the child still has difficulty learning to read, to write, and to do arithmetic, but because of his inferior achievement, the school authorities have placed him in a special class. He hates this because he speaks fluently and understands ideas better than most of his classmates. Even with the extra help he makes little academic progress, because his treatment was based on an administrative decision rather than on an understanding of the causes of his learning problems. A case of such a boy, Derrick White, who was kept unsuccessfully in learning assistance classes for 5 years until accurately diagnosed, is described in detail in the addendum at the end of Chapter 8.

Are the Professional Demands of Neuropsychology Too Heavy?

Senf (1979) has commented very clearly on the professional problems in recommending additional graduate training to the already heavy curriculum of the trainee in special education. To aid training in adult neuropsychology, developmental neuropsychology, behavioral neurology, and psychometric assessment will result in a demanding program for the graduate student and an exacting task for the curriculum planner. Hynd (1981) has discussed four possible models for teaching neuropsychology to graduate students in education, and if the two disciplines are to be merged successfully, standards of training and training programs will have to be established to assure that the population of organically impaired LD students will be served optimally.

Conclusions

The advantages and potential weaknesses of the neuropsychological approach to learning disabilities have been described. Unfortunately, more writers have presented the weaknesses of its definition and the risks in its application than have described its value; but most of the objections by those professionals who oppose it are criticisms of its clinical abuses and not of the theory itself nor of its valid clinical practice. Frequently these are educators with little or no knowledge of neuropsychology and no diagnostic experience in a neuropsychology laboratory. Clinicians and teachers with training in neuropsychology usually become enthusiastic converts when they see the diagnostic possibilities and their applications.

Neuropsychology is a well-established science with a large body of experimentally verified knowledge. These data are essential to the understanding and treatment of both the brain-damaged child and the learning disabled child with a perceptual, cognitive, or motor deficit. Underachievers with normally functioning nervous systems can usually be treated by purely behavioral or motivational means.

The term MBD, although still used by researchers in medicine and the behavioral sciences, may be confusing for the educator. Because of the lack of any organic evidence, the chaotic variability of the symptoms, and the frequent presence of some or all of these symptoms in all children up to the age of 8 years, the term is usually difficult for the researcher to validate and of little or no direct value for the educator. Borderline learning disabled children with suspected neurological dysfunction may be a more useful description.

No one theory is complete or necessarily valid, but the best available knowledge should be used to develop a theory constantly open to review and revision in light of new experimental evidence. Similarly, no one remedial practice is appropriate for treating all behavior or learning problems. For the child with a serious or subtle learning disorder, neuropsychological diagnosis for understanding the nature of the child's problem and behavior management techniques for treating it are probably the best at this point in our knowledge.

2 Prevalence Estimates and Etiology of Learning Disabilities

If the brain is indeed the principal mediating organ of behavior, and if there is a high degree of consistency across individuals in the functional anatomy of the brain, then it should be possible to establish lawful relationships involving the relative integrity of the central nervous system on the one hand and standard forms of behavior on the other.

H. Carl Haywood (1968)

The study of the incidence of disease is known as epidemiology, a term dating back to the time of Hippocrates, who devoted one of his treatises to the subject of epidemics (H. A. Skinner, 1961). More recently, attempts have been made to include specific behavioral syndromes in epidemiological studies, as well as infectious diseases, physical defects, and accident and death rates, but these attempts have produced problems and have been met with only mixed success. In the early 1970s two papers appeared (Minskoff, 1973; Walzer & Richmond, 1973) that discussed the basic problem of trying to use the epidemiological model for estimating the prevalence of learning disabilities in the public school population. There are a number of incongruities between epidemiological studies of physically abnormal syndromes and prevalence studies of behavior deviations in mentally normal individuals, and I have discussed these at some length elsewhere (Gaddes, 1976). However, the chief difference is that the definition of physical disease conditions can usually be recognized by reliable symptoms, whereas the definition of deficit behavior, such as learning disabilities, depends on the particular local description of the disability, and this varies with the professional training of the diagnostician and the budgetary limits of the administrator arranging to treat it. Because of their behavioral emphasis, it seems that "prevalence" rather than "epidemiology" is a better term to describe non-life-threatening deficit behavioral conditions.

This means, then, that to be able to count a syndrome we must first have a clear-cut definition, and to arrive at a complete definition we must be aware of the causes or etiology of the condition we are attempting to define.

At the outset, the reader should be clear about the difference between epidemiology and etiology. The first term refers to studies of a community

23

that tell us how many children are affected by a particular infectious disease or abnormal physical condition. The parallel in the present problem is to try to make a count of how many children are learning disabled in a particular community or population and of the various types of learning problems and their locations in the community. By contrast, etiology refers to the causes of the deficit condition, which in the case of learning disorders may be physical, psychological, social, or a combination of some or all of these.

Prevalence Estimates

In the mid-1960s in Canada, the Commission on Emotional and Learning Disorders in Children (CELDIC) was appointed. This multidiscipline professional group published its findings in 1970 under the title "One Million Children" (CELDIC Report, 1970). The report concluded that about 16% of all Canadian children were in need of specific remedial treatment. The writers of the report collected incidence studies of children with special needs from several countries, and their findings were as follows: Great Britain, 14%; France, 12%–14%; United States, 10%–15%; and Canada, 10%–16%. A study of reports of the Canadian Bureau of Statistics showed that in 1966 there were 6,232,000 school-age children in Canada, but only 120,720 were in special classes, or less than 2% of the group instead of the 10%–16% who needed special help (*Statistics of Special Education for Exceptional Children,* 1966; *Population 1921–1971*).

Data from the United States showed an equally dismal picture. In 1970 from 1.4% to 2.6% of all school-age children were in special classes (Silverman & Metz, 1973), but such classes were needed for about 15% of school-age children (Myklebust & Boshes, 1969).

Because of the methodological difficulties in producing a comprehensive prevalence study of LD subjects, there are very few. In fact, Cruickshank (1983) has claimed that "there is not a single adequate epidemiological study of learning disabilities in the world literature," and this is true if one is looking for a study with international application. However, it is unlikely that such a study will ever emerge because of the varieties of definitions of learning disabilities and the differing cultural demands in different countries.

Nevertheless, there is a certain reliability of estimates of severely learning impaired children, and this broad agreement among estimates from different countries suggests an organically based etiology. Rutter, Tizard, and Whitmore (1970) concluded from a study of 2300 children aged 9 to 12 years, on the Isle of Wight, that 7.9% were both mentally impaired and educationally retarded. Since theirs was a medical study, they included all *S*s who were mentally retarded (i.e., 2.5%), so this would suggest that about 5.4% of children with IQ's above 70 were educationally retarded. A much-quoted American study by Myklebust and Boshes (1969) showed that 7.5% of over 2700 third and fourth graders with IQ's higher than 90 were underachieving. These children had evidence of some type of neurological dysfunction. A more recent study (Stevenson & Richman, 1976) estimates that in the population of 3-year-old American children, over 3% have some form of language disorder and 2.3% are severely impaired in their language expression. Follow-up studies of these children showed that most of them were still having oral language and naming problems at age 9 (Stominger & Bashir, 1977). Kaufman and Kaufman (1983, p. 70, Table 3.9), studying a standardization sample of 2000 American children aged 6 to 16 years, found that 2% were speech impaired and 2.3% were learning disabled.

These data suggest that the average elementary school population may include about 15% of children who are underachieving academically. Of these, about half have some degree of central nervous system (CNS) dysfunction (i.e., approximately 7%). This means that on Table 1.1 (page 11), category 1 (hard signs) will have about 2.5% of the average elementary school population, and category 2 (soft signs) will have about 5%. These estimates appear to be both conservative and stable, and they can be useful if used cautiously and until estimates based on better data become available.

Etiology

The major causes of learning problems are (1) physiological, (2) psychological and psychiatric, and (3) sociological or environmental. The physiological causes that can most easily be identified are neurological dysfunctions, which are the main concern of this book, and genetic determinants and malnutrition. Of the approximately 15% of underachievers in our public schools, about half appear to have some type of neurological or genetic deficit and half have purely motivational problems (Myklebust & Boshes, 1969). A huge body of literature has appeared on the MBD child (Birch, 1964; Clements, 1966; Conners, 1967; De La Cruz, Fox, & Roberts, 1973; Kirk & Becker, 1963; Paine, 1962, 1965; Rutter, Graham, & Yule, 1970; Rutter, Tizard, & Whitmore, 1970; Wender, 1971, 1973; Wikler, Dixon, & Parker, 1970), and although some of these sources use the terms "minimal brain damage or dysfunction" and "learning disorder" synonymously, I do not. As described in Chapter 1, there is a recognition of a learning disability category *without neurological signs,* and I recognize that a number of children with several soft signs may not have any learning difficulties. Although children in both categories will have their learning disabilities analyzed and treated remedially, the medical data or soft signs in the MBD case may provide a more complete understanding and a better basis for prediction in prescribing treatment. The learning disabled child with no positive evidence of neurological dysfunction, once it is evident that it is not a psychological or motivational problem, may be hypothesized to have some genetic or possibly a very minimal neurological disorder, so subtle as to be missed on a standard neurological examination.

Or in some other cases, neurological function is normal and academic learning deficits may be associated with anatomical variations in brain development in different children. Geschwind (1979b) has proposed the hypothesis that in some children the normal asymmetrical structure of the temporal lobes develops differently both structurally and sequentially during fetal life. When this cerebral structure is such as to facilitate verbal processing, the child may learn to read and write with ease; when it does not, the child may have learning difficulties. This is an interesting theory because it does not imply neural pathology, but a particular structural development not conducive to a particular aptitude. As Geschwind wisely points out, we can accept a lack of aptitude for music, drawing, or athletics without associating neurological dysfunction; it is reasonable to include reading in the same behavioral model.

Malnutrition has been known for a long time to impair mental development, but little controlled research has been done, nor has the knowledge been relayed to those professionals who might make good use of it. Physicians, psychologists, teachers, and parents rarely have had any instruction in the relation between nutrition and mental development. In the past decade a number of studies have shown that malnutrition in animals (Cravioto, De Licardie, & Birch, 1966; Stewart & Platt, 1968) and at critical periods of early growth in children (Stoch & Smythe, 1968) may result in reduced brain size and impaired intellectual development. Central nervous system damage from malnutrition during the last trimester of intrauterine life or during the first year of postnatal life is usually permanent (Birch, 1970). Readers interested in pursuing this important topic further are referred to the comprehensive review by Hallahan and Cruickshank (1973, Chap. 2) or the book by Scrimshaw and Gordon (1968).

Other physiological causes of learning disabilities include endocrine gland imbalances in which one or more of the glands in this interrelated system produce too little or too much of some of their chemical secretions. The "master gland," or pituitary gland, located near the thalamus, secretes several hormones directly into the bloodstream, and at least two of these control physical growth and sexual behavior. The thyroid gland, located in the neck, secretes thyroxin, a strong chemical agent that controls the basal metabolism rate of the body, or the rate of oxygen consumption and energy output. The effect of abnormal thyroid function on physical growth has been known since the turn of the present century, and Mateer in the 1920s related an underproduction of thyroxin (hypothyroidism) with poor memory, a low IQ, overweight, and a lack of energy (see Mateer, 1935). An overproduction of thyroxin (hyperthyroidism) can produce hyperactivity, irritability, a loss of weight, and difficulty in concentrating. A marked rise in IQ and improvement in social behavior can result from competent medical treatment of the hypothyroid child.

The other endocrine glands are not usually as controllable in their relation to cognitive function, although pancreatic dysfunction, resulting in abnormal blood sugar levels, can be disruptive to academic learning, and pancreatic function may be modified by diet to some extent. Parents should be advised if their child suffers from diabetes mellitus (hyperglycemia) and the teacher should be advised of its possible behavioral effects. Too little sugar in the blood (minimal hypoglycemia) can result in word-finding difficulties, increased spelling errors, and other problems of language competence.

The other ductless glands, including the adrenals, parathyroids, pineal, and gonads, are equally important to normal physical and mental functioning, and any unusual and otherwise undiagnosed behavior that persists in a child should lead to an examination by a competent internal medical specialist. Should an endocrine imbalance be discovered, the parents, the school psychologist, and the child's teachers should be informed of its possible effects so that adequate adjustive or remedial action can be taken.

Lead poisoning is not a common cause of learning disabilities in children except in certain deteriorating housing areas. Modern house paints do not contain a lead base, but many ghetto areas with older houses, where children can peel off chips of older, lead-based paint and eat them, present a threat. Ross and Ross (1982, pp. 83–90) have provided an interesting discussion of its possible relation to hyperactivity.

Radiation stress, or the effects on children's learning of harmful fluorescent lighting and unshielded TV tubes, is just beginning to attract research attention. This has grown out of the original and interesting work by John Ott, whose early work in photography led him to experiment with the effects of natural and artificial light on plants, animals, and humans. The possibilities of its importance to physical health, mental health, and classroom learning are just beginning to be realized (Ott, 1976).

Sensory deficits, such as impaired vision or hearing, may interfere with normal academic learning, but a child with these problems, if he or she possesses at least average intelligence, can usually be taught to read and write by the use of glasses or a hearing aid coupled with special teaching methods. Most sensory deficits are "peripheral"; that is, they result from damage or dysfunction in the sensory nerves outside the brain. However, "central" visual or auditory deficits are more difficult to treat. Should the visual cortices be damaged, the child may have problems interpreting what he sees; similarly, damage to the auditory cortices can result in problems of language interpretation (receptive aphasia). Where brain damage occurs, some form of "central" processing may be disturbed and normal perception, motor response, and learning disrupted. It is these types of learning disabilities that form the chief concern of this book.

Ross and Ross (1982, pp. 100–103) have drawn attention to the possible relation between maternal drug consumption, smoking, and drinking to later obstetrical complications and hyperactive behavior in the child. Since any harmful influence on fetal development may have ill effects later, learning disabilities may be one of these.

The psychological and psychiatric factors influencing learning behavior are frequently difficult to tease out, although it is clinically evident that large numbers of children with emotional problems do badly in school. Glasser (1969) has stressed the need for love, self-worth, and successful achievement for competent learning, and the large-scale Isle of Wight study carried out in England has shown the important relationships between education and good physical and mental health (Rutter, Graham, & Yule, 1970).

Sociological factors are difficult to relate specifically to academic competence, but the studies of ghetto children show them to be at high risk for biological and social–environmental deficits (Hallahan & Cruickshank, 1973; Walzer & Richmond, 1973). Poor living conditions and malnutrition encourage and perpetuate ill health in all its aspects, physical, psychological, and social. It acts as a feedback process so that, "To him that hath shall be given and to him that hath not, even that which he hath shall be taken away" (paraphrase of Matthew 25:29). Eisenberg (1966) has shown larger numbers of poor readers in large urban centers and fewer in suburban residential neighborhoods. It seems highly likely that ghetto living produces a number of children who fit the definition of learning disabled *in some respects,* but here the etiology is more likely emotional deprivation than any primary physiological damage or maldevelopment. Many of these children respond to remedial teaching programs that include strong emotional support and academic skill training. Because their learning problems result not from a chronic neurological structural or functional abnormality but from an emotional lack that gradually is alleviated, these children may be considered as "false positive" LD children. Sometimes these cases, where the basic cause can be altered, are referred to as "learning problems" rather than "learning disabilities" (Frostig, personal communication, 1978; Gaddes, 1978a).

The reader will recognize that the above discussion has given much greater attention to the physiological causes of learning disabilities than to the psychological and social causes. This is not to imply they are more important, but to stress the aim of this book. All etiological causes are important, but by a brief acknowledgement of the psychosocial causes, we can get to the real subject of our discussion sooner.

Problems of Definition

The concept of learning disabilities has emerged within about the past 20 years, and numerous definitions have been given, depending on the professional training and experience of the person attempting the definition. Some medical doctors have stressed neurological and physical factors and made little or no attempt to relate them to classroom learning. Most psychologists and educators ignore the physical dysfunctions in learning impairment and some even deny that they exist. Some medical doctors complain that "virtually all definitions of learning disabilities exclude children whose learning problems are due to neurological handicaps" (Schain, 1972). Neither of these extreme views is accurate. There is no doubt that neurological dysfunctions are intimately involved in producing some perceptual, cognitive, and motor impairments, as this book will show, and it is true that several educators (Hallahan & Cruickshank, 1973; Myklebust & Boshes, 1969) and a large number of psychologists (Adams, 1973; Bakker & Satz, 1970; Bannatyne, 1971; Benton, 1962b; Chalfant & Scheffelin, 1969; Gaddes, 1968, 1969a, 1975, 1976; Kinsbourne, 1972; Knights, 1970, 1973; H. B. C. Reed, 1963; Reitan, 1966a; Reitan & Heineman, 1968) have stressed the neuropsychological factors in learning disorders. Most definitions include neurological dysfunctions in their descriptions (Bateman, 1964; Clements, 1966; Kirk & Bateman, 1962; Myklebust, 1963, 1973b; National Advisory Committee, 1968; Strauss & Lehtinen, 1947), although they are usually recognized as peripheral correlates of the child's psychosocial adaptation within a circumscribed educational program. In simple terms, the child's learning disability is a function of his inability to cope with the demands of the school, so that the degree of academic incompetence relative to his peers is the chief evidence that the child has a specific learning problem. Knowledge of a brain lesion will not remove the physical deficit, but it can enrich the understanding of the child's problem and thus help him or her to circumvent the difficulties imposed by the lesion.

However, the problem of categorizing children as "normal" and "impaired" implies a decision about a cutoff point above which and below which our two categories occur. A simple rule of thumb is to select children performing 2 years below their grade level on a standardized achievement test, but this is a rough method, full of many irrational and statistical invalidities. This method may select the child so seriously impaired in learning that he or she will be recognized in any event, but it will miss the borderline child, who may be superior in many abilities and subtly deficient in others. It is these borderline children who frequently have been ignored in the past and for whom a comprehensive definition and a sensitive selection technique may do the most good.

Myklebust (1967a) has recommended the use of a learning quotient (LQ) as a formula for selecting the learning disabled child. This is a measure of relationship between *learning potential* and *achievement*. A child's potential is measured by the Wechsler Intelligence Scale for Children (WISC) so that both verbal and nonverbal abilities are included in his or her evaluation, and achievement is measured by standardized educational achievement tests. With these data a child's "expectancy age" is calculated as the average of his or her mental age (MA), chronological age (CA), and grade age (GA). The last named is the average age for the children in the particular grade in which the child is placed. Having calculated the expectancy age we can now calculate the child's LQ in reading by using the following formula: LQ = reading age ÷ expectancy age × 100. Learning quotients may be calculated for any academic skill, language function, or perceptual–motor function for which there are normative data, and they are interpreted, as is the IQ, with 100 as average.

Yule has warned against the quotient model on statistical grounds and has proposed the use of a multiple regression formula instead (Rutter, Graham, & Yule, 1970; Yule, Rutter, Berger, & Thompson, 1974). Like Myklebust, he includes MA (as measured by the WISC) and CA, but not GA (grade age). Because GA would make no difference in most cases, the input to the formulas of both Myklebust and Yule is the same for the most part. However, Myklebust's selection criteria are more detailed from an educational point of view. Where Rutter and his colleagues measure educational achievement only on reading accuracy and comprehension, Myklebust's subjects are considered to be learning disabled if they fall below an LQ of 90 on only one or more of 14 measures. These include verbal IQ, nonverbal IQ, perceptual speed, spatial relations, reading (word knowledge, word discrimination, comprehension), spelling, arithmetic problem solving, auditory receptive language, and nonverbal learning (Myklebust, 1967b; Myklebust & Boshes, 1969). The advantage of such a screening procedure is that it is sensitive to minimal and subtle learning problems because of both the number of skills included and the relatively high performance quotient level of 90. As well, it supplies a mass of data significantly useful for diagnostic understanding. Whatever screening method is used for separating the "normals" from the "learning disabled," it will need to be generally agreed upon by the members of any school system, city, county, or larger area. Otherwise a widely useful definition is impossible.

Most American states have passed legislation to assure special educational programs and services for those who need them, and this move has required them to formulate definitions of learning disabilities. A comparison of these definitions shows that they include children (1) who are of near-normal, average, or above-average intelligence; (2) who have a disorder in one or more of the primary psychological processes involved in learning the basic school subjects, e.g., perception, cognition, motor responses, and/or serial order behavior; (3) who are of school age; (4) whose language development may be retarded and/or impaired; (5) whose learning disability may or may not be correlated with medically documented brain damage and dysfunction, or may be supposed to be related to minimal cerebral dysfunctions and/or genetic abnormalities or growth anomalies; (6) whose learning problems do *not* result primarily from sensory or motor handicaps, mental retardation, emotional disturbance, or environmental deprivation; (7) whose disability may show a shifting pattern, increasing with educational neglect and reducing or disappearing with successful remedial help; and (8) whose learning deficits require special remedial programs and services for educational progress.

Is IQ Related to Learning Disabilities?

Since 1963, when Samuel A. Kirk first used the term "learning disabilities," parents' chapters of the Association for Children with Learning Disabilities across the United States have accepted in their definition the exclusion of children with below-average levels of intelligence. Scientifically this is an invalid idea, but psychologically it is interesting to discover how it has come about.

In April 1963, Kirk addressed a group of parents of perceptually handicapped children and interested professionals to explore the learning problems of these children. He made an intelligently incisive and eloquent presentation (Hallahan & Cruickshank, 1973; Kirk & Becker, 1963) in his attempt to advise parents how to organize to help their children. He evidently was successful, because the day following his address a number of these parents organized the first chapter of the Association for Children with Learning Disabilities (ACLD).

In his address he stressed the need for detailed descriptions of a child's problem behavior rather than a mere attaching of labels that may satisfy the diagnostician's need for closure but do nothing for the child. His term "learning disability" reflected a more positive association about a child than "brain injured," "perceptually handicapped," and other terms current at that time.

Kirk's description of these children excluded "children who have sensory handicaps such as blindness or deafness" and those "who have generalized mental retardation'' (Kirk & Becker, 1963). It was this latter phrase that struck a chord and caused the parents to hear him say that no child with below-average intelligence was to be included. Cruickshank (1979) has called this ''one of the interesting accidents of our professional times.''

Psychologically, however, this ''accident'' is both interesting and understandable. The parents of a socially bright child who is good at art and music but impaired in learning to read and write are faced with a miserable conflict. Their common sense tells them that their child may be stupid, but their desire not to accept this painful assessment, and the fact that their child *is* better than average in so many ways, encourages them to believe he is normal. The confusion and ambivalence is a constant torment because most parents idealize their children and want to live through them. To know my child is mentally retarded is not only to frustrate but to kill my hopes and needs to project my emotional needs through him or her. To have a child whose mixed abilities I cannot understand maintains me in a continued agony of indecision, guilt, resentment, hope, despair, and love. If someone can clarify my indecision, I can be relatively free of my torment.

We can guess that Kirk's fine address did just that. He told these parents their children were not deaf or blind, mentally retarded, delinquent, or emotionally disturbed; they were just normal kids with a specific or isolated disability in perception, cognition, language development, or motor functions. Once this disability, which was no more stigmatizing than being colorblind or tone deaf, could be identified and treated remedially, the mystery of the child's learning problems was at an end. What major relief Kirk must have provided for these parents; no group therapist has likely had a greater positive effect! With the sense of relief, however, came a misguided and entrenched belief that no child with a below-average IQ could be included in the responsibilities of the ACLD.

This was unfortunate because it ignored the clinical difference between (1) primary or generalized mental retardation and (2) low IQ resulting from localized brain damage or other specific cause. Kirk did exclude the first group, but not the second. The ACLD definitions in the past have excluded both.

The Canadian Association for Children with Learning Disabilities (CACLD) has followed the lead of the American association from the first, and until 1981 it had accepted the various American definitions with the invalid and inaccurate reference to mental retardation, also, no doubt, because of its ''therapeutic'' effect. In 1977 Dr. William M. Cruickshank of the University of Michigan was asked to write a position paper for the CACLD to propose an official definition. He entitled his paper ''Learning Disabilities: a Definitional Statement'' (Cruickshank, 1979). It was a scholarly and able statement of the problem and its issues, and it ended with a formal definition that Cruickshank hoped would correct the restricted definitions current in the United Sates.

His statement included six basic principles that defined learning disabilities, but the fourth, which stated that learning disabilities can occur in "any level of intellectual function," was unacceptable by many of the parents who failed to discriminate between generalized mental retardation (which is a chronic state) and low IQ because of localized brain damage or other physiological cause that made it possible to improve the IQ level with skilled remedial treatment. These parents perceived this definition as a regression to the hopeless situation they had experienced prior to the formation of ACLD with its enlightened view of learning disabilities.

To resolve this problem, the CACLD appointed a committee to produce an acceptable definition. After considerable discussion they produced the following definition of learning disabilities, which retained the valid points in Dr. Cruickshank's statement but reworded the offensive clause:

> Learning disabilities is a generic term that refers to a heterogeneous group of disorders due to identifiable or inferred central nervous system dysfunction. Such disorders may be manifested by delays in early development and/or difficulties in any of the following areas: attention, memory, reasoning, coordination, communicating, reading, writing, spelling, calculation, social competence, and emotional maturation.
>
> Learning disabilities are intrinsic to the individual and may affect learning and behavior in any individual, including those with potentially average, average, or above average intelligence.
>
> Learning disabilities are not due primarily to visual, hearing, or motor handicaps; to mental retardation, emotional disturbance, or environmental disadvantage; although they may occur concurrently with any of these.
>
> Learning disabilities may arise from genetic variations, biochemical factors, events in the pre to peri-natal period, or any other subsequent events resulting in neurological impairment. [Canadian Association for Children and Adults with Learning Disabilities, 1981]

It seems reasonable to leave problems of primary mental retardation to the associations responsible for them, but they should not refuse responsibility for a learning disabled child with an IQ below 90 or 80 as is stated in some current definitions. Otherwise, these children will not qualify for help from either group. As will become evident later in this book, it is not difficult to discriminate a true mentally retarded child from a low-IQ LD child. The first is generally inferior on a set of neuropsychological and mental tests, and his scores usually show a good cluster. The learning disabled child, by contrast, has a number of strengths and weaknesses, so that on a similar battery, he will show a pattern of marked intertest variability. The number of normal and above-average scores and the nature of his good abilities or skills, even though his low scores may be numerous, will give the clue that he is not mentally retarded. The primary mental retardate will usually not improve mentally very much even with intensive remedial teaching; the low-IQ child with the variable pattern of skills most likely will. In some cases of the latter type, dramatic increases in IQ are possible with skilled remediation.

A North Atlantic Treaty Organization (NATO) International Conference was called in 1975 to discuss the problems of the neuropsychology of learning disorders. One of the tasks of this conference was to attempt to produce a definition of learning disorders with international usefulness. Even prior to the meeting it was evident that the concept had quite different meanings in Europe and in North America. Consequently it soon became clear that any definition was culturally bound, to some extent, and that different countries might understandably have different emphases. It was proposed (Gaddes, 1976) that each country appoint a task force or research committee to decide on a selection formula, its cutoff points, and the educational skills that should be included. With this preparation they would then be ready to attempt to produce a useful definition.

In preparing any definition of learning disabilities, it is useful to remember that there are at least three possible types (D. Kendall, quoted in Cruickshank, 1979).

1. A diagnostic and etiological definition describes the symptoms in relation to recognized or inferred causes. The CACLD definition, quoted above, is an example.
2. Educational, pedagogical, pediatric, or biochemical definition. This type defines LD within the framework of a particular discipline. Myklebust's learning quotient is an example of an educational definition.
3. Legislative or administrative definition.

   Although a purist clinician might express dismay, a judgment as to whether a child should be designated as learning disabled stems from what is essentially an administrative decision as to how many dollars are to be spent, and therefore how many children are to receive additional specialist assistance. Sometimes administrative decisions are made directly as to how many children will be recognized as learning disabled. [McLeod, 1978]

Governments may decide that if 12% of the school population is underachieving that they will allot funds for one-sixth of this group, and so recognize 2% of the total population as learning disabled. Such a definition is an example of an administrative designation, and, although it may be administratively expedient, it may be invalid diagnostically and educationally.

The definition proposed here is broad and designed to be both educational and administrative, although in-depth clinical study should precede the educational and administrative decisions in difficult or subtle cases.

Definition

A child of school age is identified as suffering from a learning disability if his or her learning quotient, as derived from the formula officially accepted in the child's school district, county, state, or country, falls below the cutoff point officially recognized. This formula should be used for selecting diagnostically those children likely to be missed by informal observation by their teachers because of the subtle or minimal nature of their educational impairments. More severe or obvious cases of learning problems may be identified by administrative selection and/or the application of the official accepted formula. Most formulae take the form of a Learning Quotient or a multiple regression model.

Conclusions

The reader will understand from the above discussion that prevalence studies in the area of learning disabilities are difficult to produce because of the lack of a universally accepted definition, because of the various professions involved and their differing diagnostic emphases, and because of the intrinsic sociological differences among different ethnic groups. In spite of these difficulties, a safe estimate of children needing remedial education services of some type seems to be between 10% and 15% in most populations.

3 The Nervous System and Learning

In modern psychology, it is now widely accepted that each kind of mental activity has a distinct psychological structure and is effected through the joint activity of discrete cortical zones.

A. R. Luria (1970)

Most teachers and clinical psychologists are reluctant to assume the responsibility of learning neurology in addition to their many other duties. However, whereas a disregard of neurological correlates is possible in the teaching of a child with a normally functioning brain, it may easily lead to misunderstanding and mishandling of the child with brain damage or some type of cerebral dysfunction. In fact, in the past, large numbers of children were misdiagnosed as "mentally retarded" because of an ignorance of some type of sensory imperception, language deficit, or motor impairment that interfered with their learning. Had they been correctly understood and a successful remedial program established early, their lives might have taken a happier and more satisfactory direction.

Most LD children are not brain damaged, but if they have persistent difficulties in academic learning it is likely that some area or areas of the brain are not functioning quite as well as they might. Because it is frequently easier to understand minimal deviations in behavior by studying severe, pathological cases, the discussion in this chapter draws heavily on cases of brain damage because so much has been learned about its impairing effects on perception and learning.

The Neurological Model of Behavior

The teacher, the parent, or anyone working with a brain-damaged or cerebrally dysfunctioning child can learn to use the neurological model of behavior profitably in educational planning. In simple form, it recognizes three processes in behavior: (1) sensory input (carried on by the sensory

36

or afferent nerves, which conduct neural impulses from the various sense organs to the brain); (2) integration, recording, recognition, storage, and retrieval of learned material (mediated primarily by the cerebral cortex and brainstem); and (3) neuromuscular–skeletal expressive behavior (effected by the motor or efferent nerves). In brief, all behavior includes input, integration, and output. If neural pathology in the sensory cortices and pathways (visual, auditory, tactile, or kinesthetic) obstructs the input, a potentially bright child may be mentally starved or frustrated for lack of mental stimulation. If neural pathology involves the cerebral cortex, the normal functions of mental integration are blocked, and if neural pathology occurs in the motor cortices or pathways a potentially bright youngster may be obstructed in learning by his or her difficulty in reciting, expressing, or establishing the motor match (Kephart, 1960/1971, 1966) so necessary to efficient learning. However, to understand these problems the clinical psychologist and the teacher must have at least a practical knowledge of the gross structure and function of the nervous system.

The study of the brain and nervous system is complex and detailed, and the reader who wishes to study in greater depth is referred to a good introductory text in neuroanatomy (e.g., Gardner, 1975; Schmidt, 1978a,b). A good text in human neuropsychology will provide basic neurological knowledge as well as research findings on the relation between brain function and behavior (Kolb & Whishaw, 1980/1984; Walsh, 1978). In this book, because we are stressing neuropsychology and its value in education, the sections on neurology are much briefer and less developed. But it is hoped that they are adequate to provide a basic understanding of brain function for the educator and/or the psychologist unfamiliar with this material.

One can recognize three broad levels of knowledge of neuroanatomy and clinical neurology and neuropsychology: (1) the pediatric neurologist typically has a detailed knowledge of neurology, a moderate knowledge of neuropsychology, and little or no expertise in special education; (2) the clinical school neuropsychologist will have a moderate knowledge of neurology, a detailed knowledge of neuropsychology, and a moderate familiarity with methods in special education; and (3) the teacher should have a simplified but basic idea of brain function, some knowledge of the most common "molar" brain–behavior relationships, and a profound knowledge of remedial procedures and teaching skills. Such a team will have an "expert" covering each of the three major professional areas of expertise, and the teacher will be able to understand the reports of the neurologist and neuropsychologist well enough to use their findings in constructing a remedial program for a particular LD student. The level of neurology described in this chapter is intended for the student in psychology and/or education who is being introduced to neurology and neuropsychology for the first time.

How Neuroanatomy is Studied

The physiological study of the central nervous system (CNS) may use any of four main approaches (Kolb & Whishaw, 1980/1984): (1) The *comparative* approach examines the various brains of organisms on the phylogenetic scale and notes the increasing structural complexity from simple wormlike animals to humans; (2) the *developmental* approach examines the increasing neurological complexity that accompanies normal growth of an individual; (3) the *cytoarchitectonic* approach examines the varying size, shape, and structure of different nerve cells (neurons) and their locations in the brain and spinal cord; (4) the *biochemical* approach is developing with new scanning techniques and is revealing new information about the electrochemical transmission of neural impulses in the brain. In this book we will concentrate on the structure, function, and developmental pattern of the human brain and make only passing reference to comparative and biochemical information, not because they are unimportant but because they are beyond the scope of this book. A list of outside references in neurology appears at the end of this chapter.

The Neuron

The various tissues and organs of the human body are composed of different types of somatic cells that make up tissue, bone, blood, muscles, and nerves. The nerve cell, or neuron, in large numbers makes up the nerves and, in part, the nerve tissue. However, the neuron differs from the other somatic cells in two basic ways. First, unlike the other cells, which are tiny membranous spheroids, the neuron possesses in addition to the cell body a sort of "aerial" or "receiver," the *dendrites,* and a sort of "ground connection," the *axon.* The neuron differs, then, in structural design from the other body cells. Like them it has a cell body with a nucleus, but in addition it has delicate, threadlike appendages, the dendrites, and the axon, which act as conductors of the neural impulses.

The second basic difference is the neuron's inability to reproduce itself postnatally. It is common knowledge that somatic cells when they are damaged can divide and reproduce themselves, and in this way the damaged tissue eventually is replaced with new cells. For example, following a hemorrhage, new blood cells are produced to replace the blood loss within a few hours. If a bone is broken it will knit. If the skin is cut it will soon replace the damage with a new patch of skin made up of newly produced epithelial cells. Unfortunately, when neural cell bodies are damaged and destroyed, they never are replaced and the person suffering this nervous system insult must continue life with a permanently reduced number of nerve cells. For example, victims of poliomyelitis have usually suffered from the destruction of motor cells, which activate the muscles, and if enough of their motor cells are destroyed a type of muscular paralysis will result. Brain damage, whether inflicted by a penetrating head injury, infection, or concussion, will mean that the person so damaged will have to meet the world with fewer cerebral cells than he or she inherited at birth. Since the average human being possesses billions of nerve cells in the central nervous system,[1] a person can afford to lose a fairly large number of neurons, provided they are not in certain narrowly localized cortical areas or are not crucially concerned with highly specific kinds of behavior. In fact, some people who have suffered rather serious brain injuries have not been noticeably impaired mentally. Hebb and Penfield (1940) reported an early case in which behavior actually *improved* following the surgical removal of frontal lobe tissue, and a study by Weinstein and Teuber (1957) revealed that a number of brain-injured soldiers who suffered mental impairment at the time of their cerebral gunshot wounds had gained back normal IQs within a few years. Milner (1975) has reported postoperative improvement in full-scale IQ in patients surgically treated because of epileptic seizures. Some of these patients made marked postoperative gains over a long period of time.

Teachers and parents of children with cerebral deficits should be reminded of the rehabilitative and adaptive tendencies of the remaining healthy tissues of the human brain and nervous system. Although many of these children may have to live with some type of permanent perceptual or learning disability, many of them will profit from an enriched educational experience almost as much as the brightest students, and most will gain to some extent.

Having drawn attention to some of the educational implications of the neuron's vulnerability, let us now return to a consideration of its structure and function. Its two basic functions include self-nutrition and transmission of the neural impulse or nerve current. It ingests nutrients from the bloodstream through its delicate cell membrane and gives off waste products, as does any living organism.

The classical view of synaptic conduction of neural impulses implies that they are received by the "branches" of the dendrites and then trans-

---

[1] Estimates of the number of nerve cells in the human brain and central nervous system range from 10 billion (Wooldridge, 1963) to 12 billion (Herrick, 1926) to 50 billion in the neocortex (Rockel, Hiorns, & Powell, 1974), and up to 75 billion in larger brains (Whishaw, 1983 personal communication). Others have estimated 10^{12} neurons in the human brain, and "the number of possible interconnections among these neurons . . . is greater than the total number of atoms making up the entire universe!" (Thompson, Berger, & Berry, 1980, p. 3). These variations in estimates result from different methods of measurement, the complexity of the problem, and whether the investigator is including all or part of the central nervous system.

mitted down the dendritic trunk, through the cell body, and on down the length of the axon to the end brush. The brushlike endings of the axon make a functional connection (synapse) with the dendritic brush endings of another neuron, or with several others, the conduction of neural energy usually being unidirectional from dendrites to axon within a neuron, and from axon endings to dendrites across the synapse. This connection is not physically direct, because while the tiny neural endings may touch or become entwined with one another, in the peripheral nervous system they are covered by an outer membranous layer, called the neurilemma, which keeps the end brushes from actual physical contact. In the central nervous system the synaptic gap is minimal (the space being about 100 A, or 10^{-10} meter).

Anatomists since the time of Golgi's researches in the 1880s have recognized two main classes of neurons (Hirsch & Jacobson, 1975, p. 110). The first are the large and distinctive neurons located in the different functional areas of the brain. They have been called Class I neurons (Jacobson, 1970), and it is these cells with their long axons that form the main neural tracts. The second class, the Class II type, have short axons, and while present throughout the nervous system, they occur in the cerebral cortex and are believed to be involved in modifiable behavior.

As well as being different in structure, they differ in their developmental patterns. The Class I, or large neurons, are usually formed first during the fetal growth of the brain, and the Class II, small neurons with short axons, develop later, some even postnatally. This pattern of neural development has special significance for the educator, the physiotherapist, and the occupational therapist, because it implies the possibility of environmental change in the structural growth and mature functioning of the nervous system.

The Class II neurons, because of their shorter axons and their presence in the human cortex and their later ontogenetic development, appear to be well suited for processing information in the nervous system, and to be "responsive to environmental influences and thus responsible for the plastic or modifiable aspects of behavior" (Hirsch & Jacobson, 1975). It seems that these structural and developmental properties of the human nervous system may very well be a basic determinant in all learning and behavior change.

The transmission of some neural impulses is primarily chemical and that of others, largely electrical. In chemical transmission, different chemicals may be secreted across the synaptic cleft, some facilitating the passage of the neural impulse and others inhibiting or blocking it. The electrochemical changes at the synapse are highly complex, and the pattern of electrical conduction more complicated than the classical view has proposed. Schmidt (1978b) has demonstrated that in the cortex, synaptic transmission sometimes may travel from an axon to another axon, and in some cases from dendrites to dendrites, and from dendrites to axon

(Schmitt & Worden, 1979). McGeer, McGeer, and Innanen (1979) have recently provided evidence of dendroaxonic transmission in the rat's brain, but in humans the whole picture is not yet clear. We do know that in the peripheral nervous system and probably in most of the human central nervous system, the conventional serial pattern of axon-to-dendrites transmission occurs, but with some of the axonless or short axon cells in some parts of the human brain there may be reciprocal synaptic arrangements (Dowling, 1979). For the school psychologist and the educator, all of this may seem confusing, but the intricate possibilities of the electrical and chemical processes of the human brain are beyond the limits of the present discussion. Regardless of the details of synaptic conduction, we know that neural impulses are conducted systematically from one part of the brain to another, and that these neural activities mediate ideas, memories, and all cognitive functions.

In order to integrate our broad knowledge of this process into a theory of learning, it is useful to note that (1) different synapses offer different levels of resistance to the passage of neural impulses; (2) chemicals are secreted by the axon, some of which facilitate the conduction of some neural impulses and some of which inhibit others; and (3) the dendrites may extinguish some weak impulses and conduct those above a certain threshold intensity. All of this means that the brain and brainstem is a three-dimensional complex of millions of interconnecting nerve cells. These cells are tiny, varying in diameter from 4 to 5 μm (a micron, or μm, is one thousandth of a millimeter) up to 50 or even 100 μm (Gardner, 1975, Chap. 3), and provide an electrochemically active network with large numbers of cells and patterns of cells producing neural impulses (i.e., neural "firing") at different time intervals.

To develop a mental picture of what goes on in the brain, the interested reader would do well to read a book on electroencephalography, that is, the study of the electrical changes that occur in the brain and cerebral cortex. These changes are detected by a sensitive electronic device, the electroencephalogram (EEG), first developed in Austria in 1926 by a psychiatrist, Dr. Hans Berger. Some of the cortical cells discharge spontaneously as slowly as 2 or 3 times per second, others at about 10 times per second, and some as fast as 12 to 16 times per second. During sleep the neural cells usually fire at a regular rate, but when the subject is awake and alert and there is a "sensory input" reaching the visual, auditory, or other sensory cortical areas, there is a speeded up and irregular pattern of neural firing superimposed on the regular spontaneous pattern. For example, a subject who has electrode connections from the scalp to the EEG machine may show an even rise and fall of electrical energy with the eyes closed. With no visual input to the subject in a relaxed state, the brain may produce *alpha* waves, which have a frequency of about 10 times per second. As Hebb (1966) has explained, "If he opens his eyes and attends to his surroundings, or if with eyes closed he is given a problem to solve, the *beta rhythm* appears: small, fast waves characteristic of the actively thinking subject.''

The EEG has been a useful clinical technique for identifying highly localized brain lesions and for understanding epilepsy. The medically trained electroencephalographer knows the normal frequencies and intensities of electrical changes ("brain waves") in different parts of the cortex, and the presence of cerebral pathology may show as a marked increase in both frequency and amplitude (spike activity). In cases of diffuse brain pathology, or even moderately localized lesions, the EEG pattern may be generalized because it is picking up changes in a broad electrical field.

Some clinicians use a grading system of i, ii, and iii to indicate minimal, moderate, and severe pathology, and most of the cases described in this book are so designated. Also, the presence of abnormally slow waves (delta waves) is common in learning disabled children. The measurements and their interpretation possess a rather marked subjective component, so that the school psychologist may need to view the EEG findings, when they are inconclusive, with healthy scientific skepticism. However, in some cases where localized pathology is clearly indicated, this information may be particularly useful, along with a large number of findings from a large and detailed battery of neuropsychological tests.

Synaptic Theory of Learning and the Neural Trace

The presence of the synaptic gap in the nervous system was discovered during the 1890s and since that time imaginative educationists and psychologists have been hypothesizing about the function of the synapse in learning.

As early as 1913 E. L. Thorndike was writing at some length on "the physiology of the capacity to learn and of readiness" (Thorndike, 1913), but because of the limited knowledge of the brain–behavior relationship at that time, what he had to say was almost the pure hypothesizing of a brilliant mind. J. B. Watson also used the idea of varying synaptic resistance (Watson, 1919, 1924) to explain the varying pathways of neural impulses during the learning of habits. Drawing on his own work with monkeys and rats, Lashley (1950) attempted to account for the "engram" or permanent change that evidently must occur in the brain and nervous system when some new idea or skill is acquired. Obviously, there must be a change in the nervous system following learning that enables the subject to retrieve it and express it, and this change must have some degree of permanence. Is this change structural, chemical, electrical, or some or all of these? Although biochemical studies have shown that protein synthesis does occur in neurons when learning has taken place, the full process is not yet completey understood. McCulloch and Brodey (1966) have written, "Whatever that process is, it must affect the future behavior of the neurons involved so as to alter the circuit action of the system." This organized modification in the brain and nervous system is called the "neural trace" or "engram" and it acts somewhat similarly to a computer program to affect future conduct.

While the neurologists, biochemists, and physiologists are attempting to unravel the mystery of the neural trace, the psychologist and the teacher need only know that some change does take place in the brain when learning occurs and that this change may be more or less permanent. The degree of permanence seems to depend on certain chemical changes, on whether the learner *intends* to remember it for a short or a long time, whether the mental image is vivid and accompanied by strong and pleasant affective overtones, and whether the learned skill is reinforced with spaced practices. Krech (1968) has drawn attention to the significance of chemical changes in the brain during short-term and long-term memory.

Short-term memory, such as remembering a phone number long enough to dial it, may depend on a reverberating cerebral circuit that decays as soon as the need for its use terminates. However, some fleeting perceptions, such as reading an exciting story, do stay with us, probably reinforced by cognitive associations and positive emotional responses. In old age, the neural and physiological processes (most likely synaptic changes) necessary to maintain the reverberating activity are seriously weakened, and as a result the senile patient has difficulty recalling an experience once his attention to it has ceased. Because the neural traces of earlier experiences are still there he can remember the events of his youth or successful middle life, but he may have forgotten already that his son visited him a half hour before.

Some children with poor short-term memories no doubt have inherited brains with inferior synaptic activities or poor conceptual imagery. These children, like the senile patient, may forget very rapidly material that has been taught to them. To overcome this, the teacher may check with the parents to make sure that the child's diet is rich in all the necessary vitamins, particularly those of the B complex. Studies have shown that temporary conditions of avitaminosis will produce a temporary condition of mental deficiency, but with adequate diet, the normal mental level may be regained within a few days (Gaddes, 1946; Guetzkow & Bowman, 1946). Within the past 10 years an increased interest has developed in the relationship between mental development, learning, and nutrition. Social and nutritional factors appear to affect mental development independently and may also show a strong interaction effect (Scrimshaw & Gordon, 1968). For those students interested in the importance of nutrition for learning, Hallahan and Cruickshank (1973, Chap. 2) have produced an interesting review.

The endocrine glands also are important determiners of motivation and mental level. Although endocrinologists are reluctant to experiment with a child's glandular functions, they can achieve dramatic changes with thyroid and pituitary feeding in particular cases. If the parents or teacher of a child with a learning disability suspects that there is a glandular deficiency they should consult a competent endocrinologist who can test the child and administer gland feeding if it is indicated.

Once the primary physical processes have been checked for possible deficit, then the teacher should attempt to teach the child so as to involve him or her positively with the material. There is physiological and psychological evidence to suggest that perceptions operating when the perceiver is happy and interested are more likely to be retained than those experienced during unhappiness and/or boredom. This would seem to be an example of psychosomatic processes in learning, and for this reason the teacher should avoid the use of sarcasm or any disciplinary technique that is likely to condition the child to dislike the material being presented or any event likely to be associated negatively with it. Glasser (1969) has written persuasively on this point: "If school failure does not exist, other handicaps can be more easily overcome." While such an approach is a purely behavioral one, it is also supported by neurological and physiological evidence.[2]

In teaching a child with identifiable neural pathology, the teacher may learn from the school psychologist, if he or she is trained in neuropsychology, something of the intensity, size, and locus of the damage or dysfunction (see Chapter 4) and, from this knowledge may be gained a better understanding of the child's strengths and weaknesses. The teacher's knowledge of cortical function and the child's aptitude pattern should provide a theoretical background with which to improvise new and particular remedial teaching techniques. This, in essence, is the model of educational neuropsychology.

Gross Structure and Functions of the Central Nervous System

The brain, brainstem, spinal cord, and peripheral nerves make up the nervous system. The chief integrating functions occur in the central nervous system, that is, the brain, brainstem, and spinal cord.

[2] Readers particularly interested in this topic should read at more length books and papers on psychosomatic medicine and related problems.

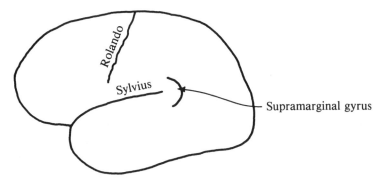

Figure 3.1. Left cerebral hemisphere showing the central sulcus, or fissure of Rolando; the lateral fissure, or fissure of Sylvius; and the supramarginal gyrus.

The cerebral hemispheres (see Fig. 3.1) form a cranial shape something like a football helmet. The outer covering, or cortex, is gray in color and is about one-eighth of an inch thick. The main body of the cerebrum is white in color and is made up of supporting and interconnecting fibers. These cerebral hemispheres, including the cortex and supporting white layers, are from 1 to 2 in. thick. The surface is wrinkled and convoluted so that about two-thirds of the cortical surface line the fissures and about one-third of the cortical surface is open to view in an exposed human brain. Some biologists have hypothesized that this design of the brain is related to human survival; to gain the same cortical surface and the same number of cortical cells, had the cortex been smooth, the human head would have had to have been as large as a basketball. But by being accordioned into its present small space, the brain is kept relatively small and an insignificant target, so less liable to external trauma.

The cortex is made up vertically of about six layers of different types of cells, and as the different parts of the cortex are examined horizontally, different cell densities are found. For example, in the motor strip (see Fig. 3.3 on page 48) the fifth cortical layer is much thicker than in either the sensory or associational areas. This layer is richer in *pyramidal cells,* so called because their cell bodies are relatively large and shaped so as to suggest a pyramid. In the parietal areas there are differently shaped cells, and in the occipital, temporal, and frontal lobes, different types of cells again. While cortical cells have been observed to differ structurally both horizontally (across the layers) and vertically (from one layer to another) there still is very little known about their various functions. The specific projection areas (vision, audition, somesthesis, and motor control) are well known, but finer discriminations for the most part are still not fully understood. Neurologists tell us that most of the afferent pathways connect into the fourth layer, which is thickest in the sensory cortex and thinnest in the motor strip (see Netter, 1962, p. 73). The nerve fibers connecting the motor cortex with the spinal cord and muscles arise mainly in the fifth layer, and the cortex is composed chiefly of interconnecting neurons, which provide neural stimulation between millions of different cerebral centers. Neurologists, conscious of the meager knowledge of the structure and function of the human brain, are hesitant to go beyond the evidence. Psychologists are less cautious. For example, Gardner (1968), an eminent neurologist, has written, "Actually, our knowledge of cortical structure is so fragmentary that any attempts to compare these units to man-made electronic feedback circuits are purely speculative." By contrast, Hebb, who is a psychologist, has followed the lead of Lorente de Nó who, in the late 1930s, first proposed the idea of "loop" or "reverberating circuits." Hebb has emphasized this concept and developed it (Hebb, 1949, 1958/1966/1972) in the idea of the "cell assembly," that is, a circuit of cells reflecting a feedback mechanism and maintaining a reverberating energy within the brain, and the "phase sequence," or a sequentially related number of cell assemblies. Hebb supports his hypothesis, pointing out that "much of the CNS, but especially association cortex and certainly closely connected subcortical structures, is filled with paths that lead back into themselves as well as leading on to other paths" (1966). This concept, growing out of histological knowledge and neurophysiological observations, has been a most useful idea during the past 25 years in attempts to rationalize brain–behavior relationships. As Hebb has warned, however, like any theory it is a tentative answer or possible explanation, and it should not be confused with established fact.

As long as the teacher can remember that the "reverberating circuit" is a useful idea to stimulate new ways of teaching a handicapped child and a productive way to stimulate imaginative teaching methods, then it will have served a useful purpose. However, this same teacher, like all of us, must be ready to discard this hypothesis when a better one appears.

In fact, evidence has already appeared to throw doubt on a theory that includes only electrical cerebral changes in memory and learning. While it has been known for a long time that the neural impulse is electrochemical in nature, its electrical properties seem to have received more attention until recently, possibly because of the invention of the cathode ray oscilloscope and other sensitive electronic devices developed since about 1920. Consequently, whereas Lashley's (1950) theory of the memory trace and Hebb's (1949) cell assembly have been useful in helping the student to conceptualize some form of energy change or action occurring in the brain during learning, they neglect the biochemical changes that occur in cerebral cells. Krech (1968) has described a popular theory positing that short-term and long-term memory involve different electrochemical processes. According to this theory a synthesis of new brain proteins is essential to the establishment of long-term memory. During the past 10 years an expanding research interest has occurred in the chemical functions of the brain cells (Schmitt & Worden, 1979), and they are beginning to be related to educational learning (Grossman, 1978; Teyler, 1978).

At this point, the student will do well to remember that memory includes both electrical and chemical changes and these probably vary as the remembered mental content varies in permanence or transience.

The Cerebral Cortex

Although the outside appearance of the human cerebrum is convoluted so as to be completely covered with gyri (convex surfaces) and sulci (fissures or deep ridges), only two of the fissures need to be learned by the nonmedical student. These are the central sulcus (also called the fissure of Rolando) and the lateral fissure (also called the fissure of Sylvius). These two fissures divide the cerebral area into the frontal, parietal, occipital, and temporal lobes (see Fig. 3.2), and as we shall see in the next chapter, each of these seems to be more or less involved in mediating particular behavioral functions.

The motor cortex, a strip about an inch wide immediately anterior to the fissure of Rolando (see Fig. 3.3), controls muscular-expressive movements and is usually called the motor strip. The motor strip of the left hemisphere controls activity of the right arm, right leg, and nearly all muscular movements of the right half of the head and body. The right motor strip, as may be supposed, dominates the left musculature. Because the two motor strips are located in the frontal lobes, motor control is a known function of the posterior parts of the frontal lobes. Damage or dysfunction of either motor strip may result in some degree of paralysis on the contralateral side.

A strip of cells just posterior to the fissure of Rolando (see Fig. 3.3) registers sensations of touch. It is called the somesthetic strip (*soma,* body; *esthesis,* sensitivity). This is the area of the brain where tactile sensations are recorded and, like the motor strips, the somesthetic strips are sensitive to the opposite sides of the body. Damage or dysfunction in

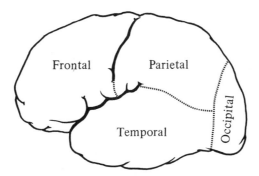

Figure 3.2.   The cerebral lobes of the left hemisphere. (© 1984 William D. West)

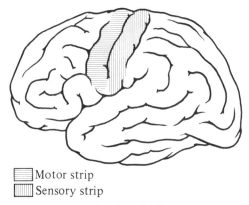

☐ Motor strip

▥ Sensory strip

Figure 3.3.   The left hemisphere showing the location of the left motor strip and the left sensory or somesthetic strip. (© 1984 William D. West)

these areas may result in anesthetic areas of the skin, poor finger localization, or disturbed body part identification while blindfolded, and this may have a serious deleterious effect on classroom learning, such as arithmetic, spelling, and any hand–eye coordination skill.

The motor and sensory strips, because of their close cortical proximity, function together. Any electrochemical activity in one strip is likely to arouse some degree of reciprocal response in the other, and this integrated function is enhanced by the fact that many sensory fibers go to the motor strip and many motor fibers go from the sensory strip. The two strips are sometimes referred to as the *sensorimotor cortex* (Calanchini & Trout, 1971), and their synthesized functions provide the neural basis for kinesthesis (awareness of the body in space and its movements); temperature awareness; muscular movement and its relation to visual, auditory, and tactile feedback; and the growth of language and mental development. Integrative processes occur in all levels and areas of brain function, but those concerned with sensorimotor integration are basic to all learning and mental function (Ayres, 1972a).

The back part of the brain houses the occipital lobes, which are centers of visual impressions. Since the optic nerves and tracts have to travel from the eyes at the front of the head to the occipital lobes at the back, any head injury has a greater chance of disturbing the visual processes. Because visual–perceptual activities are basic to most classroom learning it is important for the teacher to understand the structure and function of the optic neural mechanisms and to identify the various visual–perceptual abberations likely to occur.

The temporal lobes house the acoustic areas, and damage or dysfunction in these lobes may result in auditory imperception or distortion. Since language and speech development depend largely on exact auditory perception, temporal damage or dysfunction may result in some form of aphasia (disability of understanding or expressing language). The neuropsychological and educational problems of aphasia are discussed in Chapter 8.

The Brainstem and Corpus Callosum

The brain and spinal cord constitute the *central nervous system,* and the nerves outside this network—the cranial nerves connecting the sensory and motor systems of the head, the spinal nerves connecting the neuromuscular–skeletal systems, and the peripheral portions of the autonomic system—constitute the *peripheral nervous system.* Although both the central and peripheral nervous systems are involved in a child's learning, the discussion, in most of this book, is concerned with a study of the structure and function of the central nervous system.

The brain includes the cerebrum, with its two hemispheres, and the brainstem joining it to the spinal cord (see Fig. 3.4). If we simplify their structure, we have the corpus callosum (the broad band of fibers joining the two cerebral hemispheres) and the thalamus (which includes sensory nuclei of both vision and hearing, as well as centers of the autonomic nervous system); the brainstem includes the midbrain, pons, and medulla oblongata (see Fig. 3.5).

The Corpus Callosum

The corpus callosum is a wide band of millions of neural fibers connecting the cortices of the two hemispheres (see Figs. 3.4 and 3.5). Although the Bible has advised "Let not thy left hand know what thy right hand doeth" (Matthew 6:3), this is neurologically impossible in the case of sensory

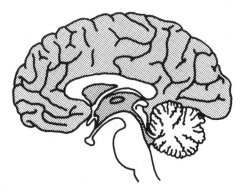

Figure 3.4. Medial view of the brain and brainstem after the brain has been cut through the midline.

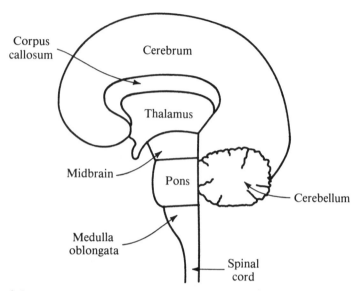

Figure 3.5. Medial view of the brain and brainstem in simplified and stylized form.

motor behavior because of the corpus callosum. If the child is taught to write with the right hand, he will be able to write with his left hand, rather badly, but without having to practice. The manual area of the left motor strip connects through the corpus callosum to the manual area of the right motor strip, and training in one of these areas is carried automatically from one to the other. Psychologists have recognized this automatic neural transmission for years as "bilateral transfer."

Not only can the right-handed child write with the nondominant hand; he finds that he can also write with his right foot in wet sand at the beach, with his left foot, with a stick in his mouth, and all with no previous practice. This type of evidence suggests that training that modifies a localized area of one hemisphere is not only carried to various parts of the opposite hemisphere (contralateral) through the corpus callosum, but to other parts of the same hemisphere (ipsilateral) through the subcortical white matter. For these reasons multisensory and multi-motor-expressive teaching techniques have had a great success because they increase the cerebral internuncial connections, thus promoting the possibility of wider cortical activity and better learning. The physiotherapist talks of "reeducation" when he or she attempts to train healthy areas of the brain to circumvent a damaged area.

Since the time of Broca's statement in the 1860s that aphasia (language impairment caused by brain damage or dysfunction) and left-hemisphere lesions are correlated, a continual search has resulted for possible structural differences that may explain the functional asymmetries. However, no clear results emerged from this century-long enquiry until very recently, about which more will be said in Chapter 7.

Normally the two hemispheres function together, but if through disease or trauma the corpus callosum is damaged or cut, various mental functions are impaired. Sperry (1964) and others have cut the corpus callosum by surgical section in animals to learn more about the specific functions of each hemisphere. Commissurotomies are carried out with human subjects to reduce or eliminate the frequency of epileptic seizures, and following such surgical procedures these "split-brain" patients are often studied in order to provide information about brain–behavior relationships of each separated hemisphere (Zaidel, 1979). If all the direct interhemispheric connections are cut the subject behaves as if he possesses two independent brains (Sperry, 1974). If the subject is taught something through the right halves of each eye (by displaying the stimulus in the left visual field) to the right hemisphere, no bilateral transfer can take place and there is no memory of the learned material in the left hemisphere. The evidence from split-brain experiments and cases of disease or agenesis of the corpus callosum are discussed in greater detail later in this book (Chapter 7). At this point, these few remarks will serve to remind the reader of the important function of the corpus callosum in interhemispheric integration, the establishment of cerebral dominance, and normal competence in reading, writing, and arithmetic.

The Thalamus

The thalamus is a particularly complex area of the midpart of the brain located beneath the corpus callosum and immediately above the brainstem (see Fig. 3.5). Medical students may spend several months studying the structures and various functions of the thalamus, subthalamus, hypothalamus, and its related parts. The teacher and school psychologist may find it useful to know that it is an important *relay station* carrying impulses from the cerebellum (see Fig. 3.5), the reticular system, and certain neural ganglia to the cerebral cortex, chiefly the association areas. In fact, all the senses but smell are processed through the thalamus before they reach their respective specialized areas in the cortex. Lower on the phylogenetic scale, the thalamus appears to be the highest organ of perception, but in humans it acts as an organ of crude consciousness between the sensory tracts and the cortex. Because most of the sensory tracts pass through the lower level of the thalamus, a thalamic lesion may result in disturbances of visual, auditory, and tactile perception.

The hypothalamus is a complex area anterior to and slightly below the thalamus. Its exact role is not completely understood yet, but we do know that as "the physiological seat of emotion" it monitors many autonomic functions. It triggers certain "thermostatic-like" mechanisms to control such functions as blood pressure, body heat, hunger, thirst, and sex, but its determination of such emotional states as anger and fear is what interests the student of human behavior. Some years ago, Masserman (1941) demonstrated immediate "sham rage" in the cat through controlled electrostimulation of the hypothalamus. Because hypothalamic lesions may cause abnormal reactions of anger or fear, the hyperactive and/or emotionally explosive child may in some rare cases be suffering from a brainstem lesion affecting the normal functioning of the hypothalamus. Behavior, at least in part, seems to result from the reflexive and spontaneous stimulation of the hypothalamus and related structures and the inhibitory learned processes emanating from the cerebral cortex. Too much hypothalamic stimulation with too little cortical (or intellectual) control presumably results in the socially obnoxious child who disregards the rights and wishes of others. The reverse pattern may result in the overcontrolled, inhibited, unimaginative child. A workable compromise would seem to be more desirable.

Not all antisocial behavior stems from organic pressures, of course. Many such cases are psychogenic, frequently resulting from a severe parental rejection pattern at home, but when a brain dysfunction accompanies explosive, disruptive behavior, as complete a knowledge as possible of the brain lesion may help the therapist, care worker, or teacher to decide on a treatment method. It may include individual or group therapy, psychodrama, environmental control, social activities, and counseling, drug therapy, or a combination of some or all of these.

The Midbrain

Immediately below the thalamus is the midbrain, a stout column of the brainstem between the thalamus and the pons (see Fig. 3.5). Its chief behavioral function is the control of cranial reflexes, such as blinking, ducking the head to visual stimulation of quick movement in the peripheral visual fields, and the pupillary reflex. Auditory reflexes, such as the startle reflex or turning the head and eyes following a loud noise, also find their stimulation here. The corpora quadrigemina, a body of four protuberances situated on the posterior surface of the midbrain, mediates these reflexes. The two upper ones, the superior colliculi, are the vestigial remains of the optic lobes and, although occipital cortices register vision in humans, the superior colliculi act to integrate incoming impulses from the visual retinae; kinesthetic input from the muscles of the eyeballs and from muscles, tendons, and joints throughout the body; and the output of impulses along the efferent motor tracts that produce the visual reflexes necessary for visuomotor coordination. As can be seen, this is a complex and delicate energy system, and a lesion or locus of dysfunction anywhere in the system may produce variations and impairments of visual perception. The two lower protuberances of the corpora quadrigemina, the inferior colliculi, provide an integration of incoming auditory impulses and kinesthetic impulses in basically the same way as the superior colliculi serve vision. Gellner (1959) has suggested that a child who can copy words but cannot use them meaningfully may be suffering from a lesion between the inferior colliculi and the acoustic areas of the temporal lobes (the gyri of Heschl). Although purely speculative, this appears to be a more logical rationale than a "general lack of mental ability" or "mental retardation" and finds its diagnostic understanding in trying to pinpoint spatially specific neural dysfunctions in the "auditory circuits." Some children labeled as mentally retarded, autistic, or dyslexic may be suffering from some disruption in visual or auditory perception because of a midbrain lesion. More or less exact knowledge regarding the locus of the lesion should lead to a better theory of the dysfunction, and this, in turn, should provide a more effective remedial educational treatment.

The Pons

Students of Latin will recognize pons as the word for "bridge," and in fact this enlarged section of the brainstem is a bridge for afferent fibers connecting the spinal cord with the cortex, for motor pathways from the motor cortex to the cerebellum, and for connections from the cerebellum to the spinal motor pathways. A tumor in the pontine area may develop in childhood and may result in visual–perceptual and visual–motor disturbances. Physical damage to the pons may result in somesthesia if the sensory fibers are cut, and in paralysis if the motor tracts are damaged or severed.

The Cerebellum

As can be seen in Figs. 3.4 and 3.5 the cerebellum is a sort of simplified cerebrum attached to the brainstem at the level of the pons. In structure it has two hemispheres, a cortex of gray matter and a middle area (medulla) of nerve tissue that is both white and gray. Unlike the cerebrum, which has irregular convolutions and different types of cells in different cortical areas, the cerebellum is lined with more regular convolutions and the cortical cells are similar throughout the surface area. They include granule cells and Purkinje cells in large numbers, and both of these possess unusually thick and complex dendritic development. These cells are interrelated synaptically, permitting a "widespread discharge following relatively limited afferent input" (Gardner, 1968).

The cerebellum acts as a filter to smooth and coordinate muscular activity. Sensory neural stimulation reaches the cerebellum from the skin, the muscles, the tendons, the joints, the labyrinth in the nonauditory part of the ear (static and position sense), the eyes, the ears, and the cerebral cortex and from the feedback of its own discharges to the cerebral cortex. Superior cerebellar function permits the graceful movements of the ballet dancer or the smooth, quick, and coordinated responses of the swimmer, sprinter, basketball player, or other athlete.

Damage to the cerebellum may cause paralysis of the arm or leg on the same side (ipsilateral) as the lesion, unlike a lesion in the cerebral motor strip, which always results in paralysis or motor disturbance maximally on the opposite (contralateral) side. Cerebellar dysfunction in milder form may result in general motor clumsiness, which in its own way may impede classroom or intellectual learning. Where the clumsiness includes a visuomotor disability even in a child of bright verbal intelligence, it frequently interferes with manual dexterity (apraxia), perceiving imbedded figures, writing, and other fine muscle performances. Brenner, Gillman, Zangwill, and Farrell (1967) matched 14 of these children in age, sex, handedness, verbal IQ, and home and school background with 14 children free of any agnosic–apraxic difficulties. The impaired group were significantly inferior on tests of spatial judgment, manual skill, spelling, arithmetic, and social adjustment. Such motor clumsiness may find its origin in dysfunctions of the cerebellum, of one of the two cerebral motor strips, or of the efferent motor pathways, or in some imbalance in one or more of the sensory neural mechanisms. Little hard evidence has emerged to relate cerebellar dysfunction directly to learning disabilities, but Dr. J. Valk, of the Netherlands, has reported some interesting findings from his neuroradiological studies of children. He has written:

> It is remarkable that the central steering center (in controlling gross and fine motor control), the cerebellum, is hardly ever mentioned as a causative factor in these coordination disorders. One of our surprises in the neuroradiological examinations of learning disabled children was the frequency in which a cerebellar atrophy or aplasia was revealed." [Valk, 1974]

He reported finding ten boys with evidence of abnormal development of the cerebellum and accompanying disturbances of fine motor control, which interfered with normal school progress.

Healthy cerebellar function contributes to normal sensorimotor integration that is basic to normal perception, motor response, and cognitive achievement. The brain stem is primarily involved in mediating gross sensorimotor activities, and the cortex is more concerned with fine motor control and mental abstractions, but successful behavior, whether largely motor or mental, requires a dynamic integration between these two levels. "Cognitive function has its tap root in the spinal cord, most of the rest of its roots in the brain stem and other subcortical structures, and the cortex assumes a mediating role over all" (Ayres, 1972a, p. 12). The cerebellum, as a primary structure in the brain stem, is necessary to all forms of normal behavior and creative imagination. Some investigators claim a correlation between cerebellar–vestibular dysfunction and poor reading, and we shall look at this relationship in more detail in Chapter 8.

The Medulla Oblongata

The medulla oblongata, the lowest section of the brainstem, is in a sense in the middle of the central nervous system. The brain is above it and the spinal cord and most of the rest of the nervous system are below it. It has more interest for the neurologist than for the educator; consequently little will be said here, other than that it is the level at which many of the sensory and motor nerves cross over to the opposite side (neural decussation) and that, in collaboration with the pons, it is the neural center for the various vital organs (heart, lungs, and digestive system).

The Peripheral Nervous System

As already explained, the central nervous system includes the brain and spinal cord. The peripheral nervous system is made up of all of those nerves outside the central nervous system, both afferent (sensory) and efferent (motor). These are (1) the cranial nerves; (2) the spinal nerves, with their sensory and motor connections; and (3) the autonomic nervous system, the neural subsystem that is intimately involved in motivational and emotion (see discussions of hypothalamic [later in this chapter] and frontal lobe function [Chapter 4]).

Twelve pairs of cranial nerves, attached to the brain and brainstem, have connections with cranial, spinal, and abdominal structures. The teacher will likely be most interested in those concerned with vision (cranial nerves II, III, IV, VI) and audition (VIII) and, if he or she suspects that a potentially bright child is impeded by visual or auditory maladjusted behavior, the teacher should refer the child for ophthalmological and/or audiological examination.

From the neck level (cervical level) to the lower extremity (sacral level) of the spinal cord there are 31 pairs of spinal nerves. Each nerve trunk includes sensory and motor nerves (see Fig. 3.6); the sensory root joins the spinal cord on the posterior (dorsal) surface and the motor root joins it on the anterior (ventral) surface. The two roots then join together inside the spinal foramen (hollow space inside the backbone designed to house and protect the delicate spinal cord) and pass out through an inter-

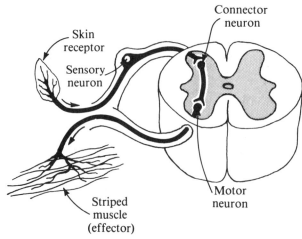

Figure 3.6. Cross section of the spinal cord showing one sensory (afferent) neuron, to represent a spinal nerve; one connecting neuron within the spinal cord; and one motor (efferent) neuron. In reality, a sensory nerve is made up of a bundle of many neurons, all conducting impulses toward the brain. Similarly, a motor nerve includes a bundle of nerve fibers that all carry impulses away from the brain. (© 1980 William D. West)

vertebral cavity on the lateral surface of the backbone. These nerves are particularly interesting because they connect to all parts of the body, carrying sensory impulses of tactile and kinesthetic impressions to the brain and distributing motor impulses to the various body muscles. Possibly the sensory and motor nerves to the hands and arms are most important in classroom learning because writing, handedness, and cerebral dominance may be better understood with an awareness of peripheral sensory and motor nerve function.

In trying to understand a child with a learning disability, the teacher should attempt to discover, with the diagnostic help of the neurologist and the consulting help of the school psychologist, whether the child's neurological damage or dysfunction is *central* or *peripheral* or both. For example, a child may be mildly apraxic and have difficulty in writing and carrying out manual tasks. If the trouble is central is may be caused by a lesion in one or both cerebral sensory or motor strips, in the motor pathways connecting the motor strip with the cerebellum, in the cerebellum itself, or in the anterior (ventral) horns of the spinal cord. The neurologist may be able to supply the diagnostic knowledge of the locus and intensity of the lesion and the psychologist, supplied with this knowledge, should be able to help the teacher develop a remedial teaching program for the child. If the trouble is *peripheral* then it may be located somewhere in the neural pathways of the arm and hand. Again, the neurologist and psychologist should supply this information to the teacher prior to his or her planning of a specific remedial program. If the dysfunction is central, it will likely distort perception or cognition or sensorimotor integration. If the dysfunction is peripheral, the impairment is more likely to affect sensory acuity or motor function, but not perceptual organization or mental imagery.

It seems highly likely that the problems of mixed laterality in many children who reverse numbers and letters occur because such children are *peripherally* left handed and *cortically* or *centrally* right handed. This concept is developed and examined in the discussion on handedness in Chapter 7.

Sensory Pathways

As already stated, neurologically all behavior includes sensory, cerebrally integrative, and motor processes. All perception and cognition depends on sensations of experience reaching the brain by the afferent or sensory nerves. If input is blocked then mental development may languish. If Annie Sullivan had failed to reach Helen Keller's mind through touch, by circumventing her blindness and deafness, then Helen would almost certainly have remained intellectually starved and mediocre, instead of developing in the superior way that she did.

In the past, many teachers have labeled some children "mentally retarded" because they could not learn as rapidly or by the same teaching techniques as most other children. Sometimes, these children have had superior minds but the sensory pathways have impaired perception in such a way as to disturb their learning. In such cases it is necessary to understand the nature of the disturbances and to develop a remedial teaching program to compensate for them.

Because visual, auditory, tactile, and kinesthetic imagery are essential to most learning, the sensory paths of these sense modes are examined briefly here. The discussion is simplified and abbreviated because the teacher needs only enough knowledge of neurological structure and function to enable a meaningful communication with the school psychologist and the neurologist. The teacher will depend on them for exact and detailed clinical knowledge; it will be his or her responsibility to take the knowledge they supply and develop a specific learning program for the child. For problems so complex, a professional team approach should provide the best results. How this team may deal with these problems is proposed in the clinical addenda following most of the chapters.

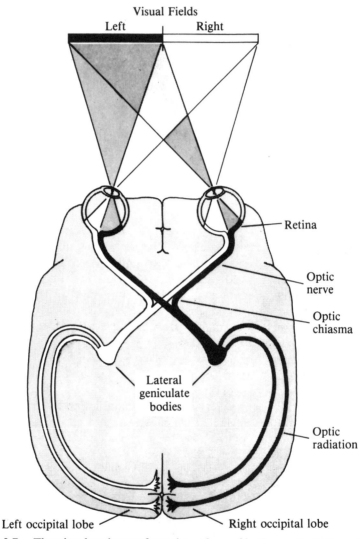

Figure 3.7. The visual pathways from the retinae of both eyes to both occipital lobes. Note that stimuli in the left visual field are registered in the right occipital lobe. Similarly, stimulation in the right visual field feeds into the left occipital lobe. (© 1980 William D. West)

Visual Pathways

The visual pathways extend from the retinae, along the optic nerves to the optic chiasma, through the superior colliculi, along the optic tracts to the lateral geniculate bodies, and finally along the optic radiation to the occipital cortices (see Fig. 3.7; also Netter, 1962, p. 63). Damage or dysfunction in parts of these pathways may produce particular types of visual field defects (see Manter & Gatz, 1961, p. 85), and brainstem, temporal, parietal, or occipital lobe dysfunction may result in visual–perceptual omissions, distortions, perseverations, rotations, misplacements, right–left reversals, and errors in judgments of size. Benton (1963b) has investigated these various types of impairments, and they are discussed in greater detail in Chapter 4.

Much research evidence supports "the doctrine that there are two visual pathways, the midbrain system (including the superior colliculi) answering the question 'where', and the geniculocortical system (including the lateral geniculate bodies and the visual cortices) the question 'what' " (Barlow, 1980). With their midbrain structures animals can locate their prey rapidly; with their visual cortices they can recognize them. When the latter are ablated in experimental animals, they cannot distinguish a carrot from a snake (Barlow, 1980) although they can focus on and locate the object. This two-process system also exists in humans. Barlow has called these two functions "the instrumental capacities of the visual system" and "the interpretive functions." If we extend these observations to the task of reading we can hypothesize that the midbrain structures are involved in scanning and the cortical areas in comprehension and interpretation. Dysfunction in one or other of these two visual pathways can affect reading and other visual skills differentially.

Auditory Pathways

The auditory pathways run from both ears to both temporal lobes, specifically Heschl's gyrus, located in the middle and upper part of the temporal lobe lining the fissure of Sylvius (i.e., the supratemporal plane). From the inner ear, sound waves set up vibratory patterns that are converted into electrochemical or neural impulses in the auditory nerve. This nerve enters the brainstem at the level of the medulla oblongata, divides, and ascends on both sides to the inferior colliculi; from here the two pathways travel by way of the medial geniculate bodies to Heschl's gyrus in each temporal lobe (see Fig. 3.8; also Netter, 1962, p. 64).

Although each ear is connected to both temporal lobes, the fibers are more strongly represented between each ear and the contralateral tempo-

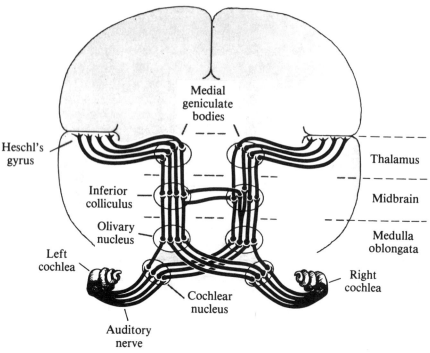

Figure 3.8. The auditory pathways from the inner ear to the cortical acoustic analyzers (Heschl's gyri). Note that the cochlea of each ear connects more strongly to the opposite side of the brain. The reduced number of neurons indicates the pathways but not the proportions of nerve fibers to each side. (© 1980 William D. West)

ral lobe. Because the left hemisphere is nearly always dominant for language, it has been found that in most people the right ear is slightly more sensitive to verbal input, and the left ear is more sensitive to nonlinguistic material, such as melodies (Kimura, 1964) and social sounds (Spellacy, 1969).

Unilateral temporal lobe lesions, if severe, do not necessarily produce deafness in one ear because of the bilateral connections of the auditory nerves, but they may produce a level of auditory imperception for certain phonetic or nonlinguistic sounds. A child with this lesion sometimes measures within the normal range on an audiometer test because he can sense individual tones across the scale at normal intensities; but because of a lack of integrated function of the two temporal lobes he may be unable to attach meaning to what is heard. This is the basic pattern in Wernicke's aphasia (receptive aphasia) that usually results from a lesion in the left temporal lobe (Fig. 3.9), and it can be devastating when it becomes confused by the teacher with mental impairment. Even worse is the diagnosis by the teacher of "failure to attend" or "unwilling to cooperate."

An example should make this clear. Some years ago a girl aged 9 was

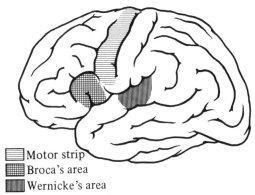

Motor strip
Broca's area
Wernicke's area

Figure 3.9. The language expressive and language receptive cortical areas of the left hemisphere. (© 1984 William D. West)

referred for neuropsychological evaluation because, as the teacher's report stated, "she cannot spell at all and we cannot teach her to read." Such severe retardation suggested the possibility that the child was mentally defective. However, on arrival she turned out to be a beautiful child, well spoken and charming in manner. On the visual and tactile tests she measured "bright to superior." In fact all her aptitudes were well above average except one, her auditory perception. Although her audiogram was in the normal range, she was unable to integrate phonetic sounds meaningfully.

Anyone who has studied a foreign language has had this experience. It is possible to hear the foreigner talking, but because of lack of experience and practice it is impossible to attach meanings to most of the sounds. Auditory *sensation* is normal in this example but auditory *perception* is defective. Once the teachers of this child understood the cause of her learning disability they stopped treating her as if she were mentally retarded, and on the recommendation of the psychologist (1) they spoke more slowly and enunciated more clearly when addressing her, (2) they abandoned phonics and taught her to spell by a visual–motor–kinesthetic method that showed some success immediately, and (3) they began teaching her to read by the same method.

Auditory imperception is almost impossible for the classroom teacher to detect, but when it occurs it can be ruinous. In Appendix A a suggested test battery is included that may help the clinical psychologist to detect danger signs. If the child is suspected of such perceptual impairment, he or she should be sent first for audiological assessment to check the possibility of a peripheral hearing loss; once normal hearing is indicated, then psychological testing on a battery of tests of auditory perception may be carried out. Such a battery might measure recognition of nonverbal "social" sounds, tonal memory, nonsense phonetic sound discrimination, and sentence repetition.

Somesthetic and Tactile Pathways

The third sensory pathway relates to the somesthetic system and the sense of touch. Physical contact with the skin or hairs triggers nerve impulses in certain specialized neurons located near the skin surface. These impulses travel along sensory nerves, enter the spinal cord through a posterior (dorsal) root, and ascend the cord and brainstem to the thalamus and somesthetic cortical strip located just posterior to the fissure of Rolando in the contralateral hemisphere (see Figs. 3.3 and 3.6). Any lesion in any part of this pathway or in the somesthetic cortex itself may result in an inability to recognize two-dimensional surface-texture patterns, such as Braille, or in a misperception of one's own fingers. The practicing clinical neurologist may look for dysfunctions in (1) light touch, (2) pressure touch, (3) localization of touch (naming the place touched), (4) superficial pain (from a pin or needle), (5) pressure pain (deep pressure or squeezing), (6) skin temperature, (7) postural sensibility (awareness of bodily position in space), (8) passive movement (knowledge of the passive movement of a limb), (9) vibration, and (10) appreciation of form by touch alone (Brain, 1960). All of these somesthetic functions are intimately involved with all learning that requires tactile sensitivity or kinesthetic awareness of body image, body movement, or manual recognition of three-dimensional forms. This last named type of perception is of particular interest to the neurologist, the clinical neuropsychologist, and the special educator. Clinical tests require the subject to palpate a three-dimensional object and match it with another one, also manually explored. Sometimes the subject may be asked to draw what he or she thinks the explored form looked like, once the blocks or objects are hidden and the blindfold is removed. This type of imagery and recognition depends on touch and kinesthesis and their cross-modal effectiveness with vision. This ability to recognize an object by touch alone (stereognosis) is believed to depend, at least in part, on the sensory strip as well as on greater areas of the parietal cortex and brain stem structures. Lesions in this area may result in defective finger localization, inferior directional sense, poor body image, and impaired academic work, depending on these neuropsychological aptitudes. In the classroom these skills include arithmetic, writing, spelling, and reading, in fact, all the "core" academic subjects. For this reason, calisthenics, the trampoline, and other techniques to exercise large body movements have been said to be related to the improvement of reading and other academic subjects (Kephart, 1960/1971).

The diagnosis of the locus or extent of a lesion in the sensory pathways or cortices is, of course, the responsibility of the clinical neurologist, but with this knowledge, interpreted by the school psychologist, the teacher is much better equipped to plan an effective remedial program for the afflicted child.

Motor Pathways

Structurally the sensory and motor pathways are somewhat similar, but nerve impulses in them, of course, travel in opposite directions. As sensations travel to the somesthetic strip just posterior to the fissure of Rolando, motor impulses are initiated in the cortical motor strip just anterior to this fissure (see Fig. 3.3). Fibers from this area connect down through the brainstem to the pons, into and out of the cerebellum, and on down the anterior horns of the spinal cord to the various exits from the cord by way of the spinal nerves. In classroom learning the motor functions most essential to success are the muscular control of the head and neck, including the eyes and speech muscles, and the hands in all types of fine muscle manipulations. Abnormal eye movements may interfere with reading, and in such a case the causes may be peripheral or central. If the lesion or dysfunction is central, possibly in the occipital lobes, the posterior part of the corpus callosum, in or near the superior colliculi, or the left angular gyrus, then the resulting dyslexia may be more resistant to remedial techniques and in any case will indicate different remedial measures. If the motor pathways are so affected as to cause manual clumsiness, the child may find academic learning, especially writing, spelling, drawing, and possibly reading and arithmetic, more difficult in spite of a superior or above-average mental capacity.

The Reflex Arc

Over 70 years ago, E. L. Thorndike (1913), proposed a psychological theory for the educator known as "connectionism" or "bond psychology." Such a theory, in simple form, hypothesized *linear* neural connections between the sense organ (receptor) and the neuromuscular–skeletal mechanism (effector) that were activated during the learning. In the 1920s Lashley's theories of mass action and equipotentiality discouraged a "telephone switchboard" view of linear neural connections and replaced it with a *field* view with an affinity for the gestalt theories popular at that time. Physiological studies with rats and nonphysiological ones with humans supported the field-theoretical view, but Hebb (1949), in attempting a neuropsychological theory, realized that both segmental cell assemblies involving linear functions and gestalt configurations including large masses of interacting neurons were likely operant. The two processes were not mutually exclusive; they depended on the level of neural integration of the behavior being studied. Geschwind (1965) also has supported a type of connectionism by showing in human aphasia cases that lesions in certain cerebral loci may result in a "disconnexion" between two essential areas and so may cause dyslexia or agraphia or both.

A simplification of the whole problem may remind us that certain fixed types of behavior (reflexes) appear to be related to the survival of the organism and are triggered by relatively simple neural pathways. These pathways may reach the spinal cord and then shunt the impulses out through the efferent route to the muscles, thus by-passing the brain. An example is the rapid retraction of the foot from a painful stimulus (stepping on a tack or hot pavement). The action occurs mechanically and involuntarily, and the subject is aware of the behavior *after* it has happened. The pupillary, salivary, dodging, and startle reflexes and withdrawal from noxious stimuli are all examples of this stereotyped behavior. Sensorimotor pathways producing reflex behavior may be only spinal or they may reach as high as the midbrain. They activate cortical cells only after their primary neural pathways have been completed.

Pavlov showed that simultaneous presentation of a "natural" stimulus and response (e.g., food and salivation) with a selected stimulus (e.g., a bell or light) can, after a few controlled repetitions, link up neurally the conditioned stimulus (the bell) with the unconditioned response (salivation). This he called classical conditioning, as students of psychology know, although not all students realize the significance of this monumental discovery. Its importance, of course, resides in the fact that mechanistic and predictable forms of behavior may be used to reinforce and direct learning. Pavlov (1928, Chap. 36) showed that conflict or "experimental neurosis" may be produced in dogs by teaching them an approach response to one stimulus and an avoidance response to another. Conflict may be produced by presenting a stimulus halfway between the two training patterns. Mateer (1918), one of the first American psychologists to apply Pavlovian principles to the training of children, discovered that conditioned responses could be more easily established in older children than in younger ones and in brighter children than in dull ones. These studies, using food as the unconditioned stimulus and salivation or anxiety as the unconditioned response, illustrated that the simple mechanism of the reflex arc could be linked to cortical centers, resulting in a learned new response, the "conditioned response." Watson (1924) in his classic studies of Albert and the rat, showed how a phobia might be produced and then eliminated by these means. More recently, Guthrie (1935) and Wolpe (1958) have used the same basic mechanisms for desensitizing phobias and managing various problems in psychotherapy.

None of this is new to the psychologist with a knowledge of the history of psychology since Pavlov's early work, but we are interested here in its neuropsychological interpretation. It is interesting to note that the relationship of brain weight to spinal cord weight becomes greater in organisms as we move up the phylogenetic scale. Whereas a frog's brain weighs less than its spinal cord, a gorilla's brain weighs 15 times as much. The human brain, with the highest ratio, 50 to 1, also possesses more cortex, which provides us with a greater variety of neural connections. A frog's behavior is predominantly reflexive and hence highly predictable. Higher order animals and humans, because of their greater neural complexity, have more varied responses to a wider range of stimuli. As the animal is more brain dominated and less spinal cord determined, its behavior becomes less reflexive, less instinctive, and more flexible and varied and, in humans, usually more intellectual. A lower animal is sense dominated (Phillips, 1969), but a human's behavior is determined not only by sensory input but also by the mediating effects of memory, practice, learning, judgment, and personal hopes and plans. Because the pattern of determinants is complex and functionally variable in human *S*s with normal brains, their behavior is not necessarily immediate following stimulation, nor is it always predictable from a knowledge of the input pattern. However, if a person suffers from some type of brain damage, or a dysfunction of some cerebral area, then the resulting behavior may be somewhat limited and hence more rigid and predictable.

The intelligent teacher with a knowledge of the child's cerebral dysfunction will try to identify his or her areas of limitation and rigidity and spheres of possible normal or superior functioning. Such a diagnostic understanding should abolish any tendency to consider the child with a learning disorder as "mentally retarded" or "mentally dull" and should avoid the dangers and prejudices of such a habit of labeling.

The clinical psychologist and the special teacher, in addition to integrating the knowledge of the reflex arc into their theoretical understanding of the child's behavior, may be interested to know of its importance in neurological diagnosis. An abnormal functioning of the patellar (knee jerk) or Babinski (plantar flexion of the toes following stroking the sole of the foot) reflexes may indicate damage or dysfunction of certain spinal centers. Cranial reflexes (e.g., pupillary reflex) may assist the neurologist to locate a brain lesion.

Cerebral Blood Supply

The arteriovenous structure and the metabolic functions of the blood system of the nervous system are more the purview of the medical student than of the teacher or the psychologist. However, there are a few points relating to them that may help the teacher to understand a child's behavior. Those wishing a more detailed explanation of this are referred to Gardner (1968/1975 [Chapter 7]) and Netter (1962, pp. 36–38), or to any good textbook on neurology. For those wishing a brief but related knowledge of the topic, however, the following explanation may suffice.

The several million nerve cells in the brain and nervous system are interlaced with an extensive network of capillaries, the tiniest blood vessels. They carry blood and oxygen to the brain; in fact, "a significant part of the oxygen used by the body is for the metabolism of the brain" (Gardner, 1975). The brain cells use oxygen at a fast rate, and if, for any reason, this oxygen supply is cut off even temporarily for a few minutes, brain cells will die. Harvey (1950) found that abnormal electrical changes occurred in the brain of rhesus monkeys within 1 minute of closing off (occlusion) the flow of blood in the middle cerebral artery. This means that almost as soon as the oxygen supply to the brain is reduced or cut off, deleterious mental changes may begin. If the blood supply is completely restored, normal physical and mental function will return, as long as the complete lack of blood to the brain is not allowed to continue more than about 6 to 8 minutes (Kabat & Dennis, 1938; Kabat, Dennis, & Baker, 1941; Weinberger, Gibbon, & Gibbon, 1940).

Military personnel who have been placed in a decompression chamber and asked to carry out simple arithmetical calculations after the oxygen content has been significantly reduced have had a first-hand experience of temporary impaired mental functions accompanying a reduced blood oxygen level. Harvey and Rasmussen (1951) also found that occlusion of the middle cerebral artery of rhesus monkeys up to 50 minutes could result in permanent neural damage, by showing paralysis in the arm and leg on the opposite side from the occlusion (hemiparesis). This added time over that found by Kabat's and Weinberger's research occurred because their studies cut off the blood supply completely. Harvey's studies occluded only the middle cerebral artery so that some blood, but not enough, was permitted to flow into the central areas of the cortex through collateral blood vessels. The studies by Kabat, Weinberger, and Harvey provide an interesting conclusion for the clinical psychologist and the teacher. A child's brain needs adequate oxygen and a partial supply can result in inferior mental functioning.

Ingvar and his colleagues in Sweden (Ingvar & Risberg, 1967) have shown increased cortical blood flow during mental activity (repeating digits backwards) as compared with a resting period with no demands for concentrated attention and mental achievement. A more detailed examination of Ingvar's experiments is presented in Chapter 5.

Although these experimental and neurosurgical phenomena do not directly concern either the psychologist or the teacher, they do help them to propose hypotheses to understand some types of congenital or developmental learning disorders. Normally the cerebral cortex is equipped with a fine net of interconnecting blood vessels that supply nourishment to all the cerebral cells. However, if a child is born with a brain in which an inadequate number of capillaries develops in one area of the cortex, then that area may suffer from an avascular growth anomaly, and mental or behavioral activities determined even in part by that cortical locus may be disturbed or impaired. For example, it is generally believed that damage to the left angular gyrus, a cortical convolution located in the middle of the left parietal lobe, is intimately involved in determining normal function in reading and writing. This is known from studies on war victims with gunshot wounds localized in this area (Russell and Espir, 1961). We may hypothesize from this knowledge that children born with an avascular left parietal cortical area may suffer from developmental dyslexia unless other cortical areas can take over its normal integrating function. Frequently, these children show an abnormal EEG in this area, and in the posterior lobes, although the disturbance is usually minimal.

While cerebral hemorrhages (strokes) usually occur in patients past middle age, children unfortunately are not free of them. A 6-year-old child, just prior to entering first grade, suddenly complained of a severe headache and became nauseated. She soon became unconscious and as a result she was rushed to the hospital, where a neurosurgeon carried out brain surgery (craniotomy). He had preoperative knowledge of a sudden cerebral hemorrhage in the left hemisphere, and during the surgery he removed the large blood clot (hematoma) and stopped the bleeding. Had this mass of waste material been allowed to remain, its pressure probably would have cut off the oxygen supply to a large number of cortical cells and the anoxia would have resulted in permanent destruction of healthy neural tissue.

Immediately following the surgery this little girl's speech was seriously impaired, but she soon regained it well enough to enter Grade 1 in November of the same year. She completed first grade by the following June but she did experience considerable difficulty with reading because her left parietal lobe had been mildly and permanently affected by the hematoma.

Ten months after the "stroke" she measured a verbal IQ of 105 and a performance IQ of 101 on the Wechsler Intelligence Scale for Children. Her vocabulary was below average, but then for the first 2 or 3 months following the cerebrovascular accident she had some difficulty understanding much of what was said to her (receptive aphasia) and this would be certain to retard her learning of new words. A year later, 23 months after the trauma, her IQ measures were about the same, but her vocabulary had improved markedly to a level average for a child of her age (8 years).

The left hemisphere damage resulted in a right visual field reduction and this complicated her reading and visual scanning in the classroom. In addition the left temporal lobe had been affected, and this resulted in some mild auditory imperception by producing some loss in the right ear in the higher frequencies. By the time this girl reached Grade 5, her brain had rehabilitated itself so well that she could now read for pleasure and was particularly competent in arithmetic and art.

Damage to a young brain is more likely to be overcome because of the growth and plasticity of new tissue. Other cases of cerebral hemorrhage and arteriovenous malformations are described in later chapters. At this point the teacher should be reminded that vascular accidents and anomalies do occur in children and some understanding of their perceptual and intellectual sequelae is necessary before the teacher can plan an adequate remedial program for a child so afflicted.

The Autonomic Nervous System

In the discussions so far the emphasis has been for the most part on the brain, thalamus, brainstem, and peripheral nerves and their relation to consciousness, cognition, perception, and learning. Most of the learning that takes place in the classroom is of this type and for this reason involves the cerebral cortex. Reflexive behavior, as described above, may involve the cortex *after* the motor response has occurred, and in this sense it is involuntary and semiconscious.

Another segment of behavior that the teacher should understand is also purely automatic and occurs with no conscious intent on the part of the behaving person. For example, one's breathing, heartbeat, digestive functions, and other vegetative activities usually occur without voluntary control. They operate separately and autonomously because they are controlled by a subdivision of the central nervous system called the *autonomic nervous system.*

Neurological knowledge recognizes two subsystems of the autonomic nervous system, the *sympathetic nervous system,* which is usually activated when energy is expended at a level above normal, and the *parasympathetic nervous system,* which is usually activated when behavior is at a normal level and energy is being conserved. Students wishing to know more about the structure and functions of the various parts of the central nervous system may consult a good introductory text in neurology (e.g., Gardner, 1975).

By contrast with the neurologist, the psychologist is interested in the role of the autonomic nervous system in human motivation and emotion. It is this function that should concern the teacher in gaining a better understanding of a child's behavior.

The conditions that throw the sympathetic nervous system into gear include fright, anger, exercise, pain, cold, infections, certain drugs, and a lack of oxygen. The two causes most interesting to the psychologist are fear and anger. These also have real significance for the psychologist and the teacher. In psychosomatic medicine any physiological symptoms, such as dermatitis (skin eruption), asthma, such gastrointestinal disorders as ulcers and colitis, and many others, resulting from prolonged anxiety or resentment, are frequently referred to as "stress disorders." Because unhappy personal relationships with those close to us are a frequent type of stress stimulus, and because stress may be relieved with successful environmental manipulation, it is important for the teacher to understand this neurochemical process, at least in basic function.

Some years ago, two medical researchers at the Mayo Clinic (Wolf & Wolff, 1942) reported an interesting and unusual case of peptic ulcer in which the stomach lining of the patient could easily be observed. The patient, a man of 56, had swallowed scalding hot clam chowder as a child. Since scar tissue resulting from the burn blocked the esophagus, the tube leading from the throat to the stomach, it was impossible for the boy to each in the normal way. From then on, he chewed his food, expectorated it into his hand, and then inserted the chewed food directly into his stomach through a fistula or opening made surgically through the abdominal wall. This physical arrangement enabled the medical scientists to observe the stomach walls through the fistula when the patient was relaxed and happy and when he was emotionally upset. They found that normally, when the man was secure and eating, the stomach lining became engorged with blood and strong digestive acids were secreted to break down the mass of food. The reader will recognize this as a physical state dominated by the parasympathetic nervous system. However, when he was angry or resentful, the same physical pattern occurred as the result of vagus nerve stimulation. This nerve connects from the medulla oblongata to the stomach and its stimulation results in the secretion of gastric juices. Because this may occur when the stomach is empty, the harsh chemicals that nature intended should mix with food now irritate the delicate mucous linings of the stomach. This may result in perforation and hemorrhage, and the irritating gastric acids may cause a peptic ulcer. If relieved of his or her anger and given milk or an alkaline diet, the patient's perforation will usually disappear.

When the man in Wolf's study suffered fear and anxiety the gastric secretion was inhibited and the rhythmic stomach contractions, normal during digestion of food, stopped. The stomach walls paled because the blood volume had moved to the extremities during sympathetic nervous system domination, and he now suffered from "nervous indigestion" with a mass of undigested food in his stomach.

A great deal of research has been done with animals to study experimental neurosis and the psychogenic production of gastric ulcers. They have been produced in rats (Sawrey & Sawrey, 1964, 1968; Sawrey & Weisz, 1956), dogs (Dykman and Gantt, 1960), cats (Masserman, 1950;

Smart, 1965), and monkeys (Brady, 1958) by subjecting the animals to prolonged anxiety, frustration, and indecision. Because a teacher who is oblivious or indifferent to the feelings of his or her pupils may create a classroom atmosphere conducive to sustained anger or fear, it is important that this whole physical and psychological mechanism be understood.

Sarcasm, intimidation, and overbearing behavior by the teacher may provide enough of a threat or irritant to the child to keep him in a mild "sympathetic" condition. This will interfere with learning if it is so acute as to be disruptive to perception and reasoning. Parasympathetic behavior is more pleasant for the child and the teacher and is more conducive to the learning process.

How Brain Functions Are Observed

The detailed knowledge of brain functions still has so many gaps that it is premature to build a complete neurophysiological or neuropsychological theory of learning. However, that is our eventual goal, and as more sensitive and exact methods appear for observing gross and subtle brain functions, we will be better equipped to produce such a theory. Already, there is a useful body of neuropsychological knowledge, and every year new truths are coming to light. Although most of the research methods are in the area of expertise of the neurological researcher, the clinical psychologist and the special teacher should have some knowledge of how neuropsychological knowledge is amassed. Following are brief descriptions of 12 neurological or physiological methods and techniques for observing the brain–behavior relationship.

Cerebral Ablations. Many years ago, Lashley (1929) demonstrated the reliable relationship between brain damage in rats and resulting mental deficit. Halstead (1947) was the first to attempt the same type of study with human subjects. Cases of required brain surgery provide the neuropsychologist with one of the best sources of knowledge by supplying two independent bodies of data—the extent of tissue damage reported by the neurosurgeon and the extent of mental deficit measured by a comprehensive battery of neuropsychological tests.

Preoperative tests are carried out and compared with the test results of postoperative procedures. The neurosurgeon reports the locus, extent, and nature of the damage and these data are examined in a correlation study to discover those relationships that provide a reasonable level of reliability. When healthy brain tissue is damaged or removed there is usually a decline in certain mental functions. However, when a benign tumor or encapsulated abscess is removed with little or no cortical damage, there may be a marked improvement in some or all mental functions.

Electroencephalogram. Electroencephalography is a method of recording the spontaneous electrical activity of the brain, which is useful in locating a brain lesion (whether it is a neoplasm, traumatically injured tissue, or an epileptogenic focus), and in the case of young children it may provide information about the development of cerebral dominance for language and the determination of handedness.

Electroconvulsive Therapy (ECT). This technique was originally introduced in the 1930s to treat psychotic behavior and, later, depression. It involves passing an electrical charge through the brain for about a half-second. More recently, with neuropsychological knowledge of cerebral asymmetry, it has been used to determine the side of language dominance. Unilateral ECT to the left hemisphere is usually followed by confusion in verbal memory, word-finding, and other signs of mild aphasia (i.e., dysphasia) for a half to a full hour. Unilateral ECT to the right hemisphere is usually followed by temporary spatial and nonverbal deficits. A patient exhibiting these signs could be supposed to be left-hemisphere dominant for language. Bradshaw and Nettleton (1983) have suggested that this approach has the advantage of providing more time than the Wada test for observation and study of the changes in behavioral and cognitive signs.

Echoencephalogram. The echoencephalogram (echo-EEG) is a device used in medical diagnosis of brain injuries. Its chief advantages are that it is quick and painless as compared with methods in which injections are used. A transducer unit is held at the side of the head, and high-frequency sound waves are directed through the skull and brain tissue. This device operates on the same principle as sonar; the sound waves are reflected back from interfaces within the skull, and any abnormalities are shown as blips on a scanning grid. While the echoencephalograph has no direct use in education it is one of the medical methods of detecting brain structure and function, and in general adds to neuropsychological knowledge.

Brain Scanning. Where the echo-EEG has only medical diagnostic value, the set of brain scanning techniques have promise of providing information that may ultimately have essential value in diagnosing learning disorders. They permit the identification of a variety of diseases of the brain, such as tumors, abscesses, blood clots, and areas damaged by reduced blood supply.

In a radionuclide brain scan the patient is given an injection of radioactive material into a vein in the arm. This procedure involves no discomfort or danger because it can be carried out with very small doses of radiation well within the limits of safety. The usual material given is 99m Technetium,[3] a purely artificial product that does not exist in nature and that gives off only gamma rays (similar to X-rays). A radiation detector that can move back and forth across the head detects the gamma rays in the brain tissue and turns them into a sort of photograph of the brain. Pathological tissue shows up as relatively dark patches, because damaged tissue shows greater radioactivity than healthy tissue. When four views of the brain (front, back, and both sides) are studied, the exact position of the abnormality may be identified.

However, a major difficulty in this conventional type of scanning is that much of the available information is lost by attempting to portray a three-dimensional body on a two-dimensional photographic plate. This means that if the X-ray beam is picking up a tumor in the brain, it is also recording all brain tissue in front of and behind the tumor, and unless the lesion differs significantly in density from the background, it may not show clearly on the X-ray plate (Hounsfield, 1973).

In early 1970s a new X-ray scanning method, computerized axial tomography (CAT or CT), was developed to overcome the weakness, described above, of the conventional methods. The CAT or CT scanner produces a narrow beam of X-rays, and as many as 160 readings of transmissions through the head may be made in one scan. The system is then rotated 1° and the process repeated for 180°; therefore 28,800 readings may be taken by each detector during a complete scan. This large body of data is analyzed by a computer that produces an X-ray picture of a "slice" of the subject's brain. This method is much more sensitive than the former brain scan methods in detecting abnormalities in soft tissue, and because the radiation is confined to the slice of brain, it avoids the problems of background interference.

This method is useful for locating tumors, abscesses, blood clots, and damaged tissue. As well as being useful for medical diagnoses, however, it holds promise for localizing cerebral dysfunctions in cases of organically determined learning disabilities (Staller et al., 1978).

In the mid-1970s the PETT scan (for positron emission transaxial tomography) was developed. While it involves injection of a radiopharmaceutical chemical in the arm and numerous successive pictures of "slices" of the brain similar to the CT scan, the biochemistry and the physics of the PETT scan are different. The CT scan uses X-rays to examine the brain and provide detailed information about its structure. The PETT scan, by contrast, involves injection of a positron-emitting substance (e.g., F-DG, a radioisotope or "tracer") that is consumed by the brain tissue at a rate proportional to that of glucose (Alavi et al., 1981)

---

[3] I am indebted to Dr. A. G. Richards, Chief Nuclear Physician, Royal Jubilee Hospital, for this information.

and enables the researcher to observe the rate of glucose consumption in different parts of the brain. The PETT scan can reveal metabolic or chemical activity as well as structure of the brain. For example, when a person's left visual half-field is stimulated with a light or object, the PETT scan will show a greater glucose consumption in the right visual striate cortex, thus providing immediate knowledge of the activity of the brain.[4]

More recently a new and revolutionary scanning technique has emerged that has a particular advantage over both the CT and PETT scanners; this is the NMR (for nuclear-magnetic-resonance) technique. This form of imaging avoids the use of radioactive X-rays and isotopes by depending on "the absorption and re-emission of radio frequency electromagnetic energy by certain nuclei placed within strong magnetic fields" (Rosen & Brady, 1983). While the levels of radiation used in both CT and PETT scanning are believed to be well within safe proportions, too much may be harmful, and NMR, while producing images comparable to those of the CT scanner, avoids any radiation risk. As well, it is proving to be of use in pediatric settings providing images of childhood neuropathology previously unobtainable (e.g., demyelination, delays in myelination, and normal development of myelination).[5,6]

Another type of brain scanning is a sophisticated use of the EEG to provide "topographic mapping and computerized display of scalp-recorded signals referred to as brain electrical activity mapping or BEAM" (Duffy, 1982). This technique, developed by Duffy and his colleagues (1979) at the Harvard Medical School, uses evoked potentials and EEG data from multichannel polygraphic recordings (from 20 to 24 recording sites on the scalp). This procedure provides such large amounts of data that visual inspection is inadequate or impossible; however, BEAM, using a computer-driven color video monitor, provides colored images of regional differences (i.e., areas of pathological tissue or dysfunction) that otherwise might have been omitted. In fact, one of BEAM's greatest uses is to evaluate functional lesions "where the CT scan is either normal or noncontributory to the clinical question at hand" (Duffy, 1982). Like NMR, BEAM is also a noninvasive technique that avoids any risk of radiation.

Angiogram. The angiogram is a medical technique that is useful for locating space-occupying brain lesions. A liquid containing material opaque to X-rays is injected into the carotid arteries and sequential X-ray

[4] Any reader wishing more knowledge about the PETT scan can find a brief and introductory discussion by Landis (1980) or a highly technical, but very interesting, account of visual, auditory, and tactile cerebral exploration using ^{18}F-DG with the PETT III scanner (Alavi *et al.*, 1981).

[5] Those readers wishing to learn more about NMR will find useful sources in Partain, James, Rollo, & Price (1983) and in Rosen & Brady (1983).

[6] I am grateful to Anthony Risser for the information about NMR.

pictures of the brain are taken as the liquid circulates in the cerebral arteriovenous system. Any distortions or avascular areas can be seen easily and this may indicate a possible neoplasm or structural abnormality. When such congenital abnormalities are discovered in growing children, this information may give clues to a specific learning disability and also indicate something about the development of cerebral dominance and handedness.

Pneumograph. Air may be pumped into the spinal meningeal space, which communicates directly with cerebral ventricles. When subjected to X-ray photography, the ventricles will appear black in contrast to the rest of the cerebrum. Any enlargements or distortions of the ventricular system can be seen easily, and this knowledge is important because generalized mental impairment frequently accompanies such structural anomalies.

Cortical Electrostimulation. Penfield and Roberts (1959), Ojemann (1979), and others have discovered a great deal about the behavioral effects of electrostimulating specific cortical loci. These experiments are carried out during brain surgery with a conscious patient who is able to report the content of mental events or memories accompanying cortical stimulation. Whereas this exciting and innovative technique enables a manipulation of the independent variable (the brain) and a subsequent observation of the dependent variables (behavior), one must be cautious in interpreting its manifestations. Delgado (1971) has warned that electrostimulation of the brain is a crude technique and varies from spontaneous neuronal activity in intensity, coding, modulation, and feedback.

Electrode Implanatation in the Brain. Mention has already been made of the enterprising experiments with animals carried out by Delgado and others in which neuronal changes are recorded during perception and motor activity, and in which motor and emotional behavior may be manipulated. These techniques, which are pointing to a closer control of the mind, may have advantages if they can assist learning (Delgado, Roberts, & Miller, 1954) but also may imply a social threat if they lead to coercive control of human behavior (Rosenzweig, Krech, Bennet, & Diamond, 1968). Many scientists, aware of the moral responsibilities of manipulating cerebral processes and behavior, have expressed such concern (Delgado, 1971). Regardless of the moral and social implications, teachers should be aware of this neuropsychological knowledge because it may provide the theoretical basis for new methods of teaching and learning in the future.

Histological Studies. Autopsy studies of the human brain frequently provide valuable knowledge of the locus, extent, and nature of a lesion. If detailed records of the patient's behavior are available, then a neuropsychological correlation of two classes of events, observed at different points of time, is possible. It was this procedure that enabled Broca in 1861 to posit the possible cortical location of the motor speech area. Déjerine (Geschwind, 1962), in 1892, developed his explanation of dyslexia by this method. More recently, Drake (1968) has provided a beautifully detailed account of a learning disabled boy who died at the age of 12 and for whom there are detailed educational, psychological, psychiatric, social, and neuropathological reports. More and more of these types of cases, although not yet numerous, are finding their way into the educational literature (Benson & Geschwind, 1969; Benton, 1964).

Use of Drugs and Chemicals. A brief reference has been made already in this chapter to the chemical nature of the neural impulse and to some experiments examining the process of interaction between brain biochemistry and behavior. One technique that is particularly useful in doing this is the Wada Carotid Amytal Test (Wada & Rasmussen, 1960) in which injections are made sequentially into the carotid artery on the side of the neck. If made on the left side, the left hemisphere, in a matter of seconds, becomes partially anesthetized or neurally impaired, and flaccidity of the right arm and leg and temporary aphasia result (when the left hemisphere is language dominant). This is a useful technique for detecting cerebral dominance for language.

In our Laboratory we began in 1968 to select those cases from our files who had had both the amytal and the dichotic listening tests administered. By 1976 we had accumulated 21 such cases, and we found complete agreement in 20 of these cases in determining cerebral language dominance using the amytal test and independently using the dichotic listening technique. This study showed a better than 95% level of agreement between the two methods. By 1981 we had accumulated 43 cases with both tests; agreement in these cases showed a 93% level. It should be noted that all of these were epileptic patients, and agreement levels for these Ss tend to be higher than for Ss with normal brain function. More will be said about this study in Chapter 7.

Biofeedback Training. A popular technique for studying brain processes utilizes the principles of operant conditioning and is called biofeedback. Its basic aim is to formulate laws of neural information processing that may help to understand relationships between brain and behavior.

When animals are studied electrodes are implanted in the occipital area or the sensorimotor cortex or the hippocampus, an area on the inside surface of the temporal lobe. The characteristic pattern of "blips" or waves is studied on a cathode ray tube following a visual or auditory stimulus or with no stimulus. A particular blip is chosen to modify, and whenever it occurs a reward is presented. After a number of such reinforcers the blip may appear with greater reliability and frequently greater amplitude. Sometimes reward is in the form of electrostimulation of the "pleasure centers" in the brain (Olds, 1956). Such experiments have shown that the delivery of reward can control discrete and minimal electrical events in the animal's brain, even though at this time the exact relation of these cerebral changes to behavior is not known.

When humans are studied, paste electrodes on the surface of the scalp may be used; hence the recordings are not as exact as those produced by electrodes implanted in the brain tissue of animals. If one wishes to increase the amplitude of one's alpha waves in the posterior parts of one's brain, the researcher may sound a tone when this occurs and tell the experimental subject. The subject's feeling of pleasure or satisfaction seems to serve as a reward, and the changes in his or her alpha waves may be reliably established. How this occurs is not yet fully understood, but biofeedback promises to be a useful technique for clinical and research theories and practices in neuropsychology.

In research it is improving knowledge about the significance of various parts of the brain waves. Electroencephalographers are able to distinguish aberrations in brain activity in conditions such as epilepsy, but they are at a loss as to what should be measured in the more subtle pathologies such as dyslexia. Biofeedback may be used to tease out those aspects of the EEG that should be measured (Walker, 1976).

Clinically, biofeedback has been used successfully to reduce the pulse rate in hypertensive patients. Possibly in the future it may enable quadraplegics to control a typewriter or motorized chair simply by their voluntarily changing their brain waves.

Summary. The reader will recognize that some of the above techniques simply record the state of the brain and others manipulate it. Regardless of this, information may be gained about the structure and function of the brain, and many deficits can be noted. Behavior is then measured by a comprehensive battery of perceptual, cognitive, language, motor, and sensorimotor tests and any behavioral deviations observed. These two sets of data are obtained from independent sources, and any reliable correlations between brain function and behavior add to our knowledge of the brain–behavior relationship. This is the essential pattern of human neuropsychology.

Neural Organization

Up to this point in our discussion we have examined segmental physiological aspects of living organisms, some small, such as nerve cells and synapses, and some larger functional units, such as arterial networks; but so far only casual references have been made to the total organization of the central nervous system and its control of human behavior.

In 1944 Herrick wrote, "Integration of bodily activities is a primordial essential; without it no living body can survive." This discussion will concentrate on the integrative functions of the brain and spinal cord, although the essential functional relations of other physiological subsystems (e.g., respiratory, circulatory, digestive, and endocrine systems) are recognized.

Functional Units

Luria (1973) tells us that "there are solid grounds for distinguishing *three principal functional units of the brain*." These are:

1. The activating reticular formation. Luria conceived of the brainstem (i.e., the midbrain, pons, and medulla oblongata) and the thalamus as working as a functional unit, the *first functional unit,* to maintain an animal's waking state. The chief function of this structure, which is organized like a nerve net, is to alert the various parts of the cortex to incoming signals. This is the chief function of the "ascending reticular system," and the "descending" fibers permit a cortical control of the brainstem. This, then, is a physiological center for attention, for screening incoming messages, and for activating various cortical areas to maximize attention and mental efficiency. A lesion or dysfunction in this area may result in distractibility and hyperactivity.

   The first function of the reticular formation is generalized arousal and the second, selective attention. Ojemann, a neurosurgeon, has found that part of the function of selective attention resides in the thalamus. By electrical stimulation of the thalamus during brain operations he can shift the patient's attention from his own internal, mental world of imagination to "what is coming in from the external world" (Calvin and Ojemann, 1980). In this connection, these writers have suggested that autism might result from a dysfunction of brain structures that result in an emphasis on "internal" attention, and a failure to attend to external stimuli. This is an interesting proposal, but Calvin and Ojemann report that anatomical studies of the brains of autistic children show no structural abnormalities either in the striatum (basal ganglia) or thalamus, the specific areas believed to control selective attention.

2. The occipital, temporal, and parietal cortices. Where the nerve net of the reticular system works in accordance with the principal of nonspecific function and gradual change, the neural structure of the three cortices in the *second functional unit* isolates the three areas of neu-

rons from one another so that each area receives discrete impulses. The occipital cortex mediates visual experience; the temporal, hearing; and the parietal, bodily sensation. Therefore, the primary purpose of this functional unit is the *reception, analysis,* and *storage* of information. Lesions or dysfunctions of any of these cortical areas can result in a variety of impairments of academic learning, as we shall see when we examine specific case histories later in the book.

3. The frontal lobes. Whereas the second functional unit is located posterior to the fissure of Rolando (central sulcus), the *third functional unit* is located anterior to it. As we have seen, the second unit mediates passive reaction to incoming information; the frontal lobes permit response to it through motor expression. Luria believed the frontal lobes were the centers for creating intentions, planning, and managing behavior in relation to one's perceptions and knowledge of the world.

Luria's concept of the vertical organization of all structures of the brain is a strong reminder that although the human cerebral cortex is necessary to our most abstract forms of thinking, the whole central nervous system contributes to it.

His concept of cortical function, based on prodigious clinical investigation, is in basic form, clear and easy to understand. In simple terms, Luria conceived of the human cortex as having (1) primary, (2) secondary, and (3) tertiary zones, distinguished by their different functions.

Primary Projection Areas. The primary projection areas are (a) the primary visual areas of the occipital cortices, (b) the primary acoustic areas of the temporal cortices, and (c) the primary sensory areas of the parietal cortices. These zones are called "projection" areas because, although they are centers for the reception of incoming neural impulses, psychologically a person "projects" subjective experience to the outside world. Whereas the visual neural processes stimulated by my pen as I write are recorded at the back of my brain in the occipital lobes, I have the experience that what I am writing is about 12 in. in front of my eyes. Similarly, the sensation of holding my pen is recorded largely in the left parietal area, but my experience of gripping it seems to be in my right hand because of the process of "projection."

These areas are called "primary" because they are believed to record only the elements of experience and not organized forms of meaningful patterns. For example, the primary visual cortices record "flashes of light, tongues of flame and colored spots" (Luria, 1973). The acoustic cortices, lining the floors of the two fissures of Sylvius, record pure tone, such as "ringing, humming, clicking, rushing, chirping, buzzing, knocking or rumbling" (Penfield & Roberts, 1959), but not meaningful sounds, such as words or melodies, and the two sensory strips record pure tactile sensations.

Secondary Association Areas. The visual association areas (Brodmann's Area 18, Fig. 3.10) are adjacent to the primary visual areas (Brodmann's Area 17). The auditory association areas occupy the lateral surfaces of the temporal lobes, contiguous to and just below the primary auditory projection area in Heschl's gyrus. Similarly, the secondary or association areas for touch are in the parietal areas bordering and close to the sensory strips.

The chief function of these secondary or association areas is to process the incoming information and to give meaning to the input. Where the neural contacts to the primary areas are mainly from the sense organs by long-axon connections in the brainstem, by contrast the neurons in the association areas have numerous short-axon connections transcortically. This means that the primary areas receive the elements of sensation and the secondary areas, which contain thousands of neural traces built up through experience, analyze and integrate the incoming messages into meaningful, recognizable perceptions and experiences.

Experimental evidence from several sources supports this concept of primary and secondary cortical function. Electrostimulation of these two zones shows much greater spreading in the association areas, and the primary zones, when so stimulated, produce elemental visual or auditory experiences, as has already been described. By contrast, electrostimulation of the secondary visual cortices produces recognizable hallucinations of "flowers, animals and familiar persons" (Luria, 1973) and of the secondary auditory cortices of familiar voices and discernible sounds (Penfield & Roberts, 1959). This is a clear example of neural integration in

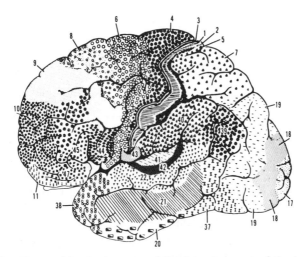

Figure 3.10. Cytoarchitectonic areas of the lateral aspect of the human brain. (According to Brodmann. *Vergleichende Lokalisationslehre der Grosshirnrinde*. Barth, 1909)

which discrete neural stimuli are organized into a meaningful experience to which the person can respond.

Tertiary Cortical Zones. Tertiary cortical zones are the areas between the various sensory association cortical areas that permit an integrated multisensory experience. In humans, language is made possible by neural interconnections between the visual and the auditory association cortices, which are located in the lower part of the left parietal lobe in most people. This neurally integrating area includes the angular and the supramarginal gyri (see Figs. 3.1 and 8.2), and it appears to play an essential function in language development, as is discussed in Chapter 8. These areas are most developed in humans, appearing in only rudimentary form even in the higher apes. In fetal development this is one of the last areas in which dendrites appear and sometimes it is slow to mature in childhood (Geschwind, 1965, Part II). These discoveries from developmental neurology suggest that both phylogenetically and ontogenetically these integrating neural structures are late to mature, and in cases of faulty development they would seem to be highly vulnerable and at greater risk in attaining mature and normal function. In cases of defective growth one might expect problems in perception, cognition, and/or motor response, which are, in fact, essential causes of learning disabilities.

Ayres (1972a) has developed an interesting theory and remediation program that is used rather widely by occupational therapists. She contends that disordered sensory integration accounts for some aspects of learning disabilities and that remediation implies improving the neural integration of the child to increase the capacity of the brain to learn, rather than drilling specific academic skills.

Functional Units and Learning

The importance of sensorimotor integration to learning and normal behavior is supported by neurological and neuropsychological clinical studies. This integration is hierarchical in design, each smaller subsystem (e.g., a cell) requiring harmonious intraorganic integration, and each group of subsystems requiring an internal consonance free of stresses or occlusions.

Certainly a deficit in integration can produce learning problems at different levels. A lesion in any one of the primary cortical projection areas or in the neural pathways leading to them can produce a partial or distorted input, making it difficult for the contiguous association areas to integrate the elemental input into a meaningful cognitive pattern. This is an example of a visual or auditory or tactile perceptual deficit.

If the primary area is free of pathology but the association area is damaged, the process of sensory analysis and integration itself is impaired, and a perceptual deficit also results, but for different reasons.

If a lesion is localized in the motor strip or strips or the efferent nerves connecting to the muscles, the child may be partially immobilized. The child's intelligence level may be above average and perceptual understanding good, but expressive abilities (spoken speech, writing, general mobility) may be impaired. An intellectually bright child with cerebral palsy is such an example.

In all of the above examples the lesions have been localized, so that normal integrative functioning of the whole central nervous system has been disturbed. If the brain pathology is more generalized, then a cognitive deficit is more likely to appear, and if it is diffuse, then some degree of mental retardation is likely.

The majority of books on educational psychology urge the teacher to deal with the "whole child," but these same books cover only psychological and social aspects. If the teacher is to deal with the "whole child" then the best neurological, psychological, and educational knowledge must be integrated. The emphasis in this book is on the first of these three, but this does not imply a disregard of the other two. The interested teacher will need to relate the knowledge presented here with his or her own psychological and educational background. Books and courses covering these two areas are numerous; books and courses covering educational neuropsychology are only now beginning to appear.

Clinical Addendum

What the Clinical Psychologist Can Do

This addendum, and those to follow subsequent chapters, presents in some detail a diagnostic approach that the clinical or school psychologist may use. It also describes how the teacher might use the information gained by the clinical neuropsychological approach. This procedure is proposed not as the only model but as a guide to school psychologists who wish to incorporate neurological knowledge into their diagnostic analyses and remedial prescriptions. Attempts to do this are not common, although increasing numbers of psychologists are expressing an interest in using clinical neuropsychology in the study and treatment of learning disorders.

It is hoped that these clinical addenda will serve as a guide to relate neuropsychological test signs to a better understanding of the LD child or adult, and to use this knowledge in preparing remedial programs. Inexperienced clinicians may follow this guide as a learning experience, if they so choose; experienced clinicians may wish to incorporate what new material they may meet into their already established clinical style.

A school psychologist wishing to use neuropsychological knowledge in diagnostic reports will soon find that neither the neurologist nor the teacher is the appropriate person to integrate the neurological, psychological, and educational data on each LD child or adult. Each of these professional people has his or her own areas of expertise, and the essential functions of the clinical psychologist include diagnosis and therapy. This means that the school or clinical psychologist will likely have to collect the diagnostic data from the neurologist, from the teacher, and from his or her own test and interview results, and then attempt to put them together into a meaningful picture. The clinical psychologist will most likely emerge as the coordinator on this team, and this clinical procedure can soon become a smoothly running operation when each member has a clearly defined role.

At first there may be problems of interprofessional communication. Medical doctors sometimes approach discussions with teachers with caution, and many teachers are timid about approaching medical doctors about professional problems. In one isolated case, an authoritarian school principal, with strong feelings about territorial rights, wrote a note to a doctor telling her "to stay out of my school, and to keep your hands off of what is none of your business." Such extreme views are not common, and teachers enjoy the opportunity to explain to the neurologist and to the psychologist the child's school problems. Periodic workshops on learning disabilities for medical, educational, and public health personnel have been popular and successful in breaking down much of the interprofessional isolationism.

Any clinical activity that promises competent help to learning disabled children will soon be submerged with referrals; hence a clearly defined admission policy is essential. All requests for our own program when it was first initiated, whether they came from parents, teachers, or medical doctors, were referred first to a qualified neurologist for a complete neurological examination, including an EEG and a skull X-ray. After about the first 3 years of the plan, we dispensed with the skull X-ray because it produced no useful information in most cases. As a replacement to the skull X-ray, the neuroradiological examination (brain scan), already described in this chapter, is a relatively new technique that has great promise for the study of children with learning disabilities (Valk, 1974).

Clinical Classifications

These classifications, first presented in Chapter 1, will be examined here in more clinical detail.

Brain Damaged

With Presence of At Least One Hard Sign. Some of these signs may be confirmed by neurosurgery, such as a subdural hematoma or a progressive lesion such as a cyst or tumor. Some may be identified behaviorally (e.g., hemiplegia) or by neuroradiological investigation (e.g., abnormal cerebral growth or atrophy of the cerebral structures). Some are identified at autopsy, and much can be learned by relating the recorded learning problems to the postmortem findings (Drake, 1968).

With No Hard Signs. Brain damage may be inferred in the absence of any hard signs, but with the presence of at least three minor indications (soft signs). These may include an EEG dysrhythmia of grade ii or iii, hyperreflexia on one side, asymmetry of sensation in hands and/or face, asymmetry of finger tapping speed between hands, asymmetry of stereognosis between hands, nystagmus, strabismus, tremor, athetoid and choreiform movements, and mild asymmetry of the skull. Some additional neuropsychological characteristics include language retardation, motor incoordination, visual perceptual deficits (e.g., rotations, reversals, inversions, defective body image) and poor right–left directional sense, but because these may be caused by developmental lag it is safer to use these only after the neurological and sensorimotor signs have been established and only with children at least 9 years old. For a fuller list of symptoms see Clements (1966).

Minimal Brain Dysfunction (MBD)

In Chapter 2 the MBD child was described briefly and symptomatically to help teachers better understand this frequently ill-defined and confusing category. Here we will examine the problems posed by this category and provide some suggestions that may be useful to the school or clinical psychologist in the understanding and treatment of children so classified.

At the outset, it is clear that the definition of MBD and the understanding of its pathology, its etiology, and any characteristic response pattern to its treatment (if such a pattern exists) are all in a state of flux. The term "minimal brain dysfunction," first formally recommended in 1962 by the Oxford International Study Group on Child Neurology, was proposed in place of the term "minimal brain damage" because it was believed by the members of the group that brain damage should never be inferred from behavioral signs alone (Strother, 1973). However, since 1962 the recognition and treatment of MBD children have attracted the attention of more nonmedically trained professionals, in particular educators and school psychologists, and this has led to a greater educational emphasis on the category. Strother (1973) tells us that "authors who write from a medical orientation prefer the term 'minimal brain dysfunction' or its equivalent, whereas those who write from an educational point of view tend to use the term 'specific learning disabilities' or its equivalent." As medical, neuropsychological, and educational researches reveal more knowledge about MBD children, the present tendency to a divided view should be replaced eventually by a common definition satisfactory to all professionals. In the meantime it will fall to the lot of the school psychologist to assess each LD child in depth and to decide on the presence or absence of soft signs.

Rutter, Graham, and Yule (1970) have suggested three groups of soft signs:

1. Signs that reflect a developmental delay, such as speech and language retardation, motor incoordination, perceptual deficits in all sense modes, impaired right–left orientation, adventitious motor overflow, and extinction or suppression of double simultaneous tactile stimulation. I would add to this, delayed or defective sequential perception and/or response. Any of these signs must be interpreted only in relation to chronological and mental age.
2. Signs that may or may not result from pathological neurological factors, such as nystagmus, strabismus, and tremor.
3. Signs of slight abnormalities that are difficult to elicit, such as slight asymmetry of tonus or reflexes, just perceptible hemiparesis, minimal athetosis, or mild asymmetry of skull or limbs.

Other signs include (Clements, 1966) EEG abnormalities without actual seizures, or possibly subclinical seizures that may be associated with fluctuations in behavior or intellectual function, and deviations in attention, activity level, impulse control, and affect. Clements has listed 99 different symptoms under 15 different classes that the school psychologist may find useful.

The confusion in defining MBD stems from the common difficulty of identifying any borderline phenomenon appearing on a continuum reflecting an intense condition that gradually decreases until there is a complete absence of it. Intense and localized brain damage in specific cortical or subcortical areas will produce predictable deficits in adult behavior with a high level of reliability (Luria, 1966, 1970, 1973; Reitan, 1959). Human subjects manifest a set of systematic brain–behavior relationships, as is explained more fully in Chapter 4. Cases of traumatic brain damage provide a rich source of neuropsychological knowledge in which the neural pathology is known and the behavioral impairment is observed. In these cases the etiological factors and their psychological sequelae are frequently clearly identified.

As we move along the continuum toward normal brain structure and function, however, we pass through a large number of children and adults who are not "brain damaged" and who, for no known reason, show many behavioral deficits similar to the brain-damaged patients, but in a much less intense way. These behavioral impairments (e.g., visual reversals, poor finger localization, asymmetry of finger tapping, and astereognosis) are the soft signs, and their presence suggests very strongly that the person's brain and central nervous system has some minimal areas of dysfunction, although a standard neurological examination may have turned up nothing.

While brain damage cannot be diagnosed completely and always conclusively on behavioral data alone, Reitan (1964b), using only neuropsychological test results, has been among the first to predict the loci of localized brain lesions preoperatively in adults, and many of his students have learned the same clinical skill with some level of success. Many neurosurgeons have found these preoperative predictions particularly useful in planning a surgical operation.

Other clinical sources that are helping to complete the mosaic picture of the MBD child are the new scanning techniques already described. They are revealing areas of brain pathology previously missed by a standard neurological examination. A patient with a reading disability because of Déjerine's syndrome (alexia without agraphia; see Chapter 9 for a full account) was found on the CT scanner to have a lesion in the left posterior part of his brain (Staller *et al.*, 1978), although the brain pathology was not evident on more commonplace methods of investigation.

In the past, some authors (Schmitt, 1975) have dismissed the soft signs as indications of maturational lag, and thus completely unreliable and meaningless for both diagnosis and prognosis. Such conclusions have usually resulted from clinical observation only. One investigator who examined this problem experimentally and longitudinally was Hern (1984). Where most studies of the stability and persistence of soft signs have covered periods of a few weeks (MacMahon & Greenberg, 1977) or up to 4 years (Ackerman, Dykman, & Peters, 1977; Hertzig, 1982), Hern followed 123 learning disabled subjects for 14 years, from elementary school age into adulthood. As well, she compared these 123 adults neurologically with 46 normal learners who were matched for age and socioeconomic status. Using a regression analysis procedure Hern found a significant relationship between 19 neurological measures at time 1 (subjects' ages between 8 and 12 years) and time 2 (the same subjects 14 years later). An R^2 of .53 was found, which corresponds to a correlation coefficient of

.73. The difference in incidence from middle childhood to adulthood showed a reduction in signs among those subjects with the greatest number at time 1 and changes in both directions for those in the midrange. Hern's findings did not support the thesis that LD children suffer from temporary maturational lag that will be overcome with time. On the contrary, she found that most LD children "do not seem to improve in their performance on a neurological examination and many show additional and different signs in adulthood that were not seen in childhood" (Hern, 1984). In addition, she found that LD adults showed more neurological soft signs than a matched control group of normal learners.

What is the school psychologist to do about so-called MBD children in the face of this evidence? First, it would seem advisable not to infer cerebral dysfunction conclusively from behavioral data alone, nor to state this in a report. As well, it should not be inferred that because the child shows a number of soft signs that he or she must be hyperactive or learning disabled.

However, if the child does have a serious learning problem and a large number of soft signs, the neurologically trained school psychologist may profit from hypothesizing what might be occurring in a particular child's nervous system, although the psychologist never mentions this to the parents nor includes it in any formal communication. Such a practice is congruent with the idea of the unity of nature and with possible later revelation of subtle brain dysfunctions in cases with only soft neurological signs. It has the advantage of encouraging a more detailed consideration of the child's case, albeit speculative; of increasing or widening the scope of logically possible diagnostic hypotheses; and of improving the probability of hitting on fruitful diagnostic knowledge. Such an approach avoids damaging the child by labeling but stimulates an in-depth consideration of a case which, at this point in our knowledge, can be only partial at best.

The school psychologist wishing further discussion on this important classification is referred to the scholarly and logical defense of the term MBD by Denckla (1978), who is a neurologist engaged in the study and assessment of learning disabled children.

In summary, the MBD classification may be useful for the physician, research psychologist, and school psychologist, although because of incomplete knowledge about its etiology at the present time its definition may vary with the discipline in which it is stated. Nevertheless, it appears to be a neurologically and behaviorally recognizable group, where private speculation by the psychologist may lead to more fruitful understanding and treatment.

Learning Disabled with No Hard or Soft Signs

These include children of normal intelligence and good health, who are usually described as having a specific learning disability or a developmental learning disability with no known cause. Orton (1928) was one of the first to study and describe the reading disabled child, although he named the defect strephosymbolia, which meant a twisted perception of the written symbols. We now know that dyslexia can result from a perceptual deficit, a language disability, or a problem in sensorimotor integration. Ayres (1972a) has written ably on this last named type. On a battery of neuropsychological tests, a person in this category may have average or better scores on intelligence, on all the perceptual tests, and in motor response, but he or she may have great difficulty in sequencing, in cross-modal tasks, in phonetic blending, or any skill demanding an integration of input and output neural functions. While all of the causes of learning problems are not known, a disturbance in sensorimotor integration seems to be present in a number of them. Genetic defects may account for some others.

The school psychologist may select these children on the basis of teacher's reports, if they are obvious, or by psychometric means, such as a learning quotient (Myklebust, 1967a) or a multiple regression formula (Rutter, Graham, & Yule, 1970), as has been discussed in Chapter 2.

Normal Controls

It is advisable for any school psychologist to collect scores of normal children on any tests he or she uses, to avoid relying completely on collections of normative data from different populations. Some collections of normative data are available (Gaddes & Crockett, 1975; Klonoff, 1971; Knights, 1966; Knights & Ogilvie, 1967; Spreen & Gaddes, 1969; Trites, 1977), but these should be used with caution unless the two populations being compared appear to be reasonably similar.

Once a child or adult is accepted for diagnostic study (in our laboratory all children in Group 1 are accepted automatically, and selected children in Groups 2 and 3), he or she is subjected to a test battery (see Appendix A), which takes between 5 and 6 hours to administer. The tests are selected to measure the person's visual, auditory, and tactile perception; verbal and spatial–constructional intelligence (WISC); motor speed; sensorimotor integration; serial order competence; short- and long-term memory; and language development.

Patterns of deficits in a child's neurological data are compared with deficits on the neuropsychological tests and from the teacher's reports of his or her classroom difficulties. Group studies are carried out to examine the possibilities of reliable correlations between these two sets of variables, as a part of the research function of the clinical or school psychologist in this setting.

The psychological and educational data are studied in the light of whether the cerebral abnormality is general and diffuse, regional (left or right, frontal or posterior), or highly localized; whether it is developmental (that is, has existed since birth) or traumatic (acquired by postnatal injury); and whether, if it is traumatic, it is of recent or long-standing occurrence.

After conferring with the parents and the child's teacher, the psychologist then writes a remedial prescription, stressing the child's strengths and weaknesses, listing the types of academic activities and skills with which he or she will likely have difficulty, and noting how these difficulties may be circumvented.

This report should be free of jargon, be in clear, ordinary language that the parents and teacher can understand easily, and include an overall diagnostic conceptual picture of the child that should help the teacher to perceive the child more accurately. It should also include a number of concrete remedial suggestions that the teacher can try.

What the Teacher Can Do

The teacher will usually have a more detailed knowledge of the child's social behavior than the school psychologist, but all signs of subtle deficits, such as phonetic auditory imperception, should be supplied to the teacher by the clinical or school psychologist.

The teacher may study the psychologist's report and build up a conceptual knowledge of the child's perceptual, cognitive, or motor deficits. With this knowledge in mind he or she should then select from his or her own professional repertoire of expertise the particular remedial approach that seems best suited to the child's needs.

A baseline should be measured before the remedial program is begun and any progress or lack of it reported to the psychologist, who may act not as an expert authority but as a consultant to help the teacher. If the child is making good progress, it is likely that the remedial approach is a valid one. If no progress is made, the psychologist in conference with the teacher should decide whether more diagnostic procedures should be carried out, whether the teaching methods should be monitored and altered, or whether there are etiological factors not yet detected.

In the next chapter a detailed discussion presents current neuropsychological knowledge and its possibility for understanding learning. Following this discussion the Clinical Addendum at the end of Chapter 4 offers more specific suggestions regarding diagnosis and remediation.

Suggested Readings in Neuropsychology

Bradshaw, J. L. and Nettleton, N. C. *Human cerebral asymmetry*. Englewood-Cliffs: Prentice-Hall, 1983.

Bryden, M. P. *Laterality: Functional asymmetry in the intact brain*. New York: Academic Press, 1982.

Filskov, S. B. & Boll, T. J. *Handbook of clinical neuropsychology*. New York: John Wiley & Sons, 1981.

Heilman, K. M. & Valenstein, E. *Clinical neuropsychology*. New York: Oxford University Press, 1979.

Hynd, G. W. and Obrzut, J. E. (Eds.). *Neuropsychological assessment and the school-age child, issues and procedures*. New York: Grune & Stratton, 1981.

Kolb, B. and Whishaw, I. Q. *Fundamentals of human neuropsychology*. San Francisco: W. H. Freeman, 1980/1984.

Rourke, B. P., Bakker, D. J., Fisk, J. L. and Strang, J. D. *Child neuropsychology*. New York: Guilford, 1983.

Spreen, O., Tupper, D., Risser, A., Tuokko, H. and Edgell, D. *Human developmental neuropsychology*. New York: Oxford University Press, 1984.

4 The Use of Neuropsychological Knowledge in Understanding Learning Disorders

All nervous centers have then in the first instance one essential function, that of "intelligent" action. They feel, prefer one thing to another, and have "ends." Like all other organs, however, they evolve from ancestor to descendant, and their evolution takes two directions, the lower centers passing downwards into more unhesitating automatism, and the higher ones upwards into larger intellectuality.

William James (1890)

In this chapter the current status of our knowledge of the brain–behavior relationship will be examined within the context of problems of cognitive function and classroom learning. This is a particularly interesting and promising area of exploration but one in which there are still many gray areas. Neurologists and neurosurgeons still are largely ignorant of the particular functions (if they do exist) of most segmental parts of the cerebrum, thalamus, and brainstem, but they do possess knowledge of some of the gross relationships of the brain and behavior, and this knowledge has relevance for the clinical psychologist and the classroom teacher. This attempt to relate neurological, psychological, and educational knowledge is a radical one and is still in its infancy. Since 1963 many professional meetings have been held in the United States and Canada to discuss learning disorders, and most of these have included neurologists as major invited speakers. These meetings have been sponsored by medical schools, associations of ophthalmology and pediatrics, and other medical specialties, as well as schools of education. This is a healthy sign, because physicians, psychologists, and educators are now likely to progress more rapidly in understanding learning disorders by pooling their knowledge and professional experience.

What follows is an attempt to synthesize current knowledge from researchers in neurology, neurophysiology, neuropsychology, and education. The student of neuropsychology should understand at the outset that the brain operates as a dynamic unitary organ when the behavioral function seems to draw on all or most of the cerebral mechanisms. At the same time it also implies a maximal processing function of one or more localized cortical areas for certain types of behavior. For example, if Broca's area (see Fig. 3.9) at the base of the third frontal convolution of the left cerebral hemisphere is damaged seriously the person may not be able to speak. Such patients may hear what is said to them and may understand its meaning, but because one of the important centers in the motor-speech function is damaged their expressive speech may be impaired. By contrast, Teuber and Weinstein (1956) found a form of behavior that seems to require normal functioning of all cortical areas. This is the ability to perceive a hidden-figure task, or to see a geometric figure hidden in a camouflaged background. Patients with left-hemisphere, right-hemisphere, bilateral, frontal, nonfrontal, parietal, nonparietal, temporal, nontemporal, occipital, and nonoccipital lesions did almost equally poorly on this test, suggesting a rather generalized cortical function to mediate successful perception of this type.

More than a hundred years ago the famous French neurologist, Flourens (1794–1867), hypothesized that "one point excited in the nervous system excites all the others; one point enervated enervates them all; there is a community of reaction, of alteration, of energy . . ." (Boring, 1957). This unitary function of the brain he named "action commune." The localized functions of the brain he called "action propre." It is interesting that neuropsychological evidence currently appearing still tends to support Flourens' early insights, although with more precise knowledge.

Shure and Halstead (1958) have described this situation thus:

> At one extreme are the theories which argue for a very fine division of the cortex with a corresponding distribution of psychological functions. On the other side are those which argue for the concept of the brain as a dynamic unitary organ with a corresponding diffuse representation of intellectual ability in the cerebrum.

At our present level of neuropsychological knowledge there is value in studying the brain as a whole and recognizing the behavioral effects that accompany both specific and localized brain lesions. Kurt Goldstein, an eminent German neurologist who studied the mental effects of brain injuries in German soldiers in World War I, developed a holistic theory not only of brain function, but of total behavior. In comparing the atomistic study of parts and the holistic approach, he favored starting with an examination of the whole organism, then dissecting, but always keeping the total function at the center of interest. In this connection he wrote,

> For us there is no doubt that the atomistic method is the only legitimate scientific procedure for gaining facts. Knowledge of human nature has to be based on phenomena disclosed in this way. But is it possible to proceed from material gained by the use of this method to a science of the organism as a whole, to a science of the nature of man?

If the organism were a sum of parts which we could study separately, there would be no difficulty in combining our knowledge about the parts to form a science as a whole. But all attempts to understand the organism as a whole directly from their phenomena have met with very little success . . . because the organism is not a sum of parts. [K. Goldstein, 1940]

Riese, in explaining Goldstein's work, has written,

Goldstein denied neither the significance of structures nor the possibility of cerebral localization. He only wanted to relegate both within their own limits. He was searching for a constructive formula of those functions which are accessible to cerebral representation and localization. . . . Cerebral activity, he said, is always a total one, but always with ever-changing regional accents . . . [Riese, 1968]

In brief, this means that the brain functions as a whole, but many specific behaviors impose more demands on different cerebral parts. Consequently when a lesion occurs in a particular cerebral locus, behavior that draws heavily on the normal functioning of that area or areas joined by that locus may suffer. However, this does not mean that that particular form of behavior is determined exclusively by the particular locus under study. Hughlings Jackson, the eminent British neurologist, realized this 100 years ago and his theoretical insight was re-expressed by Weisenburg and McBride (1935/1964) when they wrote "the aphasic symptoms are the result of the activity of the uninjured parts of the brain, for dead tissues cannot produce kinetic phenomena."

This means, then, that the knowledge of the locus of a brain lesion may help us to predict a particular behavioral deficit, and vice versa, but this does not necessarily support an exclusively localizationist or structural view of brain function and behavior. Knowledge of generalized or localized cortical dysfunction can provide the diagnosing clinical psychologist with different types of information that can help the special teacher to design an effective remedial program.

Adult and Child Neuropsychology

Just as child behavior differs from adult behavior in quality, complexity, and abstractness, so too, do brain–behavior relationships differ from child to adult. But how they differ is only partially understood because developmental neuropsychology is still a new science; a few clinical studies appeared following World War II (Strauss & Lehtinen, 1947; Strauss &

Kephart, 1955; Cruickshank, Bice, Wallen, & Lynch, 1957), but most research in this area has appeared since about 1960.

Adult neuropsychology preceded child studies by more than a century, both because adult patients were more numerous and hence more available and because they were more easily understood. While no problems in human neuropsychology are simple, at least the adult brain and its correlations with behavior are reasonably stable after about midadolescence. By contrast, the brain of a child grows very rapidly to about age 9 (see Fig. 4.1), and the cognitive and behavioral functions dependent on this

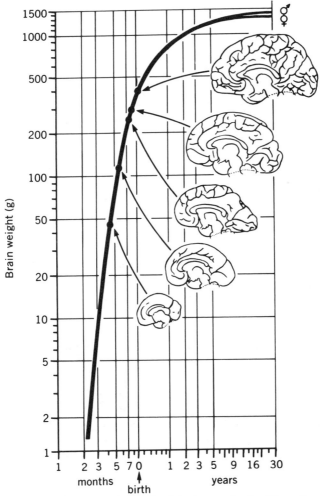

Figure 4.1. Pre- and post-natal growth of the human brain. (From Lemire, R. J., Loeser, J. D., Leech, R. W., & Alvord, E. C., *Normal and Abnormal Development of the Human Nervous System.* Harper & Row, 1975. Adapted from Larroche, J. C., in Falkner, F. (ed.), *Human Development.* Philadelphia: W. B. Saunders, 1966. With permission of the authors and the publishers.)

cerebral growth show a comparably rapid development. While adult norms of brain and cognitive functions are relatively static, those same measures in children change from month to month.

To understand the degree and quality of mental impairment associated with cerebral damage or dysfunction, it is essential to be able to compare the performance of normal subjects with that of brain-damaged subjects. One of the first researchers to draw attention to this need was Hebb (1942a), but his collections of normative data related only to brain-damaged adult patients (Hebb, 1942b; Hebb & Morton, 1943). By the late 1940s a few people were becoming interested in the neuropsychological problems of children, but these early investigators made only clinical studies and supplied no normative data. Probably the first person to do this was Benton (1959); he provided normative data on finger localization and right–left orientation on sizeable samples of children (approximately 40 at each year) aged 6 to 9 years inclusive. Another investigator at that time was Wake, who provided normative data for finger localization for children at each year from age 6 to 12, with group samples ranging from 52 to 126. His data can be found in Benton's book (1959, p. 69).

However, most books and studies of clinical neuropsychology included only adult subjects, and in 1959 Reitan produced the first summary of test signs of brain dysfunction in adults as measured by the Halstead battery (Reitan, 1959). Having done this, he then turned his attention to producing a comparable battery for children (Reitan, 1964a), which enabled him to examine in some detail the differences between children and adults. In 1974 he published what was up to that time probably the most comprehensive examination of child neuropsychological findings using the Halstead–Reitan battery (Reitan & Davison, 1974; 7 of the 12 chapters examine neuropsychological studies of children). These, and findings by other researchers, will be described in appropriate places throughout the book, but a few of these differences and similarities follow:

1. Because the human brain is near to adult size by age 9, and some cognitive skills are at or near adult levels of competence, "the attempt to compare the patterns . . . of older children with . . . neuropsychological studies of adults may very well be fruitful, but this does not seem to be the case with younger children" (Rourke & Gates, 1981). Reitan (1974a), Boll (1974), and our own experience support this. The transition between "younger" and "older" children appears to be about age 10 for many cognitive and behavioral skills. "For example, adult levels of auditory phonetic discrimination for nonsense syllables are reached by age 10, visual–manual reaction times do not improve significantly after age 11, and most basic language skills reach an adult level by age 13" (Gaddes, 1983). But the child of elementary school age is still increasing cognitive and behavioral skills by emerging from

a sensorimotor–concrete–operational pattern to a level of intellectual abstract conceptualizing at about a mental age of 11 (Piaget, 1952).

2. Unilateral brain damage or dysfunction will impair the contralateral sensory and motor functions similarly in adults and children of all ages (Reitan, 1974a).

3. However, lateralized brain lesions show some differences in their effects on cognitive abilities. Unilateral brain damage or dysfunction in adults will result in a pattern of left-hemisphere language impairment and right-hemisphere nonverbal impairment, but this relationship is not as clear in very young children and preadolescents. The reasons for this are not completely understood, but organic and psychological immaturity and the plastic adaptive qualities of the developing brain appear to be essentially involved.

Some early research, using behavioral criteria to select left- and right-hemisphere damaged child subjects (Reed & Reitan, 1969), and others using EEG selection techniques (Pennington, Galliani, & Voegele, 1965) failed to find the typical adult pattern, but most studies in the past 20 years of both normal and brain-dysfunctioning children have supported a cerebral asymmetry for cognitive functions and an asymmetrical deficit behavioral pattern related to it.

In the past, most selections of unilaterally damaged child patients had to be made on the basis of either behavioral or EEG signs, both of which methods will produce an unknown number of false positives. Where detailed neurosurgical information is available in young children the condition of exclusive unilateral dysfunction can be more firmly established, and the typical adult pattern of verbal impairment with left-hemisphere dysfunction and spatial–constructional deficit with right-hemisphere dysfunction can be observed in most cases. Such a case from our own files (Vera Brown, pages 299–301) of a 6-year-old child with left temporal surgery, showed an immediate problem with all verbal skills and a superior ability in the graphic arts. This split did not show itself in the VIQ–PIQ pattern as explained on page 300; but this case is a good example of how children may differ qualitatively from adults. Making inferences about brain function with children younger than about 10 years is much more difficult than with similarly injured adults, because there is "a far larger number of potentially interfering and confounding factors than . . . with adults" (Boll, 1974, pp. 91–92). No doubt, the new brain scanning techniques will provide more and better knowledge about the nature of functional asymmetry in the developing brain of the young child. It seems safe to accept that unilateral cerebral dysfunction in young children will be associated with a split or imbalance in verbal and spatial–constructional abilities similar to the adult pattern, but "cognitive functions, while becoming increasingly complex during development, may become increasingly tied to one or the other hemisphere'' (Rourke, Bakker, Fisk, & Strang, 1983, p. 59). More will be said about the development of cerebral asymmetry in Chapter 7.

Neuropsychological Tests

In a school system it is usual for the school psychologist or person responsible for selecting and administering diagnostic tests to assume responsibility for examining and evaluating the validity, reliability, and appropriateness of the tests to be used. This type of judgment depends on a theoretical knowledge of test construction and administration, and, normally, teachers and many educational administrators are not trained to this level of knowledge and must depend on the decisions of the school psychologist or chief psychometrician.

For this reason, those responsible for testing programs will need to know how neuropsychological test batteries have been validated. As well, teachers may be interested to read this section, although, because their areas of expertise and responsibility are principally pedagogical, they usually are not required to make responsible decisions pertaining to test selection.

A within-child model of diagnosis implies a systematic examination of a child's cognitive skills, psychological structures, social environment, and attitudes to and perceptions of that environment. Such a study can include casual social observation; controlled social observation; reports by parents, teachers, medical practitioners, speech pathologists, and other professionals; and batteries of psychological tests.

In this section the use of neuropsychological tests in educational diagnosis will be examined. The use of any types of psychological tests implies some basic rules:

1. The tests used should possess a reasonable measure of validity. That is, they must make a reasonable measure of what they claim to measure. The reader will discover that neuropsychological tests may have differing levels of efficiency depending on whether they are used to localize a brain lesion or to predict a learning disability. Measures of concurrent validity are usually higher than those used for prediction.

2. Tests should be reliable or show a high level of consistency in their measurement over time.

3. The battery should be appropriate. Many psychoeducational batteries are too limited. A common battery is a Wechsler (WISC-R), a Bender–

Gestalt, and maybe a draw-a-person or a Frostig test. Such a battery would take about 2 hours to administer, and this would seem to indicate a generous portion of the psychologist's time and a liberal amount of test findings. The school administrator, untrained in the problems of psychometrics, might misguidedly feel satisfied that his or her district was supplying an above-average caliber of diagnostic services. For the child with a minimal or moderate auditory imperception, however, such a battery as we have described would miss the crucial causal factor in his or her learning problem. Because the information from this battery is not likely to help the teacher solve the child's subtle auditory learning deficit, it is, in a sense, time and money "down the drain," and the school administrator should be aware of this. Unless the test battery is designed to tap all or most of the possible problem areas it will be inefficient and expensive. If it taps most of the problem areas it will be expensive and time consuming, but it will most likely produce some useful diagnostic knowledge. Competent neuropsychological assessment procedures are time consuming but useful; mediocre test services are usually worse than none at all, in that they usually produce little or nothing of worth and hence are a waste of money.

4. Some test batteries are redundant and hence too long. It is not difficult to find cases of children who, because of a persistent learning disability, have been tested and retested during their school experience. Frequently the child's file, which is usually thick, will contain several Wechsler tests done at different points in time and 10 or 12 educational achievement tests. There may be five or six in reading and several in arithmetic and spelling. A resumé of all these findings may produce very little information other than that the child is of average intelligence and cannot read, write, or do arithmetic very well. The teacher already knows this, but because of the redundancy and narrowness of the tests, little of use emerges from this expensive exercise. Again, the school administrator should be aware of this.

5. In our view, a neuropsychological test battery provides a more thorough and more systematic examination of a child's perceptual, cognitive, and motor abilities, and with its use there is less chance of missing the causal factor or factors of the child's learning problems.

Reitan validated his tests empirically during the 1950s (Reitan, 1955b, 1958, 1959), and in a series of original experiments (Reitan, 1964b) he showed that, when supplied with 112 adult patients with five different categories of medically known brain damage [(1) left frontal lesion, (2) left posterior, (3) right frontal, (4) right posterior, and (5) diffuse brain damage], he could localize the damage correctly in 88 cases (78.6%), and very closely in another 15 cases (making a total of 92%). When asked to test 100 patients in which 50 were medically diagnosed as brain damaged and

50 were normal, Reitan independently picked 96% of the brain-damaged patients correctly. All of these studies were blind; that is, they took place without prior knowledge of the medical diagnosis. In these experiments Reitan showed that his test battery had a high level of empirical validity in detecting cerebral dysfunctions.

In the next 10 years, from 1960 to 1970, this method of neuropsychological identification of brain dysfunctions became more refined and in wider use (Reitan, 1966b) and it is now becoming known in educational circles (Hynd & Obrzut, 1981; Rourke, Bakker, Fisk, & Strang, 1983). Some writers in the area of learning disabilities have claimed that no valid psychological tests yet exist to detect either brain dysfunctions or learning disabilities (Coles, 1978), but such writers must be unaware of the 30-year-old work of Reitan and many other research neuropsychologists (A. Smith, 1975; Teuber, 1964; Teuber, Battersby, & Bender, 1960) or they fail to relate it to the diagnostic problems facing the special educator.

Drawing maximally on Reitan's work, Russell, Neuringer, and Goldstein (1970) have outlined in detail a "key" approach for describing the localization, type of lesion, and degree of lateralization of brain dysfunctions. A Smith (1975) has developed his own test battery for a study of the nature of the mental impairment rather than an emphasis on lesion localization.

To summarize, the neurologist and/or neurosurgeon can gain medical knowledge of the locus of a brain lesion by using radiological and other techniques and sometimes by direct observation during brain surgery. The neuropsychologist may predict the locus of the brain lesion by observing the pattern of cognitive and behavioral deficits as shown on a battery of neuropsychological tests and, by correlating these findings with the medical data, can recognize certain reliable brain–behavior relationships. Clinical psychologists, wishing to acquire this diagnostic skill, may find it best to learn the principles of neuropsychological assessment with adults first (Lezak, 1976/1983; Reitan, 1959; Reitan & Davison, 1974; Russell, Neuringer, & Goldstein, 1970). Once having learned this procedure thoroughly, they are better prepared to approach the more complex assessment demands of children (Hartlage & Hartlage, 1977; Hynd & Obrzut, 1981; Reitan & Davison, 1974; Rourke, 1975, 1978b, 1981; Rourke, Bakker, Fisk, & Strang, 1983).

Once a body of principles (i.e., reliable human brain structure–function relationships validated empirically) has been established, then neurological inferences may be made with the neuropsychological test data alone. For years, neurologists have been localizing brain lesions prior to brain surgery on the basis of behavioral data. For example, the location of visual field defects (right or left, half fields, quarter fields, etc.) can tell the neurosurgeon prior to surgery where, in the optic nerves or tracts or occipital lobes, a brain lesion is most likely to be found and where he or she should explore (Manter & Gatz, 1961, p. 85). Because most patients with brain dysfunctions never come to surgery, the major part of diagnostic work by neurologists employs this method.

Since most learning disabled children with cerebral dysfunctions also never come to surgery, it soon became evident to clinical neuropsychologists that this would be an invaluable diagnostic method for a better understanding of the possible causal patterns of their learning problems. Reitan, as we have shown, in the early 1960s began to recommend this method to educators (Reitan, 1966a) and many of his students have incorporated it into their learning theories (Doehring, 1968) and promoted its use in special education (Gaddes, 1966b, 1968, 1969a, 1975, 1978a; Knights, 1970, 1973; Rourke, 1975, 1981). The research of Satz and many other neuropsychologists has shown that sensorimotor and perceptual deficits, as measured by neuropsychological tests, are closely correlated with academic learning disabilities (Matthews & Folk, 1964; Matthews & Kløve, 1967), and that in young children they are reliable predictors of future learning disabilities (de Hirsch, Jansky, & Langford, 1966; Eaves, Kendall, & Crichton, 1972; Satz, Taylor, Friel, & Fletcher, 1978; Spreen, 1978).

The locus of lesion (left or right, frontal or posterior), whether it is focal or diffuse, whether, if it is a tumor, or it is intrinsic (i.e., within the brain tissue) or extrinsic (sitting on the cortex), whether it is progressive (e.g., a tumor) or is subsiding (e.g., aftereffects of a stroke or hemorrhage), all of these qualities will affect cognitive functioning differently. To relate these variables with any degree of reliability requires several years of training in neuropsychological assessment. If the school psychologist without this level of competence, or the educator or speech pathologist or other professional person, uses neuropsychological tests for screening learning disabled children, this is a justifiable procedure, but it should not be described as "neuropsychological screening," and any reference to brain dysfunctions should be carefully avoided. It only becomes a neuropsychological assessment in a primary sense when it is related to empirically derived medical data or draws on the tested clinical experience of a highly trained clinical neuropsychologist. If educators and others will be careful in their use of these test techniques they will avoid the devastating and logical criticisms of the misuse of tests (Coles, 1978).

Arthur L. Benton, at the Medical School, University of Iowa, and Otfried Spreen, of the University of Victoria, have developed an interesting battery of tests to tap various neurosensory functions. In addition, Spreen and Benton have produced a detailed Aphasia Screening Test that has already been translated and standardized in a number of foreign languages, and normative data are available for children (Gaddes & Crockett, 1975) and for adults (Spreen & Benton, 1969/1977). No attempt will be made here to recognize all the researchers producing neuropsychological test batteries, but the following list may be useful: Ayres (1972a), Bannatyne (1971, Chap. 14), Benton (1962a, 1963b, 1967, 169a, b, c, 1972),

Kløve (1963), Knights (1971, 1973), Reitan (1955b, 1956, 1959), Reitan & Davison (1974), Rourke, Bakker, Fisk, & Strang (1983), A. Smith (1975), Spreen (1969), and Spreen and Benton (1969/1977). The work in our own laboratory draws heavily on the Halstead–Reitan and Spreen–Benton batteries (see Appendix A).

Cerebral Laterality and Behavior

As already explained, the brain is divided by the longitudinal fissure into the left and right hemispheres, and although these two halves appear histologically almost similar, or as "mirror mates," they are dominant for different types of behavior (particularly intellectual and cognitive behaviors) and equipotential, although contralateral, for most sensory and motor functions. A simple example of differential lateral control is the dominance of the left hemisphere for language in most people (even most left handers) and the dominance of the right hemisphere for visual–spatial perception. An adult with a left-hemisphere lesion will usually obtain significantly lower scores on the Wechsler verbal tests than on the performance tests; a subject with a right-hemisphere lesion will usually show the reverse pattern, with lower performance scores (Reitan, 1955a). B. Milner (1968), a neuropsychologist at the Montreal Neurological Institute, demonstrated this laterality effect with an interesting study, in which she showed that patients with left temporal lobe lesions manifested demonstrable impairment of verbal memory but performed normally in remembering and recognizing faces in a delayed matching task. The right temporal lesion patients, by contrast, had great difficulty in remembering the same set of faces in a collection of photographs, although they showed no impairment on tests of verbal recognition and recall. Fedio and Mirsky (1969) showed the same laterality pattern with children aged 6 to 14, with unilateral epileptiform discharges localized in the left or right temporal lobe.

In the classroom a left-hemisphere lesion is more likely to impair performance in language, reading, writing, and verbal conceptualizing. By contrast, a right-hemisphere dysfunction is more likely to affect academic subjects drawing on spatial imagery, such as arithmetic, art, geometry, map reading, drafting, industrial arts, and sewing. While a teacher will not use this type of evidence to localize a cerebral lesion (the neurologist will attempt that), if he or she is supplied with the knowledge of the locus and intensity of the lesion, the teacher can make sounder predictions about the child's potential ability and, with experience, may develop a more effective remedial program.

This recent neuropsychological insight of laterality of cerebral function and specific behavioral dominance has grown out of many researches, but one of the most interesting and definitive techniques used to examine this problem is the Wada Amytal Test. In the late 1940s, Dr. Juhn Wada, a research neurosurgeon, during studies on epileptic seizure mechanisms, injected sodium amytal and metrazol into the carotid arteries of human subjects. The left carotid artery runs up the left side of the neck and supplies blood to the left cerebral hemisphere; the right internal carotid artery does the same for the right hemisphere. Wada discovered that if the patient's left carotid artery was injected with amytal the subject usually became aphasic within a few seconds as a result of the effects of the drug in the cerebral blood stream. For several minutes, while the inhibiting effects of the drug were affecting the left cortical hemisphere, such patients, if they were completely left-hemisphere dominant for speech, were unable to speak, to understand what was said to them, to read, or to write. The patients might, however, be able to carry out nonverbal tests with cartoons successfully. Following right carotid amytal injection most patients may retain their speech and language functions but lose their visual–spatial perceptual competence temporarily (B. Milner, 1966). Because the mental impairment is short lived, usually about 3 or 4 minutes, if there were no risk of organic damage, this technique might provide a possible avenue for studying academic performances dominantly controlled by one or the other cerebral hemisphere and specific memory functions.

In other studies, B. Milner (1966) has carried out research with Wada's test to investigate short-term memory effects, temporary dysphasia, temporary facial agnosia, and retrograde amnesia, but so far this research technique has not been directed at classroom learning problems, except indirectly.

Visual–perceptual functions show a cortical laterality, and so do auditory functions. The dichotic listening technique was introduced by Broadbent in England in 1954, and includes the simultaneous stimulation of both ears with different auditory messages. When the stimuli are verbal and balanced for initial consonant and equal length (e.g., "six" and "sin"), it is interesting that most people hear the word fed into the right ear, and tend to suppress the word stimulating the left ear. Kimura (1961a, b) was the first to relate the technique to cerebral asymmetry of function. Prior to this, Broadbent had thought that the functional imbalance was caused by a successive perceptual activity of the two ears. Kimura concluded from her study that both temporal lobes were essential to perception of verbal material, but that the left temporal lobe was more important. Because it is known that the auditory pathways from each ear are physically more strongly represented in the contralateral temporal lobe, Kimura reasoned that right ear perceptual preferences occurred in most dichotically stimulated subjects because the left hemisphere is dominant for speech in most people. Although dichotic listening is not directly useful to the teacher of the child with a learning disorder, it has real value for the clinical psychologist in providing information regarding the hemispheric asymmetry and possible language dominance of the child. The clinician may need to supply this information to the neurosurgeon who is considering the possibility of removing temporal lobe epileptogenic foci; even when surgery is not considered, it may provide useful evidence regarding the cerebral dominance of a child who reverses letters in spelling or digits in compound numbers.

The research of the 1950s discovered the basic pattern of cerebral functional laterality as has been described above (Reitan, 1959), but at that time, and throughout the 1960s, it was believed by most to be a stable and fixed phenomenon. By the end of the 1960s it was concluded by most neuropsychologists that verbal stimuli in most cases were processed by the left hemisphere and pictorial or nonverbal stimuli by the right. Dozens of experiments in the visual, auditory, and tactile fields were reported, using a tachistoscopic half-field technique, dichotic listening, and stereognostic procedures (Bryden, 1960a, b, 1963; J. Davis & Reitan, 1966; Kimura, 1964, 1966, 1967; Kløve, 1959), and laterality studies became a major preoccupation with numerous neuropsychologists.

During the 1960s there had been occasional reports of contradictory findings but these were not satisfactorily explained because they were not clearly understood at that time. With the 1970s came findings that revealed that lateral function was not rigidly tied to verbal and nonverbal processing, but that the brain reacted dynamically in terms of age (Bakker, Teunissen, & Bosch, 1976), sex (Buffery, 1976), stimulus complexity (Umilta, Bagnara, & Simion, 1978), and stimulus modality (A. E. Davis & Wada, 1977). These ideas are discussed at more length in Chapter 7.

Frontal Lobes

Cortically the frontal lobes include the brain tissue anterior to the fissure of Rolando and above the front parts of the temporal lobes. Below the outer layers of the cortex is the white neural tissue, which provides hundreds of thousands of interconnections to various areas of the opposite cerebral hemisphere (contralateral) and to various areas of the same hemisphere (ipsilateral). These numerous connections are believed to permit the variability and flexibility characteristic of rapid mental calculation, active imagination, and abstract conceptualizing.

The limbic system is located underneath and on the inside surfaces (the mesial surfaces) of the frontal and temporal lobes. This is a complex network of brain structures (cingulate gyrus, hippocampus, amygdala, uncus, etc.) concerned with self-preservation (feeding behavior) and race preservation (sexual behavior; MacLean, 1959). The intellectual functions that may be determined by this subcortical system, at least in part, are only just coming to be recognized. Many years ago, Jacobsen (1935) found that monkeys suffered impaired memory in delayed response tasks when both of their frontal lobes were surgically removed. B. Milner (1954) attributed short-term memory deficit to lesions of the hippocampi, and Kimble and Pribram (1963) related it to control of serial order behavior. The whole matter of sequential behavior is one that the teacher should consider carefully. When it is normal, the child may speak fluently, spell correctly, and read and write smoothly. When it is not, the child may stammer, stutter, or mix the order of words in a sentence and may have great difficulty with spelling, reading, and writing. Many children with frontal lobe dysrhythmias have these learning problems, and when this occurs special remedial measures are necessary. More is said about this in Chapter 5.

The cortical motor strip, immediately anterior to the fissure of Rolando, is functionally the only clearly defined part of the frontal lobes. The left motor strip controls the voluntary muscular action of the right side of the body and vice versa. Figure 3.9 illustrates the motor speech area (Broca's area) and the left motor strip. A severe lesion in Broca's area may produce mutism, and a mild electrical dysrhythmia may result in an articulation problem (dysarthria). If the child is right handed and has a mild dysrhythmia in the manual area of the left motor strip, he or she may have trouble writing and drawing because of a resulting manual clumsiness. Sometimes this type of interference in a child's learning is confused with mental dullness, when, in actual fact, his or her intellectual potential may be normal or above average. Muscularly awkward children may be mentally bright but impaired in classroom learning because so much of it requires motor-expressive activities. The teacher should try to decide whether the child's dysfunction is maximally sensory (input), intellectual (integration), or motor (output), or a fairly evenly distributed combination of two or three of these. If the dysfunction is in one motor strip, it is almost certain to show itself in motor impairment on the contralateral side of the body.

If, however, the lesion or dysfunction is in the frontal cortices anterior to the motor strips, it is more difficult to identify the behavioral effects related to these areas. In the past, there has been a common belief that the frontal lobes are the seat of our highest intellectual processes, but neuropsychological research within the past 20 years has shown ambiguous results on this point. Whereas Halstead's research (1947; Shure & Halstead, 1958) has supported the hypothesis that the capacity for abstract thought is mediated more by the frontal cortices, Teuber's (1959, 1964) research throws real doubt on this and suggests that the "belief in the crucial dependence of higher intellectual functions on the integrity of the frontal lobes may have historical rather than logical reasons" (Teuber, 1959). As was explained earlier, Luria hypothesized that the fontal lobes, particularly the left prefrontal areas, enabled humans to plan and carry out their intentions, although some clinical research with localized lesion cases (left frontal, right frontal, left nonfrontal, and right nonfrontal) has failed to support his contention (Drewe, 1975). It is more generally agreed that bilateral frontal damage results in a reduced ability to plan and follow through, as well as deficits in "recent memory," weakened ability for mental abstraction, personality alterations, diminished concern for the future, impulsiveness, mild euphoria, and lack of initiative and spontaneity (Benton, 1968). In his own research Benton found verbal fluency impaired most by left frontal damage, as did B. Milner (1964), but verbal learning, which was severely affected by bilateral frontal damage, showed very little effects from unilateral frontal lesions. Spatial imagery was more impaired by right frontal damage than by either left or bilateral frontal damage. Temporal orientation was not affected by unilateral frontal damage but was impaired by bilateral damage. This pattern was largely similar for explaining proverbs. This evidence suggests that bilateral frontal damage can be seriously impairing emotionally, but that effects are much reduced for intellectual skills, especially if the damage is one sided. It seems likely that the post-Rolandic areas of the brain are more vitally concerned with the sensory processes in verbal learning and academic skills.

In fact, individual cases have been reported in which patients with bilateral frontal damage have performed almost normally. Historically one of the most celebrated was the case of Phineas P. Gage, a young Vermont railwayworker, who in 1848 suffered a bilateral frontal lobe injury in a blasting accident. A pointed crow bar, flung by the concussion, entered the left side of his face, passed through and upward, and emerged from the top of his head slightly to the right of the median line. On recovering from his head injury, he traveled with a road show and earned a good living for himself and his manager, although he suffered an explosive temper and other marked personality changes (Coleman, 1956).

Teuber (1959) has reported the case of a man with a bilateral frontal pistol wound who "attacked one of the classical tests of concept formation [a modified Weigl card sorting test] with immediate and correct analysis of the three principles (color, form and number) built into the test." In our own research we have studied a man of bright mind and superior administrative abilities who suffered damage to his right frontal lobe. For several years he was a successful personnel manager in an industrial firm employing 2000 workers. Unfortunately, at the age of 52 he developed a large benign tumor in his right frontal lobe that had to be removed surgically. Although he still measured a verbal IQ of 136 on the Wechsler Adult

Intelligence Scale and talked fluently about all topics to do with his work, it was necessary for the management to retire him because of a loss of the ability for subtle judgment, and for the understanding of fine nuances of meaning in evaluating and handling social group situations. Shure and Halstead (1958) concluded from their studies that whereas the frontal lobes contribute most to mental abstraction, all cortical lobes are involved. No doubt the right frontal damage that this man suffered was just enough to "take the edge off" his formerly very sharp mind.

B. Milner (1963) reported an interesting study which suggests that the dorsolateral parts of the frontal lobes are more important than other cortical areas to abstract tasks requiring mental flexibility and rapid *shift* to a new conceptual principle. Lesions in this area were more devastating to this task than those in any other cortical lobe or even the orbitofrontal (the parts of the frontal lobes at the extreme forward part of the brain and the undersides immediately above and behind the eyes) and temporal lobes together.

The evidence from the above research suggests that the frontal lobes are not necessarily the locus of our highest intellectual functions, but they may be concerned with mental abstraction and flexibility of mental adaptation to new principles, visual scanning of complex pictures or objects (Karpov, Luria, & Yarbuss, 1968), visual–postural tasks (Teuber, 1959; Teuber & Mishkin, 1954), social judgement, emotional control, planning, and motivation. Their damage seems to reduce the overall level of abstraction but not enough to make any difference necessarily to IQs measured on a group test (Weinstein & Teuber, 1957).

Occipital Lobes

In the posterior part of the brain are the occipital lobes (see Fig. 3.2), which are the cortical centers for visual experience. Area 17 in each occipital lobe is the primary visual sensory center, but the cortical areas immediately anterior to this are believed to be the visual association centers that provide "meaning" to what one sees. However, before discussing the evident relationship between the cerebral optic mechanisms and visual experience, it will be well to study the design of the cerebral optic mechanisms.

Figure 3.7 shows that the left occipital lobe is connected, by a circuitous route, to the left side of each retina. Similarly, the right occipital lobe is connected to the right side of each retina, and by this design the connections from the eyes contradict the usual contralateral connections of the sensory and motor tracts. That is to say, both eyes are connected to both occipital lobes; the usual contralateral design between hemisphere and the body does not hold. Light waves entering the eye stimulate a photochemical reaction in the retinal cells, the rods and cones. This process triggers neural impulses that travel along the optic nerves to the optic chiasma, which is located just in front of the pituitary gland. Here there is a partial decussation or crossing over of the nerve fibers so that fibers from only the nasal side of each retina cross to the other side. From the optic chiasma this new organization of nerve fibers travels to the lateral geniculate body, a sort of "junction box" in the thalamus. Here the optic fibers sweep forward and downward and then loop back along the outside area of the temporal lobes (the optic radiation) to the linings of the calcarine fissure, a part of the longitudinal fissure in the occipital lobes. It seems likely that the broad distribution of the optic pathways through every cerebral lobe is related to the sensitivity of many visual tasks to damage in any area (e.g., a figure–ground test; Teuber and Weinstein, 1956; Cruikshank, Bice, Wallen, & Lynch, 1957). The student wishing a more detailed description of the structure and function of the visual mechanisms may see other sources (Gardner, 1968/1975; Gregory, 1966; Manter & Gatz, 1961, p. 84; Netter, 1962, p. 63).

Although the visual pathways are clearly defined and microelectrode studies in the occipital cortices are beginning to reveal a good deal about the point-to-point stimulation from retinae to visual cortex, overall cerebral function is just beginning to reveal itself in neuropsychological research.

The laterality effect of the right hemisphere, possibly the right temporal lobe, in visual–spatial perception has already been mentioned. Kløve and Reitan (1958) studied 36 adult patients who were unable to copy a Greek cross without distorting the spatial configuration (see Fig. 4.2). Their results showed that the patients who had difficulty copying the Greek cross also did poorly on the performance tests of the Wechsler–Bellevue scale, tests that also demand visual–spatial–manual skills. Dysphasic patients did poorly on the Wechsler verbal tests, and a third group of patients with both difficulties had low scores on both parts of the Wechsler. The consistent inferiority of right-hemisphere lesion cases in

Figure 4.2. Attempts by three patients to copy the Greek cross (shown at left) in which the spatial configuration was distorted. (From Kløve & Reitan, *American Medical Association Archives of Neurobiology and Psychiatry*, 1958, *80*, 708–713. With permission of the authors and publishers.)

visual–spatial tasks (Benton, 1963b; Kløve, 1959; Reitan, 1955a) implies that the occipital lobes have a stronger functional relationship with the right side of the brain in most subjects, especially the parietal and temporal lobes, when a person is looking at nonverbal stimuli such as a map, studying a mechanical diagram, viewing a blueprint of a house plan, doing geometry, and attempting routine arithmetical calculations. The last-named task possesses a strong visual–spatial component; it requires one to write digits vertically in order to add; to write digits in a particular horizontal and vertical relationship in order to subtract, multiply, and divide; and to scan horizontally left and right from a decimal point. These procedures may be relatively simple for a child or adult with a healthy brain and a high IQ, but they may be difficult or almost impossible for the bright youngster with a right-hemisphere lesion.

An example should make this clear. A 17-year-old boy, whom we have followed for the past 14 years, suffered, during birth, damage to the middle part of his right hemisphere. As a result he has always had a mild weakness of the left hand and foot. In addition, the permanent damage to the right temporal lobe is so severe that it evidently impairs his visual–spatial perception so that he cannot copy a simple Greek cross. Art work has always been painful for him, although because his left hemisphere is both intact and superior, he has always done well in reading, social studies, science, and language and verbal arts. Algebra has not caused him too much trouble, but geometry, because it is spatial, has been impossible. This boy, when first seen, was counseled away from spatial activities and toward verbal ones. As a result, he completed high school, took a typing course, and is successfully employed as a clerical worker in a government office. His initial Wechsler IQs were performance, 69 and verbal, 110. Over the years these measures have shown a marked stability, and as a young man in his late 20s, he still is unable to recognize or interpret geometric figures.

This and many other cases suggest that our traditional school system, with its emphasis on reading and language skills, favors the child with a superior left hemisphere. A poor right hemisphere, as in the above case, may be a frustration, but it may not be a major academic handicap.

In Chapter 3 reference was made to Benton's (1963b, p. 5ff) categories of visual–perceptual errors common in a task of visual memory. Because it is important that clinical psychologists and teachers be aware of these, a brief description of them follows.

Omissions and Additions. When a person studies a geometric pattern for 10 seconds and then attempts to draw it from memory, he or she may omit one of the figures or part of one. Patients who have shown this difficulty have frequently had posterior cerebral dysrhythmias, suggesting that certain registration centers in the occipital and parietal lobes or some part of the optic mechanisms may be dysfunctioning or structurally lacking. In such a case it is possible that certain parts of the design are never accurately perceived and that the pattern finally reaching the occipital cortices has certain gaps, blind spots, or scotoma. Damage to the primary visual cortex may produce the same results. Obviously, the child can only remember what is impressed on his or her visual cortex and, if this lacks parts of the original pattern, reproduction will be inaccurate. The neurologist describes the process of memory as "neural storage." If the brain is healthy and whole it is well equipped to store a memory accurately with its transient electrical phase sequence and protein changes in the neural cell bodies; but if it is damaged or dysfunctioning these electrochemical processes are less efficient.

Visual scanning may be difficult either peripherally (ocular muscle weakness) or centrally with a frontal lobe lesion (Karpov, Luria, & Yarbuss, 1968). Efficient scanning is necessary for accurate perception, memory, and reproduction, and if the clinical psychologist detects this trouble he or she should help the teacher devise suitable remedial measures to assist the child.

A child with defective perception and memory who is trying hard to succeed and hence overcompensates may add details that were not present in the original stimulus.

Distortions. A figure may be reproduced inaccurately by simple substitution (e.g., of a pentagon for a hexagon). Again this may result from dysfunction of the posterior part of the brain (usually some part of the parieto-temporo-occipital area) or the frontal lobes. As usual, there is a greater incidence of right-hemisphere lesions. When the cerebral dysfunction is disruptive enough, the child cannot copy the simple figure, even though he or she is given unlimited time (see Fig. 4.3).

Perseverations. K. Goldstein (1939, 1942), in his study of head-injured veterans of World War I, described their tendencies of mental rigidity and perseveration. This may result from the patient's simplified perception and memory and increased stereotypy of response because of his impaired cortex.

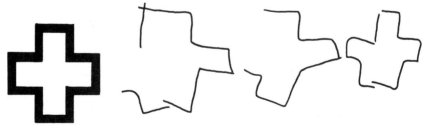

Figure 4.3. Three attempts to copy the Greek cross at the left by a 17-year-old boy with a congenital right-hemisphere medial lesion. Note the difficulty with the left side of the figure and the lack of continuity of lines.

Rotations. The fact that a subject will view a design and reproduce it in a rotated position is intriguing but so far inexplicable. For example, on the Benton test, where one is required to draw from memory a geometric design after viewing it for 10 seconds, a subject may draw the design accurately except that it is rotated to the right or left 45°, 90°, or 180°. Occasionally rotations of less than 45° may occur, and this can happen with either memory reproductions or copying.

One of the most interesting cases of this in our own laboratory was a 15-year-old girl who suffered a cerebral hemorrhage in the deep tissues of the right occipital lobe. A neurosurgeon evacuated the large blood clot (intracerebral hematoma) with a small incision in the posterior part of the right parietal lobe. He was careful not to cut tissue in the occipital cortex because this might have resulted in "central blindness," showing itself in a dysfunction of the right halves of the two retinae, and a resulting left visual field reduction or some degree of blindness. Surgery was carried out in early January 1965 but within a week another craniotomy was necessary to clean out the same right occipital–parietal area. This second treatment was successful and 4 weeks later the girl was ready for testing. A large and detailed battery of tests was carried out, among which was the Benton Visual Retention Test. She was able to remember the general shape and detail of 8 of the 10 diagrams, but there was a consistent tendency to rotate her drawings about 30° clockwise. This rotational tendency necessitated scoring those patterns as mistakes. This gave her a correct score of 4 out of 10 with 6 rotations. Six weeks later she was tested again and the rotational responses had disappeared and her correct score was now 6.

Three years later she developed seizures from complications following her brain surgery and, when tested on the Benton Visual Retention Test, she now had a correct score of 7, but two rotations had reappeared. On Benton's Embedded Figures Test, on the first testing a month after her surgery she showed great difficulty keeping her pencil on the dotted lines. She tended to draw her line to the right of the actual dotted line she meant to copy. This also seemed somewhat similar to her rotational tendency in a clockwise direction on the Benton Visual Retention Test, and with the normal rehabilitation of her brain following surgery this visual–motor impairment disappeared within 6 weeks on both tests.

This case provides evidence that is particularly interesting in the consideration of visual rotational responses. Why did this girl rotate the diagrams when tested soon after her surgically imposed brain damage? Also, why did she consistently rotate the figures to the right and outline figures with the pencil to the right of the dotted lines she was attempting to copy? Why had this visual–motor impairment disappeared on the next testing, which was 9 weeks after the second craniotomy?

Hypothetical answers can be proposed that may help the clinical psychologist and the special teacher to consider this problem more fully. It is possible that in this case, since the right occipital lobe was not functioning normally and this resulted in a reduced left visual field, there may have been an unconscious attempt to compensate for this imbalance and the girl distorted her perceptions so that the left side of the figures seemed, in retrospect, to be higher. Likewise, since the left occipital lobe was normal and operating with greater energy than the right, possibly the incoming images actually were tilted slightly to the right. Regardless of the cause, it is interesting to know that within 6 weeks her brain rehabilitated itself well enough to return her perception of horizontal to normality. When the seizure problem developed later with an epileptogenic focus in the right temporal lobe, the rotational tendency returned, but not seriously.

Visual rotations can also appear in an adult following a penetrating head injury. A man referred for neuropsychological evaluation had suf-fered a very severe head injury in which the left side of his skull was crushed. The frontal, temporal, and parietal lobes on the left side were all damaged, with the greatest injury in the left frontal lobe and temporal pole. A right temporal–parietal burr hole was made, indicating that there may have been some damage from pressure on the right side of the brain. On the Wechsler Block Design Test, which requires the subject to build a mosaic design while looking at the pattern, he rotated pattern 3, 90°, pattern 6, 180°, and pattern 10, 45°. All rotations were clockwise.

If a child is having difficulty with reading, map drawing, arithmetic, geometry, or any other spatial academic task, the possibility of visual rotation should be checked. The clinical psychologist may use a matching test, a copying test (e.g., Bender–Gestalt, Benton, Graham–Kendall), a visual retention test (Benton), the Block Design Test on the Wechsler, or any other suitable test in his or her repertoire. The teacher may notice the tendency in the child's art work, printing, or writing of numbers, and if it appears serious, the child should be referred for neurological and psycho-logical evaluation.

Visual Scanning. It must be remembered that visual perception proba-bly never depends exclusively on the occipital cortices but includes a transcortically integrated function of these areas and other parts of the cerebral cortex and brainstem. A common neurological view, as already described, considers the occipital lobes (Area 17) as centers of visual sensation, but the parietal cortices bordering Area 17 as necessary to visual understanding and meaning. A study of a patient with a right pa-rieto-occipital lesion (Karpov, Luria, & Yarbuss, 1968) showed that he still possessed normal active searching movements, but he lacked ability to synthesize what he saw. When presented with a detailed picture, Re-pin's "Unexpected Return," depicting the return of a prisoner to his family after many years of imprisonment, the patient, although previously familiar with this picture, which is famous in Russia, was unable to relate the parts. He commented: "This is a rather well known picture but I don't remember it. I don't remember its contents, as though I never paid attention to it before . . . I think a father is returning home to his family after being away . . . his children are sitting . . . he himself . . . the woman, probably the mother . . . on the wall there are pictures, icons. . . ." From this patient's report it can be seen that he was able to perceive individual objects but was unable to integrate these meaningfully. This is a sort of partial visual agnosia, and the patient was helped when the clinician asked specific questions, such as "How old is each person? How is he dressed?"

This case has relevance for the psychologist since some understanding of the more severe pathological cases, such as the one just described, will help the clinical or school psychologist to a better diagnostic evaluation and the special teacher to a better remedial plan. The special teacher will rarely have a student with severe neuropathology, but children with minimal occipito-parietal dysrhythmias occur in some classrooms. Such children may have difficulty in producing meaningful stories about pictures, although the sensitive psychologist would need to experiment to discover whether this reflected a visual perceptive or linguistic deficit. Remedial measures with these children can include practice in looking at discrete objects, then two objects together with helpful questions from the teacher, cross-modal reinforcement with visual–tactile and visual–auditory associations, and finally increased multiple stimuli.

Temporal Lobes

The lateral cortical surfaces of the temporal lobes, as can be seen in Fig. 3.2, include the lateral surfaces of the cerebrum below the level of the fissure of Sylvius. The posterior boundaries, both between the parietal and between the occipital lobes, are arbitrary and are based on a localization of special functions. The surfaces are roughly similar in location to the ear protectors in a football helmet. A comparative neurological study of subprimates and primates, including humans, reveals that the temporal lobes do not occur in subprimates. The fissure of Sylvius, and its inner vertical surface (the temporal operculum), is just beginning to appear in small animals, such as the shrew and marmoset; it is more invaginated in monkeys; and is most deeply developed and differentiated in humans (Sanides, 1975).

On the undersurfaces of the temporal lobes, the inside or mesial surface next to the brainstem, are a number of different structures, known collectively as the *limbic system*. These include the hippocampus, amygdala, and uncus, which in humans have functions that are just beginning

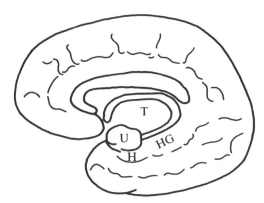

Figure 4.4. A simplified medial view of the human brain showing the location of the uncus (U), hippocampus (H), hippocampal gyrus (HG), and thalamus (T).

to be understood (see Fig. 4.4). In fact, B. Milner (1954) reported that until her study of the functions of the temporal lobes in humans, completed in 1952, there were no such studies in the scientific literature. Whereas temporal function in subhuman animals had been studied, humans had been neglected.

The chief perceptual function of the temporal lobes is hearing. The acoustic areas of the auditory cortices are in Heschl's gyrus, or the superior temporal gyrus on the floor of the fissure of Sylvius. Connections from each ear go to both auditory cortices (see Fig. 3.8) so that unilateral temporal lobe damage does not cause deafness in either ear, and normal function of both ears provides the subject with cues for auditory localization. Because hearing is essential to the normal development of speech and because in most subjects the left hemisphere is dominant for language, normal temporal lobe function and left-hemisphere action are necessary for a child's learning to speak, read, and write normally. When the left hemisphere is damaged or dysfunctions, there may be impairment in the child's language development (aphasia), and when there is inferior temporal lobe function on one or both sides, he or she may suffer from some degree of auditory imperception or agnosia. Such disorders are often confused with mental retardation by the inexperienced clinical psychologist or special teacher. Aphasia is discussed at greater length in Chapter 8.

B. Milner (1967) has reported an interesting study in which 38 patients with temporal lobe lesions were given the Seashore Measures of Musical Talents. In all 38 patients the left hemisphere was dominant for speech; 22 had left-side lesions, and 16 right. The Seashore test includes six subtest measures of pitch, loudness, rhythm, time, timbre, and tonal memory (Seashore, Lewis, & Saetveit, 1960). The fact that the right hemisphere is more involved in the perception of nonverbal material (Kimura, 1964; Spellacy, 1969) was supported by the fact that the left-hemisphere lesion cases showed no change preoperatively and postoperatively for such stimuli when sections of the left temporal lobe were surgically excised. All pre- and postoperative changes occurred only in the right-hemisphere lesion cases and the most marked impairment was in the perception of timbre changes and the memory of sequential tonal patterns. Subsequent research suggests that this may result because the right hemisphere is specialized for the analysis of harmonic information (i.e., the number and complexity of overtones) rather than a general ability for the perception of music (Sidtis, 1980). As well, hemispheric specialization should not be considered as an immutable single dominant function; by increasing the complexity of the stimulus and the strategies of the perceiver, it is possible to produce a right ear advantage for tones and a left ear advantage for words on the first trials, but with continued trials, the expected ear advantages will emerge (Sidtis & Bryden, 1978). Because each ear is physically represented more strongly on the opposite side of the brain than on the same side, and a sound delivered to one ear alone excites more neural activity on the opposite side than in the same side (Rosenzweig, 1961), the right ear, in most children, is slightly more sensitive to verbal material and the left ear to nonverbal material (Kimura, 1964; Spellacy, 1969), as has already been noted in the discussion of cerebral laterality effects.

Although both temporal lobes are involved in auditory perception, the left one is more concerned with verbal learning and the right with storage of nonverbal information regardless of the modality of presentation. Left temporal lesion cases have been found to be relatively poorer in verbal associative learning (Meyer & Yates, 1955) and for story recall (B. Milner, 1958). By contrast, right temporal lesion cases have shown disturbances in pictorial comprehension (B. Milner, 1958).

B. Milner (1958) has also found that left temporal lobe lesions affect verbal memory whereas right temporal lesions affect memory for nonverbal material.

Information regarding the relation of memory and temporal lobe function has come largely from four research methods: (1) autopsy studies of patients who, in their final months or years, have developed serious memory deficits; (2) observations of memory loss after surgical removal of various parts of the cerebral cortex; (3) electrical stimulation of the human cortex in conscious patients during brain surgery; and (4) the use of the Wada amytal technique (mentioned earlier in this chapter) to produce temporary amnesia in conscious patients. Milner has drawn attention to the fact that Bekhterev, the famous Russian physiologist and contemporary of Pavlov, was the first to suggest (in 1899) "that the mesial parts of the temporal lobes might play a critical role in human memory processes" (B. Milner, 1966). He examined the brain following autopsy of a patient whose most striking behavioral abnormality had been a severe memory impairment. The brain cutting revealed a bilateral softening or deterioration of cerebral tissue in the region of the uncus, the hippocampus, and the adjacent mesial structure of the temporal lobes. Milner, in the same publication, lists a number of clinical studies in which hippocampal damage and memory disorder appear to be related. Most of these studies, however, have included some form of infection (encephalitis) and the resulting tissue damage has been diffuse and poorly defined. While such studies are valuable in providing gross neuropsychological relationships, they lack the exactness that results from studies of more homogeneous experimental samples.

In this regard, evidence from studies of patients after surgical removal of parts of the cerebral cortex is more definitive. In the early 1950s W. B. Scoville, a neurosurgeon, carried out some new experimental operations on the mesial surface of the temporal lobes in an attempt to alleviate certain psychotic symptoms. Frontal lobotomies had shown some undesirable behavioral effects and it was important to discover whether fractional lobotomies would be successful in alleviating psychosis. For example, it had been found that undercutting of the orbital surfaces of both frontal lobes (i.e., the area above and behind the eyes) actually did have a favorable therapeutic effect in psychosis without any new signs of personality deficit. Because the orbital frontal surfaces and the mesial temporal cortices are closely related, it was hoped that surgery in the mesial temporal area might have the same salutary effect. Scoville and Milner (1957) have reported that when the mesial or inside surfaces of both temporal lobes are undercut in the hippocampal area, severe impairment of recent memory results. When only the uncus and amygdala were removed bilaterally no memory impairment occurred, although the relation of these structures to memory is not clear. Their studies led them to conclude that the anterior hippocampus and hippocampal gyrus were critically related to recent memory, but their removal, with the lateral temporal cortices left intact, did not impair early memories or habitual memory, technical skills, general intelligence, or perceptual abilities. Such cases also showed no deterioration in personality such as is seen in more complete bilateral temporal lobectomy. Their studies suggested that the lateral temporal cortices are needed for long-term memory, but that the mesial temporal areas, particularly the hippocampus and hippocampal gyrus, at least on one side, are crucial to short-term memory.

However, if a memory test includes a series of line drawings of common objects that are chosen so that they can be categorized as to physical shape or lexical category, normal subjects will organize them either way. But subjects with unilateral right temporal lobectomy grouped the pictured objects according to lexical category, and those with left temporal lesions grouped the objects as to their shape (Moscovitch, 1979). This type of evidence reminds us that verbal memory draws on both hemispheres, and may make more or less use of the right hemisphere depending on the degree of semantic or visual imagery involved in the memory performance (Paivio & Linde, 1982).

The third research technique is that of electrostimulation of the cerebral cortex. Wilder Penfield's studies at the Montreal Neurological Institute during the 1930s and 1940s, reported in the 1950s, provided considerable new knowledge using this technique. The details of how this was done have been described by Penfield and Roberts (1959). With a local anesthetic to reduce discomfort from the incision, the patient remains conscious during the early part of the operation so that he or she can report any sensations or experiences as they occur following cortical electrostimulation. Penfield found that in one patient, stimulation of the posterior cortex with a weak current could produce a false sense of familiarity regarding her present experience. In many patients suffering from temporal lobe epilepsy the phenomenon of "déjà vu" is not uncommon. When different points on the temporal cortex were stimulated, previous experiences, such as the patient's place of work, a scene from a play, her small son's voice, in fact any experience stored in memory, were revived. However, these experiences were more vivid than normal remembering and Penfield has reported (Penfield & Roberts, 1959), "The patients have never looked upon an experiential response as a remembering. Instead of that it is a hearing-again and seeing-again—a living-through moments of past time." Penfield's findings have also been repeated and extended by other researchers (Mahl, Rothenberg, Delgado, & Hamlin, 1964; Ojemann & Whitaker, 1978; Ojemann, 1979). This evidence suggests that the electrical activation of memories in the brain may be somewhat similar to the action of a tape recorder. A story, a song, or some pattern of meaningful material may be permanently stored on the tape in a magnetized pattern. When this pattern is appropriately stimulated the original material may be retrieved as many times as it is wanted. This concept of the brain depicts it as an electrochemical repository of experiences neurally stored for future reference. It is interesting to note that only the temporal lobes produced these "flashback" experiences when stimulated; no such responses resulted from stimulation of any of the other lobes.[1]

The Wada technique, the fourth method for studying the relationship between brain function and memory, has already been described. While it was originally developed to establish hemispheric dominance for speech prior to therapeutic surgery for severe epilepsy, it has been useful in demonstrating transient memory disorders produced by this method of single hemispheric anesthetization. Wada's original technique (Wada & Rasmussen, 1960) was to have the patient lie on a bed with the forearms up in the air and the fingers either moving constantly or gripping the examiner's hand. The knees were drawn up with the feet near the buttocks, and the patient was asked to begin counting as the injection was made into the carotid artery in the neck. If made on the left side, the left hemisphere soon became anesthetized or maximally affected, and the arm and leg on the opposite side (contralateral) would slump to the bed. This

[1] The reader is referred to an excellent, inexpensive paperback on cortical electrostimulation: W. H. Calvin and G. A. Ojemann, *Inside the Brain,* New York: Mentor Books, 1980.

flaccidity of the contralateral limbs and the cessation of counting would usually occur by the time the injection was completed. The ipsilateral arm and leg (i.e., those on the left) would remain in the air and could be moved voluntarily to command, although the patient was unable either to speak or move his right arm or leg. The aphasia (inability to speak) and the right hemiplegia (paralysis of the right limbs) usually was complete for a period of from 1 to 3 minutes, after which time normal speech and voluntary limb movement gradually returned as fresh blood replaced the drug in the left hemisphere. When the injection was on the language nondominant side (i.e., the right side in most people), the patient was able to speak, read, and write, but unable to remember and interpret pictorial material accurately (B. Milner, 1958) during the period of the left hemiplegia. Although this technique has great value for studying cerebral dominance, for providing preoperative information to the brain surgeon, and for shedding light on the phenomena associated with amnesia, we are concerned, at this point, with its help in providing evidence for the importance of the temporal lobes in memory functions.

In summary, unilateral temporal lesions of the left hemisphere may result in difficulties of verbal recall and the understanding and retention of verbally expressed ideas (receptive aphasia). In dichotic listening experiments with normal subjects, it is usual for more words to be recognized by the right ear (contralateral) than by the left (ipsilateral), because most people are left-hemisphere dominant for language (Kimura, 1961a, b). However, this normal pattern is disrupted in cases of unilateral temporal lobe damage; in these cases better dichotic perception for speech stimuli may occur in the ipsilateral ear (Berlin, Lowe-Bell, Cullen, Thompson, & Stafford, 1972) when both ears are stimulated at normal and similar intensities. When the ipsilateral ear is stimulated below threshold, then the contralateral ear may approach normal function (Berlin, Lowe-Bell, Jannetta, & Kline, 1972).

Right temporal lesions are usually accompanied by impairment of spatial perception and imagery and the comprehension of pictorial material. Children with temporal lobe seizures tend to be more impaired than normals in stereoscopic vision (Webb & Berman, 1973). Whereas unilateral temporal lesions result in relatively mild or moderate memory deficits, bilateral damage to the hippocampal areas produces severe and generalized loss of recent memory.

Epilepsy and Brain Function

In this section the normal and epileptic activity of the brain and its possible relation to behavior and classroom learning are discussed. Because most epileptogenic foci or lesions causing focal epilepsy occur in the temporal lobes, the mental effects of epileptic activity in the brain, especially if accompanied by brain damage, are usually similar to those just discussed in the section on the temporal lobes. If, however, the epilepsy is generalized, the mental effects are more likely to be global.

The human cerebral cortex is made up of an intricate three-dimensional network of billions of nerve cells, each having the capacity of self-firing several times per second. In the normal brain an integrated rhythmical pattern is produced, each cell generating a neural impulse in a smoothly timed sequence so that the impulses feed into other cells and other circuits in such a way that normal rhythmic patterns can be detected on the electroencephalogram (EEG). Sensory inputs, whether visual, auditory, or tactile, show themselves as volleys of electrochemical or neural impulses traveling to the brain along the optic, auditory or cutaneous nerve pathways. Light waves impinging on the retinae stimulate the retinal cells, which in turn trigger neural impulses in the optic nerves, leading to the occipital lobes. Sound waves vibrating the ear drums in turn stimulate the sensitive hair cells of the inner ear (organ of Corti), which also trigger neural impulses in the auditory nerves, leading to the acoustic areas in the temporal lobes. Similarly, all sensory input is converted into irregular patterns of neural impulses, which are superimposed on the regular rhythmic patterns of spontaneous self-firing in the brain.

Sometimes, however, because of injury, disease, pressure, or lack of oxygen, an area of the gray matter may discharge volleys of impulses irregularly. Such an area may develop into a self-discharging electrochemical unit, or *epileptogenic focus*. Penfield has described this phenomenon thus: "In such an area or focus, excess electrical energy is formed and so, from time to time, unruly mass discharges may be released" (Penfield & Roberts, 1959). Such an explosive discharge may produce an epileptic seizure or fit and may be large or small depending on the extent and intensity of discharge. If it is minimal (petit mal) the patient's eyes may turn up involuntarily for a few seconds resulting in brief inattention, but there is no loss of consciousness except possibly for a second or two. Such small seizure conditions may interfere with a child's concentration and productivity in school and may be undetected by a teacher with no knowledge of these conditions.

Because of the minimal signs of petit mal, they are often ignored or misinterpreted by teachers and classmates. Because the child so afflicted may appear to others as inattentive, disinterested, and mildly incompetent, he may be the butt of jokes from other children and the focus of adverse criticism from the teacher. Even some medical doctors have been known to fail in recognizing the condition and have referred the child for psychological assessment and treatment because of incorrigible and disruptive behavior, when, in fact, a thorough medical examination by a competent neurologist should have been the first step.

Even though most teachers have encountered epilepsy, some are insensitive to and ignorant of its nature and may misinterpret the child's behavior as resulting from mental retardation or some form of emotional disturbance. Such treatment only serves to alienate the child in a hostile environment, to encourage emotional problems, and to aggravate all forms of learning.

Grand mal attacks are more intense, they involve a loss of consciousness, and possess a typical behavioral pattern. Many victims of grand mal epilepsy experience an *aura,* which warns them of the imminence of the attack and enables them to sit down or lie down in a relatively safe place. Some patients have no aura and hence no warning. The nature of the aura differs in patients and may include brief mutism, involuntary motor movements, a "strange" feeling probably emanating from organic changes, some type of hallucination, or localized pain. Several children we have seen have complained of "feelings like needles" in the upper middle part of the abdomen just prior to a grand mal seizure. "The convulsion proper may begin with a loud cry, but this is more absent than present. Consciousness is lost either immediately after the aura or at the very beginning of the attack" (Brain, 1960).

With loss of consciousness the patient falls to the ground and goes into a muscularly rigid state (tonic phase), during which the jaws are clenched and breathing ceases for a few seconds or usually not more than half a minute.

This is followed by rhythmic contractions of the muscles (clonic phase) during which the patient may bite his tongue, foam at the mouth, and fling his arms and legs out. During this period he may injure himself, but gradually the jerking movements grow weaker and finally cease. He may remain unconscious following the seizure for periods up to half an hour, and on regaining consciousness he may be fatigued and may sleep for several hours.

As in the case of petit mal, grand mal also produces the same social problems for the child or adult so afflicted, but they may be more intense. Sometimes teachers and others are fearful of the possibility of a grand mal seizure, and they imply rejection of the child either directly or indirectly. Sometimes even parents will not fully accept their epileptic child and this will certainly affect the child seriously and adversely. The physician should explain the condition fully to the parents and stress that it "is not contagious, and that there is no reason why the child should not mix with others. . . . Children with epilepsy should go to school. If their intelligence is normal, they should go to a regular school. It is important that the principal and teacher know of the problem so that they can take appropriate steps in the event of a seizure" (Robb, 1981, p. 64). Victims of epilepsy will have numerous questions about schooling, occupational training, and social behavior (jobs? marriage? etc.). A well-informed counselor should be consulted so that the epileptic patient will not limit his opportunities unnecessarily.[2]

---

[2] The United States Department of Health and Human Services has produced an excellent monograph for counselors: P. Robb, *Epilepsy, a manual for health workers.* Bethesda, MD: NIH Publication No. 82-2350, September 1981.

Various authorities have attempted to classify the epilepsies but because of their variability of etiology and description this is a difficult task. Many introductory books include the categories of petit mal, grand mal, psychomotor, and Jacksonian epilepsy. The last-named, first described by Hughlings Jackson, the famous nineteenth century British neurologist, consists of a twitching of one side of the face or of a finger or arm on one side of the body. The motor activity gradually spreads in intensity and extent to include the whole side of the body. An interesting discussion of the epilepsies for classroom teachers has been made by Folsom (1968) and by Haslam (1975).

Although these classifications may be expedient in the clinic, a classification having more useful information for the neuropsychologist may be in terms of whether the epilepsy is (1) *generalized* or (2) *focal,* as suggested by Hess (1966). In cases where a chain reaction of neural overexcitability spreads to include most or all parts of the brain there may be no brain lesion and hence no mental deficit when the patient is free of seizures. As is well known, many mentally superior professional people have suffered from grand mal seizures. Julius Caesar, Lord Byron, Swinburne, Dostoevsky, and Guy de Maupassant, to name a few, are known to have suffered from epileptic attacks. Some forms of epilepsy are believed to originate in the brainstem or central parts of the brain (centrencephalic epilepsy), possibly in the subcortical, mesial, and basal surfaces of the frontal lobes (Hess, 1966). The generalized symptoms may result from the deep location of the point of origin and its spreading effect as it travels to the cerebral cortices.

Focal epilepsy, by contrast, is stimulated by a lesion or epileptogenic focus located on or near the cerebral cortex, which may be congenital (e.g., a cerebral growth anomaly) or a tumor or a scar resulting from actual brain tissue damage. Birth injuries, cerebral infections (e.g., encephalitis), or severe trauma followed by permanent neural destruction may produce various types of *post-traumatic epilepsy.* War and traffic head injuries have accounted for thousands of these cases, and "by far the most common form of focal epilepsy in the adult is temporal epilepsy" (Hess, 1966). A study of school-age children (aged 6 to 14 years) with either temporal lobe or centrencephalic epilepsy showed the expected verbal–spatial split in those children with unilateral temporal lobe disease. The split was not evident in the children with centrencephalic epilepsy, presumably because they possessed bilateral disturbances. However, they had difficulty in tasks demanding sustained attention (Fedio & Mirsky, 1969), possibly because of electrical disturbances in the brain stem.

Some examples should make this clear. For experimental purposes epileptogenic lesions have been surgically imposed on monkeys (Seino & Wada, 1964) and following the imposition of the brain lesion the animals were found to be inferior to normal monkeys in learning a spatial delayed and a delayed alternation problem. In humans, focal epilepsies have been shown to be related to inferior performance on tasks that regularly depend on the normal functioning of the cortical area locating the lesion.

A 40-year-old man seen in our laboratory had fallen down a flight of stairs and suffered a severe injury to the right side of his head. Neurological examination indicated the presence of a massive right-sided hematoma (large mass of blood resulting from a brain hemorrhage) and a craniotomy was carried out in order to evacuate the blood clot and free the brain from the abnormally increased cerebral pressure. Brain surgery revealed that the right temporal lobe was severely lacerated, and this extended back almost to the occipital lobe. Within a few months post-traumatic epileptic seizures began, although this man had had no history of convulsions at any time prior to his head injury. The EEG revealed a moderate to severe dysrhythmia in the right fronto-temporal region, which resulted in two types of seizures: generalized convulsions that rendered the patient unconscious (grand mal) and a focal type of seizure involving the face and throat. Anticonvulsant medicines had reduced the grand mal attacks to about two a year, but he was bothered by the minor spasms affecting the right face and sometimes the left arm and leg.

A detailed battery of neuropsychological tests revealed that this man obtained a verbal IQ on the Wechsler Adult Intelligence Scale (WAIS) of 108 but a performance IQ of 91. He had great difficulty with the tests requiring visual–spatial perception. Adaptive behavior in terms of inductive and deductive reasoning was impaired, and visual perception of figure and ground was below average. Auditory perception was normal, which suggested that the healthy left temporal lobe maintained normal function or that the acoustic area of the right temporal lobe was spared. Three-dimensional construction of a model with blocks was slow and included minor errors, suggesting mild right parietal involvement (Benton, 1968). This man's most marked mental symptom following his injury was his faulty short-term memory, which was a constant handicap. At work he would forget to carry out some duty he had been asked to do, and unless he wrote everything down and referred to the list frequently, he was constantly in trouble both at work and in his personal life. He still possessed an above-average verbal intelligence that resulted in considerable insight into his condition. This type of case is a reminder that certain seizure cases and those with a combination of above-normal, normal, and subnormal behaviors are difficult for most people to accept. These fluctuations of normality create much more tension than do the consistent shortcomings of the mentally retarded child: Others know what to expect from him or her (Ross & Ross, 1976/1982).

Although it is known that particular individuals with idiopathic epilepsy (i.e., epilepsy without known causes) may be mentally superior, as already mentioned, two neuropsychologists at the University of Wisconsin Medical Center, Kløve and Matthews, have made several interesting studies of large numbers of epileptic patients of different etiologies. Prior to their studies, most investigations had concluded that "the IQ's of institutionalized epileptics are generally lower than those found in non-institutionalized epileptics, and that the IQ's of non-institutionalized are comparable to those in the normal population" (Kløve & Matthews, 1966). Their study did not support this, chiefly because along with the Wechsler test (WAIS) they used the Halstead battery of tests, which is more sensitive than are standard intelligence tests to behavioral changes resulting from brain damage (Reitan, 1956). Halstead based his theory of testing on investigating "biological intelligence" (i.e., behavior depending more on adaptive abilities and sensorimotor functions) rather than "psychometric intelligence" (i.e., behavior heavily loaded with verbal learning and long-term memory). Measures of the former show greater deficits following cerebral organic damage; measures of the latter show greater resistance to brain damage, possibly because of the greater degree of overlearning. Consequently, Kløve and Matthews found that when they compared four matched groups, (1) a control group, (2) a group of verified brain-damaged patients without epilepsy, (3) a brain-damaged group with epilepsy, and (4) a group of patients with epilepsy of unknown etiology, the controls, as would be expected, were significantly superior to the other three groups on most measures. Group 4, the idiopathic group, was next, and the two brain-damaged groups were poorest. Of these two, the brain-damaged group with epilepsy was slightly better than the brain-damaged group without epilepsy, but the differences were not significant. This study, with sizable groups ($N = 51$ in each of the four groups) suggests that epilepsy in the majority of cases impairs most intellectual and sensorimotor functions, but when it is accompanied by verified brain damage impairment is worse. In another study, Matthews and Kløve (1967) found no differences between the test performances of controls and patients with psychomotor epilepsy of unknown etiology (i.e., automatic behavior for which the patient is usually amnesic). These patients performed at significantly better levels than did patients with major motor seizures of unknown etiology. However, a teacher, ignorant of the nature of psychomotor epilepsy, might reasonably misinterpret a child's mental confusion that typically accompanies this form as inattention, stupidity, or incorrigibility. It is important that all teachers familiarize themselves with the various types of epilepsy so as not to misunderstand the behavior of children so afflicted.

In summary, it seems that epileptic patients of unknown etiology (idiopathic) may or may not suffer mental deficits.

Seizure conditions without any brain damage frequently do not impair learning except temporarily at the time of the seizure. Therefore an abnormal EEG by itself cannot necessarily be regarded as evidence of a disturbance causing learning disorders. In fact many epileptics with grossly abnormal EEG's are highly intelligent and have no particular

learning problems, . . . the evidence suggests that epilepsy is one manifestation of cerebral dysfunction, which, when no tissue damage occurs,
may not impair learning at all, except temporarily. When epilepsy occurs
with evident brain damage, the location and extent of the lesion rather
than the seizures, are chiefly responsible for the impairment of learning
and behavior. [Gaddes, 1972]

Those patients with post-traumatic epilepsy will most likely suffer behavioral impairments in relation to the locus of the cerebral lesion. Most of
these involve temporal lobe lesions or dysfunctions, and as a consequence the behavioral and mental effects are usually related to defective
temporal lobe function.

Parietal Lobes

The parietal lobes, like the temporal lobes, appear to be essential cortical
processing areas for a great variety of distinctive behavioral functions,
and lesions in these areas may produce a number of specific sensory and
cognitive deficits.

Each parietal lobe is cortically bounded as follows: anterior boundary,
fissure of Rolando, or central sulcus; superior boundary, longitudinal fissure; inferior boundary, fissure of Sylvius; and posterior boundary, the
occipital lobe. Arbitrary boundaries between these natural borders are
indicated graphically by dotted lines in Fig. 3.2. Just posterior to the
fissure of Rolando is the postcentral gyrus that is known as the *somesthetic strip* and is the primary receiving area for tactile sensations from all
parts of the body. Because the tactile sense is the first sensory modality to
develop prenatally (about the 49th prenatal day) compared with the vestibular (90–120 days), visual (180 days or earlier), and the auditory (210
days or earlier) (Gottlieb, 1971), its longer history appears to provide it
with a special value in sensorimotor remedial procedures, as we will see
later in the book. Just as the motor strip or precentral gyrus is located on
the anterior or frontal boundary of the fissure of Rolando and is contralaterally and inversely vertically related to motor functions in the body from
head to feet, so the somesthetic strip in the anterior parietal lobe is similarly contralaterally and vertically connected to the tactile receptors
throughout the body.

If the left hand is stimulated by a fine nylon hair (esthesiometer) it is
usually maximally recorded in the right somesthetic strip, but a lesion in
this area may reduce, obliterate, or distort the tactile input. The somesthetic strips are the primary projection or sensory areas of the two parietal

lobes, and their normal function is essential to competent neuromuscular coordination and control. The remaining part of the parietal lobe has been considered in the classical conception to be an "association area" or one of the so-called "silent areas" of the cortex, but neurological and neuro-psychological research during the past 40 years has done much to dispel its silence.

The first major monograph on the parietal lobes was published in 1953 by Dr. Macdonald Critchley, the eminent British neurologist, and his book still has value. More recent publications by neuropsychologists (Kolb & Whishaw, 1980/1984; Luria, 1973; Walsh, 1978) will provide detailed discussions of the neural structures and psychological functions mediated by these cortical areas. They are interconnected with the fron-tal, temporal, and occipital lobes, and to various subcortical centers in-cluding the thalamus, the striatum, the midbrain, and spinal cord. These neural connections with all of the primary and association cortical areas and brainstem centers make possible a delicate integration of spatial imag-ery with all other sensory experiences, verbal and nonverbal memory, and language and motor functions.

Disorders of Tactile Recognition

The thumb, index finger, other digits, and the hand are all represented in the two sensory and motor strips (Fig. 3.3). This provides the experienc-ing subject with the ability to recognize form by touch alone. For exam-ple, if sandpaper figures are placed under a screen, the child may feel or palpate them and form a mental image from this source alone. This ability to recognize two-dimensional objects by touch alone is known as *ste-reognosis* and may include two-dimensional stereognostic recognition, such as reading Braille or figures outlined by differences in surface tex-ture, or three-dimensional stereognosis, such as recognizing blocks by touch and replacing them in a form board (see Fig. 4.5). This latter type is also called *haptic recognition*. When lesions occur in the somesthetic strip and the parietal cortices adjacent to them, the person may experi-ence difficulties in tactile recognition in the contralateral hand. With bilat-eral parietal lesions, stereognostic deficit may be experienced in both hands.

Stereognosis is an important sensory and perceptual source for all types of learning. The baby explores his world first by touch both with his hands and his mouth. By repetitive synchronization with the visual and auditory correlates of an object, the infant gradually learns to develop two- and three-dimensional visual perception. He learns to recognize his mother by the feel of her arms and face against him, the sound of her voice, and the visual topography of her face and figure. No doubt, olfac-

Figure 4.5. An 11-year-old girl attempting the Tactual Performance Test from the Halstead–Reitan battery. This makes a measure of three-dimensional stereognosis or haptic recognition and imagery. Reprinted with the permission of the Professional Press, Inc., *The Journal of Learning Disabilities*.

tion and other senses reinforce this recognition, but it seems certain that touch, vision, and hearing are the major sense modes in his learning. As he grows, he learns to recognize books, dogs, chairs, tables, spoons, tricycles, and hundreds of other objects by feel, appearance, and sound, when sound is involved. Unconsciously he begins to use his stereognostic knowledge independently or almost separately, when he hops on his tricycle and puts his hands on the handlebars and feet on the pedals without looking. He may learn to play the piano or finger a violin without visual cues. Later, as an adult when he drives a car, he will manipulate many hand and foot controls without taking his eyes off the road and he will learn to recognize a dime and a quarter in his pocket by palpating them. Dressing himself will become a complicated but largely automated daily routine largely dependent on stereognosis.

In the classroom, the child with a parietal lesion may have trouble with stereognosis and hence have difficulty in learning to spell, write, read, or do any academic skill drawing on reading and writing. Such a child, if mentally bright, may show a superiority in discussions, oral composition, and dramatics, and because of this brightness he or she may learn to spell and read through a visual–auditory match. Such a learning process makes less use of the tactile and kinesthetic input.

However, such a case is rare. It is much more common to find the child with impaired visual perception or auditory perception, or both, but with average or better than average tactile imagery and recognition (stereognosis). This type of child will often have a muscular clumsiness resulting in a "visual–motor disability" (e.g., difficulty copying spelling words from a book or the blackboard, hitting a nail with a hammer). To teach this child it is usually better to subordinate the visual and auditory experiences to the tactile. This type of child may be taught to spell by a technique emphasizing tactile–motor input (e.g., using a tactile alphabet, writing in damp sand with the index finger, writing spelling words in finger paints, with a felt pen, or on the typewriter). For many years, the Montessori system has stressed a multisensorimotor approach in learning to spell, read, and write, and no doubt much of its success is because tactile recognition is grosser and more primitive than both visual and auditory perception and arises earlier in the child's developmental history. Most teachers of special education have discovered over the years that teaching a child with learning disabilities frequently succeeds when a tactile emphasis is coupled with visual and auditory recognition. Ideally, the child's body image should include a smoothly synthesized input pattern of visual, auditory, and tactile stimuli.

Parietal dysfunction may result in graphesthesia (i.e., inability to recognize numbers traced with a stylus on the fingertips or palms of the hands), in poor judgment of weights, in an inability to localize the point of tactile stimulation, finger localization (Benton, 1959), confusion in recognizing two-point simultaneous stimulation, and a number of specialized sensations to touch and pain that usually may be more interesting and valuable to the diagnosing neurologist than to either the clinical psychologist or the special educator. The neurologist draws heavily on almost pure sensory functions to localize lesions and make diagnoses of neurological dysfunction. The special educator, by contrast, is not primarily concerned with pure sensory data (e.g., can the child hear pure tones at certain intensities? What is the child's threshold of auditory sensation? What is his or her tactile threshold?) but with learning disabilities for specific types of academic material. The neuropsychologist, although interested in both these areas, is primarily concerned with perceptual, cognitive, and motor functions and how they are related both to neurological structure and function and to behavioral impairment. For example, the neurologist may be able to state that a child has a left parietal lesion; the psychologist can say that the child has impairments in directional sense, finger localization, stereognosis in the right hand and poor body image; and the teacher knows that the child is a poor speller and reader. His remedial learning program should be constructed around the data supplied both by his teacher and the psychologist, both to avoid remedial programs based largely on trial and error and to develop instructional techniques based on both neuropsychological and educational data.

Neuropsychological Theories of Tactile Recognition

The classical view of astereognosis is that it is a form of tactile agnosia. According to this theory, perception requires two successive processes: first, the primary registration of simple elements of sensation or tactile awareness, and second, the integration of these elements into meaningful whole patterns that may be related to past experience and that are essential to perception and recognition. In the parietal lobe, sensation was supposed to have taken place in the postcentral gyrus or somesthetic strip and perception to have taken place in the "association areas" of the middle and posterior parietal lobes. As Teuber (1965) has pointed out, "The classical doctrine of agnosia was simple and eminently teachable," but recent research has thrown genuine doubt on this simple and structural view.

When the subject is unable to be sure if he has been touched on the hand, or his tactile threshold varies very unevenly across his hands or from finger to finger, then astereognosis may be suspected because of such a severe sensory defect. One cannot interpret when one cannot be aware. If a child possesses normal tactile sensation and still is impaired in perceiving differences in surface, roughness, texture, size, form, and pattern, then the classical view of astereognosis is untenable. Such cases, although rare, suggest that the processes of sensation and perception are separated and that different cerebral structures mediate them. Semmes (1965) has investigated this possibility but has found no support for the view that the "tactual association area" mediates shape discrimination selectively. She found that lesions in the parietal lobes did produce impairment in this perceptual ability, but so did cortical lesions that spared the parietal lobes and the motor strips. In addition, Semmes carried out an ingenious search for a nontactual factor in subjects with tactile sensory defect. As a result, she found no significant correlation between astereognosis and hand-grip strength, finger tapping, intelligence as measured by the Army General Classification Test, ability to categorize on a sorting test, and dysphasia. She also found no correlations between spatial orientation and roughness, texture, and size discrimination, but she found a high correlation between spatial orientation as measured by route finding on a map and shape discrimination, and this relation held whether the maps were explored visually or tactually. From this evidence Semmes concluded that visual and tactual orientation are both related to stereognosis. When she examined the association between visual–spatial orientation in subjects with no tactile sensory defect, and also in subjects with a sensory defect of both hands, an interesting finding emerged. Those with sensory defect of the *left* hand only showed a difficulty of stereognostic recognition, but those with a *right* hand defect were no different from those with no sensory defect of either hand. Because the right hemisphere is more involved in spatial perception, it seems logical that this functional asymmetry between the two hands should show itself, and it is interesting to know that this spatial function includes shape discrimination (stereognosis) as well as visual–spatial orientation. Semmes concluded that:

> The spatial factor (i.e., directionality in space) might enter into all performances which require appreciation of spatial arrangements, regardless of the modality transmitting the information. It is possible that this factor might be more important in tactual than in visual form perception, however, since in the case of objects palpated, the spatial arrangement of the elements (and hence the form) must usually be reconstructed from a temporal series of partial impressions, rather than being simultaneously given as in vision. [Semmes, 1965]

In this regard it is interesting to note that almost all auditory perception is sequential and has to be decoded in the brain as it is received, as in listening to a melody or in understanding oral speech. This requires a normal serial order function of the brain, but more will be said about this in Chapter 5. Nevertheless, whereas most visual perception usually involves the scanning of stimuli that are "simultaneously given," as in looking at an object or a map, some visual perceptual processes require successful serial order cerebral functioning, such as in reading, walking, and driving a car. Luria (1973) has described in considerable detail the holistic and simultaneous spatial sensations of visual perceptions and the temporal sequential neural input of verbal–auditory speech. This led to a popular and simplified model among some professionals that described the left hemisphere as mediating sequential processes and the right hemisphere as subserving holistic perceptions. Das and his colleagues (Das, Kirby, & Jarman, 1979) developed this idea with a model of simultaneous and successive cognitive processes.

Disorders of Spatial Imagery

We have seen from Semmes' research, described above, that stereognostic perception, particularly shape and pattern recognition, seems to be strongly related to spatial orientation. Although much of spatial perception includes vision and has been discussed earlier in this chapter, many nonvisual functions believed to depend on the parietal lobes are also involved. Benton (1969a), in discussing disorders of spatial orientation, has listed the following: (a) the inability to localize objects in space; (b) the inability to estimate the size of objects; (c) the inability to judge the distance of objects from the observer; (d) the impaired memory for the location of objects and places in recalling the spatial position of furniture in a room after leaving it; (e) the inability to trace a path or follow a route from one place to another, as from one's hospital room to the physiotherapy room, or on a map from New York to one's home or to a named city; (f) reading and counting disability to the degree that reading and counting require the comprehension of a spatiotemporal directional stimulus sequence; (g) the incapacity to relate spatially separated objects or events to each other; (h) visuoconstructive disability as indicated by impairment in viewing a model and constructing an identical one when supplied with all the blocks (Benton, 1969b); (i) disorders of the body schema, such as defective identification of the right and left body parts and impaired finger localization. These functions fall into two broad categories, those concerned with body awareness or *personal space,* and those having to do with the perception of objects in space, *extrapersonal space,* although they are functionally interrelated and appear to feed into one another. Parietal lobe lesions may disturb the body image and hence impair some or all of the above-listed spatial functions.

Gerstmann's Syndrome

Between 1924 and 1930 Josef Gerstmann published several papers in which he related focal disease in the dominant parietal–occipital region (in the left hemisphere in most subjects) to a constellation of four behavioral deficits, namely right–left disorientation, bilateral finger agnosia (the somesthetic inability to indicate accurately which fingers have been touched by an experimenter), agraphia (the inability to write), and acalculia (the inability to carry out arithmetical calculations). While there appears to be a tendency for these four deficits to occur together in patients with left parietal disease, they sometimes appear in isolation or in partial groupings. This inconsistency led Benton (1961) to question the validity of the Gerstmann syndrome. He tested the hypothesis that if the four deficits comprised a natural constellation then they should show stronger associations among themselves than with symptoms outside the syndrome. In comparing them with constructional praxis, reading, and visual memory, he did not find that they clustered any more than other combinations. From this evidence he concluded that the Gerstmann syndrome was an artifact of selective perception. Nevertheless, the four behavioral deficits described by Gerstmann do seem to be related to left parietal dysfunction, and the syndrome is a firmly established concept in clinical neurology. Whether or not the Gerstmann syndrome is exclusive of other disabilities, it is a useful descriptive label because these symptoms so frequently occur with parietal pathology, particularly when it occurs in the language-dominant hemisphere.

Visual Defects

In the discussion of the occipital lobes earlier in this chapter, descriptions of cases with visual defects resulting from lesions in the parieto-occipital areas were presented. It is interesting to note that parietal lesions themselves may produce various visual defects for at least two reasons. First, the posterior parietal cortices bordering on the occipital lobes are intimately involved with vision. Second, the optic radiations, as they bend back from the lateral geniculate bodies, travel through the subcortical white matter of the temporal and parietal lobes and terminate in the upper and lower lips of the calcarine fissure. Although the optic radiations do not lie in the parietal cortical tissue, they do occupy the white matter immediately below the angular gyrus on each side, and there is considerable evidence to suggest that lesions in the left angular gyrus result in dyslexia (Benson & Geschwind, 1969; Russell & Espir, 1961), and unilateral parietal disease may result in agnosia and neglect of one-half of the extrapersonal space. For example, such a patient, if asked to make a freehand drawing of a daisy, may draw petals on only one side, neglecting them on the side contralateral to his or her parietal damage or dysfunction. Other visual defects that may result from parietal pathology are central or cortical blindness, hemianopia (possessing only half visual fields), difficulty in color naming, visual agnosia for objects, facial agnosia (common in senile patients, who may have difficulty recognizing members of their own families), loss of three-dimensional or stereoscopic vision, dyslexia (discussed in Chapter 8), the inability to retrieve memories of visual images, and many others.

Warrington, James, and Kinsbourne (1966) found that drawings by adult patients with known brain pathology were impaired by unilateral lesions on either side, but each side showed different types of errors. Left-hemisphere lesion cases tended to widen all angles (e.g., in drawing a cube) and to put in fewer details in a freehand drawing (e.g., of a house). The right-hemisphere lesion cases tended to reduce all angles, to show more asymmetry in their drawings, and to "doodle" or build up complex geometrical figures (Warrington, James, & Kinsbourne, 1966). Right parietal damage may impair the visual perception of fragmented figures, figure–ground discrimination, recognizing common objects when reproduced larger than life size, and recognizing an object in an unconventional view (e.g., photograph of a pail in side view and from above into its interior; Warrington & Taylor, 1973).

Apraxia

The inability to carry out specific neuromuscular acts at will is called *apraxia* and it appears to result from abnormal parietal function. *Ideational apraxia* is the inability to demonstrate how to use a common object, such as a hammer or toothbrush, when it is placed before the subject. The ideational motor patterns necessary to such demonstrations evidently draw markedly on the parietal lobes. *Ideomotor apraxia,* by contrast, is the inability to perform an intransitive gesture, such as saluting, waving goodbye, or pretending to comb one's hair with an imaginary comb. DeRenzi, Pieczuro, and Vignolo (1968) in Italy found ideational apraxia to be associated with left-hemisphere lesions, usually parietal. The reader will realize that ideomotor functions are essential to carrying out voluntary behavioral acts. Miming, for example, demands this, so that one might conclude that superior parietal function, among other cerebral superiorities, is essential to a successful career in acting. A common need in this regard is *dressing praxis,* or the tactile and kinesthetic awareness essential to putting on one's clothes. Small children are usually unable to put on their clothes without help until about the age of 4 or 5, as every parent and kindergarten teacher knows, not because they lack the physical strength, but because they lack the necessary ideomotor images. In senility, with the breakdown of parietal cortical cells, old people also suffer from *dressing apraxia* and need help as they did as small children.

The Integrating Function of the Parietal Lobes

In the previous chapter the "tertiary cortical zones" were described as:

> the zones of the posterior regions of the brain that lie at the boundary between the occipital, temporal and postcentral regions of the hemisphere, where the cortical areas for visual, auditory, vestibular, cutaneous and proprioceptive sensation overlap. [Luria, 1973]

The reader will realize that the parietal lobes are the center of all of this cortical organization. The transcortical connections of millions of short axons provide the physiological bases for an analysis and synthesis within a sensory projection area (e.g., within the visual or auditory cortex) and an integration between these areas (e.g., cross-modal function). Many writers have considered the angular gyrus and the immediate cortical areas to be vital in mediating these intersensory functions (Benson &

Geschwind, 1969; Déjerine, 1892; Geschwind, 1965), lesions of these areas do not produce disturbances specific to vision, audition, or tactile sensation but do disrupt the integrated reception and analysis of information. Probably the most common behaviors disrupted in this way are reading, writing, and all forms of perception involving spatial imagery. Neuropsychological studies of adult patients with parietal damage, when compared to patients with lesions in the frontal or temporal cortices, have shown them to be impaired on all cross-modal matching tasks, even though each sense mode by itself was functioning normally (Butters & Brody, 1968). These same investigators concluded that auditory–visual cross-modal tasks depended more on the left parietal lobe, and more is said about this in Chapters 8 and 9 in discussing the neurological bases of reading and writing. Nonverbal spatial reversible operations (e.g., You are to make your stick pattern look to you like mine looks to me.) appear to draw more on the right parietal lobe. The "left may be more crucial than the right for cross-modal associations while the right plays a slightly more dominant role than the left in the performance of spatial rotations" (Butters, Barton, & Brody, 1970).

The discussion so far has devoted greater attention to cortical integrative functions but, as explained in Chapter 3, cerebral organization occurs vertically (e.g., from spinal cord to brainstem to cortex) and horizontally (between two sides of the spinal cord, brainstem, thalamus, and the two cerebral hemispheres).

Ayres (1972a) has made a detailed presentation of the relation of neural integration and learning. She stresses that living organisms utilize intersensory integration as a basis for adaptive behavior. Many years ago, Stratton (1897) demonstrated that after several days of wearing a reversible lens, he became adapted to the initial visual rotation of the environment and was able to walk about and behave in a normal manner. Ayres (1972a), using this type of evidence, concludes that "presumably the visual, tactile, and proprioceptive inputs are reassociated through intersensory integration in order to enable an adaptive response." She advises the improvement of visual and auditory perception through vestibular stimulation and other sense modalities, a neurological rationale supported by the successes of Montessori (1912), Kephart (1960/1971), and many other special educators using a multisensorimotor therapeutic approach.

Hyperactivity

It seems highly likely that Strauss and Lehtinen's (1947) influential book, *Psychopathology and Education of the Brain-Injured Child,* was largely responsible for establishing the belief among many professionals that all brain-injured children are hyperactive and distractible. In fact, the term "Strauss syndrome" was coined to describe the hyperactive and distractible child, and many people during the 1950s and early 1960s used circular reasoning to conclude that such children were also brain damaged. Since hyperactive and distractible children usually have poor academic success in school, some educators and psychologists consider them common correlates and possibly causes of learning disabilities.

Hyperactivity may be defined either quantitatively or descriptively. Those researchers who define it as "a level of daily motor activity which is clearly greater than that occurring in children of similar sex, mental age, socioeconomic and cultural background" (Werry, 1968) are faced with the serious weakness that there are no activity level norms for children against which to compare the child under study (Ross & Ross, 1976/1982). To derive these, the total amount of daily movement would need to be recorded on large samples of children at each age level. Schulman, Kaspar, and Throne (1965) did this in a very well-controlled study, but their population was limited to 35 mentally retarded male students in a school in the Chicago area. Their ages ranged from 11 years to 14 years 11 months, and their IQs from 50 to 80. Activity was measured with an actometer worn on the wrist, and distractibility by four perceptual and cognitive tests. Although this study used objective measures to define hyperactivity, the normative data were limited to a small and specialized population and obviously were invalid for general use.

Those who attempt to describe hyperactivity verbally suffer from the same normative lack, and they are usually forced to use subjective reference points. This has led to the common observation that hyperactivity is recognized as a function of the ability to tolerate noise and activity by the adult supervising the child. It is a commonplace occurrence that some teachers will rate a child as incorrigible whom other teachers rate quite positively.

Whereas hyperactivity is difficult to define, both quantitatively and descriptively, for research purposes, it can usually be recognized socially. The hyperactive child shows a high motility level and inappropriate behavior so that he or she is constantly in conflict with the social environment.

The causes may be either constitutional or psychological or a mixture of both of these. Although no primary genetic evidence has yet been identified as producing hyperactive behavior, studies of animal breeding and human familial and twin studies strongly support a constitutional etiological theory.

Schulman, Kaspar, & Throne (1965), with the first study of total daily activity, concluded that "there is a basic tendency to activity level which is an inherent property of the organism." This was basically a homeostatic theory wherein the organism was constantly attempting to compensate for too much or too little activity; periods of overactivity were followed by relative inactivity, and periods of controlled inactivity (e.g., the structured program of a classroom) could lead to marked restlessness. Ross and Ross (1976) report that Winston Churchill's hyperactivity as a school boy led his teachers in one school to let him leave the classroom at regular intervals to run around the school grounds. Such a practice implies a homeostatic theory of activity.

Following traumatic brain damage animals and humans may become more active. One of the first controlled studies with animals was reported by Lashley in 1920. He measured the behavior of rats on activity wheels and found that those with imposed cerebral lesions were more active postoperatively and more active than nonoperated rats, although the experimental animals showed a wide variation of response. Children following encephalitis (brain infection) frequently develop an increased tendency to activity, irritability, and distractibility. Neuropsychological studies of violent and nonviolent delinquent adolescents have shown significantly more test signs of impaired brain function and organically based impulse problems among the violent group, as compared to the nonviolent group (Spellacy, 1977). The same finding showed itself in a neuropsychological discrimination between violent and nonviolent adult men (Spellacy, 1978). Considerable neurological and neuropsychological evidence exists to show conclusively a causal relation between violent behavior and damage to specific areas of the brain, frequently the limbic system, which includes the "cingulum, the hippocampus, the thalamic and hypothalamic nuclei, and the more complex masses of the basal ganglia, midbrain, and amygdala" (Mark & Ervin, 1970). Whereas hyperactive children are rarely violent, many children with thalamic lesions, limbic dysfunctions, or temporal lobe dysrhythmias suffer from an unusually restless type of behavior. It seems that their engines are constantly racing and cannot be induced to idle except by medical intervention. Metabolic and endocrine disorders (e.g., hyperthyroidism), toxic conditions, food allergies, sensory disorders, maturational lag, psychoneurosis, personality disorder, and psychosis (Ross & Ross, 1976/1982) are other correlates and possible causes of hyperactivity. It is clear that some of these are traumatically neuropsychological, some are constitutional, and some are psychosocial in origin.

Many hyperactive children possess no primary physical deficit but develop a characteristically aggressive response to their world because of basic anxiety. The environmental causes of hyperactivity may be socially based in either the home, the school, or the community. The child with rejecting or unreliable parents may lack the opportunities at home for learning social control, and this may lead him or her to a defensive and manipulative approach to the world. Such children soon learn that most adults have little tolerance to their aggressiveness, so that it becomes a ready method for getting attention and warding off neglect. In school they may become restless when the academic task becomes too difficult, and a skilful matching by the teacher of the difficulty level to the child's ability for success may be a primary psychosocial control of disturbing behavior in the classroom.

Management of hyperactive children may be purely psychosocial or include drug treatment or both. The first area of investigation should be the child's behavior in an attempt to see if the psychopathology appears to originate in the home. Is it the result of a poor home situation, marital problems, sibling difficulties, poor housing, etc.? The mode of psychotherapy will depend on the training and preference of the therapist but it may include parent and child counseling, parent training, behavior therapy alone or in combination with other treatment methods, modeling, and any one of a group of popular therapeutic approaches. Whatever the technique, the aim is to reduce the child's hyperactivity and to improve his or her self image and relationship with the social environment.

Drug therapy for hyperactive children is a professional practice abused by some, managed with skill by some others, and showing little agreement among professionals. The "spectrum of dissent" (Ross & Ross, 1976/1982) stretches from complete and militant avoidance of drug treatment for children to claims of complete success with its use and implications of criminal neglect for withholding it from children who allegedly need it. Much of this confusion seems to have developed from poorly designed research, a loose interpretation of data, or an ignorance of psychological theories and practices by some of those urging drug therapy as a quick panacea. However, some impressive research in the past decade has done much to clarify the picture. Methylphenidate has been shown to be more effective than thioridazine in improving attention to a picture recognition task in emotionally disturbed children, and a peak dosage for improving social behavior of most children is slightly higher, between .5 and 1.0 mg/kg, than the .3 level for peak cognitive function (Sprague & Sleator, 1976). It now seems clear that stimulant drugs do not enhance memory or facilitate state-dependent learning (Aman & Sprague, 1974), and drug effects on paired associated learning, although significant, appear to affect selective attention more than memory or learning *per se* (Connors, Eisenberg, & Sharpe, 1964). Conners has also shown that "a variety of improvements on tests of visual and auditory perception, discrimination, and learning are largely attributable to attentional factors rather than specific improvements in those functions" (Conners, 1976). Conners' Teacher Rating Scale (Conners, 1969) for use in drug studies with children has been used in abbreviated form by many researchers, including Sprague and his colleagues (Sprague & Sleator, 1976), with both the child's teacher and parents. It has been found useful in providing a longitudinal and itemized measure of the child's behavior.

Prescribing stimulant drugs for children includes serious side issues, both physical and social. Ross and Ross (1982, pp. 197–220) have provided a valuable discussion that includes the potential dangers of all drugs (the possibility of leading to habits of drug abuse, growth suppression, cardiovascular effects), the chemical straightjacket effect (i.e., imposing a state of reduced affect that affects all behavior), and the mixed effects on classroom learning. All careful and comprehensive studies of drug treatment of hyperactive children have shown that it is not a treatment with unqualified success for all children. It seems to vary with the age of the child, the child's basic biochemical pattern, whether the treatment is short-term or long-term drug intervention, the care and skill of the medical researcher, and the competence and creative imagination of the teacher. It is not a procedure to be practiced carelessly or with little informed preparation.

Douglas and her colleagues at McGill University in Montreal have produced a large number of carefully controlled experiments. As a result of their many studies, Douglas believes that hyperactive children typically (1) ignore subtle but salient stimuli in the environment, (2) have poor inhibitory control, and (3) possess an impaired ability to sustain attention. She has found these children poor at most sensorimotor tasks, but good at choice discrimination tasks if a normal mental set is established. From this evidence she feels that all treatment should be directed at their inattention and impulsivity and should stress cognitive learning more than contingency learning, but for best results both should be used (Douglas, 1978).

In summary, it is important to remember that the syndromes of hyperactivity and learning disabilities are different. A child may suffer from both, but not necessarily.

1. The child whose brain is dysfunctioning, especially cortically, may suffer from perceptual deficits, cognitive impairments, and sensorimotor integration difficulties. *This is the primary LD child.*

2. The hyperactive child may have a normal and healthy brain and central nervous system but because of environmental and emotional frustrations he or she may be hyperactive. This may produce inattentiveness and impulsivity, which interfere with learning. *This is the child whose learning problem is secondary to the hyperactivity.* Such children *can* learn if their anxiety can be reduced and their attention improved (Douglas, 1976; Meichenbaum, 1976).

3. The hyperactive child may be hyperactive because of a brainstem or limbic dysrhythmia and may suffer from a perceptual, cognitive, or integrative deficit. This child's learning disability implies both primary and secondary components, and treatment will need to recognize both of these.

Environment, Learning, and the Brain

So far in our discussions we have examined cases of brain damage or dysfunction and how these pathological processes can result in deficits in behavior. This influence is from *brain to behavior*. But the brain–behavior relationships *are not unidirectional;* they imply a two-way process. While the influence of brain changes affect behavior potently and immediately, environmental influences can affect structural and functional changes in the brain, although many of these may be minimal and subtle and take considerable time.

Probably the quickest environmental alteration in the brain and CNS occurs in classical conditioning. Pavlov working with animals (1928) and Watson working with children (1919) showed that fear can be established in two or three associations with a loud noise. While the exact nature of the neurological change was not clear, the involuntary fear response that followed the cue, after a few treatments, seemed to be evidence that a change had taken place in the CNS and that it was persisting.

More recent research with animals has shown that environmental stimulation can result in increased growth of brain structures, and, conversely, prolonged environmental deprivation can modify and reduce cerebral growth. In one such experiment (Rosenzweig, 1966), litters of rats were divided at the time of weaning (about 25 days postnatally) and kept either in an enriched or an impoverished enviornment. In the enriched situation the animals were housed in groups of 10 to 12 to a large cage that had ladders, activity wheels, boxes, and platforms. The rats in this group were given free play and formal training sessions. These animals enjoyed stimulation from their cagemates, their supervised training, and their complex environment. Each of these rats had a littermate assigned to the impoverished condition where the animals were in solitary confinement in small cages with solid walls. No training or stimulation was given these animals and they were deprived of any social contact with any other animals. After 80 days the animals were sacrificed and their brains examined. The 130 littermate pairs shows that overall, the cortex of the enriched rats weighed 4% more than the cortex of the impoverished rats ($p < .001$) and was also thicker. As well, certain enzymes that facilitate the production of neurotransmitters at the synapse were more plentiful in the brains of the enriched rats. "An enriched environment after weaning increases, respectively, the number of dendritic spines and the dendritic branching of cells in the rat cortex" (Berlucchi & Buchtel, 1975). "This type of evidence suggests that rather than being fixed and pre-determined, neural mechanisms are responsive to and capable of being shaped by a variety of external factors" (Kirk, 1983a).

Let us now move up from rats to monkeys for an example of how experience can modify the brain's wiring. From the retinal cells (rods and cones) in the primate brain to the visual cortex, neural impulses travel along a tract of six synaptically connected neurons. In these optic pathways, impulses come from stimulation of either the left eye or the right. The slightly different views of the world from each eye are not merged until after the impulses reach the sixth-order nerve cell in layer IVc of the visual cortex (Calvin & Ojemann, 1980, p. 121). Cells in the layers above this, the outer cortical layers, contain neural cells sensitive to input from *both* eyes, and it is in these layers that convergence takes place and stereoscopic vision is made possible. Calvin and Ojemann (p. 122) have described an experimental situation in which a frosted contact lens is alternated daily from one eye to the other in an infant monkey, thus making normal binocular vision impossible. The cortical cells that are wired to respond to both eyes never get a chance to react normally; instead they become habituated to one eye or the other. If in the monkey's adolescence or young adulthood (about 9 months of age) the contact lens is discontinued, the ability for both eyes together to stimulate the cortical cells is almost completely lost, permanently. Evidently the early months postnatally are critical to ensure normal and optimal environmental modifying of the brain's wiring.

While radical experiments are possible with subhuman animals, they are not with human subjects. However, "studies of . . . a number of species will provide some basis for tentative extrapolation of the curves of phylogenetic development through chimpanzee to man" (Hebb & Thompson, 1954). Such extrapolation has obviously led to the infant stimulation programs practised in children's hospitals and recommended to young parents. This area of investigation provides some of the neurological knowledge on which to develop theoretical models of learning for the normal child and adult, and rehabilitation procedures for those suffering from various types of CNS damage and/or dysfunction.

Summary

This chapter, in retrospect, may seem paradoxical. It set out to stress the unitary action of the brain and then supplied evidence for lobular and hemispheric specialization, *but the reader will understand that brain function is both holistic and localized*. Although Flourens in the first half of the nineteenth century believed in the unitary activity of the brain, after 1850 there developed an increasing belief in specific cerebral localization. This view was reinforced by the continued influence of phrenology; Broca's celebrated discovery in 1861 of the relation between mutism, or expressive aphasia, and a lesion in the third frontal convolution of the left hemisphere; the improvement of the microscope, and the consequent increased knowledge of nerves and neural connections; and the discovery by Hughlings Jackson in the 1860s of the relation between unilateral cerebral disease and one-sided convulsive movements on the contralateral side of the body. In 1870 Fritsch and Hitzig electrostimulated the cerebral hemispheres of dogs and learned a great deal about the behavioral relationships of the motor strips. This led to a large number of similar studies in other animals, including monkeys and, later, humans, and by 1900 the projection areas of the cortex were known, i.e., the motor strips, somesthetic strips, acoustic areas, and visual centers of the occipital lobes (Tizard, 1959).

In psychology and physiology from about 1890 to 1930, Pavlov's reflexology, J. B. Watson's behaviorism, and E. L. Thorndike's connectionism dominated North American psychological thought. This approach conceived of nervous action as *linear* and mechanistic (the telephone model) and it tended to favor a localization view in neuropsychology. However, as is well known in the history of psychology, the imaginative researches of the Gestaltists and the brilliant work of Karl Lashley during the 1920s were among the major influences in support of unitary function of the brain. Lashley's work spoke forcefully against a segmental cerebral function. Although he started his studies under Watson about 1914 and hence believed that the linear reflex arc was the unit of all behavior, Lashley's researches after 1917, when he first met Franz, led him to the belief that behavior might be controlled by widely separate cerebral loci and prompted him to produce his theory of cortical *equipotentiality* and *mass action*. Although *projection function* (i.e., the action of the three sensory and one motor cortical areas) is localized, even it shows some within-area variability in the rat. For example, even in the motor strip the same center at one moment may stimulate a finger, at another time another finger, and at yet another time the shoulder. He concluded that *projection function* is localized, although not rigidly, but *correlation function* (i.e., the neural action of the remaining association cortices) is not.

Judson Herrick (1944) wrote:

> Integration of bodily activities is a primordial essential; without it no living body can survive. . . . No local activity of sensorimotor type can be carried on by well-insulated autonomous reflex arcs as these have been conventionally described. *There are no such reflex arcs in the amphibian nervous system.* There are reflexes, because of a pathway of preferential discharge, but there is a spreading effect, and accompanying the response there is also excitation of much nervous tissue not involved in the overt action.

Hebb (1949) was one of the first psychologists to see the efficacy of accepting both concepts, Herrick's "pathway of preferential discharge" (a kind of connectionism) and the field action of the cell assembly. Geschwind (1965) more recently has proposed the concept of the "cerebral disconnexion syndrome" in explaining aphasia, apraxia, dyslexia, and agraphia. Essentially this is a more recent version of earlier connectionist models, in which destruction of transcortical or subcortical pathways joining two functional centers in the cortex produces an isolation of those centers or impairs the normal interaction between them. Coulter, a pediatric neurologist, uses this same concept to explain learning disabilities in children. He proposes that "functional hypoconnection of cerebral cortical regions important for cognitive growth could result from relative underdevelopment of specific cerebral association fiber pathway systems necessary for learning. Hypoconnection could reflect decreased myelination, axodendritic underdevelopment, synaptic dysfunction or neurotransmitter abnormalities" (Coulter, 1981). In simple language, this means that a lesion in one cerebral locus may incapacitate two or more other centers remote from it, even though the tissues of those centers themselves may be healthy and undamaged. In spite of this complex and dynamically variable action of the brain, a lesion in a particular locus tends to have a reliable result.

Diffuse left-hemisphere dysfunction is likely to impair verbal abilities and cause them to be inferior to visual–spatial and constructive functions. However, localized left-hemisphere lesions, depending on their location, may have little or no effect on verbal skills. A 12-year-old boy seen in our laboratory had the front third of his left temporal lobe removed surgically, and postoperatively he obtained a WISC verbal IQ of 116 and a performance IQ of 97 even with left-hemisphere language dominance. Because no language areas of the left hemisphere were seriously affected by the surgery, he still retained much of his preoperative verbal superiority, but because he had to learn to write and manipulate objects with his left hand following a postoperative hemiparesis on the right side (partial paralysis of the right hand), his slowness on coding and object assembly pulled down his performance IQ. This is a good case to caution us against making quick or superficial diagnoses from knowing the site of the lesion. The verbal–spatial–left–right dichotomy usually holds in adults and older children, but a focal lesion requires more knowledge before statements can be made about probable behavior. Similarly the neuropsychologist cannot deduce the side of the lesion *only* on the basis of a verbal–performance imbalance on the WISC.

Although parietal lobe lesions usually impair the subject's directionality, this does not always hold. In our laboratory we have encountered two adult patients with space-occupying parietal lesions who both pre- and postoperatively obtained perfect scores on Benton's Right–Left Orientation Test. Such seeming contradictions require more knowledge of the exact locus of tissue damage and the quality of performance on the test.

Another patient, aged 20, following the surgical removal of her right parietal, temporal, and occipital lobes, was still able to do simple route-finding problems and locate major cities on a map of North America, although her spatial–perceptual abilities were impaired. Her WAIS performance IQ was only 77, although she could still obtain a near-superior verbal IQ of 117.

The above two cases, while contradicting what we would expect using the classical model of brain function as a basis of prediction, are useful as a caution against quick and simplistic diagnoses. In both cases, more knowledge accounted for the seeming paradoxical behavior, in the form of localized lesions that spared essential neural pathways and compensatory learning strategies acquired by the patients.

Clinical Addendum

What the Clinical Psychologist Can Do

Using a detailed battery of neuropsychological tests has the advantage that it provides numerous measures of sensory, cognitive, motor, sensorimotor, and serial order behaviors. The psychologist familiar with such a battery soon learns to read the test profile and to hypothesize that the cerebral area of dysfunction is likely central or peripheral, cortical or subcortical, and diffuse, regional, or highly localized. He or she proposes a diagnostic hypothesis from this knowledge of specific brain–behavior relationships.

Let us look first at an adult case of traumatic head injury. This young man had successfully completed the freshman year of university so it seems safe to conclude that, pretraumatically, he did not suffer from a severe learning disability.

Clinical Case Findings

Male; age 21 years; tests administered 3 months posttraumatically.
Wechsler Adult Intelligence Scale: Verbal IQ, 95; range of verbal subtest
    scores, 8–11; performance IQ, 59; range of performance subtest scores, 4–5.
Halstead Aphasia Screening Test: Verbal responses, average to above average;
    drawings, inferior.

Visual Perception: Visual–motor tasks, poor; imbedded figures, weak.
Nonverbal sound recognition and phonetic discrimination, poor; oral repetition
   of sentences, normal.
Stereognosis: Right hand, near normal; left hand, inferior.
Finger localization: Right hand, one error; left hand, three errors.
Right–left orientation: Very poor, many reversals.
Finger tapping: Right hand, slow; left hand, inferior.
Discussion: The test data suggest that this young man suffered a very severe
   head injury, with bilateral dysfunctions but maximal impairment in the right
   hemisphere.

These tests were administered 3 months after the injury, and the fact that
he still showed so much perceptual and motor impairment tells us that the
injury was very severe.

Even so, there are some hopeful signs. The fact that he could score in
the normal range (although in the low side of that range) in spatial inductive and deductive reasoning (Halstead Category Test), in commonplace
arithmetical problems (Wechsler arithmetic) and abstract verbal conceptualizing (Wechsler similarities) is strongly suggestive of large areas of
healthy cortical tissue that were spared. In addition, this above-average
performance on the Weschsler Comprehension subtest provides some
evidence of retained integrative mental functions.

The signs of impairment are many. The consistent relative inferiority
on the Wechsler performance scores, the visual perception tests, and the
many inferior scores on the left hand are typical of right-hemisphere
damage and resulting dysfunction. However, the left hemisphere did not
escape completely because his verbal IQ of 95 is much lower than measures made when he was in elementary school (Grade 3 IQ, 112; Grade 6
IQ, 115). Also, his inability to do serial order tasks (Wechsler Digit Span
and Digit Symbol; Seashore Tonal Memory; Reitan Trail-Making Test) is
strongly suggestive of left-hemisphere damage and/or dysfunction. As
well, both hands were below average in their performances on the Benton
Stereognosis Test, Benton finger localization, Benton Right–Left Orientation Test, finger tapping, and hand-grip strength.

Medical History

The deductions about brain damage so far in this case have been made
purely from the psychometric data. Let us see how this is complemented
by the medical history. The neurologist reported: "This young man was in
an automobile accident in 1963 in which he suffered a depressed skull
fracture in the left frontal area. He was brought into the hospital in a
completely comatose state and was completely unresponsive even to

painful stimuli (pinpricks in his hands and feet). His arms and legs showed a neuromuscular rigidity (hypertonicity) that indicated bilateral brain damage. He was unconscious for almost 3 weeks, and when he first regained consciousness he was mentally confused.'' His speech was slurred and still was when he was tested 3 months later. He was hospitalized more than 2 months, and when he was finally able to walk, his gait was unsteady and poorly coordinated. His EEG showed generalized bilateral disturbance with greater dysrhythmia in the left frontal and right parieto-temporal–occipital areas.

Combining the information of both the medical and neuropsychological data, it seems almost certain that the severe impact to his head on the left frontal side of his skull had a *contra-coup* effect in which the concussion traveled through to his right hemisphere where most of the damage occurred. The left frontal damage seems to be related to his slurred speech (Broca's area) and his problems with sequencing, and the right-hemisphere damage is most likely correlated with his poor visual–spatial–constructional skills.

Follow-up

This young man was clinically followed for 6 years with periodic test measurements and is still contacted intermittently in connection with his occupational placement. On the Wechsler he showed the following pattern of improvement:

	Verbal IQ	Performance IQ
July 1963	Accident.	
October 1963	95	59
March 1964	106	89
October 1964	102	91
November 1965	100	94
August 1969	112	90
Mean	103	84.6

On the last Wechsler (WAIS) administered, in 1969, his above-average scores were:

Arithmetic	15
Comprehension	14
Vocabulary	13
Information	12
Similarities	12
Block design	12
Verbal IQ	112
Performance IQ	90

All other subtests were below average, presumably from the permanent brain damage. However, the general test profile shows him to be verbally mentally bright.

He still suffers from minimal balance problems, although he has learned to waterski again, something that he enjoyed prior to the accident. His speech is permanently slurred and this has proved a handicap in job interviews because it has sometimes been mistaken for mental retardation and/or drunkeness. This young man took several years to adjust his vocational aims from a professional level to a type of work he could enjoy and at which he could be successful. He could handle his first job as a filing clerk because of his above-average verbal intelligence, but he disliked the tedious routine and the confinement of an office. Preferring outdoor work he took a professional gardening course, and eventually he was hired as a gardener by a city parks board. He has subsequently married and made a good adjustment to his injury.

A Cautionary Note to the School Psychologist

In this chapter the major part of the discussion has focused on cases of brain damage or localized cerebral dysfunction, because an introduction to organically based LD students is easier to understand with these types of cases. While they have been selected because of their pedagogical usefulness, the reader will remember that they occur in only a minority of cases (probably 2% to 3% of the elementary school population). Such cases fit our category 1 (see Table 1.1). The subjects in the second category (MBD) most likely have CNS lesions or dysfunctions, but as we have already seen, it is frequently difficult or impossible to be sure. Category 3 contains subjects with no evidence of brain lesions, and they include most of the LD children seen in a large elementary school. This means that while most LD children have no clear evidence of specific brain lesions, they may exhibit subtle perceptual or motor deficits that suggest possible cerebral dysfunctions, and to analyze a minimal learning problem it is often useful to understand more severe cases of impaired cognitive processing. As we have observed before, the school psychologist with a competent knowledge of normal brain function and dysfunction will likely be better prepared to propose realistic hypotheses for remediation. But we must be reminded that conclusive brain lesions occur in a minority of LD cases, and the school psychologist should guard against looking for brain damage or neural pathology in every case of academic underachievement.

What the Teacher Can Do

The case of traumatic brain damage in an adult described above, will likely be of more interest and use to the teacher of high school, college, or an adult rehabilitation center. We have chosen adult cases to examine first because they do not have the complicating developmental changes that are typical in childhood. Even so, many of the same remedial measures used with children are useful with traumatically brain-damaged adults because their cognitive skills may have been temporarily repressed and constrained at a childish level.

In the case of our young man, there were several positive indications for the remedial teachers and therapists. The chief of these were (1) his cheery personality and his cooperative acceptance of direction (frequently right-hemisphere lesion cases react surprisingly euphorically), (2) his above-average verbal intelligence, and (3) his supportive family.

The program of remediation included speech therapy; exercises to improve visual discrimination, visual–motor speed, and accuracy; phonetic discrimination and oral verbal memory; tactile–kinesthetic (or haptic) recognition; large- and small-muscle activities to enhance his sensorimotor integration; and reading and writing. Specific remedial activities have not been listed because they should be selected in each case by the therapist and/or remedial teacher, but the areas needing attention were indicated by the neuropsychological test battery. As well, the teachers and therapists were provided with the medical and neuropsychological findings, and the expected pattern of competent and deficit behaviors. This supplied a better basis for their ongoing program evaluation of the case and the possible prognosis. His increase in verbal IQ from 95 to 112 6 years later suggests that the activation of his brain and neuromuscular system may have had some restorative value.

5 Perceptual Disorders

. . . the input is never into a quiescent or static system, but always into a system which is already actively excited and organized. In the intact organism, behavior is the result of interaction of this background of excitation with input from any designated stimulus. Only when we can state the general characteristics of this background of excitation, can we understand the effects of a given input.

Karl S. Lashley, *The Hixon Symposium* (1948)

The education of children with perceptual handicaps . . . is the most technical of all aspects of teaching. It cannot be taken for granted that any teacher can teach these children on the basis of the usual teacher preparation or special education teacher preparation programs. Teachers of children with perceptual developmental problems must be skilled diagnostic and educational technologists as well as excellent teachers.

William M. Cruickshank (1975)

Teachers characteristically have directed their pupils to "pay attention" or "settle down and concentrate" when they have wished to communicate a new idea or concept. The simplistic implication is that if the pupil pays attention to the statements of the teacher (that is, opens up his receptive apparatus in some unexplained way) he will learn. Unfortunately the process of learning is not that simple.

Since the beginning of the gradual integration of neurological, psychological, and educational knowledge in the early 1960s, it has become useful for both psychologists and teachers to use the neurological model of behavior for diagnostic understanding. As described in Chapter 3, in this model there are three regions or areas of neurophysiological functions: (1) sensory nerve function, (2) cerebral or brain function, and (3) motor nerve function. The first of these includes the afferent nerves leading from the sense organs (chiefly the eyes, ears, and touch receptors in the skin) to the brain. Once the various nerve patterns reach the brain they are decoded, integrated, and reorganized; some are stored, others are retrieved from the brain's data bank. Finally, they are encoded into the nerve pattern to travel down the motor nerves to the muscles, tendons, and skeletal connections. Observed behavior is actually the neuromuscular activity resulting from the expression of the nerve patterns traveling along the motor or efferent nerves to the effectors. The behavioral correlates of these neural events are (1) sensation, (2) cognition, and (3) response. Although this mechanistic view of behavior is useful for diagnostic trouble shooting, it must be remembered that all behavior is holistic and involves all three areas interacting and operating simultaneously. More will be said about this later in the chapter.

Sensation

It may be useful for the special educator to have a clear and workable concept, although a simplistic one, of sensation, in contrast to perception. Sensation may be thought of as the sensory awareness of simple elements of experience in the "distance senses" of seeing and hearing and the "skin senses" of touch, warmth, cold, and pain. Examples of these stimuli are spots of light on a screen, a tone on an audiometer, or the pressure of a fine nylon hair on a finger. In such experiences the subject has only to report when he or she has the sensation of the light, or the tone, or the physical pressure. These stimuli can be started at a weak level of intensity below the threshold of sensitivity (i.e., subliminally) and increased systematically to a level where the subject will report first being aware of the stimulus. In such a situation, known as the study of psychophysics, a known physical intensity is related to a reported subjective experience. In neuropsychology this can be a useful technique for inferring the presence and locus of a brain lesion.

Hebb (1958/1966/1972) has described the neurological substrate of sensation as involving the activation of receptors "and the resulting activity of afferent paths up to and including the corresponding cortical sensory area" (1966). He views sensation as a "one-stage" process that is little affected by learning, if at all. It implies a simple neural process from the particular sense organ to its appropriate projection area in the cortex, with a minimal amount of stimulation of association cortical area. The automatic perception of figure and ground appears to be nativistic and a sensorily determined unity, mediated by the inherited structural and functional characteristics of the nervous system (Hebb, 1949). Two examples may make this clear. Newborn infants appear to fixate an object held above them, and perception can be elicited by varying its brightness, color, or movement. Fantz originated an ingenious experimental method for observing this process:

> The infant's eyes are observed through a $\frac{1}{4}$ inch hole in the center of the chamber ceiling. To provide an objective criterion of fixation, the stimu-

lus and lighting conditions are adjusted so that tiny images of the targets are clearly visible to the observer, mirrored from the surface of the infant's eyes. [Fantz, 1961]

Fantz infers that when the reflection of a particular target is directly over the center of the pupil, the infant is looking at that particular target.

Our second example circumvents the lack of verbal report from infants by referring to clinical reports of initial vision in adults following surgical operation for the removal of cataracts existing since birth. These cases are not numerous and frequently are incompletely reported, but Hebb (1949) has described several, in particular one examined by Senden (1932). Evidently these patients immediately after the bandages are removed from their eyes can see an object or simple geometric design, such as a square, but they cannot learn to name it without several weeks of repetition. In other words, they can sense a figure against a background but they cannot perceive and remember small distinguishing features until many repetitions have occurred. This may give the teacher of the dyslexic child some insight into the problem and generate more tolerance for the child who has no difficulty in pointing to particular letters and words, but who cannot remember their meaning in spite of frequent remedial drill.

While these types of research and clinical findings may be interesting to the teacher, their practical value is indirect. What is useful is to know whether or not the child with the learning problem is free of any sensory deficit. For example, a dyslexic child may perform normally on the ophthalmologist's tests of visual acuity, and in fact he usually does; but one can only infer from this that his reading problem does not stem from visual dysfunctions as measured by the usual visual tests. Since the child's problem is not in the visual tracts, one can presume that it is primarily central or neuropsychological, genetic or social. It is not a problem of sensation, then, but of perception.

Less frequent is the child who shows normal hearing on an audiometric test but is unable to perceive phonetic differences. One girl seen in our laboratory showed near-normal auditory sensation and high nonverbal intelligence but was "deaf" to almost all words, even her own name. Again, this was a problem of almost normal sensation with auditory imperception.

Perception

By contrast with sensation, perception implies recognition, discrimination, and understanding of what one is aware. Where, in our definition of sensation, the subject had only to report awareness of a spot of light or a tone, in perception he must now recognize the form of an object, such as a chair; a graphic symbol, such as a letter or word; or a stream of speech sounds as meaningful language. It is the product of repeated experiences and motor responses to the environment. The child must be sensorily aware of an object, must store an image of this object in the form of a neural engram somewhere in the brain, and must react to the object and retain a memory of his reaction to it. Then, when next confronted with it, he compares the immediate sensation of the object with his active memory of it; in this way the child can recognize it and decide how to deal with it in relation to its immediate environment and to his own wishes at the time. Sensation and perception, while closely allied functionally, differ in that sensation implies only restricted afferent neural function and is dominated by sensory control. By contrast, perception, although initiated by sensation, includes numerous cortical neural exchanges and is not dominated by sensory input. Hebb has shown that it "normally requires a sequence of stimulations, and . . . an internal sequence of mediating-process activities; it is very much influenced by learning, and its relation to stimulating events is highly variable" (Hebb, 1958/1966/1972).

In sensation, the same stimulus produces the same experience and the same response (Hebb, 1972, Chap. 12). Two examples will illustrate this. First, the reflex arc, described in Chapter 3, is an example of rigid stimulus and response; second, a spot of light impinging on the retinae of a normally healthy subject will arouse excitations of a spot of light in the occipital lobes. In these cases no perception or interpretation of the situation need take place. It is pure reflex action or mechanical registration.

In perception, there may be a variable response in terms of the subject's experiences and wishes. By contrast with the rigidity and invariance of response in sensation, in perception "the same stimulus can produce different perceptions and different stimuli the same perception" (Hebb, 1966). It is commonplace knowledge that the same Rorschach card will produce various descriptions from a number of viewers and that a movie or play will arouse in different members of the audience reactions ranging from disapproval to enthusiastic admiration.

Neuropsychologically we might hypothesize that the two processes, sensation and perception, require sensory nerve tracts and appropriate projection areas of the cortex, but in perception wider cortical activation occurs, presumably to provide greater association of meaning and integration of wider cortical, neural (H. Davis, 1964), and circulatory changes (Risberg & Ingvar, 1973).

It is important that teachers have clear and distinguishable concepts of sensation and perception so as not to fall into the trap of thinking that the dyslexic child who performs normally on a visual acuity test is free of all visual difficulties. Frequently teachers, deceived by this seeming paradox, have concluded, "It can't be his vision because his eyes are OK," and they have tried to look elsewhere for causes, or they have abandoned the search as insoluble. An eye chart will not reveal perceptual rotations nor an audiometer, a phonetic imperception. Accurate information about the child's modes of perception is essential to the diagnosis of his learning problem.

Attention

It is well known that humans are bombarded by numerous and various environmental stimuli, but only some of these stimuli are accepted and responded to. Because "attention involves the selection of specific information by the organism . . . it is logical to expect it to be associated with selective facilitatory processes in the brain" (Hernández-Peón & Sterman, 1966). In fact, it seems to be determined by basic neural structures and characteristic functions of which the school psychologist and the special teacher can be aware.

The first of these is the brainstem, reaching upward from the medulla oblongata to the thalamus and the cortex. The sensory nerves connecting into the thalamus branch out, some going directly to their particular sensory nuclei and thence to the appropriate sensory area of the cortex—visual, auditory, or tactile. The others, several million of them, connect through the thalamus to all parts of the cortex. The function of the main branch is to provide perceptual cues, and the function of the remaining fibers to the nonspecific cortical areas is believed to be an "arousal system" (Hebb, 1972). The reticular activating system appears to have two functions, arousal and selective attention. While neurophysiological research has confirmed the "arousal" function (Moruzzi & Magoun, 1949) there is not complete agreement on how the brain selects particular objects on which to focus attention while ignoring all others, but this seems to include the inhibition of receptors (Hernández-Peón, Scherrer, & Jouvet, 1956), the acceptance or inhibition of sensory input (i.e., "gating," P. M. Milner, 1970) by both the brain stem and the cortex, the amount of experience and knowledge, and the strength of motivation of the person attending.

The upper part of the brain stem mediates arousal and regulates sleep. Various parts of the thalamus control the shift of attention from the internal to the external world, and, like the cerebral cortex, the left side of the thalamus is more involved with verbal perceptions and the right thalamus more with visual–spatial input. "The selective attention mechanism seems to be the system turning different brain areas on and off to the external or internal world" (Calvin & Ojemann, 1980, p. 97). These writers have proposed the interesting speculation that malfunctioning of the selective attention system could lead to a weak ability to hold attention on external stimuli (e.g., instructions of a teacher) so that attention could easily be diverted by other external or internal stimuli (i.e., distractibility). This pattern of behavior will be familiar to any experienced teacher as typical of many LD children. Many of them manifest chorea (i.e., minimal involuntary twitching movements of the hands and/or the face) and other neurological signs that might be the result of malfunctioning of the thalamus or striatum (Calvin & Ojemann, 1980).

Where the gross structure of the reticular formation is believed to regulate the incoming neural stream from the receptors to control attention and concentration, single cells function in particular ways to direct it. Some exciting researches in the last two decades have provided strong evidence to suggest that specific cortical cells respond to specific environmental stimuli. In the visual sphere, Hubel and Wiesel (1959; Hubel, 1963) have shown that some cortical cells in the cat's striate cortex react to vertical lines of light but not to horizontal or sloping ones. They have discovered that some cells are turned "on" by particular forms and contiguous cells are inhibited. The "on" and "off" groupings of cells were found to be mutually antagonistic and to possess not a random distribution and function but an orderly arrangement in the cortex. These were microelectrode or single-cell studies and provided information to support the idea of a one-to-one relationship from retinal pattern to visual cortical coding. Morrell (1961, 1967) has found that some cells in the visual cortex, but not all, are subject to stimulation by temporary connections. These particular cells, which initially reacted to a specific light stimulus, could be primed to respond to a temporally contiguous sound stimulus. This evidence suggests that some cortical cells are unique in their responses and others are more general. Some may be feature-detecting cells (Pribram, 1971) and others may be more concerned with arousal functions and with more general tasks of perception and interpretation.

For the teacher, it is interesting to know whether "feature-detecting" cells, or indeed any large groups of cortical cells, can be modified by experience. At Cambridge University in England a number of researchers (Blakemore & Cooper, 1970; Blakemore & Mitchell, 1973) raised kittens in complete darkness from birth, except for periods in cylindrical chambers with walls painted in black and white vertical stripes. They found that the critical sensitive period for modifying brain growth in kittens is from 3 to 14 weeks of age, and the 28th day seemed to be the time of peak sensitivity. Microelectrode studies of control animals showed large numbers of visually unresponsive cells, and many with no orientational preference at all. However, the experimental animals all showed the majority of the cells in the primary visual cortex responding over a narrow range of orientation strongly biased to vertical. It was interesting that they found no degeneration of unused cells and no regions of silent cortex. Kittens raised in an environment of horizontal stripes appeared blind to vertical contours when they were released in a normal physical environment of tables and chairs. Neurons from the "horizontally" raised cat showed orientational preference for reaction to horizontal lines ± 20°, and neurons from a "vertically" raised cat showed a preference for vertical orientation. In a normal environment "They always followed moving objects with very clumsy, jerky head movements and they often tried to touch things moving on the other side of the room, well beyond their reach . . . they often bumped into table legs and they scurried around" (Blakemore & Cooper, 1970). Teuber (1975) in trying to replicate Blakemore's work found no such unequivocal results, but reported evidence of kittens raised only in an environment of strobe light patterns developing "no directional" cells in their brains. This impaired their development of normal visual form recognition although they responded positively to strobe light stimulation.

Although all of these studies are inconclusive, they do suggest that the child's brain probably develops cortical cells, some of which are specific to various perceptual patterns and some more general in their functions and responses. Animal studies show that neural patterns of function may be altered in very young animals, but knowledge of neural plasticity of children's brains is less clear. Even so, we might hypothesize that children raised in nonliterate environments might have greater difficulty in learning to recognize letter forms, and to read and write, than those who were raised with books and stories, although this would be difficult to test in most cases because of the negative attitudes transmitted by illiterate parents.

The psychologist will recognize that the physiological processes of arousal and selective attention described above are responsible for what has been called in psychology, "mental set," that is, the attitude of preparedness that enables a person to react to a meaningful pattern of significant cues and to ignore the "background noise." Understanding possible reasons for its impairment should lead to greater tolerance of the distractible learner and to better methods of improving his ability for competent attention.

Lateral Asymmetries in Perception

We have already seen that brain damage and/or dysfunction in the left hemisphere usually impairs verbal skills, and dysfunction in the right hemisphere, visual–spatial competence. In this section we shall look at some research studies designed to examine the hemispheric differences in subjects with *normal* brains, when they are confronted with visual stimuli or subjected to auditory excitation. In other words, we shall look at the innate perceptual tendencies of the normal brain.

Before we examine some experiments in visual perception we should be reminded that the left half of each retina connects into the left occipital lobe, and the two right halves to the right occipital lobe (Fig. 3.7). This means that if the left halves of the retinae are stimulated, only the left cerebral hemisphere is affected, and by stimulating only the right retinal halves there results only right-hemisphere processing of the neural input. If the two hemispheres possess innate tendencies to treat verbal and spatial material differently, as the lesion studies have suggested, then it should show itself in controlled experiments with normal brains. A visual stimulus in the left visual field, that is, to the left of the midline, will excite points in the right half of each retina because the incoming light rays cross in the lens. Similarly, objects in the right visual field will impinge on the left half of each retina (Fig. 3.7).

To study this process a subject is seated before a white screen with a fixation point or X in its center. The subject is asked to fixate the X and report what he sees as visual stimuli are flashed on the screen in either the left or the right field for short periods of time, usually between 100 and 200 milliseconds (one-tenth to one-fifth of a second).

In the 1950s it was discovered that when stimuli were presented rapidly on a tachistoscope (a device for presenting very rapid visual stimuli under highly controlled conditions) to either the left or the right visual field, verbal material was usually reported more accurately from the right visual field (Heron, 1957; Mishkin & Forgays, 1952). At that time this was interpreted completely in terms of learned scanning habits acquired through reading. However, Dr. Doreen Kimura, a Canadian psychologist then at McGill University, first proposed that this asymmetry was caused, at least in part, by the more dominant participation of the left hemisphere in the processing of words and letters (Kimura, 1961b), and this neuropsychological interpretation, added to what was already known of perceptual learning, resulted in a great body of research into perceptual asymmetries (Dimond & Beaumont, 1974; Kimura, 1959, 1961a,b, 1966, 1969, 1973a; Kimura & Durnford, 1974; Kinsbourne & Smith, 1974).

This discovery of the possible relation of cerebral dominance and perceptual asymmetry in the right and left visual fields and the right and left ears was a major accomplishment in the acquisition of neuropsychological knowledge, and the interested student might like to read Kimura's early paper (1959), in which she tried to explain the right visual superiority only in terms of increased facility in reading. She sensed that some other force was at work, because she concluded that the neural feedback model of learned eye movements "cannot be the complete explanation" (Kimura, 1959). However, within 2 years she had concluded from her dichotic listening studies and her work with temporal lobe lesion cases that the crossed auditory pathways are more efficient (Kimura, 1961a).

To understand this, the student must be reminded that each ear connects to both temporal lobes, but the crossed neural pathway or the connections to the contralateral hemisphere are more strongly represented than those to the ipsilateral temporal lobe (Fig. 3.8). Kimura (1961b) wisely extended her conclusions from the auditory to the visual sense mode. "If the relation suggested here between the identification of verbal stimuli and the hemisphere at which they arrive is correct, one might expect a similar effect with visually presented verbal material." Once the importance of cerebral dominance, as well as learning, was invoked to explain perceptual differences for verbal and nonverbal visual and auditory stimuli, many of the previous unexplained discrepancies could be understood.

In further studies, Kimura (1966) showed a superior right-hemisphere function or left visual field superiority for spatial material. She has provided not only an excellent summary of her work in left visual field superiority for dot enumeration and right field superiority for letter identification, but she has reported (Kimura & Durnford, 1974) better left field recognition of geometric forms; sex differences for spatial localization, with males showing a significant left field effect; better binocular depth perception in the left field but no differences for monocular depth perception; and a slightly better identification of line slant in the left visual field.

The student new to these ideas must realize that functional hemispheric asymmetries are not rigidly and exclusively determined by verbal and nonverbal input. As we have already shown in Chapter 4, other variables are also at work such as attention (Kinsbourne, 1975c), expectancy (Spellacy & Blumstein, 1970), the level of intellectual complexity or difficulty (Buffery, 1976), the age of the child (Bakker, Teunissen, & Bosch, 1976), stimulus complexity (Umilta, Bagnara, & Simion, 1978), and stimulus modality (Davis & Wada, 1977). These ideas will be explored again in Chapter 7 and throughout the book.

Visual Agnosia

Because it is frequently easier to understand small behavioral imperfections within the normal range by examining the grossly abnormal, we will look briefly at a severe and somewhat rare clinical example of impaired or distorted visual perception. Although not all neurologists agree on a definition of the visual agnosias, they are disorders of perceptual recognition caused by dysfunctions of higher cerebral nervous activity. Frederiks (1969a) has described the syndrome of "the impaired recognition of an object which is sensorially presented while at the same time the impairment cannot be reduced to sensory defects, mental deterioration, disorders of consciousness and attention, or to a non-familiarity with the object.''

Benson and Greenberg (1969) have reported the rare case of a man with normal visual fields but severely impaired form recognition. At the age of 25 this young man suffered permanent and diffuse brain damage as the result of inhaling carbon monoxide fumes from a leaking connection in an army shower room. Prior to this accident he had been physically normal and healthy. Following his brain injury he could name colors and appeared to follow moving visual stimuli, but he could not recognize by vision alone familiar objects placed before him. He was able to walk along hospital corridors and avoid furniture, although his movements were jerky and awkward. His understanding of spoken speech was normal and his tactile form recognition (stereognosis) was unimpaired. Visually he was unable to recognize large letters or numbers on a blackboard, although he could name them if he watched them being drawn slowly. This suggests that he was using proprioceptive cues rather than visual ones to perceive the form of the letter.

His recent and long-term memory, his speech (both comprehension and spoken), and his ability to repeat sentences were all normally intact. Although he could name colors he was unable to identify objects, pictures of objects, body parts, letters, numbers, or geometric figures on visual confrontation. He could, however, identify objects by touch, smell, or sound. He was totally unable to copy letters or simple figures, a condition which is partially similar to a severe case of developmental agraphia.

He was unable to select his doctor or family members from a group until they spoke, and he identified his own image in a mirror as his doctor's face. This case illustrates a highly selective visual–perceptual impairment, the inability to recognize forms of familiar objects and letters. Since this ability was normal prior to the brain injury we can conclude that the association cortical areas essential to visual form recognition were most likely permanently destroyed.

This case of visual agnosia reminds us rather forcibly that brain damage or dysfunction can impair the ability for normal visual recognition of commonplace objects, persons, and letters. The last named will interest the remedial teacher because it proposes a possible primary cause of dyslexia. However, not all cases of visual object agnosia are dyslexic, nor are all dyslexics suffering from some form of visual–perceptual impairment.

Levine (1978) has reported a particularly interesting case of a woman who, in her late 50s, developed a brain tumor in the lower posterior subcortical part of her brain. The tumor, a space-occupying progressive type, pressed on the right occipital lobe with such force as to displace it laterally to the right and down onto the cerebellum to produce an awkward gait. To remove the tumor, the surgeon was forced to cut into the occipital lobe at both its upper (by the falx) and lower (by the tentorium) extremities. Following this surgery, the woman was unable to recognize by sight her own relatives, her doctors, and hospital ward personnel. However, her speech was fluent, her comprehension of language excellent, and her reading competent with large print.

It seems likely that Benson and Greenberg's case was occipitally *bilaterally* damaged because the damage was diffuse, so that both visual reading and object recognition were impaired. Levins' case, by contrast, was severely damaged by surgery in the right occipital lobe, which produced the visual object agnosia, but since the left hemisphere was spared, reading, speech, and language were intact.

In Chapter 8 we will examine the neurological causes of dyslexia at more length.

Auditory Imperception

We have already referred briefly to two cases of auditory imperception, in Chapter 3 and previously in this chapter, but because this process is essential to normal academic learning, we will examine the consequences of its dysfunction more thoroughly here.

First, the teacher and the diagnostician must be clear in understanding that auditory imperception may result from neural damage or dysfunction in (1) the peripheral auditory nervous system, resulting in deafness or some degree of hearing loss; and/or (2) the central auditory tracts in the brain and auditory cortex, resulting in some type of auditory agnosia.

Because subtle forms of hearing loss are often missed and are nearly always at least a partial source of a learning disability, it is imperative that at the outset a competent audiometric test be carried out. If the child is obviously hard of hearing, a technical aid may compensate for his difficulty, and if the child's brain functions are normal he should be able to learn at a normal or near-normal level. In this case the physiological deficit is *peripheral,* not *central,* so that the correction of sensory input will provide the child with a normal learning situation.

Some estimates of hearing deficits resulting in classroom learning problems have indicated that most are caused by "high frequency hearing losses associated with a sloping configuration of audiogram" (Schain, 1972); and that these are sometimes associated with some degree of speech disturbance. However, Wepman (1975) warns that no research has been reported verifying this assumption. Once the teacher is advised of the presence and nature of the hearing loss, he or she should be able to obtain direction regarding the management of the case from the speech therapist or school psychologist.

Although cases of sensorial or peripheral deafness are more common, cases of *central* deafness, when they occur, are more devastating in their disruption of learning. These are the cases of auditory agnosia for speech, nonverbal sounds, and music, and they include the inability to recognize or decode auditory stimuli, although hearing may be intact (Frederiks, 1969a). Whereas neurologists and audiologists may provide a more elaborate and definitive classification, the teacher and clinician may find it more practical and expedient to concentrate attention only on those aspects of auditory perception and imperception that are strongly related to classroom learning. These are (1) language and speech perception, the deficit being known as receptive aphasia; (2) the perception of nonverbal environmental sounds, such as a fire bell, whistle, handclapping, the deficit being known as auditory agnosia; and (3) the perception and enjoyment of music, the deficit being known as amusia.

At this point auditory imperception for speech will not be discussed, because sensory aphasia will be examined in Chapter 8. However, neurologically, it is interesting to note that this appears to result from a brain lesion or dysfunction in Wernicke's area of the dominant hemisphere (Luria, 1966).

By contrast, it appears possible that nonverbal sound recognition may depend more on the nondominant hemisphere, although as symbolic processes are drawn on for more subtle understanding and apperception, it seems certain that both hemispheres are increasingly involved, especially committing the first and second convolutions of both temporal lobes (Frederiks, 1969a). In fact, all or most tasks of auditory perception of so-called nonverbal stimuli include some degree of verbal mediation. The Spreen–Benton Sound Recognition Test (Spreen & Benton, 1969/1977) requires the child to name the source of the sound after listening to a tape of a cat meowing, a church bell ringing, people clapping, etc. For an aphasic child, a multiple-choice form is used that allows the child to avoid the word-finding task by pointing to a picture in an array. Even in this form of the test, which is designed to minimize the language aspects of the situation, there is symbolic content that is likely to include some degree of verbal activity. Probably, the only nearly pure nonverbal auditory stimulus is music, and what clinical evidence exists suggests that a motor amusia (the inability to sing and imitate a tune) may result from a right frontal lesion, in roughly the mirror position of Broca's area. Receptive amusia (the inability to recognize a tune or appreciate music) appears to include the temporal lobes bilaterally (Wertheim, 1969). For a person to sing a song with words, both hemispheres contribute. Wada (Wada, Clarke & Hamm, 1975) has demonstrated this neatly in a simple clinical test. After he injects sodium amytal into the patient's left carotid artery, he asks the patient to sing "Happy Birthday." If the patient is left-hemisphere dominant for language, as most people are, he will be able to hum the tune but not produce the words. When the same patient after right-side amytal injection is asked to sing the same song, he will recite the words of "Happy Birthday" in a monotone, unable to produce the tune. Wada has found this asymmetrical pattern in the majority of the patients he sees.

A survey of the literature of auditory imperception shows that most, if not all, patients also have some signs of receptive aphasia, or difficulty in understanding spoken speech. However, rarely a case occurs wherein the patient cannot recognize simple environmental sounds but has no problems either in understanding or expressing language. Such a case was reported by Spreen, Benton, and Fincham (1965).

This was the case of a 65-year-old man who had suffered a right-hemisphere stroke resulting in impairment of his left arm and left leg (left hemiparesis). The hemiparesis gradually disappeared during the following 6 months, to be followed by left-sided clonic seizures. His right side was not affected during these seizures, indicating that he was suffering from a unilateral lesion in the right half of his brain. The seizures were successfully managed by the administration of anticonvulsive medication. During the next 2 years he was hospitalized from time to time because of frontal headaches, emotional personality changes, a difficulty in walking, and a mild left visual field defect. An EEG showed abnormal activity chiefly over the right temporal area.

On neuropsychological testing his overall intelligence was in the dull normal range, but he had most difficulty with visual–spatial tasks, performances usually impaired by right-hemisphere dysfunction. Finger localization was normal for the right hand but inferior for the left, although detailed language testing revealed no signs of aphasia. His worst performance was in sound recognition; he was unable to recognize a machine gun, knocking on wood, a door banging, handclapping (applause), and water running. Although he was tested several times during the 18 months prior to his death, he persisted in showing this severe deficit in auditory recognition. Nevertheless he could do arithmetic relatively well and he showed no disturbances in reading, writing, or carrying on normal conversation.

At autopsy a large area of deteriorated tissue was found in the right frontal, temporal, and parietal lobes. The left hemisphere and the corpus callosum were normally healthy.

The evidence provided by this case, as well as those studies of right temporal lesion cases being inferior in tonal memory (B. Milner, 1962) and in dichotic recognizing of melodies and tonal qualities (Kimura, 1964; Spellacy, 1970; Spellacy & Blumstein, 1970), suggests that nonverbal sounds are processed mainly by the right cerebral hemisphere, but as they involve greater verbal mediation both hemispheres become increasingly activated. By contrast, the left hemisphere is more sensitive to spoken speech.

Sequencing

The neurological mechanisms underlying serial order behavior are only just beginning to be understood. An early experiment with monkeys (Kimble & Pribram, 1963) suggested the left hemisphere (specifying the left hippocampal area) as being dominant in the control of serial order processing. Lashley wrote in 1948 that the study of language and the evidence that the brain readies or prepares the words in a sentence just prior to their expression suggest that "some scanning mechanism must be at play in regulating their temporal sequence" (Lashley, 1951). However, he admitted he had no answer regarding the nature of this selective mechanism or its location in the central nervous system. In our own laboratory we have produced a mechanism to present moving lights sequentially to study its usefulness in detecting brain damage in human patients (Gaddes, 1966a, 1969b). In an early study (Gaddes & Tymchuk, 1967) we found that left hemisphere lesion cases were inferior to right hemisphere lesion cases in remembering the sequentially presented light patterns. As well, frontal lesion cases performed worse than those with posterior lesions. This study suggested the left frontal cerebral areas as being important in controlling serial order functions.

A more recent study on split-brain patients (D. Zaidel & Sperry, 1973) required the subject to palpate two or three three-dimensional nonsense figures and some familiar household objects, and then to reproduce from memory the objects in correct order. "The left hemisphere was found consistently to be superior to the right in patients with complete section of the forebrain commissures, regardless of stimulus type or sequence length, and in agreement with the general association between language and temporal order." Such a finding leads one to wonder whether the left hemisphere is usually dominant for language because it genetically is supplied with the scanning mechanism that regulates temporal ordering. If this is true, then the left hemisphere is better equipped, but not exclusively so, to provide meaningful order to language perception and expression than the right hemisphere. However, this is not to say that the right hemisphere is illiterate, because some recent findings have shown it to have some limited language functions (Gazzaniga & Hillyard, 1971; E. Zaidel, 1973).

No doubt the researches of psychologists into this phenomenon (Bryden, 1960a, 1967; Epstein, 1963; Gottschalk, 1962, 1965; P. M. Milner, 1961) interested professional educators, because within the last 15 years, the mention of serial order functions, both perceptual and motor, has been increasing in books on remedial education (Johnson & Myklebust, 1967; Kephart, 1960/1971, 1964; Myers & Hammill, 1969; Valett, 1973) as a recommended corrective procedure, but with no proposed empirical justification. Since all behavior occurs in a temporal continuum, and because serial order can easily be identified in classroom learning, tasks such as reading, spelling, and adding, it is logical to believe, on an a priori basis, that facility in sequencing skills is essential to academic learning.

The chief reason that little rational support has been given to the promotion of remedial sequencing drills for learning disabled children is that very little research pertinent to this question had been carried out until recently. In the late 1950s, as the result of the interest and stimulation of D. O. Hebb, a number of graduate students and researchers at McGill University (Bryden, 1960a, 1962, 1966, 1967; Gottschalk, 1962, 1965; Heron, 1957; Kimura, 1959; P. M. Milner, 1961) carried out a number of valuable studies into the logical and orderly arrangement of thought and action, which Lashley (1951) described as "the most complex type of behavior that I know."

A few educational references have provided research evidence for or attempted to investigate the relationship between sequencing ability and academic achievement. Chalfant and Scheffelin (1969), in an able review of research findings relative to cognitive dysfunctions in children, have discussed sequencing in auditory perception; however, no comparable discussion occurs for the visual or haptic sense modes, although these are implied under "visual scanning and tracking" and tactile recognition of "movement patterns." A carefully controlled study of serial order ability in good and poor readers was done at McGill University by Wiener, Barnsley, and Rabinovitch (1970). They investigated the skills of good and poor readers on sequencing and nonsequencing tests in the auditory, visual, and tactual modes. No differences were found between the performances of good and poor reader groups on the ability to sequence, as measured by their test battery. This, of course, does not mean that sequencing ability is unrelated to success in academic achievement. It either means that the types of sequencing demands that they used were not strongly related to reading and writing skills, or that nonverbal serial order tasks typically are more tenuously related to one another than serial order verbal tasks. All of the tasks of Wiener, Barnsley, and Rabinovitch were nonverbal perceptual in each of the three sense modes.

Other researchers who have studied the significance of sequential processes in academic learning include Das, Kirby, and Jarman (1979), Denckla (1979), Leong (1975, 1976), Mattis (1978), and Senf (1969).

Probably the first comprehensive study of temporal order perception and reading was made by Bakker (1972) in The Netherlands. He investigated the visual, auditory, and haptic serial order perception of normal and learning disturbed children aged 7–11 years, inclusive. Bakker defined his terms carefully; for him succession implied the presentation of two identical stimuli (e.g., tones or light flashes) with a time interval between. By contrast, temporal order (or sequencing) implied the ordered succession of stimuli that were different so that they could be identified singly (e.g., tones of different pitch). Bakker has recognized two types of response to serial order stimuli: (1) imitation and (2) explication. Repeating digits forward is an example of imitation, because the subject can merely echo the sound pattern with little cognitive awareness of the numbers. Repeating digits in reverse order is an example of explication, since the subject must recognize the position of each digit and indicate the serial order of each number. It would seem that, neuropsychologically, imitation is mediated largely unconsciously and subcortically, whereas explication demands selective attention and memory, and presumably a larger cortical function.

Bakker's research, completed in the late 1960s, led him to conclude that *verbal* sequential tests discriminate between good and poor readers, and that *nonverbal* sequential tests do not. However, his nonverbal tests, which required the child to look at series of pictures, were not timed. The Dynamic Visual Retention Test or DVRT (Gaddes, 1966a), because it is designed to present patterns of lights at various speeds with light exposures and between-light intervals as short as 100 milliseconds (one-tenth of a second), provided the opportunity to test the possibility that *speed of sequencing* was an important causal factor.

Consequently two pilot studies, one with eight severely retarded children and the second with eight adult dyslexics, showed that when these subjects were matched for Wechsler performance IQ with normal readers that as the light sequences were speeded up the dyslexics in both groups were inferior. In the child study, the LD and control children performed significantly differently on the DVRT ($p < .001$) a test ostensibly designed to be a *nonverbal* visual sequential task (Gaddes, 1982). A tachistoscopic sequential presentation of single letters at slow and fast speeds, although a *verbal* sequential test, did not discriminate between the good and poor readers. The same basic findings were obtained in the adult study.

These findings were contrary to Bakker's general conclusion, and there are reasons for the differences. While the DVRT appears to be a *nonverbal* test (i.e., series of lights on a screen), the child is asked to count the lights to help him or her identify the changed light in the second sequence. As well, the rapid speeds (100 msec) subject the child to cerebral processing functions unlike the slower viewing tasks of Bakker's research (1 minute or no limit).

The knowledge of sequencing has progressed since the late 1950s from a fixed idea about the cerebral locus of the sequential scanner to a much more dynamic view. In 1963 Efron wrote, "temporal analysis of sequences, interval and simultanity is performed in the left hemisphere in right-handed *S*s, as well as in the majority of left-handed ones" (Efron, 1963). The previous year Milner had located the perception of sequential tonal patterns as a right-hemisphere function (B. Milner, 1962). In 1967, I thought it was in the left hemisphere (Gaddes & Tymchuk, 1967), and by the early 1970s a synthesis of numerous sequential studies from lesion cases, dichotic listening and tachistoscopic half-field studies, carotid amytal injections, electrophysiological studies, split-brain experiments, comprehensive batteries of neuropsychological tests, and longitudinal studies of aphasic patients, traumatically brain-damaged persons, and those with developmental learning disabilities was taking place. Bakker (1972) produced an improved concept of sequential cerebral function. Where most of the researchers of the 1960s had thought the scanning center had a fixed location in the brain, Bakker concluded that it could be left either left- or right-brained depending on whether the stimulus was verbal or nonverbal. Research findings during the 1970s enable us to conclude that:

1. Visual sequential perception is sensitive to brain dysfunction anywhere in the brain.

2. It is a discrete ability and, although associated with normal perception and memory, it possesses its own functional integrity and can be independent under certain conditions. For example, a child presented with the letters T, X, A serially at a very fast speed on a tachistoscope may report all three letters correctly, but in the wrong order. This would seem to indicate that the child's perception and memory are normal but his or her cerebral ordering defective.

3. It is task specific, varying with the degree of verbal or nonverbal quality, the level of difficulty of the task, and/or the sense mode involved.

4. There is no fixed cerebral locus for sequencing. Both hemispheres are involved depending more or less on the nature of the sequential task, the experience and training of the subject, and his or her intentions and planned strategies.

What has all this to do with LD children? It should help the clinical or school psychologists to improve his or her diagnostic understanding of the child. In cases where the loci of cerebral dysfunction are known, it should help to conceptualize the delicate, dynamic, and adaptive pattern of cerebral serial order functioning. Its relation to remediation is not clear yet, although one study (Gaddes & Spellacy, 1977) compared seven nonverbal and verbal sequential tasks with success in reading, spelling, and arithmetic and showed by correlational analysis a stronger relation between the verbal tasks and academic success than between the nonverbal tests. Measures of sequential skills were made in Grade 2 and Grade 5 to provide information on developmental changes. The first multivariate analysis of the Grade 2 data showed a significant relationship between success in reading and recognizing differences in light patterns at a slow speed. The evidence from this study suggested that "verbal serial order tasks for Grade 2 students are only a little more strongly related to academic success than nonverbal sequential skills when speed is introduced in the presentation of the latter" (Gaddes, 1982).

Reading in Grade 2 showed the highest correlation with the DVRT[1] at the slow speed. Reading in Grade 5 showed three steps that produced significant multiple correlations. These were with the Visual Expressive Test[1], the Auditory Expressive Test[1], and the DVRT at the slow speed. These findings suggest a shift from an emphasis on slow visual decoding at the Grade 2 level to a more integrated auditory and visual processing (see Fig. 5.1).

Spelling showed different patterns of involvement with nonverbal sequential skills (see Fig. 5.2). A multiple regression step-up analysis of Grade 2 data showed significant correlations with the DVRT at the slow speed, the Visual Expressive Test, the Auditory Expressive Test, and the DVRT at the fast speed.

Analysis of the Grade 5 spelling data showed that children in this age range prefer the DVRT at the fast speed. Because their visual scanning skills have improved since Grade 2, the fast speed is more satisfying and less tedious for most of them, as is any task administered at a speed well below the level of comfortable achievement. Significant correlations were found between success in spelling and achievement on the DVRT at the fast speed, the Auditory Expressive Test, and the DVRT at the slow speed. These correlations were considerably lower than those for reading,

[1] For a description of the five nonverbal sequential tests, see Appendix, page 411.

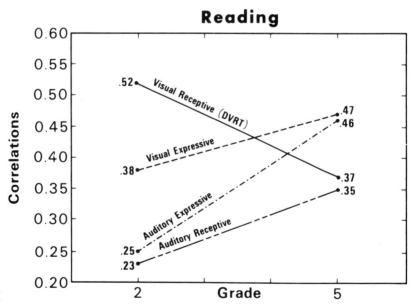

Figure 5.1. Progressive changes in correlations between reading and various sequencing processes from Grade 2 to Grade 5. (From Gaddes, 1982; with permission of Syracuse University Press.)

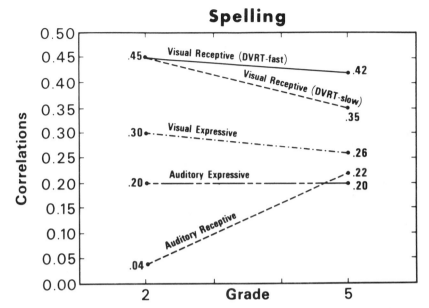

Figure 5.2. Progressive changes in correlations between spelling and various sequencing processes from Grade 2 to Grade 5. (From Gaddes, 1982; with permission of Syracuse University Press.)

and one reason is likely the failure of the nonverbal tests used in this study to tap the kinesthetic–sequential motor skills so essential to writing and spelling.

When testing arithmetic achievement it is important to examine both oral skills and written ability, because they appear to draw on different patterns of cognitive skills and neuropsychological processes. In this study we were interested to learn how nonverbal sequential skills related to competence in both oral and written arithmetic.

Oral arithmetic at the Grade 2 level produced significant correlations (see Figs. 5.3 and 5.4) with three of the tests, the DVRT at the slow speed, the Auditory Receptive Test, and the DVRT at the fast speed. Written arithmetic at this grade level showed only one significant correlation and it was with the DVRT at the slow speed. These findings suggest that the 7-year-old in our schools may be primarily concerned with the spatial aspects of numbers and "possibly oral arithmetic frees the child to give his attention more to number concepts, and hence the stronger relation of both auditory and visual sequential processes" (Gaddes, 1982).

A multiple regression step-up analysis of the Grade 5 arithmetic data showed significant correlations with the Auditory Receptive Test, the DVRT at the slow speed, and the Auditory Expressive Text. "The evident ascendancy of the auditory sequential skills may mean that the older child conceptualizes arithmetic more in oral and subvocal language, and

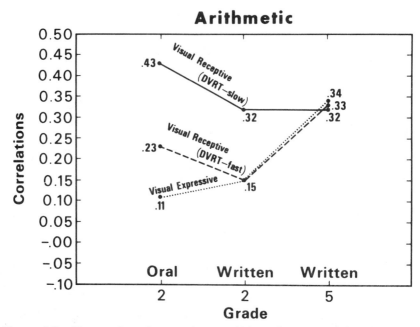

Figure 5.3. Progressive changes in correlations between oral and written arithmetic and visual sequencing processes from Grade 2 to Grade 5. (From Gaddes, 1982; with permission of Syracuse University Press.)

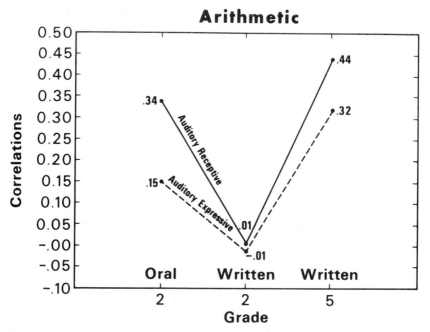

Figure 5.4. Progressive changes in correlations between oral and written arithmetic and auditory sequencing processes from Grade 2 to Grade 5. (From Gaddes, 1982; with permission of Syracuse University Press.)

has now automatized many of the visual–motor skills required in reading and writing" (Gaddes, 1982).

This evidence suggests that remedial drills probably should include verbal material first, because it is more strongly related to academic skills, and then nonverbal sequential drills should be introduced. If this is true, it would not agree with Ayres' thesis (Ayres, 1972a) that one should develop the brain's ability to learn rather than teach specific skills. However, our evidence derives only from correlational data and hence cannot infer causal relations regarding remediation. To validate any remedial program requires an experimental examination of its remedial drills under controlled conditions.

Electrical Changes in Attention

In the discussion on attention earlier in this chapter something was said of the possible specific function of some cortical cells in perception and the evident more generalized function of other cells. At this point we will examine some research evidence of electrical changes in the brain during attention, perception, and mentation, in order to increase the clinician's and the teacher's conceptual picture of the learning disabled child's neural functions. Let us look first at experiments with animals, and then at some with human subjects.

Some years ago a fascinating experiment in the attentional changes in the auditory tracts of a cat (Hernández-Peón, Scherrer, & Jouvet, 1956) drew attention to the possibility of neural suppression in the afferent nerves long before the impulse neared the auditory cortex. The experimenters implanted electrodes in the cochlear nucleus of a cat. While this is a part of the inner ear, impulses stimulated by sounds still have to travel the full distance through the brain to the auditory cortex before they are decoded. When spasmodic clicks were sounded near the cat, this initiated neural impulses in the cochlear mechanisms and along the auditory nerve to the auditory cortex. The EEG connected to the cochlear nucleus showed obvious "blips" of amplitude two and three times that of the ongoing wave pattern. In other words, the auditory clicks showed immediately on the EEG as large spike waves. However, when two mice in a closed bottle were placed in front of the cat, his attention was riveted on the mice, and now the clicks produced markedly reduced blips on the EEG. The researchers report, "they were practically abolished as long as the visual stimuli elicited behavioral evidence of attention." When the mice were removed the blips returned to their previous amplitude, and we can imagine that the cat was hearing the clicks again. An olfactory stimulus and a shock to the cat's paw that attracted its attention had the same suppressive effect.

Another and more recent researcher who has investigated electrical changes in attention in animals is E. R. John, who has studied single-cell firing patterns in different parts of the cat's brain. His findings seem to contradict a "switchboard" or connectionist view of the brain and throw doubt on the possible presence of "feature extractor" cells. Instead, he has found that learning and attention activate large numbers of neurons in different parts of the brain in a coordinated way by the spatiotemporal characteristics of the stimuli that happen to be present during a learning experience (John, 1972). John's researchers are ingenious, technically complex, and beyond the scope of the present discussion. However, his studies of the electrical changes in cats' brains during learning are innovative and informative. He fitted an experimental cat with an instrument with several microelectrode connections to different parts of the brain. When the cat was stimulated visually with a steady flicker, seven different parts of its brain showed minimal electrical activity. These were the visual cortex, the lateral geniculate body, the mesencephalic reticular formation, the nucleus centralis lateralis, the ventral hippocampus, the dorsal hippocampus, and the posterior suprasylvian cortex. In other words, electrical activity appeared simultaneously in the occipital and temporal cortex, the brainstem, and the limbic system. At this point the cat was taught that milk could be obtained whenever a lever was pressed, and that on a different flicker frequency he must not press the lever. Microelectrode patterns from the same seven cerebral loci showed a change in pattern and amplitude following anticipation of the visual stimulus as a particular cue for food. John's work is important in that it supports a unitary rather than localizationist view of the cat's brain function, and it provides detailed information of the electrical changes in individual cerebral cells following the establishment of a newly learned pattern of behavior. Recently, John and a number of other researchers have found marked changes in the EEG tracings of humans when clicks have been sounded (i.e., an auditory evoked potential) and they have been asked to attend to them and then to ignore them by reading a book.

The type of research done by Hernández-Peón and his colleagues in the 1950s was mainly with animals and it led them to conclude that selective attention and selective perception, when viewed neurophysiologically, involved a blocking of unattended sensory impulses before they reached the cortex. In the experiment with the cat and the mice, discussed above, the electrode was connected to the cat's cochlear nucleus and hence was picking up electrical events in the cat's peripheral nervous system, not its brain.

During the 1960s and 1970s considerable research has been done with human subjects; this has led researchers to revise their view that the neurophysiological changes that control "attention" are not peripheral, but are central, including electrochemical events in the brainstem (the reticular system) and in the cortex itself. With human subjects it has been possible to obtain better control of "attention" than in the animal studies.

Näätänen has carried out an interesting experiment (Näätänen, 1970) wherein his human subjects were asked to listen to loud and soft clicks. These were alternated and spaced sequentially 1 second apart. His subjects attended to the loud clicks against a background of soft clicks, and vice versa. This meant that the attended clicks became the "relevant" stimuli and the unattended the "irrelevant." There were 50 clicks of each intensity. Five of the 50 relevant stimuli differed slightly in intensity from the remaining 45, and the subject's task was to detect these "target" clicks. He concluded from his observations that there was somewhat generalized cortical activation preceding the relevant stimuli and this caused an enhancement of the evoked potential in the brain resulting from the clicks. This generalized cerebral electrical activation was in agreement with E. R. John's findings, discussed above.

Other studies have shown greater electrical cerebral responses to numbers flashed on a screen than when the screen was blank (Chapman & Bragdon, 1964) and even imaginary events have been investigated neurophysiologically. Human subjects equipped with long-term gold electrodes implanted in their brains showed clear-cut electrical activity even when a stimulus was expected but did not occur (Weinberg, Walter, & Crow, 1970). These writers concluded that "the emitted potentials (resulting from unrequited expectation) resembled those evoked when real stimuli were presented . . . suggesting that they may reflect memory processes corresponding to the perception of real events."

The experiments described above are segmental, neurophysiological, and remote from ordinary social behavior, but the knowledge gained from these kinds of studies can help us to conceptualize the possible defects in a learning disabled child's behavior. A lesion or dysfunction in the brainstem or cortex may impair the delicate energy system necessary to normal selective perception. Normal cerebral function may result in systematic neural blocking so that the child engrossed in an exciting book or an interesting TV program may not hear his mother call him to dinner. This seems to imply that the attended stimuli (book or TV) provides enhanced cortical activation and the unattended stimuli (mother's voice) is inhibited in its cortical function. All of this may make the teacher more aware of the behavioral complexities that are demanded when he or she commands the child to "pay attention."

Cerebral Blood Flow and Changes in Attention

As has been explained in Chapter 3, the cortical cells throughout the cerebral areas are constantly supplied with oxygen and nutrition through the cerebral arterial system. Occlusion of any part of this system may result in the starved cells dying after a few minutes, because of anoxia, as was shown by the experiments by Harvey with monkeys (Chapter 3).

In this section we will give our attention to some recent and highly original research carried out by Ingvar and his colleagues in Sweden (Ingvar & Schwartz, 1974). By an ingenious intraarterial technique they were able to measure the cortical areas with the greatest blood volume at any one time. With changes in mental activities the blood volume shifts, and these changes could be observed.

Figure 5.5 shows the left hemisphere of a number of subjects (the diagram is a cumulative one) at rest where the blood volume tends to be largely in the medial and frontal areas. When the subject was asked to read, the blood volume shifted more to the parietal and temporal areas, although the frontal lobe still retained an above-average blood volume. Talking produced much the same kind of blood volume shift from a pre-

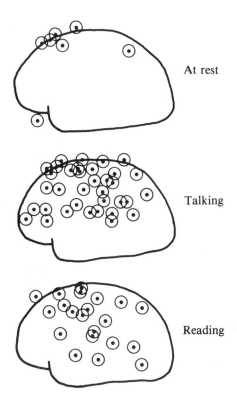

Figure 5.5. Regional cerebral blood flow during rest, talking, and reading. Only peaks more than 25% above the mean hemisphere flow are shown. (After Ingvar & Schwartz, 1974. With permission of the authors and Oxford University Press.)

dominantly left frontal concentration to a wider distribution over the frontal, parietal, and temporal areas.

Some studies investigating verbal and nonverbal auditory stimulation have found significant increases in blood flow over the left posterior Sylvian region for both verbal and nonverbal input, but "a trend for verbal activation to evoke a wider area of flow increase than the nonverbal task" (Knopman *et al.*, 1980).

Another study by Dabbs and Choo (1980) used skin temperature over the ophthalmic arteries to be an index of carotid blood flow. Subjects examined were : (1) left handed but wrote with their hand in an upright position; (2) left handed but wrote with the hand inverted; (3) right handed; (4) superior in verbal skills; and (5) superior in spatial skills. The mean blood flow temperatures suggested that in group (1) there was a tendency for more blood to go to the left hemisphere; in group (2) more blood to the right hemisphere; group (3) was like (2); group (4) was like (1); and group (5) was like (2) and (3). A summary of their findings suggested that "more blood goes to the nonverbal side of the head, with this effect tempered by individual differences in ability. The two types of left-handed subjects, opposite to one another in lateralization of cerebral function, were opposite also in major blood flow. The relationship to ability seems to indicate more blood flow associated with more robust cognitive function" (Dabbs and Choo, 1980).

This evidence is particularly interesting in that it supports a unitary cerebral action because all cortical areas include a healthy blood supply. With particular behaviors, however, there is a sensitive and rapid shifting in blood volume to accommodate and provide dominance for specific acts, such as talking and reading.

Summary

This discussion of the neurological evidence of the LD child's perceptual functions and dysfunctions should improve the reader's understanding of the breadth and subtlety of problems that prevent normal learning. It is invaluable for the clinician and teacher to have a delineated conceptual view of the scope of these prolems. Behavior is viewed holistically, but for purposes of study, sensation, perception, attention, lateral perceptual asymmetries, and sequencing have all been examined separately. Recent researches measuring cortical electrical and arterial changes during attention have been described briefly to provide a dynamic picture of this very complex behavior.

Clinical Addendum

In this section we will look at two cases with evidence of fairly clearly defined regional cerebral dysfunction, one with left-hemisphere dysfunction and one with right-hemisphere impairment. Both children had suffered these deficits since birth so that their mental and psychological development had been shaped by these abnormal neurophysiological conditions. One of these children has been described briefly in Chapter 4, but here we will examine this case in more detail.

These two cases have several advantages for the teacher and the psychologist in their attempts to integrate neurological information and behavioral data. They each show clear laterality effects, they were each seen initially at about the same age (12 and 13 years), they each showed interesting perceptual problems, and they have been followed for more than 10 years.

Case I: Left-Hemisphere Dysfunction

Sam, birth date 1954, was referred by a neurologist to the neuropsychological laboratory when he was 12 years old because of poor academic school performance and a history of epileptic seizures. Sam was the second oldest of three children and his prenatal and birth history were normal. However, at the age of 6 weeks he developed meningitis and apparently convulsed at that time. He was quite ill but made a good recovery and remained well until the age of 6, when he developed the second convulsion. On this occasion this was a right-sided seizure (his right arm and right leg were activated in involuntary clonic movements). In a few moments the seizure involved both sides of the body, which suggested that the epileptogenic focus was in the left hemisphere and stimulated the right side of the body; the cerebral electrical storm gradually spread bilaterally throughout the brain, and the seizure became generalized. Two EEGs carried out previously supported this by showing a severe dysrhythmia in the central temporal area of the left hemisphere. An EEG done just prior to our seeing Sam showed the continued presence of a grade iii spike activity in the left frontotemporal area.

At age 7 Sam was placed on anticonvulsive medication, which was largely successful. At age 7 he suffered a minor episode in which the right side of his mouth drooped and his right hand twitched.

His development appeared to be normal except for his language. He was a nice looking boy, even tempered and easy to manage, but he spoke very little. He had great difficulty saying anything until after the age of 2, and even when we saw him at age 12, he only answered when spoken to, and then very meagerly.

The psychometrician wrote: "He is extremely uncommunicative but not surly, simply withdrawn." He enjoyed the performance part of the Wechsler (WISC) and even smiled occasionally during the completion of the Block Design Test. However, on the verbal tests he had trouble. He had a peculiar habit of cupping one hand over his mouth when he was speaking, as if he were embarrassed to have any one see him talk. On the Vocabulary test he used only a minimum of speech and when asked, "Go on, tell me more," he usually remained mute. He never said "I don't know" or "I can't," he just sat waiting passively for the tester to make the next move. He did not appear to have any articulation problems; what little he did say was pronounced correctly.

On the initial Wechsler (WISC) he measured a verbal IQ of 87 and performance IQ of 110. On the verbal tests he measured average on Arithmetic and above average on repeating digits back, but on all those subtests using words he did very badly.

On the performance tests his achievement was at a very superior level on the Block Design subtest (spatial imagery), and he obtained very good scores on Picture Completion (identifying small errors or omissions in line drawings) and Object Assembly (a jigsaw puzzle task). His visual memory and tactile perception were good, but he had difficulty with the auditory–perception tests for both language and nonverbal stimuli.

His sensorimotor skills, manual reaction times, finger tapping, finger localization, and right–left orientation were all good. His hand-grip strength was weak in both hands; this finding is frequent in cases with neurological damage or dysfunction somewhere in the central nervous system.

The Psychologist's Role

This boy, because of his poor verbal abilities, had never done well at school and in fact had been kept in a slow learners' class for the first 6 years of his school life. The test findings showed that whereas he had a definite impairment in spoken speech, in reading, his word recognition was normal for his age, as was his written arithmetic. As well, he was quite superior in tasks involving spatial imagery, spatial analysis and construction, and visual perception for detail.

It was quite clear that this boy considered himself intellectually inferior and suffered strong feelings of personal inadequacy and social isolation. It was explained to him that although he did not talk very much, he should be aware that he was quite superior in the kinds of skills that led to mechanical work, construction, architecture, and engineering.

From a neuropsychological view, Sam was a classic example of left-hemisphere dysfunction with his poor verbal skills and his strong right-hemisphere (spatial–constructional) abilities.

A letter to the boy's school principal described the history of meningitis, mentioned the left-hemisphere dysfunction as related to his weak verbal skills, but stressed his superior spatial abilities and his average performance in arithmetic deductive reasoning. The letter said in part: "He should do very well reading maps in geography, interpreting blueprints and mechanical drawings, and doing geometry when he reaches that stage. In these areas he is a bright boy." This was an attempt to alter the image of Sam, which likely had developed because of the verbal emphasis of most school programs, and to draw attention to specific areas his teachers might explore if they had not already detected them. The letter ended with a request for a normal placement for Sam: "May I suggest that I think that a boy as potentially bright as this, may profit from placement in a regular class, with daily remedial drill in reading and spelling."

The School

The principal and Sam's teacher were interested enough in the reports and suggestions that they visited the laboratory to discuss further the management of Sam's case. On the basis of the evidence, they decided to move him into a regular class and teach him reading and spelling with an emphasis on visual–motor aspects rather than phonics. He read silently better than aloud because of his motor–speech difficulties, so his teacher decided to stress silent reading.

When Sam returned the next year for evaluation the Wechsler (WISC) showed a phenomenal improvement in his performance scores. His verbal IQ measured only 80, but his performance IQ was now 132, better than 99% of other children his age. He also showed a little improvement in the Information, Digit Span, and Similarities subtests, but his overall verbal abilities were still below average. It seems reasonable to conclude that, because the school authorities moved Sam into a normal class, began to think of him in different terms, and to use remedial measures based on his strengths, he became at least partially emancipated from his former feelings of inferiority and alienation.

By the time Sam reached Grade 9 he elected an "occupational program" that stressed drafting, mechanics, and industrial arts. He completed this program and on graduation entered an apprenticeship in auto-mechanics.

There are a number of interesting points that emerge from Sam's case and are worthy of note. First, there was clear evidence of electrical dysfunction in his left temporal lobe near the Sylvian fissure. Since this disturbance was strong enough to produce epileptic seizures and appeared to involve Wernicke's area (see Fig. 3.9) at least in part, this would lead us to examine his phonetic auditory perception. In fact, on our first administration of the Halstead Speech Perception Test, he had real problems discriminating nonsense phonemes (e.g., weech and weej), and his error score out of 60 phonemes placed him more than one standard deviation below the average score of normal 12-year-olds. It seemed reasonable to assume that this auditory imperception was related to his retarded speech development, his poor spelling, and his slow reading. Also, the fact that three EEGs, administered intermittently during his first 12 years of life, all showed a grade iii disturbance in the left Sylvian area, suggested strongly that a permanent lesion, possibly scar tissue, existed in Sam's left temporal lobe. Although this speculation should not excuse his teachers from trying to teach him to speak, read, and write, it could reduce their feelings of frustration if his verbal progress was unusually slow. Herein lies one of the greatest values of neurological knowledge in understanding and managing learning disabled children: *the better opportunity for prediction.*

The next year, when Sam was 13, we retested him on the Meikle Consonant Perception Test. This is a purely auditory perception test that requires the child to answer "same" or "different" to two nonsense phonemes and a few words, presented on a tape recorder. This time Sam's score placed him more than two standard deviations below the average score of normal 13-year-olds and enhanced our tentative prediction the previous year that Sam had a chronic temporal lesion that would always interfere with his reception and expression of oral language.

When he returned at age 20 for a recheck, the left temporal disturbance still showed itself, but Sam had gained considerable success in his drafting and mechanical courses as a substitute for his weak academic achievement, and while still quiet and somewhat submissive, he was developing signs of adult assurance in his apprentice training.

Case II: Right-Hemisphere Dysfunction

Until Will (birth date 1953) was 13 years old, when we first saw him, no one had ever attempted to relate his neurological impairment (a mild left hemiparesis) and his learning problems at school. Because they did not impair his verbal abilities, Will did reasonably well in the core academic subjects except when spatial skills were required. As a consequence, he was frustrated and anxious, wondering whether he were really stupid. His parents also were confused, and they became somewhat defensive and hostile toward the school for not helping their only son more.

Will's birth was about 2 months premature and he was in an incubator for 7 weeks. When he began to stand at about 18 months, it was noted that he could not put his left foot flat on the floor. A diagnosis of mild cerebral palsy was made, with spasticity in the left arm, leg, and face.

An EEG carried out when he was 13 years old showed a minimal dysrhythmia in the right occipital, parietal, and motor strip areas. Hand grip was normal in the right hand and inferior in the left.

The Psychologist's Role

The Wechsler (WISC) showed a verbal IQ of 110 and a performance IQ of 69. He was severely impaired on the Block Design, Picture Completion, and Maze Tests. He could not draw the Benton geometric diagrams from memory except very poorly, and his attempts to copy a Greek cross were sketchy, incomplete, and uneven (see Fig. 4.3). Although his visual and tactile perception were poor, his auditory perception and memory for both verbal and nonverbal material was superior.

His impaired spatial skills had made art, paper construction, map reading, and interpretation of diagrams in arithmetic and science a real punishment. Will reported, "I hated all art work from Grade 1. If the teacher showed us how to fold a paper, the others could do it, but mine was never right." Arithmetic was also difficult because of the many spatial demands in the first few grades (vertical columns in adding, reading right and left from the decimal, diagonal columns in multidigit multiplying and long division).

Following the testing, Will's father who had brought him for testing very reluctantly and somewhat defensively, was counseled. The relation between Will's left hand and foot weakness with the right half of his brain was explained, and the further relation of this and spatial imagery. Will's success in reading, language, social studies, and science (only the reading parts, not the maps or diagrams) was explained in terms of his superior left hemisphere. This simplistic model was something the father could understand and welcomed, in that it objectified Will's learning problems and removed the confusion, frustration, and feelings of possible guilt. He left the laboratory expressing his gratitude and offering to bring Will back any time.

Two years later we saw him again, at which time he measured a verbal IQ of 106 and a performance IQ of 71, still the same verbal–spatial split, because Will's right hemisphere was chronically damaged and hence his spatial skills permanently restricted. The degree of this impairment could only be revealed by longitudinal observations over a period of time.

At 15 Will was still severely handicapped in any task requiring spatial imagery, visual perception for small detail, visual–manual integration, visual figure–ground perception, and visual memory. As well, his hand-grip strength was very weak in both hands, and the sensory and motor functions of his left hand were inferior. His auditory phonetic discrimination was still good and his immediate verbal memory as measured by the Spreen–Benton Sentence Repetition Test, almost superior. Fortunately, Will was right handed, and since his left hemisphere was above average in processing verbal material, he had no problems in spelling.

During later adolescence, Will was seen twice very briefly, but his verbal superiority and spatial inferiority still showed itself. At 23 he was tested more fully, and his Wechsler (WAIS) verbal IQ measured 110 and his performance IQ only 68. It was interesting that on the Information Test purely verbal questions were answered well, but when direction, distance, or measurement were involved he "had no idea." When asked the distance between Paris and London he said, "Oh, 2000 miles. I have no idea." When asked where India was located, he hesitated a long time and then said, "Oh, in the south half of the hemisphere." He had no concept of the population of Canada, nor of the number of seats in the legislature, nor the temperature at which water boils. However, he was able to answer all the pure verbal questions from history or literature.

He still had great difficulty on the Block Design Test, being unable to do even the simple patterns without a demonstration first, and in some cases even then he could not analyze the design spatially and construct it. On the Benton Visual Retention Test (visual memory and visual–motor skill) he performed at the level of a borderline mental defective. On the Halstead Finger Tapping Test he did well above average with the right hand, but increasingly poorly with each trial with his left.

It was clearly evident that Will's lateralized pattern of competence and failure was still with him into adulthood.

The School

Will was in Grade 7 when we first saw him. He did well in English and the verbal aspects of all subjects where reading and writing were required. His achievement in arithmetic was extremely poor, but it seemed certain that much of this failure stemmed from his lack of confidence and spatial difficulties. Consequently Will's father was advised to encourage oral arithmetic and to watch for difficulties when he was confronted with geometry in a later grade. Although Will was not told of this possible future learning problem (because our prediction might have been wrong), I asked Will's father to advise any of his teachers to contact me if they ran into a problem they could not solve. Two years later, when Will was in

Grade 9, I received a call from his mathematics teacher who sounded desperate. He complained that although Will seemed like a normally bright boy, he was hopeless in geometry. He could neither interpret nor draw a simple geometric figure, although he could handle algebra. This made no sense, said the teacher, until it was explained in terms of left- and right-hemisphere function. "Very interesting," said the teacher, "but what am I to do? One half of the Grade 9 mathematics courses includes introductory geometry, and the other half algebra." In conference with the junior high school principal they decided to redraft Will's program. He took English, Latin, and French and avoided geometry from then on. As a result, he graduated from high school with a plan to be a high school language teacher, but when faced with 5 years of university studies he decided against it. Instead, he attended a business college and learned typing, filing, and bookkeeping. Because of his cheery personality he is a typist–receptionist in a public library, where he is fairly free of spatial problems. As a result he is successfully situated in his job, and last year was happily married.

Summary Comment

The two cases of Sam and Will point up some important considerations for the educational management of children with *unilateral* brain dysfunction.

1. Because most elementary school programs stress the teaching of verbal skills, most teachers teach more to the left hemisphere than the right. For the child who is bilaterally normal this is no problem.
2. The child who suffers left-hemisphere dysfunction is frequently treated unfairly by the school system. His skill in drawing, construction, sewing, map drawing, and singing are frequently more or less ignored since problems in reading, writing, and spelling are so apparent. Although Sam was globally superior intellectually to Will, he never was able to complete high school in the present system and had to be assisted, at the age of 20, by a government agency for the handicapped to help him find placement in an apprenticeship.
3. By contrast, the child who suffers right-hemisphere impairment is frequently treated normally because he can usually handle the verbally loaded core subjects. The fact that he cannot draw, sing, or read maps is not considered serious as long as he can pass in reading, writing, and arithmetic. This means that the *present school system tends to discrim-*

inate unfairly against the child with unilateral left-hemisphere dysfunction and to favor the right-hemisphere lesion child because he usually has a better chance to satisfy the demands of the system.

4. To counter this injustice, the school psychologist can draw attention to the child's left- and right-hemisphere skills attaching importance to all of them. Eventually, with this type of input more teachers will learn to respect the poor reader with a performance IQ of 148. As well, from this information they may derive new insights in how to teach reading to such a child.

5. Both cases presented here suggest that learning impairments resulting from chronic brain lesions are likely to be permanent. This does not mean that remediation should not be attempted, but dramatic positive results cannot be expected in most cases at the age of 12 or 13 and older.

6. Early detection of brain dysfunctions and learning disorders should lead to more successful remediation because of the greater plasticity of the young brain.

7. At present, some school systems neglect and/or maltreat children with aphasia, subtle sequencing problems, or spatial difficulties resulting from unilateral brain damage or dysfunction. An increased knowledge of the neuropsychology of learning disabilities should better prepare school psychologists to understand these children and to assist teachers to help them. With this increased understanding and better directed remediation the school system can learn to treat these children with greater competence and justice.

6 Sensory and Motor Pathways and Learning

Movement is in fact the basis for the development of personality. The child, who is constructing himself, must always be moving. Not only in those large movements which have an external aim, such as sweeping a room . . . but also when the child merely sees, or thinks, or reasons; or when he understands something in relation to these thoughts and sensations—always he must be moving . . . [This idea] will unlock for you the secret of the child's development.

Maria Montessori (1912).

In Chapters 4 and 5 a review was made of research evidence providing knowledge of various cerebral cortical activities and their possible behavioral correlates. When damage or dysfunction occurs in the cortical layers or the neural connections between various cortical areas, it usually impairs the specific sensory, intellectual, or neuromuscular behaviors maximally dependent on these loci.

In this chapter we will examine the possible behavioral deficits or learning disorders that may result from cortical lesions in the somatosensory and motor strips, in the sensory or motor pathways of the peripheral nervous system, or in the interconnecting pathways in the cerebrum linking these two major systems. Defective tactile form perception is known as *astereognosis;* defective motor accuracy and control is called *apraxia.*

The Sensory and Motor Systems

The afferent neural pathways that mediate proprioception (awareness of the body in space and internal bodily states) and stereognosis (awareness of extrapersonal or environmental objects by touch alone) are depicted in Fig. 6.1. As explained in Chapter 3, impulses from the cutaneous receptors travel along sensory neurons to the spinal cord, where they enter through dorsal roots (see Fig. 3.6) and then extend vertically to the medulla oblongata, where most of them cross over to the opposite side (neural decussation); they then continue vertically to the thalamus and finally to the somesthetic strip on that side. Proprioception and stereogno-

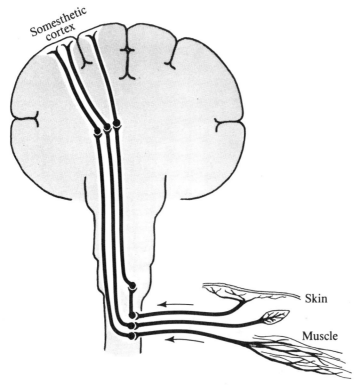

Figure 6.1. Simplified diagram of the sensory (afferent) pathways from skin and muscle to the sensory or somesthetic cortex. Note the contralateral connections. (© 1980 William D. West)

sis involve much more complicated spinal and lateral pathways, but Fig. 6.1 provides the reader with simplified and grossly accurate information about the sensory pathways that supply information about the hand movements in writing, spelling, drawing; fingering a musical instrument; or any other fine manual activity involved in academic learning.

Figure 6.2 shows a simplified representation of the efferent or motor neural pathways from the motor cortex to the neuromuscular system. Impulses originating in the motor strip travel down the efferent pathways to the midbrain level, where they cross over to the other side (neural decussation); they then enter the cerebellum and go out to the pons, down the anterior or ventral horns of the spinal cord, out through a ventral root (see Fig. 3.6), and along motor neurons of the peripheral nervous system to muscle tissue. The cerebellum acts a a sort of "filter" to provide smooth and accurate action of muscle groups. Dysfunctions in the cerebellum, the sensory or motor pathways, or the sensory or motor areas of the cerebrum may result in awkward motor behavior that may interfere with normal learning. For example, a cerebral palsied young adult with a

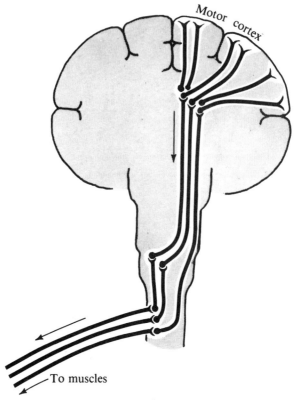

Figure 6.2. Simplified diagram of the motor (efferent) pathways from the motor cortex in the left hemisphere to the muscles of the right arm and hand. (© 1980 William D. West)

verbal IQ of 130 may be unemployable because of severe spasticity of the speech and hand muscle systems and involuntary movements (athetosis) of the head and hands. Other examples are *apraxia,* the inability to imagine a motor act and carry it out, and *ataxia,* an incoordination of neuromuscular action. These impairments and their relation to learning are discussed later in this chapter.

Although it is convenient to think structurally of afferent nerves (*ad fero,* to carry toward), interconnecting cerebral nerve networks, and efferent nerves (*ex fero,* to carry away from), the teacher must keep in mind that all of these structural systems work as one and that dysfunctions in any one of them may impair stereognosis or body image (proprioception). Even so, there are techniques that the clinical or school psychologist may use to try to isolate the part of the system giving the greatest trouble.

An example may make this clear. Suppose that a child obtains an inferior score on the Benton Visual Retention Test where he is required to draw a series of geometric designs following a 10-second exposure of each design. Is this child's poor performance because he cannot perceive the designs, cannot remember them, or has a motor disability (apraxia) and cannot control the pencil well enough? Is it because of areas of skin anesthesia in his fingers and hands, because of reduced stereognostic help in his drawings, because of some or all of these, or because of some other problem completely missed by our examination? We can tease out some of this information by the following procedure:

1. Suppose that the *multiple-choice form* of the Benton Visual Retention Test, administered a few days after the usual drawing administration to minimize possible memory effects, tells us the child's perception and memory of the diagrams is normal. This suggests that the trouble may be a motor one and not a perceptually receptive problem.

2. The esthesiometer, an instrument wherein graded fine nylon hairs are applied to the fingers and hands, tells us that the child's tactile sensitivity is normal and hence there are no insensitive areas of the skin.

3. The Halstead Finger Tapping Test reveals a normal tapping speed for the child's nondominant hand, but a severely slowed tapping speed in his dominant hand, thus strengthening the tentative diagnosis in (1) above that this child suffers from a manual–motor disability. Remedial drills, in this case, would stress activities to improve motor skills and muscular integration. The teacher could feel reasonably confident that the child's visual–spatial perception of geometric designs was within normal limits, but his motor expressive abilities were more impaired.

Sensorimotor Integration

In Chapter 3 we presented the classical concept of the reflex arc which, as expressed by Sherrington in 1906 and Watson in 1914, implied a linear input and output neural pathway between receptor and effector. Although Sherrington talked about a *simple reflex,* he realized it was a part of the whole nervous system "because all parts of the nervous system are connected together" (Sherrington, 1906) and he admitted that "it is probably a purely abstract conception" and "is a convenient, if not a probable, fiction." Years later Herrick (1944), taking the same view of spreading activities in the nervous system, denied the very existence of reflex arcs in the amphibian nervous system (see Chapter 4).

John B. Watson, the founder of the school of behaviorism, was satisfied to be more restrictive in his concept of the reflex arc. To him it was purely linear, being "an actual chain of nerve cells (and their fibers) running from each sense organ to the central nervous system (the brain and spinal cord) and out from the central nervous system to the muscles and glands" (Watson, 1924). This simplistic and linearly mechanistic view of sensorimotor neural conduction, the "classical view" of reflexes, was perpetuated by psychologists for many years after neurologists knew it to be inaccurate. We now know that all of the input mechanisms of the amphibian are controlled by the central nervous system (CNS) via feedback loops. Just as the "response" of a furnace (production of warm air) controls the thermostat and turns the furnace off, thus cooling the air until it again triggers the thermostat to reactivate the furnace, so many control mechanisms operate in the human body to maintain a number of homeostatic processes within normal ranges. These are examples of the simple feedback loop, and the nervous system is equipped with a large number of these. In walking, the efferent control of the foot and leg swinging through the air provides ongoing and rapidly changing information to the brain about the sensory awareness of the foot and leg in space. In other words, the input or perceptual content is constantly monitored by the changing motor activity or efferent control. The same process is true of reading; the muscular eye movements across the page provide judgment regarding the speed with which one can attend and comprehend the material on the printed page. Should there be even a slight deficiency in the speed or accuracy of neural conduction in any part of the input, integrative, or output mechanisms in the CNS, a child may have difficulty in learning to read.

How input from muscle tissue is fed into the dorsal root of the spinal cord to be integrated with the afferent information from the skin receptors has been explained more fully by Pribram (1971).

As well, there are *feedforward* processes (Pribram, 1971) that seem to affect perception and may be similar or related to the attention and preparatory "set" mechanisms discussed in Chapter 5. Teuber has described these processes with original insight, suggesting that "perhaps the greatest difficulty in understanding the frontal lobes (and we might add the brain) has been the classical tendency to start all considerations of brain function from the sensory side, and to proceed in the familiar fashion from the sensory to the motor" (Teuber, 1964). Teuber proposed that we should examine the cerebral processes which discharge from motor to sensory structures and prepare them for an anticipated change. This process he named a "corollary discharge."

Not only are the sensory and motor functions necessary to perception and learning, but they must be well integrated in a well-balanced and smoothly running energy system. Many years ago, P. Weiss (1941) demonstrated the continuous, although uncoordinated motor activity of muscle tissue when that balance is interrupted. He surgically removed an animal's limb and kept it alive in a pool of nutrient fluids maintained at body temperature. Because all normal sensory input was removed, only the motor twitching, resulting from the incessant neural firing of live tissue, remained. Hebb concluded from this that "sensory activity is essential to the regulation of central firing but not essential to initiating it'' (Hebb, 1949). In this case there were no afferent fibers but only efferent ones, and hence no sensory control, but only internal spontaneous stimulation. Lashley's expression of this basic neurophysiological knowledge appears in the quotation prefatory to Chapter 5: input is always into an actively excited system.

Sensorimotor integration may be examined with a visual–manual and an auditory–manual reaction time test. The child is asked to press a telegrapher's key as quickly as possible when a red light appears or an auditory tone sounds in headphones. Reaction time has been investigated for the past 100 years, but interest in its relation to cerebral dysfunction is more recent, dating from World War I. Controlled studies with matched groups of normal and brain-damaged adults have shown the brain-damaged group to be slower with both simple and choice reaction time tasks to a visual stimulus (Blackburn & Benton, 1955) and much greater variability of response (Benton & Blackburn, 1957). When adult subjects are motivated by providing them with verbal encouragement and immediate feedback regarding their level of achievement, more of the brain-damaged subjects showed increased improvement than the normal controls, although both groups reacted positively to the effects of motivating instructions (Blackburn, 1958). When the instructions included information of both success and failure in a choice reaction time task, significant acceleration in scores occurred for both adult brain-damaged and normal control subjects for both types of information (Shankweiler, 1959).

When the same types of studies were done with 60 elementary school children (age range, 7 years 7 months to 9 years 4 months) it was found that motivating instructions, in the form of verbal urging and informational feedback, produced a significant acceleration in reaction time (Owen, 1959).

Up to this point we have discussed single motor performances and brain functions, but much behavior includes several motor activities occurring simultaneously (e.g., walking and talking). If the brain is required to mediate two concurrent motor performances, the degree of interference of one performance by the other, or the degree of independence of the two motor skills, will depend on which parts of the brain are controlling the two performances, and how near or far apart are these areas transcortically. If a subject is carrying out two activities simultaneously that are programmed by the same cerebral hemisphere, these motor acts will tend to be inferior to two acts each mediated by separate hemispheres. For example, when adult subjects are asked to speak and balance a dowel rod on the right and then on the left index finger, more interference occurs in right-sided balancing than left (Kinsbourne & Cook, 1971). Finger tapping is also decreased more in the right hand than left with concurrent verbal tasks (reciting a nursery rhyme, reading words silently, and solving anagrams silently). The pattern of difference between the hands is more pronounced for familial dextral subjects than familial sinistral subjects, and the difference increases with the complexity of the verbal task (Kee, Bathurst, & Hellige, 1983). This effect occurs also in kindergarten children (Kinsbourne & McMurray, 1975), although more exacting verbal tasks must be used with adults because of their better automatizing of finger tapping skills. Kinsbourne and McMurray (1975) have suggested that "the present methodology appears to offer a simple and convenient way of ascertaining the lateralization of the control of expressive speech in children (and probably also of other forms of vocalization)." This method is simpler and more directly available than dichotic listening and might be considered by the school psychologist with limited experimental apparatus.

Basic Research in Tactile Perception

An esthesiometer is an instrument designed to stimulate the skin in a graded way to enable the experimenter to measure the threshold of pressure sensitivity. This type of measure may be done singly and provide information about pressure sensitivity and/or the ability to localize the source of pressure. Likewise, two points on the skin may be stimulated simultaneously to provide information about two-point discrimination or extinction or obscuration of one stimulus during a double stimulation. In our own laboratory we measure only pressure sensitivity of the fingers and sometimes extinction, because these seem to be more important to the types of neuropsychological processes related to classroom learning problems.

The teacher of children with learning problems will not normally carry out pure research, but the information coming out of researches in this area is related to normal learning. It should help the teacher enrich his or her concept of the child's idiosyncratic behaviors in a learning situation.

Since tactile and manual proprioception seem to be intimately involved in learning to write and spell, and more tenuously to read, it is interesting that controlled studies of linear tactile perception of direction have shown that in normal subjects it is slightly more accurate on the left hand than on the right hand of right-handed subjects (Benton, Levin, & Varney, 1973). These findings support the results of studies of subjects with unilateral right-hemisphere lesions; it was found that a large number of these subjects show bilateral impairment, but that patients with left-hemisphere disease may show a deficit only in the right hand (Carmon & Benton, 1969; Fontenot & Benton, 1971). With the child with normal brain functions the left and right hand differences are so small that the teacher can normally ignore them. However, if it were known that the right-handed child has identifiable left- or right-hemisphere dysfunction, the possibility can be expected of some manual awkwardness or inferiority that may show itself in errors of copying from the blackboard, frequent misspellings, untidy writing, or poor spacing and scanning.

The diagnostician soon becomes aware that two-dimensional tactile recognition (such as reading Braille letters or palpating sandpaper letters on a flat surface) is a different process than haptic or proprioceptive recognition of a three-dimensional object (e.g., putting one's fingers and hands around all sides of a block or other object; see Fig. 4.5). The first requires maximal stimulation of the skin receptors in the finger tips, and the second includes not only that but a much greater proprioceptive involvement of the muscles of the fingers, hand, and arm. Because the second perceptual task implicates many more muscle patterns in its three-dimensional activity, it is reasonable to infer that different patterns of cortical neurons are activated, and likely more of them. Many years ago this difference between tactile and haptic functions was demonstrated by showing that discrimination of passive movement (e.g., stroking the hand) was not affected by anesthetizing the overlying skin and muscles (Goldscheider, 1898). In this same experiment it was shown that with strong faradic current through the joints (the receptors for proprioception are the muscles, tendons, and joints) the thresholds for detection of movement were increased. This same phenomenon has been demonstrated more recently without pharmacological blocking. Levin (1973) has shown that when fingertip tactile sensitivity is changed by a covering with a foam rubber pad, no difference occurs in the efficiency of a proprioceptive task requiring precise manipulation of a button within a specified range of distance. This was true for both younger (age 19.9 years) and older (age 56.7 years) subjects. This information suggests that body-image and proprioceptive defects will be more seriously impairing than poor finger tactile sensitivity in learning manual–motor classroom skills. Put another way, restricted sensory deficits (in this case, tactile sensitivity in the fingers) are probably not as important to learning as perceptual organization (in this case, somesthesis and stereognosis).

Basic Research in Motor Functions

Electrostimulation of the motor strip in animals was first done a little more than 100 years ago. These types of experiments demonstrated the contralateral connections of motor tracts, as well as localized functional areas in the motor strips themselves. More recently, it has been found

(Hunter & Jasper, 1949) that by stimulating various parts of a cat's thalamus a number of excitatory and inhibitory types of behavior may be produced. One of the most interesting of these is the "arrest reaction" in which the animal can be made to stop and "freeze" in midaction, whether eating, walking, or pursuing a mouse. A more dramatic example of the arrest reaction was produced by Delgado when he stopped a charging bull by remote control electrostimulation of its brain (Delgado, 1971). These examples remind the diagnostician and the special teacher that motor acts, both excitatory and inhibitory, are controlled by delicate electrochemical changes in a complex neural circuit originating in the sensorimotor strips of the cortex and ending in the neuromuscular system of the effectors. Any slight dysfunction in any part of the circuit may interfere with the afferent integrating processes of the brain and so result in a disturbance of the body image or ideomotor patterns necessary to initiating motor responses. Such dysfunctions may show themselves as apraxias, body-image deficits, and forms of motor aphasia (i.e., problems in expressive oral speech).

The Apraxias

A person "is apraxic when he is unable to act, although the systems through which he carries out his actions are intact (i.e., when there is neither paralysis, ataxia, nor abnormal movements), and he presents no marked intellectual disturbance" (De Ajuriaguerra & Tissot, 1969). A 10-year-old girl seen in our laboratory was unable to touch her fingertips behind her back, although the action was demonstrated several times for her. In order to please the tester, she eventually placed her hands on her hips. This girl walked and talked normally, but because of a biparietal dysfunction her spatial abilities were severely impaired, and she was unable to imagine or produce the ideomotor patterns necessary to guide her fingertips kinesthetically into the correct position. One child, who watches the dancing teacher demonstrate a series of steps, may imitate the whole movement correctly and rhythmically after one demonstration. Another child may want to see it repeated three or four times and have his or her own feet guided through the dance step before managing it slowly but successfully. The first child is quick to acquire the cortical–muscular pattern; the second lacks this aptitude, although neither child is paralyzed, ataxic, palsied, nor mentally retarded. Every drill sergeant is plagued with clumsy recruits, whom he relegates to the "awkward squad." These are the individuals who need more repetitions to acquire the cortical engrams and their correlative symbolic spatial patterns necessary to the required motor act. Just as a computer needs a readymade program to produce a particular solution or response, the human nervous system requires a repertoire of ideomotor programs on which it can draw. Sometimes the apraxic person may have difficulty carrying out an intransitive act related to his own body, e.g., salute, blow a kiss, pretend to clean his teeth or comb his hair. Sometimes such a person may be awkward in dealing with objects in his environment (i.e., carrying out a transitive act), such as hammering a nail, batting a ball, writing with a pencil or constructing a model. Preschool children who cannot put on a coat are suffering from "dressing apraxia," but as their nervous systems develop they reach a level of neural maturity where they can produce the necessary symbolic patterns. By age 6, most children, if they have been taught, can put on a coat because they have acquired the sequence of complex cortical and neuromuscular processes necessary to the act. In old age, senility may cause a breakdown in cortical and central nervous system structures so that the old person may have regressed to a dressing apraxia and cannot put on his clothes without direction or assistance.

Body-Image Deficits

The clinical investigation of a body image or body schema began about 1890, so it is a relatively recent concept in neuropsychology. The first theories stressed "coenesthesis" or the coordinated input of kinesthetic or muscular sensations. This view, however, ignored the *spatial* aspects of the body image, and it was Head and Holmes (1911) in England who first presented a theory that attempted to account for the temporal and spatial aspects of the awareness of one's body in space. They proposed that the body schema was a function of comparing the position or posture at any moment with the preceding one, and this comparison was supposed to be preconscious. In this view, a person is continuously building a schema that is constantly changing; therefore Head and Holmes named it a "plastic schema." In the past it has been believed that disturbances in the body schema are correlated with defects in right–left orientation and finger agnosia, but one more recent report (Poeck & Orgass, 1971) has failed to find any supporting evidence for this claim. In fact, the evidence found by Poeck and Orgass throws doubt on the usefulness of the concept of body schema itself since measures of its presence and/or nature are contaminated by both verbal and nonverbal factors. In spite of the methodological problems of measuring or detecting the proprioceptive awareness of one's own body in space, most researchers, teachers, psychotherapists, actors, and athletes find it a very real concept, essential to the learning and performances of their particular professional concerns. A recent description of the normal body schema depicts it as "the peripheral, schematically conscious, structured, plastically bordered spatial perception of one's own body, constructed from previous and current (especially somesthetic) sensory information" (Frederiks, 1969b). To understand the types of minimal impairments frequent in some learning disabled children, it may help to look briefly at the clinically pathological extremes resulting from moderate to severe brain damage and/or dysfunction. These include the loss of perception of one-half or one part of the body. When this experience is conscious, the experience may be similar to that of an amputee, although there is no amputation. When the hemiasomatognosia is nonconscious, the patient simply ignores one-half or one part of his body and behaves as if it did not exist. Sometimes a patient, because of brain dysfunctions, is unaware of his limb paralysis and cannot be persuaded of its existence even through logical demonstration. Others are unable to localize the parts of their bodies touched by the examiner, or to name them. A finger localization test can be used to investigate this (Benton, 1959) and to relate it to academic performance in the classroom (Satz et al. 1978). The phantom limb phenomenon, when it results from cortical damage or dysfunction, is an obvious perversion of the body image, as is the uncommon tendency of some patients to perceive the size of their body parts inaccurately. It is sometimes easier to understand subtle variations in normal behavior by being aware of the many abnormal conditions that sometimes occur. Later in the chapter we will look at performances on tests of finger identification, right–left orientation, and other tactile and motor responses and their relationships to successful or disabled classroom learning.

Cortical Electrostimulation

As we saw in Chapter 4, electrostimulation of the cerebral cortex was first attempted by Fritsch and Hitzig in Germany in 1870. They exposed the brain of a dog under light anesthetic and touched areas of the motor strip with an electrode delivering a minimal electric current. This produced motor responses in the contralateral legs. By the 1920s, the famous German neurosurgeon Otfrid Foerster was treating cases of traumatic epilepsy in human subjects (many of these were war injuries) by excising the epileptogenic scar tissue. He was also using the technique of cortical electrostimulation to explore the brains of his patients prior to the actual cutting.

In 1928, Wilder Penfield went to the University of Breslau to study with Foerster, who was professor of neurology and neurosurgery and president of the prestigious German Society of Neurology and Psychiatry (Penfield, 1977). On his return to Montreal, Penfield established the Montreal Neurological Institute where he refined the technique, and during the 1930s and 1940s "cortical mapping" became an established diagnostic procedure for the surgical treatment of epilepsy and the incidental study of brain function (Penfield & Roberts, 1959).

During brain surgery the patient remained conscious, all probable pain being controlled by local anesthesia. An electrode applied to the cortical sensory strip (postcentral gyrus) was charged with a weak electrical current. The voltage strength would gradually be increased until the patient reported the presence of a bodily sensation. This was taken to be the threshold strength for sensory functions for that patient, and it provided a guide for the stimulus strength of the motor strip (precentral gyrus) in order to activate an involuntary motor activity (e.g., movement of the fingers or hands). Usually the stimulus strength to activate motor activity was greater, sometimes twice that of the sensory threshold strength. Stimulations in different cortical areas may produce either an inhibition of specific movements, a temporary paralysis during the stimulation, or an activation of activity that the patient cannot resist. Interference with the motor speech areas may cause a temporary interruption with naming a series of objects, counting, reading, and writing. This impressive and imaginative clinical research may help the clinician and the special teacher to conceptualize and better understand problems of stammering, stuttering, articulation, word finding, spelling, writing, and sequential motor speech.

Since the 1950s cortical mapping has been adopted by numerous neurosurgeons in other centers. A few, like Penfield, have used it to increase our knowledge of brain function. One of these, George Ojemann, at the University of Washington in Seattle, has collaborated with a professional team of neurophysiologists (Calvin & Ojemann, 1980) and neuropsychologists (Ojemann & Whitaker, 1978; Ojemann & Mateer, 1979), and he and his colleagues have produced a valuable collection of papers for the clinical neuropsychologist and the student of the human brain.

Sensorimotor Functions and Learning

Because the myelination of cortical cells in the sensory and motor strips and the occipital lobes is most advanced at birth (Flechsig, 1927) this may explain why the infant during the first few months of life explores his world largely through his tactual sense mode. He finds the object by sight but explores it by touch with hands and mouth. This has led some educators to propose that the child's tactile sense is his most primitive, and historically most practiced; hence it is the one to use as a basis for remedial teaching when that is indicated. The small infant learns about the three-dimensional environment by integrating what he sees with what he can touch and move.

Many professional educators have made use of this observation in both their theories and practices, but one of the earliest and most influential in this century was Maria Montessori, an internationally recognized Italian scholar. It is notable that her first strong academic interests were in mathematics and this led to technical training in engineering, then in biology, and finally in medicine. She became the first woman to complete a medical degree in Italy (1896), and it was this background that was to alert her to the importance of the biological bases of behavior and learning in her long career as an influential educator. After several years of practical experience in medical practice and treatment of feebleminded children, she returned to the university to prepare herself for education of the normal and subnormal. She studied philosophy, psychology, pediatric neurology, and the theories and methods of Itard and Seguin, both of whom had devoted their lives to the treatment and education of the retarded. With her training in rigorous scientific principles, physiology, neurology, psychology, philosophy, and the special education of the feebleminded and her strong humanistic drive to help children, both normal and impaired, she was one of the best prepared educators of her time. So convinced was she that the teacher must consider the child completely, in terms of his physical and mental inheritance, that she never made the error of viewing the child only in behavioral terms but emphasized that the child's intellect was intimately bound up with his body, particularly with the nervous and muscular systems. Although Montessori's methods were developed prior to the emergence of modern neuropsychological knowledge, she was convinced of their value. She believed that "the hand is the instrument of the brain" and that the education of the child demanded an activation and an interaction of these two. She talked about the sensorial foundations of intellectual life and recommended sensorial, mainly tactile and visual, contact with objects in the initial stages of learning about them. To teach the abstract concept of "triangularity," she would give the child a triangular block that he could handle and fit into a form board. When this skill was mastered, the child was then shown printed cards with silhouettes of triangles (with the inside spaces filled in). When the child could recognize these as triangles he was then shown line drawings of triangles; finally the child was taught the verbal abstraction of the concept, the description of a triangle (i.e., a plane figure enclosed by three straight lines). In other words what he first experienced tactually, and then visually, he now was able "to see" mentally (Standing, 1962). Like Piaget, Montessori proposed a developmental pattern in which the child at first learned about the environment unconsciously, simply by being moved about in it, but later, conscious learning occurred through repeated manipulation and tactile and motor exploration of environmental objects. By this time the hand had truly become the instrument of the brain, and it was through this manual activity that the child enriched his experience and developed himself (Montessori, 1965; Standing, 1962). The reason for introducing Montessori in this chapter is to remind ourselves that successful remedial teaching practices have always made use of tactile and visual–manual activities, and that their value has been recognized in many developmental theories.

Piaget, in his theory of child development, proposed the sensorimotor period as the first stage of growth ranging from birth to about 2 years of age (Phillips, 1969/1975, 1975 edition, Chap. 2); this sensorimotor interaction provided the child with increasing information about the world. Some of the child's responses are automatic or reflexive (or unconscious in Montessori's theory) and some provide variable patterns of interacting.

> Sensorimotor space begins to evolve right from the child's birth, and together with perception and motor activity it undergoes considerable development up until the appearance of speech and symbolic images.
> . . . This sensorimotor space is superimposed upon various pre-existing spaces such as the postural, etc., though it is by no means a simple reflection or repetition of them. [Piaget & Inhelder, 1956]

As students of Piaget will know, he developed a highly detailed theory of visual perception and its relation to haptic experience. Like Montessori, he drew attention to the perceptual and conceptual processes in cognition, but he proposed a more refined and sequential analysis of the small child's responses to perceptual or sensorimotor space. All understanding of the physical environment includes both sensory awareness and the imaginary recall of objects in their absence, and perception in its complete sense means an interaction of these two processes. Where these two provide a smooth reciprocal function, perception occurs with a sense of familiarity, ease, and confidence. Where these two do not, such as in viewing a formless, abstract painting, the perceptual response may bring with it a sense of incomprehension, frustration, and insecurity. Piaget has expressed this as follows: "It (perception) completes perceptual knowledge by reference to objects not actually perceived" (Piaget & Inhelder, 1956).

The first exhaustive developmental observation of a child's haptic perception, it seems, was carried out by Piaget. He discovered, in studying the child from 2 to 7 years, an unfolding and self-revealing pattern. Below the age of 2 years 6 months, experimentation with hidden figures is limited. From then up to $3\frac{1}{2}$ or 4 years, the child can recognize haptically familiar objects (such as a ball, scissors, or spoon) but not geometric euclidean figures (such as a square, circle, or triangle). This is an interesting finding which suggests that haptic recognition (i.e., three-dimensional stereognosis) is not only easier but developmentally earlier than two-dimensional stereognosis or very thin abstract forms. In this same connection, clinical neuropsychologists and speech therapists are aware that aphasic patients with word-finding problems may be unable to name pictures of objects (i.e., two-dimensional ones) but may be much more successful when these same objects are handed to them to examine (i.e., three-dimensional ones). More will be said about the understanding and treatment of aphasia in Chapter 8.

At the preschool age of $3\frac{1}{2}$ to 4 years, Piaget found the beginnings of haptic recognition of shapes, but "curiously enough, the shapes first recognized are not euclidean but topological" (Piaget & Inhelder, 1956). He found that the child at this stage could distinguish open from closed forms (e.g., O and C) but could not distinguish a square from a circle since both are closed, and straight lines and angles are still not identified. The poor haptic recognition in the early years is correlated with relatively passive tactile exploration, which frequently provides only chance discoveries.

As the child matures, his tactile–kinesthetic exploration becomes more vigorous and searching so that, by $5\frac{1}{2}$ to 6 years, he begins to identify abstract forms, with much hesitation, such as the rhombus and trapezium. Between age 6 and 7 the child becomes much more methodical in such tactile–kinesthetic exploration and he now can discriminate among complex forms, for example, a semicircle, a diamond, and a star. It is at this age that we begin to study children in the Victoria laboratory, and we find that they can replace the blocks in a six-block version of the Seguin formboard, although with a great variability of performance (Spreen & Gaddes, 1969).

While the theories of both Montessori and Piaget were developed before the emergence of modern neuropsychological knowledge, both theories either stressed or implied the importance of the biological bases of behavior, the presence of mediating organic processes, and the necessity of adapting to the environment. However, whereas they recognized the important presence of underlying physiological processes, their primary concern was with the behavioral phenomena, which is the proper province of the teacher and school psychologist. To become aware of the neurological correlates of tactile perception, we must go to the research neuropsychologist. It is interesting that when Luria describes the topic of "tactile perception" he first describes the brain structures mediating it. When explaining "disturbances of tactile synthesis," Luria (1966) wrote, "These disturbances (i.e., tactile agnosia or astereognosis) may arise from lesions of the parietal areas of the cerebral cortex, areas constituting the cortical portion of the cutaneo-kinesthetic analyzer. . . ." By this "analyzer" he meant the sensory strip just posterior to the fissure of Rolando and the adjacent parietal cortex. He reports damage to these cortical areas resulting in disturbed body image, poor finger localization, impaired cutaneous localization, inaccurate perception of the direction of a line drawn on the skin, and astereognosis, even though in some cases tactile awareness was intact. Luria has written at some length not only on disorders of tactile perception, but also on visual imperceptions and the many varieties of visual–motor disorders. Any remedial teacher would do well to study this material, which is supplied with many graphic examples (Luria, 1966, pp. 134–153).

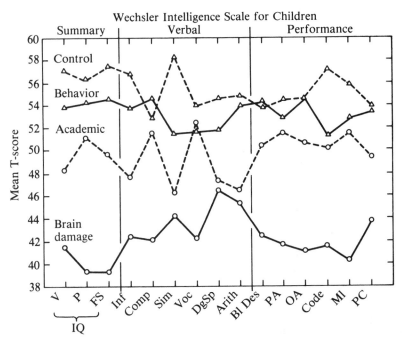

Figure 6.3.   Graphic presentation of mean performances on the Wechsler Intelligence Scale for Children for a control group, a brain-damaged group, and minimal brain-damaged groups with academic deficiencies and school behavior problems. (From Reitan & Boll, 1973. With permission from the authors and The New York Academy of Sciences.)

Many educators have recommended a perceptual–motor or motor emphasis or a sensorimotor integration model purely on behavioral evidence (Ayres, 1968, 1972a, 1975; Barsch, 1965, 1966; Cratty, 1967, 1968; Cruickshank, 1975; Fernald, 1943; Freidus, 1964, 1966; Getman, 1966; Kephart, 1960/1971, 1966, 1975; Kirk, 1966; Strauss & Lehtinen, 1947; Valett, 1973), but if these remedial prescriptions are examined with the additional knowledge offered by neuropsychology, the teacher will become prepared with a more comprehensive understanding of the functions of somesthesis and its role in classroom learning.

Neuropsychological Findings

Having presented a neuropsychological model of the sensorimotor structures and functions in learning, the next step is to relate test findings of these behavioral processes to success and failure in academic learning.

Probably no one has been more active and productive than Ralph M. Reitan during the past 30 years in the use of neuropsychological test findings for identifying and localizing brain lesions. In addition, during the past 20 years he has carried out several valuable researches to compare normal and learning disabled children with medically documented brain-damaged subjects of the same age. In one study (Reitan & Boll, 1973) he subjected four groups of children (mean age 7.3–7.5 years) to a large battery of intellectual, educational, and neuropsychological tests and compared their group differences. The groups included 25 normal controls (none had ever failed a grade in school or ever been referred for academic or behavioral problems), 25 who were brain damaged, 25 who were referred for academic and learning difficulties but not behavior problems, and 19 who were referred for school behavioral difficulties. In any school population it is almost certain that all of these types of children are represented and must be dealt with by teachers.

Reitan and Boll found that on the Wechsler (WISC) the brain-damaged group performed consistently more poorly than the other three groups and, of these three, the group with academic deficiencies (that is, the learning disabled group) was the poorest. This same order of performance, the controls best, the behavior disorder group next, then the learning disabled, and finally the brain-damaged group worst, also held for academic measures (reading, spelling, and arithmetic as measured by the Wide Range Achievement Test), visual–spatial skills, motor functions, tactile perception, and incidental memory (Fig. 6.3). The control and "behavior" groups were very close and their scores on most tests were, for the most part, not statistically significantly different. While such a study concerns itself with group performance levels on various skills and hence tells us nothing specific about a particular child, it does suggest the strong possibility of subtle cerebral dysfunctions in the case of the learning disabled child. Certainly, the group test results show such a child to be closer in behavior to the known brain-damaged subjects than either the normal control or behaviorally disturbed child. It is quite possible that the child with poor social control is a product of family pressures or other psychosocial forces, whereas the child refractory to normal learning and motivational procedures may be suffering from chronic intrinsic conflicts stemming from organic dysfunctions. Reitan and Boll's study, combined with our own clinical experience, has led us to the view that many or most of the learning disabled children are suffering from the same kind of sensorimotor, perceptual, and cognitive disabilities as the brain-damaged child, although to a lesser degree, regardless of the absence of conclusive evidence of neurological damage or dysfunction.

Table 6.1 summarizes the findings of a computer survey of the files of 154 children referred to our laboratory because of moderate to severe learning disorders. These children ranged in age from 8 to 15, and about 70% were boys and 30% girls. They were selected by computer from our

Table 6.1 Percentages of Learning Disabled Children, Aged 8–15, Scoring Below Average and Below One Standard Deviation on a Number of Sensorimotor Tests

Test	N	Dominant Hand		Nondominant Hand		Both Hands		Range (%)
		$\bar{X}$ (%)	<-1 SD (%)	$\bar{X}$ (%)	<-1 SD (%)	$\bar{X}$ (%)	<-1 SD (%)	
Esthesiometer	20 boys and girls	95.0	95.0	100	85.0			87.5–100
Stereognosis	80 boys	72.8	46.4	70.4	44.6			20.0–96.0
	25 girls	65.5	40.9	74.0	59.1			0.0–100
Tactual perception	44 boys					45.5	31.3	19.2–66.4
	15 girls					46.2	25.9	0.0–100
Hand grip	61 boys	91.8	65.6					90.0–93.3
	21 girls	90.5	61.9					75.0–100
Finger tapping	19 boys and girls	78.9	63.0					60.0–100
Visual–manual R.T. [a]	56 boys	78.6	57.1	78.6	57.1	78.6	57.1	50.0–100
	26 girls	76.9	46.1	61.5	38.5	69.2	42.3	25.0–100
R–L orientation	83 boys					59.0	51.8	18.2–100
	22 girls					54.5	45.4	0.0–100

[a] The complete name is "Visual-Manual Reaction Time Test." (The child hits a key as soon as he sees a light.)

files in Category 3 (see Table 1.1), that is, *learning disabled children with no clear neurological signs.*

An examination of the data summarized in Table 6.1 reveals that: (1) Although the neurologists found no clear-cut neurological findings of abnormality, most of these children performed at a level below average on most of the sensorimotor tests listed here, in the same way that brain-damaged children do. (2) Although most of the learning disabled children were inferior on sensorimotor tasks, a few of them achieved normal scores in a few instances. (3) While the numbers of subjects in some age groups were small, especially in the case of the girls, this tended to make the ranges greater (e.g., from 0 to 100%), but even so the average performances were inferior except in the case of the Tactual Perception Test. It is useful to note that the Esthesiometer Test and Dynamometer (hand grip) were failed by the greatest number of learning disabled boys and girls. These tests are also sensitive indicators of central nervous system damage or dysfunction.

In summary, then, we can conclude that inferiority in a sensory, and/or a motor, and/or a sensorimotor integration task is a sensitive indicator of central nervous system dysfunction and a reliable correlate of learning disorders. This type of evidence supports the hypothesis that cases of learning disabilities with negative neurological examinations may nevertheless be suffering from minimal and subtle neurological damage or dysfunction.

Clinical Addendum

An examination of some clinical cases of parietal dysfunctions should help the clinical or school psychologist to improve diagnostic skills, and hence remedial prescriptions, and the special teacher to a more comprehensive understanding of the child with sensorimotor, body-image, and spatial difficulties. Let us look first at a case from the medical literature and then at two from our own files.

Three Cases of Parietal Dysfunctions

Case 1

Benton (1969a) has described an early case, reported by Badal in France in 1888, in which a young woman possessed preserved central visual acuity but suffered severe impairment of the sense of space. Although her visual acuity was normal, she could not find her way about in her own house. She could read letters, numbers, and familiar words, but because of her loss of directional orientation she was unable to spell or read serially. She also suffered from a dressing apraxia and was unable to draw either from copy or from memory. Benton concluded that "it seems probable that this patient suffered a cerebrovascular insult with bilateral parieto-occipital involvement . . ." (Benton, 1969a).

Case 2

Some years ago a neurologist referred to us a 6-year-old boy who had a problem of poor coordination and hyperactive behavior. His mother reported that he was easy to raise, he walked early, and he developed speech at the normal time. The parents, both young (the father was 24 and the mother 20 at the time of Mark's birth), reported that they noticed the hyperactivity by Mark's second birthday. In school his poor coordination showed itself in an inability to draw, cut with scissors, and carry out normal manual activities. In addition he was distractible, excitable, and easily frustrated. The neurological examination revealed one minimal and one major finding: involuntary movements of his hands and feet, and a grade iii dysrhythmia in the left cerebral motor region, respectively. Because Mark was right handed this had a seriously disturbing effect on his writing and manual skills.

Our test examination showed Mark to be an alert, likable boy. Throughout the 5 hours of testing he showed no signs of distractibility, since in the testing laboratory he was on a one-to-one situation. There were no clear signs of "hyperactivity" so that these reported behaviors seemed to be more related to situational and psychological factors than to organic ones.

On the Wechsler (WISC) he measured a verbal IQ of 118 and a performance IQ of 105. He had superior scores on the Vocabulary, Digit Span, and Similarities subtests but had only average scores on Picture Arrangement and Coding, because of his moderate apraxia. On the Benton Visual Retention Test he neglected the peripheral figures in the right visual field, which suggested that the left-hemisphere disturbance, although centered in the left motor strip, must also have affected the left visual tracts minimally. Other than the minimal right visual field neglect, his visual perception was intact, as were also his auditory and tactile recognition. He showed a slowness with his right hand relative to his left on visual–manual reaction time, finger tapping, and hand-grip strength. The parents reported that in running or climbing he showed a slight awkwardness in his right arm and leg.

In the report to Mark's teacher it was stressed that he was a bright, eager little boy whose reported hyperactivity was likely related more to situational frustrations than to any perceptual problem. Since the school knew that Mark had been referred to a neurologist, this report made it clear that "there is no conclusive evidence of brain damage, but because of a slight unevenness of electrical function in the left side of his brain, he will likely always have a certain awkwardness of manipulation in his right hand. This means that he may be slow in writing and carrying out many manual tasks requiring speed and fine precision."

A year later, on recall, we found that Mark's learning problems had largely disappeared. His teachers realized his potential brightness and the specific nature of his manual apraxia, and they allowed for this in their dealing with him. His "hyperactivity" disappeared and was replaced by an image of alert, energetic interest in learning.

A follow-up interview, when Mark was in Grade 9, showed him to be a bright, well-adjusted adolescent, with A grades in mathematics and science. His handwriting was still slow and awkward, but he had learned to live with it and to compensate for it successfully.

Case 3

Donald is one of the most extreme cases of "spatial disorientation" in a child that one is likely to see in 30 years of teaching. He was first referred for testing by a pediatric neurologist when he was 10 years old, because of seizures (both petit and grand mal) and severe learning disabilities.

Donald's mother reported no unusual health history with him until the age of 5, when he developed a brain infection (encephalitis), followed first by staring spells and later by occasional grand mal seizures. Anticonvulsive medication was prescribed with fairly heavy doses to control the frequency of the seizures, and Donald's EEGs were abnormal from then on. They showed bilateral spike activity in the left frontal and parietal lobes and in the right parieto-temporal areas. At age 7, Donald showed a WISC verbal IQ of 91 and a performance IQ of 86. His spoken language was normal but he could neither read nor write, and he had great difficulty with spatial (e.g., Block Design on the WISC) and sequential–visual–motor tasks (e.g., Coding on the WISC). Donald not only suffered from a poor sense of direction, but he also showed awkward coordination in hopping and skipping. The evidence from the EEGs suggested strongly that there were bilateral dysfunctions in the motor and sensory strips as well as some areas of the parietal lobes.

At age 10, Donald measured a WISC verbal IQ of 74 and a performance IQ of 52. His poorer mental measures would seem to have stemmed from the effects of the heavy medication program. Although he tried to cooperate in the testing situation, he yawned continually and usually fell asleep on arriving home from school in the afternoon. Since learning is related to the degree of "motivated activity" (Montessori, 1965), the drug-imposed reduction of Donald's activity seemed to result in an impoverished school experience. Although detailed remedial exercises were proposed, Donald made little or no progress for the next 2 years, either because his teachers gave him inappropriate instruction or because he was unable to profit from it on account of his imposed lethargy.

Observation during testing focused on Donald's ability to perceive visual forms and to draw them or to react to them spatially. He was able to copy a square and a triangle reasonably well, although he hesitated to do this at first. After drawing them he was able to name them correctly. It was interesting to observe that whereas his speech was normal, his vocabulary was very limited because of his learning problem. When shown a Greek cross, he made a vertical line and was unable to do anything more. Even when urged to continue, he was unable to scan it, analyze it, and draw it. Evidently he had not yet acquired the necessary cortical engrams or the ideomotor images.

In stereognosis he had great difficulty in recognizing forms with his left hand, although performance with the right hand was a little better. This supports the hypothesis that while there was pathology in both hemispheres, it was more pronounced in the right. His inferior spatial imagery correlated with this supposition, and his normal expressive speech supported normal or near-normal functions in the motor–speech tracts of the left hemisphere.

Donald's auditory–linguistic abilities were among his best. When we saw him a year later at age 11, he was able to recite the complete alphabet correctly, but he could not remember the visual form of some of the letters, and his visual scanning was so chaotic that there was no semblance of straight lines (Fig. 6.4).

Motor activities requiring spatial scanning were impossible. He could not imitate a sequential pattern of tapping a series of blocks, no matter how many times or how slowly the tapping sequence was repeated. Hopscotch was impossible for him and he was unable to touch his fingers behind his back, although this was demonstrated several times. Nevertheless, he was neither paralyzed nor ataxic, and he walked normally.

Donald's mother reported he had fluctuating success in dressing himself. Sometimes he suffered from severe dressing apraxia and at other times there seemed to be little or no problem. Such fluctuations in behavior suggest biochemical changes (possibly dietary or transitory blood chemistry imbalances).

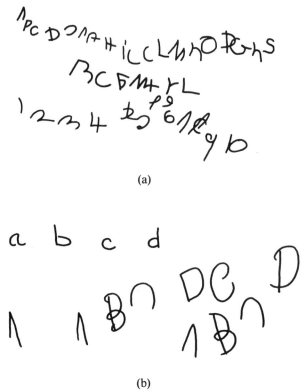

(a)

(b)

Figure 6.4. **(a)** Donald's spontaneous writing of the alphabet and numbers (age 11 years, 3 months), and **(b)** his copying of four letters that had been named for him.

His spatial disorientation in extrapersonal space had been chronic since his encephalitis. He got lost in his own house and had difficulty finding the bathroom or his own belongings in his bedroom. When sent for something in the backyard he sometimes could not find the kitchen door in order to return to the house. In three test sessions in our laboratory (totaling about 18 hours) over a period of 18 months, he never learned to find his way from the testing room to the hall where his mother was waiting, although all of the other children we have seen (over 2000 up to that time) learned this on their first visit.

What Donald's Teachers Might Do

A teacher confronted with a child as severely impaired as Donald will have a monumental task, and he or she will need as much help as possible in the form of professional information and suggestions. There were two basic problems that Donald's teachers faced: (1) the mental lethargy and reduced attention resulting from the heavy medication program and (2) the chronic visual–motor–spatial deficits resulting from the bilateral parietal brain dysfunctions.

Let us look at the first of these. If Donald were hospitalized and taken off his anticonvulsive medication, it seems highly likely that his IQ would measure 20 or 30 points higher. However, in his case, because the parents were afraid that severe seizures would cause more brain damage, this was not tried, and his teachers had to struggle to teach him with his drug-imposed mental sluggishness. This is frequently the cruel dilemma of the epileptic child; the advantage of being seizure-free is often at the cost of functioning at a mental level much below his or her potential.

In cases such as these it is advisable for the pediatric neurologist, the teacher, the school psychologist, and the parents to meet to clarify the possible risks of removing the child from or markedly reducing his or her medication dosage to a level where the child can profit more from remedial education. When this is done, then "baseline" measures on psychological and educational achievement tests should be carried out after the reduction of the drug dosage and prior to the remedial program. The teacher or psychologist, in obtaining baseline measures, should take special care to wait long enough after the withdrawal of medication to be sure there are no residual drug effects; otherwise the spurious baseline measures will operate to the child's disadvantage. Intermittent testing during the months ahead will permit comparison with the baseline measures and inform the teacher whether or not the remedial measures are effective.

The second problem relates to Donald's chronic learning deficits. Before attempting to devise a remedial program, all available evidence will be assembled to provide a conceptual model of what is likely going on when Donald views the world or tries to acquire ideas about it through reading and writing.

Diagnosis

Most current educators are now recommending a diagnostic approach based on a neurological model of input, cerebral integration, and output (Kirk, 1966; Valett, 1973) as already recommended in the initial chapters of this book. The following diagnostic discussion is based on this model.

Sensory and Perceptual Functions

Visual Perception. The teacher will want to know answers to the following questions. Does Donald perceive his environment visually in such a chaotic way that it is virtually impossible to teach him to read or write, or is his visual perception normal, but his visual memory defective? Likewise, are both these functions reasonably normal, but his visual–motor abilities so defective that he is unable to reproduce drawings or writing in an average way for a boy his age? On the Benton Visual Retention Test, which required him to copy 10 geometric diagrams, he obtained zero scores at ages 9 years 11 months, and 10 years 5 months; he was unable to draw any of the designs although the average child of this age can draw from memory (a more difficult task than copying) four designs at age 9 and five designs at age 10 (Benton, 1963b, p. 46). On the third testing, when Donald was 11 years 3 months old, he completed one of the designs successfully. This was Card 3, which was fairly detailed; it included two linked circles in the center of the card with a small square in the right peripheral area. There were some parts of the other cards drawn correctly, but no part marks are allowed. To compare this with his verbal memory of the designs, the multiple-choice form of the Benton Visual Retention Test was administered twice, and both times he remembered two of the 10 designs he had seen on the initial viewing. This evidence suggests that his visual memory when free of drawing or motor demands was accurate, although inferior for his age. When asked to draw something, Donald's scanning and visual spacing was so impaired that he was unable to draw what he could remember.

This hypothesis was also supported by the evidence from drawing and writing. When asked to draw a square and a triangle, he could do this satisfactorily, although he required a great deal of urging and encouragement to do it. Evidently, the scanning required to draw these basic figures was simple enough to permit him to draw them. The Greek cross, however, which analytically is made up of five squares of equal size, was beyond his abilities to translate into accurate motor patterns. At age 9 years 11 months he drew one vertical line; at age 11 years 3 months he made two more complicated attempts, but neither resembled a Greek cross (Fig. 6.5). It is interesting to note that he did perceive the analytical fact that the cross was made up of rectangular spaces, but his severely impaired spatial orientation made it impossible for him to scan the figure mentally and to arrange the arms in their correct spatial relationships.

Figure 6.4 shows his writing of letters and numbers. At first he was asked to write the alphabet and the numbers from 1 to 10 from memory. A scrutiny of his writing shows that his auditory–linguistic knowledge was completely accurate, but his visual–graphic transposition produced many errors. The letter A lacks the crossbar, as it does everywhere on that sheet. On B, he remembered only the top eliptical form and neglected the bottom one. C and D are satisfactory. E is reversed and lacks the crossbar, as did A. F also lacks the crossbar. G is correct except that it is reversed *and* inverted. H and I are acceptable. J is reversed. K lacks the vertical line. L, M, N, and O are recognizable. P and Q are linked because of his poor spacing, and Q lacks closure. R is a lower case letter, and S is acceptable. T lacks the left half of the top crossbar, and U, which is

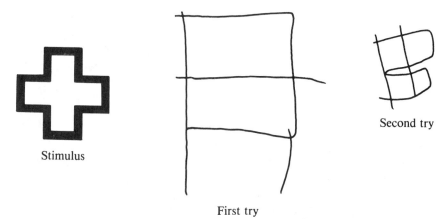

Stimulus

Second try

First try

Figure 6.5.   Donald's attempts to copy a Greek cross (age 11 years 3 months).

rotated, is joined to it. V is rotated and resembles U rather than V. He needed two tries at W, the second being successful but inverted. X and Y are recognizable and Z lacks the top crossbar. When we look at the numbers, they are all there, but in some cases badly deformed: 1, 2, 3, 4, 6, 7, 9, and 10 are recognizable; 5 has an extra inverted 6 on it, which suggests he wrote it over the 6, unable to space it separately. He needed another three tries on 6, but it is notable he was aware of the reversal and inversions on the first two tries and corrected himself successfully on the third try. Figure 6.4b gives us some useful information about his abilities to copy. The psychometrician wrote the four *lower case* letters, a, b, c, and d, on the sheet and asked Donald to copy them. Because most of the visual–graphic–motor patterns that he had mastered were capital, or upper case, letters, he wrote the four letters in that form. Again, however, he neglected the crossbar on A on all three tries and reversed C. B and D are satisfactory. This information tells us that he was able to *read* lower case letters, but because of his severe spatial disorientation he did not have confidence that he could copy what he saw. Instead, he transcribed the *concept* of what he read into a *motor pattern* with which he had some familiarity.

We tested his visual discrimination of "larger than" and "farther and closer" and found these completely successful for commonplace environmental objects.

In summary, the test evidence suggests that Donald's perception had some degree of accuracy and that it could be helped by mnemonic devices, and his visual–perceptual attention improved by multisensorimotor exercises. The exact nature of these is described later under remediation.

Auditory Perception. Donald's phonetic discrimination was in the normal range, as was his verbal memory in repeating sentences back on the Spreen–Benton Sentence Repetition Test. Dichotic listening suggested that he was markedly left-hemisphere dominant for language, which was fortunate in that neurological examinations had indicated his left hemisphere to be less affected than his right. His speech abilities appeared normal in ordinary conversation, in his ability to recite the alphabet and numbers, in naming objects he could not draw, and in sentence repetition. Because oral speech was one of his relative strengths, it was exploited in his remediation program.

Stereognosis (Tactile Form Recognition). Because of his biparietal disturbance, Donald's tactile recognition was not good in either hand, but it was better with his right hand because of the relative superiority of his left cerebral hemisphere. Because he was strongly right handed this was fortunate and permitted his spatial orientation to be encouraged through a manual–spatial set of exercises.

Intellectual Abilities

Intelligence quotients are essentially useless in diagnosing the mental abilities of children on heavy medication programs, but intelligence test results are useful if viewed qualitatively in the light of the pharmacological influences. On our three test sessions, he obtained verbal IQs of 74, 63, and 58, and performance IQs of 48, 44, and 45. The diminishing verbal IQs indicate not a progressively deteriorating brain condition but a partially impoverished educational experience resulting from difficulty of attention except in a "one-to-one" instructional situation and from the mental lethargy caused by the drugs. Because of his near-normal speech skills his WISC vocabulary conceptual abilities measured almost in the normal range. However, arithmetic was inferior because of his spatial deficits, and general information, comprehension of commonplace problems, and memory for digits were extremely poor because of his inability to read and learn normally. All of the WISC performance tests were inferior because of their heavy spatial loadings. This information suggests a major part of Donald's learning should occur through conversation and discussion, and that reading, writing, and spelling should be assisted through multisensorimotor–spatial reinforcement.

Motor Skills and Sensorimotor Integration

Donald's finger tapping was neuromuscularly fluent but slow, presumably because of the drugs. Reaction times to a light and to a tone were his best measures, in this group of tests, although they were slow and hence below average for his age. Donald's hand grip in his right hand was better than in his left, but still below average, and his finger localization was inferior on both hands. His performance on the Benton Right–Left Orientation Test was defective, showing poor directional identification of his own body parts and of objects in extrapersonal space. Since all of these skills are believed to draw heavily on parietal function, the poor scores on these sensorimotor tests are not surprising. At the same time, they are not discouraging because his neuromuscular integration appears to be normal and this is a good basis for motor learning.

Remediation: What to Do to Help Donald

Since Donald was a happy, reasonably well-adjusted youngster, the primary therapeutic responsibility was to help him circumvent his specific learning disabilities, once the depressing effects of the medication program could be reduced. Obviously when a child manifests chronic emotional symptoms stemming, at least in part, from the frustrations he suffers from learning problems, then the teacher must devise ways of minimizing the effects of the perceptual and/or motor deficiencies but also must try to help the child to resolve poor emotional habits and attitudes and to develop a better level of self-acceptance. In Donald's case, it seemed that a remedial program to help the first aspect of the problem could have no other effect on his self-esteem but to improve it. Basically, however, his learning problems were not maximally "emotional"; Donald was cheery and well adjusted with his peers, his teacher, and his family.

Donald's remedial program included the following cognitive and behavioral skills:

1. A medical readjustment of his medication program to maximize attention.
2. Visual processes.
   a. Visual memory. Donald was shown nonverbal stimuli (actual commonplace objects first, then line drawings of objects) in increasing numbers and asked to report on or describe them. This report was requested immediately following the removal of the stimuli, then after 5 seconds, after 10 seconds, etc. Following this, the same procedure was done with geometric figures, then single letters, words, phrases, and short sentences. Any remedial teacher will have a repertoire of exercises to improve visual memory. The inexperienced teacher has many sources to draw on (Cruickshank, 1961, 1977; Myers & Hammill, 1969; Rosner, 1979; Valett, 1973).
   b. Visual–motor skills. A large variety of hand–eye coordination exercises were carried out *after* Donald had practiced the motor skill with his eyes closed. This was to eliminate the disturbing effects of his visual–spatial deficits in the early stages of learning. At this stage his drawing of simple objects was severely impaired (Fig. 6.6).

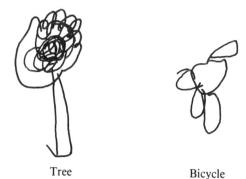

Tree   Bicycle

Figure 6.6. Donald's attempts to draw two common objects (age 11 years 3 months).

3. Auditory processes. Although his conversational speech was unimpaired, Donald was given practice in talking, memorizing and reciting poetry, and taking part in classroom plays. This not only provided language development for him but gave him an opportunity to gain success in one of his behavioral strengths. Some use of a tape recorder assisted him in learning to spell and to read.

4. Validation of remedial measures. A case as difficult as this needs constant monitoring and evaluation to discover whether the methods are appropriate and what progress, if any, is resulting. Donald's teacher will need to be supplied with a great variety of remedial suggestions and the patience and interest to make ongoing measures of possible progress.

Progress Report on Donald

Figure 6.7 shows the marked improvement in Donald's writing after only 8 months of training in a special center for severely learning disabled children. He entered this special school at the age of $11\frac{1}{2}$. He was taught to read by a modified Gillingham method because his auditory language was good. Essentially the procedure made use of phonics coupled with multisensory stimulation. By the end of his second year he read at a Grade 5 level, slowly, but accurately for the most part. His progress in both reading and spelling was rapid.

His writing within 2 years has progressed from chaotic inaccuracy (Fig. 6.4) to legible and well-spaced writing (Fig. 6.8). Three sentences were dictated, and other than one visually misspelled word (tier), a lack of periods, and a capitalized first word in the third sentence, they are written neatly and intelligibly. He was taught to write using dark-lined paper and

Dictation

Marry

Other

Minute

Heavy

Front

Awake

Teacher's stimulus
drawings

Donald's attempts
to copy them

Six

Twenty-four

One hundred and ninety-two

Sixty-seven

Figure 6.7. Donald's writing and drawing after 8 months of intensive remedial teaching (age 12 years 10 months).

with his eyes closed or averted. This made use of a strong tactile–auditory match and avoided the disturbing effects of his poor visual perception and memory. Initially grid paper was tried but was visually more confusing than lined paper, so was abandoned in favor of heavy lined paper which worked successfully.

Donald's arithmetic was still very weak. At the age of 13 he could add and count, but other skills were unreliable. No doubt the strong spatial component in elementary written arithmetic has been a serious impediment. Figure 6.7 shows how his good auditory memory and impaired visual scanning produced "logical errors" in writing to dictation multi-digit numbers with internal zeros. He has since learned to write such numbers correctly with the aid of skilled remedial teaching.

Jim likes foot ball
he will take the pig skin and hug it to him

I have a flat tier on my bike
Mike will help me fix it
we will ride down hill for home

Figure 6.8. Donald's writing to dictation after 17 months of intensive remedial teaching (age 13 years 8 months).

Because his oral speech is fluent and competent, Donald's written English is reasonably good. Once he learned to space his letters and write on lines, he showed an ability to compose short stories and write them at about a Grade 5 level. His spelling includes "phonetically correct errors" because of his good auditory memory but weak visual memory (see Fig. 6.7).

His spatial orientation has improved with training since he embarked on the special remediation program. When he first arrived at the school he was continually lost unless someone accompanied him to the washroom, gymnasium, crafts building, or dining area, because each of these was in a separate building. Since Donald's biparietal damage made it difficult for him to produce mental schemata of the buildings and school campus, his teachers helped him to develop proximal cues in the environment. After a few weeks he was able to walk independently on the campus, until the first snowfall! That morning he was found completely confused about 100 yards away from the school. He has since been taught a number of routes by walking with him from A to B, where Donald hid a bag of peanuts or chocolate. He was then accompanied back to A and left free to find his way back to B. The reinforcement of the hidden reward, plus the sensori-motor action of hiding it, plus verbalizing the cues as he walked the route, all seemed to have combined to help Donald learn some common routes on the campus of his school, around his home, and in the small town where he lives.

At present Donald is a cheery 13-year-old who can read and write at about a Grade 5 level, can manage Grade 2 arithmetic, and has learned to overcome his spatial-orientation deficit to a marked degree. He is well motivated to learn and continues to show progress, particularly in the language arts.

7 Hemispheric Specialization, Handedness, and Laterality

The main theme to emerge from the foregoing facts is that there appear to be two modes of thinking, verbal and non-verbal, represented rather separately in right and left hemispheres respectively, and that our educational system, as well as science in general, tends to neglect the non-verbal form of intellect. What it comes down to is that modern society discriminates against the right hemisphere.

R. W. Sperry (1973)

Until recently it was thought, perhaps somewhat simplistically, that a right-handed person was necessarily left-hemisphere dominant for language, and similarly a left-handed person was right-hemisphere dominant for language. Now it is known, from neuropsychological researches over the last 30 years, that this is not so and that the whole question of the relation between handedness and hemispheric specialization is highly complex and variable within certain limits. However, before we examine the relationship between cerebral function and handedness, let us look at these two behavioral processes separately.

Cerebral Dominance

Over 20 years ago a conference was held at Johns Hopkins University School of Medicine at which the topic "Interhemispheric Relations and Cerebral Dominance" was discussed. A number of eminent neurologists and neuropsychologists were invited to present papers on their research, and these papers and their discussions were subsequently published (Mountcastle, 1962). During the 3 days of the conference a total of 11 scholarly presentations was made and valuable discussions followed these papers, but because the members of the group could not agree on a definition of cerebral dominance, none was given. Although this important neurological and behavioral phenomenon was named in the title of the book, the subject index did not contain the term anywhere.

Such is the difficulty of describing what happens in the brain tissue when a particular area of the cerebral structures seems to dominate or control some particular form of behavior. Although unable to explain how the brain provides selective control, we can describe it behaviorally, and some of its neuropsychological relationships.

Following the discoveries by Dax in France in 1836, Broca in 1861, and others at that time that aphasia was a result of disease of the left hemisphere, the belief developed that the left hemisphere in most people was dominant, because it seemed to influence and direct language functions. So concerned were neurologists in attempting to identify the "leading" or "major" hemisphere that the "minor" hemisphere was considered subordinate and vaguely inferior in function. In fact, it is only recently that scientific attention has been directed to study the "nondominant" hemisphere; as a result, evidence has appeared to suggest it possesses its own dominance, particularly for nonverbal functions (Benton, 1965), although it is not exclusively nonverbal (Gazzaniga & Hillyard, 1971; Kinsbourne, 1975a; E. Zaidel, 1973). During the past 30 years there has been a growing realization that the two hemispheres work together, possessing a reciprocal and interacting variety of hemispheric specialized functions.

We know, for example, that a child born with a defective left temporal lobe, particularly if the defect affects Wernicke's area, will most likely have a shift of the language functions to the right hemisphere, and he or she will learn language with the normally "minor" hemisphere. The child may still be right handed if the left frontal lobe and motor strip are healthy and operative. This means that the two hemispheres share control of different behavioral functions in different ways, depending on the locus of the healthiest cerebral tissue. Luria has described this dynamic cerebral function thus: "The dominance of one hemisphere in relation to speech functions proved not to be so absolute as was supposed, and research showed that the degre of dominance varied considerably from subject to subject and from function to function" (Luria, 1966). Not only that, but it seems possible that language dominance may alter following traumatic brain injury. One study of 25 right-handed adult traumatic aphasics with left-hemisphere damage showed that as they recovered and improved in language use, cerebral dominance gradually became more firmly established in the *right* hemisphere (Pettit & Noll, 1979). Cummings, Benson, Walsh, and Levine (1979) have reported the case of a middle-aged man with global aphasia following a massive left-hemisphere stroke who showed a partial recovery from his aphasia over a 3-year period. They attributed his language improvement to a gradual transfer of language dominance. They concluded: "Right hemisphere language function may underlie much of the recovery from aphasia after injury of the left hemisphere" (Cummings, Benson, Walsh, and Levine, 1979). This evidence supports a "shift in dominance" hypothesis and a dynamic concept of brain function.

Before we look at the functional relationships between the cerebral hemispheres and language and handedness, let us first define our terms.

Definition of Cerebral Dominance

We have already commented briefly on the difficulty of explaining cerebral dominance, and if we cannot explain it, it will be difficult to define. Operationally we know *what* happens (at least in gross terms) when one area of the cortex is maximally involved with a contralateral motor function, but we do not know completely *how* all this happens. We know that the pyramidal or motor tracts from one side cross over, mostly at the medullar level (see Fig. 6.2), but the physiological controls that direct the neural energy in the appropriate amounts and to the precise peripheral locations are not yet understood. A. Meyer, drawing on the writings of Hécaen (1969), Subirana (1969), and Clarke and Dewhurst (1972), has written "The underlying structural and physiological substrates of dominance are so far unknown" (A. Meyer, 1974).

Since at this point in our knowledge we cannot define cerebral dominance completely, let us list what we do know about the functional relationships among cortical activity and speech, brain, and handedness.

1. Cerebral dominance, until about 25 years ago, usually referred to the language mediation of the left hemisphere, along with a silent or "minor" right hemisphere. Neuropsychological research during the past 20 years has produced a concept of bilateral function with each hemisphere specialized for different forms of information processing. The left hemisphere in most people is more efficient in processing serial order perceptions, cognitions, and motor responses (Geschwind, 1975; Kimura, 1976; Mateer & Kimura, 1976), and for logical, sequential analysis. Because spoken and written language fit this analytic–temporal sequential mode of processing, it tends to be regulated by the left hemisphere.

    The right hemisphere in most subjects is better suited to process spatial and holistic material that is recognized instantly rather than sequentially. The perception of spatial relationships, whether visual, auditory, or tactile, depends largely on this type of cerebral processing. Because spatial–perceptual–constructional tasks fit this type of processing, they tend to be regulated by the right hemisphere.

    But because most perceptions include both linguistic and spatial aspects, any ongoing cognitive process will include bilateral functions that vary in relative emphasis from moment to moment. Throughout the following discussion, when we use the term "cerebral dominance" we will mean "hemispheric specialization" of *either* hemisphere. In each instance, it will be indicated whether the dominance (i.e., special-ization) relates to language, spatial, perceptual, or other cognitive or behavioral functions, and whether it is a left, right, or bilateral cerebral process.

2. Cerebral dominance for speech is central, unconscious, and beyond the ordinary control of the subject.

3. There seems to be an association between handedness and speech lateralization, but it is not yet fully understood. In almost all right-handed and over half of the left-handed subjects cerebral dominance for speech is in the left hemisphere.

4. Right handers usually show little or no evidence of bilateral language dominance. About 95% of them are left-hemisphere dominant for lan-guage, and about 5% are right-hemisphere dominant. By contrast, left handers are more variable. About 61% are left-hemisphere language dominant, about 20% are bilaterally controlled, and about 19% are right-hemisphere dominant for language (Segalowitz & Bryden, 1983). However, it should be understood that all of these figures are *estimates* and that individual studies show a marked variability in their esti-mates. For example, in a recent study of five patients showing bilateral speech representation as determined by the Wada sodium amytal speech test (Strauss & Wada, 1983), four of the patients (or 80%) were right handed. This type of evidence is a continued reminder that all estimates made by different researchers using different selection crite-ria, and studying groups of subjects with varying types of cerebral dysfunctions, cannot be accepted as final, nor as a basis for uneqivocal interpretation of the brain–behavior patterns of single cases.

5. Although handedness for writing and fine manual–motor movements develops with a preference for the right hand in most children, it can be changed. A left-handed child can be trained to write with the right hand, and right-handed subjects who have lost their right hands by amputation or accident have learned to write successfully with the left. This suggests a basic difference from speech in that the lateral prefer-ence for handedness may be peripherally imposed, is conscious, and is within the ordinary control of the subject (Subirana, 1958).

6. The behavioral manifestations of dominance are at both the cerebral and effectoral levels.

Phenomena considered to reflect cerebral asymmetry directly have been traditionally classed as "cerebral dominance" phenomena, while phe-nomena which appear to be only indirectly related to cerebral asymme-try of function have been classed as "lateral dominance" phenomena. More specifically, cerebral dominance has been generally used to refer to asymmetry of functions primarily resident in the cerebral hemispheres, e.g., language and perceptual functions. Lateral dominance, on the other hand, has referred to peripheral asymmetry of function manifested by lateral preferences at the effector level, e.g., handedness and footedness. [Higenbottam, 1971]

The term "cerebral dominance" can imply the involuntary domination of brain functions that the subject cannot perceive. The term "lateral preference" can imply the voluntary choice of hand or foot action that the subject can perceive.

Determinants of Dominance

Physiological Determinants

Structural Asymmetries. Since 1861, following Broca's statement of left-hemisphere dominance for speech, numerous researchers have sought for structural differences between the two hemispheres to account for the prodigious disparities in function. Some investigators have found differences in volume and length of the carotid arteries on each side, in the weight and complexity of the two hemispheres, in the varying number of Betz cells, and in the asymmetries of the two temporal lobes. While many researchers have found differences, which usually favored the left hemisphere, some found none, and even the differences that were discovered were so small (Von Bonin, 1962) as to be "unable to answer how to correlate these small differences with the astonishing disparities in function in the two sides of the brain" (Subirana, 1969). Since 1968, belief in the structural differences has been increased by the finding of Geschwind and Levitsky (1968) that of 100 adult brains studied histologically, the planum temporale was larger on the left in 65%, on the right in 11%, and equal in 24%. Wada has studied not only the brains of adults, but also the brains of neonates and fetuses. He has reported that "the left temporal planum was larger than the right in the majority of both the adult and the infant brains" (Wada, Clarke, & Hamm, 1975). Wada's data showed a larger left planum in both adults and infants in roughly 90% of the cases. Geschwind and Levitsky had reported left planum superiority in only 65% of the cases, but when they added the 24% of the cases showing equality between the hemispheres, they had a group with a left planum temporale either equal to or larger than the right homologous area in 89% of their cases. In a study of only 10 brains by Von Economo and Horn, reported by Wada, a similar pattern of 90% of cases showing an equal or larger left planum was found. Witelson and Pallie (1973) studied the brains of 14 infants and 16 adults and reported "that the left-sided area was statistically significantly larger in the neonate, as in the adults."

The report by Wada, Clarke, and Hamm, the most comprehensive study yet attempted to include infant as well as adult brains, and the other smaller studies described above, all indicate that structural asymmetries begin to show themselves and become measurable by the 29th week of gestation. This imbalance shows an equal or larger planum temporale on the left side at birth in about 90% of the cases and suggests that the temporal asymmetry precedes speech and language development, a conclusion impossible from the earlier studies of only adult brains. In this regard Witelson and Pallie (1973) concluded, "it is suggested that this neonatal asymmetry indicates that the infant is born with a pre-programmed biological capacity to process speech sounds."

However, the relationship between planum asymmetry and functional lateralization is not a simple one. Amytal studies show that about 88% to 90% of the population have left-hemisphere speech dominance, yet the left planum temporale is larger than the right in about 70% on the average. In some samples this measure is as low as 55%. Obviously there is a discrepancy here. Witelson (1983) has provided a detailed and useful critique of the problems relating to this issue that the clinical neuropsychologist will find valuable. While there appears to be a possible relation between planum asymmetry and language dominance, it is not clear at this point, and a full understanding will have to await further research.

Other possible structural asymmetries were reported by Yakovlev and Rakic and described by Benson and Geschwind (1968). They found that in most fetal and newborn brains, the pyramidal tract (the motor nerve fibers connecting from the motor cortex to the muscles) from the left hemisphere began to cross to the right side of the spinal cord *before* the motor fibers from the right hemisphere. Not only was the neural decussation from left to right earlier, but the *size* of the pyramidal tract on the right side of the cord was larger. Kertesz and Geschwind made the same finding regarding the initial decussation of the left pyramidal tract in the human adult (Benson & Geschwind, 1968), and these authors concluded that "the demonstration of a larger pyramidal tract in the right cord suggests that hand preference may depend upon increased innervation available to one side of the cord, which leads to finer digital control on that side."

More recently, Geschwind (1979a) has reported a difference in the angle of the Sylvian fissure in right- and left-handed people (the fissure on the right was angled up more sharply in 67% of right handers) and in the width of the frontal lobes (the right frontal lobe was wider in 70% of right handers). Left-handed people tended to show little differences in these measures. Ratcliff, Dila, Taylor, and Milner (1980) studied 59 patients with amytal to establish the side of speech dominance and also used carotid angiograms to examine the asymmetry of the angle of the posterior Sylvian branches of the cerebral blood vessels. Their findings were basically similar to those reported by Geschwind (1979a), that is, that for right handers the angle is higher and wider on the right and a little lower and more acute on the left. They found that the left handers were more atypical for both Sylvian angle and side of speech dominance. These writers concluded that the "measure of the posterior Sylvian asymmetry is related to cerebral dominance for speech in the sense that it is present in association with left-hemisphere speech but significantly less marked in the presence of atypical speech representation" (Ratcliff, Dila, Taylor, & Milner, 1980). To account for the lack of complete agreement among cerebral language laterality, Sylvian angle, and handedness, they invoked a model of inheritance of both handedness and cerebral language dominance proposed by Annett (1972). According to Annett's theory, hand preference is determined by two factors: (1) a genetic predisposition in favor of right hand superiority, which is present in the majority of the population, and (2) chance, which affects the minority who for some reason have not inherited the genetic tendency to shift. "The majority of the population, in whom the shift factor is present, will be biased in favor of right handedness, left hemisphere speech, and a narrower left Sylvian arch. The minority, lacking the shift factor, will be unbiased with respect to all three variables which will be randomly and independently determined" (Ratcliff, Dila, Taylor, & Milner, 1980). This is an interesting and acceptable theory that makes use of genetics and chance and accounts for the observable facts.

In another study McRae, Branch, and Milner (1968) reported a longer left occipital horn in the ventricular system in right-handed people, and a longer right occipital horn in about half of the cases of left handers. The behavioral significance of this is not yet known, but it may be a part of the process of revealing many more anatomical asymmetries that at some time may show themselves to be functionally related to handedness, cerebral dominance, and other behavioral and functional asymmetries.

Genetic Determinants. Possible genetic determinants of cerebral dominance have been studied using handedness as the indicator, but because there is not a perfect correlation between the hand and contralateral hemisphere, findings from such studies have not been conclusive. Theories growing out of these kinds of studies range from a denial of innate factors to an emphasis on them. Although the causes are masked there are data which suggest that genetic factors are involved. Subirana (1969) has reported that 46% of offspring from 31 pairs of homozygotic left-handed parents were also left handed, whereas only 2.1% of children from two right-handed parents were left handed. The proportion rose to 17.3% when one parent was left handed. These findings, which may be genetically determined, do not, of course, rule out environmental influences.

An interesting theory linking handedness, cerebral dominance, and genetic factors is that of Annett (1964). She proposes that handedness is genetically determined by a dominant (D) gene pattern and a recessive (r) one. Dominant homozygotes (DD), that is, those children who have inherited dominant handedness genes from both parents, are consistently right handed, with language dominance in the left hemisphere. Recessive homozygotes (*rr*), that is, those children who have inherited recessive handedness genes from both parents, are consistently left handed, with language dominance in the right hemisphere. Genetically these children are "pure" right handed and "pure" left handed, respectively, and except when they suffer traumatic brain damage they have no unusual learning problems. The heterozygotes (*Dr*), that is, those children who have inherited a dominant handedness gene pattern from one parent and a recessive one from the other parent, are usually right handed and left-hemisphere dominant for language, but they may use either hand for skilled abilities and develop speech in either hemisphere.

Annett makes the interesting proposal that if genetic determination were the only cause of handedness, then the distribution of "pure" right-handed, hybrid right-handed, and "pure" left-handed people would reveal a binomial distribution. In every 100 subjects $[8^2 + (2 \times 8 \times 2) + 2^2]$ there would be 64 (*DD*) pure right-handed, 32 (*Dr*) right- or left-handed, and 4 (*rr*) pure left-handed ones. However, genetic determiners are not the sole cause, because cerebral dysfunctions and social learning are organic and functional influences that may intrude unsystematically on the effects of genetic programming. These variables then may cause shifts in normal language dominance in cases of early unilateral brain damage or dysfunction and/or deliberate training of a child to write with the hand opposite to his or her natural preference.

This model has the advantage in that it explains why most left-handed people are less consistent (i.e., they show more mixed handedness, footedness, and eyedness) than most right-handed subjects. However, some left-handed people are consistent. By this theory, the inconsistent left-handed subjects are heterozygotes (*Dr*) and the consistent ones recessive homozygotes (*rr*). Traumatic damage to the central or peripheral nervous system may result in the use of the alternate hemisphere or limb, but only heterozygotes, according to Annett's theory, can shift dominance to compensate for injuries. Homozygotes injured in the dominant hemisphere will be unskillful with either hand and may be subject to speech disorders. "Although there is some indirect support for this position, the mechanisms still remain obscure" (Satz, 1972).

It is clear from this discussion that while there may be conclusive genetic determiners of handedness, an individual child may vary from his or her inherited predisposition if traumatic injury or forcible training intervene to disrupt the theoretical binomial distribution proposed by Annett, which is reasonably close to her findings in a study of 1226 subjects (Annett, 1970b). Satz (1972), in a theoretical discussion of pathological left-handed patients, has shown that half of all manifest left-handed subjects have signs of brain dysfunction, particularly mental retardation and/ or epilepsy.

Coren and Porac (1977) surveyed more than 5000 years of art works, scoring instances of unimanual tool or weapon use in 1180 photographs and reproductions of drawings, paintings, and sculpture. They covered the period from 15,000 B.C. to 1950 A.D. in seven different geographical regions (e.g., Central Europe, Mediterranean Europe, Africa, etc.) and found that 92.6% were right handed with no trend toward increasing right handedness, and no differences among regions. These researchers concluded: "Thus, as far as the historical record takes us, man appears to have always been right-handed" (Coren & Porac, 1977).

A more speculative but still useful approach is through historical ethology that draws on probable genetic mechanisms and environmental influences, rather than emphasizing one or other of these etiological determiners exclusively. Using the assumption that humans have always been right handed, at least since recorded history, Calvin (1983) has proposed "a fanciful reconstruction of events" to account for left-brain–right-handed writing and general right handedness. He has suggested that when humans began to write, about 5000 years ago, they first chiseled symbols into hard rock, but because of right handedness, there was a tendency to chisel from the easier side of the tablet (the right side) to the more awkward side (the left). The right-to-left sequence of ancient written languages, such as Hebrew, has sometimes been explained in this way. Later, when ink or dyes were first used to write on skins or papyrus, writing was presumed to have switched to a left-to-right sequence to avoid smearing the ink.

But the above fantasy is based on the assumption of the right handedness of the majority of the population, and we have to wonder how this preference developed.

Some manual skills, as Calvin has described, can be done with both hands (e.g., clubbing), but throwing a rock is necessarily one handed. Present surveys show that about 90% of the population throw a ball right handed. To account for this, Calvin has looked to the phenomenon of maternal heart beat. He has proposed (1983), as have others before him (Huheey, 1977; Salk, 1973; Wyeth, 1880, quoted in Harris, 1980), that because the mother's heartbeat is loudest on the left side, and because it has a soothing effect on the infant's behavior, a mother usually carries her infant on her left arm. This common custom, supported historically by surveys of hundreds of pictures of madonnas and their children, may have resulted from imprinting (Salk, 1973). Calvin has suggested that millions of years ago women were the chief hunters for food, so they soon learned to throw rocks to kill small animals at a distance. Modern studies of the great apes show the females to be better hunters and more competent in handling tools. Women in some primitive cultures are still active hunters, and maternal left armedness obviously left the right arm free to throw. After many centuries, the better hunters survived (natural selection) and tended to increase the proportion of right-handed genes in the population. However, there was always a minority who preferred to use the left hand for throwing and to hold a child with the right arm.

As well, it is likely that the left hemisphere was always programmed for better sequential perceptual analysis and more precise motor response. If this were so, it could account for the more accurate throwing of prehistoric woman and the better left-brain–right-hand pattern in writing.

Brain Damage and/or Cerebral Dysfunction. Since the research use of the Wada Amytal Test and the Dichotic Listening Test for determining hemispheric language dominance, it has been demonstrated that most right-handed people have speech represented in the left hemisphere and they rarely have bilateral speech. Some years ago Milner, Branch, and Rasmussen (1964), using the Wada test, showed that of 48 right-handed adults, 90% were left-hemisphere dominant for language, none was bilateral, and 10% had language represented in the right hemisphere. A group of 44 adults with no history of known brain injury but who were either left handed or ambidextrous was found to be left-hemisphere dominant for language in 64% of the cases, bilateral in 16%, and right-hemisphere dominant in 20% of the cases. In a study of 27 left-handed and ambidextrous subjects who did have a history of early left-hemisphere damage, the investigators found speech in the left in 22% of the cases, bilateral speech in 11%, and right-hemisphere speech in 67%. These data reveal two important findings: (1) Early left-hemisphere brain injury will shift language to the right hemisphere in a large number of cases (in the Milner, Branch, and Rasmussen study cited above there was a shift in the most deviant sample, from a norm of 90% left-hemisphere dominance to only 22%, or a shift to some degree of right-hemisphere processing of 68% of the cases); and (2) even in spite of early left-hemisphere damage 22% of the cases retained their language dominance in the injured hemisphere. Why this is so is not yet clear, although it may be because the speech areas have been spared, or it may be that homozygotes and heterozygotes react differently to brain damage (Annett, 1964). Whatever the cause, in large numbers of the learning disabled children it is evident that a shift from the language-dominant hemis′ ⸴e has not occurred. Examples of some of these are included in the Clinical Addendum at the end of this chapter.

Handedness and Cerebral Blood Flow. Using skin temperature over the ophthalmic branches of the internal carotid arteries as indexes of blood flow to the two sides of the head, Dabbs and Choo (1980) found that cerebral asymmetry as indicated by side of blood flow is related to handedness. "It has been found that among right-handed subjects the right side of the brain has more blood flow, higher blood pressure, a wider frontal lobe, and more protrusion of frontal bone" (Dabbs & Choo, 1980). Their findings indicate that more blood goes to the nonverbal side of the head, and suggest that spatial mental functions involve slightly more blood flow than verbal functions. As well, these researchers studied two types of left handers, those with upright handwriting posture, and those with inverted or "hooked" handwriting posture. The "hooked" group, like the right handers, showed more right-sided blood flow, while the "upright" group involved slightly more on the left side. While these differences are small, they are quite reliable and seem to be part of the related pattern of cerebral asymmetry and handedness.

Training

Environmental influences can change handedness, as has been demonstrated many times. Right-handed subjects who have lost their right hands traumatically have learned to write with their left. A Norwegian friend of mine reported that all children in his school in Norway during the 1930s wrote with their right hands, since no one was allowed to write with the left hand in those days. Benson and Geschwind (1968) have reported that Déjerine in France in 1912 commented that he had never met anyone who wrote with the left hand. It may be that left-handed writing was accepted to a greater degree in North American than in European schools at that time.

Although a parent or teacher can shift handedness by training, it seems improbable, if not impossible, that cerebral dominance for speech can be shifted in this way. As we have already seen, even early left-hemisphere damage will not shift speech dominance in a large number of cases, even though the child would seem to gain markedly should the shift take place. Some writers have suggested that writing with the right hand by a left-handed person may shift speech dominance to the left hemisphere, but there is no neuropsychological evidence that this has ever taken place. This is not to say that it should not be tried, if there is strong behavioral or other evidence that the child should write with the right hand. The child's improvement in learning, when it occurs, would seem to be caused not by a shift in cerebral dominance, but by an improvement in the neural communication between the right hand and the cortical language centers, be they in either hemisphere or in both hemispheres.

Behavioral Manifestations of Cerebral Dominance

Language

Because about 95% of humans have left-hemisphere dominance for speech and language functions, whether they are right or left handed, a teacher can expect most of his or her pupils to have left-brain language dominance. However, it must be remembered that while most people are left-hemisphere dominant for language, they are not exclusively. The right hemisphere may also contribute, though to a lesser extent, to language functions. If the child is right handed then he or she is nearly always left brained for speech, but not always. Very rarely a right-handed child may be *right* brained for language, and unless the teacher is advised of this, the child's poor academic achievement, if it results from this conflict, may be credited to laziness, inattention, or some other undesirable sign that may be secondary to his or her unusual cerebral condition. Such cases are rare, but two from our files are described in the Clinical Addendum at the end of this chapter, one in which a boy suffered from a subtle learning problem and one in which a girl was a good student.

At present, the most reliable technique for detecting cerebral language dominance is a combination of a neurological investigating technique (the Wada Amytal Test) and a neuropsychological assessment technique (the Dichotic Listening Test). This clinical combination may not be available to most teachers, but any serious school or clinical psychologist can acquire a dichotic tape and add the technique to his or her repertoire of clinical skills.

However, the clinical or school psychologist with no previous experience with the dichotic technique must guard against accepting without question its indication of cerebral language laterality. The Wada Carotid Amytal Test, a reliable indicator of cerebral speech dominance, shows that about 90% of the adult population are left-hemisphere language dominant and about 10% are right dominant (Milner, Branch, & Rasmussen, 1964). But studies employing the injection of amytal always include patients with some type of cerebral pathology or dysfunction; because it is an invasive technique, the amytal test is rarely used on normal subjects. Studies of normal subjects with the dichotic listening technique often show about 70% to 75% right ear advantage (REA), and if the test is being used as an indicator of cerebral laterality of language, there is an obvious discrepancy between known language dominance and that suggested by the dichotic procedure. Satz (1977), using a Baysean analysis to examine the expected relationship between cerebral speech dominance and ear asymmetry in 100 hypothetical right handers, concluded that the technique used as a diagnostic indicator is "both unwarranted and reckless" (Satz, 1977). It may "give a false sense of quantification of the underlying cerebral factors" (Colbourn, 1978).

Nevertheless, there are some redeeming features in this picture. The dichotic technique shows a high level of agreement with amytal findings in the same subjects being examined for medical reasons. In our laboratory we have studied 43 epileptic patients, all of whom had both the amytal and dichotic tests. There was agreement in 40 of these cases between the dichotic predictor and the amytal indicator of language laterality. Geffen, Traub, and Stierman (1978) studied 35 adult patients, 31 of whom were being treated with ECT (electroconvulsive treatment, often popularly referred to as "shock treatment") because of severe depression, and 4 epileptic patients who were administered the amytal test. The electric shock was administered unilaterally on successive days to each hemisphere, and the degree of dysphasia following the treatment was measured by an aphasia test. The side producing the greater degree of language confusion was presumed to be the language-dominant hemisphere. Two patients showed themselves to be bilateral for language and were eliminated in the final analysis of the results. In the remaining 33 patients, there was complete agreement between the two neurophysiological techniques and the dichotic assessment in 32 patients. This means that in the Geffen, Traub, and Stierman study, the dichotic method was valid in 96.8% of the cases, and in our own study there was agreement in 93%. These findings suggest that the dichotic listening technique is a reliable indicator of cerebral language laterality in patients with brain pathology, but with normal subjects there may be an error rate as high as 20% in predicting individual cases.

How can the clinical or school psychologist guard against making erroneous conclusions on single cases?

1. The subject's ear dominance scores (i.e., difference score, $R - L^1$) can be compared with the group findings of a number of subjects on the same test, evaluated in reference to a statistical probability criterion before inferences are made. Wexler, Halwes, and Heninger (1981) have proposed using a χ^2 statistical significance criterion to increase the diagnostic accuracy of single cases.

2. A test of substantial length should be used because the REA may be increased by presenting more pairs before recall or by using words rather than digits (Bryden, 1964). Many tests use 40 groups of three pairs of words (i.e., a total of 120 words).

3. The test should be administered *at least twice* to check on the reliability of the results. Wexler, Halwes, and Heninger (1981) found with their 33 subjects a test–retest correlation (Pearson r) of .91. If the R − L score is consistently high on both administrations the clinician, without the availability of the amytal test for cross validation of the results, nor the time to calculate a validity measure based on statistical probability, may infer, with a strong degree of probability, that the language

---

[1] The difference score is some form of R − L (i.e., the number of stimuli identified correctly by the right ear minus the number identified by the left ear). Some researchers prefer not to use raw difference scores (i.e., R − L), but to calculate a laterality quotient (e.g., R − L/R + L), or in addition, a total errors score (i.e., the number of pairs minus the number correct, n − (R + L)). These types of scores imply a *degree* of cerebral language laterality depending on the size of the difference score. Some researchers have argued that because of causal factors other than hemispheric assymetry (e.g., input asymmetry and attentional variables), the degree of laterality is not indicated by dichotic scores, and that it is important to recognize *only* REA, LEA, or RE = LE. A proponent of this view, Clark (1981), score LEA as 1; RE = LE as 2; and REA as 3. This type of scoring ignores the possibility of degree and indicates only the side or neutrality of ear preference. A huge literature in dichotic research has accumulated since 1961, and the reader can find various scoring procedures and their respective rationales.

dominance of the subject is in the left hemisphere. If, however, the R − L difference score is close to zero, then no conclusive diagnosis can be made without a cross-validating check, but the subject can be suspected of bilateral language dominance or mixed left or mixed right cerebral laterality.

4. The clinician, in using dichotic data alone for detecting cerebral language dominance, should accept it as a *suggestion,* not a conclusive indication, of probable brain function. It should be kept in mind that ear preferences may or may not change with age (Bryden & Allard, 1981), with sex (Bryden, 1970), with the frequency of use and concreteness of words (Dodwell, 1964), with the syntactic meaning of groups of words (Gray & Wedderburn, 1960), with the meaningfulness and emotional arousal of different words (Emmerich *et al.*, 1965), and with the spatial direction of the auditory stimulus (Pierson, Bradshaw, & Nettleton, 1983). However, if difference scores are consistently high on successive administrations, and they can be related to behavioral and medical data (when it is available), the dichotic procedure can be a useful added technique to the armamentarium of the clinician. But the careful clinician must guard against simplistic interpretations of dichotic experiments, because "not all behavioral asymmetries are necessarily related to the differing functions of the two hemispheres" (Bryden, 1982).

Hand Preference

While the clinical methods described above are reasonably reliable for detecting cerebral dominance, they may not immediately be available to the classroom teacher. One method that is available may be used casually as a peripheral but not conclusive indicator; that is, hand movements during speech. Kimura has carried out some imaginative and interesting research in which she showed that right-handed subjects who were left brained for language tend to make many more free hand movements (e.g., any hand or finger movement that is free of their body) with their right hands while speaking (Kimura, 1973b) than with their left. Self-touching movements in these same subjects (e.g., scratching, running fingers through the hair) was greater in the left hand. When left-handed subjects were examined (Kimura, 1973c), free hand movements were greater for the left hand, but the differences between the two hands were not as great as for the right-handed subjects. Related to this knowledge are some interesting newer findings reported by Moscovitch (1980). He has found that Kimura's findings hold only when the speaker is discussing nonemotional material, but when he or she becomes emotionally moved by the subject matter so that his facial expression reflects his feelings, there is no contralateral hand preference for activity. Because the right hemisphere is usually more involved with emotion, it seems that the greater bilateral involvement obliterates the hand preference activity. Presumably the left-hemisphere activity (language) is cancelled out by the right-hemisphere activity (emotional expression).

Kimura maintained strict controls to avoid observer biases, which would not be normally possible for a classroom teacher, and for this reason this method for identifying cerebral dominance in the classroom is not strongly recommended except as an interesting peripheral observation to help the teacher conceptualize what may be occurring in the learning disabled child's central nervous system. If the child is right handed, makes the majority of free hand movements with the right hand during speech, and has most or all lateral preferences on the right, then any serious learning problem, if one exists, is likely to result from causes other than cerebral–manual conflict. In contrast, if the child is right handed, makes about equal numbers of free hand movements during speech, and shows signs of considerable mixed laterality and serious learning problems, then the possibility of cerebral–manual conflict should be followed up with a referral to a school psychologist with the competencies to investigate it. The same type of referral should be made for the left-handed learning disabled child with mixed laterality. Whether the child should be changed in handedness depends on his age, the seriousness of the learning problem, and the consensus of his parents, teachers, and other professionals after a careful neuropsychological behavior analysis. More will be said about this problem in the addendum at the end of this chapter.

Left Handedness

Most mothers recognize the usual indifference to handedness in their infants and small children. During the second year of life most children are as likely to use their push-spoon in either hand, but if the mother consistently offers it to the child's right hand, within a period of time he or she will usually become habituated to hold it with the right hand.

However, some children, from the very start, are highly resistant to training that discourages their left handedness, and these cases are probably the genetic left-handed children, those who are right brained for language and naturally superior with their left hands. There is also the possibility that they are left handed because of brain damage or cortical dysfunction somewhere in the left hemisphere, a condition that may have existed since birth or early infancy. Many years ago, Gordon (1920) recognized two categories of left-handed people: those he called "natural" and those he called "pathological." Hécaen and de Ajuriaguerra (1964) have reported Subirana's finding "that the percentage of right- or left-sidedness of children from a high social level is different from that of orphans placed in an institution," and Mayet, as early as 1902, "remarked upon this frequency (of left handers) in idiots and in epileptics." In 1952 Hordijk found, in a study of 4307 school children, 15 times as many epileptics in left-handed families as in those that were clearly right handed. A large number of studies have shown that left handedness "probably exists to about twice the extent in the markedly retarded as in normal subjects" (Hordijk, 1952), although this difference cannot be completely attributed to left-hemisphere pathology. As well as being less competent with the right hand because of left cortical inferiority, the retarded child may be exposed to fewer social contacts and be less able to profit from those he does experience.

Satz (1972), in a noteworthy study of pathological left handedness, recognized the higher probability of left handedness in brain-damaged samples (an increase from 8% among normals to 17% in brain damaged); the high probability ($p = .81$) of left-hemisphere lesions, regardless of pathological or natural left handedness; the greater chance of pathological left handedness following early brain injury; the greater chance of right-hemisphere dominance for language following early left-brain damage; the lack of shift of language dominance in patients with no evidence of early left-brain injury; and the difference between pathological left handedness, which is the result of injury, and natural left handedness, which presumably is the result of genetic and cultural determinants. Satz also made the important observation that occasionally there are cases of pathological right handedness, but these are rare and likely to be ignored in a right-handed world. Only careful genetic and neuropsychological examination would reveal such a case, but if a teacher suspects this possibility, he or she should seek competent diagnostic help.

Whether left handedness decreases with age or whether it is constant throughout childhood is still questionable. In 1964 Hécaen and de Ajuriaguerra wrote:

> Among 10,000 children tested, Ballard (cited by Bloéde) found 4.1 percent left-handed in a group 4 to 14 years of age as against only 2.7 percent in a group 8 to 14 years of age. Likewise, Johnson, in a dynamometric test of 57 children $5\frac{1}{2}$ to 13 years old, found a left-handed superiority in 16 of them, but a year later control tests showed only a single case of superiority of the left hand. Heinlein's studies, carried out in a more systematic way, also confirm this decrease of left-handedness with age.

At the same time, Annett (1964) remarked that "the well-documented decline in the incidence of left handedness with increasing age is accounted for by supposing that the dominant gene increases its control during growth." However, it is interesting to note that when she put this idea to the test (Annett, 1970a) she found that the distributions of hand preference and relative manual speed were unchanged in children aged

$3\frac{1}{2}$–8 and 9–15 years. Boys in the younger group showed clear left handedness in 6.1% of the cases, and in the older group in 6.0%. Girls in these two age groups showed frequencies of 1.9% and 4.4%, respectively, a tendency in the reverse direction and also numerically different from the boys. However, she did find that mixed and left preferences were more frequent in boys than girls.

What does this seemingly conflicting evidence tell us?

1. Any results in an experiment are a function of the type of tests used. In the case of Johnson's study, hand-grip strength, as measured by a dynamometer, is a gross muscular function and improves as finer muscular skills are acquired. However, it should be remembered that although 5- and 6-year-old children tend to prefer their stronger hand, they may shift to their other hand for writing when they enter school if they discover that using the other hand improves the quality of their handwriting.

2. Ballard's study included 10,000 children, whereas Annett's included 219, but we are not told the nature of Ballard's tests. It is possible that some of them included tests of strength rather than fine neuromuscular coordination. Annett's tasks are described, and all required manual dexterity and specific neuromuscular control. Annett's evidence strongly suggests that:
   a. Hand preference is established at least by age $3\frac{1}{2}$.
   b. Proportions of right-, mixed-, and left-handed subjects among boys and men remain constant.
   c. Girls show a little variation but the cause of these differences is not clear.
   d. Consistently left-handed children in her sample showed a superiority in vocabulary and those with mixed handedness were more variable.
   e. There was an excess of mixed-handed children among those of lower IQ.

Many early researchers (Hécaen & Sauget, 1971; Milner, Branch, & Rasmussen, 1966; Satz, Achenbach, & Fennell, 1967) consistently found a greater tendency to bilateral language dominance in left-handed subjects as compared with left-hemisphere dominance in most right-handed subjects. However, the relationship of cerebral dominance and language development is examined in more depth in Chapter 8.

Levy (1974) has made an interesting discovery in the understanding of left-handed subjects. She observed a right-handed writer, T.N., who wrote with his hand inverted in the manner common to many left-handed people. Although he had always written with his right hand, he was ambilateral for some manual activities and left handed for throwing a ball.

Levy investigated three groups, right-handers (Group R), left-handers who wrote normally (group L-N), and left-handers who wrote with the hand inverted (group L-I), and found evidence which strongly suggests that the L-I group members were ipsilateral for their left language dominance and left-handedness, whereas the L-N group members were not. This evidence appears to be in basic agreement with the hemispheric blood flow patterns and handwriting posture reported above (Dabbs & Choo, 1980).

Mirror Writing

It is generally agreed that mirror writing (that is, writing whole words, phrases, or sentences from right to left with all letters reversed and in correct sequence) occurs in all or most cases in left-handed individuals (Benson, 1970; Benson & Geschwind, 1968; Hécaen & de Ajuriaguerra, 1964). This seems to occur because the human body is symmetrical, but only in the vertical plane. For this reason the small child may have difficulty learning left from right. However, Benson (1970) has pointed out that because "there is no symmetry in the horizontal plane" the small child has little or no difficulty learning up and down on his own body, because the differences are obvious.

It is evident that it is easier to draw a line from left to right with one's right hand and from right to left with one's left hand. One moves out from midline because it is easier to pull a pen than push it. Hécaen and de Ajuriaguerra (1964) have recognized that "the left-handed child has to push his pen instead of pulling it," and because his centrifugal movements are easier and more harmonious than his centripetal movements (those moving toward the center), the left-handed child can more easily write from right to left. Requiring him to write from left to right immediately imposes neuromuscularly awkward demands.

While the above explanation may account for the neuromuscular aspects of mirror writing, it does not explain the cognitive process involved. How is it that only a few left handers produce mirror writing but most do not? A study reported by Hécaen and de Ajuriaguerra (1964) suggests that this ability is a function of age and maturity of the central nervous system, and that dyslexics (those with CNS dysfunctions) are less able to do it. Put positively, this evidence suggests that the mirror writer is free of brain lesions and can conceptualize spatially in reverse in a flexible, mature, and reliable way. Harris (1980) has pointed out that Leonardo da Vinci and Lewis Carroll, both mentally superior, were accomplished mirror writers, "but there is no evidence that (either of them) were ever *confused* about spatial direction, or that their practice of mirror writing was anything but strictly controlled" (Harris, 1980, p. 61).

Herron (1980) has combined our knowledge of upright or "noninverted" left handwriting position, inverted position, and mirror writing.

When the left hand in the noninverted position writes from right to left, mirror writing is produced. The inverted left hand will produce mirror writing *upside down,* but the letters will be in the normal left-to-right sequence (Herron, 1980, p. 244).

Few cases have been reported in the literature, but Benson (1970) has described an 8½-year-old boy who was *strongly left handed* and whose immediate family had four sinistrals. On entering school he was a mirror writer, but this trait disappeared completely by the end of first grade. However, he did possess a developmental dyslexia, although he had normal intelligence. This case indicates the independence of mirror writing and developmental dyslexia in some cases but does not necessarily indicate a freedom from brain dysfunctions.

Although reversing letters is common in 6- and 7-year-olds, and this is mirror writing at a single letter level, cursive mirror writing is not common. Its cause is not known, but Benson (1970) believes the various theories can be reduced to three major hypotheses:

1. An early theory posited the existence of two writing centers, one in the language dominant left hemisphere and the other in the right. If the right hemisphere is dominant, then mirror writing, according to this theory, will result. However, the facts do not support this, because Annett's consistent left handers should all be mirror writers initially if this theory were true.

2. Bilateral differential cortical visual imagery has been a more popular theory. According to this view, two separate visual images are formed with the right-hemisphere image a mirror reversal of the left. In most cases, because the left hemisphere is dominant, the right-hemisphere image is suppressed; but if the right hemisphere is dominant, mirror writing will occur. Benson's objection to this theory, on the grounds that mirror writers should also copy drawings reversed, seems questionable for two reasons. First, mirror writers act spontaneously when they are producing the sinistrad (reversed) form; if asked to copy writing or printing they can do it, although awkwardly. Second, drawings of common objects normally have no "correct" direction, as do letters and sequences of letters. Also, the fact that strongly left-handed children are forced to write with their right hands, are consistently slower and less proficient in their handwriting than normal right-handers suggests they are slowed by the frustrations of having to adapt to the more complex cerebral circuits and the normally suppressed visual image. Orton was the first to propose this theory, which was based on extensive studies of the writing of left-handers (Orton, 1937, pp. 99–110).

3. Benson prefers the theory of mirrored motor patterns in the two hands. According to this view, mirror writing is normal for left-handers but is

usually suppressed because the output is socially meaningless and hence not reinforced.

It seems likely that both visual imagery and motor patterns are involved since mirror writing disappears with age. Moreover, "masked left handers" can frequently improve their handwriting if shifted to the left hand even as late as age 11 (Orton, 1937) or 15. Two cases of ambidextrous individuals reported by Orton (1937, pp. 106, 108), whose best writing was sinistrad with the right hand, appear to flout the mirror motor theory and be supported by the hemispheric visual imagery theory. Both subjects were older (11 and 21) and both were mentally bright.

The teacher faced with the problem of poor handwriting and frequent spelling errors should obtain the following information before deciding on a remedial program:

1. A detailed measure of handedness on a well-constructed inventory (examples will be given at the end of this chapter).
2. Manual–motor tests of both hands.
3. Examples of writing with both hands.
4. A comparison of the child's drawings of simple forms, such as a square, triangle, star, or cross, from copy and with his or her eyes closed after studying the figure for a few moments. This last test will give some information on whether the visual–motor relation is disturbed and whether motor skill is better when the visual input is withheld.
5. Measures of writing speed and legibility from standardized handwriting tests.
6. A comparison of the child's cursive writing with his or her printing. Cursive writing tends to help mirror writers overcome their problem, but this is not always the case (Durbrow, 1963). Grace Fernald, in her training school, encouraged the child to write a word cursively and without interruption. This approach is based on a belief that *whole* cortical and muscular patterns are being established in the central nervous system.
7. Evidence of the child's language cerebral dominance.

Handwriting is not a simple learning task. As well as being essentially related to cerebral dominance, there are many other functions that must be sequentially integrated with handwriting, such as visual scanning, right–left orientation, sequencing, motor development, spatial imagery, visual–motor coordination, visual form recognition, and all or most of the complexities of speech and language development.

Interhemispheric Functions

Throughout this chapter we have been examining the lateral asymmetries both in the internal processes of the central nervous system and in the external manifestations of human behavior. In such a discussion there is a real temptation to refer to "left-hemisphere abilities" and "right-hemisphere skills" as if these functions existed completely independently. Of course, they do not, and in any normal, healthy brain whatever occurs in one hemisphere is affected by the other one, this influence being mediated largely through the corpus callosum. Kinsbourne (1974, Chap. XIII) has described the possible competitive, compensatory, and collaborative effects of the homologous areas of the two hemispheres where one hemisphere is maximally involved in behavior (e.g., speech) and where both hemispheres are equally involved (e.g., auditory localization).

Since the early 1950s, neuropsychologists have recognized that the two cerebral hemispheres mediate different functions, and this concept has been well established by unilateral lesion studies (Reitan, 1955a), and more recently by blood flow studies (Risberg, Halsey, Wills, & Wilson, 1975) and positron emission tomography (i.e., PETT scan; Gur et al., 1983). These findings over a 30-year period have indicated that in most adults the left hemisphere is more competent in handling verbal and linguistic tasks, while the right hemisphere is better with visual–spatial–constructional and other nonverbal skills. This concept of hemispheric specialization has appealed to many psychologists and educators, but like all new ideas that at first appear clearly defined, it may be interpreted by enthusiastic clinicians and applied workers too simplistically and with little understanding.

Let us look at this problem first with adult subjects. Bryden, Hécaen, and DeAgostini (1983) examined 270 adult patients with unilateral brain

Table 7.1 Association between Aphasia and Spatial Disorders in Patients with Unilateral Brain Lesions

	Left-Handed				Right-Handed			
	Left Lesion		Right Lesion		Left Lesion		Right Lesion	
	Aphasia	Spatial	Aphasia	Spatial	Aphasia	Spatial	Aphasia	Spatial
Men	35.6%	6.8%	9.7%	31.7%	39.5%	7.0%	0	63.3%
Women	39.3%	3.6%	8.3%	33.3%	37.0%	14.8%	6.6%	30.0%

After Bryden, Hécaen, & DeAgostini, 1983. With permission.
Number of Subjects: Men: right handed = 73; left handed = 100; total = 173
                                     Women: right handed = 57; left handed = 40; total = 97

lesions; 140 left handers and 130 right handers. From the neuropsychological test results, each patient was classified as aphasic or not, or showing a visual–spatial disorder or not. If the left–right hemispheric specialization pattern, described above, is valid in all cases, then we can expect to find all of the left lesion cases impaired in language and the right lesion cases visually–spatially impaired. But this is not what Bryden and his colleagues found. Some of their major findings follow:

1. Of all the 173 men in the study, 21% showed *both* language and spatial deficits; 23% of all the 97 women showed both deficits. These findings could suggest that in some cases the same hemisphere can be superior for both verbal and nonverbal processing (Bryden, 1973), or that more than one-fifth of this sample had bilateral control of both language and spatial skills and that damage to either hemisphere could affect both abilities. Obviously these findings do not support the simplistic view of this concept that is so prevalent in the popular press and in some educational publications.

2. Of the 73 right-handed men, left lesions produced aphasia alone in 39.5% of the sample, and right-sided lesions produced spatial problems in 63.3%. No deficits of either type were found in 37%, no doubt because the locus of cerebral dysfunction was outside the language centers of the left hemisphere, and/or anterior to the temporo-parietal areas of the right hemisphere. However, the interesting findings in the left lesion group are the 7% who suffered only spatial problems.

3. Of the 100 left-handed men, left-sided lesions produced aphasia alone in 35.6% of the sample, and spatial problems in 6.8%. Right-sided lesions produced spatial deficits alone in 31.7% of the sample and aphasia in 9.7%.

4. Of the 57 right-handed women, 37% of the left-lesion cases had aphasic signs alone, and 14.8% had only spatial problems. Thirty percent of the right lesion cases had spatial problems, and 6.6% had aphasia alone. No deficits in either function showed in 47.4% of the sample.

5. In the group of 40 left-handed women, left-sided lesions produced aphasia alone in 39.3% of the cases, and only spatial disorders in 3.6%.

Bryden, Hécaen, and DeAgostini concluded that "aphasia is more frequent with posterior lesions in the left hemisphere of right handers, and spatial disability is more frequent with posterior lesions in the left hemisphere of left handers, and in the right hemisphere of right handers" (Bryden, Hécaen, & DeAgostini, 1983). "The majority of individuals will show language and visuospatial functions in opposite hemispheres even though the two are causally independent of one another" (p. 254). Bilaterality occurs only in left handers for both verbal and spatial functions and in both sexes.

This evidence makes it clear that a simplistic left–right dichotomy of cerebral function in adults is not the case. While the *majority* of right handers fit the right–left pattern fairly closely, the left handers, especially those with a history of familial left handedness, show a great deal of variability in cerebral organization.

The left hemisphere in most adults is more proficient in mediating verbal, sequential material, motor skilled performances, the analysis of verbal ideas, and the storage and use of "well-routinized codes" (Goldberg & Costa, 1981). The right hemisphere is better adapted to handle visual–spatial–three-dimensional imagery, holistic or intermodal integrations, and to process new material. Goldberg and Costa (1981) have proposed that the right hemisphere plays an essential role in the initial stages of learning, when the material is new and unfamiliar. The left hemisphere gradually takes over the processing as learning becomes coded in established neural patterns and expressed in familiar mental concepts.

The investigations of hemispheric asymmetry during childhood are relatively new, most studies having appeared since 1960. Researchers divide themselves into two groups on this issue: (1) Those who consider that the two hemispheres are neutral in infancy and permit language to develop bilaterally during the first 2 years. Then, according to this view, language dominance develops gradually until early adolescence when it reaches its mature form. An influential proponent of this view was Lenneberg (1967). (2) Those who hypothesize that cerebral lateralization is potentially established during fetal development, and that structural and behavioral asymmetries are present from birth. Kinsbourne (1975b) is a strong proponent of this view. More will be said about developmental cerebral organization in the next section and later in the book because knowledge of its functional patterns should aid in the better understanding of learning during childhood development, and to choices of teaching or remedial methods.

Sex Differences in Laterality

Recent evidence from a number of neuropsychological studies strongly suggests that women characteristically are more proficient with their left hemispheres and men with their right. If this is true, it should have significance for special education. McGlone and her associates at the University of Western Ontario have carried out investigations that tend to support a sex difference in hemispheric specialization (McGlone & Davidson, 1973; McGlone & Kertesz, 1973) and other researchers have made similar findings (Buffery, 1976; Hobson, 1947; Kimura, 1969; Lansdell, 1962; Sandström, 1953; Wechsler, 1958; Witkin, 1949).

Because there does seem to be a reliable female verbal superiority and a male spatial superiority, this pattern suggests that a "specialization of the right hemisphere for nonverbal functions may be advantageous for space perception, and that males more often than females have this type of neural organization" (McGlone & Kertesz, 1973). Other studies (McGlone & Davidson, 1973) have shown that when a task can be performed by either left- or right-hemisphere mechanisms, males are more likely to use their right hemispheres, whereas females are more likely to use their left. In brief, this means that depending on the sex of an individual, she is more likely to use a verbal strategy to solve a problem, and he is more likely to use a nonverbal strategy, where either is possible.

Buffery (1976) studied boys and girls at each year from age 5 to age 9 and found a preference by both sexes to process easy-to-verbalize problems more by the left hemisphere, although the asymmetry was more pronounced in the girls, especially as they grew older. However, when he presented problems that were difficult to verbalize, both sexes used their right hemispheres predominantly for processing them. He also found that cerebral asymmetry for cross-modal analysis, particularly with spatial material, emerges later in boys (at about 8 years) than in girls (at about 7 years). This evidence suggests several possible practical applications that need experimental investigation. In general we might expect girls up to the age of about 8 to be more competent than boys in following purely verbal instructions, and boys to be better in understanding spatial diagrams or pictorial material. It may also mean that if an idea is difficult for the child to grasp by verbal explanation alone, he or she should be provided, as much as possible, with accompanying graphic material related to it, because the level of difficulty is a determiner of the child's cognitive strategy and hemispheric emphasis.

In a research with normal adults Buffery (1976) found sex differences in those with signs of mixed laterality. His sample included 100 women and 100 men students at Oxford and Cambridge Universities who, we can safely assume, had no serious learning disabilities. Even so, his evidence showed 8%–19% with ipsilateral hemispheric dominance and eyedness and handedness. Buffery has concluded that his findings "are contrary to any simplistic hypothesis of crossed laterality being a sufficient condition for learning disorder" as proposed by Delacato (1963). Among the women he found 13% with dominance and handedness on the same side and among the men, 8%. When dominance and eyedness were examined, 14% of the women showed an ipsilateral pattern and 19% of the men. Mixed hand and eye dominance was found in 23% of the women and 28% of the men. Buffery rightly points out that since "a sex difference in cerebral asymmetry of function has been demonstrated in adults which is similar to that found in children, an explanation in terms of a transient lag in male development is not appropriate." It would seem that the elementary school's emphasis on acquiring verbal skills may give girls an advantage, which boys later overcome when problem material enables them to exploit their spatial facility.

Townes, Trupin, Martin, and Goldstein (1980) studied the relation between a large number of neuropsychological skills and academic success in 230 kindergarten and 226 Grade 2 children. During the 3-year period from age $5\frac{1}{2}$ to $8\frac{1}{2}$, marked improvement was made in most of the neuropsychological variables (motor, perceptual, conceptual, and language skills), and these researchers found the test findings useful in understanding each child's pattern of cognitive strengths, and in planning an instructional program for him or her. They found the girls superior in verbal reasoning, language skills, and serial–perceptual matching. Boys were superior on tests of spatial memory and motor skills. Because the school program from the earliest grades is heavily loaded with verbal demands, it was suggested that "boys are at a developmental disadvantage with respect to academic achievement during early elementary school years" (Townes, Trupin, Martin, & Goldstein, 1980). Drawing on Witelson's work (1977), these writers suggest that normal-reading boys processed verbal information in the early stages using linguistic strategies, while dyslexic boys preferred a spatial strategy.

Teachers of the early grades are constantly impressed by the greater facility of girls than of boys at reading, and whereas this is generally true, the verbal superiority does not include all language skills. In our laboratory, a study of 353 normal boys and girls, aged 6–13, was made to examine their language development on 20 subtests of the Spreen–Benton Aphasia Battery (Gaddes & Crockett, 1975). It was found that girls in this age range were *not* superior to boys in most language skills as measured by the battery. No sex differences were found in 11 of the 20 subtests, and these included visual naming, description of the use of an object, stereognosis in both hands, sentence repetition, repeating digits forward and backward, constructing sentences with a number of supplied words, identification of objects by name, identification of objects by descriptive sentence, and reading names of objects and pointing to them. All of these tasks can use a strategy that is maximally verbal or nonverbal, so that in the light of the neuropsychological studies cited above, it seems likely that boys and girls, possibly using different tactics, achieved the same levels of success.

In those nine tests where girls did show a superiority it was only a transient or isolated advantage in seven of them. These included copying writing, oral reading, reading descriptive sentences and pointing to objects, visual–graphic naming, writing to dictation, and articulation. By age 9 boys were able to match the girls' performance.

On only two subtests did the girls show any prolonged superiority. These were in word fluency and spelling. Present knowledge suggests that primary age girls *do* possess better abilities in reading and writing, but that boys may match their level of verbal achievement in most basic skills by using a different strategy, which likely draws more on spatial or pictorial analysis.

The research of Bakker, Teunissen, and Bosch (1976) has shown that in the first three grades cerebral dominance for language seems to be established sooner in girls than boys. He found that at the Grade 3 level, girls read well maximally with their left hemispheres, whereas boys were bilateral and slower; Grade 2 girls were bilateral readers and boys did not develop unilateral reading until Grade 5 or 6. An investigation of reading strategies by these children across grades showed that right dominant readers are slow but accurate in their reading, whereas left dominant readers tended to be fast but careless. These findings suggest that girls pass through the successive laterality–reading stages faster than boys, and that boys may get stuck more frequently than girls in the early stages of learning to read. This type of neuropsychological evidence is beginning to provide a better understanding of the verbal superiority of girls in the early grades.

These researches draw attention to the assumed development of cerebral dominance. The idea that the small child's brain is probably bilateral for language at first and gradually shows an increasing lateralization was given credibility by Lenneberg with his influential book in 1967. He proposed that in most children there was a progressive increase in the role of the left hemisphere and a gradual decrease in the role of the right hemisphere. The so-called "Lenneberg hypothesis" described this developmental process as beginning in infancy and becoming complete by puberty. Another similar view saw this development occurring more quickly and maturing by the age of 5 (Krashen, 1973), but some recent research has thrown possible doubt on this popular belief and supports the view that the human cerebral hemispheres are specialized both structurally and functionally in infancy. A persuasive proponent of this view, Marcel Kinsbourne, has even suggested that the concept of progressive lateralization be rejected (Kinsbourne, 1975b). Hiscock (1979) has presented evidence of a right ear advantage in dichotic listening studies in preschoolers, school-age children, and adults. From this he concluded that if dichotic listening measures a fixed function of the brain, and if this is lateralization for language, then it would seem that this function is already established by the age of 3 and so does not develop. Kinsbourne and Hiscock (1978) have made an impressive case against the concept of progressive lateralization, citing evidence from studies of anatomy, neurophysiology, developmental psychology, handedness, and neuropsychology. However, the case is far from closed because of methodological problems and some conflicting and some unexplained evidence. The school psychologist may want to keep abreast of the investigations in this area and the special teacher may want to be aware of the developmental behavioral evidence.

Before we leave the subject of hemispheric specialization, let us look at some commonplace examples of its effect on our social behavior. Printers and poster artists have customarily placed pictorial figures in the top left area of a poster and a standard printed message in the top right corner.

Experience has shown that, other things being equal, this format usually is more successful in attracting attention. In the theater, play directors will tell you that the most dramatic entrances are made from the theatrical right side of the stage (the viewer's left). At a lecture on the Peking Opera, which has established traditions for about 1000 years, it was explained that entrances were always from the audience's left, and the exits always on the right side of the stage. Presumably the slight superiority of the right hemisphere in processing spatial–pictorial input may have been the underlying neural mechanism that determined these customs. And this commonplace phenomenon seems to have experimental support. Right handers in some studies prefer pictures with a rightward-balance and left handers prefer leftward-balance (McLaughlin, Dean, & Stanley, 1983). These researchers concluded that "aesthetic preferences for asymmetric pictures seem determined by the direction of cerebral assymetry."

Conductors of bands and symphony orchestras nearly always enter from the left side of the stage (the viewer's left), as do also the soloists, and lecterns for lecturers who comment on slide or film shows are nearly always placed at the left side of the screen. These customs, no doubt, have grown out of intuitive feelings of artistic taste, but could these judgments of appropriateness have been defined by the relatively better spatial processing of the right hemisphere in most people?

These observations may mean that it is better to place the teacher's desk at the left front corner of the class room, and any notices on the right end of the front blackboard. Bakker and Van Rijnsoever (1977) have actually studied the effects of auditory–spatial asymmetries in the classroom. They set up two loudspeakers in the middle of the left and right walls. Pairs of words, some differing in initial consonants, some differing in final consonants, and some identical, were presented from one or other of the loudspeakers. They found that those children seated in the middle of the classroom made fewer errors, that discrimination of different phonemes is better for most children when projected from the right, and of identical phonemes, it is better when they are projected from the left. This is one of the first studies to apply the knowledge of dichotic and monaural listening to classroom management.

Summary

Teachers have known for years that a number concept can be more easily acquired by using blocks or other concrete objects to count. No doubt this is helping the child to use *both* hemispheres in this learning process. In our own work with left-brain damaged adults of normal intelligence we have found that reading is facilitated when objects are left casually on the table, if they are pertinent to the sentence being read. Some times the traumatically dyslexic adult is unable to read, "Show me a large yellow square," when the table is bare, but he can read it successfully when a large number of colored tokens, of various shapes and sizes, are spread out. Possibly the spatial stimulation interacts with the impaired verbal skills to assist them. This phenomenon has been demonstrated experimentally by presenting peripheral words tachistoscopically along with target words to read. Laterally presented words were found to bias the perceived meaning of target words presented in the center of the visual field. When the target word was a homograph (i.e., it had two or more meanings, such as *box*) the peripheral words, though not consciously read and not reported because they were beyond the fixation point, were found to influence the reader's perceived meaning (Bradshaw, 1974). If target words are preceded by words with semantic associations, they may be read faster than if preceded by words of unrelated meaning (Meyer & Schvaneveldt, 1971). This phenomenon is partially similar to the production of paralexias by deep dyslexics (deep dyslexia is discussed in Chapter 8).

The brain's functions are extremely complex, and many or most are not yet understood, but this may be the basic mechanism in learning in an enriched environment. An Armenian friend of mine was born and raised in Egypt, where he learned Armenian at home and French and Arabic at school and on the street. At the age of 17 he left Egypt to settle in the United States. Twenty-five years later he and his wife decided to return to Egypt for a visit, but prior to the trip he wondered how he would converse because he had long since lost his Arabic. In fact, he could remember hardly any words, but on landing at the Cairo airport he found a competent working knowledge of the language came back to him with surprising facility. Is it possible that the appropriate environment stimulates the brain more completely and more efficiently?

In summary, this means that the child learns specific cognitive skills with different parts of the left or right hemispheres, but learning may be facilitated by activating *both* hemispheres in the process. Skilled remedial teaching requires an imaginative and experimental approach to arrive at ways to maximize this bilateral activity.

Clinical Addendum

Measures of Handedness

So far in this chapter handedness has been described as left and right. Annett's theory allowed for a "mixed" category between the two extremes, but this was not elaborated. Here, we will examine this problem with more care because, as any experienced teacher or school psychologist knows, few people are completely right or left handed, if a large number of manual activities are examined.

Lateral preferences (hand, foot, and eye) may be assessed by personal examination and by questionnaire where an examination is not possible. Most examinations will require the subject to carry out a variety of performances to demonstrate how to handle a large number of objects not present, and actually to write with each hand, to sight through a paper funnel, to hold a toy rifle, and to squeeze a dynamometer. In addition, sensory and motor tests are made of each hand to discover lateral differences in sensory and motor efficiency. On the test used in our laboratory, a possible score of 140 indicates right handedness and complete right-sided superiority on all tasks; a score of 70 indicates ambilaterality; and a zero score implies complete left sidedness. These kinds of tests are interesting and produce a lot of data, but such inventories possess only face validity, as handedness is defined solely in terms of test scores. There is no conclusive evidence that they are the same thing. White and Ashton (1976) have examined the structure, with factor analysis, of a modified version of the Edinburgh Handedness Inventory (Oldfield, 1971), a widely used examination. They extracted a major factor, which they called "handedness," and a second minor factor that seemed to be related to "mental imagery," because they included items that related to the non-preferred hand and required the person to "experiment" mentally.

It is the responsibility of the school psychologist to be knowledgeable about cerebral dominance and handedness and to select the best lateral preference inventory based on this knowledge. A major literature is available in this field with which the psychologist will want to become familiar (Annett, 1964, 1970a, 1972, 1974; Bradshaw & Nettleton, 1983; Briggs, Nebes, & Kinsbourne, 1976; Bryden, 1977, 1982; Hécaen & Sauget, 1971; Hicks & Kinsbourne, 1976a,b, 1977; Kimura, 1973a; U. Kirk, 1983a; Levy, 1969; Levy & Nagylaki, 1972; Molfese, 1973; Rourke, Bakker, Fisk, & Strang, 1983; Satz, 1972, 1973; Segalowitz, 1983; Spreen et al., 1984; Wada, Clarke, & Hamm, 1975).

Three Cases of Varying Hemispheric Specialization and Handedness

Jim Lane

Jim was 10 years old when we first saw him because of a developmental language disability and weak arithmetical reasoning. His mother reported nothing remarkable in his medical history; he always appeared bright and mentally quick until he entered school, when he immediately ran into obvious difficulty in learning to read and spell. As a result, Jim had become quiet and socially cautious at school, but there were no serious behavior problems. His family was highly supportive, and his grandmother, a retired teacher, helped him with his reading.

Our tests showed him to have a verbal IQ of 105 and a performance IQ of 115 (WISC), but his grade-point averages on the Wide Range Achievement Tests (WRAT) were: reading (single-word recognition), 3.3; spelling, 2.9; and arithmetic, 3.9. Because Jim, at the time of testing, was 9 years 11 months old, to be academically *average* he should have obtained grade-point averages of about 5.5.

His family doctor, who was very interested in the possible neuropsychological variables that might be related to Jim's learning problem, reported that she thought he showed mixed handedness and footedness. Until the age of 8 he wrote with either hand and his reading and writing were full of reversals.

A family history revealed that Jim's father was ambidextrous but was forced to write with his right hand when he went to school. *Both* of the paternal grandparents and the only paternal uncle were left handed. This familial pattern of left handedness would seem to be related to Jim's early manual indifference and led us to anticipate the results of the Dichotic Listening Test with genuine interest. It was impressive, then, to find that the test suggested fairly strongly that Jim was *right*-hemisphere dominant for language (right ear preference, 10 and left ear preference, 34). These finding suggested a cerebral–manual conflict, in that he was right handed and probably right-hemisphere dominant for language. This meant that if our hypothesis were true, Jim had to initiate his language concepts in his right hemisphere, shunt them to the left motor strip, and then convey them to his right hand for writing. This unusual circuitous route is frequently correlated with spelling problems.

To examine this hypothesis further we looked closely at Jim's handgrip strength (which was weak in *both* hands, although a little stronger in the right), his finger tapping (which was about 10% too slow in *both* hands, although the right hand was better than the left), his finger localization (which was perfect in the left hand and had two errors in the right) and his visual–manual and auditory–manual reaction times (which were slow for *both* hands to a visual stimulus, but which showed a relative *left*-hand superiority to both visual and auditory stimuli). All these indicators together point to the possible hypothesis that Jim was intended to be left-handed by genetic determination, but because of a minimal brain dysfunction in the sensory and motor strips of both hemispheres, his handedness was weak and confused in developing and ended in a conflict pattern.

We were now faced with the problem of whether or not to change his handedness. We decided against it because of his age and the learned establishment of his right hand. Because Jim's tactile and phonetic recognition were strong we recommended a remedial teaching program that stressed these two sense modes. On spatial tasks he was superior (Raven's Matrices, better than 95th percentile) and on a picture vocabulary test he measured an IQ of 118 (approximately 88th percentile).

Although the neurologist's examination turned up no positive findings, the neuropsychological tests revealed minimal but definite signs strongly suggestive of brain dysfunction in the sensorimotor strips bilaterally. It is highly likely these dysfunctions contributed to Jim's indifferent handedness, his brain–hand conflict, his developmental dyslexia, and his spelling apraxia.

A stress on tactile and auditory instruction showed an improvement in his reading and spelling after only 6 months.

Marie Farrell, Age 9

Having looked at a case of ipsilateral cerebral dominance and handedness that appeared to be related to Jim's learning problems, let us now look at a case in which the same brain–hand pattern coexisted with no learning problems. In fact, Marie measured a verbal IQ of 124 and was an excellent student in Grade 4. She did extremely well in arithmetic and all the language arts and was highly motivated and interested in school.

She was referred to our laboratory for neuropsychological assessment prior to possible brain surgery to reduce or eliminate a severe seizure condition. Her mother reported a complete absence of epilepsy in either her husband's or her own family, yet Marie began to show periods of unconsciousness as early as 18 months. At age $2\frac{1}{2}$ she complained of stomach aches "like a needle" in her stomach. At age 6 the grand mal seizures began but fortunately they occurred only at night. During a seizure she would put her left hand on her stomach and the fingers of her right hand in her mouth, and during the unconscious period she would babble incoherently. These periods lasted about 30 seconds but she did not always lose consciousness. The seizure frequency varied from once a week to once a month.

Marie showed herself to be strongly right handed, right eyed, and right footed. An EEG revealed severe electrical disturbances in the left temporal lobe, and the amytal and Dichotic Listening Tests suggested right-hemisphere language dominance. Our dichotic measures showed her to have a left ear preference for words and a right ear preference for music (nonverbal auditory stimuli). This was congruent with the amytal test findings of right-hemisphere speech dominance.

How can we account for this atypical neurological pattern? It seems highly likely that genetically, Marie was intended to be left-hemisphere dominant for language and right handed. Because the left temporal lobe was abnormal, and because she was heterozygotic (if Annett's theory is true), her brain shifted the language functions to the right hemisphere in infancy. However, since the pathology was highly localized to the left temporal lobe and the left motor strip was healthy, her right handedness, eyedness, and footedness remained.

Evidently this little girl's brain reorganized its functions so successfully that her cognitive achievements were superior. The only difficulties she showed on the neuropsychological tests were a slowed visual–manual reaction time and some minimal awkwardness in remembering and drawing geometric designs. However, these subtle impairments appeared to be sensitive test indicators of her brain pathology, which, because of its localized nature, did not interfere with her superior academic achievement. Marie's case reminds us not to jump to the conclusion that handedness and brainedness on the same side necessarily produce a learning disability, particularly because the two hemispheres respond in a compensatory way.

This case draws our attention to an important point. It seems certain that it is not the brain–hand conflict itself that produces a learning disorder. If it did, Marie would not have been a competent student; but she was. The learning problems stem from the diffuse or uneven cortical dysfunction that has produced the ipsilateral pattern of language dominance and handedness.

Sara Fraser, A Case of Reported Mirror Writing

This little girl was referred for neuropsychological assessment in March 1982, because of mirror writing and difficulty in following directions involving written work. At the time of her referral, Sara was 7 years old and in first grade.

At the end of kindergarten in June 1981, the school psychologist had reported that her large muscle coordination was good (balance, throwing, and catching were normal), but she was unable to copy designs. She had a speech problem (poor articulation) and mixed laterality (she threw and caught a ball with her right hand, but drew and colored with her left). After several demonstrations of skipping, she was unable to imitate it.

In first grade she had learning problems from the beginning, although a Wechsler test (WISC-R) administered in October of that year (1981) showed her to have a verbal IQ of 114 (better than about 82% of 6-year-olds). Her speech was unclear until age 4, and during kindergarten and her first grade years she continued to have speech therapy to improve her articulation problem (dysarthria). She had trouble learning to pronounce her own name correctly until she was 5 years old. Reading was poor and spelling chaotic, and she had difficulty in written arithmetic but not oral counting and number facts. She reversed several digits when writing them. She frequently did not follow oral instructions well although her academic achievement level showed considerable variability from day to day.

Handedness

Sara was strongly left handed for writing and drawing and always had been, although both parents and all four siblings were right handed. This pattern strongly suggests pathological left handedness.

I Neuropsychological Assessment (March 1982)

Verbal Abilities. Her strong verbal IQ of 114 was corroborated by high scores in Sentence Repetition, Word Fluency, following oral instructions (Token test), and tactile naming. Her ability in oral arithmetic was good (WISC-R subtest = 13), but Sara's written arithmetic in school was inferior because of her poor motor abilities. Her oral vocabulary on the WISC-R was superior (subtest score = 14).

Handedness. The lateral dominance examination confirmed her strong left handedness and left eyedness. Her footedness was mixed; she kicked a ball with her left foot, but stepped on an imaginary bug with her right. Her hand grip was stronger in her left hand although both hands were weak. Her finger tapping speed showed the same pattern; her left hand was faster than the right, but both hands were slower than the 7-year average (Spreen & Gaddes, 1969). Sara's visual–manual reaction times were better for her right hand (her nondominant hand) and her auditory–manual reaction times were slow for both hands. Her printing was large and poorly controlled, and her perception of right and left, both on her body and in extrapersonal space, was inferior. These findings indicate that as well as a spatial–perceptual problem, there is a motor disability, and the unsystematic pattern of laterality suggests that the sensorimotor strips on both sides may be involved.

Memory. Sara's ability to draw geometric designs on the Benton Visual Retention Test was poor, but on the Multiple Choice Form she did very well. Her scores on the Embedded Figures test were also superior. This suggests that her nonverbal memory *per se* was above average, but that her motor disability impaired her performance on the drawing version of the Benton VRT.

Childhood Allergies. Sara's mother reported that the birth was normal, but that Sara was slightly jaundiced. However, it soon became evident that she reacted with stress to a number of stimuli. Her eyes have little tolerance to bright light, and nutritionally she was and is allergic to dairy products, oranges, apples, and tomatoes. Since age 2 Sara has had a skin eczema and scalp irritation, and certain soaps and perfumes aggravate the condition. Three of her siblings are allergic to the same foods, so a family pattern of food allergies is evident.

Test Behavior. Sara is a pretty little girl who was alert and cooperative throughout the test sessions, although at times she appeared to have lapses of attention. She is the middle child of five in a supportive and affectionate family. Mrs. Fraser is intelligent and genuinely interested in Sara's progress, and while she realizes that Sara is "different" from her other children in learning, she is careful not to communicate this to her.

Summary and Recommendations. Sara's problems included difficulty with manual speed and dexterity, an attentional deficit, a visual–motor disability, an inferior directional sense with poor body imagery, and a possible hand–brain conflict (i.e., left-hemisphere language dominance and written left handedness).

We found that while Sara was referred to us as a mirror writer, in fact, she did not write whole phrases or sentences in reverse. She did, however, reverse about half of the digits, especially under pressure on a speeded test, and she reversed a number of short words and many single letters. She suffered from a problem of severe spatial confusion. To help her overcome these problems we recommended the following:

1. Body image and large muscle exercises (e.g., "Simon Says").
2. Small muscle activities (e.g., writing spelling words in damp sand with simultaneous multisensorimotor exercises).
3. The use of color coding (e.g., red sticker on left hand, and green sticker on right hand to learn left and right; Sara should be taught to relate this to navigation lights on boats, ships, and airplanes).
4. The use of color coding to learn letters in writing (e.g., *d* faces left and is red, *b* faces right and is green, etc.).
5. Tactile reinforcement in learning left and right.

Medical Referral. Because of her allergy condition, her attentional lapses, and her variability in speech and intellectual competence from day to day, we referred Sara to an internal medical specialist in August 1982. All biomedical tests (e.g., urinalysis, PKU screening, etc.) were negative, and genetic studies showed normal chromosome appearance.

In September 1982 Sara entered Grade 1 for the second time. The school authorities believed that she was not ready for Grade 2, so she was placed in a first grade class with another teacher. We argued that conceptually she was ready in that her verbal intelligence level was better than about 82% of her classmates, but that her learning was disturbed by her spatial and motor problems. Since these were not primary elements of intellectual capacity, but mechanistic processes of its expression, and as such could be improved with skilled remediation, we urged the school to promote her to Grade 2 and provide daily remedial training for her learning disabilities. We likened the situation to failing a mentally bright cerebral palsied child because his writing was untidy and his speech unclear. However, on the basis of performance, not potential, Sara was directed to repeat Grade 1.

In March 1983, during Sara's second year in first grade, Mrs. Fraser was contacted for a progress report. Wondering if Sara would be bored and frustrated in having to endure the same material again, we were pleased to hear that she was enjoying school. The work was well within her grasp and she was acting as the teacher's aide in helping some of the other children who were having problems in learning the academic material. Sara's mother reported that Sara excells in long-distance running and that she could run the 1 kilometer run with the Grade 5 students. This repeat year has given Sara a better opportunity to establish herself as an important member of her group. Socially, it has improved her by increasing her self-confidence, but Mrs. Fraser said, "I know that she is not being challenged and I realize that she may not be equipped to meet the stiffer academic demands next year in Grade 2."

This case illustrates a common problem, whether or not a potentially bright child in the early grades should be kept back because of a perceptual–motor disability. No one can predict this with certainty because of the impossibility of repeating the alternative choice with the same child at the same age. However, we can study specific cases like Sara's and learn from them. Consequently we have followed her case with genuine interest and will continue to do so.

II Neuropsychological Assessment, July–August 1983

Sara was still cheerful, but restless during the testing, and she still had difficulty giving prolonged attention to assigned tasks. She frequently made careless errors because of a failure to perceive the stimulus accurately. For example, she was inaccurate in counting items and copying designs.

Intelligence. Her Full Scale IQ on the WISC-R was not much changed from a year ago (down from a 70th percentile level to a 65th percentile level). The biggest change was a marked decrease in Verbal IQ (down from 82nd percentile to 70th percentile), and an increase in Performance IQ (from 45th percentile up to 60th percentile). An examination of her verbal subtest scores showed that only two tests were down, Arithmetic and Vocabulary. A year ago her arithmetic score depended largely on counting and providing simple number facts. This year it is beginning to depend more on number concepts, and her poor directional sense may be impairing her achievement.

Memory. Last year on the Token Test she followed oral instructions very well. This year she dropped from a 90th percentile level in 1982 to a 10th percentile level. This variability appeared to result from Sara's distractibility. However, her ability to remember geometric designs and draw them improved from a 20th percentile level to a 50th percentile level.

Perception and Sensorimotor Tests. Sara's auditory perception of language sounds (phonetic discrimination) was weak. It dropped from a 40th percentile level in 1982 to a 20th percentile level in 1983. Her visual recognition of embedded figures (geometric figures against a camouflaged background) also decreased markedly, but this appeared to be due to carelessness. Her right–left orientation for both personal and extrapersonal space was very confused. Her finger localization showed slight improvement in both hands.

Sequencing. Her inability to imitate skipping, in April of her kindergarten year, alerted us to the possibility of a sequencing problem in reading and writing. In both test sessions (in 1982 and 1983), Sara was unable to tell which light in a sequence was different from a standard pattern; in fact, even during the second test session when she was 8 years 4 months old, she was unable to understand the instructions, although some 6-year-olds and most 7-year-olds can do this test successfully.

All of these findings indicate that Sara still had serious problems in spatial and directional orientation, maintaining attention on a task, and sequential perception and motor response. Her teachers were urged to continue a program of sensorimotor activation in learning to spell, to encourage Sara to use a typewriter to increase her sequential skills and her attention in learning to spell, to have Sara use a tape-recorder to learn the auditory aspects of spelling, and board games such as Parcheesi to practice sequential preception and more accurate visual attention. Her teachers, of course, drew on their own experience to provide a varied academic remedial program.

Sara's Mother's Report (1983)

"Sara has now completed two years in Grade 1 and repeating it was not very stimulating. There were no major problems as there had been during the first year, but there were no real challenges either. She still reverses numbers when under pressure of a speed test. Her speech varies; some days her articulation is good, other days very poor. It will be interesting to see how she deals with the new work in Grade 2."

Allergies and Learning Disabilities. Geschwind (1983) has reported that childhood allergies such as hay fever, asthma, and eczema tend to occur with abnormal frequency in families of dyslexics. He has also found significant interrelationships with food allergies, disorders of the immune system, left handedness, childhood migraine, and developmental dyslexia. More will be said about these biological associations with left handedness in Chapter 8.

In spite of the negative findings of the biochemical tests in 1982, an association between Sara's allergies, her left handedness, and her learning problems will continue to be considered as a tentative possibility for understanding her behavior.

Sara's Mother's Report (March 1984)

"She is doing well in Grade 2. At first she slipped from the top reading group, but in November they began giving her more remedial help and she is back up now. She likes her teacher (a man) very much. Her speech is clear now; the speech therapist 'graduated' her from therapy in October (1983). The reversals have disappeared from her writing, unless she is tired or hurried. Her writing is neat if she takes time; she can write well. She still needs help with her spelling, but the school believes that will be an ongoing process. She is enjoying school, and while not at the top of her class, she is progressing satisfactorily."

When questioned about Sara's allergies: "I keep her on a pretty strict diet. I have found that she can drink milk if I scald it, without developing eczema."

Summary

At this point in Sara's life she is learning to cope successfully with her learning problems. Neuropsychological assessment techniques identified her specific deficits although they did not reveal their cause(s). However, this approach permitted a successful remedial program to be developed. Possibly in the future, improved neurological and neurochemical assessment procedures may disclose the etiological mysteries of cases like Sara's.

The Clinical Classifications of Handedness

There is no conclusive evidence to point to an exact classification of handedness, but the following may be useful and is strongly supported by current research findings.

1. Pure right handers. These subjects are consistently right sided in all their lateral preferences and strongly left-hemisphere dominant for language. On a Dichotic Listening Test they will probably show a strong right ear preference for verbal stimuli. If they show no neurological signs of brain dysfunction and have at least average intelligence, they should be free of any specific learning disabilities. If they are under-achieving academically, the chances are high that their problem is purely motivational and not organic. According to Annett's theory they make up 64% of the general population.

2. Pathological right handers. These children are rare and may be missed because they are operating in a right-handed world. They are brain-damaged subjects who genetically were intended to be left handed and right-hemisphere dominant for language. Because of the disturbing effects of the cerebral dysfunction, which is maximally in the right hemisphere, they tend to be right handed (i.e., the right hand is controlled by the healthy left hemisphere), but unfortunately the language dominance remains in the defective right hemisphere. They may suffer from specific learning problems, depending on the locus of the damage. Since many of these children go undiagnosed, we have no way of knowing their frequency, but it is probably much less than 1% of the population.

3. Mixed right handers. These children use their right hands for writing and nearly always are left-hemisphere dominant for language. However, because of brain dysfunctions in various loci of the right or both hemispheres, they tend to show a mixed laterality for manual skills other than writing and for eyedness and footedness. As beginners in school they manifest a high incidence of letter reversals in writing, and they show impairment in perceptual and motor skills. In Annett's theory these children would be heterozygotes with brain damage superimposed. Most of them suffer some type of academic learning problem. They may be discriminated from the pathological right hander by careful neuropsychological diagnostic study.

4. Pure left handers. These children are assumed to be natural or genetic left handers. They normally have right-hemisphere dominance for language and are consistently left sided in their lateral preferences. When they are free of brain dysfunctions, they should be as free of specific learning disabilities as the pure right handers. According to Annett's genetic theory they may make up about 4% of the population.

5. Pathological left handers. The majority of these children were genetically intended to be right handed, but because of brain dysfunctions in various loci of either the left or both hemispheres they have used their left hand for writing and some manual skills. However, they are nearly always characterized by mixed laterality for various manual skills and for eyedness and footedness. Their cerebral dominance for language is on the left in about one-half of the cases, and bilateral, to some degree, much more than groups of right-handed subjects (Hécaen & de Ajuriaguerra, 1964; Luria, 1966; Milner, Branch, & Rasmussen, 1966; Shankweiler & Studdert-Kennedy, 1975; Subirana, 1958; Zangwill, 1960). Deficits are common in right–left orientation, body image, visual perception, and visual–motor skills.

Most children with organically based disabilities come from Groups 3 and 5, that is, the mixed right handers and the pathological left handers. They seem to make up about 7% of the elementary school population, according to the data of Mykelbust and Boshes (1969).

Continuum of Cerebral Lateralization

We have already drawn attention to the fact that handedness does not manifest itself in discrete groupings. The above five classes of handedness are major constellations of hand–brain organization, but detailed handedness examinations, as we have already shown, reveal a continuum from very strong right sidedness, through degrees of mixed laterality, to marked left sidedness.

Recent neuropsychological research has supported Hughlings Jackson's early caution (in 1874) that cerebral dominance is not absolute. It is evident that dominance for speech is bilateral in many cases, and that a continuum of lateralization for speech perception exists from complete left-hemisphere dominance, through various degrees of bilaterality, to complete right-hemisphere dominance (Shankweiler & Studdert-Kennedy, 1975). These two researchers measured this relationship on a series of handedness measures and on a dichotic consonant–vowel syllable test.

Numerous researches have already been noted that indicate a tendency for earlier left-hemisphere proficiency of little girls, and for earlier right-hemisphere competence of little boys. These abilities frequently include better verbal, sequential, or analytical skills attributed to the left hemisphere, and better spatial, imaginative, and holistic ones attributed to the right (Bogen, 1975). These findings suggest that women may use their brains more bilaterally than men when confronted with certain types of spatial problems and that they may be lateralized in the left hemisphere earlier for language than men (Buffery & Gray, 1972). It has been suggested that this earlier language lateralization and possible bilateral function accounts for their better recovery from traumatic aphasia in some cases. However, this whole matter is not clear because Buffery (1976), in studying 100 male and 100 female students at Oxford and Cambridge Universities in England, found a greater laterality for handedness and dichotic ear preference in females than males. It seems highly likely that the response of either sex is a function of the task being faced. Van Duyne, Bakker, and De Jong (1977) found that under normal conditions in a dichotic listening experiment girls in the primary grades recalled more words than boys with their right ears (left hemisphere) but under the condition of proactive inhibition boys and girls recalled the same number of words with their right ears (left hemisphere).

Although the whole matter of cerebral bilaterality and sex differences is not yet clear, many studies have shown that girls show a superiority in verbal fluency that seems to be present from infancy, earlier speech than boys, better articulation, fewer grammatical errors, and the production of longer and more complex sentences (Buffery & Gray, 1972). This advanced language ability in girls may result from some subtle cerebral structures and functions not yet identified, and it may be that this earlier language learning provides a stronger defense against cortical disorganization in aphasia. Whereas many women show a better recovery from traumatic aphasia, this is not always the case (Kertesz & McCabe, 1977).

The reader who wishes to pursue this topic further may find some pertinent papers in books by Bradshaw and Nettleton (1983); Bryden (1982); Heilman and Valenstein (1979); Herron (1980); Kirk (1983b); Kolb and Whishaw (1980/1984); Maccoby and Jacklin (1974); Miller and Lenneberg (1978); Ounsted and Taylor (1972); Pirozzolo (1979); Rourke, Bakker, Fisk, and Strang (1983); Segalowitz (1983); Segalowitz and Gruber (1977); Spreen *et al.* (1984); and Wittrock (1980a).

Should Handedness Be Changed?

Every first-grade teacher is faced with the problem of whether a left-handed child should be changed to write with his or her right hand. This has already been discussed theoretically in the main body of the chapter.

Here we shall describe a simple educational procedure that any teacher can carry out to examine a left-handed child's handedness and writing.

This little examination can be carried out with a left-handed 6-year-old as soon as he can write all the numbers from 1 to 10 and as early as possible in the fall term of first grade. Obviously these two limitations are interrelated.

Ask the child to write the numbers from 1 to 10 as fast as he can. Note the number reversals (e.g., ς for 2, ε for 3). Then say, "Now let's try it with the other hand. I know you don't write with that hand, but let's see if you can write the numbers 1 to 10 with that hand." If the child has been writing on a sheet of paper, then turn it over so that he cannot see what has already been written. If the child has written on the blackboard, either rub off what has been written or move to another part of the blackboard so the child is unable to see his first sample. If the left-handed writing is frequented with reversals and the right-hand writing is free of them, then we should question whether there is a manual–cerebral conflict present. The child should be referred to the school psychologist for detailed study, including a lateral preference examination (Barnsley & Rabinovitch, 1970; Harris, 1958; White & Ashton, 1976) and a Dichotic Listening Test (Kimura, 1961a,b, 1967; Satz, Achenbach, & Fennell, 1967; Zurif & Bryden, 1969). The decision to change should only be made after the neuropsychological evidence strongly suggests the child is left-hemisphere dominant for language and a better speller with his right hand, and after a thorough discussion with the school psychologist, the teacher, the child's parents, and the child himself.

Some References on Handedness Examinations and Inventories

Bryden, M. P. Measuring handedness with questionnaires. *Neuropsychologia,* 1977, *15,* 617–624.

Crovitz, H. F. & Zener, K. A. A group test for assessing hand- and eye-dominance. *American Journal of Psychology,* 1962, *75,* 271–276.

Harris, A. J. Harris tests of lateral dominance: Manual of directions for administration and interpretation, 3rd Ed. New York: Psychological Corporation, 1958.

Oldfield, R. C. The assessment and analysis of handedness: The Edinburgh Inventory. *Neuropsychologia,* 1971, *9,* 97–113.

Raczkowski, D., Kalat, J. W. & Nebes, R. Reliability and validity of some handedness questionnaire items. *Neuropsychologia,* 1974, *12,* 43–47.

White, K. & Ashton, R. Handedness assessment inventory. *Neuropsychologia,* 1976, *14,* 261–264.

Footedness Laterality

Footedness laterality measures have their own tested methods of measurement. See Vanden-Abeele, J. Comments on the functional asymmetries of the lower extremities. *Cortex,* 1980, *16,* 325–329.

8 Language Development, Aphasia, and Dyslexia

It is known that the study of the function of separate parts of the brain began with observation of cases of speech pathology.

A. R. Luria (1964)

. . . there are major and fundamental differences between rules of language and rules of games. The former are biologically determined; the latter are arbitrary.

Eric H. Lenneberg (1967)

The concept (of aphasia) always has entailed both physiological and behavioral facets; this is one reason for its being difficult.

Helmer R. Myklebust (1971b)

Probably the most compelling argument in favor of professional educators including neuropsychological knowledge in the understanding and treatment of children with learning problems is the close relationship between brain structure and function and the development of language. As Lenneberg (1967) has shown, the rules of language are biologically determined, because "all behavior, in general, is an integral part of an animal's constitution." It is related to structure and function, one being the expression of the other. Psychologists for many years have been interested in this dynamic interaction. "If a behavior sequence matures through regular stages irrespective of intervening practice, the behavior is said to develop through maturation and not through learning" (Hilgard, 1948). Put more simply, some forms of behavior result simply because the animal grows older. Maturation must always precede learning, for all learning, and particularly for this discussion, verbal learning, is biologically dependent.

A simple example of this principle is the emergence of speech in the human infant. Not only does language first appear at about 9 months, but the same phonetic sounds begin to appear in different children regardless of their geographical or cultural location. This means that until the speech centers in the cortex and the necessary sensory and motor tracts in the central and peripheral nervous systems have matured, the child is unable to produce words. No matter how potentially bright is a 6-month-old

251

child, and no matter how skilled the teaching, it is impossible to teach him or her to talk. Six months later, when his brain is older, the child now can produce two or three words. Not only that, but there is some system to the appearance of the sounds he can utter, because "the onset of speech is regulated by maturational development of certain physiological and perceptual capacities" (Lenneberg, 1966). This development is complete in most children between the ages of 5 and 7 years, so that by this age the phonetic repertoire is complete; of course, the child will continue to learn new words beyond this age, but no new phonemes in English. To acquire language normally the child must learn to hear and discriminate different phonetic sounds and to recognize the subtle auditory speech cues that occur in a temporal sequence. As well, he or she must master the motor skills of articulation and motor–speech expression and, finally, must build up "the store of linguistic knowledge that eventually forms the basis for both the production and reception of speech" (Fry, 1966).

In English there are over 40 phonetic units for the child to master, some relatively simple to produce because of the earlier cortical and neuromuscular maturational changes, and some much more difficult, presumably because of the later developmental changes in the human brain and central nervous system. Lenneberg (1966) has told us that "man's brain-maturation history is unique among primates" and determines the onset and development of language.

A child's first utterances will includes those phonetic sounds easiest to produce, and these usually include p, b, m, n, d, t, and the vowel a (as in sofa), although he or she may use only three of these at first. For example, one child may say "mama" and "dada," thus using only three phonemes in his or her first recognized words that emerge from the babbling stage, a period usually lasting 4 or 5 months prior to the first word. Another child may first use p, m, and a, and say "papa" and "mama." These variations will occur because of different environmental demands, but all children, regardless of culture, will tend to produce the same earliest phonetic sounds. For this reason, the names for the parents are composed of sounds from the early list. North American children usually call their parents "mama" and "dada," which later become "mum" or "mom" and "dad." German children say "papa" and "mama," and "Vati" and "Mutti" before they articulate the final form of "Vater" and "Mutter." Their grandparents are called "Opa" and "Oma," later to become "Grossvater" and "Grossmutter." French children say "papa" and "maman." Russian children say "mama" and "papa," and "baba" for the grandmother. Chinese children use "pa" and "ma," although the more formal Mandarin forms are "foo" and "mo."

A little later, the child learns to master k, g, f, w, and s, and much later, sometimes 4 or 5 years later, the more difficult sounds, such as j, l, r, h, th (as in thin), th (as in this), sh (as in she), n (as in sing), and finally, probably the most difficult blend in English, thr (as in thrift). The 2- and 3-

year-old who has not yet learned to master these difficult phonetic sounds will adapt his or her speech to the use of the simpler sounds. The 18-month-old child may call his or her older sister Janet, "Dan'dan," and her older brother Stephen, "Dee-dee." Rachel may call herself "Ay-oh" at first, and Neill refers to himself as "Neeno." The 3-year-old, when asked his age, will almost certainly say, "I'm free." Because cortical development in all children, regardless of color or race, seems to be similar, then their first words are likely to be similarly phonetically based. This is an example of what Lenneberg (1967) called "behavioral specificity." Whereas some behaviors are similar across species because they are structurally determined, others are unique to some individuals because they are specifically trained. Specificity results in a common repertoire of basic speech sounds across all humans, and plasticity in the different languages of different cultures. Both processes coexist.

Lenneberg has shown a remarkable degree of regularity in the emergence of language. Single words begin about the eighth or ninth month and show the same developmental pattern of increase whether the child is raised in Austria, Great Britain, or the United States. The emergence of two-word phrases among British children showed a pattern similar to the other two languages and about 10 months later than the first single words in all three.

Normal Language Development

How language develops is not fully understood but it depends on the maturing of cortical cells (Lenneberg, 1967), social reinforcement (B. F. Skinner, 1957), and social learning (Piaget, 1965). A large number of theorists have described the development of language, and most recognize the importance of perceptual reception, understanding, adaptation, imitation and expression. The infant, in order to learn language, must have normal hearing for a wide variety of speech sounds and he or she must be able to observe visually the gestures of the speaker and to sense the emotional tone accompanying the verbal utterance. All of these processes involve decoding and understanding. The child then imitates the sounds of words he has heard and learns to formulate them to express the ideas and feelings he wants to communicate. Bannatyne (1971, Chap. IV) has provided a useful summary of a large number of theorists on the acquisition and development of auditory–vocal language in infancy and childhood.

What we have described includes the three basic processes in acquiring oral and written language: (1) Phonological processing. This refers to the recognition and muscular–motor production of language or phonetic sounds. (2) Semantics. The understanding of the meaning of single words. (This can be measured by a vocabulary test.) (3) Syntax. The systematic arrangement of words in a meaningful sentence structure. (A knowledge of syntax is needed for speaking or writing grammatically correct sentences.)

Myklebust's (1964) developmental hierarchy of the human language system includes the above three linguistic processes in a practical and useful model. It conceives of the development and acquisition of language proceeding from meaningful auditory experience to motor-expressive behavior. In detail, the behavioral stages are as follows:

1. Birth to 9 months. The child hears language and gradually begins to understand it. He develops an "inner language" or a conceptual understanding that is largely nonverbal.

2. Up to 12 months: auditory receptive language. The infant learns to comprehend much of what is said and, by 9 months, is beginning to imitate specific words, usually "Muhmuh, buhbuh, dada," and similar easily produced sounds, which later may become enunciated as "momma," "baby," and "daddy."

3. From 12 months to about age 7: auditory expressive language. This stage includes the auditory perception of words and the motor–speech imitation of them. This is the period of the development of oral speech and a passive vocabulary of about 3000 words.

4. Age 6 and up: visual receptive language (reading). On entrance to school the child must learn to acquire an auditory–graphic match between what he knows auditorially and the printed or written representation of speech. This demands a cross-modal integration.

5. Age 6 and up: visual expressive language (spelling and writing). Where reading is a receptive process, in which the child recognizes letters and words and attaches auditory meaning to them, writing is a reversed process. To write, the child must convert the verbal idea into an oral word, analyze it phonetically, and translate the word into a motor–manual–linguistic pattern that is socially understood.

This scheme is useful for the teacher because it recognizes the order in which language is learned, but it is important to remember that this whole perceptive, motor, integrative process is reinforced by the *meaning* that language conveys. Lenneberg (1964) has reminded us that "understanding is more significant for language development than the capacity for making speech sounds."

Because the acquisition of language involves visual and auditory perception, verbal abstraction, understanding, imitation, and motor–speech expression in a correct sequence, all of the brain parts subserving these various behavior processes will need to be functioning normally for the child to learn to listen, to talk, to read, and to write. The next section describes the speech centers in the brain and considers how their dysfunctions may lead to a verbal learning disorder.

Language and the Functional Anatomy of the Human Brain

The language cortical circuits have been known for a little more than 100 years. In 1861 Broca, a French neurologist, identified the area in front of the left[1] motor strip that controls the muscles of the face, jaw, tongue, and speech muscles. This area is known as Broca's area (see Fig. 8.1) and is the cortical center largely involved in the articulation and expression of spoken speech. In 1874, Carl Wernicke, a young German neurologist, published his first paper, which identified the superior lateral surface of the left temporal lobe as the cortical area for decoding oral speech. It was Wernicke who made the assumption that the two areas, Broca's and Wernicke's, were connected. We now know this to be true, the two areas being connected by a subcortical bundle of fibers known as the arcuate fasciculus (see Fig. 8.1). Geschwind (1965, 1972) has proposed the very logical theory that if a person is asked to repeat a word, he hears it and decodes it in Wernicke's area and relays the auditory pattern, by way of the arcuate fasciculus, to Broca's area, where the necessary cortical changes take place for the word to be pronounced. As Geschwind (1972) has pointed out "this model may appear to be rather simple, but it has shown itself to be remarkably fruitful," and it has been supported by numerous clinical and autopsy studies.

The classical model of language representation in the human cortex of the left hemisphere has been developed since the conceptual establishment of Broca's area in the 1860s and Wernicke's area in the 1870s. By 1890, William James described in some detail the classical cortical areas involved in aphasia. These included the auditory linguistic receptive cortex (Wernicke's area) in the posterior portion of the superior temporal gyrus (usually the left); the motor speech area (Broca's area) in the inferior frontal gyrus; the arcuate fasciculus joining the Wernicke and Broca areas; the motor and sensory strips in the pre- and post-Rolandic gyri; the supramarginal gyrus located around the posterior extremity of the Sylvian fissure; and the angular gyrus in the parieto-temporal region. This model

---

[1] Since about 94% or 95% of the population are left-hemisphere dominant for language, the discussion of brain processes includes only left-hemisphere function.

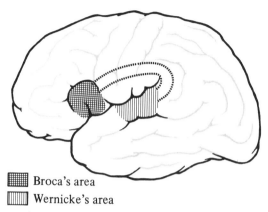

Figure 8.1. Receptive auditory speech cortex (Wernicke's area) and motor-expressive speech cortex (Broca's area or contiguous tissue) showing the subcortical connections (arcuate fasciculus) between the two speech areas. (© 1984 William D. West)

(see Figs. 8.1 and 8.2) has survived for a century, although early on it became evident that some cases with known lesions did not respond as predicted by this theory. Two possible reasons for these discrepancies are: (1) Most brain lesions are not highly localized so that while the focus of the brain dysfunction might be known, the extent of its "distance effects," named *diaschisis* by von Monakow in 1911 (A. Smith, 1975), were frequently unrecognized. (2) The theory, which was originally based

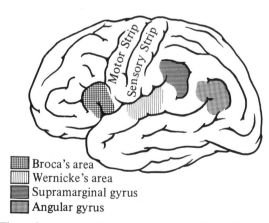

Figure 8.2. The primary speech centers in the left cerebral cortex. (© 1984 William D. West)

on studies of brain lesions exclusively, assumed that the brains of all humans were structurally and functionally identical.

We know now that there is great variability among subjects. This new knowledge has come largely from cortical electrostimulation and brain scan studies, which are much more exact indicators of brain function than trying to infer it from the atypical behavioral signs that follow traumatic brain damage.

Cortical electrostimulation of conscious patients undergoing brain surgery was first done in 1909 by Harvey Cushing, the eminent American neurosurgeon (Ojemann & Whitaker, 1978), and was well established by Wilder Penfield and his associates in the 1930s and 1940s (Penfield & Roberts, 1959). In fact their discoveries led to the identity of a new language cortical area, the supplementary motor area, not previously detected from behavioral studies of brain-injured patients. More recent studies (Fedio & Van Buren, 1974) have led to the conclusions that "much anatomic variability seems likely in the language association cortex" and "the detailed functional anatomy of our brains may be as individualized as is the detailed anatomy of our faces" (Ojemann & Whitaker, 1978).

For example, three patients studied by Ojemann during craniotomy showed a great variability (see Fig. 8.3). Patient A showed naming errors when the normal function of Broca's area was interrupted with electrostimulation (filled circle in Fig. 8.3) but no naming errors when Wernicke's area was electrically interrupted (open circles in Fig. 8.3). This is what we would predict using the classical model of cortical language representation. But patient B does not show as clearly localized a picture. Stimulation of this patient's Broca's area produced naming errors, as we would expect, but so did one spot in the temporal lobe. Patient C was even more atypical; stimulation of Broca's area produced naming errors, but so did Wernicke's area, and spots in the parietal and frontal lobes. Cortical electrostimulation of large numbers of patients show expressive language deficits when Broca's area is stimulated; but among some patients, areas remote from Broca's area may also produce the same language disturbances (Fedio & Van Buren, 1974; Ojemann & Whitaker, 1978).

This same variability is shown quite clearly when a composite picture is made of brain scans of a number of patients with expressive aphasia. When 14 patients with Broca's aphasia had their CT scans superimposed (Kertesz, Lesk, & McCabe, 1977) they showed a wide area of variability (see Fig. 8.4). While the focus of dysfunction centered on Broca's area, some of the patients showed additional pathology in areas quite remote from it.

In summary, this means that the localizationist model of language representation in the human brain, established in the last quarter of the last

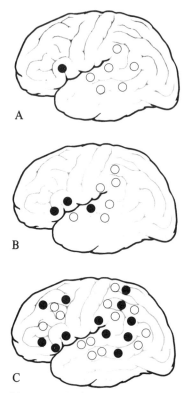

Figure 8.3. Mapping of language centers with electrostimulation in three different patients. Filled circles are sites where stimulation produced naming errors; open circles are sites with no errors. (Adapted from W. H. Calvin and G. A. Ojemann, *Inside the Brain,* Mentor Books, 1980, p. 28. With permission of the authors and the publisher.)

century, is no longer tenable. While there is a strong tendency for expressive language to involve cortex contiguous to Broca's area, and for receptive language to include Wernicke's area in most people, in some subjects additional functional cortical areas may be involved.

Subcortical Connections

While the cortical language areas are essential to normal linguistic function, so too are certain vital centers in the brainstem. In Chapter 3 the cortical connections with the thalamus were described (see Fig. 8.5), and it has been found, by subcortical surgical procedures and the new brain scanning techniques, that when localized lesions occur in the left thalamus, frequently deficits in language and short-term verbal memory may

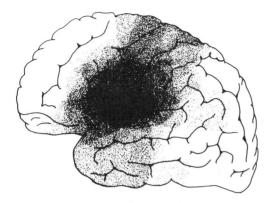

Figure 8.4. A composite diagram of the brain scans of 14 patients with Broca's aphasia superimposed. Note the concentration of pathology in the region of Broca's area, but also the diversity of some of the cases. (From Kertesz, Lesk, & McCabe, *Archives of Neurology,* 1977, p. 594. With permission of the authors and the publisher.)

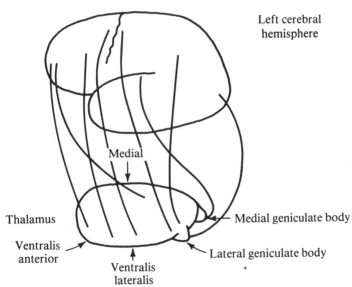

Figure 8.5. A diagrammatic representation of some of the many connections from the left half of the thalamus to the cortex of the left cerebral hemisphere. The thalamus is drawn proportionately larger than life (actually it is made up of two ovoid masses about 4 cm or 1½ in. in length). Many more fibers connect from the thalamus to the cortex than is shown in this simplified drawing, and another large number of fibers connect from the cortex to the thalamus. This is a good reminder of the important involvement of the subcortical structures in cognition and learning and the complexity of the neural circuitry.

result (Ojemann, 1975). When isolated lesions occur in the right thalamus, deficits in visuo-spatial memory and arithmetic calculations may occur (Ojemann, 1974). Ojemann has hypothesized that thalamic electrostimulation acts as a "specific alerting" circuit "that directs attention to verbal material in the external environment, while simultaneously blocking retrieval of . . . material from either short-term or long-term memory" (Ojemann, 1983).

For the student wishing a detailed neurophysiological explanation of the thalamocortical radiations, a fine graphic presentation is made by Netter (1962, Plate 47, p. 72), and discussions are available in any good text in neurophysiology (Schmidt, 1978a, p. 58ff.; Schmidt, 1978b, p. 252ff.).

When the brain mechanisms that subserve language functions are normal and healthy, the child, if motivated to do so, can learn to read, write, and spell with little difficulty. However, if these brain centers are damaged, diseased, or structurally malformed, the child will have difficulty in acquiring language skills, the degree of difficulty correlating directly with the severity of dysfunction and the locus of the damage. When the dysfunction is in the language centers and is mild, the child is said to have a specific learning disability involving reading and the language arts; when it is severe, he or she is said to have aphasia.

Aphasia

Why Include Aphasia?

It may seem irrelevant to introduce the study of aphasia in a book designed for educators, but I do it for three reasons. This book is intended for clinical psychologists, school psychologists, and *special* educators, and these professionals need all the information they can get to help them hypothesize about the possible causes of the subtle learning problems of their students. Since most learning disabilities include language deficits, it is highly probable that a mild form of childhood aphasia is involved. Because it is easier to understand a borderline form of pathology by studying its fullblown form, this is my first reason for including a study of aphasia in this chapter. My second reason is to assist rehabilitation therapists who are faced with teaching severely brain-injured children and adults. Traumatically brain-injured adults frequently have been neglected by society once they have been discharged from the hospital, with the conclusion that they have recovered from the medically treatable sequelae of their injuries. More recently, long-term treatments and occupational training centers are being established to meet the needs of the traumatically brain-injured adult. The teaching personnel in these centers will profit from an understanding of aphasia.

My third reason is probably the best. A great deal is known conclusively about aphasia and, by tying a theory of dyslexia to a theory of aphasia, we are on tested ground. Those school psychologists who are knowledgeable about the theories and clinical manifestations of aphasia are more thoroughly equipped to provide better diagnoses and predictions than are those with no systematic knowledge of language development or impairment.

Definition of Aphasia

What is aphasia? It is the loss or impairment of the use and/or understanding of language resulting from some type of brain injury or dysfunction. When it affects spoken language it is medically described as aphasia; when it affects reading it is called alexia or dyslexia; and when it affects writing it is called agraphia. Educators may prefer other terms for deficits in reading and writing, but the medical terms imply accompanying brain dysfunctions.

The classifications of aphasia are almost as numerous as the researchers attempting to make them. However, in most clinics aphasia is usually dichotomized into *expressive* or motor aphasia when the patient is impaired in formulating speech, and *receptive* or sensory aphasia when the patient has difficulty understanding what is said to him. In spite of there being no clinical evidence for motor aphasia by itself (Pribram, 1971) this broad division has been and is still current in most clinics. This suggests that some type of comprehension difficulty is a part of all the aphasias, even the so-called expressive aphasias. Benson (1979) has provided an excellent discussion of aphasia and has supplied a chart with most of the major classifications since 1885 (Benson, 1979, p. 28). He also presents his own preferred classification, which is based on those aphasias in which repetition is seriously disturbed and those in which it remains intact (p. 39). The presentation here will be kept at an introductory level so that the reader with little or no clinical experience of aphasia can follow the discussion with profit.

Receptive Aphasia

The most severe aphasic disorder includes an inability to carry on inner language functioning, and hence a difficulty in perceiving oneself with any clarity. Johnson and Myklebust (1965) have described the development of inner language as the first linguistic step in the hierarchical development of language. This occurs during the first few months of life in the preverbal stage of cognitive development. The infant has meaningful, pictorial experiences (e.g., he reacts with enthusiasm to the sight of the bottle at feeding time) but has not yet learned to associate verbal symbols or words with these experiences. Gradually the infant learns to integrate experiences in all the sense modes and to attach nonverbal symbolic meaning to them. A dog or cat remains at this stage of development of *inner language*. Once this stage of cognitive understanding is reached in the human infant, however, he or she is ready to develop receptive and expressive language as described above. "Because of this developmental hierarchy, no child speaks until he has learned the meaning of words. . . . Input precedes output" (Johnson & Myklebust, 1965).

This description indicates the basic priority of *inner* and *receptive language*. An inability to interpret one's own subjective experiences is called *central aphasia* and because of its severity it is difficult to diagnose. No doubt it is sometimes confused with childhood autism or psychosis.

From reports of Annie Sullivan's first struggles with Helen Keller, it seems that Helen as a child was subject to explosive temper outbursts and socially meaningless behavior similar to that of an autistic child. Once she learned to interpret her world and herself by tactile language symbols, her potentially superior mind developed and her disorganized behavior disappeared. It seems possible that she may have moved out of a condition similar to *central aphasia* in which she could not communicate with herself, to one in which, through verbal symbols, her mind took on order and clarity.

Receptive aphasic children may be able to understand their own mental lives but have difficulty understanding what is said to them or remembering specific words they wish to use. In one of the forms of receptive aphasia, *amnesic aphasia,* the adult patient cannot remember the name of an object he can describe (anomia). For example, when shown a key he may say, "I know what it is but I can't tell you. You do that with it (makes a twisting motion with his hand) in a door to open it. It's a lock, no, but that's close." When the therapist supplies the word the patient will say, "Yes, a key." We have all had this experience when tired; we cannot find the word for the idea we wish to express.

The typical adult with a receptive aphasia will have a left temporal lesion (in Wernicke's area) and a number of behavioral symptoms, including a word-finding difficulty (anomia), impoverished verbal content, and frequent paraphasias. Paraphasias are of two types: (1) verbal substitutions and (2) nonsense words (neologisms) or mixtures of two words. Examples of substitutions are "chair" for "table" or 6 when one conceptually intends 8. We have all had such verbal slips when we are fatigued; these types of errors suggest that the cortical mechanisms have triggered the wrong readymade cortical circuit. Abnormal mixtures of words are limitless and when they dominate the person's speech it may be referred to as "jargon aphasia." Such a patient, when asked to describe a key, might say, "Kay (pause), that's what I want, it's dorent—I'm in the floor, door. It's all away." Whereas the receptive aphasic's speech is fluent and generally manifests normal grammar and articulation, it sounds like "double talk." Very little is communicated and much of it is confused. The condition appears to stem from the inability of the person to mobilize the words he or she needs in the correct order, and to attach the appropriate conceptual meanings to them. Ojemann has produced most of these types of speech errors by electrostimulating the left thalamus (Ojemann, 1975).

Military personnel subjected to decompression chamber experiments will have had these same difficulties when the oxygen content of the air was severely depleted. Potential aircrew members during World War II were frequently tested for their ability to do simple arithmetic calculations as the air pressure was systematically reduced to simulate flying conditions in a nonpressurized cabin. Frequently, most people began to find difficulties in concentrating above 10,000 ft (simulated), and as the air became more rarefied it became increasingly difficult to remember the conceptual meanings of numbers. This type of mental impairment in fact was an artificially imposed and temporary receptive aphasia. As soon as the air pressure was returned to normal, the word-finding and conceptual associations of the testees returned to their intact functional level.

Motor Aphasia

The so-called motor aphasic might answer, when asked to name a key, "Bay—no! Day—no! Cow—no, no! Kay—no!" He may hit on the right word or may never get it until the therapist supplies it. In any case, motor aphasia includes the understanding of words but the inability to produce them fluently and accurately. The motor aphasic's failure to say the word is not caused by an inability to say it, since he may be able to produce it when prompted, or on other occasions. In any case there is no impairment in function of the tongue, teeth, lips, or vocal cords in most cases. When there is a problem of peripheral articulation this is known as *dysarthria*. Such a patient may or may not be completely free of aphasia. A bright person with poor articulation because of a harelip is an example; he or she is dysarthric (has poor articulation) but is not aphasic.

The motor aphasic has difficulty in producing, in his own imagination, the exact sensorimotor pattern prior to pronouncing the word. Many normal students mispronounce the word "statistics" because they have never taken the care to analyze it and therefore cannot imagine its correct muscular form. Consequently they may hurry over "stastistics" knowing it is not quite correct, but not knowing how to correct it. The motor aphasic patient may have enough damage or dysfunction in the left hemisphere to render him unable to produce the desired word, although his understanding and intent are quite clear. These patients understand language reasonably well, but their speech may be elliptical and telegraphic. Their language may be devoid of connectives, articles, and small parts of speech, like that of a 2-year-old learning to talk.

Conduction Aphasia

If there is a lesion in the arcuate fasciculus (see Fig. 8.1) so as to disconnect Broca's from Wernicke's area, a particular disability results—the inability to repeat what is said to one. Because Broca's area is intact, speech is fluent and unimpaired, and because Wernicke's area is intact, comprehension of oral speech is complete. However, the ability to repeat oral language on command is grossly impaired because of the disconnection of the verbal mobilizing area and the motor speech area. This syndrome is known as *conduction aphasia.*

Although it is unlikely that so impaired a child would be found in the public school system, an inability to repeat sentences accurately by many children is not uncommon. An understanding of the neural mechanism underlying conduction aphasia and the awareness that some school children might have minimal dysfunctions in their arcuate fasciculi or cortical areas of their left hemispheres, should lead to greater tolerance by the teacher of poor performances on a sentence repetition test. All well-developed aphasia batteries include such tests, which can easily be administered by a school psychologist to measure a child's competence in this skill. If a consistent weakness appears in the child's ability on the sentence repetition test relative to the other tests in the aphasia battery or to the norms for that particular age, this could strongly suggest an organic basis. Such a hypothesis would contraindicate such diagnoses as "lazy, isn't trying, needs to settle down," which are all too frequent in these types of cases. Normative data are available for children aged 6–13 on a 26-sentence form of the Spreen–Benton battery (Spreen & Gaddes, 1969) and a 22-sentence form (Gaddes & Crockett, 1975).

Isolation of the Speech Area (Mixed Transcortical Aphasia)

A particularly rare form of aphasia can occur when the speech area is isolated from the rest of the cortex (see Fig. 8.6), and the lesson to be learned from this type of case has significance for understanding normal brain function. Benson (1979) has called this condition "mixed transcortical aphasia." Geschwind, Quadfasel, and Segarra (1968) have reported

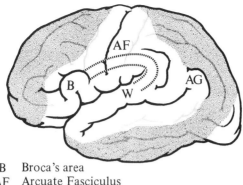

B   Broca's area
AF   Arcuate Fasciculus
AG   Angular gyrus
W   Wernicke's area
▨   Deteriorated tissue

Figure 8.6. A pattern of cortical deterioration that results in cortical isolation of the healthy speech areas of the left hemisphere. Geschwind, Quadfasel, and Segarra have reported such a case. (© 1984 William D. West)

the case of a young woman brain damaged by carbon monoxide poisoning and studied for 9 years prior to her death. Postmortem examination revealed a remarkable lesion that isolated the speech area from the rest of the cortex. "A detailed study of serial whole brain sections showed intactness of auditory pathways up to and including Heschl's gyrus, of Wernicke's area and Broca's area and of the arcuate fasciculus connecting these two cortical regions, of the lower Rolandic cortex and of corresponding portions of the pyramidal tract." Also, both the limbic system and the reticular structure of the brainstem were intact. However, extensive cortical deterioration was present in the prefrontal, upper and posterior parietal, and inferior temporal cortices, thus sparing the essential cerebral mechanisms for the production of speech but isolating them from a total healthy cortex.

Behaviorally, she never spoke spontaneously and she appeared to have no understanding of oral speech. However, she could repeat, parrotlike, what was said to her, and she could complete certain phrases and familiar and rhyming statements begun by the examiner. She could also learn to sing a song by imitation. Since the brain damage was outside the speech and auditory areas, she could recite speech mechanically, but with no understanding. Thinking requires the whole cortex to feed into the cortical speech production areas. By themselves these areas have no more understanding of their speech production than a tape recorder, record player, or talking mynah bird.

This type of clinical evidence would seem to point a widespread cortical stimulation in order to develop language skills. No doubt this is why a multisensorimotor approach is remedially successful with most children.

Developmental Aphasia

All of the above discussions have related to traumatic aphasia in adults. In these cases the adults had already acquired normal or superior language use prior to their brain damage. That is, they lost something that they had already acquired.

In childhood aphasia there is a different pattern. Here, because of maldevelopment or injury to the language centers of the central nervous system prenatally, perinatally, or postnatally during the first year of life, the child is unable to develop or has difficulty in developing a normal understanding and use of language. However, because of the plasticity of his brain, this child may adapt to the neuropathological condition he has inherited either by becoming right-hemisphere dominant for language or by developing a bilateral shared dominance. For this reason the loci of cortical lesions in children may show a pattern different from that of the adult. In this case Broca's area, Wernicke's area, the arcuate fasciculus, and the acoustic area (Heschl's gyrus) of the left temporal lobe are usually impaired in whole or in part and in differing degrees.

So different is childhood aphasia from adult aphasia, both behaviorally and cerebrally, that Bender (in West, 1962) has suggested that knowledge of adult aphasia first may blind us to a clear understanding of the syndrome in children. The plasticity of the child's brain enables him to overcome both the number and the severity of language impairments, which in an adult with the same cerebral pathology would likely be more serious. The reader, and particularly the school psychologist, is referred to an interesting and informative discussion by Drs. Lamar Roberts, Richard L. Masland, and Lauretta Bender regarding this problem (in West, 1962, pp 45–51).

Children with normal hearing and intelligence who fail to acquire oral speech have been recognized at least as early as 1825, when Gall published a treatise on the function of the brain and each of its parts (Wilson, 1965). Myklebust (1971b), in his scholarly review of childhood aphasia, records a continuing interest in the subject since Gall's early publication and the use of the term "congenital aphasia" by Broadbent in 1872. Myklebust draws attention to Binet's early work in 1908, in which Binet identified the four basic operations in language development, understanding, speaking, reading, and writing. Binet noted, "and each of these operations may be suppressed separately by a cerebral accident" (quoted by Myklebust, 1971b).

While a few special schools have been interested in treating aphasic children since the establishment of the first such department at Central Institute for the Deaf in St. Louis, there was no wide interest in their diagnosis and teaching until Myklebust's important book in 1954 (Wilson, 1965).

During the 1950s progress was made by a number of investigators in refining the terminology and classification system. These contributions led to a recognition of these children as being mentally normal, having normal hearing and no evidence of cerebral palsy or obvious disease, but showing a marked delay in the development of speech.

Because the normal acquisition of speech is through auditory sensation and perception, imagery, symbolization, and conceptualization (Myklebust, 1954), it is not surprising that the most impressive gains in the understanding and treatment of aphasic children were made in special schools for the deaf. In fact, developmental aphasia in some cases may reveal a mixed picture of brain damage and partially defective hearing. In small children, because of their inability to introspect and to follow complex instructions, it is frequently difficult or impossible to be sure whether the child suffers only from auditory imperception or weak auditory sensation, or both. The case of Kathleen, discussed in the Clinical Addendum to this chapter, illustrates the difficulty of this type of differential diagnosis and reveals how the child's normal aging can facilitate it.

Teachers of special classes and psychologists and therapists in rehabilitation centers will certainly have to teach some aphasic children. An awareness of the common symptoms may help the teacher to recognize the problem and the school psychologist to make a differential diagnosis.

Traumatic or Acquired Aphasia in Childhood

In the above discussion of developmental aphasia, we included, in one of the etiological classifications, traumatic brain damage prior to the age of 1 year. After that age the child begins to acquire language, and any left-hemisphere damage between age 2 and puberty, normally referred to as acquired or traumatic childhood aphasia, will interfere with language habits already learned. During growth and development the brain-injured child experiences language learning (from his social environment) and language interference (from his brain injury). Earlier researchers reported fairly rapid recovery from traumatic aphasia for preschoolers (Lenneberg, 1967) but slower recovery for children between 4 and 10 years of age. For adolescents and adults, traumatic brain damage nearly always left obvious speech deficits. However, while younger children, because they frequently learned to speak fluently again, appeared to make complete recoveries from their aphasias, more recent long-term studies have shown that most of these children carry chronic and subtle aphasic symptoms into adulthood, and formal verbal learning is nearly always difficult for them.

Denckla (1979) has reported that, in her clinical experience, there seem to be very few cases of acquired aphasia in young children; in a period of 7 years as director in a large neurological institute, she saw only seven such cases under the age of 10. While this is true, there are many children with early left-hemisphere damage who can be described as "aphasoid," and who are somewhat inept in most types of verbal learning and linguistic expression. These children probably make up a large number of those labeled as learning disabled.

Severe left-hemisphere damage in preadolescence frequently is followed by recovery of spoken language in a year or two, but much slower recovery of reading and writing skills. Adolescents and adults tend to recover the latter more quickly, presumably because of the greater degree of practice and overlearning. The case of Robbie Yates (discussed later in this chapter) is a good example. He was injured at age 3 years 9 months, and by age 6 his oral speech appeared normal to a casual observer. However, his reading and writing skills were chronically inferior even with skilled remedial teaching.

A reluctance to speak is common among most aphasic and some aphasoid children. Denckla (1979) has proposed that this may result from the child's relative inexperience and lack of practice in learning "the articulatory rules and social habits of speech" as compared to the adult aphasic. As a consequence, the lack of language knowledge (which draws heavily on the posterior left hemisphere) is not enough to produce a normal volume or quality of language even though the mechanisms of motor speech (in the left frontal lobe) are intact. The case of Sam (in Chapter 5, page 170) illustrates such repressed verbal expression.

Readers wishing a more thorough examination of traumatic or acquired childhood aphasia may find useful discussions in Denckla (1979, pp. 537–540), Lenneberg (1967, pp. 145–150), and Myklebust (1971b, pp. 1181–1217).

Common Symptoms of Developmental Aphasia

Language Retardation. Although language retardation is the primary symptom, it is essential to remember that not all impaired speech is aphasic. The most common causes of inferior speech development in children, other than aphasia, are peripheral hearing loss, mental retardation, emotional disturbance, social deprivation, and/or a peripheral articulation problem. By the time the child reaches school age it is usually possible to make a differential diagnosis of developmental aphasia versus some other nonaphasic syndrome, but sometimes the aphasic child may be mistakenly labeled as mentally retarded or emotionally disturbed, when in fact the child may be potentially mentally bright or superior.

Receptive Signs. Receptive signs include poor auditory perception. The child can hear sounds but cannot decode them meaningfully. This usually results from cortical damage to Wernicke's area (Luria, 1973) and may include the auditory projection pathways connecting from the medial geniculate nuclei (Benton, 1963a) and possibly the parieto-occipital areas

(Landau, Goldstein, & Kleffner, 1960). Benton (1963a) feels that "the most extreme degree of disability is shown by children who show 'auditory imperception.'"

Central Processing Defect. If damage or dysfunction occurs in the left inferior parietal or parieto-temporal–occipital area, adults may have difficulty in associating individual words or ideas into a meaningful whole. They have difficulty understanding sentences, and for this reason this condition has sometimes been called "semantic aphasia" (Luria, 1973). Because it also may include poor memory and defective association of abstract concepts and symbolic thinking, it has also been called "central aphasia." Considerable clinical evidence exists to localize brain lesions in aphasic adults, but few cases of children with developmental aphasia have come to postmortem study. Three who have are described below, and whereas the language areas are generally similar in location to those in adults the impaired behavioral responses are less intense and may show a greater degree of recovery.

There is also evidence that aphasic children are slower to process auditory sequential stimuli, both verbal (Tallal & Piercy, 1974) and nonverbal (Efron, 1963; Lowe & Campbell, 1965; Tallal & Piercy, 1973a,b).

Expressive Signs of Childhood Aphasia

1. Little or no expressive speech with near-normal understanding.
2. Telegraphic speech. There is an absence of connectives (articles, prepositions, conjunctions) and a presence of what Benton (1963a) has called "syntactical poverty." This lack may also show in the child's writing.
3. Articulation may be normal or near normal on repetition but poor in spontaneous speech.

Personality Disturbance. Since the development of language enables one to control oneself and one's environment, any retardation in language in a child with average intelligence may serve only as a frustration and source of anxiety. It is common to find the aphasic child subject to temper tantrums, mood swings, hostility, destructiveness, apathy, and/or a desire to be left alone. It seems highly likely that some children who are diagnosed as "autistic" are in fact aphasic, because their social behavior improves as their language is developed.

The Neurology of Developmental Aphasia

Because it is generally accepted, even by the most enthusiastic behaviorists (B. F. Skinner, 1938), that aphasia is a direct result of brain damage or dysfunction in the speech centers of the dominant hemisphere (Luria

1966, 1973), it seems essential for the school psychologist and useful for the special teacher to know something about the possible neurological deficits of the aphasic child. A major literature exists on the aphasic adult (Bay, 1964; Brain, 1961; Geschwind, 1965; Lhermitte & Gautier, 1969; Weisenburg & McBride, 1935/1964) and these findings indicate a strong reliability in locus of lesion and behavioral sequelae in normal adults who have suffered injury to the speech centers (Luria, 1966, 1973).

However, in the case of children, the clinical literature is not as rich and the behavioral deficits are more varied. Because much can be learned from in-depth studies of individual cases, these appear throughout the book.

Probably the most complete clinical report yet made on a child with developmental learning disabilities is that by Drake (1968), in which he reported in detail the medical history, the physical and neurological examination, the psychiatric findings, the educational record, the psychological test results, and the neuropathological report of a boy who died suddenly at the age of 12 and whose brain came to postmortem study. Billy was a likable boy of average intelligence who was subject to marked mood swings, some "dizzy spells and blackouts," and trouble with most academic learning. He was retarded in reading and had difficulty remembering what he read; he had some problems with arithmetic, spelling, and writing; he was slow in learning to tell time (he learned after he was 11 years old); and he showed extreme slowness in completing homework assignments. In the sixth grade he read at a fourth-grade level, and his word analysis and spelling were at the fifth-grade level. Arithmetic was about 1 year retarded.

A postmortem examination of his brain showed abnormal growth of the parietal cortices *bilaterally* and poor development of various parts of the corpus callosum. As well, there was an unusual and abnormal pattern of cortical gyri or convolutions. Subcortically there were abnormal structures of the blood vessels and displacement of some of the subcortical cerebral cells. In view of this major disorganization of Billy's brain, it is remarkable that he learned to read at all or to show any academic progress. Lenneberg (1968) has described such a process by concluding "the child with a perinatal cerebral injury only gradually 'grows into his symptoms,' and that both lesions and symptoms have their own ramified consequences." More simply, it might be inferred that the congenitally brain-damaged child learns to make the optimal compromise between structure and function. Because his brain is young he can shift to the healthier parts with greater freedom than can the traumatically brain-damaged adult.

The first autopsy study of a child with developmental aphasia (Benton, 1963a) was reported by Landau, Goldstein, and Kleffner (1960). This 6-year-old boy seemed mentally bright but had almost no understanding of spoken language. His speech was a chaotic mass of jargon and he resorted to gestures in order to communicate. After 3 years of special speech training he developed a moderate vocabulary and learned to say simple sentences. He also learned to read and write simple material and arithmetic at about the first-grade level. During those 3 years his nonverbal IQ rose from 78 to 97, which suggested average nonverbal intelligence. Audiometric testing showed normal hearing in the right ear with a possible high frequency loss in the left. These findings eliminated the possibility of a hearing loss to account for his language retardation and suggested localized cerebral damage and dysfunction.

This hypothesis was supported with the postmortem findings following the boy's sudden death at age 10. Autopsy study showed considerable evidence of inadequate growth of the cortical layers in *both* temporal lobes. Because this growth anomaly was *bilateral,* it was difficult for the boy's brain to shift his defective Wernicke's area to the other side. The posterior portions of the parietal, temporal, and occipital lobes were reduced in size on both sides, and the medial geniculate nuclei, connecting the auditory nerves to the Heschl's gyri on both sides, were severely degenerated. It seems highly likely that the registration of language sound patterns in his brain were so distorted that learning to understand oral speech was impossible for him except to a limited degree, and only with specialized language training.

In commenting on this very interesting case, Benton (1963a) draws attention to the fact that comparable lesions in adult patients would have produced central deafness. Again, however, it seems that this boy responded to the special speech training by using whatever healthy cerebral tissue he possessed. This type of evidence supports the belief in skilled remedial teaching as early as possible, to exploit to its fullest the plasticity of the child's brain.

Roberts (1962) has reported a very interesting case of a little girl whom he followed from age 6 until her death in her early adolescence. Her development was normal until the age of 15 months, when she incurred a high fever associated with convulsions and the development of a right hemiparesis. The seizures continued and could not be controlled by medication.

Examination at age 6 showed a smallness of the left side of her cranium and the right side of her body. She had a mild right hemiparesis, which indicated pathology in her left cerebral hemisphere. Her oral speech was so garbled that only her mother could understande her, and her attempts to vocalize normal phonetic sounds were quite abnormal in most cases. She developed an idiosyncratic speech with a consistent meaning for herself.

An EEG showed spike discharges over the left side of her brain mainly in the parietal area. Brain surgery revealed diffuse atrophy of the left hemisphere especially in the parietal lobe, which was surgically removed.

Treatment of Aphasic Children

Two of the early major contributors in the field of treatment of developmental aphasia are Helmer R. Myklebust, who worked extensively with deaf and aphasic children for many years, and Mildred A. McGinnis, a gifted teacher who worked for more than 40 years at the Central Institute for the Deaf in St. Louis, and latterly at the Pathway School in Norristown, Pennsylvania.

Mykelbust (1971b) has stressed the importance of a competent identification and diagnosis of the aphasic child. It is important, as has already been stated, to differentiate the aphasic from the mentally retarded, hard of hearing, or emotionally disturbed. A deficit in auditory language may be recognized during the preschool years, whereas aphasia may not be suspected until after the completion of first grade, or not recognized as a chronic problem until the third or fourth grade. The diagnosis will provide information regarding auditory perception, comprehension, integration, and expression, thus indicating the pattern of deficits and relative strengths the child may have. The diagnostic procedure lies in showing a significantly inferior ability in auditory language relative to his or her nonverbal intelligence level, hearing, emotional adjustment, and motor ability. The study of the child with language retardation must include both a detailed audiometric examination by a qualified language pathologist and a comprehensive battery of psychological tests (Myklebust, 1954), and I would add neuropsychological tests. Myklebust (1971b) recommends an exhaustive evaluation of the child's perceptual processes, which include his ability to give attention; his rate, intensity, and duration of response to both verbal and nonverbal, meaningful and nonmeaningful, and rhythmical and nonrhythmical auditory stimuli; his sound recognition and phonetic discrimination; and his ability for auditory figure–ground recognition, perception and manual production of rhythm, and intersensory perception. For many years, Myklebust has recognized the importance of intraperceptual and interperceptual functioning. In his own research he has used cross-modal tasks as one of the most sensitive behavioral tests of the presence of brain damage, or particular cortical dysfunctions.

As well as perceptual processes, verbal functions must be carefully evaluated. These include auditory verbal memory, comprehension and integration of language, verbal memory using both methods of recognition and recall, and motor expressive functions. How all of this is done clinically is discussed by Myklebust in summary but detailed form (1971b) and in full detail (1954). The school psychologist not thoroughly familiar with the clinical evaluation of childhood aphasia is well advised to study these and other sources.

Remediation is highly individualized, being determined by the child's particular strengths and weaknesses in perception, auditory memory, comprehension, integration, recall, and expression. Myklebust for a long time has emphasized the importance of including both verbal and nonverbal skills in evaluating any child with a learning problem, and he has given these two functions equal weight psychometrically in his formula for the learning quotient (Myklebust, 1967a). For the evaluation of the potential abilities of the aphasic child this is particularly important.

Although there is great variability among aphasic children, Myklebust stresses certain basic homogeneities. The first of these is that input precedes output. The child's understanding of a word should be assured before one attempts to teach him to say it. Similarly he should be able to read a word before being taught to write it. A second basic assumption is: Do not use the multisensorimotor approach indiscriminately. It is necessary first to find out the child's perceptual strengths and weaknesses and any possible motor deficits. An unsystematic use of multistimulation may interfere with learning in some cases. "Overloading may be deleterious to attention, orientation, motivation, and in rare instances may cause severe fatigue, if not seizures" (Myklebust, 1971b).

Myklebust's approach is extremely practical and is based on a sound knowledge of learning principles, neurology, neuropsychology, and classroom teaching of children with special needs.

Mildred McGinnis' approach, which she called the association method, has many differences. She reports (1963) that "the opinions, suggestions, and judgments contained in this book are based upon the author's accumulated first-hand experience of daily contact over a period of forty years with the problem of assessing and teaching children with deficiencies in the ability to communicate orally." Miss McGinnis was a gifted and very successful teacher and she concerned herself only with the behavioral aspects of oral communication, and not the organic deficits underlying the child's aphasia.

From her experience with hundreds of children with communication disorders she developed a clear clinical judgment that enabled her to differentiate the aphasic child from the deaf, mentally retarded, autistic, emotionally disturbed, or the child with delayed speech. Her book illustrates each type of differential diagnostic problem with a large number of detailed clinical case studies.

The association method is systematically adhered to and if "one step is by-passed a gap in learning becomes apparent, and the steps must be retraced" (McGinnis, 1963). The aphasic child is first trained to develop attention to directions, and then to say and read 50 common nouns. This begins with single sounds; sounds are then combined to form the whole word, and finally, activities are used to associate meaning with the word. This is primarily a phonetic and articulatory attack leading to reading and then writing. Once the 50 nouns are mastered, the next stage provides the development of an increased memory span by teaching simple sentences using the familiar nouns. From here the training increases the knowledge of concrete nouns and moves on to abstract ideas and more complex grammatical forms of language.

By contrast, McGinnis stresses a teaching method, whereas Myklebust stresses a thorough neuropsychological analysis of the child's ability that will indicate a particular teaching program for that child. McGinnis' book is a rich compendium of opinions, suggestions, and judgments drawn from her own experience, but there are no references to research. Myklebust is a vigorous researcher himself and his writings are thoroughly documented with numerous references to current research studies in neurology, psychology, and special education. The writings of both writers have their special value for the new worker in the field of childhood aphasia. One comprises the insights and practical recommendations of one of the major living scholars in this field, and the other the detailed first-hand account of a particularly gifted teacher.

Dyslexia

Up to this point we have considered only auditory receptive and expressive speech. Let us now look at written receptive language (reading) and at its defective form, dyslexia. Money (1962) has written, "the reading defect may represent loss of competency following brain injury or degeneration; or it may represent a developmental failure to profit from reading instruction."

Definition of Dyslexia

In 1968 the World Federation of Neurology proposed the following two definitions of dyslexia (Critchley, 1970):

1. Specific Developmental Dyslexia: "A disorder manifested by difficulty in learning to read despite conventional instruction, adequate intelligence, and socio-cultural opportunity. It is dependent upon fundamental cognitive disabilities which are frequently of constitutional origin."
2. Dyslexia: "A disorder in children who, despite conventional classroom experience, fail to attain the language skills of reading, writing and spelling commensurate with their intellectual abilities."

These definitions raise several points: (1) The reading disability may stem from congenital deficits, i.e., may be "developmental," or (2) it may result from postnatal traumatic brain damage after the child or adult has acquired the skill of reading. These types of reading deficits, that is, those resulting from central nervous system damage or dysfunction, have been termed "primary reading retardation" (Rabinovitch, 1959). Rabinovitch proposed two categories of reading retardation, primary and secondary. Primary reading retardation resulted from "a basic disturbed pattern of neurologic organization." He did not include traumatically brain-injured cases in either category. For him the "primary" cases were due to some biochemical imbalance or chronic neurological deficit that resulted in what we now call "specific" or "congenital" reading retardation. Secondary reading retardation describes the cases in which the potential ability "to learn to read is intact but is utilized insufficiently." Causes of this may be environmental (e.g., limited schooling) or internal (e.g., negativism). In this book "primary" will refer to all physiologically determined cases of reading retardation (both traumatic and developmental). Our "secondary" category is similar to that of Rabinovitch. The primary forms may include, as well as brain dysfunction, mental retardation, genetic defect, autism, and aphasia. Cultural and educational causes of reading problems have been labeled "secondary reading retardation." These may include hostile family climate, parental rejection or neglect, and social or educational deprivation. Calling reading problems "primary" when they result from organic dysfunctions does not imply a greater importance than the "secondary" emotional ones, but they are more refractory to conventional teaching methods because of central processing dysfunctions. The psychiatric or "secondary" group retains an intact capacity to read (Quadfasel & Goodglass, 1968) which can function normally when the emotional conflicts are resolved. For this reason, the remedial teacher will want to know at the outset whether he or she is dealing with an "organic" or "purely motivational" type of reading problem. This knowledge will indicate a basically different remedial approach depending on the causal pattern of the reading deficit.

More than 20 years ago, Money (1962) pointed out that "medicine and pedagogy have been slow to come together" in the study of dyslexia. This professional parallelism has given way to a greater blending of these two disciplines in the last few years mainly because of dramatic advances in neurological research (e.g., CT, PETT, and NMR scanners), the investigation of possible organic correlates of dyslexia by histological examinations (e.g., Galaburda & Kemper, 1979; Galaburda & Eidelberg, 1982), the advances in assessing functional cerebral asymmetries, the marked increase in neuropsychological studies of dyslexia and other learning problems, and the greater availability of these findings in psychological and educational journals. Up until the mid-1970s, most educators and school psychologists attributed reading failure exclusively to psychogenic causes; neurological factors were seldom considered.

By the beginning of the 1980s the significance of the brain in learning was at least recognized, if only superficially understood, by large numbers of educators and school psychologists. They were gradually becoming aware of convincing evidence in some cases and in others, of knowledge with peripheral usefulness in the better understanding of linguistic impairments.

Let us look at some of this evidence. The first neurological evidence correlated with the inability to read came from adults suffering cerebral strokes. The various categories of reading retardation that we shall use in this discussion follow:

A. Primary reading retardation (alexia or dyslexia)
   1. Adults
      a. Traumatic dyslexia
      b. Developmental dyslexia
   2. Children
      a. Traumatic dyslexia, after $1\frac{1}{2}$ or 2 years of age
      b. Developmental dyslexia, when trauma was prenatal, occurred at birth, or occurred postnatally before $1\frac{1}{2}$ years of age
B. Secondary reading retardation (weak motivation because of poor environmental influences).

Terminology

Many educators prefer a term such as "reading retardation" to the term "dyslexia." In fact, in some teacher training colleges the term "dyslexia" has been banned as undesirable. The young teacher may find this confusing because the term continues to be used by some educators, the medical profession, and the press. Consequently, a brief commentary on this problem may help to clarify it.

The terms "alexia" and "dyslexia" receive different definitions from different writers. *Webster's New Twentieth Century Dictionary* (2nd Ed., 1968) defines "alexia" as the "inability to read, caused by lesions of the brain; word blindness," and "dyslexia" as "the loss of power to grasp the meaning of that which is read." The implication here, although it is not specifically stated, is that the reading disability in alexia is caused by brain damage but in dyslexia is unknown. Benson and Geschwind, both neurologists, accept this classification with greater definitive specificity. For them, "alexia refers only to *acquired* defects in contrast to dyslexia, a term designating an *innate* or constitutional inability to learn to read" (Benson & Geschwind, 1969).

Many educators use the term "alexia" to indicate a complete or very severe inability to read, and "dyslexia" to mean a mild dysfuncton or moderate retardation in reading, but this use of the words to indicate a degree of severity of the same condition has been rejected by some neu-rologists (Quadfasel & Goodglass, 1968). Obviously this confusing situa-tion in naming a phenomenon they are all studying has resulted from a lack of communication between educators and neurologists. Neurologists in the past have made a greater effort to share their knowledge with educators (Binet & Simon, 1908; Montessori, 1965; Orton, 1937; Critch-ley, 1970) than the other way around. There are a few notable excep-tions, such as Myklebust, but many psychologists and educators, im-pressed with the value of neuropsychological data, have been told by many of the Educational Establishment that it is irrelevant to the educa-tional process. That contribution is a poor return for the wealth of knowl-edge neurology has to offer education.

Let us look at the evidence.

Primary Reading Retardation in Adults

Traumatic Dyslexia

In Chapter 4 we described the Wada Amytal Test. It will be remembered that following injection to affect the left hemisphere, the patient for sev-eral minutes is unable to speak, to understand what is said to him or her, to read, or to write. The patient's understanding of nonverbal tasks is normal or near normal, but he or she is temporarily aphasic, *dyslexic,* and agraphic. In our study of dyslexia, we are primarily concerned with this patient's temporary inability to read because of the chemical effects on the left-hemispheric cortical centers essential to reading. As fresh blood replaces the drugged supply, the patient's normal ability to read returns after a few minutes. Thousands of amytal tests have been carried out in most parts of the world since 1948, when this technique was first devel-oped by Dr. Juhn Wada in Japan. The response to this procedure is highly reliable for predicting the side of speech dominance. It is evident that when the cortical "reading centers" are rendered powerless by controlled chemical means, reading is temporarily impossible, although visual recog-nition of nonverbal stimuli is usually normal and intact. However, al-though this clinical experiment tells us that there is a reliable causal relationship between the normal functioning of the language-dominant hemisphere and the ability to read, it does not tell us *what parts* of the hemisphere are vital.

To discover this we can go to another type of clinical study, the study of localized lesions. One of the best of these is the impressive report of Russell and Espir (1961) in England in which they examined the medical reports of almost 1200 men suffering brain wounds during World War II. Most of these men were injured during the invasion of Normandy in 1944, and they reached hospital in Oxford a few days after being wounded. The brain wounds were mostly caused by small fragments of metal from shrapnel or high-explosive shells so that they usually produced highly localized lesions. Russell and Espir developed a system for recording the site of the lesion or wounds. A tracing was made of the lateral view of the skull, and X-ray information was transferred to this outline drawing. They then composed a cumulative tracing of all those men suffering aphasia and those free of it. The two tracings were basically complementary to one another, the one being the negative of the other. The aphasics suffered injuries to Broca's area, the inferior part of the left motor strip, the related parts of the sensory strip (controlling the speech muscles and right hand), the left angular gyrus, and Wernicke's area. Left-hemisphere wounds not causing aphasia were outside the speech areas, in the prefrontal cortex, lining the longitudinal fissure, and in various scattered loci. Of the aphasic subjects, and these made up about one-third of the total sample, we are particularly interested in those in whom reading ability was impaired. In their Chapter XIII on alexia, Russell and Espir report seven cases with graphic information regarding the brain damage on the lateral brain tracing outline. Six of these showed lesions in the left parietal cortex near to or involving the angular gyrus and one with left anterior parietal damage. It is interesting that this last case, several years after his injury, regained his ability to speak and he could read accurately, although slowly. From the tracing of this man it appeared the angular gyrus was spared.

Another source of evidence comes from the work of Norman Geschwind in Boston. He has written at some length on the anatomical basis of language and has pointed out that the angular gyrus and the supramarginal gyrus do not appear in subprimate species. They appear only in rudimentary form in the higher apes (Geschwind, 1965). In neural development these areas are among the last to myelinate, and some evidence exists to show that this region matures structurally very late, often in late childhood. Geschwind believes, from this neurological knowledge, that the angular gyrus is in evolutionary terms a new association area interconnecting other cortical regions. Put more simply, it seems to function as a "junction box" interconnecting the visual, auditory, motor, and sensory cortices. As explained in Chapter 3, this transcortical interconnecting center appears only in humans and provides an integrating neurological basis for language. "Early language experience, at least, most likely depends heavily on the forming of somesthetic-auditory and visual-auditory associations, as well as auditory-auditory associations" (Geschwind, 1965). This means that the acquisition of speech requires an ability to form cross-modal associations, and because only humans possess these transcortical connections, inner language develops in subhuman forms, but not speaking, reading, or writing as do in humans.

A. R. Luria, the famous Russian neuropsychologist, has made a monumental contribution to the study of language development using neuropsychological knowledge. His first major work to be translated into English, *Higher Cortical Functions in Man,* was published in 1966, and since that time several of his translated books have appeared. In Chapter 3 we have presented his ideas on the functional organization of the human brain, but here we shall concentrate on his conception of dyslexia.

In reading Luria one is immediately impressed with the depth and breadth of his thinking. He gives an integrated concept of reading, writing, and language and objects to those classical neurologists who discussed these matters as entirely separate processes. For Luria, reading and writing are special aspects of speech activity, although their "psychological structure and functional characteristic . . . are considerably different from those of oral speech" (Luria, 1970). When there is a disturbance in language functions (i.e., aphasia) there are also disturbances of reading and writing, and Luria considers these the most common symptoms of traumatic aphasia.

In analyzing speech and reading, Luria points out that in oral speech a person usually speaks spontaneously and unself-consciously, whereas in reading, he must be able to carry out a conscious auditory analysis of syllables from the written or printed page. In reading, the letters representing the sounds of words are supplied directly to the reader, who must translate them into a correct acoustic pattern or word. The reader then recognizes the sound of the word and associates its meaning. This is what Luria (1970) calls "acoustic analysis and synthesis," and this process is disturbed and impaired with lesions in the left temporal lobe or Wernicke's area (Luria, 1970, 1973).

Phonetic analysis and synthesis of words are only the first stages in reading. The first grader may sound out "c—a—t" and then synthesize or blend the three sounds into the monosyllable "cat," but as these processes become automatized, the child soon learns to recognize whole words as visual ideograms. The experienced reader recognizes words from the general contour of the word or from its major letters. As well, the context of meaning in the sentence may facilitate the recognition of the word. Only when the reader encounters a new or difficult word does he need to revert to phonetic analysis and synthesis, otherwise familiar words are read by direct recognition.

Luria's examination of the dyslexic patient is based on this systematic analysis of the psychological structure and function of the reading process (1970, p. 349):

1. Recognition of individual letters. The subject is asked (a) to choose identical letters in a list and (b) to read letters aloud from both written and printed pages. Failure on task (a) indicates a disturbance of the visual perception of single letters (i.e., literal alexia), but the person may have no trouble recognizing common objects, only letters. This inability to perceive written or printed symbols results from lesions in

the parieto-occipital zones of the dominant left hemisphere (Luria, 1973). Failure on task (b) may result from either an impaired visual recognition of the letter as in (a) and/or an auditory imperception leading to an impaired ability to associate the appropriate phonetic sound.

2. Reading simple and complex syllables. The patient is asked to read syllables varying in phonetic complexity, e.g., "ba, mo," and "bat, mit," and "bake, mote." This test will show whether the subject can pronounce the syllable as a whole or has to spell it out letter by letter.

3. Reading simple and complex words. Three simple tests are used with single words: (a) the recognition of familiar words, such as the subject's own name; (b) silent reading of less familiar words, some of which will require phonetic analysis; (c) reading aloud words requiring phonetic analysis. Failure on (a) may indicate a failure to recognize words regardless of their familiarity (verbal alexia). This may result from disturbed visual form recognition or, if the recognition of letters is intact, the subject may be unable to remember their meaning (literal amnesia).

4. Reading sentences. Sentences are provided with various structures, some deliberately designed to provide a set or context to assist the interpretation of the word. Other sentences lack such a facilitating set, and this enables an understanding of the various strategies the reader employs.

Lesions of the primary and secondary visual cortices result in visual alexia, both literal and verbal. Such lesions may also result in a reduction of the "reading field" (Luria, 1970); that is, the patient may be unable to perceive more than two or three letters at a time. This seems to be a lack of simultaneous organization of visual material, and to overcome this defect the patient may recite the letters one by one, then recognize their auditory pattern and identify the word. In other words, he carries out the process of word synthesis not in the visual mode but in the auditory mode. It will be noted that although Mrs. Stanley, described in the following section, Alexia Without Agraphia, suffered an almost complete loss of single letter recognition; she could recognize the same words instantly if they were spelled orally to her. Although her visual word recognition and synthesis was almost completely lacking, her auditory word synthesis was intact. This is the characteristic pattern of the "Déjerine syndrome" as will be explained in the later section. Visual–perceptual disturbances in reading, or optic alexia, always result from lesions of the occipital and occipito-parietal cortices, or what Luria calls "the visuo-gnostic systems" (Luria, 1970).

Different types of reading problems result from disturbances of the speech processes, especially the auditory analysis and synthesis of words. Traumatic temporal lobe lesions in children may be more devastating than in adults because children have not had as much time to automatize the reading process. Since there is a disruption of the acoustico-gnostic systems, the patient is not able to resort to phonetic analysis to interpret the word. The adult who has had more time to perfect the process of direct visual recognition has a greater repertoire of sight words and hence is less disturbed by traumatic temporal lobe damage. This means that the child with a dysfunctioning left temporal lobe will have to learn to read by a visual–motor method. This by-passes the acoustic features of the word, and while this approach is ultimately slower than a phonetic method, it provides some immediate success for the child.

Auditory analysis, as well as aiding in the identification of letters, syllables, and words, also provides an ability of *inner articulation* (Luria, 1970). If one is asked to pronounce the word "sister" covertly, that is with the mouth closed and no lip movement, the awareness of each letter and phoneme is introspectively muscularly clear. This process occurs in normal hearing subjects during silent reading. However, a person with *afferent motor aphasia* (i.e., lacking normal sensations of muscle activity) who has lost the inner articulatory ability, will have difficulty with both reading and writing. Such a person will misread and confuse letters because he or she has lost their phonetic meanings. This person will resort to a lot of guessing in order to be able to recognize some letters or parts of most words by visual recognition but will not have the advantage of phonetic analysis to establish their correct identities. Luria believes that afferent motor aphasia results from a lesion in the left sensory strip, affecting the kinesthetic sensations in the face, lips, and tongue (Luria, 1973) and that sensory aphasia or acoustic agnosia (phonetic auditory imperception) results from lesions of the secondary areas of the left temporal lobe, i.e., Wernicke's area.

Efferent or *kinetic motor aphasia* has a different psychological and neurological structure and function from afferent motor aphasia. It has two types, both of which result from lesions in the left (dominant) motor strip or pre-Rolandic area. The first involves lesions in the inferior zones of the premotor strip (i.e., the cortical motor centers for the face and speech muscles). In contrast to afferent (kinesthetic) aphasia, patients with lower motor strip lesions have no trouble in inner articulation of single letters, and they can pronounce individual sounds but cannot blend sounds smoothly into words. Consequently their speech is blocked and grotesque. Although this type of aphasia interferes mainly with expressive language, both oral speech and writing, it may also impair reading.

Premotor lesions also interfere with smooth, integrated sequential motor responses and, if deep at the subcortical level, may result in an inability to inhibit sequential motor actions, such as tapping. This latter phenomenon is known as elementary motor perseveration (Luria, 1973).

In summary, Luria's concept of dyslexia makes a detailed psychological analysis of the structure of language and the integration of visual, auditory, tactile, and motor sensations involved in the complex process of reading. He relates systematically the various loci of lesions producing the numerous defects that contribute to an inability to read normally. All of his evidence is drawn from careful clinical studies of traumatically brain-damaged adults.

Electrostimulation mapping of the human cortex during craniotomies under local anesthesia has led Ojemann to conclude that cortical organization for some language functions (e.g., naming or word-finding) has a mosaic pattern. He has found that "when a response has been reliably evoked, the transition from the site where that response occurs to one where it does not occur is often quite abrupt, appearing over a distance of a few millimeters" (Ojemann, 1983, p. 136). Naming, short-term verbal memory, and reading usually have separate stimulation sites outside of Broca's area "where all speech output and all types of facial mimicry are altered" (p. 139). Outside of the motor speech area, he found syntactical errors in reading resulted from stimulation of the peri-Sylvian region and certain spots on the lateral surface of the left temporal lobe. These findings have corroborated the involvement of the classical language areas of the brain but have added more definitive information. Electrical stimulation mapping has provided evidence suggesting that language is mediated in the dominant hemisphere of both the cortex and the thalamus. The peri-Sylvian region appears to be a control center for speech and reading, short-term verbal memory, phonetic discrimination, and sequential motor responses. All of these processes are essential to successful reading, and dysfunctions at any of the sites mentioned can be presumed to produce dyslexic symptoms.

Having now looked at evidence of neurological causes of reading disability from Wada (Canada), Russell and Espir (England), Geschwind (United States), Luria (Russia) and Ojemann (United States), let us look at some common classifications of dyslexia in adults following traumatic brain damage. Benson and Geschwind (1969) have described these syndromes in more clinical detail.

Hemialexia. While hemialexia is a somewhat rare type of reading disability, I include it because it is a powerful reminder of the close causal relationship between specific types of brain function and successful reading ability. Geschwind (1965) has written very clearly and convincingly on this syndrome. To understand it clearly one must be reminded of the primary visual tracts, which connect to the language decoding areas of the left hemisphere. The two eyes connect to the two occipital lobes, and the neural impulses stimulated by printing or writing are then shunted to the left angular gyrus and then to the left temporal lobe (Wernicke's area) for verbal interpretation (see Fig. 8.7). The right occipital lobe, which registers visual sensations from the left visual field, is connected to the left angular gyrus by a band of fibers that passes through the posterior part

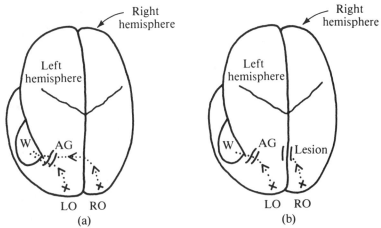

Figure 8.7. Two views of the human brain showing slightly more of the left hemisphere, including the left temporal lobe and Wernicke's area (W). **(a)** Normal cerebral function during reading. The visual stimulus (written or printed letter X) in the right visual field is registered in the left occipital lobe (LO), and the X from the left visual field, in the right occipital lobe (RO). Both occipital areas feed into the left temporal lobe through the area of the angular gyrus (AG) for phonetic analysis. **(b)** A lesion in the splenium (posterior part of the corpus callosum) that blocks passage of neural input from the right occipital lobe (RO). Only input from LO (hence stimuli from the right visual field) is processed. This is the phenomenon of hemialexia, or the ability to read material only when it is shown in the right visual field.

of the corpus callosum. This posterior part of the corpus callosum is called the splenium.

The first reported case of the cutting of the splenium during brain surgery was made by Trescher and Ford in 1937 (Benson & Geschwind, 1969), and it was discovered that the patient postoperatively suffered from a permanent unilateral reading disturbance. He was unable to read anything placed in his left visual field, but reading was normal for printed material placed to the right of his midline. However, it was particularly interesting to note that vision for nonverbal stimuli was normal in *both* full visual fields. The authors concluded that the right occipital lobe was isolated from the left angular gyrus by their cutting of the splenium, thus obstructing the verbal–visual input from that visual cortex. Because the connection of the left occipital lobe to the left angular gyrus was intact, all printed stimuli reaching it from the right visual field were decoded normally. A large number of similar cases in which the splenium has been cut or destroyed by a pathological condition (Maspes, 1948; Gazzaniga, Bogen, & Sperry, 1965) have since been reported, and they provide evidence to support the left visual field reading problem in hemialexia.

However, while destruction of the splenium in an adult patient will produce hemialexia, failure of the corpus callosum to develop from birth does not. Several patients with congenital callosal agenesis have been studied and found to react differently than comissurotomized adult patients. Two siblings (aged 9 and 18 years) with total agenesis of the corpus callosum were studied (Sauerwein & Lassonde, 1983) and found to be able to recognize both letters and geometric designs tachistoscopically and to compare them when presented simultaneously in one visual half-field and in both. This type of presentation required the subjects to process both verbal and nonverbal material intrahemispherically and interhemispherically. Sauerwein and Lassonde found that their acallosal subjects did not differ substantially from normal-IQ and IQ-matched controls, although they tended to respond more slowly. The ability of the subjects to react to bilaterally presented stimuli demonstrated their ability to cross-integrate visual information. To account for this the researchers proposed residual secondary commissures located lower in the brain stem, and/or cerebral reorganization in terms of abnormal hemispheric specialization. Regardless of the exact cause, this does demonstrate the marked difference in the results of traumatic damage in normal adulthood and fetal damage or agenesis. As is well known, early brain injury is less damaging than later because of the plasticity and adaptability of the developing human brain.

Alexia without Agraphia: The Subject Cannot Read but Can Still Write. One of the most interesting cases of acquired reading disability in an adult is the "Déjerine syndrome" known by neurologists since 1892 but generally unknown by most teachers and psychologists. Geschwind (1962) has presented a detailed explanation and discussion of Déjerine's famous case along with a number of very interesting line drawings reproduced from the original report. This is the classic case of *pure word blindness without agraphia,* and all school psychologists not familiar with the syndrome could profit from reading Geschwind's account. To see one of these patients is very compelling and quickly lays to rest the delusion that all reading problems are psychogenically produced.

Very briefly, Déjerine's case described an intelligent man of 68 years who suddenly discovered he could not read a single letter. He was sent for ophthalmological examination but his eyesight was within the normal range. He spoke fluently and understood all spoken speech normally. He could name objects perfectly (i.e., there was no word-finding difficulty) and he could identify his morning newspaper but he could not read anything in it, even its name.

His writing was perfect, both to copy and to dictation, but once he had written, he was unable to read what he had just written. Whereas he could not decode writing or print visually, he could identify and recognize letters both tactually and auditorially. If his fingers felt the letters of a tactile alphabet, or if a word was spelled orally to him, the patient had no difficulty in decoding the words presented. Although he could not read letters visually, he had no problem with Arabic numerals or complex written calculations. He could not read musical notation but could write musical notes to command. His ability to sing and play instruments was normal. From the time of the cerebrovascular accident that had caused his sudden dyslexia, he suffered from a right hemianopia. This, of course, implied a left hemisphere dysfunction, which was to be expected as a language function was impaired.

About 4 years later he suffered a second cerebrovascular accident (stroke) which left him with paraphasic speech and a sudden loss of his ability to write. He died 10 days later and Déjerine performed an autopsy within 24 hours of his death.

Two major lesions were found in the brain, the 4-year-old lesion and the recent one. It was possible to discriminate these by their different discolorations and the presence of atrophied tissue in the older lesion. Examination of the brain enabled Déjerine to conclude that the presence of alexia with the ability to write was caused by localized damage of the left occipital lobe and the splenium, with sparing of the left angular gyrus (see Fig. 8.8). This meant that no visual–verbal input could reach the angular gyrus because the left occipital lobe was destroyed and the right occipital lobe, although normal and healthy, was isolated from it (Geschwind, 1962, 1965; Benson & Geschwind, 1969). At the same time, the left temporal acoustic analyzer (Wernicke's area) was still normally connected to the sensory and motor strips, so the man had no difficulty interpreting words by the tactile and auditory modes, nor in expressing

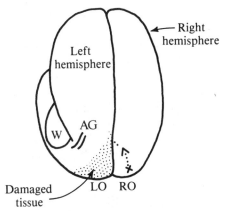

Figure 8.8. View of the human brain from above, showing the area of damage resulting from a hemorrhage of the left posterior cerebral artery. The primary visual cortex of the left occipital lobe and the splenium are damaged, thus destroying visual input from the left occiput (LO) and blocking input from the right side (RO). This is the basic neurological pattern of the Déjerine syndrome, in which a person is unable to read but can still write and interpret spelling words through auditory and tactual presentation.

them in speech and writing. In other words, the oral speech and writing cortical circuits were still intact.

The second hemorrhage 10 days prior to his death damaged the angular gyrus, thus disconnecting Wernicke's area from the sensory and motor strips. This appeared to cause the aphasic speech and his inability to write.

Mrs. Stanley, aged 66, seen in our laboratory, exhibited the classic signs of the Déjerine syndrome. On a visit from her home in London, England, she suddenly suffered a cerebral hemorrhage, presumably of the left posterior artery. Although a highly intelligent woman, she suddenly discovered she could not read, but she could write normally. In fact, she wrote long letters to her friends in England that were perfectly spelled, but she was unable to proofread or reread them. She could recognize letters moderately well if her hand traced them in the air or on the page, and she was quick and accurate to identify all words spelled orally to her.

To test the possibility of her regaining her ability to read, she was seen twice a week for 2 hours each for remedial teaching, for a 4-month period. She was highly motivated and she tried very hard but she still could not read any words. Toward the end of the 4-month period she learned to read five or six letters sometimes but her performance was erratic and unreliable.

I asked her to write "London," which she printed in a large, firm style. She could point to each letter and identify it if she spelled the word orally, but if I started her on the second letter without her noticing, she identified the letters quite wrongly and was surprised to find she ran out of letters one from the end. In other words, her oral spelling, both receptive and expressive, was quite intact because, presumably, the left angular gyrus was spared, but her optic dyslexia was permanent. It is possible to speculate on the cause of this and similar cases because of the large number that have come to autopsy examination since 1892.

Alexia with Agraphia: The Subject Cannot Read or Write. Although the previous syndrome, alexia *without* agraphia, is not common, alexia *with* agraphia is frequent in left-hemisphere stroke cases. Structurally the difference in the two syndromes stems from the sparing of the angular gyrus in the first instance and the destruction of it in the second. Déjerine discovered this in 1892 at the autopsy study of his famous case. The hemorrhage that occurred 10 days before the man's death destroyed his angular gyrus and as a result the writing circuit was erased. Put another way, the Wernicke's area was disconnected from the manual writing area in the left motor strip.

This deficit has been observed numerous times since Déjerine's report, and all cases that have come to postmortem have shown damage or destruction of the angular gyrus, with accompanying alexia and agraphia. There is frequently a mild receptive aphasia, because damage to the angular gyrus can sometimes affect Wernicke's area, which is nearby. Mrs. Stanley had mild word-finding problems that she found frustrating, and even picture identification and naming was slow.

Aphasic Alexia. Patients suffering from a severe receptive (Wernicke's) aphasia will have great difficulty understanding the conceptual words spoken by others. Similarly they will have difficulty bringing meaning to the printed word. Motor (or Broca's) aphasia may interfere with the ability to produce inner articulation. While the perceptual and cognitive aspects of reading may not be impaired, the expressive functions in normal reading are lacking or distorted.

Just as the aphasic patient produces paraphasias in his speech (i.e., he substitutes the wrong word for the desired word, e.g., "table" for "chair"; or a neologism or fabricated nonsense word in place of the desired word), some dyslexics when reading aloud may misread a word and substitute a different one for it (paralexic error). The important point to note in both paraphasias and paralexias is that they possess a *semantic relationship* with the desired word (e.g., "chair" for "table", or 6 for 8), or they have a rhyming and semantic association. The aphasic patient who recognized a key but could not name it, said, "Kay, . . . it's dorent [probably a contraction of "door" and "not"]. I'm in the floor [floor rhymes with door, which semantically is related to the desired word, key]. It's all away" (the subject knows all the words are wrong).

Paralexias have been known since 1928 (Marshall & Newcombe, 1980), but a systematic study of them has only existed since the mid-1960s, and a name for this syndrome, *deep dyslexia,* was originated in the early 1970s. The patient with deep dyslexia is an adult who, after acquiring reading skills, suffers traumatic damage to the language dominant hemisphere, and manifests semantic errors while reading aloud (e.g., "act" is read as "play"), derivational errors (e.g., birth → born), visual errors (e.g., saucer → sausage), misreading functional words (i.e., articles, prepositions, conjunctions; e.g., his → she, or for → and), and inability to read nonwords (e.g., wep → wet). Deep dyslexics read concrete and high-imagery nouns best, then adjectives, then verbs, and function words the poorest. They often complain that "the small words are the worst" (Marshall & Newcombe, 1980).

Attempts to provide a neuropsychological theory for deep dyslexia have included drawing on our knowledge of right-hemisphere reading. Coltheart, Patterson, and Marshall (1980) have proposed a model that includes integrated hemispheric specialization. They summarize it thus: "When the deep dyslexic is asked to read a word aloud, then his problem . . . is this: orthographic input to a right hemisphere linguistic system is possible, but speech output is not; speech output from a left hemisphere linguistic system is possible but orthographic input is not. If so, the task of reading aloud will require (a) orthographic input to a right-hemisphere reading system, followed by (b) transfer from the right hemisphere to the left of information which can be used (c) to select from amongst the phonological forms of words stored in the left hemisphere that form which corresponds to the word being looked at" (p. 352).

This theoretical proposal has much to recommend it. Some split-brain experiments have shown that the separated right hemisphere is superior to the left in reading calligraphy and numbers (E. Zaidel, 1973) and it is unable to speak. Bliss Symbolics, a form of picture writing, can frequently help a severely cerebral palsied child with maximal damage in the left hemisphere to learn to read and write using the Bliss symbols. Presumably this makes use of the better right hemisphere and avoids the damaged left one.

Some, but not all, aphasics may produce paralexias during oral reading. To investigate this phenomenon Landis, Regard, Graves, and Goodglass (1983) studied 20 male aphasic patients with left-sided lesions resulting from unilateral vascular disease. The size of lesion in each case was examined by CT scan. About half the sample produced paralexias; the average lesion size of the paralexic group was almost triple that of the nonparalexic group. Most of those patients without paralexias had lesions maximally in the frontal areas, and the two paralexics with the smallest lesions had them in the angular gyrus area. These researchers concluded: "This suggests that semantic paralexias and right hemisphere reading can appear following smaller lesions in specific anatomical sites. Large lesions would, of course, be likely to include such sites" (Landis, Regard, Graves, & Goodglass, 1983).

For a full discussion of deep dyslexia and paralexic errors in reading, the reader should consult Coltheart, Patterson, and Marshall (1980).

Developmental Dyslexia

An unknown segment of the adult population is unable to read, or they read so minimally that they hide it as a personal disgrace or sign of inadequacy. These people are of average or superior intelligence level so that their disability is even more mystifying and humiliating to them. Some of them have successful careers in business, athletics, or construction work; and they are on constant guard to keep their secret, because reading is so commonplace in modern Western society that they know many people would consider them stupid if their disability were known.

The evidence regarding acquired dyslexia from traumatically brain damaged adults that began in the early 1890s with Déjerine's autopsy studies, while interesting and definitive, cannot be used to explain the disability of all congenital nonreaders. However, when the first such case was reported by Morgan in England in 1896, he used Déjerine's evidence to hypothesize that a 14-year-old boy who was academically bright but had great difficulty in learning to read and write probably suffered from an underdeveloped angular gyrus. This was a logical association, to reason from a known cause of reading disability to an unknown, and it is still a temptation for the neurologist or neuropsychologist who has worked with any one of the types of traumatic dyslexics included in the preceding discussion. But most cases of developmental dyslexia, subjected to a standard neurological examination, show no signs of neurological pathology, and many of these subjects possess unusual talents in other areas. These are the children who may be gifted artists, superior mathematicians, or charismatic social leaders. As adults many of them have become successful business people, artists, or scientists. The fact that Albert Einstein was said to be dyslexic is well known. According to "the family legend when Hermann Einstein asked his son's headmaster what profession his son should adopt, the answer was simply: 'It doesn't matter; he'll never make a success of anything'" (Clark, 1971).

It soon became evident in the early part of this century that among the population of dyslexics there were too many with superior intellects and special talents, and many more with normal levels of intelligence, to accept an etiology of brain damage or cerebral atrophy for all of them. This led to a search for some type of brain dysfunction without identifiable brain damage that might interfere with the complex neuropsychological processes demanded by reading.

The first influential proposal was that of Orton (1925, 1926, 1937) who suggested that incomplete cerebral dominance may be the major cause of developmental reading retardation. Since Orton's proposal, many researchers have also described dyslexia as having a single cause, though these causes varied from brain dysfunctions, to genetic, to linguistic origins (see Table 8.1). This group of theorists viewed dyslexia as a unitary syndrome, being generated by one class or group of determinants.

By the 1960s dualistic theories began to appear (see Table 8.2) and since about 1970 most of the multicausal theories have been produced (see Tables 8.3, 8.4, and 8.5). As Malatesha and Dougan (1982) have indicated, "One major controversy in the field involves the question of the nature of dyslexia—whether it is a unitary phenomenon or represents a group of disorders" (p. 70).

While reading as a neuropsychological process is only partially understood, and hence a conclusive theory is not yet possible, there is a great mass of clinical evidence to suggest several subtypes that stress different cerebral structures and hence possess different patterns of psychological processes. This evidence suggests that any view of dyslexia describing it as a unitary syndrome is highly suspect. Benton and others have advised against "perseverating in the present strategy, which assumes that all dyslexic children suffer from the same basic deficiency" (Benton, 1975, p. 39).

Since the late 1970s much new knowledge relating reading to brain

Table 8.1   Etiological Factors Used in Viewing Dyslexia as a Unitary Syndrome

I. Cerebral dominance hypothesis
   1. Orton (1937)
II. Maturational lag of cerebral organiza-
   tion
   1. Bender (1958)
   2. Delacato (1959)
   3. Smith & Carrigan (1959)
III. Perceptual–motor deficiency
   1. Drew (1956)
   2. Kephart (1960)
   3. Cruikshank (1968)
   4. Frostig & Maslow (1973)
	IV. Genetic trait
	   1. Hermann (1959)
	V. Language deficiency
	   1. Vellutino (1979)
	VI. Deficits of the parietal re-
	   gion
	   1. Jorm (1979a)

(From Malatesha and Dougan, 1982, with permission of the authors and Academic Press, Inc.)

function and dysfunction has come from experiments in cerebral blood flow, brain scanning, cortical electrostimulation, histological studies, and correlational studies in biopsychology. The first three techniques have already received brief explanations; their findings suggest that dysfunctions in any part of the cerebral cortex (particularly on the left), and anywhere in the brain stem (particularly in the thalamus and cerebellum) may result in impaired reading.

Autopsy studies of the brains of dyslexics have only recently appeared (Drake, 1968; Galaburda & Kemper, 1979; Galaburda, 1983). These histological examinations have revealed abnormal neural tissue growth. Drake reported excessive numbers of neurons in the subcortical white matter, which is abnormal. Galaburda and Kemper (1979) studied the brain of a 20-year-old left-handed male dyslexic and found an abnormal amount of white matter in the whole left hemisphere and evidence of disordered neuronal migration in the left peri-Sylvian area.

The brain of a 14-year-old dyslexic (Galaburda, 1983) also showed abnormal growth. Collections of neurons were found in layer one of the cortex, and in the subcortical white matter of the left hemisphere, a condition not seen in normal brains. By contrast, the right hemisphere appeared architectonically normal and mature. Galaburda's findings suggest that the brains of developmental dyslexics may have acquired anomalous lateralization, and that their left hemispheres contain structural distortions.

Geschwind (1983) has reported an interesting association of food allergies, immune disorders, left handedness, and childhood migraine among developmental dyslexic children (mostly males) and their families. The biological aspects he related to brain development by proposing the following hypothesis: It is known from fetal studies that the right hemisphere tends to grow faster than the left, but in dyslexics there appears to be a slowed migration of neural cells to the language areas of the left hemisphere. This slowing of the left may produce compensatory growth of the right hemisphere, thus resulting in left handedness and superior spatial and artistic skills.

During intrauterine life the male fetus produces huge quantities of testosterone, a male sex hormone, and Geschwind suggests that this may retard the growth of the left hemisphere in males. He points out that his hypothesis possesses some empirical support in animal studies, in which testosterone injected into rats and birds has shown resulting brain changes. Excessive testosterone may also result in impaired migration of cerebral nerve cells, and in disturbances of the immune system. While this theory is far from complete it does point to a possible relation among biochemical processes, neural brain growth, and developmental dyslexia.

Mr. Darwin. Mr. Darwin was referred to our laboratory at the age of 32. He was a fine looking man with an engaging manner, successful in managing his own logging business. The only word he could read and write was his own name, because he needed to sign checks in the management of his business, and he could recognize and name about 12 individual letters.

Table 8.2 Postulated Dyslexic Classification: Two Subtypes

I. *Visual and auditory types*
  1. Johnson & Myklebust (1967)
    a. Visual dyslexia
    b. Auditory dyslexia
  2. Bakker (1979); Pirozzolo (1979)
    a. Visual–spatial group
    b. Auditory–linguistic group
  3. Kinsbourne & Warrington (1963)
  a. Language retardation group
  b. Gerstmann's group dyslexia

II. *Other types*
  1. Zangwill (1962)
    a. Dyslexia in normal hemispheric specialization
    b. Dyslexia in incomplete hemispheric specialization
  2. Prechtl (1962)
    a. Specific brain lesions
    b. Nonspecific brain lesions
  3. Rabinovitch (1968)
    a. Primary reading retardation
    b. Secondary reading retardation
  4. Bannatyne (1971)
    a. Genetic
    b. Minimal neurological dysfunction

(From Malatesha and Dougan, 1982, with permission of the authors and Academic Press, Inc.)

He had attended a small rural school during the 1940s and because he could not read he was left to look at picture books while the other children completed their academic exercises. He could read arabic numbers and was able to do simple arithmetical calculations at about the Grade 5 level, and this had enabled him to manage a small logging business, hire skilled help, do his own bookkeeping, solicit business, and direct the whole operation. In 1966, when we first saw him, his business management was so successful that he earned half again as much that year as the local high school teachers at the top of the salary scale (i.e., with an MA degree and at least 10 years experience). This was particularly impressive because he could not read "cat."

Being a gregarious fellow he mixed socially a good deal, and this necessitated the development of a number of social coverup strategies .When he was in a restaurant with a number of people he would pick up a menu and pretend to read it for a few moments and then pass it to one of the others. When the waitress came to take their orders he would listen to what the others requested and either pick the most appealing order from what he heard or order a standard dish that was certain to be available. Since he could read numbers he was able to read price lists, which was of some help.

The neurologist who referred Mr. Darwin originally reported that although he complained of frequent headaches, his neurological examina-

Table 8.3 Postulated Dyslexic Classification: Three Subtypes

I. *Clinical observation and study*	b. Slow reader
1. Bateman (1968)	c. Mixed type
a. Good visual memory but poor auditory memory	5. Ingram, Mason, & Blackburn (1970)
b. Good auditory memory but poor visual memory	a. Audiophonic
c. Mixed	b. Visuospatial
2. Smith (1970)	c. Mixed
a. Deficiency in sequencing ability	6. deQuiros & Shrager (1978)
b. Deficiency in simultaneous ability	a. Visual–perceptual handicap
c. Mixed	b. Visual–auditory handicap
3. Quadfasel & Goodglass (1968)	c. Vestibular and proprioceptive integration handicap
a. Symptomatic reading retardation	7. Birch (1962)
b. Specific reading disability	a. Visual–auditory integration impairment
c. Secondary reading retardation	b. Visual–kinesthetic integration impairment
4. Nicholls (1968)	c. Visual–tactual–kinesthetic integration impairment
a. Congenital or developmental dyslexia	

(Continued)

Table 8.3 *Continued*

II. *Neuropsychological profiles*
1. Mattis, Rapin, & French (1975)
   a. Language disorder
   b. Articulatory–graphomotor disorder
   c. Visual–perceptual disorder
2. Aaron & Baker (1982)
   a. Posterior dyslexia
   b. Anterior dyslexia
   c. Central dyslexia

III. *Factor-analytic studies*
1. Doehring & Hoshko (1977); Doehring, Hoshko, & Bryans (1979)
   a. Language deficit
   b. Phonological deficit
   c. Naming deficit
2. Petrauskas & Rourke (1979)
   a. Auditory–verbal memory deficiency
   b. Sequencing, finger localization deficiency
   c. Psychomotor skills impairment

IV. *Reading and spelling patterns*
1. Boder (1973); Boder & Jarrico (1982)
   a. Dysphonetic
   b. Dyseidetic
   c. Mixed dysphonetic–dyseidetic
2. Mann & Suiter (1978); Jordan (1977)
   a. Auditory deficiency
   b. Visual deficiency
   c. Manual deficiency

V. *Computerized brain scan*
1. Hier, Lemay, Rosenberger, & Perlo (1978)
   a. Left parieto-occipital region wider than right
   b. Right parieto-occipital region wider than left
   c. No difference between the left and the right regions

VI. *Alexia research*
1. Benson (1977); Albert (1979)
2. Marshall & Newcombe (1973)
   a. Visual dyslexia
   b. Surface dyslexia
   c. Deep dyslexia
3. Kremin (this volume)
   a. Pure alexia without agraphia
   b. Literal, deep and/or phonological alexia
   c. Surface dyslexia

(From Malatesha and Dougan, 1982, with permission of the authors and Academic Press, Inc.)

tion and EEG were both normal. His skull X-ray was completely normal. His neuropsychological test findings were also unremarkable. He measured a verbal IQ of 88 and a performance IQ of 106 on the Wechsler Adult Intelligence Scale. His general information was inferior and his vocabulary below average because of his dyslexia, but his diagnostic understanding of commonplace problems (Comprehension) was near superior. His visual, auditory, tactile, and motor scores were all in the normal range, so his pattern suggested a man of above-average intelligence with a specific reading disability. Because the neurological and neuropsychological examinations revealed no deficits, his reading failure may have been genetically determined or the result of a minimal and

Table 8.4 Postulated Dyslexic Classification: Four Subtypes

I. *Clinical observation*
   Mattis (1978)
   a. Language disorder
   b. Articulatory–graphomotor disorder
   c. Visual–perceptual disorder
   d. Sequencing disorder
II. *Genetics study*
   DeFries & Decker (this volume)
   a. Visual–spatial deficiency
   b. Short-term memory deficiency
   c. Reading disability without the above two deficiencies
   d. Mixed
III. *EEG study*
   Hughes (this volume)
   a. Positive spikes
   b. Excessive slow occipital waves
   c. Sharp waves or spike discharges
   d. Diffuse or generalized asymmetry

(From Malatesha and Dougan, 1982, with permission of the authors and Academic Press, Inc.)

subtle cortical dysfunction too minute to show on a standard neurological examination. The fact that his two sons were also poor readers, but his daughter was not, reinforced the possibility of a familial pattern in the male members.

Because the neurological and neuropsychological tests were negative we felt confident in recommending a multisensorimotor remediation program. This proved to be successful, because when he returned a year later he could read 200 words correctly and had learned good methods of phonetic attack, although he still occasionally confused the sound of "i" and "e." On the Gates–McKillop reading test he could read at the early Grade 3 level and his perception of visual and auditory sequential stimuli had improved markedly.

On his third visit to our laboratory, $2\frac{1}{2}$ years after we had first seen him, Mr. Darwin could read about 500 words and was reading the newspaper headlines and brief bits of news reports. Tachistoscopically he could read single letters at half a second and most common words from the Dolch lists (Dolch, 1945) at 1 second (e.g., dish, sister, brother, wife, pen). Within another year he was able to read at a fifth grade level and to write well enough to fill out a job application.

It seems almost certain that Mr. Darwin's reading problem resulted from some undetermined constitutional source (possibly a subtle neurological deficit or a genetic defect) because he was so refractory to normal teaching methods as a child and so had suffered educational neglect in the school system.

Table 8.5 Postulated Dyslexic Classification:
Five Subtypes

I. Keeney (1968)
   a. Specific developmental dyslexia
   b. Secondary dyslexia
   c. Slow reader or bradylexia
   d. Acquired dyslexia (alexia)
   e. Mixed
II. Denckla (1977)
   a. Global–mixed language disorder
   b. Articulatory–graphomotor disorder
   c. Visual–perceptual disorder
   d. Dysphonemic–sequencing disorder
   e. Verbal learning (memorization) deficiency

(From Malatesha and Dougan, 1982, with permission
of the authors and Academic Press, Inc.)

Reginald Simmons. Reginald Simmons was referred to us because of an inferior ability to read. This case is an interesting comparison with Mr. Darwin; whereas no abnormalities showed in either Mr. Darwin's neurological or his neuropsychological examination, in Mr. Simmons' case, the neurological exam was negative but very specific left-hemisphere signs showed on the neuropsychological exam. Both men were 32 years of age when first referred and both men were competent athletes. In fact Mr. Simmons was a professional hockey player.

On the neuropsychological test battery Mr. Simmons showed himself to be of average intelligence level but left handed and most likely left-hemisphere dominant for language (right ear preference, 26; left ear preference, 5). Figure 8.9 shows the significant findings in brief summary. His tactile form recognition (stereognosis), finger localization, and tapping speed were all poor with his right hand, although normal with his left. As well, his right–left orientation and sequencing abilities were poor. All of these signs point to possible minimal dysfunction in the medial part of the left hemisphere (particularly the left sensory and motor strips). Because nothing showed on the neurological tests, this lesion, if it exists, must be minimal and subtle but potent enough to make him use his left hand. The dichotic findings suggest that normally he should have been right handed.

Since his auditory perception was good, a modification of the Gillingham method was used in conjunction with a color-coding system. At the beginning of a remedial program (6 hours per week) he read at a grade-point level of 4.2 on the Gates–McKillop test, so he was not severely alexic to begin with, as Mr. Darwin was. After 3 months of special tutoring he measured at the grade 7.0 level. The presumed lesion would seem to have retarded his sequential skills with visual and auditory tasks and visual–motor abilities.

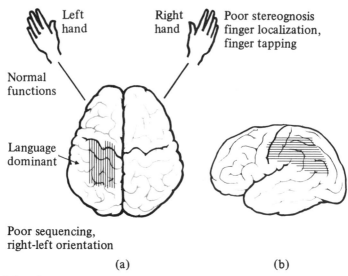

Figure 8.9. Case of Mr. Simmons showing neuropsychological signs of possible minimal left-hemisphere dysfunction: (a) top view of his brain with arms outstretched; (b) the left hemisphere with the inferred lesion shaded. (© 1984 William D. West)

Summary. These two cases of developmental dyslexia in adults provide some interesting clues to guide us. First, whereas the traumatically damaged adults had highly specific reading deficits that showed a close relation to the locus of damage and a reliability of prediction, the adults with developmental dyslexia as a group were highly variable both neurologically and behaviorally. This would seem to result, in the first case, from a normal nervous system being damaged after the cortical language centers had been locked in, whereas in the second case, the child during his or her development was using the functional areas of the brain and making the optimal compromise. Consequently, the child or adult with developmental dyslexia will need to be studied in great detail both neurologically and behaviorally, and a remedial program constructed making a maximum use of this knowledge. This is in basic agreement with Myklebust's (1971b) recommendation for the treatment of children with developmental aphasia.

Primary Reading Retardation in Children

Traumatic Dyslexia

Quadfasel and Goodglass (1968) have made the point that brain damage incurred between birth and about the age of 2 years (i.e., prior to the acquisition of established speech) and damage incurred after 2 years may have some unique differences. One would expect the first type to be similar to developmental dyslexia, and the second to be increasingly specific, the older the child at the time of injury. To examine this point three children are presented here who suffered brain injuries at the ages of 22 months, 3 years 9 months, and 6 years 9 months.

Max Pearson. This boy had been hit by a car while playing on a residential street in front of his home. He was 22 months old at the time of the accident. When he was picked up he was unconscious and blood was issuing from his left ear. He made a good recovery and was discharged from the hospital 10 days later.

His head injury left him with a squint in his left eye that was later medically corrected, and the neurologist found some minimal signs of left-hemisphere dysfunction ("He hopped less well on his right foot than on his left") and the EEG showed a generalized grade iii dysrhythmia.

We saw him first when he was 6 years old, and in the next 3 years we made the following Wechsler (WISC) measures:

Age (years)	Verbal IQ	Performance IQ
6–1	86	99
8–4	80	108
8–5	82	104 (Tested in another clinic)
8–11	72	96
Average	80	101.75

By themselves these findings were congruent with inferior left-hemisphere function. This conclusion was reinforced by a relatively inferior performance with the right hand on hand-grip strength, finger tapping speed, and stereognosis. In addition, his ability on sequential tasks (largely a left-hemisphere function) was also poor.

At age 6 his handedness was mixed even for writing, but by our last testing (age 8–11) he was writing consistently with his right hand and the dichotic test suggested that he was markedly left-hemisphere dominant for language but not strongly so (right ear preference, 18; left ear, 8). By this time he was in Grade 3 although he was beginning his fourth year of school. While mildly aphasic (he could not follow oral instructions except in small bits), he learned to read at a level that his teacher considered "average" for the class. His arithmetic was very weak because his abilities for abstraction were so poor. Socially, Max was well adjusted, he spoke well to adults, and he gave an impression of normal alertness, which would tend to obscure his "invisible disabilities." However, studies of his development suggest that as an adult he will most likely be employable, because of his cheery personality, in some type of unskilled work.

Considering the seriousness of Max's head injury, his brain had made a remarkable adjustment. He is minimally aphasic to oral instructions, has learned the mechanics of reading, but has weak comprehension. The early brain damage has impaired his competence in arithmetic much more. Although he can write numbers neatly, his very weak conceptual ability has impaired him seriously. Had an adult of average intelligence received this pattern of brain damage, he would almost certainly have become aphasic and alexic but retained most or all of his ability in simple arithmetical facts. Max's pattern is in the reverse direction, no doubt because of the bilateral functional reorganization following his brain injury.

Robbie Yates. This boy was struck by a car at the age of 3 years 9 months and sustained bilateral, diffuse brain damage, with greater injury in the left hemisphere. Because oral language is becoming pretty well established by this age, the average child having an active vocabulary of about 1400 words (M. E. Smith, 1926, adapted by Thompson, 1962), we can logically expect his language development to be impaired.

The neurological and neuropsychological evidence indicated bilateral damage resulting from a violent closed head injury. This type of injury reduces the possibilities of compensation by preventing the child from using healthy tissue, as is possible by a localized injury. At age 4 years 10 months his Stanford–Binet IQ measured 63, mainly because the tester had so much difficulty communicating with Robbie. He was quiet and extremely noncommunicative.

At age 7 years 11 months, when we first saw him, he was unable to read anything. The school put him on a multisensorimotor remedial program, purposely not stressing phonics, but including them, because his phonetic discrimination was not strong. By the time he was 11 years 5 months, he could read slowly and he was able to sound out and blend three- and four-letter words competently. Because of a mild receptive aphasia, it was necessary for the teacher to speak slowly, at a tempo Robbie could decode. Wechsler (WISC) measures at age 11 years 4 months showed a verbal IQ (VIQ) of 72 and a performance IQ (PIQ) of 94. Two months later he was tested again for medical–legal reasons and his WISC measures were VIQ, 75 and PIQ, 90. The permanent lesion in his left hemisphere, which by this time had existed for almost 8 years, was showing itself in a pattern of chronic verbal inferiority and relatively better, but not strong, spatial–constructional skills. His teachers, in a special school for brain-damaged and aphasic children, understood this and developed a remedial program and set of expectations Robbie could manage successfully. As a result, he made slow but steady academic progress and a healthy and normal social adjustment.

Vera Brown. This little girl was normally healthy and happy until she suddenly suffered a spontaneous cerebral hemorrhage at the age of 6 years 9 months. This occurred the day before she was to enter Grade 1, so that fortuitously this case provides a pattern of normal preschool health with all formal academic learning being impaired by the effects of left-hemisphere brain damage.

Vera was playing with some other children on the day of the subarachnoid hemorrhage, when she felt ill, was nauseated, and became unconscious. She was rushed to the hospital, where her skull was opened and a large hematoma was evacuated and the bleeding stopped. The bleeding originated in the inferior left parietal–occipital area, and until it was stopped it caused some permanent damage in the left temporal–parietal-occipital region.

One of the obvious sequelae of this damage was a right visual field defect, which, when Vera was learning to read, caused her to have to move her head a great deal, because her restricted visual field extended from the vertical midline to the normal left extremity. To make it easier for her in school we advised her teachers to seat her at the right side of the classroom.

Vera spent 6 weeks in a hospital recovering from the brain surgery and 2 weeks at home, and she was ready to enter first grade by early November. Although the other first graders had a 2-month start on Vera, she caught up enough to pass into Grade 2 the following June. Her mother, a primary school teacher, was unusually skillful and supportive in helping her learn. Even so, she had great difficulty in learning to read, and an analysis of her weaknesses showed that they included a below-average vocabulary (a mild anomia) and poor phonetic discrimination, although an audiometric test showed her hearing to be normal. As well, she had difficulties in visual sequencing, spatial imagery, visual–motor speed, and rhythmic sequential tapping.

Vera's mother reported that she was one of the most promising students at the end of kindergarten the previous year, but at the end of Grade 1 she slipped to an average level (see Table 8.6).

Table 8.6 Kindergarten and First Grade Achievement: Vera Brown

Name	Kindergarten (pretraumatic)	Name	Grade 1 (posttraumatic)
Vera	*High*	Richard	High
Richard	High	Susan	High average
Susan	High average	*Vera*	*Average*
Louise	Low average	Louise	Low
Gordon	Low average	Gordon	Low

Ten months after her brain injury we tested Vera for the first time and found a Wechsler (WISC) verbal IQ of 105, a performance IQ of 101, and difficulties in reading, writing, and all the language arts. Her mother's persistent and skilled help no doubt had a great deal to do with Vera's steady progress during the next few years.

The next year, about 22 months after her cerebrovascular accident, we found a WISC verbal IQ of 103 and performance IQ of 96. The drop in the performance IQ resulted mainly from an inferior score on the Picture Completion Subtest. Her hemianopia was making it difficult for her to scan pictures thoroughly and notice some small details. Reading was still a problem, but Vera was doing well enough that she was almost keeping up to the average of the class. With all her remedial help at home she rated "low average," which was a passing grade.

About 3 years went by before we saw her again. By this time she was beginning Grade 6, and her mother reported that during the previous summer she began to read spontaneously for her own pleasure. The intensive remedial work in the language arts during the past 5 years was beginning to pay off, because her vocabulary was now above average and her teacher reported that she wrote interesting stories with a competent choice of words. She did well in arithmetic and very well in art. In fact, she took private lessons in drawing because she showed a special artistic talent.

Vera's musical ability remained defective. Her mother reported that "she cannot carry a tune and her sense of rhythm never has returned."

Academically, Vera did moderately well in Grade 7, but in high school she had many difficulties because many of the high school teachers *did not believe she had a learning problem.* In Grade 10 she was able to keep up in the English course with tremendous effort, which usually meant 3 hours of homework each night.

At the end of Grade 10, Vera's mother wrote:

> Looking back, I feel sure, as a teacher, that we should not have put Vera into grade one immediately after recovering from her brain hemorrhage. Speaking as a primary teacher, we find children who have had a great deal of hospitalization before six years of age are really not ready for grade one. Also, we must remember how disoriented children with sudden brain damage are. They need time to adjust to their old world before embarking on a new venture.
>
> How many adults who have had a stroke would one recommend to start a new job one month later—especially one that requires a new set of values, and a lot of new language skills?
>
> Very has managed "to keep up to her grade level," whatever that means, but I feel she has done this at the loss of her social development. She feels she is dumb and has few close friends, but she has never been one of the crowd, any crowd.
>
> I would suggest to parents of children who have sudden brain damage

to be very careful of the school placement of their children when they return home from hospital. Doctors and most other professionals encourage you to think that these children are normal, but they are not, in the sense that they cannot cope immediately with their new life. They need help in the transition from their memory of their former life and the acceptance of their new impaired one. I don't mean that they should be treated as invalids, but only helped to recover from the shock, in the same way we allow adults.

Also, I want to suggest that some sort of help be available to the parents, perhaps through the Association of Children with Learning Disabilities. Everyone forgets what a shock it is for them. I think so much stress is placed on the medical aspects of the case the psychological ones are overlooked. Once the child is free of the hospital, everyone writes "finis" to the case. There is much emotional adjustment to be made by both parents and child, and some counseling would be welcome.

The frustrations of the brain-damaged child and his or her parents are usually obscured to society and are just as "invisible" as his disabilities. As a result, some teachers deny the existence of the so-called learning disability and frequently blame the parent for trying to manipulate the school. More will be said of the roles of the child, the parent, and the teacher in Chapter 10.

Developmental Dyslexia

In the past, the child with a congenital reading problem was usually referred for an ophthalmological examination. Because reading obviously requires visual functions it was believed that dyslexics must have some deficit in the structure or functions of their visual systems. In almost all cases the dyslexic is normal or superior in reading an eye chart. The ophthalmologist or optometrist with this evidence will report that the child's vision is normal, and this seeming contradiction has only added to the etiological mystery of dyslexia. However, as more became known about brain structure and function, a preference for a *central* or brain dysfunction to account for reading problems became established, and *peripheral* or visual deficits have come to be recognized as rarely associated with retarded reading.

One exception to this view has been expressed by Pavlidis (1979). His research indicated "that dyslexics' erratic eye movements are present not only during reading but also in other non-reading tasks such as trying to follow moving lights." However, other researchers have been unable to replicate Pavlidis' findings (Brown *et al.*, 1983). Pavlidis is still answering his critics (1983) so this issue is not clearly resolved. At this stage, in our knowledge it seems safe to recognize that many dyslexics do not show any peripheral dysfunctions and most cases appear to involve central causal factors.

Frequently, a child with a severe reading problem reveals no deficits on a neurological examination. If he or she possesses normal intelligence, is free of any sensory deficits and is well motivated, the only remaining cause appears to be a genetic one. Drew (1956), Hallgren (1950), Hermann (1959), and Sladen (1970) all have provided support for a genetic theory of dyslexia. A more recent report by a team of behavioral geneticists provides evidence that might link specific reading disability to chromosome 15 (S. D. Smith, Kimberling, Pennington, & Lubs, 1983). They found a lod score of 3.241 where a score of 3.0 is traditionally accepted as significant. A lod score is a measure of linkage between a specific behavior and a particular locus on a designated chromosome.

When no deficits show on a neurological or neuropsychological test, this does not necessarily mean the person is free of some slight but crucially located dysfunction, as was described in the case of Mr. Simmons. Prior to the neuropsychological findings, nothing had ever been found that might account for Mr. Simmons' dyslexia, so he was left to think he was stupid. Counseling, based on interpreting these findings, was basic in improving his own self-image.

Children brain injured prenatally, at birth, or up to about the age of 2 years constitute a subgroup of developmental dyslexics. Numerous studies have appeared for the past 70 years relating perinatal events as precursors of learning and reading disabilities. Balow, Rubin, and Rosen (1975–1976) have reviewed more than 30 of these studies and conclude that ''it is most probable that some neurologic function or functions mediate between perinatal factors and later reading ability.'' They point out wisely that abnormal perinatal conditions likely only have a long-term impairing effect to the extent that they have permanently damaged neurological functioning. This can explain why many premature babies or infants suffering anoxia at birth have no learning problems; presumably their perinatal discomfort was temporary enough not to result in a neurological insult.

When the injuries are severe and bilateral, as they were in the cases of Max and Robbie, the reading retardation is permanent and only partially responsive to therapeutic teaching. Probably most children with chronically severe reading difficulties have had early brain injury or some obscure genetic anomaly that interferes with normal reading. At present, the best diagnostic and remedial approach to the treatment of these children is to discover as much as one can about the child's perceptual, intellectual, motor, cross-modal, sequential, and sensorimotor skills. Ideally the school psychologist should be equipped to do this and to supply this detailed information to the teacher, who, in collaboration with the psychologist, develops a tentative remedial program. Such a program is always tentative, contingent on regular and ongoing evaluations of its effectiveness.

Secondary Reading Retardation

This category includes children of average or superior intelligence level; normal sensory, motor, and cognitive abilities; a normal and healthy central nervous system; and no genetic defects, but who are underachieving in reading and academic learning. When tests have removed the possibility of any seriously impeding organic causes, then the logical origin would seem to be psychological and environmental determinants. What are the family pattern, sibling relationships, parental attitudes, the subcultural view of reading (lazy, effeminate, second or third rate), and television viewing habits? The etiology of this type of reading retardation is primarily psychological and social, and skilled methods of behavior management coupled with proven methods of teaching reading usually are all that are needed to correct the problem.

Behavior modification techniques, of course, can also be successful with the child with brain damage and/or a specific reading disability, but a careful neuropsychological analysis is needed first to help in devising a prescription for teaching. This can help to provide a more effective learning climate for the child and reduce the chances of frustration by trying to reinforce a type of behavior that may be impossible or difficult for him.

Mrs. Semmes was referred to our laboratory because she was unable to read. An attractive young woman of 31, she was happily married with two young children but constantly frustrated by her problem. A neurological examination was completely normal, and neuropsychological study revealed average intelligence with no defects in perception, motor, sensorimotor integration, sequencing, or oral language.

The story of her childhood read like something out of Dickens. She was orphaned at the age of 5 years and placed in a residential school operated by a religious order of women. Finding her a bright and active child, they soon had her working all day, washing floors or windows or doing whatever had to be done. She was a strong girl and evidently considered more useful on the housecleaning staff than in school; and because she had no family to defend her rights she was never sent to class. This continued until she was 16 years old, when she ran away and married, to escape her unhappy life. This first marriage did not survive long, but by the time she was 22 she married Mr. Semmes, who provided a stable and happy marriage.

At the age of 31 she heard of the experimental program in our laboratory and sought help. She was put on a remedial program that employed visual, auditory, tactile, and motor association and reinforcement. Within a month she was able to read a large number of words on the Dolch lists and was excited by the fact she could now read street and traffic signs. By the end of 3 months she could read at a Grade 5 level and could spell about 200 words with a fairly strong level of assurance.

This case is the classic Cinderella story, and her dyslexia was purely the result of educational neglect. Our own studies, although covering short training periods so far, have shown that many non-brain-damaged adults, when strongly motivated, can be taught to read at a rate of 1 year's progress for each month of training. How permanent the results are will not be known without further training and evaluation.

Individual Studies of Dyslexia: What Do They Teach Us?

So far in this chapter we have examined individual cases of children and adults who have suffered unusual reading problems. The reader may find some of these cases interesting as case histories but still feel no closer to a confident diagnostic and remedial approach. To clarify a neuropsychological model of dyslexia, the following summary of neuropsychological signs is proposed.

A Neuropsychological Analysis of Dyslexia

The reading circuits in the brain are extremely complex, including specific centers usually in the left-hemispheric cortex with thalamic connections to other subcortical areas. There are most likely as many types of dyslexia as there are loci of cerebral lesions in this circuit and its contiguous brain tissue. Figure 8.10 is a simplified diagram showing the cortical areas of the left hemisphere that are strongly involved in mediating reading, spelling, and writing. Following are the various processes involved in reading, with their cerebral functional correlates.

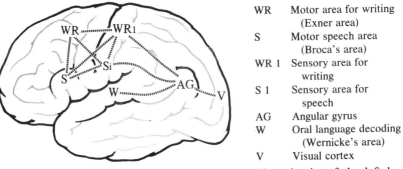

WR	Motor area for writing (Exner area)
S	Motor speech area (Broca's area)
WR 1	Sensory area for writing
S 1	Sensory area for speech
AG	Angular gyrus
W	Oral language decoding (Wernicke's area)
V	Visual cortex

Figure 8.10. Cortical reading, spelling, and writing circuits of the left hemisphere (simplified). (© 1984 William D. West) This is the classical view of the language centers in the cerebral cortex; it does not recognize the variability among human subjects (see discussion on page 257ff.). Therefore it cannot be accepted as valid for every case.

Visual Letter and Word Recognition. Lesions in the left occipital–parietal cortices and the splenium may produce a visual agnosia that results in literal dyslexia or an inability to recognize individual letters and associate their linguistic meanings (Benson and Geschwind, 1969; Geschwind, 1962; Luria, 1970, 1973). The term used for verbal dyslexia has been "word blindness" since before the turn of this century, but Orton (1937) correctly pointed out that the term "is somewhat misleading since the (alexic) individual . . . can still see the word but the grasp at sight of the meaning of the word is gone."

Visual Searching and Scanning. Visual searching and scanning, so essential to normal reading, can be impaired by lesions in the right parieto-occipital region (Karpov, Luria, & Yarbuss, 1968) and in the dorsolateral areas of the frontal lobes (Luria, 1973).

Figure–Ground Perception. Figure–ground perception, necessary for letter and word recognition, may be disrupted by cortical lesions anywhere in the cortex (Teuber & Weinstein, 1956) or in the frontal lobes, in particular (Luria, 1973). Although figure–ground perception of pictorial material has been known for a long time to be inferior in brain-damaged children and adults (Cruickshank, Bice, Wallen, & Lynch, 1957; Strauss & Lehtinen, 1947; Werner & Strauss, 1941), visual agnosia for letters while other vision remains normal attracted little attention until Orton (1937), Geschwind (1962), Johnson and Myklebust (1967), Myklebust (1967a, 1971a, 1975a), Luria (1970, 1973), and many others began to report significant research studies in this field. Since letters and words must be perceived against a background of writing or print the same perceptual function seems to be involved, although the cognition of pictures and of letters stresses opposite hemispheres.

Visual Sequential Perception. Visual sequential perception essential to the reading process (Gaddes, 1982; Gaddes & Spellacy, 1977; Leong, 1975) is interrupted with lesions to the left frontal lobe or the left motor strip (Luria, 1973).

Phonetic Auditory Discrimination. A child with auditory imperception may be suffering from some degree of peripheral deafness (a lesion or dysfunction located somewhere between the eardrum and the medial geniculate body), or some degree of central deafness (a lesion or dysfunction in the dominant Heschl's gyrus or Wernicke's area). Frequently, a child may have a normal perception of pure tones on an audiometric test (Heschl's gyri are functioning normally) but he cannot discriminate "deer" and "dare" when presented auditorially on a tape recorder (possible evidence of a lesion or dysfunction in Wernicke's area). Luria has described this phenomenon clearly: "in local lesions of the secondary zones of the left temporal lobe in man [i.e., the Wernicke area] the ability to distinguish clearly between the sounds of speech is lost'' (Luria, 1973). The reader will recognize this as a basic causal factor in sensory or receptive aphasia.

Most reading involves some degree of recoding from the visual to the auditory modality. Any receptive aphasic impairment in comprehension at the individual word level is likely to result in a corresponding difficulty in reading. Indeed, Wernicke (receptive) aphasic patients usually show similar difficulties in reading as in auditory comprehension.

Auditory Memory. As has already been discussed, standardized sentence repetition tests can be used to detect this possible defect in a child's repertoire of skills. Left temporal lesions can produce this (Luria, 1973). Short-term verbal memory can be disturbed by electrical stimulation at various sites in fronto-parieto-temporal cortex of the left hemisphere (Ojemann, 1983).

Auditory–Verbal Understanding. Luria (1973) has described clearly the process of auditory perception of a sentence, followed by a simultaneous survey of the words, ordering them into a logical scheme, and extracting the meaning. As sentences proceed from simple subject–verb forms to complex logical–grammatical relationships, there is an increasing demand on this ability. Following oral instructions that become more and more complex is an example of this ability, which is impaired by generalized dysfunctions in the left temporal, parietal, and occipital areas. The Token Test designed by DeRenzi and Vignolo (1962), is a useful clinical test for measuring this ability in aphasically impaired adults (Spellacy & Spreen, 1969; Spreen & Benton, 1969/1977), in normal children up to the age of 10 years (Gaddes & Crockett, 1975), and in language impaired children of any age.

Understanding oral speech depends on a number of prerequisite skills. Some children and adults of normal or above-average intelligence are unable to process rapidly presented nonverbal tones (Lowe & Campbell, 1965; Tallal & Piercy, 1973a). They also have difficulty in decoding certain subtle phonological cues (Tallal & Stark, 1983) and organizing rapidly incoming linguistic concepts systematically. Certain LD children may be able to cope with classroom demands if the teacher will slow the tempo of oral delivery when giving instructions. See the case of Chris Jamieson in the addendum at the end of this chapter.

Auditory Sequential Skills. It is artificial but analytically useful to extricate the sequencing abilities, because they are an essential part of auditory–verbal understanding. Examining auditory receptive and auditory expressive processes in children suggests that the auditory sequencing skills, subordinate to the visual sequencing skills in Grades 1 and 2, increase in importance so that by Grade 5, visual and auditory expressive skills seem to dominate the reading processes in both sense modes (Gaddes, 1982; Gaddes & Spellacy, 1977).

Repetitive Speech. Since oral reading requires a repetition of verbal concepts originating from an extrapersonal source, the simple ability to repeat words may be a very small aspect of the complex reading process. A child with a minimal conduction aphasia may be impeded in his learning to read. A standardized articulation test can measure this ability, although it is useful to watch for competent imitation on the test coupled with inferior articulation during spontaneous speech. It is possible this is a sign of a mild expressive aphasia. The Spreen–Benton Articulation Test is useful for measuring 6-, 7-, and 8-year-olds (Gaddes & Crockett, 1975). Difficulty in articulation so that literal paraphasias are produced may result from lesions in the left inferior sensory strip (Luria, 1973). Any good sentence repetition test is useful here; the Spreen–Benton Test has the advantage of normative data for children (Gaddes & Crockett, 1975) and for adults (Spreen & Benton, 1969/1977).

Mattis, French, and Rapin (1975), in a study of 82 carefully selected dyslexic children, found that almost half of the developmental dyslexics in the study (i.e., 48%) suffered from problems of articulation and poor visual–motor skills. This was their major deficit; language problems affected 28% of this group and visual–spatial deficits only 14%. Because the mean age of these children was between 11 and 12 years, the findings of Mattis and his colleagues support the evidence of the increased importance of *expressive*-motor processes after 5 years of school over receptive-perceptual ones in reading.

Word Fluency. The ability to recite the letters of the alphabet (Satz, Taylor, Friel, & Fletcher, 1978) and the ability to produce words fluently usually correlates positively with reading ability. Tests of word fluency and sentence construction can be useful in evaluating this skill (Gaddes & Crockett, 1973).

Right–Left Orientation. A number of researchers have reported a conclusive relationship between directional confusion and reading retardation (Benton, 1958, 1959) and the Benton Right–Left Discrimination Test has been found to discriminate good and poor readers (Hundleby, 1969). The lambchop test of direction sense is also useful for investigating this (Bannatyne, 1971, p. 626; Silver & Hagin, 1975; Wechsler & Hagin, 1964). Bilateral parietal lesions will usually produce a directional deficit (see the case of Donald, Chapter 6).

Tactile Sensitivity. There is considerable evidence that the sensory and motor areas of the cortex are among the first to be myelinated and in that sense they are neurologically older than most of the rest of the brain. It seems highly likely that this is a major contributing factor to the fact that the infant's first learning is sensorimotor (Piaget & Inhelder, 1956; Phillips, 1975). Many educators consider tactile learning "primitive" and hence particularly potent in reinforcing cross-modal skills. For this reason it is useful to know whether the input mechanisms for sensorimotor activity are functioning normally, and to find this out a test of tactile sensitivity can be useful. To do this an esthesiometer may be used. This is a series of plastic rods, each equipped with a nylon hair of decreasing diameter. The nylon hairs are applied to the subject's fingers or palm in order of size, using a method of ascending and descending stimulation. In this way, the threshold of tactile sensitivity may be measured for each hand. Norms for children are available (Spreen & Gaddes, 1969) and a deficit in one hand can indicate possible dysfunction in the contralateral sensory strip, the parietal lobe, or the sensorimotor area. A deficit in the right hand frequently is associated with poor reading because both draw on the left parietal cortex (see the case of Mr. Simmons).

Tactile Form Recognition (Stereognosis). Clinical tests of stereognosis are believed to draw strongly on the sensory and motor strips largely on the side contralateral to the exploring hand (Reitan, 1959). Since sensory and motor processes are reciprocal and interacting, "they are expressed in the single word *sensorimotor* and cannot be considered separately in analyzing the problems of the learning disabled child" (Ayres, 1975). Numerous educators stress the importance of sensorimotor development in their remedial prescriptions (Ayres, 1975; Bannatyne, 1971; Barsch, 1967; Beery, 1967; Cratty & Martin, 1969; Frostig & Maslow, 1970; Kephart, 1966) and experimental investigation has indicated markedly improved scores on word recognition and oral reading by those learning disabled children receiving remedial activity designed to enhance specific types of sensory integration (Ayres, 1972b). These activities have included proprioceptive, vestibular, tactile, thermal, somatosensory stimulation, and motor activity. The Benton Stereognosis Test is a useful and inexpensive test for exploring visual–motor integration in children, and normative data are available for children aged 8–15 years (Spreen & Gaddes, 1969).

Finger Localization. Awareness of which finger has been touched, both when the subject can see the finger being touched and when a screen obscures his view, is mediated by the sensorimotor strips and the contiguous parietal cortices on the contralateral side. Studies of finger localization in mentally defective, in brain-injured, and in normal children have shown the first two groups to be inferior to normals (Benton, 1959). However, a subject's impairment in this perceptual skill appears to be related to the locus of the cerebral damage. Some mental defectives may achieve perfect scores on a finger localization test (Strauss & Werner, 1938) and we have seen dozens of cases of localized brain-damaged children with no deficit in this area. This would seem to imply that in these cases the sensorimotor and parietal areas essential to this skill have been spared.

In our own clinical analysis of learning disabled children and adults we have found a frequent correlation between retarded reading and defective finger localization in both hands or, particularly, the right hand (the case of Mr. Simmons is an example). Because reading and finger localization of the right hand draw primarily on left parietal function, a dysfunction in this area can affect both behavioral skills. It is highly significant that in a 6-year longitudinal study of 442 children from kindergarten to Grade 5, Satz and his colleagues found the finger localization test to have the best predictive value regarding competence in reading of any of a large battery (Satz, Taylor, Friel, & Fletcher, 1978). More is said about this important study later in this chapter.

Visual–Manual Reaction Time. When a subject is asked to watch a signal light and to press a telegrapher's key as fast as possible following the appearance of the light, it seems certain, from knowledge of clinical neurology, that a large circuit is involved in the brain. The right-handed person sees the light, and the neural impulses travel along the optic nerves and tracts and through the thalamic level of the brainstem to the occipital cortices. The situation is recognized and responded to by presumably large cortical areas, the "decision" is concentrated on the manual area of the left motor strip, and the right hand is stimulated to press the key. A test that activates so many areas of the brain is likely to be more sensitive to random cerebral dysfunction. For this reason, a visual–manual reaction time test has been used for many years to examine both brain-damaged and mentally retarded subjects. Brain-injured subjects have been found to be significantly slower than normal controls for both simple and choice reaction time tasks (Benton & Blackburn, 1957). When brain-injured subjects with unilateral lesions were studied, their reaction times for *both* hands were slower than normal, but the hand contralateral to the lesion was the more impaired.

Because of the complexity of neural involvement and the certain activity of the posterior cortices, the chances are increased that the child with slow visual–manual reaction times is also suffering from brain damage or dysfunctions in parts other than the immediate visual–manual circuit described above. If that is so, and the left parietal lobe is involved, the child may be suffering from some of the Gerstmann signs, which could be a part of a larger syndrome that could include receptive aphasia or dyslexia (Benton, 1977).

Normative data for visual–manual reaction times are available for children aged 6–12 years (Spreen & Gaddes, 1969), and they are useful for providing evidence that indicates chronic brain dysfunctions producing a continuing impairment to normal reading.

Auditory–Manual Reaction Time. One may use an apparatus in which an auditory signal is given to each ear singly, using earphones. It is then possible to ask the subject to press the telegrapher's key with his right hand or left hand in response to a tone in his right or left ear. This produces reaction times from six different sensorimotor combinations: (1) right ear–right hand, (2) right ear–left hand, (3) left ear–right hand, (4) left ear–left hand, (5) both ears–right hand, and (6) both ears–left hand. It is interesting that the average reaction times for normal adults on this test are about 75 milliseconds faster than for the visual–manual reaction time test. No doubt this is because of the much shorter cerebral circuit. The auditory stimulus is picked up in the eardrum and has to travel to the temporal lobes. By comparison with the visual circuit described above, the auditory–manual circuit is about half the length or less.

There are no data relating reading retardation with poor performance on this test, but diagnostic knowledge from it can help to understand the cerebral functioning of a child or adult. For example, a right-handed subject with left-hemisphere dominance for language and normal hearing would be expected to have the fastest reaction time to his right ear–right hand combination, or to his both ears–right hand pattern. If the subject does not, he may be suffering from a left-hemisphere lesion or dysfunction that may be related to the retarded reading.

Hand-Grip Strength. Normative hand-grip strength data for children aged 6–12 years are available (Spreen & Gaddes, 1969) and are useful for indicating the presence of nonlocalized brain damage or dysfunction. Clinical experience has shown that large numbers of traumatically brain-damaged adults, especially when the brainstem is injured, do poorly on this test regardless of their muscular development. No relation is known directly between hand grip and reading, but because thalamic connections are involved in language in an integrating function (Ojemann, 1983; Penfield & Roberts, 1959), it seems logical to speculate that thalamic and brainstem damage may impair reading. We know from thalamic electrostimulation studies that object-naming, mental arithmetic, and verbal recall are impaired when the left thalamus is stimulated (Ojemann, 1975).

Lateral Preferences. In Chapter 7 the problems of cerebral dominance and handedness were discussed at some length. At this point, it is sufficient to observe that when there is a conflict between manifest handedness and cerebral dominance there is usually, but not always, a reading problem. There are more reading problems among left handers, but when they are competent readers it may be that they are "pure" left handers (i.e., genetically intended to be left handed and right-hemisphere dominant for language), or that they are partially bilateral for language, or that they compensate with a superior intellect, or that the lesion producing the left handedness is outside the language areas. The school psychologist needs to know the dominance–handedness pattern, and with detailed neuropsychological data he or she can describe the unique cerebral pattern and prescribe a remedial program in collaboration with the special teacher. Each case is different and needs to be understood on the basis of its own evidence.

Sequencing. I have already referred to visual and auditory sequencing and their relation to reading and assisting in localizing a brain lesion. However, sequencing in its relation to reading is much more comprehensive. Bakker (1972), a neuropsychologist in Amsterdam, carried out an exhaustive developmental study on over 400 Dutch children aged 6–8. He recognized four types of serial order behavior: (1) verbally imitating (i.e., receptive or perceptual), (2) nonverbally imitating, (3) verbally expressive, and (4) nonverbally expressive. He examined temporal sequences in these four categories and three sensory modes, visual, auditory, and haptic. He found that temporal order ability was clearly related to age and that girls at ages 6 and 7 were superior to boys. Between 7 and 8 years, girls were almost equally good in sequential recall tasks in all three sense modes; by 8 and until 11 their haptic sequencing fell off and they emphasized visual and auditory sequencing. Girls showed a superiority in recalling temporal sequences when all three sense modalities were grouped, but from age 9 to 11, boys matched their performance exactly. Bakker concluded that "the temporal perception of verbal and of verbal codifiable stimuli is mediated by the language hemisphere" (i.e., the left hemisphere in most people).

As has been explained earlier in this chapter, the faster the speed of presentation of tests of both verbal and nonverbal stimuli, the more sensitive are they to impaired sequential processing. I have discussed this problem in some detail elsewhere (Gaddes, 1982).

Cross-Modal Integration. In Chapter 3 we presented Luria's classical model of lobular brain function. The reader will remember that these include (1) the primary or projection areas of the cortex, which contain neurons that are highly specific and react to visual, auditory, and tactile stimuli; (2) the secondary or association areas, which are contiguous to the primary areas, and provide a synthetic function leading to an understanding of the perceived stimulus in a particular sense mode; and (3) the tertiary zones, or "the zones of overlapping of the cortical ends of the various analysers," as Luria (1973) called them.

As an illustration, the sounds of oral speech are recorded in Heschl's gyrus of the left temporal lobe (primary area); these sounds are decoded in the auditory speech analyzer, called Wernicke's area (secondary area), and it is related to visual input in the occipital lobes by way of the angular gyrus (tertiary area).

Geschwind has clarified the importance of the interconnections in the human brain among the three basic perceptual and motor areas and credits this cortical association with our ability to acquire speech. In subhuman animals each sensory area is largely connected to the subcortical limbic system; the visual, auditory, and tactile cortices have few transcortical interconnections. In humans, however, the left parietal cortex is a vigorous and flexible association center, connecting the primary, secondary, and motor areas. "In man, with the introduction of the angular gyrus region, intermodal associations become powerful" (Geschwind, 1965). Because animals have no arcuate fasciculus they have no oral speech, and because their intermodal associations are weak by comparison with humans, their conceptual language is limited and their reading ability almost nonexistent. "The ability to acquire speech has as a prerequisite the ability to form cross-modal associations" (Geschwind, 1965).

The probable function of the angular gyrus in reading has already been explained (Geschwind, 1962, 1965; Orton, 1937). Neural associative dysfunctions always impair learning. For this reason, a learning disabled child may score normally on individual tests of visual, auditory, and tactile perception, but if he or she cannot switch quickly from one to another of these, this may be the key to the disability and the index to its remediation. The importance of intersensory perceptual functioning in the learning of children has been recognized for a long time (Ayres, 1972a; Birch, 1964; Myklebust, 1971a; Myklebust & Brutten, 1953) and its malfunctioning as a sensitive indicator of cerebral cortical damage and/or dysfunction (Myklebust, 1963).

The discussion so far has described the classical model of language brain function with its emphasis on cortical activity. While normal cortical function is essential to competent linguistic processing, the appearance of subcortical surgical procedures and the new brain scanning techniques have recently revealed that isolated lesions in the left thalamus can disrupt normal language reception and expression. Ojemann (1983) has hypothesized that left thalamic stimulation directs attention to verbal stimuli in the *external* environment, while at the same time blocking retrieval of material from both short-term and long-term verbal memory (i.e., the *internal* environment). Electrostimulation of the right thalamus provides a similar "gating" function with visual–spatial stimuli and visual–spatial memory. "This thalamic-specific alerting mechanism may well play a major role in learning. . . . When the mechanism is active, the type of material present in the external environment will be more readily retained, but material of the same type already in memory is less readily available" (Ojemann, 1983). When more is known about this possible interior–exterior–thalamic relationship, it may be an important step to understanding childhood autism.

It is obvious from this new type of evidence that has begun to appear within the last decade that attention and cross-modal integration involve both horizontal mechanisms (transcortical) and vertical ones (cortical–thalamic–cerebellar).

Summary

Neuropsychological knowledge can direct us to the various possible causes of dyslexia. As already indicated, there are probably as many types of reading impairment as there are loci of brain lesions, but most studies suggest that behaviorally they may include abnormal language development and competence, impaired perceptual skills (in all three sense modes), poor motor-expressive abilities, disturbed sensorimotor integration, faulty sequencing, and mixed cerebral dominance and lateral preferences.

Mattis, French, and Rapin (1975) studied 113 children referred for neurological and neuropsychological assessment. They were diagnosed as (1) brain damaged and (2) dyslexic with no evidence of brain dysfunctions (i.e., developmentally dyslexic). When these 113 children were divided according to their reading ability, three groups emerged: (1) brain-damaged readers, $N = 31$; (2) brain-damaged dyslexics, $N = 53$; and (3) non-brain-damaged or developmental dyslexics, $N = 29$. The reader will recognize this last named group as similar to Category 3 in the grouping system described in Chapters 1 and 3. Mattis' study found few neuropsychological differences between brain-damaged and non-brain-damaged poor readers, a finding also made by Black (1973) with a younger group. This suggests the possible presence of undetected CNS dysfunctions in some of the developmental dyslexic group that may reveal themselves with the development of more sensitive neurological instruments, such as the new scanners, although there is yet little conclusive supporting evidence for this (Benton, 1975).

Mattis and his colleagues found that their 82 dyslexic children were impaired in (1) language (anomia, poor comprehension of oral instructions, weak sentence repetition, and phonetic imperception), (2) articulation and motor-expressive skills (sound blending, copying geometric figures), and (3) visual–spatial skills (matching complex spatial designs, drawing geometric designs from memory, and a relatively inferior performance IQ on the WISC). It is interesting that the distributions of these deficits among the 82 dyslexic children were (1) language, 39%; (2) articulation and visual–motor skills, 37%; and (3) visual–spatial perceptual disorders, 16%. Because the types of language problems they found are also common aphasic symptoms (e.g., word-finding problems and sentence repetition and oral comprehension difficulties), this emphasizes the need to use aphasia screening methods in the assessment of learning impaired children. Later Mattis (1978), in agreement with Denckla (1977), added an additional clinically observed syndrome, a "sequencing disorder" syndrome that appeared to affect about 10% of developmental dyslexics.

However, a neurological approach by itself is not enough. The educational neuropsychologist is only one member of a diagnostic team that may include the child's teacher, a neurologist, and, where appropriate, a neurosurgeon, a pediatrician, a social worker, and a speech therapist. It is unlikely that these people will always find it convenient to meet as a group, but detailed reports should be provided for the child's file from all of them, and a social history will be supplied by the parents. Since remediation is a psychoeducational process, all relevant information should be directed toward that goal.

Developmental Aspects of Reading

E. E. Gibson (1965) has provided a sequential model for learning to read. Based on her experimental findings and clinical observations, the stages in a child's mastery of reading include: (1) learning oral language during the preschool period, (2) learning to differentiate visually graphic symbols, (3) learning to decode letters to sounds, and (4) developing the use of higher order units of language structure (e.g., several letters to produce a word, several words to produce a phrase or sentence). She studied children at every year from age 4 to age 8 and found that visual discrimination of letter forms improved with age. Although this was to be expected, different types of visual discriminations showed faster or slower developmental patterns. Recognizing a closed figure or one with a break was the easiest visual detail for 4-year-olds (about 16% made errors) but by 8 years the errors had dropped to zero. Line to curve figures were next in difficulty (about 38% of 4-year-olds made errors) but by 8 years the deficient group had dropped to 5%. Rotations and reversals, during this age range, reduced from error scores of 45% to ones of about 4%.

Satz has drawn on this evidence (Satz & Sparrow, 1970; Satz, Taylor, Friel, & Fletcher, 1978) to propose a theory of neurological maturational lag to account for cases of specific developmental dyslexia. These children, by contrast with those with identifiable brain damage or dysfunctions, "fail to acquire normal reading proficiency despite conventional instruction, socio-cultural opportunity, average intelligence, and freedom from gross sensory, emotional or neurological handicap" (Satz & Sparrow, 1970). It is important to remember that while the child with specific developmental dyslexia is free from gross neurological damage as shown on a neurological exam, this, of course, does not exclude the possibility of very minimal neurological brain dysfunctions. As well, there may be a further possibility of a genetic deficit that in some way interferes with normal reading.

Very briefly, Satz' theory assumes that reading disabilities reflect a lag in cerebral maturation, which in turn delays differentially all those skills that are characteristically predominant at different ages. In younger children visual–perceptual and cross-modal sensory integration develop as typical of this age range (preschool to puberty). During middle childhood and early adolescence, language skills, verbal abstraction, and formal logic normally emerge. According to Satz' hypothesis, those preschool children who are delayed in perceptual–motor development will be retarded in learning to read. Although many of these children will eventually learn the early skills if given enough time, they will lag on conceptual–linguistic skills and require extra time to acquire them, if they ever do. "In this theory, developmental reading disabilities are seen as disorders in central processing, the nature of which varies with the chronological age of the child" (Satz, Taylor, Friel, & Fletcher, 1978).

Satz and his colleagues followed 442 boys from kindergarten through Grade 5. Of a large number of tests administered early in the kindergarten year, five showed themselves to be powerful predictors of reading problems for the next 6 years. These were (1) finger localization, (2) visual recognition–discrimination, (3) Beery Visual–Motor Integration Test, (4) alphabet recitation, and (5) the Peabody Picture Vocabulary Test. Initially the children were divided into four criterion reading groups using a discriminant function analysis computed on classroom reading level. This analysis provided the following groupings: (1) severely retarded, (2) mildly retarded, (3) average, and (4) superior. By combining the first two groups, it was evident that 120 children, or 26% of the kindergarten children, were retarded in reading readiness. By the end of Grade 2, reading achievement tests showed agreement with the initial measures at the beginning of kindergarten of 89% of the severely retarded group and 94% of the superior group. This evidence indicates that in Satz' large sample, most of the superior readers were still in the top category and most of the severely retarded readers had not improved. In fact, there were now 144 children or 34% falling in the reading disability group. A few children from both extreme groups moved toward the center, but most did not. By the end of Grade 5, of the 49 severely retarded readers in Grade 2, three improved to the average group and six improved to the mildly retarded group, but 30% of the average readers were now retarded. Of the 62 mildly impaired readers in Grade 2, three improved to superior readers by the end of Grade 5, eight improved to average, and 24 deteriorated to the severely retarded group. This showed almost no improvement in the problem readers (severe and mild) between Grades 2 and 5, and a 30% chance that average readers in Grade 2 decline to become problem readers by Grade 5. The initial tests predicted the superior readers accurately, in that 97% of them continued to be reading at grade level or above at the end of Grade 5.

Satz, Taylor, Friel, and Fletcher concluded, "these findings, while generally discouraging for children having reading problems in early grades, are compatible with four recent longitudinal follow-up studies using generally smaller samples" (Muehl & Forell, 1973; Rourke & Orr, 1977; Trites & Fiedorowicz, 1976; Yule & Rutter, 1976). His data showed a steady increase in the incidence of both the severe and mild groups from the beginning of kindergarten to the end of Grade 5. The increases were most marked during the first year (kindergarten) and the last (Grade 5).

Another longitudinal study covering the 6-year period from kindergarten to Grade 5 was carried out by Spreen (1978). It differs from Satz' study in that it included more children (N = 1282) but fewer predictor tests (N = 4). The four tests included the Peabody Picture Vocabulary Test (Dunn, 1965), the Revised Visual Retention Test (Benton, 1963b), the Coloured Progressive Matrices (Raven, 1965), and the teacher's five-point rating scale to predict the future reading ability of each child. Achievement tests in reading, writing, arithmetic, science, and social studies made up the criterion variables. Spreen found the best predictors were the PPVT and the Benton VRT; he reported an accuracy of prediction rate ranging from 63% to 86%.

More recently (1983) Spreen has reported on a 15-year follow-up study of 191 young adults (median age almost 25 years). These young people had been assessed in our laboratory originally at the age of about 10 years. Spreen has reported a large body of data on neurological status, neuropsychological assessment, educational achievement, and personal and occupational adjustment. All measures were compared by categories 1, 2, 3, and 4 (see Table 1.1, page 10). Spreen found that retarded readers at age 10 tended to be retarded readers at age 25. On the Peabody Individual Achievement Test (PIAT) Reading Comprehension, he found that the subjects in Category 1 (brain damaged; N = 55) were reading at a Grade 8.0 level; Category 2 (MBD; N = 59) at Grade 9.2; Category 3 (learning disabled with no neurological signs; N = 26) at Grade 9.8; and controls (N = 51) at Grade 12.5.

Frauenheim and Heckerl (1983) followed 11 severe developmental dyslexics for about 17 years. At age 11 their mean verbal IQ was 84, and at mean age 27 (range 25–30) their mean VIQ was 85. Their mean performance IQ's at these two ages were 105 and 104. Their reading achievement scores showed a similar reliability. Their childhood grade level for reading at age 11 was 1.9; by mean age 27 it had increased to only 2.6. As adults, these dyslexic subjects still had severe deficits in associating sounds with symbols, they read at a painfully slow speed, and they still reversed some short words. The authors concluded: "Patterns of skill weaknesses and cognitive abilities, as measured by academic and psychological tests, have remained remarkably consistent over a period of approximately seventeen years'' (p. 345).

These findings can be explained by a neurological model; the chronicity of both neural dysfunction and reading achievement, despite remedial teaching, are causally related. The increase in the incidence of reading retardation probably results from the inability of the dysfunctioning brain to handle material that makes increasing demands in complexity and flexibility.

While such evidence is discouraging in showing retarded readers likely to remain below average in reading skill, it in no way implies the uselessness of remedial teaching. That short-sighted view produced the adult dyslexia in the cases of Mrs. Semmes and Mr. Darwin and in numerous other adult dyslexics. Had their teachers understood that, as children, they needed the best remedial teaching, they would have been slow but competent readers now, and all would have avoided the personal frustrations and unhappy experiences that haunt the nonreader in our society.

Linguistic Awareness and Reading

The reader will recognize that this chapter has described reading as a process initially of perceptual decoding of small units, then of larger units, and finally recognition of the meaning associated with the stimulus material. Such a concept views the process of learning to read as a continuum from single-letter recognition through more complex perceptual–motor skills, to rapid understanding of large semantic units.

There are many reading specialists who are offended by such a simplistic model because there is considerable evidence that a child's understanding of the nature and purpose of reading is an important precursor to successful reading (Ayers & Downing, 1979), that reading includes both an analytical and an impressionistic phase, and of a socially conditioned knowledge of the grammatical structure of language, which may be unconscious (Mattingly, 1979) or conscious (Chomsky, 1979). There are a few specialists who stress understanding of the semantic content and claim that the teaching of decoding skills, as practiced by most teachers, is an impediment to the normal and natural process of learning to read (Doake, 1979). Certainly all of these stresses on the *understanding* of oral and written language are valid, and the fragmentation of language in teaching initial reading skills is probably unnecessary for the bright child with a *normally functioning* brain and central nervous system. As we have seen from numerous clinical cases in this chapter, however, neuropsychological deficits may impair perceptual–motor skills, which, in turn, interfere with understanding.

The models proposed by reading specialists on linguistic awareness and meaning imply an unstated premise of normal central nervous system structure and function. Consequently they do not normally address the types of neuropsychological problems discussed in this chapter, which may affect from 5% to 7% of all readers.

Summary and a Perspective

Experienced reading teachers may find the discussion in this chapter too physiological and too remote from the real concerns of teaching reading. They may find too much emphasis on the mechanisms subserving decoding skills and an avoidance of the daily remedial procedures that are the reality of the classroom. It is true that reading includes a functional synthesis of perceptual–motor processes and a cognitive organization of semantic and syntactic determinants. A purely behavioral approach to reading that is stimulating and catches the interest of the learner is all that is needed for most children. But there are frequently three or four children in every Grade 2 or 3 class who do not respond to this teaching method and who need more intensive diagnostic understanding. This minority of LD children frequently suffers from deficiencies in basic processes (e.g., auditory imperception or sequencing) and these are related to specific neurological deficits (Mattis, French, & Rapin, 1975). While it is useful diagnostically to identify these deficiencies we must not lose sight of the holistic process of reading, what Maria and MacGinitie (1982) call "the complex and interactive nature of the reading process." Neuropsychological knowledge may be essential in understanding many reading-retarded children and adults, but we still need the skilled remedial teacher who uses this knowledge to provide competent task analyses and to cultivate successful learning strategies.

Clinical Addendum

Kathleen: A Case of Auditory Imperception

When a child has difficulty understanding what is said to him or her, it may be caused by (1) peripheral deafness, either partial or complete; or (2) central deafness resulting from damage or dysfunction in the auditory brain centers; or (3) a mixture of these two in differing degrees. When the comprehension of language is seriously impaired in an otherwise bright youngster, it is usually a difficult diagnostic task to identify exactly the quality of the etiological picture. If the child is young, only tentative diagnoses may be possible, and the clinician may have to wait until he is older and more mature before additional qualitative information is available. This was the pattern in our study of Kathleen.

Age 2. She was diagnosed as peripherally deaf by a medical doctor.

Age 4. An audiologist found that she had normal hearing for tones produced on an audiometer. However, she continued to behave as a deaf child, which was to be expected whether the deafness was peripheral or central.

Age 6. When she entered school her family doctor prescribed a hearing aid. Evidently he either disagreed with the diagnosis of the audiologist 2 years earlier, was ignorant of it, or was prescribing a "shotgun" type of therapy with the hope that he was increasing the probability of a helpful treatment.

Her teachers were frustrated because she made no response to oral instructions. She was unable to learn to read and write but she could copy printed words very well. Her teachers were sure she was not mentally retarded because she was socially alert and pleasant, but they did not understand her learning problem and they were confused regarding how to teach her.

Her first grade teacher reported that when she came to school, Kathleen hardly spoke at all. She tried to attract her teacher's attention by pulling her sleeve and pointing at things. Most of the children in the class helped her, but they soon stopped this in order to see whether Kathleen would start to talk. This seemed to work, although her speech was "flat" with little or no intonation, and her vocabulary was very limited. However, right from the start she showed an interest in all the classroom activities, she was never restless, and she always paid attention. Her first grade teacher showed perceptive insight by writing, "She seems to be quite intelligent."

Kathleen was socially well adjusted and played happily with the other children. On the playground she seemed to gain in confidence, became outgoing and active, and was frequently boisterous and noisy.

One of her second grade teachers reported:

> It was very difficult to teach her as she had learned to depend on the other children for answers, and she kept her eyes on them. In her efforts to get her written work done she became an expert at copying other children's work. One quick glance could provide many answers, but she would become frustrated and defensive if her neighbours decided to cover their work. She was unable to write a sentence of her own to describe a picture.
>
> To get her attention, I would have to grasp her by the arm and cup her chin in my hand in order to make her watch my lips. She spoke with a very nasal tone and omitted final consonants. When reading orally she could get some of the basic words in the Grade One reading vocabulary, but not enough to read a whole sentence. She was able to find word clues to answer some comprehension questions.

It seemed obvious that Kathleen was potentially mentally bright but starved for vocabulary, verbal concepts, and normal language development because of her deafness.

Age 8½. After a 5-hour battery of psychological, neuropsychological, and educational tests on her first visit to our laboratory we concluded that:

1. Kathleen was conceptually superior with nonverbal ideas. On the Halstead Category Test, which explores the child's abilities in inductive and deductive reasoning with spatial tasks, Kathleen obtained the highest score in 10 years that we had ever recorded with an 8-year-old. Instructions were given by visual demonstration, and she was quick to follow them.

2. She was above average in interpreting pictorial and visual–spatial material. Her WISC performance scores were: Picture Completion, 13; Block Design, 13; Object Assembly, 15. The Coding test produced a score of 11 and the Picture Arrangement Test a score of only 6. Her impoverished vocabulary seemed to impede her ability in the last-named test and this was confirmed on a repeated test 10 months later.

3. She was deaf to almost all language sounds. She could recognize her name if she could lip read, but not if the speaker was out of sight. She also wrote to dictation, by lip reading the words, "car, cow, baby, horse, dog, and cup." She misspelled the following dictated words:

"schoop" for "spoon," "tolbe" for "table," and "chir" for "chair." At this testing she was wearing her hearing aid, which she preferred not to use, around her neck. It was rather dirty and neglected, so we suggested that in light of the audiologist's report, it was of no use, and that Kathleen should stop wearing it. This she was happy to do.

4. She had difficulty with some of the serial order tasks, which was consonant with left-hemisphere dysfunction.

5. She was inferior with her right hand in both visual–manual reaction time and stereognosis. These findings also correlate with left-hemisphere pathology.

The neurological tests, including an EEG, were completely normal, so that Kathleen's brain lesion, wherever it was, was likely subcortical, or if cortical, so minimal as not to show on a standard neurological examination. Following this first testing, we advised the referring family doctor that we believed Kathleen was not peripherally deaf but suffered from a dysfunction in Wernicke's area or in the auditory nerves leading from the brainstem to the left Heschl's gyrus. Her teachers were advised to use a visual–motor approach, as if she were deaf. Central deafness was explained to them, but the remedial teaching approach is largely similar whether the deafness is central or peripheral.

Age 9½. At our second testing, 10 months after the first, Kathleen still spoke very little, and when she did her voice was nasal and monotonous. In the interim since the first testing, her teachers had taught her to read and write a large number of words using the visual–tactile method. Since they had concentrated on nouns, in order to increase her vocabulary, her reading of verbs, adjectives, and adverbs was inferior for a girl of her age and potential intelligence level.

Because more than 3 years had passed since her last audiometric test, we requested an updated one with the hope that her improved abilities in understanding and communication would provide a more accurate measure. Her family doctor carried out a test and found a severe hearing loss in both ears on all frequencies, but because of the complexity of this case he recommended further studies done by a specialist.

Age 11½. A complete audiometric examination was carried out, and a severe loss was found in both ears. Following this test Kathleen was fitted with a very sensitive hearing aid in her right ear. She immediately adjusted it and indicated pleasure at hearing sounds such as clapping hands, a clock, scissors, and her own voice. She obtained an average 40-dB amplification of the frequencies 250–4000 Hz. In simpler language, this means that her hearing was improved from a severely impaired level of deafness to a level bordering on normal hearing.

The word discrimination score did not show any significant improvement with the hearing aid. Either aided or not, her understanding of words was at only a 45% level. This evidence supports the presence of a central language deafness or phonetic imperception.

This case illustrates the difficulty of attempting a differential diagnosis of peripheral versus central deafness with a young child. In the early examinations of Kathleen the diagnoses swung from one to the other with regularity. At age $8\frac{1}{2}$, when we first saw her, we concluded she suffered from central deafness and the hearing aid should be dispensed with. The final tests, done when Kathleen was $11\frac{1}{2}$, showed all of us to be wrong, that in fact she was impaired by *both* peripheral and central word deafness. The fact that the high-grade hearing aid improved her hearing of nonverbal stimuli but not words revealed this. The important point in any such case is to continue to make tentative diagnoses and to continue to revise one's knowledge in the light of improved information.

Age 14. My most recent visit with Kathleen was in her junior high school classroom, where I observed her in regular academic activities. When I arrived, she was acting in a small skit written by the students producing the play. Her lines were brief, but she spoke them fairly clearly using a visual cue to time her lines.

She can converse much better than when I had seen her last, but her speech is telegraphic. Her teachers reported that she is an excellent athlete, but her main problem is in the language arts. There are major gaps in her vocabulary that make it difficult for her to read and write. Basically this is a receptive aphasia producing an aphasic dyslexia. Kathleen has many gaps in her understanding of verbal concepts, and her teachers often stumble on these. They recently discovered she misunderstood "knee," thinking it was synonymous with "leg." She had been taught to write "leg" with her teacher pointing to a picture of a person's leg, and "knee" in the same way. Evidently her teacher had unwittingly pointed to the knee in both cases.

Kathleen is a pretty girl and well liked by her companions in school. It is difficult, at this point, to imagine how her deafness will affect her adult life. In the meantime her teachers are working hard to develop her language skills to help her adjust to a normal and happy adult life.

Derrick White: A Case of Mild Receptive Aphasia

Derrick was 9 years 7 months old when first seen by a young psychologist in private practice. A large battery of tests were administered and the psychologist reported that Derrick scored in the average to superior range on the sensorimotor tests and that he had difficulty with most of the verbal tests. On the Wechsler (WISC-R) he measured a verbal IQ of 96, a performance IQ of 90, and a full-scale IQ of 92.

Derrick was a healthy, nice-looking boy, popular with his peers, and a better-than-average athlete. However, he had had difficulties with academic work from the beginning of Grade 1. The teachers told his mother that Derrick had a learning disability, and it was for this reason that she had sent him to the psychologist. However, the psychologist told her very little that she did not know already, and he provided no suggestions of what to do about Derrick's frustrations at school.

His mother then sent Derrick to see a pediatric neurologist who found Derrick to have normal hearing and no abnormalities on the formal neurological examination. He reported, "The general physical examination likewise was within normal limits." He referred Derrick to our laboratory for an assessment of his learning problems and a recommendation for remedial follow-up.

Educational History

In kindergarten Derrick first showed signs of being upset. This surprised and mildly alarmed his parents because, until then, he had always been a happy and sunny little boy. The parents attributed it to the fact that they moved in the middle of the kindergarten year and Derrick had to enter a new class in a different school in midyear.

However, in Grade 1 he continued to be frustrated and unhappy, and his teacher reported that "his semantic skills are poor." In Grade 2 Derrick was placed in a "learning assistance" class because his language skills, both reading and writing, were so poor. By the end of Grade 2 he was much behind his peers and was being teased by them. In Grade 3 he was the top scorer on his class's soccer team and was popular with his classmates on the playground, but with typical 9-year-old behavior they teased him unmercifully for being in the "dumb class." He begged his parents to get him out of the learning assistance class, so they hired a tutor who met Derrick twice a week for remedial help.

At the beginning of Grade 4 the school agreed to put Derrick back into a regular class full time, but by late November he was falling behind and he was returned to the learning assistance class, which he hated. At the same time he was captain of the soccer team and was the best sprinter in his class. Physical education and art were his only successes in school. It was in this year that the parents sent him to the psychologist.

By the fall of his Grade 5 year Derrick was approaching a crisis. At home there were increasing episodes of frustration, bouts of tears, and begging to be freed from the special class. His mother in turn, was requesting additional homework so that between the extra time with his tutor, Derrick had almost no time to himself, and he was developing a strong hatred for school.

It was at this time that the parents took Derrick to the pediatric neurologist. He recognized the presence of the learning disability and wisely analyzed the situation in which the boy found himself—a school setting that was unhappy for Derrick but where the teachers casually minimized the seriousness of Derrick's learning problems, and his home, which was supportive but where his parents were obviously distressed by his learning problems and his poor achievement. The ambivalence of his peers added to Derrick's misery and resulted in model behavior at school and violent outbursts at home. The neurologist remarked in his report: "I think that this cannot go on much longer before there will be a breakdown." It was at this point that Derrick was referred to our laboratory.

Analysis of Derrick's Problem

In the spring of his Grade 5 year we first saw Derrick who by now was 11 years old. He was a fine-looking, well-spoken, and personable boy, who was sociable and pleasant. The school had placed him every year for 5 years in a learning assistance class for part of the year. Obviously this was not working because Derrick was still having trouble with arithmetic, reading, spelling, and writing.

Because the neurological examination was clear it was evident that we were dealing with a Category 3 case (i.e., LD with no evidence of neurological deficit). We then subjected Derrick to a detailed battery of neuropsychological tests, academic achievement tests, and the full Spreen–Benton Aphasia Battery. It was the latter, along with some of the verbal memory tests, that gave us the clue to the mystery of Derrick's learning and resulting behavior problems.

Test Results

On the sensorimotor tests (e.g., finger tapping speed, reaction time, tactile sensitivity, hand-grip strength) Derrick's scores were all above average. This was expected because of his good athletic abilities.

The Wechsler Test (WISC-R) gave him a verbal IQ of 101 and a performance IQ of 96, so we knew that he was at least mentally average. Two of his low scores (Digit Span and Picture Arrangement) are particularly vulnerable to anxiety, so it seems very likely that his real mental potential under optimal conditions is above average.

The Peabody Individual Achievement Test (PIAT) showed Derrick not to be below grade level in reading. Because he was tested in March of his Grade 5 year, any score at or above 5.6 was not below average. Derrick measured 5.6 on Word Recognition and 6.8 on Reading Comprehension. Other measures were below average: Mathematics, 4.9; Spelling, 4.1; and General Information, 4.7.

The memory tests and aphasia battery revealed the basis of Derrick's problems. He had difficulty following oral instructions, but when he understood clearly what was wanted, he frequently had a perfect score on most subtests. He was unable to process *auditory sequential language* at a fast speed. However, if we slowed our tempo of speech, he usually had no trouble.

Because of his strong desire to succeed, Derrick would give an answer based on what he *thought* was said. For example, when asked to construct a sentence with the words "drive—street—car", he misperceived the words and said, "There was a drive-in at McDonald's and there was an accident in the street." Note the paraphasia, "drive-in" for "drive," and the omission of "car." When he was advised to listen again to the three words and they were delivered at a slower pace, he produced a correct sentence.

On the memory tests he did well on Sentence Repetition, better than average in drawing geometric figures from memory, and very well remembering paired-associated nouns. These findings contraindicate a primary memory deficit and suggest that his problem is one of semantic and syntactic comprehension. When he was asked to listen to short stories and then report what he could remember, he produced gross distortions and paraphasic associations that rendered his scores inferior. After listening to a story of a ship that struck a mine, he described "a man who struck it rich" and an accurate fragment about people in life boats who were rescued. He made no attempt to relate the paraphasic phrase and the correct episode; he simply reported them.

Derrick's teacher early in Grade 5 soon recognized that he would ask for her oral instructions to be repeated immediately after she had given them. She found this understandably irritating, and, crediting it to inattention, she refused to repeat her instructions. Had Derrick been too careless to give concentrated attention, the teacher's strategy might have encouraged him to learn to attend more accurately. But since he suffered from a minimal receptive aphasia, it simply had a devastating effect on his learning and his self-confidence, and he kept getting further behind.

In the tactile naming test he also produced some paraphasias, namely, an "egg-beater" a "can opener." When he was asked what it was used for, he continued the distorted association by saying "to open cans." On the Boston Naming Test, he named pictures of common objects at a normal level for his age, but when we tried a few items above his age level and provided him with a phonetic cue, he produced a nonsense word (e.g., target word, "muzzle"; oral cue, "mŭ"; Derrick's response, "mout." (It is interesting to note that "mout" and "mouth" are phonologically close, and "muzzle" and "mouth" possess a semantic association.) It seems likely that Derrick produces many paralexias during his unsupervised reading (see the discussion of deep dyslexia earlier in this chapter).

Analysis of the Problem

Why, after 5 years in school, was Derrick's academic record so poor? Basically it was because no in-depth diagnostic examination had been done until the spring term of his Grade 5 year. The school each year for 5 years had assigned him to a learning assistance class and this remedial program had been determined by *administrative decision* rather than on the basis of diagnostic understanding of Derrick's cognitive structure and his learning strategies. This is not to dismiss administrative decisions completely. In most cases they need to be the *first* decision, but *no child should be left for 5 years in a program that is not working*. If it is not working within a very short time the child should be studied in depth and experimental teaching programs should be developed, based on the collected diagnostic knowledge. The results of the teaching procedures should be continually monitored and assessed and readjusted in terms of their success or failure.

Evidence from Derrick's Social Behavior

When I explained Derrick's problem with processing oral instructions, his father looked relieved. "That explains his confusion at lacrosse," he said. He explained that because Derrick was so successful in soccer, he had taken him this year with one of his friends to a lacrosse coach. At the first practice the coach explained the rules to the two boys and Derrick's father could see that Derrick looked more and more confused, while his friend followed the instructions with no difficulty. During play Derrick made several errors because he did not understand the rules. By the second practice a week later, the errors had diminished, and by the third practice Derrick had a complete understanding and was a valuable member of the team. When we saw him 6 months later he was the established top scorer and a valuable player.

Remedial Program

Derrick's basic learning problem is a slowness in processing large quantities of sequential material, especially oral material. Instructions should be presented (1) at a slower tempo, and (2) in bits or single ideas.

His tutor, with this knowledge, organized a detailed program of remedial measures in arithmetic, reading, and spelling, drawing on multisensorimotor exercises and multiple activities to improve his language development.

A follow-up one year later in April of his Grade 6 year showed steady improvement for Derrick. His Grade 6 teacher is keen and interested, and he is aware of the nature of Derrick's learning problem. The mild aphasic tendency to confuse oral messages is a constant handicap, but Derrick compensates by doing well in written work that he can prepare in advance. It is possible that he may have to tape some lessons when he enters Junior High School. This will give Derrick the opportunity to replay and repeat some lessons as they become conceptually more complex. He now understands that he is not stupid and his attitude toward himself has improved markedly in the last year.

9 The Neuropsychological Basis of Problems in Writing, Spelling, and Arithmetic

Man's language systems, the auditory and the written, develop sequentially according to a patten determined phylogenetically and ontogenetically, neurologically and psychologically.

Helmer R. Myklebust (1965)

The indispensable instrument of the writer is not so much the pen as the left cerebral hemisphere.

Oliver L. Zangwill (1976)

In this chapter is a discussion of the processes of writing and spelling as the logical sequence to the discussion in Chapter 8 of reading and reading problems, because a child who "has difficulty in the comprehension and use of spoken or read language, . . . will probably have difficulty learning to use written language" (Chalfant & Scheffelin, 1969). The reader will remember that according to Myklebust's developmental hierarchy of language skills, written language is the last to be acquired and is only learned normally if all of the preceding stages have been successfully established. Not only is writing the last language function to be acquired, but it is practiced and used least, even by highly educated people. This may account for its being the first language skill to suffer following any type of diffuse brain damage or deterioration. It is a common observation that most elderly people lose their ability to write letters while still retaining the competence for normal simple conversation.

Arithmetic, while primarily concerned with quantitative concepts and their interrelations, also depends on verbal understanding and communication, although on a comprehensive battery of neuropsychological tests, the skills necessary for success in arithmetic and in language show significantly different patterns (Rourke & Finlayson, 1978). But let us look first at writing and spelling.

D. W. Reed (1970) has pointed out that whereas speech in some form is probably more than a half-million years old, writing is only about 5000 years old. As well, although all present human societies have oral languages, many still have no system of writing, and in our own society all

328

normal adults are able to speak, but only a very few can write with the same level of competence.

Although oral speech is normally acquired spontaneously and without conscious effort, the ability to communicate by writing not only comes later but as the result of conscious effort and intensive study. "From the very beginning written speech is a voluntary, organized activity with the conscious analysis of its constituent sounds" (Luria, 1966).

The Process of Writing

Learning to speak and to write differ because they depend on different psychological and neurological processes. Whereas reading is a perceptual–cognitive process that begins with visual stimuli in the *outside* environment and ends with a meaningful interpretation of those stimuli within the cerebral cortex, by contrast, writing begins with an idea and an intent to communicate that originates *within* the brain and ends with a psychomotor act (writing) that leaves a tangible record (the written message) in the outside environment. In a simplistic sense, reading and writing are reverse neuropsychological processes.

The traditional view of writing assumes that written language is dependent on spoken language, i.e., that phonological encoding occurs in writing. This model, presented by Chalfant and Scheffelin (1969), includes a task analysis of the hypothesized psychological processes involved in writing (see Table 9.1). Following the decision to communicate a message by writing, one decides on what one wants to say and then mobilizes the message in a syntactically acceptable sequence. One then puts pen to paper and begins to retrieve the graphic-language symbols (i.e., letters) that correspond to the auditory-language signals (i.e., words) one has in one's mind. Whether writing from dictation (i.e., having the oral words supplied externally by another person) or writing spontaneously (i.e., generating the words mentally), one initially must analyze the word phonetically letter by letter. The small child first learning to write a spelling list will usually sound each word analytically as he writes it. Once the child has identified the phonetic sound of a letter or phoneme, he then has to remember the shape of the optic structure (i.e., the grapheme or letter) and initiate a sequential pattern of neuromuscular activities that will produce the correct letters in a particular visual–spatial pattern. As the child learns to write words as higher order wholes he eventually begins to produce an automatized motor skill in which the oral phonetic analysis for all those words he has mastered are inhibited and a spontaneous free-flowing muscular activity, the writing of a literate adult, is substituted.

Table 9.1   Encoding Graphic Language Symbols: A Task Analysis

---

  I. Intention
      (*a*) Possess the need to communicate
      (*b*) Decide to send the message in graphic form
 II. Formulate the message
      (*a*) Sequence the general content of the message
      (*b*) Retrieve the appropriate auditory-language symbols which best
           express the intent of the communication
III. Retrieve the graphic-language symbols which correspond to the selected
     auditory-language signals
IV. Organize the graphic–motor sequence
      (*a*) Retrieve the appropriate graphic–motor sequence
      (*b*) Execute the graphic–motor sequence for producing the graphic-
           language symbols

(From Chalfant, J. C., & Scheffelin, M. A., *Central Processing Dysfunctions in Children,* NINDS Monograph No. 9. Bethesda, MD: U.S. Department of Health, Education, and Welfare, 1969, p. 111.)

This traditional view of writing appears valid on an introspective basis, but in recent years it has been challenged on the basis of experimental findings in studies of aphasic patients by psycholinguists and neurolinguists. Where the traditional view of writing assumes a dependence of graphemic functions on phonemic processes (the dependence hypothesis), neurolinguistic evidence suggests that these two systems can be independent of one another (the independence hypothesis). Friederici, Schoenle, and Goodglass (1981) studied 12 male aphasic patients with tests of oral naming of pictures of common objects, written naming of the same pictures, and picture–word matching. They controlled the high and low frequency of the words, the high and low frequency of the phoneme–grapheme rules of each word, and the length of words, whether one, two, or three syllables.

The Broca's aphasics ($N = 8$) showed a marked variability in that half of them were significantly better in written than oral naming, and the other half showed the reverse pattern. The Wernicke's aphasics ($N = 4$) showed no difference in these skills. These findings suggest a possible dissociation of oral and written production, although any conclusions must be viewed with skepticism because of the small sample sizes. These researchers concluded that "in aphasia, at least, the independent functioning of the graphemic system is hard to disprove" (Friederici, Schoenle, and Goodglass, 1981). But they agreed that in normal writing "for written-word retrieval both pathways, the phonologically mediated and the direct pathway" can be used. It seems highly likely that the phonological accessing of words is a left-hemisphere function, and that direct accessing of graphemes from the mental lexicon is largely a right-hemisphere function. In non-brain-damaged subjects it seems likely that both systems are used both alternately and together, while in some left-hemisphere-damaged subjects there may be a tendency for the two systems to be independent.

Lesion studies (Luria, 1966) of adults with writing disorders indicate that the language centers of the left hemisphere, the occipito-temporal–parietal areas bilaterally, and the left manual–sensorimotor strips, are all intimately involved with written language. No doubt the total cerebral cortices are responsible for creating and planning the message, but these auditory–visual–motor areas seem to be largely responsible for the mechanical production.

This neuropsychological information can account for the fact that all writing disorders fall into three etiological categories: (1) those with an aphasic basis, (2) those with an auditory or visual perceptual deficit, and (3) those with a motor disability or apraxia (Chalfant & Scheffelin, 1969; Luria, 1966; Myklebust, 1965). These categories are not necessarily mutually exclusive and many subjects suffering from dysgraphia may have a syndrome with basically only one of these or a combination of two or all of them.

Dysgraphia and Aphasia

Localized lesions of the "speech area" of the left hemisphere typically produce an aphasic disturbance of both oral and written language. Penetrating brain injuries, closed head injuries, tumors, abscesses, intracerebral hematomas, and vascular accidents are common causes. Left-hemisphere "strokes" may result in transitory or permanent disability in writing. Such a disability is a frequent symptom of traumatic aphasia and led Luria to observe (1970) that "writing disorders accompany almost every form of aphasia."

We will begin by examining some cases of traumatically brain-damaged adults, and then look at some cases of dysgraphic children.

Adults with Dysgraphia

Left Anterior Temporal Lobe Excision and Damage in Broca's Area

John Hall. John Hall was a bright young man, who on completion of high school, entered the Air Force and was allocated to the Military Police Branch. He was friendly and pleasant and he got along well in the security force.

At the age of 29 he developed severe headaches and a number of signs of a neurological problem. Neurosurgical examination revealed the presence of a cyst embedded in the anterior part of the left temporal lobe, and because of an abnormal arteriovenous malformation, a large piece of the frontal part of the left temporal lobe was removed. Because this did not destroy Wernicke's area, John's understanding of oral speech was normal, but because the frontal and inferior temporal area was affected by the surgery, his speech was postoperatively plagued by a serious word-finding problem and an unreliability of oral expression. He usually knew what he wanted to say but another word would come out. In oral arithmetic he frequently would conceptualize one number and say another, although he was aware of his aphasic problem.

Enough brain damage had resulted to affect both his reading and writing. We saw him for assessment 6 years postoperatively when he was 35 years old. At that time he measured a grade-point average (GPA) in reading (single-word recognition) of only 2.2, and in spelling of only 4.0. He was well above average in spatial tasks (right-hemisphere function) and this seemed to help his written arithmetic, which measured a GPA of 6.1.

His ability to name simple objects and write their names was impaired (see Fig. 9.1). When shown a toy pistol he wrote "gun" correctly. For a plate he wrote "pain" (paraphasia). For a lightbulb he wrote "bunb," (another paraphasia, both of which indicated he was having difficulty in the sequential production of the correct letters). "Screwdriver" was almost correct except for the missing last letter. "Sponge" and "ruler" were both misspelled, although he recognized them and named them correctly in oral speech. For "eggbeater" he said "mixer" and wrote "bake." This is another spontaneous substitution. For "spring" he wrote "snoug" (paraphasia), which he recognized as incorrect and stroked it out.

Following the list of names, he tried to write two sentences to dictation. These were: "This is a very nice day" and "This brick building was built last year." His attempts had omissions of words, substitutions, and misspellings (see Fig. 9.1).

The next two sentences, "I am very hungry" and "The color of the walls is green," were both copied correctly. His visual–spatial skills were good and it seems likely he was drawing on his right hemisphere to copy these sentences as spatial patterns rather than samples of sequential language.

His handwriting postoperatively was large but well-enough formed and was different in style from his writing prior to the brain damage.

John Hall's dysgraphia is a good example of a language deficit resulting from his aphasia and it contains some paralexias, with semantic associations, of the type described in Chapter 8 in the discussion of deep dyslexia.

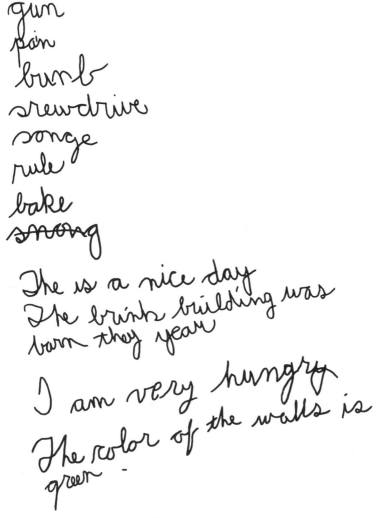

Figure 9.1. Samples of John Hall's writing to dictation and to copy. See text for the discussion of these samples.

Mary Galloway. Following a head injury from a traffic accident, Mrs. Galloway was seen for neuropsychological assessment. She was 34 years old at the time of testing, which was 2 years after the accident. Her brain injuries affected the left frontal part of her brain and her cerebellum, so that she was very unsteady on her feet and her speech was slurred. Her articulation was so impaired that naive observers were likely to interpret her as mentally retarded. In fact her verbal intelligence was better than about 77% of other adults so that Mrs. Galloway found this most frustrating (see Fig. 9.2).

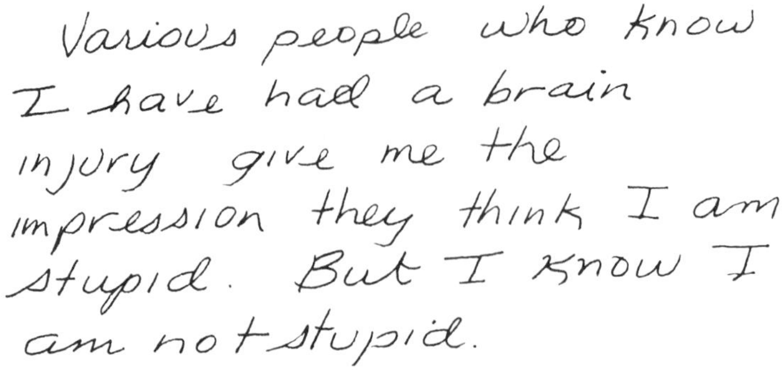

Various people who know I have had a brain injury give me the impression they think I am stupid. But I know I am not stupid.

Figure 9.2. Sample of Mrs. Galloway's post-traumatic spontaneous writing.

This case contrasts with that of John Hall. Where he suffered from aphasia, Mrs. Galloway's language was completely intact. Her spoken speech was severely dysarthric (inarticulate) but her written expression was normal (Fig. 9.2). The brain injury had resulted in her writing being larger than it had been previously (see Fig. 9.3) and she now needed lined paper to guide her, but her writing was neat and legible and its content well organized.

Summary. Agraphia in traumatically brain-damaged adults may result from lesions or dysfunctions in (1) Wernicke's area or contiguous parts of the left temporal lobe, (2) the occipital lobes or the left parieto-occipital area, (3) the motor strip or premotor area, or (4) the left sensory strip or the left parietal lobe. No one has written in as much clinical detail as Luria

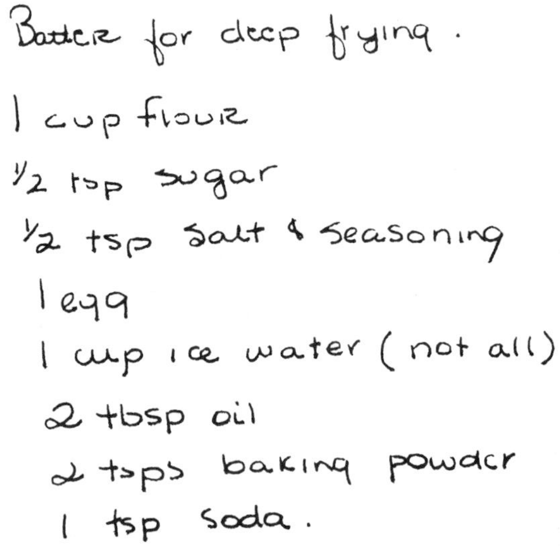

Batter for deep frying.
1 cup flour
½ tsp sugar
½ tsp salt & seasoning
1 egg
1 cup ice water (not all)
2 tbsp oil
2 tsps baking powder
1 tsp soda.

Figure 9.3. Sample of Mrs. Galloway's writing prior to her head injury.

on the neuropsychology of agraphia, and his clinical studies have led him to believe that: (1) Lesions in the left temporal lobe impede subjects in writing to dictation, although they can still write overlearned motor stereotypes such as their own signatures (Luria, 1973); (2) lesions in the two occipital lobes or in the left parieto-occipital lobes result in an inability to write either to copy or to dictation, since there is an inability to imagine or remember the visual form of letters (Luria, 1970, 1973); (3) lesions in the left sensory strip may produce mirror writing (Luria, 1970); and (4) lesions in the left motor strip or premotor area can produce a motor perseveration that may cause repetitions and omissions of single letters (Luria, 1973). This last syndrome leads to problems of chaotic spelling, e.g., "Abbr" for "Abner."

Agraphic and Dysgraphic Children

One of the first investigators to examine the act of writing using neuropsychological knowledge was Myklebust. In 1973 (Myklebust, 1973a) he pointed out that whereas the development and disorders of oral speech and reading in children have been investigated "by many workers representing a variety of disciplines, only meager attention has been given to written language." To correct this neglect he produced two volumes: The first (Myklebust, 1965) investigates the problems of writing in the brain-damaged, dyslexic, aphasic, deaf, mentally retarded, emotionally disturbed, culturally deprived, and educationally neglected child. The second volume (Myklebust, 1973a) examines the written language of normal and exceptional children and provides diagnostic and remedial procedures. Few writers since Orton (1937) have provided as knowledgeable a presentation of the neuropsychological aspects of written language in children as Myklebust, and his two well-detailed volumes provide a clear analysis of the psychological processes involved in writing.

English writers, of course, have concerned themselves about the structure of language and the elements of written style ever since the advent of creative writing. But only recently have multidisciplinary groups of English scholars, psychologists, linguists, neurolinguists, and educators attempted its joint analysis (Gregg & Steinberg, 1980). By conducting psychological experiments to examine a tentative theory of writing and by embedding it in computer technology, Collins and Gentner (1980) have expressed the hope of eventually producing a predictive theory of writing, but they admit that that day is still far off. Bereiter (1980) has proposed looking at the development of writing skills within a theoretical framework that he calls "applied cognitive-developmenal," but like most writers in this field he directs his analysis to the development of normal learners. While this is important, much additional information can be gained by studying learners with both traumatic injuries and developmental problems.

Psychomotor Disorders

Paralysis of the Dominant Hand. Paralysis of the dominant hand, because of either left-hemisphere damage or peripheral injury, forces the child to write with his nondominant hand. Since control must now travel from the language dominant hemisphere through the corpus callosum to the motor strip of the nondominant hemisphere and then down the pyramidal tracts to the nondominant hand, writing with this hand usually is less fluent and more awkward. Many years ago, Orton (1937) showed examples of writing of a 15-year-old boy. He was not paralyzed, but he was genetically left-handed and had been forced to write with his right hand, and his right-handed writing at age 15, although a product of 8 years of training, was more cramped and less legible than his spontaneous writing with his left hand, which nature had intended (see Fig. 9.4). Such evidence suggests that children forced to write with the nondominant hand

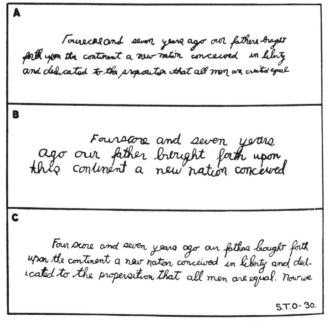

Figure 9.4. Samples of writing of a 15-year-old boy who was originally left handed but who was forced to write with his right hand. (A) An example of his right-handed writing when first examined. (B) His left-handed writing at the same time. It was more legible but much slower (half as fast). (C) The effect of 2 months' training of the left hand for writing. In this time it had acquired the same speed as the right hand. (After Orton, 1937.)

for any reason, including paralysis, are likely to be dysgraphic. Those who continue to write with the affected hand, because the paralysis is mild, will likely be dysgraphic because of the minimal motor interference.

Cerebellar Ataxia. Cerebellar ataxia is a condition of neuromuscular coordination that may affect any motor activity, including walking and manipulating. When it affects the hands, the legibility of writing may be impaired, although the spelling and sentence structure may be normal or near normal. Myklebust has provided an excellent case of this with a sample of the subject's writing (1965, p. 17). From our own files, Chuck Becker is a good example. When he was 10 years old, Chuck received a severe head injury in an automobile accident, in which, among other things, he received a severe blow to the back of his head. He was riding in the back seat of the family station wagon, and on impact, a heavy metal box packed on the rear deck of the car was hurled forward, hitting Chuck in the base of his skull. So severe were his injuries that he remained unconscious for a period of 3 months, and following that his recovery was slow and partial. Because of injury to his cerebellum his gait and manual control were both severely impaired. In fact, he fell down so much in the early stages of his rehabilitation that he was required to wear a protective helmet. As well as the injury to the back of his brain he also sustained a contra-coup effect, which centered in the left frontal cerebral area. This showed itself in an articulation problem (dysarthria) and a manual difficulty in his right hand, which was both sensory (reduced manual sensitivity) and motor (paralysis). For more than 2 years after his injury he was unable to recognize forms of blocks with his right hand (astereognosis) and to write. On our fourth testing session with Chuck, which was $2\frac{1}{2}$ years after his injury, he was able to attempt the Coding subtest on the Wechsler (WISC) for the first time, but symbols were poorly drawn and one square was omitted. At age 13 he could spell words orally at an above-average level for his age as measured by the Wide Range Achievement Test, but he could not write them. The psychometrician wrote the words to Chuck's dictation. He learned to write again later that year, at the age of $13\frac{1}{2}$ years. He wrote: "I wish to announce something. I can now write" (see Fig. 9.5). His first writing, while grammatically correct, was briefer in content and larger in size than it had been pretraumatically, 4 years before (see Fig. 9.6).

By the age of 16, $6\frac{1}{2}$ years posttraumatically, Chuck could write the symbols more firmly in the Digit Symbol subtest of the Wechsler (WAIS) but he was so slow that he obtained a very poor score (scaled score, 6). It was his poorest score. His best score was on Arithmetic (scaled score, 12). He attended a remedial school for about 7 years, during which time his writing showed slow improvement (see Fig. 9.7).

An examination of his writing from his first attempts at age $13\frac{1}{2}$ to the last sample at age $21\frac{1}{2}$ shows a steady improvement in his ability to com-

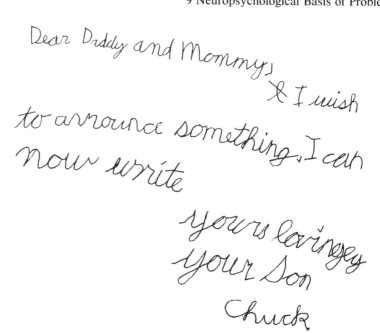

Figure 9.5. Example of Chuck Becker's first writing $3\frac{1}{2}$ years posttraumatically (age $13\frac{1}{2}$ years).

pose verbal ideas and to increase their variety and level of social insight. Because of his permanent cerebellar damage he will always be apraxic, and this is reflected in a cramped and jerky style in his penmanship. In spite of his rather extensive brain damage, Chuck has shown a persistent determination to gain independence like any normal young adult (see Figs. 9.8 and 9.9).

EEG Dysrhythmia in the Dominant Motor Strip. The case of Mark, described in detail at the end of Chapter 6, illustrates a case of agraphia that was caused purely by a motor disability (apraxia). The dysrhythmia was highly localized in the upper left motor strip (Exner's area, see Fig. 8.10) so that motor speech was normal, but fine movements of the right hand were abnormally slow. It should be noted that clinical evidence does not reliably support a highly localized motor writing area, as Exner proposed in 1881, but at least the manual area of the left motor strip in Mark's case was electrically disturbed enough to produce a mild manual apraxia resulting in slow but accurate writing.

Delayed Visual Feedback. Delayed visual feedback can produce a transient dysgraphia by introducing an abnormal delay between the act of writing and the appearance of the script. Van Bergeijk and David (1959) carried out an ingenious experiment to investigate the visual–motor pro-

Dear Mommy + Daddy,
I hope you had
a nice trip to
San Francisco:
I met Don and cince then
I went to a movie and
fishing.
Your loving son,
XOXOXO
Chuck

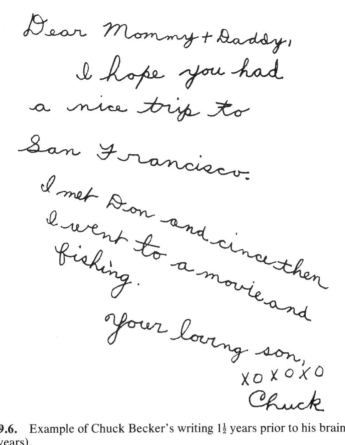

Figure 9.6. Example of Chuck Becker's writing $1\frac{1}{2}$ years prior to his brain injury (age 9 years).

cesses in writing, using a technique similar in design to delayed auditory feedback. Because it is well known that delaying a speaker's auditory awareness of his own speech will interfere with his normal fluent speech, Van Bergeijk and David asked subjects to write words on a *telewriter*, a device that can reproduce the person's writing on a separate viewing screen. Normally, the kinesthetic and visual experiences in writing are

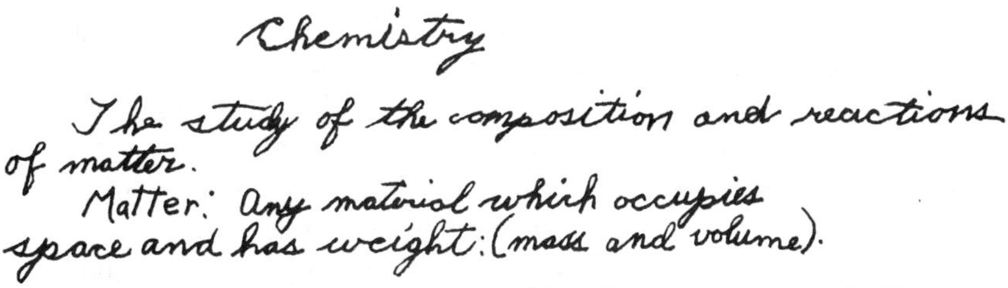

Chemistry
The study of the composition and reactions
of matter.
Matter: Any material which occupies
space and has weight: (mass and volume).

Figure 9.7. Sample of Chuck Becker's writing $4\frac{3}{4}$ years posttraumatically (age 15 years).

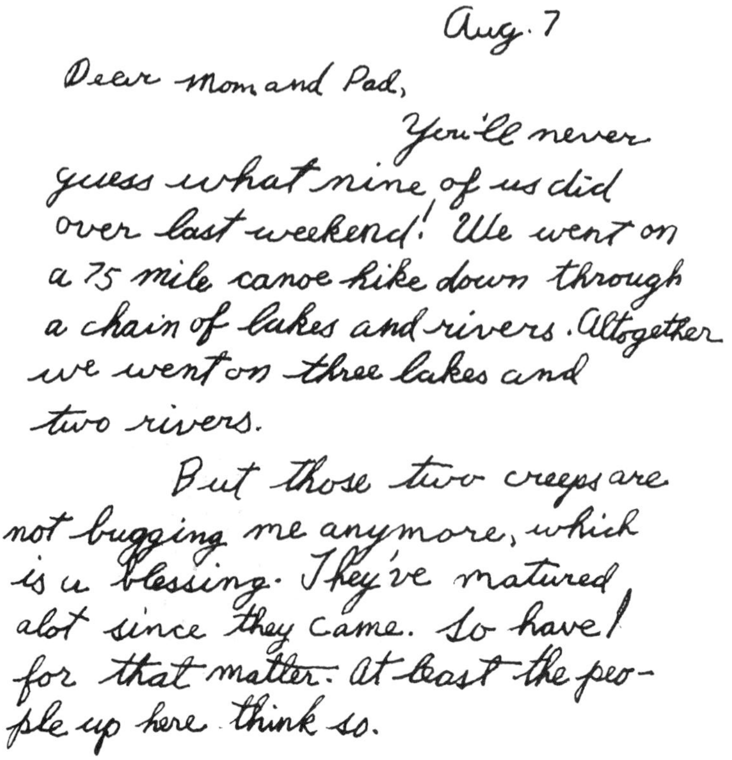

Aug. 7

Dear mom and Dad,

You'll never guess what nine of us did over last weekend! We went on a 75 mile canoe hike down through a chain of lakes and rivers. Altogether we went on three lakes and two rivers.

But those two creeps are not bugging me anymore, which is a blessing. They've matured alot since they came. So have I for that matter. At least the people up here think so.

Figure 9.8. Sample of Chuck Becker's writing 7 years posttraumatically (age $17\frac{1}{2}$ years).

simultaneous, but the telewriter permitted the experimenters to delay the visual input by 0 (no delay, or normal conditions), 40, 80, 150, 270, and 520 milliseconds. In terms of neatness, writing deteriorated monotonically with increased delay. As the delay was increased, errors of omissions, duplications, and substitutions (i.e., spelling errors) appeared. Frequently extra letters or wrong letters were inserted when the subjects were instructed they were to be scored on speed and neatness.

This experiment is an interesting reminder of the importance of the cerebral motor patterns in writing. They are integrated with visual input, visual imagery, visual and auditory memory, cerebral sequencing, language structure, and a number of other psychological and brain processes. Whenever one of these systems is disturbed, the behavioral product (writing) may also be impaired.

Occasionally, a brain lesion may disrupt the visual–motor integration of a dysgraphic child's ability to copy written material; such children write better when they cannot see what they are writing. For example, in the above experiment of Van Bergeijk and David, the subjects could easily have escaped from the effects of the telewriter by writing with their

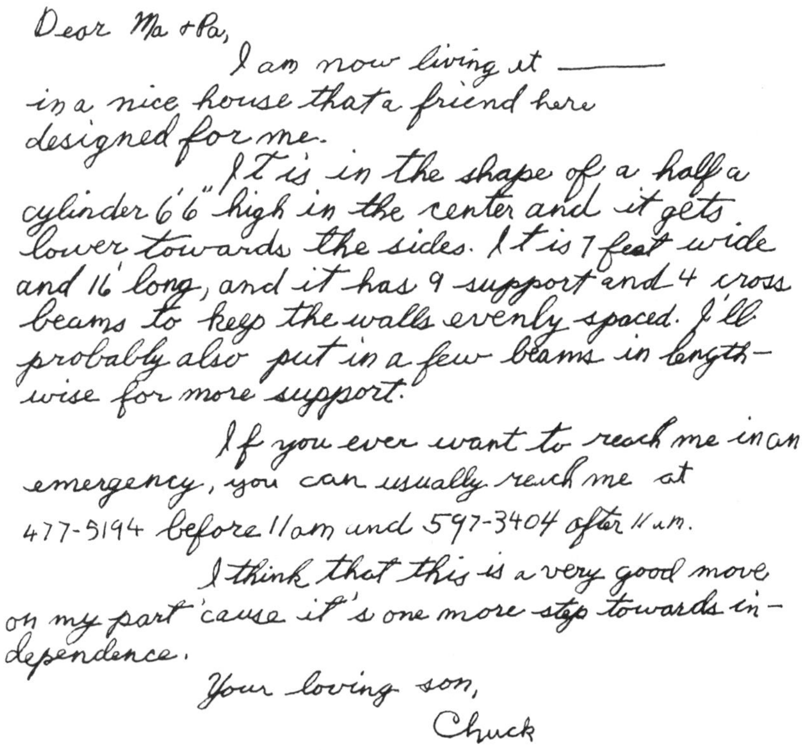

Dear Ma + Pa,
  I am now living at _____
in a nice house that a friend here
designed for me.
  It is in the shape of a half a
cylinder 6'6" high in the center and it gets
lower towards the sides. It is 7 feet wide
and 16' long, and it has 9 support and 4 cross
beams to keep the walls evenly spaced. I'll
probably also put in a few beams in length-
wise for more support.
  If you ever want to reach me in an
emergency, you can usually reach me at
477-5194 before 11 am and 597-3404 after 11 a.m.
  I think that this is a very good move
on my part 'cause it's one more step towards independence.
      Your loving son,
        Chuck

Figure 9.9. Example of Chuck Becker's writing 11 years posttraumatically (age 21½ years).

eyes closed. In our laboratory some years ago, we saw a 10-year-old boy who was unable to copy correctly from either the blackboard or a page near at hand. It was discovered that when his hand was shielded so that his writing was screened from view, his writing improved markedly both in neatness and in accuracy. Most remedial teachers have reported similar cases.

Visual Processes in Writing

We have already been introduced to the visual–motor processes in the above discussion. Here we will note that visual copying of letter forms is a primary function in the initial learning to write, but as the motor engrams become established they gradually become less strongly associated with the visual–perceptual aspects of writing and more strongly related to the visual and auditory imagery of the child and developing a knowledge of language.

As Luria (1970) has pointed out we investigate a person's writing by examining his ability (1) to copy written or printed material and (2) to write spontaneously. The first tests the level of visual–motor competence in writing, and the second taps all the concomitant psychological and neurological processes necessary to successful adult writing.

If the agraphic child can copy sentences accurately and neatly, then we know that the visual–motor integration necessary in writing is intact. This will then direct us to look at his auditory phonetic discrimination, oral verbal memory, auditory sequencing, abilities for syllabication and/or phonetic blending, or the possibility of an aphasia.

If the child's visual–motor integration is defective so as to produce visual–spatial disturbances in writing, a brain lesion most likely exists bilaterally in his parietal–occipital lobes, or unilaterally in the same area of the language dominant hemisphere (Luria, 1973). The writing of Donald, shown in Fig. 6.4, Chapter 6, illustrates his poor visual memory for the letter forms and his chaotic visual scanning. Figure 6.7 shows his marked improvement after 8 months of skilled remedial teaching.

Poor visual memory can lead to poor visual learning, defective writing, and chaotic spelling. So many deficits suggest the possibility of wide-spread or diffuse brain dysfunction, and it is typical of the chaotic speller of normal intelligence. Every teacher has had these students; they some-times appear even at the university level, although the less bright have usually dropped out before this to seek a less frustrating line of activity.

In Chapter 7 we observed that it is easier to draw a line from left to right with one's right hand, and from right to left with one's left hand. This is even more pronounced if one attempts a series of loops in continuous form like cursive writing. How then do Israelis write from right to left because most of them are right handed? The answer seems to be that Hebrew does not include a cursive style of writing; each letter or grapheme is spatially independent so that it is as easy to write in either direction. It is interesting to note that adult patients with progressive neurological deteriorating diseases frequently abandon cursive writing for printing in the last stages of their illnesses (Ferguson & Boller, 1977) because isolated letters are easier to produce. These observations can provide greater insights into the writing of children who tend to produce many reversals, to mirror-write, and to produce other left-right writing disorders. The educational diagnostician will need to look at handedness, cerebral dominance, and the relative frequency of errors in cursive and printed writing.

Carl. Carl was 7 years old when we first saw him and 11 years old when he wrote his mother from camp (Fig. 9.10). His birth had been a difficult one and he was cyanosed at 6 weeks (a "blue baby" because of lack of adequate oxygen in the blood). At the age of 1 year, seizures first appeared, which seemed to be clear evidence of a brain lesion or lesions in the medial parts of the brain, near enough to affect the motor strips.

By the age of 7 the seizures were well controlled with anticonvulsive medication, and although he had numerous learning problems in first

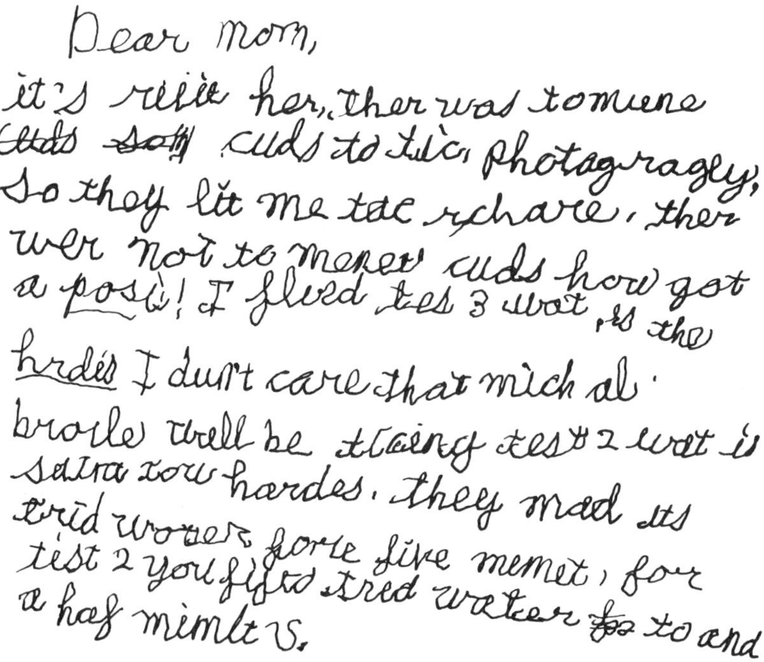

(Mother's Translation)

Dear Mom,

It's raining here. There were too many clouds to take photography so they let me take archery. There were not too many clouds, have got a picture. I failed test 3, what is the hardest. I don't care that much although I will probably be taking test 2 that is second to hardest. They made us tread water for five minutes for test two. You first tread water two and a half minutes.

Figure 9.10.   Sample of writing of Carl Morris, age 11.

grade, Carl was a likable and socially bright little boy. His Wechsler (WISC) showed a verbal IQ of 91 and a performance IQ of 89. He did well on the Block Design test (spatial imagery of nonverbal figures) but badly on all the other visual–perceptual tests. His memory for words (sentence repetition) and numbers (digit span) was weak. His auditory recognition of nonverbal sounds (e.g., a church bell, people clapping), normally an easy test for average 7-year-olds, was done poorly by Carl. His right–left orientation was so poor as to be in the defective range. Obviously, then, Carl had numerous deficits, poor visual memory, poor auditory memory, a defective visual–sequential ability, and an impaired directional sense. His oral language was normal for his age and his ability for productive ideas much above average.

Because his perceptual, intellectual, and motor deficits suggested diffuse minimal brain damage, and because his oral language and social development were good, Carl made steady progress on a remedial program that stressed puzzles and card games to improve his arithmetic and multisensorimotor drill to teach him to spell and write.

Pearson Morsby. Pearson Morsby was referred to our laboratory when he was 11 years old. His teacher knew that he was not mentally retarded but could not understand why he could not read above a Grade 1 level. In writing, his own name was his only accomplishment. Arithmetic was his best academic area, but his sight vocabulary was about 45 words. His memory was poor from day to day and this included a difficulty in remembering the shape of individual letters (poor visual memory). He also had difficulty associating phonetic sounds with specific letters because he could not remember their shapes. He had no problem repeating auditory stimuli.

Detailed neuropsychological testing revealed a developmental aphasia with an aphasic dyslexia. At a special remedial school they began by trying to teach Pearson the letters of the alphabet, but after 4 months he was still able to write only some of the letters and his recall of most of the rest was erratic. Because he was musical, the teacher decided to try singing. When it was put to the tune of "Baa-baa black sheep," Pearson learned the alphabet perfectly in 3 days.

Neuropsychologically this may be understood in terms of laterality. Because his brain dysfunction almost certainly must have been in the left hemisphere, or bilaterally in the occipito-parietal areas, when his language learning was shifted through singing to the right hemisphere he was able to learn the alphabet quickly. His teacher also encouraged him to sing the letters while writing and this improved his writing markedly.

Pearson was left handed although left-hemisphere dominant for language, and his sensorimotor skills were poor in his right hand. This is the picture of a "pathological left-hander" with probable dysfunction in the left temporal–parietal area.

Examples of Pearson's writing on his arrival at the special school are shown in Fig. 9.11. His marked improvement resulted from a detailed knowledge of his strengths and weaknesses and a skilled remedial use of his abilities. After 4 years of remedial teaching, Pearson was able to return to a special program in a public high school, where he can read and write accurately, but slowly, at a seventh-grade level.

Auditory Processes in Writing

Peripheral and Central Deafness. The case of Kathleen presented at the end of the previous chapter illustrated peripheral and central deafness. Until she was fitted with a suitable hearing aid she was unable to hear clearly the phonetic patterns of words, and hence did not possess the

Dictated words	Writing of Pearson
go	
cat	c a t
in	i n
boy	b o y
and	a n d
will	
make	h
him	h
say	s a h
cut	c' t
cook	c
light	n

Figure 9.11. Pearson Morsby's attempts to write to dictation, age 11½.

auditory mental images necessary to reconstruct the sequential syllables prior to translating them into the correct graphic-motor pattern.

Janet was a child of above-average intelligence with no particular academic learning problems. In Grade 3 she developed an infection in both ears, which resulted in a moderate peripheral deafness. Following recovery from the infection she returned to school, but a residual deafness persisted. This meant that she missed much of what was said in school and she was unable to gain very much from the phonics instruction. Gradually her hearing returned to normal and by Grade 7 she measured normally on a phonetic discrimination test, but her spelling has continued to suffer from her hard of hearing period, so that as an adult she still produces original spellings of many infrequent words. Obviously this type of case can be remedied with skilled teaching with a basic phonetic approach since her hearing is now normal.

Auditory Sequencing. Francis Martin was referred to our laboratory early in his freshman year, because of a serious spelling and writing problem. His verbal IQ on the Wechsler (WAIS) was 121, so it was not surprising that he liked to read and he enjoyed school. However, neuropsychological testing revealed a persistent weakness in all the sequencing tests, including auditory sequencing. While he enjoyed lively conversation on a topic with verbal ideas because his understanding was superior, he was unable to write essays because his spelling deficit impaired his level of language expression. His reading on a standardized test was only average and his spelling, atrocious.

Samples of his writing to copy (Fig. 9.12a) and his writing to dictation (Fig. 9.12b) prior to remedial teaching, and a spelling list of 20 words reveals numerous errors (Fig. 9.13). His performance 6 months later (Fig. 9.14) showed a marked improvement.

Because Francis' sequential skills were weak, his tutor gave him practice in serial order exercises in all three sense modes. Because Francis possessed a stronger auditor imagery than visual, the tutor stressed an auditory–tactile match in learning to write the spelling words, and he drew partially on Boder's teaching method for dyseidetic spellers (Boder, 1971). The tutor soon discovered that in spite of Francis' breezy, friendly manner, his spelling deficit was a constant worry to him and a threat to his self-confidence. With this insight the tutor worked on Francis' self-image, and the total remedial effort paid off in a brief 6 months. Francis went on and completed a BA degree in history.

Diagnosis and Remediation of Spelling Disability

To a person who has learned to spell with no difficulty, it seems incredible that any bright person might be unable to do what seems so common-

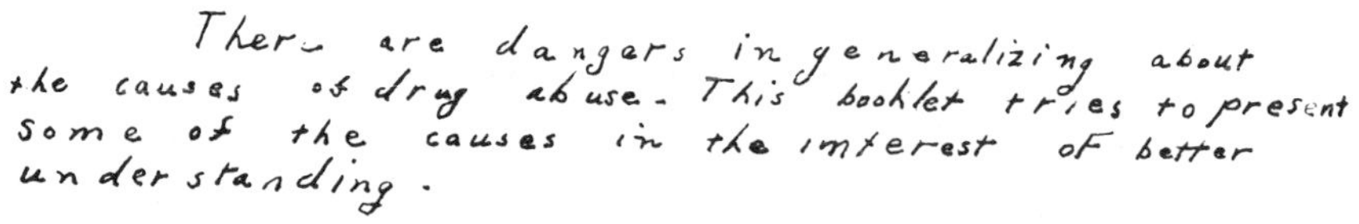

(a)

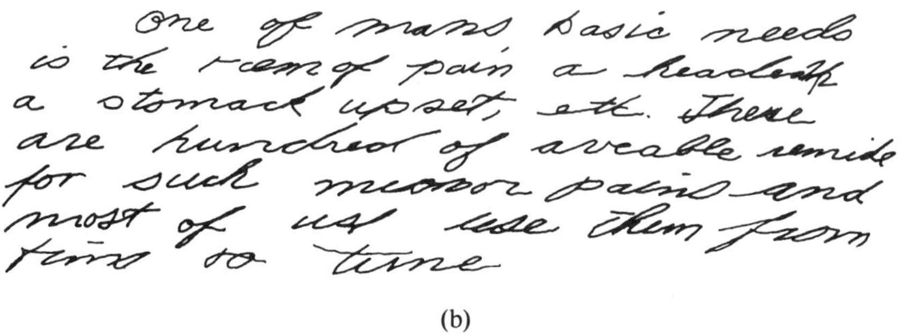

(b)

One of man's basic needs is the relief of pain — a headache or a stomach upset. There are hundreds of available remedies for such minor pains and most of us use them from time to time.

(c)

Figure 9.12. Samples of Francis Martin's writing prior to remedial teaching program. (a) Writing to copy; (b) writing to dictation; (c) text & dictated paragraph.

September 1972

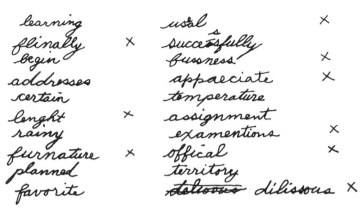

Figure 9.13. Sample of Francis Martin's written spelling prior to the remedial teaching program.

place. However, once an analysis of the whole complex process involved in written language has been done, it begins to become more believable.

There are probably as many causes for a spelling deficit as there are loci of brain lesions in the language circuits. Very simply, however, the cause will stress (1) a language deficit (aphasia); (2) a visual–perceptual

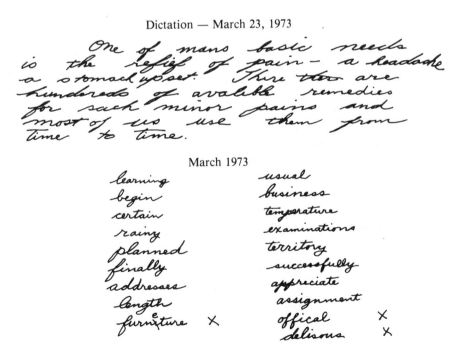

Dictation — March 23, 1973

March 1973

Figure 9.14. Samples of the same dictated paragraph and spelling list after 6 months of remedial teaching.

dysfunction; (3) an auditory–perceptual problem; (4) a motor–expressive sequential impairment, or (5) a combination of two or more of these.

While it is useful for diagnostic purposes to isolate language, visual, auditory, and motor processes, in reality that is a misrepresentation because all of these are integrated functions of *one process,* human behavior.

Vellutino (1978), in a thorough examination of developmental dyslexia, concluded that basic language deficits are the main causes of reading retardation and that perceptual–motor and sequencing impairments are secondary manifestations of verbal deficiencies. He points out that the child who has difficulty in relating the meaning of words to their acoustic patterns, in recognizing the phonetic structure of speech, and in understanding the grammatical or syntactical forms of language, will not only have difficulty in reading but also in writing. Regardless of their relative etiological value, certainly competence in phonological recognition, in semantic processing, and in syntactic comprehension are essential to normal reading and writing, and any remedial program should include them all as ultimate goals.

Much attention has already been given to visual and auditory perceptual processes in reading, so only a brief comment will be made here. In writing, the tactile–somesthetic functions take on more importance since a person can read without writing skills and can write without direct visual cues. Nevertheless, phonetic analysis is still needed to direct the manual–motor activity of writing legibly and spelling correctly. The recent interest in left-hemisphere trauma and profound reading difficulties (deep dyslexia) has been extended to writing and spelling. A patient, aged 57 years, who suffered a left cerebrovascular accident at age 47 and who was diagnosed as a deep dyslexic, also exhibited the same linguistic errors in written and oral naming and writing to dictation (Nolan & Caramazza, 1983). These researchers have proposed that any linguistic performance requiring lexical mediation (e.g., reading, writing spontaneously and to dictation, and oral and written naming) may exhibit the typical symptoms of deep dyslexia. This same patient could copy and repeat single words correctly because, as Nolan and Caramazza hypothesized, an intact phonological processing system can by-pass lexical mediation and be accessed directly by auditory input. One can repeat or echo a word without semantic understanding.

Before leaving a discussion of writing, a brief look at the "motor theory" of speech perception should be useful. This model of motor speech perception and production found its early beginnings in the work of Hughlings Jackson (1958), who was more concerned with the cortical representation of *movements* than the localization of *muscle* connections in the brain. More recently Luria (1973) has developed this idea by discriminating a simple motor *function* (e.g., electrostimulation of a point in the left motor strip may produce an involuntary muscular contraction in a finger of the right hand) and a *complete functional system* (e.g., writing, talking, walking, etc.). No behavioral movement is controlled only by efferent motor impulses traveling from the motor strips to the muscles; as well, there is a steady flow of afferent impulses providing feedback information about the location in space of the moving limb and the nature of its movement (kinesthesis). Hebb (1958) observed that all behavior is under sensory direction linked with an internal series of mediating processes and a constant feedback from muscle responses. With this model he proposed the "cell assembly" (i.e., the repeated stimulation of a number of neurons induces lasting cellular changes—the neural "trace"), and the "phase sequence," a complex and dynamic combination of a number of cell assemblies. The phase sequence provides the neural substrate for perception, motor response, and all intellectual activity. For Hebb, the awareness of body movement is important in perception, but "motor activity in itself cannot possibly explain the organization of perception, [but] nevertheless . . . it has an essential role" (Hebb, 1949, p. 83). This model has been adapted to explain speech perception (Liberman, Cooper, Shankweiler, & Studdert-Kennedy, 1967) as mediated by speech production. Since the speaker has acquired "all the mechanisms for putting language through the successive coding operations that result eventually in the acoustic signal," Liberman and her colleagues assumed that language encoding and decoding are *one process* "with appropriate linkages between sensory and motor components" (p. 452). Such a theoretical model is supported by the success of educational remedial programs that stress sensorimotor integration (Ayres, 1972a, b; Montessori, 1964). Nauta, the great neuroanatomist, has observed "that the brain builds its mental activity system either in parallel with or perhaps even with the *same* pathways as its motor systems" (reported by Denckla, 1983, p. 40).

The reader may have thought that we have wandered far from a discussion of writing and spelling, but in the remediation of any form of impaired or undeveloped behavioral skill, the exercise of neuromuscular *movement* is important to improve perception, understanding, and expressive response, whether that response is oral or written. All behavior is a holistic system of input, integration, and output, and the best type of remediation will activate all areas of this system. In diagnosing a spelling problem, the diagnostician needs to survey the behavioral skills and to decide on the areas of dysfunction and the correlative behavioral deficits. Because the writing process requires a phonetic analysis of the flow of speech, examining the child's auditory skills is a good place to start.

Auditory Processes and Aphasic Signs in Oral Speech

1. Is the child's hearing normal on an audiometric test? Has he ever had a history of ear infections and periods of partial deafness?
2. If his hearing is normal, can he perform normally on a phonetic discrimination test?

3. Can he recite all the letters of the alphabet?

4. Can he associate all of the phonetic sounds of all of the letters?

5. Is his auditory memory normal on a digit span test and a sentence repetition test?

6. Can he follow detailed oral instructions? (e.g., Token test)

7. Can he name common objects without hesitation?

8. Can he describe the use of common objects?

9. Word fluency: How many nouns can he produce in one minute?

10. Can he construct a meaningful sentence if given three words?

11. Can he read new words using phonetic analysis?

12. Can he blend syllables into words?

13. Does he have any obvious articulation problems? Did he when he was growing up?

14. Can he write single letters to dictation? Can he write one-syllable words to dictation?

15. Can he analyze a word phonetically aloud? Can he explain how he does this?

16. If you spell a word aloud can he tell you what it is?

17. Is his auditory sequencing normal?

Once the diagnostician has identified the auditory skills that are giving trouble, then remedial drills can be selected to strengthen them.

Visual Processes

1. Can the child look at pictures of commonplace objects and match them with a similar picture? (The 1916 Stanford–Binet test used this procedure with a number of animal pictures.)

2. Can he name each picture? (e.g., any picture vocabulary test)

3. Can he match geometric figures?

4. Can he name geometric figures?

5. Can he read all the letters of the alphabet?

6. Can he write all the letters of the alphabet?

7. Can he read words and sentences at his expected level?

8. Can he copy sentences accurately from the blackboard or a book?

9. Is his figure–ground visual perception normal?

10. Can he remember figures on a visual retention test (VRT)? (e.g., Benton VRT)

11. Is his visual sequencing normal?

12. Can he identify right and left on a person facing him or on a picture of a person?

13. Is his visual–motor performance normal: (e.g., Frostig tests)

Tactile Processes

1. Can the child write while blindfolded or with his hand obscured?

2. Can he "read" letters and numbers "written" on his palm or back with a stylus?

3. Can he trace letters and then write them correctly?

4. Can he recognize and name, by touch alone, common objects placed in his hand? If he can name an object by sight but is unable to name it by touch he is said to be suffering from "tactile aphasia." This may occur when the somesthetic areas of the parietal lobes are isolated from Wernicke's area and the occipital lobes. It may also occur in a lateralized way with a lesion of the corpus callosum that isolates the two somesthetic areas (Geschwind, 1965, I, pp. 287–290).

5. If an object that is similar to one of a group of objects scattered on the table is placed in the child's hand, can he match the two objects, i.e., the one he feels with the one he sees? This is cross-modal matching. If he can do this but cannot name the objects, the somesthetic and occipital cortical areas must be normally connected, but the speech areas isolated from both of these areas.

6. Is his tactile recognition much better in one hand than the other? Is it normal? (Spreen & Gaddes, 1969).

Aphasia

Any detailed aphasia battery includes a large number of auditory, visual, and tactile tests already included in the above three sections. However, using a battery such as the Spreen–Benton battery (Spreen & Benton, 1969/1977) has the advantage of providing normative data for children aged 6–13 years for each of the 20 subtests and an overall profile of the child's language development (Gaddes & Crockett, 1975). The Illinois Test of Psycholinguistic Abilities (Kirk, McCarthy, & Kirk, 1968) is also useful in providing some of this same information.

Motor-Expressive Processes

In spelling, the motor-expressive acts that are of greatest importance are manual (writing) and articulatory (oral speech). The diagnostician will want to know:

1. What is the child's finger tapping speed for each hand? Are they both normal? If not, which one is not? What is their relative pattern?

2. What is the child's hand-grip strength for each hand? Is there a difference between hands? What is the pattern?

3. Is his motor sequencing normal? Can he imitate tapping patterns?

4. Is his spontaneous speech clear and free from articulation problems?

5. Can he imitate words on an articulation test?

6. Is his oral reading smooth and accurate?

Intersensorimotor Integration

It is obvious that spelling requires a subtle and smoothly running integration of a large number of neurological and psychological functions. A knowledge of the locus of a brain lesion or an area of cerebral dysfunction may help the diagnostician, the school psychologist, or the special teacher to understand an uneven or isolated behavior in a child with a writing or spelling problem. For example, Geschwind's explanation of tactile anomia resulting from a disconnection of the sensory strip and the speech areas is logical and should direct the diagnostician to stress a visual–auditory–motor prescription. It is difficult to teach spelling to a child with this type of defect, but if a skilled remedial program is begun early he can be taught by stressing his strengths.

Numerous multisensorimotor methods for teaching spelling have been used for many years (Fernald, 1943). Writing letters on the child's back (Blau, 1968) and having him or her sound them phonetically is an attempt to link the somesthetic and auditory centers of the brain. Asking the child to write his spelling words in damp sand with the index finger while he sounds the word simultaneously reinforces the tactile (granular feel and temperature differential), auditory, and visual sense modes with the manual–motor activity. This exercise attempts to build engrams linking the occipital, temporal, parietal, and motor strip areas that are crucial to correct writing.

If the diagnostician can provide the special teacher with a clear inventory of the child's strengths and weaknesses, and a prescription of remedial procedures that he or she believes on an *a priori* basis should be successful, then the teacher may select from his or her own repertoire of remedial techniques. Once a clearly defined diagnostic understanding of the child's strengths and weaknesses is made available to the special teacher it is an easy task to select a battery of remedial techniques that would seem, on a basis of logic, to be suitable. Any experienced teacher already has developed an armamentorium of teaching skills to draw from.

Developmental Agraphia

Within the neuropsychological model, a congenital deficit in writing is simply a form of developmental expressive aphasia. Typically, there is an impaired ability to express oneself in writing without any disorder of the peripheral speech mechanisms or the writing hand and arm (Orton, 1937). Children suffering from a developmental agraphia are retarded in learning to write "because the necessary areas of the brain do not develop in the normal manner, or at the usual rate" (Myklebust, 1965).

If born with a dysfunction, even very minimal, in the left motor or premotor area of his brain, the child will likely have problems of awkward or slow handwriting and/or sequential problems in spelling. Minimal dysfunctions in the posterior parts of the child's brain may result in poor letter and word recognition. Temporal lobe dysfunction in the language-dominant hemisphere may result in poor phonetic discrimination and any number of aphasic symptoms. Diffuse and minimal brain dysfunctions are likely to impair the cross-modal integration relating these different cortical areas. Behaviorally this may result in poor handwriting, defective spelling, and/or inferior linguistic expression. The child whose penmanship is untidy but who can spell and write written language normally for his or her age is no real problem. The "nonspeller" and the child who cannot generate verbally expressed ideas and commit them to paper are definitely educational responsibilities.

Nelson and Warrington (1976) have examined two groups of "nonspellers": (1) those retarded in both reading and spelling, and (2) those retarded only in spelling. Both of these groups are of interest in the consideration of developmental spelling agraphia. In a study of 121 of these children, these authors found a pattern of lower VIQ on the WISC for the dyslexic–spelling retardates, and no significant difference between VIQ and PIQ for the spelling-only retardates. It will be remembered that in the single case of Francis Martin, reported above, his VIQ was 121 and his PIQ 102. In other words, this chaotic speller who was an above-average reader was not impaired in either verbal or performance IQs, a finding in agreement with Naidoo (1972).

Nelson and Warrington grouped the spelling errors of their subjects in three major categories: (1) order error (i.e., defective sequencing), (2) phonetically inaccurate (i.e., the addition or omission of an unrelated or necessary phoneme), and (3) phonetically accurate (i.e., cases in which the phonetic structure was maintained but with inappropriate graphemes, e.g., cucumber spelled Qcomeber). The reading plus spelling retardates made more phonetically inaccurate errors than the spelling-only retardates, which is similar to the case for adults who have received brain injuries resulting in dysphasia. Although we cannot translate the behavior deficits of traumatically brain-damaged adults directly to learning disabled children, it seems obvious that the spelling deficit of the dyslexic nonspeller is "one aspect of a more generalized language retardation" (Nelson & Warrington, 1976).

A more recent study with large sample groups (Finucci et al., 1983) examined 483 children in Grades 3 to 12 divided into four groups: (1) 69 disabled readers with an average age of 11.5 years; (2) 85 school-age siblings of the disabled readers in group 1; (3) 88 adolescent disabled readers from the Gow School with an average age of 16.2 years; and (4) 241 normal controls with an average age of 13.9 years. These researchers classified spelling errors as (1) phonetic errors included attempted words that could be pronounced to sound like the test word, e.g., *nachur* for *nature*; and (2) dysphonetic errors included three subgroups, those with omitted, added, or interchanged syllables. The reader will note that these classification names differ from those of Nelson and Warrington in that the names imply an exclusive impairment of auditory processing, when, in fact, the second group appears to include some errors of visual sequencing and visual memory. While the names differ, the types of spelling errors are basically similar in the two studies.

In brief, Finucci *et al.* concluded that (1) the type of spelling error is independent of sex; (2) in good readers IQ has little effect on the proportion of dysphonetic errors; (3) for the disabled readers IQ made a difference in the proportion of dysphonetic errors; and (4) disabled readers as a group are more likely to produce dysphonetic errors than are normal readers.

The spelling-only retardate is an interesting child because, as already reported, he or she may not be impaired at all either in the WISC VIQ or PIQ when compared with normal controls. Such a child may read normally and possess no signs of a generalized language weakness. Because Kinsbourne and Warrington (1964), in an earlier study of brain-damaged adults, had found that on an oral spelling task those with dysphasia were more likely to produce phonetically inaccurate errors and those with finger agnosia made more sequential errors, Nelson and Warrington (1976) expected they might find the same pattern in spelling disabled children. They did, in part, in that the reading disabled nonspellers made phonetically inaccurate errors, but the spelling-only children made no more sequential errors than the poor readers. They did, however, make significantly fewer phonetically inaccurate errors than were made by the reading plus spelling retardates.

The evidence from the above studies, and our own clinical evidence of spelling-agraphic subjects suggests the following tentative conclusions:

1. The dyslexic nonspellers, whether adults or children, will also manifest a number of dysphasic symptoms. These may include a dysnomia, an impoverished vocabulary, poor phonetic discrimination, or any of the usual symptoms of aphasia.

2. The child or the adult who is retarded both in reading and spelling will tend to make phonetically inaccurate errors more than any other.

3. The adult nonspeller-only may read at a normal level or better, but will show poor sequencing or defective letter order and phonetically accurate errors. He or she may also exhibit a mild finger agnosia and other

behavioral signs of sensorimotor lesions (e.g., tactile sensitivity, finger tapping, finger praxis).

4. The child who is retarded only in spelling but not reading will demonstrate more phonetically accurate errors but may or may not show sequencing problems in letter order.

5. Subjects with left temporal lesions may have problems in both reading and spelling, producing phonetically inaccurate errors in their written language.

6. Subjects with left motor strip lesions may have problems in spelling but not reading, making sequential and/or phonetically accurate spelling errors.

Although there is already a body of evidence to suggest the validity of these hypotheses, more clinical research is needed until we understand more fully the neuropsychological relationships underlying agraphia and spelling disability.

Arithmetic

"On the one hand, a great deal is known about mathematics, far more than any learning disabled child or professional working with the child will ever have to know. On the other hand, very little is known about disabilities in mathematics, less about effective measurement and diagnosis, even less about effective intervention, and still less about children who manifest problems in mathematics" (Cawley, 1981). Most educators agree that there is a relative lack of adequate research into, understanding of, and development of validated remedial programs for children and adults with particular difficulty with arithmetic. Like any scientific study, new knowledge will come from various relevant sources. In this section we will examine briefly some findings from clinical physiology and neuropsychology that promise to enrich what the educator already knows. We will look at (1) the neuropsychological–cognitive aspects of the learner, and their relation to some basic arithmetical functions, and (2) the educational environment and the learner's emotional–social perception of and response to it.

The following discussion includes an examination of (1) an acquired disorder of calculating ability in adults as a result of traumatic brain damage (this is known medically as acalculia), and (2) developmental arithmetical retardation in children. While teachers are concerned almost exclusively with the second of these, an examination of the first may aid an understanding of both.

Arithmetical Functions

In any clinical–psychological study of a learning disorder, it is necessary to make a task analysis of the particular learning behavior and relate this to a neuropsychological examination of the learner. First, then, we will investigate some basic processes involved in mathematical calculation and then look at evidence of impairment resulting from known brain lesions or cerebral dysfunction.

Number Concept

The normal adult, when told the number "seven," can produce a mental concept that has meaning for him in terms of quantity. Seven can be represented concretely with seven environmental objects, but the normal adult also associates with the word "seven," an abstract concept that he can manipulate as realistically, and much more easily and quickly, than he can the concrete objects. In periods of malnutrition, extreme fatigue, or illness or following brain damage or dysfunction, a person may be unable to produce or have great difficulty in producing the necessary symbolic operation to give meaning to a perceived number.

Soldiers subjected to decompression chamber experiments were rendered temporarily aphasic when the oxygen content of the air was reduced below certain critical levels (see Chapter 8). If asked to write "seven" they could usually do it because of the overlearned motor stereotype involved, but they might have great difficulty in trying to remember what the quantity "seven" meant.

This type of evidence tells us that there is a relation between acalculia and aphasia, that the perception and writing of numbers is more resistant to the debilitating effects of aphasia than their abstract conceptual aspects, and that competent abstraction depends on healthy metabolism in the brain.

Relative Value

Although number concept demands an association of a meaningful mental image, numbers are rarely, if ever, used in isolation. Social behavior makes constant demands to decide, for example, How far am I from that? Is this bigger or smaller than that? Is its increase linear or erratic? How do I walk through this room full of furniture? As Cohn (1971) has pointed out, "Interacting organisms must be aware of inhomogeneities in their environment in order to make necessary physical adaptations." Put in simpler terms, a person must be able to count, to judge relative size, and to estimate immediate distances in order to move about and carry on a normal social life, since mobility implies a three-dimensional spatial perception of the world. In fact, Luria (1966, pp. 158–162) gives great emphasis to the close relationship between arithmetical operations and spatial imagery and spatial concepts.

Some years ago I was interested in exploring the relation between the vividness of number imagery, which was spatial, and competence in arithmetic. This investigation was initiated by a sophomore student who had unusually vivid number imagery. He thought of the digits on the circumference of a circle with one at 6 o'clock and the numbers from 1 to 9 and zero arranged clockwise and in correct numerical order. As well, each number was in a different color, 1 was always white, 2 blue, 3 yellow, and so forth. If he thought of any number it always had the same color, and this was consistent even with multidigit numbers. He was surprised when I told him that everyone had his or her own system for imagining numbers; until then he had assumed that everyone conceptualized numbers in color on a circle as he did. It would seem reasonable to think that anyone who could visualize numbers so vividly would have an advantage in learning arithmetic, but as it happened this student had had great difficulty getting through the freshman course in mathematics.

To investigate the problem, the arithmetic scores from the college admissions test of 147 freshmen were correlated with their responses on a questionnaire designed to investigate their number imagery. These responses were dichotomized as "vivid" or "unclear." Most respondents who used number imagery saw numbers from left to right in a straight line, a few saw them in circles, and very few associated color with them. A large number were unable to describe any kind of visual or spatial number imagery, or it was so vague as to be relegated to the "unclear" category. A biserial correlation between the 147 arithmetic scores and the two classes of number imagery showed a correlation close to zero. In other words, as many students with vivid as with vague imagery did well, and those with poor scores also came equally from the two groups. Those with vivid number imagery claimed it helped them to calculate, but those with no definitive imagery who were skilled mathematicians could see no real meaning in the question. Sir Francis Galton, himself a brilliant mathematician, possessed no visual number imagery. In a fascinating discussion of "Number Forms," he wrote, "I see no 'Form' myself" (Galton, 1907).

Although vivid visual number imagery appears to be unrelated to success in arithmetic, basic spatial skills are related. Luria (1966) has found that lesions of the parieto-occipital areas of the brain result in impaired spatial imagery and in acalculia, and Hécaen (1962) includes the "spatial type" of dyscalculia as one of the three major categories of the disorder.

Electrostimulation of the left and right thalamus has been found to impair arithmetic ability differentially (Ojemann, 1974). Left thalamic stimulation tended to accelerate the rate of counting backwards and to increase calculation errors. Right thalamic stimulation tended to slow the counting rate and to increase calculation errors. Ojemann believes that the right thalamus is related to somesthetic and spatial functions, and it may have a role in number reading. This seems quite likely because the right thalamus and the cortex of the right hemisphere are structurally interconnected and the disconnected right hemisphere has been found better than the left in reading calligraphy and numbers (E. Zaidel, 1973). This could explain why most dyslexic subjects, who cannot read words, can usually read numbers (see the case of Mr. Darwin, page 291ff.). Bradshaw and Nettleton have provided a brief but detailed summary of a number of studies investigating arithmetic and the right hemisphere (Bradshaw & Nettleton, 1983, p. 155).

It is obvious that written arithmetic contains many spatial demands. Multidigit numbers must be written horizontally from left to right and spaced evenly. Addition sums usually are written in vertical columns, and the answer is measured from the decimal to the left, the units, tens, hundreds, and thousands having their value indicated by their spatial position. Multiplication and long division demand not only horizontal and vertical spacing but oblique spacing to the left in multiplication and to the right in long division.

To aid a child to develop a number concept the teacher may place objects spatially on the table or mark "tallies" on a sheet. The spatial ability appears to be related to the concepts of larger than, smaller than, farther, closer, and all relative measures. Cuisinaire rods and other concrete number-teaching aids are designed to assist the learner to improve spatial imagination, relative value, and number concept.

Accurate Reading of Numbers

Making detailed clinical studies of many traumatically brain-damaged adults, Luria (1970, p. 358) devised a systematic examination to estimate the degree and nature of acalculia. The educator may find this type of investigation useful because it relates arithmetic impairment to brain dysfunctions. Luria checked the subject's ability to read numbers in the following procedure: (1) He would ask the person to count aloud and then ask him to stop. This was to establish whether he has the memory for numbers and whether he can recall them in the correct order. (2) Having established that the subject knows the names of the numbers, Luria would attempt to discover whether he knows the quantity associated with each one by showing the subject a number of objects grouped together on the table and asking him how many there are. (3) Having established the subject's ability in (1) and (2), the next step was to discover whether he could read one-digit numbers accurately. The subject was shown a card with a single digit written or printed on it and asked to point to the group of objects on the table having the same number. This established the ability to read single numbers and recognize their value. (4) To discover whether the subject could write single digits, Luria would point to one group of objects among several of differing sizes and ask him to write the number of objects. (5) The above four tests relate to the reading and writing of single digit numbers. If the brain-injured adult is competent on all these tasks then Luria would examine his comprehension of the decimal system and success in reading multidigit numbers. The impaired person was asked to read orally multidigit numbers with zeros in them (e.g., 201, 1010, 2006). (6) Another test to discover the subject's understanding of numbers was to ask him which of two numbers is larger. Pairs such as 601 and 598 or 1000 and 978 test whether the subject understands the decimal system or whether he is looking at the largest single digit. (7) Presenting the two numbers, such as 16 and 61 or 573 and 375, and asking the subject if they are equal or not reveals at least three cognitive or perceptual defects. If pairs of numbers such as the above are perceived as equal, this may mean that the subject is dyslexic for numbers (a visual agnosia caused by an occipital–parietal lesion bilaterally or unilaterally on the dominant side), that his spatial abilities are impaired (a biparietal lesion), or that he is unable to conceptualize the quantities of such numbers (a receptive aphasia resulting from a left temporal lobe lesion and/or generalized bilateral dysfunction). (8) Having established all of the above skills, the next step was to examine the patient's ability for the basic automatic number skills. The addition, subtraction, and multiplication tables were examined. If the brain-injured adult has these processes intact, it is almost certain that his brain injury is in the areas peripheral to those parts of the nondominant hemisphere that mediate directional orientation and spatial skills, or outside of the speech areas in the dominant side. If the subject is partially impaired, it is likely he is dysphasic with a left temporal lesion. If the aphasia causes the subject to think of one number and say another (similar to the case of John Hall) dysfunctions are likely in the left temporal lobe and may be affecting the arcuate fasciculus and the motor–speech areas. It is important to observe the methods used by the patient to express the automatized number facts. Does he or she write them (visual–motor)? Does he recite them (oral speech)? Does he write them and elicit minimal speech movements (visual–auditory–motor–verbal)? (9) The next step was to see whether the subject can use these facts in situations that have not usually been memorized. Luria suggested starting by asking the impaired adult to subtract a single-digit number from a two-digit one, e.g., 41 minus 6. Such a task requires "that several components be present in the field of consciousness at once" (Luria, 1970). A more complex problem requires the subtraction of a two-digit number from another two-digit number, e.g., 83 − 19. Successful completion of these kinds of problems assures the diagnostician that the patient's number facts are intact and that he or she can conceptualize to handle two differing number quantities and carry out the mental imagery necessary to the particular computation. (10) Sequential calculations demand an ability to remember answers from preceding problems and to use them as a basis for a subsequent operation. Common examples are taking 7s from 100 or adding or subtracting a long series of numbers presented orally. Success in these types of tasks demonstrates a facility in basic number facts and a flexible number imagery necessary for varying operations and numerical relationships. (11) The last stage was to present problems requiring the ability for both inductive and deductive reasoning. The brain-injured adult may show some difficulty here, even though he or she has been successful in the reading and writing of numbers and the automatizing of basic number facts. Abstract reasoning is believed to draw on the whole brain, at least the whole cortex and specific subcortical mechanisms (Ojemann, 1974), so that lesions anywhere in the cortex or thalamic area are likely to increase mental rigidity and hence reduce rapid adaptive intelligence.

Luria's studies of traumatically brain-damaged adults led him to conclude that damage to the language dominant parieto-occipital areas may result in alexia for numbers or a confusion of one number with another. This is a somewhat rare occurrence, the dyslexic individual usually being able to read numbers. A lesion in the left temporal lobe may result in a difficulty in attaching conceptual meaning to spoken numbers, and this type of patient can usually read numbers normally but has difficulty writing long numbers because of a deficit in inner speech.

Clinical vigilance usually shows a combination of poor number reading and writing and calculation and arithmetical reasoning, no doubt because they all draw markedly on the left hemisphere (Hécaen, 1962). Spatial dyscalculia results largely from right-hemisphere lesions and acalculia involving all of these impairments implies bilateral dysfunctions.

While it is invalid to translate findings of acalculia in traumatically brain-damaged adults to children with developmental number retardation, it should be useful to use Luria's clinical diagnostic procedure to examine the cognitive deficits in their disability.

Developmental Number Retardation

The neuropsychological model of the basic causes of disturbances in arithmetical operations (i.e., spatial, visual–gnostic, and auditory–gnostic) is useful in helping us understand how normal number skills develop and how to diagnose a developmental number retardation. Although we are concentrating on neuropsychological deficits in this discussion, it is obvious that there are other psychological and environmental reasons for poor arithmetical achievement, such as anxiety, cultural attitudes, or poor teaching. Because of its uncompromising structure and function, arithmetic seems to stimulate anxiety in students more than reading, writing, and artistic endeavors. In arithmetic, reality is imposed rigidly on the child, and if he cannot meet its demands, he has failed. In creative drama, the child creates his own reality, so that in that sense he cannot fail. However, assuming that the child is reasonably happy and secure in the classroom setting, is motivated to learn, and is taught imaginatively, and still is unable to learn arithmetic as well as might be normally expected, a developmental disability may be suspected. The teacher or diagnostician will then proceed to carry out a task analysis to determine the areas of trouble.

The precise origin of developmental dyscalculia is not known, because, like developmental aphasia, it is less clearly defined than in the acquired or traumatic type in older children or adults. However, the few cases that have come to postmortem suggest very strongly that it is related to the abnormal or underdevelopment of the parietal, temporal, and occipital cortices on both sides and the intracerebral mechanisms with hearing and language.

In Billy's case (Drake, 1968), described in Chapter 8, he was reported to have "some trouble with arithmetic" and a table of his achievement from Grade 1 through Grade 6 showed him to be near or slightly below average each year. However, his spoken language was normal, as was his spatial imagery (WISC Block Design score 9 at age 10, and 10 at age 12). His visual perception for small details as measured by the WISC Picture Completion subtest was 11 at age 10, and 9 at age 12. In oral arithmetic, as measured by the WISC Arithmetic subtest, he measured only 6 at age 10 (which is poor), and 9 at age 12 (which is low average). The evidence from this case suggests that with normal auditory language, and average visual–cognitive and spatial skills, Billy, in spite of his biparietal and callosal underdevelopment, was able to manage classroom arithmetic for his age at a near-average level. Put another way, he was not aphasic, and his spatial and visuocognitive skills were near normal.

The second case (Landau, Goldstein, & Kleffner, 1960), also discussed in Chapter 8, concerned a boy who seemed mentally bright enough but had no speech. At age 6 he measured a performance IQ of 78, and 2 years later, after specialized teaching in a class for aphasic children, his performance IQ measured 97. At this time, at the age of 8, he could count to 5 (something that is common to many preschoolers) and his number concepts were poor. By the age of 9 he could add and subtract numbers up to 10, an achievement normally reached before the end of first grade. At age 10 he measured an educational quotient of 76, but no information was provided regarding his arithmetical skill. By comparison, this boy showed progress much inferior to Billy's, and probably the major contributing factor was his aphasia. We are provided with no detailed information about either his spatial imagery or his visual–perceptual competence, as we were in the case of Billy, but it seems safe to conclude that they were average because his last performance IQ measured 97. This evidence suggests that developmental problems in auditory language probably are more devastating to arithmetical competence than is a deficit in any other psychological process, because it impairs inner language, conceptual growth, and incidental learning.

Cohn (1968) has provided some interesting case histories with data from neurological examinations. He concludes that developmental dyscalculia is manifested by (1) malformed, frequently reversed, or large number symbols; (2) dyslexia; (3) inability to sum single integers; (4) inability to recognize operator signs and to use linear separators; (5) failure to read accurately the correct value of multidigit numbers because of their order and spacing; (6) poor memory for basic number facts; (7) failure to "carry" numbers where appropriate; and (8) inaccurate ordering and spacing of numbers in multiplication and division. The reader will recognize the close relationship between this list of behavioral deficits and Luria's sequential examination of acalculia in traumatically brain-damaged adults.

Arithmetical Aptitude, Nonverbal Learning, and Social Adjustment

One of the first to recognize the important relationship between nonverbal learning and social adjustment was Myklebust (1975b) who produced many new insights pertaining to this reciprocal association. Because all learning implies both verbal and nonverbal processes, and because the verbal aspects of learning have attracted most attention in the past, Myklebust examined nonverbal intelligence and its relation to academic achievement. Nonverbal learning, in addition to including spatial–constructional skills, temporal estimates, the knowledge of body parts, and directional sense, also implies social perceptions of oneself and of others. Competent social understanding is intimately related to personal independence and greater comprehension of the subtleties of social interactions. Myklebust has proposed that because a weak ability for social perceptions limits one's inner experience, and because this has an impoverishing effect on all deductions and adaptive learning, it is reasonable to conclude that nonverbal learning disorders "are more debilitating than verbal disabilities" (Myklebust, 1975b). He argues that while both verbal and nonverbal skills contribute simultaneously to normal information processing in social perceptions, verbal deficits may have little effect on nonverbal experiences, but nonverbal impairments can produce serious distortions in social perceptions. People so impaired may have fluent speech but may be indecisive, emotionally immature, and socially dependent. Examinations of large samples of children supported his hypotheses. Academically failing students of normal intelligence possessed significantly poorer nonverbal skills on a battery of performance tests. These children were less able to produce time concepts; to orient themselves in space; to make judgments of size, speed, height, and laterality; to identify body parts; to carry out motor activities smoothly; and to behave in a socially mature way. A discriminant function analysis showed a large number of performance tests to discriminate between LD and normal children.

As we have already seen, the cognitive functions involved in arithmetical calculations (i.e., number concept, relative value, and accurate reading of numbers) draw heavily on basic spatial skills, abilities essential to success on all or most performance tests. Strang and Rourke (1983) found that a group of children whose arithmetic scores on the Wide Range Achievement Test (Jastak & Jastak, 1965) were at least 1.8 years higher than their reading and spelling scores on the same test, had a mean performance IQ (PIQ) on the WISC (Wechsler, 1949) of 107.2 and a mean verbal IQ (VIQ) of only 92.27. Another group with the reverse pattern (i.e., reading and spelling scores more than at least 2 years higher than arithmetic) had a mean VIQ of 102.2 and a mean PIQ of 87.93. Differences in both cases were highly significant. With these findings these researchers concluded that, "It would seem clear that the deficient nonverbal concept-formation and reasoning abilities found to be characteristic of Group 3 children [i.e., those with VIQ > PIQ] contribute in some way to their social inadequacies" (Strang & Rourke, 1983). They also found that on the Halstead Category Test (a test of inductive and deductive reasoning using geometric figures in spatial relationships) the Group 2 children (i.e., those with PIQ > VIQ) tended to improve with experience while Group 3 children did not benefit to the same extent.

Myklebust has provided a number of detailed case histories to illustrate individual examples of his group findings that led him to conclude that, "No longer is it feasible to consider deficits in learning only in psycholinguistic terms or only in any other terms that overlook the nonverbal aspects of experience" (1975b). These comprise not only social comprehension and nonverbal reasoning, but should also include emotional and motivational aspects. This means that the social behavior and learning strategies of the learner should be included in a comprehensive examination of cognitive structure and development.

Drawing on Luria's model of the functional organization of the brain (see Chapter 3, page 77ff.), Das, a student of Luria, and his colleagues have developed a theory of intelligence that sees *coding* and *planning* as the basic cognitive functions (Das, Kirby, & Jarman, 1979). Within coding they include Luria's concepts of *simultaneous* and *successive* processing. By coding, Das, Kirby, and Jarman recognize the cognitive functions of

Luria's second cerebral functional unit or block, that is, the reception, analysis, and storage of information. Physically this block of the brain was conceived by Luria to include the post-Rolandic areas. Like Luria, Das, Kirby, and Jarman see planning and executive direction as the principal funciton of the frontal lobes. To summarize, "The three blocks of the brain are concerned respectively, with arousal, coding, and planful behavior" (Das, Kirby, & Jarman, 1979). Intelligent behavior is conceived as including an adequate level of arousal (Block 1), comprehensive knowledge (Block 2), and a competence in creative thinking, planning, and decision making (Block 3). A weakness in any one or more of these can lead to inferior learning.

An example of simultaneous processing is looking at a map or geometric figure, where all parts of the stimulus can be perceived at once. An example of successive processing is listening to or reading human speech, where each part is perceived serially and the whole meaning is not conveyed until the end of the sentence. As well, serial processing has been attributed largely to left-hemisphere function and simultaneous processing largely to the right.

This model of cognition, while not complete, has been useful for examining academic achievement because coding and planning are involved in all learning tasks, although some types of learning stress one more than the other. For example, learning a ten-word vocabulary list does not require much planning; it depends primarily on verbal memory and retrieval. Arithmetical facts are memorized and coded, but using them in problem solving requires decision making and planning (i.e., adaptive intelligence).

Kirby and Ashman (1984) have examined the possible relation between planning skills and achievement in mathematics. They see some aspects of the ability for planning susceptible to instructions, and its weakness as one of the causes of poor academic achievement in LD children. By a factor analysis they found four types of planning that emerged from the tests that they used: a scanning factor, both visual (e.g., mazes) and verbal (e.g., word fluency); a rehearsal factor (specific to digit span tasks); a clustering factor (specific to semantic categorizing of common objects); and a metacognition factor employed in open-ended situational problems. They compared the arithmetic scores of 121 Grade 5 students with their scores on a battery of planning tests and concluded that the scanning, or selective attention factor, is the best predictor of mathematical achievement, followed perhaps by metacognition.

The few research studies cited here point to a possible relationship between "social intelligence" and mathematical ability, and while much more study of this relationship is needed to clarify it, these studies may alert the educator to the recognition of much broader cognitive and behavioral attributes in mathematical competence than has been formerly and generally realized.

Piaget and Luria

Probably no one has examined the development of the child's cognitive growth in more depth than Piaget, and no one has studied in more detail the neuropsychological relationships of cerebral dysfunction than Luria, so that a comparison of their work should prove useful.

Although Piaget was not primarily concerned with establishing normative data for children, all of his studies revealed an emerging cognitive complexity determined by the biological growth of the child. "Piaget's early academic training was in zoology, and his theory of cognitive development is rooted firmly there" (Phillips, 1975). The biology of the growing human brain and its relation to learning is just beginning to be understood. As recently as 1950 Lashley admitted an inability to find any difference in brain structure following learning (Lashley, 1950), but since then histological evidence has appeared (Conel, 1939–1963) to reveal a marked change in brain structure with growth and experience. Although the total number of neurons in the central nervous system is almost complete at birth and continues to increase only for a very short period postnatally, the work of Conel has shown a marked increase in dendritic arborization at the age of 3, 15, and 24 months postnatally (see Fig. 9.15). Although it is evident that the engram or neural trace accompanying learning is not an increase in

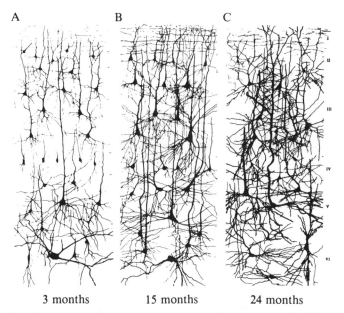

Figure 9.15. Drawings of sections from the cerebral cortex of children aged 3, 15, and 24 months. The increased growth of interconnections and the thickening of the dendrites can be observed with age. (From the work of Conel, A, 1947; B, 1955; C, 1959. With the permission of Dr. Karl H. Pribram.)

neural cell bodies it may result from (1) neural growth of growth cones or amoeboid-like structures on the tips of dendritic branches; (2) the increase of neuroglia, nonneural tissue that supports the neurons; or (3) biochemical changes at the synapse or within the neurons, which possess some degree of permanence (Pribram, 1971).

Regardless of the physiological etiology of the neural trace, Piaget's work possesses literally hundreds of examples of cognitive change from perceptual naiveté to logical abstraction, and from simplicity to mental complexity, that parallel the development of the brain and nervous system. In studying the mental imagery of the child at ages 5, 7, and 11 years and at the adult level, he found a progressive decrease in errors in copying a 20-cm rod, and after imagining rotating it 180° or seeing it in another indicated position (Piaget & Inhelder, 1971). In studying the development of the child's concept of number, a problem particularly pertinent to the present discussion, Piaget is interested in the establishment of the concept of permanence (conservation) of a number or quantity. Just as he had found that the infant in his first months discovered the permanence of perceived objects when they were out of sight, the realization of a permanent number concept emerges between the ages of about 4 and 7 years. This cognitive process must develop before the child can reason in arithmetic because "a number is only intelligible if it remains identical with itself, whatever the distribution of the units of which it is composed" (Piaget, 1941). Initially the child perceives quantities perceptually "in the sensible universe." At the age of 4 or 5, most children have no idea of the conservation of quantity regardless of its change in shape. If two containers of identical size and shape are filled with exactly identical quantities of liquid, the child at this age will say the two quantities are similar because he *sees* the two levels the same. If the contents of one of these containers is poured into a tall narrow container, however, the child will now say it contains more liquid than the other, because he can *see* the level of the liquid much higher.

By about the age of 6, children begin to become less perceptual and more conceptual and will begin to give answers that show an unresolved conflict between what they see and what they think. By the age of 7 most children understand that the quantities of liquid are conserved "irrespective of the number and nature of the changes made" (Piaget, 1941).

This same pattern of cognitive development can be demonstrated with continuous quantities (liquids) and discontinuous quantities (such as beads or beans). A 5-year-old confronted with two glass containers of similar size and shape filled with equal numbers of identical beads will say the quantities are similar, again because he can *see* the levels are the same. However, if the beads from one container are poured into a tall narrow one, he will say it now contains more beads than the other container. When questioned, he will say that a necklace made from the beads in the tall container will be longer than a necklace made from the beads in the other one. When the beads from the tall container are poured back into the original one, the 5-year-old will state that a necklace now would be the same length as the other one. In other words the quantities, according to the child at this stage, will increase and decrease because of their *perceived* sizes. By the time they are 6 years old, most children realize that the numbers of beads remain constant regardless of the shapes of their containers, and that necklaces made from two equal quantities of beads, regardless of the shape of their container, will be the same lengths.

Because Piaget was primarily interested in studying the intellectual growth of normal children, his experimental evidence parallels normal brain development. To examine the effects of brain dysfunctions on the pattern of cognitive growth he described, we will look at a few Piagetian experiments carried out with mentally retarded subjects.

"Piaget sees the mind as a dynamic system which, en route to maturity, passes through qualitatively different levels of integration" (Robinson & Robinson, 1976) as opposed to a view of the mind as possessing a fixed structure that acquires new knowledge and skills. The Piagetian view not only gives more hope to the retarded child but gives us more information about his intellectual development. It will be remembered that Piaget proposed four major developmental periods: (1) the sensorimotor period, extending from birth to about 2 years, is marked by reflex, sensory, and motor activity; (2) the preoperational period, extending from about 2 to 7 years, is marked by the beginning of symbolic thinking, although it is characterized by perceptual rather than conceptual processes; (3) the period of concrete operations, extending from age 7 to 11, is typified by a rapid development of number and spatial processes and an understanding of mechanical cause and effect; and (4) the period of formal operations, extending from age 11 to 15, is marked by a rapid expansion of symbolic thinking, abstract conceptualizing, and the improved ability to carry on inductive and deductive reasoning. Since mental life is mediated by the brain and central nervous system, then brain-damaged subjects may be expected to function at a level lower than normal for their age. Research, both within Piaget's laboratory and in other centers, with mentally retarded subjects has shown this to be true. Inhelder (1968), a colleague of Piaget, found the profoundly mentally retarded adult as fixated at the sensorimotor level of intelligence. The moderately retarded adult reached the preoperational stage of intuition but usually could develop no further. The mildly retarded adult, usually the trainable and educable subject, reached the level of concrete operations, and the borderline mentally dull subject might master a limited repertoire of the simpler forms of mental abstractions. Independent work carried on in centers other than the Geneva Laboratory have been largely confirmatory, although some researchers have not found all mentally impaired subjects to fall into the stages in a clear-cut way. This is understandable in terms of present neuropsychological knowledge: Spotty or localized brain damage may impair many mental functions and leave others to function at an above-average level because the cerebral areas vital to their operation may have been spared.

The three major causes of a developmental number retardation and dyscalculia, that is, deficits in language (auditory–gnostic), reading (visual–gnostic), and/or spatial imagery, can be understood within the Piagetian model of development. Auditory language or oral speech is largely developed during the first two periods, reading and writing and automatic handling of numbers in the third period, and abstract reasoning in mathematics in the final period, during adolescence. This developmental model also fits the usual curriculum pattern of the elementary and junior high school. The first grader arrives, at the age of 6, with an oral vocabulary of about 2500 words or more; he or she still is largely "magical" and subjective in his thinking and is unable to deal with temporal abstractions. During the next 4 or 5 years the child learns very rapidly to read and write and to master hundreds of number and verbal facts and to understand spatial diagrams and maps. By junior high school he is learning to solve problems in arithmetic that require adaptive thinking, to manage problematic abstractions in algebra, and to resolve spatial theorems in geometry. All of this requires a normal and healthy bilateral cerebral function; any brain damage or dysfunction, whether localized or diffuse, may impair some or all of these psychological processes.

Although most of Luria's clinical experimentation had been with brain-injured adults he drew liberally from the work of Piaget and a large number of Russian investigators to put together his theory of the ontogenetic formation of the concept of number and of arithmetical operations. He recognized the visual, spatial, and finally conceptual aspects of number processes in that order as the child grows, but he stressed that "in the latter stages the concept of number and arithmetical operations retain their spatial components" (Luria, 1966).

If a child suffers from cerebral agenesis in the parts of the brain largely responsible for spatial perception and spatial imagery (these parts in the traumatically brain-damaged adult are always in the temporo-parieto-occipital systems), then he may be unable to scan or imagine points in asymmetrical space "which are essential for correct calculation" (Luria, 1966). Arithmetical operations become difficult or impossible through loss of their spatial coordinates.

In our laboratory we have found significant correlations of .43 between arithmetic and sequential memory of light patterns at the Grade 2 level and one of .32 at the Grade 5 level (Gaddes & Spellacy, 1977). This was measured by the Dynamic Visual Retention Test, a device that illuminates patterns of lights on a plain screen. To do this test successfully the child must imagine a set of spatial coordinates on the bare screen against which he or she must compare the location of the lights being illuminated. While sequential memory may be related to arithmetical competence, it seems almost certain that the spatial skills demanded by the test are also strongly involved.

Luria's model of arithmetical acquisition parallels Piaget's. This model comes largely from his study of brain-damaged adults, but it is based on his observations of the order in which number operations disappear with brain damage. It would seem reasonable to believe that they appear during normal growth in the reverse order, and clinical observation supports this. The preschool child begins with material objects, which he or she can handle arranged in space, and later acquires the number facts from visual and manual contact with the objects. When the child learns to write numbers this leads to the formation of tabular calculation, and following this automatized learning through oral recitation and writing in a particular spatial arrangement, he finally learns to think symbolically with numbers and to reason abstractly.

This model also fits the curriculum of the elementary and junior high school. In Grades 1–4 inclusive, the child is largely concerned in automatizing number facts and writing the calculations in correct spatial pattern. By Grades 5 and 6 he begins to read and contend with problems the calculations of which depend on correct mechanical function but in which choice of method is not automatic but deductive. Some children who may have been adequate in arithmetic up to Grade 4 may begin to fall down because their abilities for logical abstraction are inadequate.

In Chapter 4 the case of a 17-year-old boy, born with a medial right-hemisphere lesion, was described. Although he was above average in the language arts, he had extreme difficulty with art, reading maps in geography, arithmetic, and anything demanding spatial analysis or synthesis. When he reached high school he could manage algebra at a passing grade but geometry was impossible for him. This evidence suggests that his inarithmetria was not a result of inferior reasoning abilities, otherwise he could not have succeeded in algebra, but a result of his severely impaired spatial skills. Certainly, this case can be understood in the light of Luria's model and provides a special case of normal language and reading skills, but defective spatial abilities. In this case, the boy's deficit, in only one of the major etiological areas, was enough to produce a severe anarithmetria but an average calculation ability in algebra, which is a type of quantitative reasoning expressed in verbal rather than numerical symbols.

10 Remediation, Therapy, and the Learning-Disabled Child

Thus, man's brain shapes freedom. Through ever more effective innovations in the rules for social interaction, man's brain frees him from fear. Through ever improving methods of production and distribution, man's brain frees him from want. Through ever growing powers to perceive and plan, man's brain frees him for love and fun.

Man's brain does this and always has. We share the promise that it always will, though slowly and by steps with pain. For that is how we learn.

Karl H. Pribram (1964)

In remediation planning, we must recognize the ways in which the learning disability influences the child's pattern of motivation, not only the ways in which motivational factors might be influential in complicating the effects of the learning disability. This is the essence of the psychoneurologic approach to intervention.

Helmer R. Myklebust (1975a)

Although remedial measures have been described throughout this book, this chapter is devoted to a more systematic examination of possible treatment measures for the child or adult with learning problems.

Teachers are primarily practitioners and usually are more interested in what to do about a child's learning disorder than in spending time looking for causes. Whereas this approach may be admissable for the busy teacher, the school psychologist should take time to be experimental and help the teacher with suggested new remedial alternatives. In the past, it has not been unknown for a teacher to apply the same remedial method to all his or her students. One young teacher recently told me, "I find the Gillingham method the best for my children." Unfortunately one of her students with a subtle form of receptive aphasia and auditory imperception was unable to learn to read under her energetic and well-meaning efforts. She failed to realize that a phonetic system, such as the Gillingham method, although successful for the majority of children, is almost useless with a child who cannot discriminate phonetic sounds. With more knowledge she would have had a better chance of success with this boy.

370

A second common pattern is the teacher who learns two or more methods of teaching reading or some other academic skill. When faced with a learning disabled child this teacher tries every technique in his or her repertoire in a "shot gun" attack. This approach need not include any diagnostic understanding of the child's learning problem, and frequently does not; it does include a blind trial of one technique after another until the teacher's repertoire is exhausted. With luck, one of these methods may have happened to mesh with the child's needs, and he or she begins to show improvement. Without this kind of luck the teacher is defeated and the child may be abandoned to "busywork," sarcasm, or neglect, all of which compound his personal problems.

A third pattern, and the one recommended here, includes an educational, psychological, and social analysis of the child, a task analysis of the skills to be taught, and a periodic evaluation of the possible progress. The psychological analysis should include both physiological and behavioral data.

Cognitive Processes and Cerebral Organization

A knowledge of normal brain function can direct the diagnostician to examine all or most psychological processes involved in learning. In other words, we can *let the knowledge of brain structure and function direct us*. If we start with the occipital lobes, we will need a battery of tests to tap the various visual–perceptual skills such as figure–ground, form recognition, letter and word recognition, visual memory, visual sequential memory, and visual–motor speed and accuracy, to name a few. If we then move to the temporal lobes, we will want to know about auditory perception of verbal and nonverbal stimuli, auditory sequential memory, dichotic listening, oral and written language, verbal memory, spatial imagery, etc. The parietal lobes should direct us to enquire into tactile form recognition, tactile sensitivity, finger localization, directional sense, body image, tactile naming, etc. The frontal lobes should remind us to check motor speed and accuracy, hand-grip strength, motor speech, and a variety of motor, postural, and movement skills (Ayres, 1972a; de Quiros & Schrager, 1978). As well, as we have seen in Chapter 9, frontal lobe function should remind us to examine visual scanning (e.g., mazes), selective attention (e.g., cognitive scanning of the lexicon, or personal active vocabulary, in a word fluency test), and planning (mobilizing and organizing ideas into a useful and systematic pattern). Even a small battery of "planning" tests can be useful to indicate cognitive functions usually missed or insufficiently assessed by standard intelligence tests (Kirby &

Ashman, 1984). A consideration of the two cerebral hemispheres should direct our attention to the expected balance of language and spatial-constructional skills, and the sensorimotor cortex should suggest examining kinesthetic sensations, visual–manual and auditory–manual reaction times, and any skill integrating "spatial, kinesthetic, and language information to motor formulation and movement" (Calanchini & Trout, 1971). A neuropsychological knowledge of normal brain function can direct attention to normal processes in all the various perceptual and motor skills instrumental in academic competence. In understanding abnormal behavior it is essential.

One of the most inclusive concepts of normal brain function and the relation of central processing deficiencies to children's learning problems is that of Rourke (1982). Drawing on the model of normal brain function proposed by Goldberg and Costa (1981), Rourke has presented a tentative theory to understand better "central processing deficiencies in children." Although some researchers have held that ontogenetically cerebral hemispheric organization proceeds from the left to the right hemisphere, Rourke, following Bakker (1979), Goldberg and Costa, and others, holds the reverse view. This seems to be supported by naturalistic observation of small children who, during their first year of life, appear to be observing and interpreting their world *nonverbally* and pictorially. Then, at about 12 months of age, when they have had time to learn some simple interpretations of their environment, they begin to code these in vocal utterances. Some observers have interpreted this as "filling the right hemisphere first" with broad, nonverbal concepts, and when small children have reached a certain level of simplistic understanding, they then begin to develop speech. Presumably the first process is mediated largely by the right hemisphere and the second by the left. Rourke has explained all common forms of learning disabilities in terms of the right hemisphere subserving novel experiences that involve global, nonverbal concepts. "Right-hemisphere systems provide the content for concepts whereas left-hemisphere systems are particularly geared to their articulation, elaboration, and stereotypic application" (Rourke, 1982). Because reading is at first a novel experience, it may be mediated initially by the right hemisphere, but with practice the graphemes, which at first were unfamiliar, are related to the already established speech pattern of phonemes. As the process of reading becomes automatized, it is seen as drawing less on right hemisphere function for decoding and more on left. Rourke sees the right hemisphere then free to analyze, organize, and synthesize the conceptual content of what is read, that is, the essence of comprehension. This model can explain why some children can decode and read orally at a normal speed for their age, but whose comprehension is limited or inadequate. These children presumably have adequate left-hemisphere functions to mediate normally automatized reading, and either deficient or partially inaccessable right-hemisphere activity to provide successful conceptual understanding. Using this model of normal brain function with localized or regional dysfunctions, Rourke also accounts for the child who can learn to read by the "look–say" method but later has difficulty with phonetic decoding and resulting impaired comprehension; this same child frequently understands the same material very well when it is read to him by someone else at a normal speed. As well, Rourke has examined the phonetically accurate and the phonetically inaccurate spellers; various subtypes of empirically derived reading disabled children; and the acquisition of arithmetical skills, both routinized and calculable. Rourke presents his model as tentative and limited by areas of present ignorance of the detailed cerebral functions and the psychological processes involved in children's learning and its disorders. Nevertheless, it seems to be one of the most promising theoretical frameworks available at present to explain the clinical findings of LD children and to provide a basis for their remediation.

Luria, in his studies of brain-damaged adults, recognized (1) the *psychological structure* of an act, and (2) the organized cerebral activity mediating that particular behavior. The first is the observed behavior (e.g., the child learning to write "mat" may sound each letter singly, remember its visual form, and draw each letter laboriously). The cerebral areas subserving these various activities are becoming more accessible to observation with the appearance of the many brain scanning and other new investigative techniques.

Remediation drills change not only the psychological structure of a given operation, and this is what concerns the remedial teacher, but also its cerebral organization. With repeated exercise, desired skills can be automatized with presumed neural traces established to enable a repetition of the skill at a desired time in the future. Luria believed that well-automatized forms of mental activity are based on quite a different cerebral control system from newly acquired ones, so that all new learning implies a reorganization of it with the old learning, and a parallel reorganization of the various cerebral structures underlying these different skills.

The neuropsychological model of diagnosis and remediation as practiced by Luria, Reitan, Myklebust, and many others is summarized in Table 10.1. Columns A and B include the neuropsychological information obtained on a particular child or adult. The school psychologist may use his or her broad knowledge of the discipline to relate the neurological information in A with the behavioral evidence in B, and to judge the possible chronicity of the learning disability and its response to remediation. Column C contains a detailed task analysis of the desired academic skill, and the discrepancies between specific points in B and C will provide the clues for the choice of an appropriate therapeutic procedure by the teacher and the school psychologist.

Any learning task can be analyzed by observing systematically and in detail how an "expert" completes the task. An expert, in this case, is

Table 10.1. The Neuropsychological Model of Diagnosis and Remediation

Neuropsychological Information		
Neurological Data	Psychological Structure of the Child	Task Analysis
A	B	C
Information from neurologist *re* locus, intensity, and nature of identifiable brain dysfunction, or lack of such evidence	Information from neuropsychological test battery *re* which perceptual, cognitive, and motor skills are normal and which defective	List of perceptual, cognitive, and motor skills needed for successful achievement of the academic skill under consideration (e.g., reading, spelling, arithmetic)
Brain dysfunction	Learning disability	

anyone who performs the task efficiently and successfully. "Task analysis has very little to do with instructional methodology. It has everything to do with figuring out how people go about doing certain tasks" (Johnson & Morasky, 1977, p. 272). Of course, it may provide the basis for directing the teacher to include the skills, decisions, and strategies necessary for success.

However, while it is highly likely that chronic perceptual, cognitive, or motor deficits are the most common causes for failure to learn in school-age children, the factors described in Table 10.1 do not account for all underachievers. Some children fail because of ineffective learning strategies (Torgesen, 1977), inattention, weak self-confidence, poor motivation, and a lack of a strong intent to learn. Others fail because of a mixture of perceptual deficits and motivational weaknesses. Other students, with neither of these deficiencies, may perform at a mediocre level because of a lack of originality or creative imagination. Students of this type may be able to perform well enough on tests of highly structured material that they have mastered, but they may feel defeated when faced with an open-ended problem that requires mental procedures of trial-and-error, independent choice and decision, and restructuring and reorganization of present knowledge. Students of this type may be able to master the routinized number facts, but be intimidated by arithmetical problem solving that demands a flexible interaction of several conceptual processes operating simultaneously and sequentially. Such students may lack adequate adaptive intelligence either because of inheritance or unimaginative teaching.

This means that the school psychologist must exercise a sensitive insight in his or her interpretation of the test findings in column B, Table 10.1. The psychologist can guard against diagnostic invalidities by testing the possible chronicity or transience of a deficit symptom (e.g., repeating the test at another time) or being aware of those behavioral skills that are more vulnerable to the effects of anxiety or less appealing or more threatening to the testee (e.g., a finger tapping test is usually more interesting to the academically underachieving subject, and also more reliable than a problem-solving task designed to measure an ability for deductive or inductive reasoning). As Torgesen has pointed out, a better understanding of these motivational factors in learning will be useful in deciding on remedial measures. I will comment on this again in the discussion at the end of this chapter on the treatment of the hyperactive and distractible child.

What Is Meant by Remediation?

Remediation implies a controlled balance between the impaired learner's abilities and the demands of his environment, and this is true whether the learner is a child or an adult. If this balance is finely tuned, the learner can be led to acquire new academic and social skills and to continue to be stimulated and satisfied. If the demands are too easy, the balance is too lax and the learner becomes bored; if the demands are too difficult, the balance is too strained and the learner is frustrated, distracted, and increasingly disinterested. A strong disturbing force in either the learner or his environment will shift the balance of diagnostic attention by demanding more understanding in devising compensatory treatment of the source of disturbance. Two examples should clarify this. A 10-year-old boy is referred because of failing grades in school and an uncontrolled temper at home and at school. Analysis of the problem shows a stable, supporting family, but medical evidence of a marked EEG dysrhythmia in the boy's left temporal lobe. This electrical disturbance very likely may be related to his temper outbursts and his poor achievement in the language arts. These findings can lead to a medical consultation, a prescription of an appropriate medication to reduce the temper outbursts, and a psychoeducational treatment of the boy's aphasoid symptoms. Another case may show normal physical health but a family pattern of emotional conflict and marital strife. Here the attention is directed more to the environmental side of the equation, and a balance is sought by attempting to resolve the disturbing family situation and to train the child to understand the problems and to learn some compensatory skills.

Remediation Procedures

Numerous instructional methods and training procedures for LD children have been recommended for the last 80 years, if we begin historically with Maria Montessori. Some of these symptoms have stressed training in perceptual–motor skills, multisensory activities, language development neurolinguistics, phonics exercises, structured cognitive training, ego psychology and the improvement of the self-image, and cognitive and motivational strategies. The proponent of each of these methods frequently recommends his or her system with an emotional fervor that reflects a stronger relationship with professional prejudices than with the objective behavior of the child.

The fact is that none of these procedures by themselves is complete and adequate for dealing with all LD children. The superiority of any one method over another has not been generally demonstrated, and we need all of these procedures and some not yet developed, if we are to deal successfully with every LD child.

The development of neuropsychological knowledge in the last 30 years has had a very real influence on the understanding and treatment of learning disabilities. In the 1950s and early 1960s, neuropsychologists were primarily concerned with discovering reliable relationships between localized brain lesions and specific psychological measurements (Reitan, 1959). In special education this was reflected in an emphasis on perceptual–motor dysfunctions and learning disorders (Cruickshank, 1966; Strauss & Kephart, 1955). By 1970 cognitive psychology was drawing on the new insights from neuropsychology (e.g., cerebral asymmetry) and enriching the understanding of both normal and abnormal brain function. By the early 1980s, Myklebust was able to write: "No longer do we accentuate entities such as perceptual–motor deficiencies. . . . we now recognize that learning disabilities derive from alterations of cognitive processes and that these alterations result from dysfunctions in the brain" (1983). The recognition of two major types of learning disabilities, those deriving from verbal and those from nonverbal dysfunctions, is a major step in their understanding and treatment.

Thirty-five years ago ideas of learning were generally considered in two camps, *association* (behavioristic) and *field* (mentalistic) theories (Hilgard, 1948). By the 1980s this basic dichotomy still held, but many psychologists at present see the mentalistic or cognitive group as having two divisions: (1) pure cognitive psychology stressing perception and cognition, and (2) a *cognitive–neuropsychological* approach stressing the use of neurophysiological knowledge to enhance an understanding of cognition and social behavior (Gaddes, 1983). Some theorists and practitioners are recommending the use of "behavioral neuropsychology," a merging of both views, to deal with academic learning problems (Horton,

1981), and this is a practice that already has shown considerable promise (Scull & McNie, 1980).

Diagnosis

A careful diagnostic analysis of the child's perceptual, cognitive, motor, and educational skills is made prior to any consideration of a remedial program. If there are strong behavioral indications of possible cerebral dysfunctions, a complete neurological and neuropsychological examination is carried out. Even if there are no such indications, a neuropsychological test battery may still be useful because of its thorough coverage of the child's psychological abilities. Also, it might reveal some soft signs not previously detected, or in their absence it can provide evidence of the child's cognitive strengths and confirm the purely motivational nature of his learning problems.

Neuropsychological assessment may contain two levels of examination: (1) Screening. This includes the evaluation of groups of children on a brief battery of tests shown to have a high level of predictive validity for selecting "at risk" LD children. Such a test battery is only a scanning instrument, and "scanning does not imply diagnosis" (Silver, 1978); at best, it will only select those subjects with the deficit that the battery is designed to identify, and having done that, the learning-impaired children so designated may be referred for in-depth diagnosis. It has a number of methodological problems that should be observed by anyone planning to construct or use a screening battery (de Hirsch, 1971; Hynd, Hayes, & Snow, 1982; Jansky & de Hirsch, 1972; Satz & Fletcher, 1979; Silver, 1978). (2) Diagnosis. Most referrals of children for diagnostic study come from parents or school personnel concerned about the child's obvious learning problems. LD adults who come (they are usually severe developmental dyslexics) are either self-referred or urged by a concerned spouse. This means that only a minority are referred from screening programs. Clinical assessment programs vary and will reflect the clinician's theoretical preferences and applied training. For children, the most commonly used test batteries are the Halstead–Reitan tests (Reitan & Davison, 1974; Selz, 1981), the Spreen–Benton tests (Benton, Hamsher, Varney, & Spreen, 1983; Gaddes & Crockett, 1975; Spreen & Benton, 1977), and composite batteries of well-established tests. Composite batteries frequently lack a systematic conceptual framework but have the advantage of flexibility. New tests may be added with the discovery of new insights, and modified batteries can be adapted to differing behavioral patterns of specific children. This approach is recommended by Obrzut (1981, p. 249) and is used in our own laboratory. Golden (1981) began research in 1980 to adapt the Luria tests for children. Early data based on small samples appear to be encouraging, but it is too early to know the value of this battery until more validation studies are completed and the battery has been successfully used in other centers. Useful discussions of assessment of children can be found in Hynd and Obrzut (1981) and Rourke, Bakker, Fisk, and Strang (1983, Chap. 5).

Assessments of adults, while they sometimes are directed to developmental learning disorders, are more frequently concerned with the study and rehabilitation of brain-damaged patients, monitoring the course of progressive neurological diseases and the effects of traumatic damage or neurosurgery, providing information on psychiatric patients with and without underlying neurological disorders, and detecting neurological dysfunctions in their early stages of development. For further discussions the reader is referred to Benton, Hamsher, Varney, and Spreen (1983) for an instruction manual for the Spreen–Benton tests, to Lezak (1983) for an updated and comprehensive discussion of the whole field and to Reitan and Davison (1974) and Russell, Neuringer, and Goldstein (1970) for explanations of the Halstead–Reitan battery.

Motivation to Learn

The remedial procedure recommended here is a "success model" of learning, which implies that a desire to learn must precede the learning process. White (1959) considered the child's level of competence in dealing with his environment essential to total motivation, and the desire to interact with the environment to be neurogenic. Directing the child into appealing activities at a level he can manage with satisfaction is the first step in remedial teaching and in improving the child's self-evaluation.

Incentives

A detailed explanation of the principles of delivering reinforcement in behavior therapy is beyond the scope of the present discussion, but it is important to recognize that because the LD child will be asked to try to master skills that will be difficult for him or her, the child will need to be "paid." In adult behavior, activities that are intrinsically pleasurable are usually done with no extrinsic reward (e.g., recreation). If adult society wants a particularly unpleasant or dangerous task done, however, it is usually necessary to pay someone to do it.

Any one teaching method, no matter how successful with a majority of students, will be inappropriate and even detrimental for those children constitutionally unsuited to it. This is true of behavior modification techniques as well as of other methods, and this should serve as a caution to those educators who consider any method, including behavior modification, a cureall for all learning problems. For example, the Distar method for teaching reading is motivationally well designed, using a behavioral approach, but it is unsuited to a child with a serious or moderate auditory imperception. The Gillingham method, like any phonics procedure, although successful with most children, is also ineffective with the same type of child. Motivating a child to try to do something he or she is neurologically unable to achieve can only lead to frustration and a lack of interest in learning. Motivational methods, using behavior therapy, are desirable and useful with most children, but they must be used diagnostically and selectively.

Task Analysis

A simple rule of thumb in teaching is: Teach it globally, and if that does not work, break the task into smaller segments that the child can deal with successfully. In Chapter 6 was the description of Montessori's method of teaching the concept of triangularity by analyzing the learning procedure of the normal child from concrete to functional to abstract concept. She first taught the idea using simple concrete forms and then two-dimensional line drawings of varying complexity. No doubt imaginative teachers have always analyzed the skill to be learned and resorted to small segments when that was indicated. The modern teacher has the advantage of a much more detailed inventory of the child's skills to match against the task analysis summary.

Some years ago, Lenneberg and a group of colleagues embarked on an interesting analysis of reading-disabled children using neuropsychological findings from adult aphasics. The reasoned that because aphasia studies of brain-damaged adults have produced a prodigious literature, that this knowledge might be useful in understanding dyslexia in children (Brown, 1976, p. 28). They recognized that traumatic aphasia in adults and developmental dyslexia in children have obvious differences, but also it is not unreasonable to expect some degree of similarity. Lenneberg assumed that many aphasic patients with left cerebral vascular accidents (i.e., strokes) have reasonably normal language competence, but because of specific "neurological interference mechanisms" they cannot remember or express certain words. It is common for stroke patients to know what they want to say but be unable to do so.

In the study of adult aphasics (Lenneberg, Pogash, Cohlan, & Doolittle, 1976) the investigators manipulated five variables: (1) degree of abstraction of material; (2) degree of familiarity of material; (3) size of the stimulus field; (4) sequential timing of tasks; and (5) order of presentation. They then observed the type of errors in understanding made by the adult aphasics. They discovered that the patient frequently was able to answer the questions when certain neuropsychological interference mechanisms were removed. Some of these error patterns were: (1) simultanagnosia (the inability to comprehend a large number of stimuli at once); (2) perseveration (repeating a correct response inappropriately to subsequent questions); (3) catastrophic reaction (response with agitation and defeat; a negative response to subsequent items following failure on early items); (4) depression; (5) fatigue (an inability to sustain attention for long periods of time); and (6) arousal (variations in attention from time to time). These interference mechanisms are all related, but for analyzing the learning situation it is useful to consider them separately and as aspects of simultaneity and sequencing.

Brown and Lenneberg were interested to discover the reasons why a subject knows an item at one time and not at another; and if these conditions can be identified, can they be varied? If they could isolate these interference mechanisms and control them, it might lead to a better understanding and treatment of reading-impaired children with left-hemisphere dysfunctions. In fact, the five variables, if manipulated, do enable many aphasics to do better. By reducing the abstraction level, by providing the learner with relevant information, by presenting information in small bits, at a slowed tempo, and with items graded from easy to increasing difficulty, we can facilitate learning for both the adult aphasic and the organically dysfunctioning reading-impaired child.

With delayed readers who will eventually read satisfactorily by about age 9, Brown (1976) recommends patience and emotional support by the teacher rather than intensive remedial drills because this type of child will read anyhow, once his nervous system has had time to mature. The conclusions from these types of studies not only relate sound pedagogical practices with clinical knowledge of aphasia, but they imply that much of what we know about teaching many LD children can be useful for cognitive training of traumatically brain-damaged adults.

Train the Brain or Teach the Child What You Want Him to Learn?

To teach the retarded reader to read, do you only improve brain function, or do you drill the child in the specific perceptual and cognitive skills needed to read? Proponents of both views are equally enthusiastic in recommending their theoretical and remedial beliefs. Let us look at the evidence.

Training the Brain. The view that recommends the exercise of the brain and sensorimotor systems to improve their capacity to learn has a highly respectable history. It grew out of an awareness of the integration of neuromuscular functions and cognitive ideas. Maria Montessori, as we have already seen, 80 years ago produced a theory and practice based on motor training, self-direction of the child during his or her learning, and the integration of cognitive development with the "education of the senses" (Montessori, 1964). More recently Kephart, Barsch, Cruickshank, Johnson, Myklebust, and many others have made perceptual and motor training a keystone in their practices of treating LD children. Sometimes in extreme cases, poor readers have been removed from regular instruction in reading to crawl around a gymnasium and engage in an intensive motor-training program, with the unfortunate consequence that at the end of the training period, because of educational neglect, they are frequently even further retarded in reading. Such abuses of sensorimotor training are practiced by teachers or others with no real understanding of its functions and potential educational value.

One of the most articulate and best developed programs of sensorimotor training for LD children is that of Dr. A. Jean Ayres (1972a). Ayres is both an occupational therapist and psychologist and has developed a detailed battery of perceptual, motor, and psycholinguistic tests (1976), the findings of which she uses to infer central nervous system dysfunctions. She strives to improve neuromuscular function with exercises to increase sensorimotor integration at all levels of the nervous system. "If the brain develops the *capacity* to perceive, remember, and motor plan, the ability can then be applied toward mastery of all academic and other tasks, regardless of the specific content" (Ayres, 1972a). It is interesting that in her chapter "The Art of Therapy" in her book on learning disorders no mention is ever made of specific academic remedial measures. The whole discussion centers on the improvement of sensorimotor accuracy and efficiency. Her book has had a considerable influence on occupational and physiotherapists in clinics with orthopedically and mentally handicapped children, where these therapists' chief responsibility is to improve brain function and motor skills. It is for someone else, presumably a special teacher, to teach the child to read and write.

Teach the Child What You Want Him to Learn. The proponents of this view range from some who minimize the value of sensorimotor training to those who encourage training in both basic behavioral skills *and* academic skills. Critchley and Critchley (1978) have used neurological knowledge to throw doubt on the usefulness of sensorimotor integration training for the alleviation of dyslexia. They take the stand that "there is no logical place in the curriculum for elaborate systems of motor training," on the grounds that reading and writing are functions of the whole brain, whereas motor skills principally involve the limited cortical areas of the sensory and motor strips. Anatomically and functionally their statements are true, but they do not necessarily disprove the value of sensory and motor training as a preparation for academic learning.

Although most remedial programs include drilling the requisite skills for successful academic achievement (e.g., Bannatyne, 1971; Cruickshank, 1961, 1975, 1977; Downing, 1964; Fernald, 1943; Freidus, 1966; Frostig, 1975; Gillingham, 1965; Gillingham & Stillman, 1936; McGinnis, 1963; Myklebust, 1965; Scull, 1978; Stott, 1970; Strauss & Lehtinen,

1947; Valett, 1973), many, if not most, special educators believe there is value in perceptual and motor training and teaching cognitive and verbal skills.

To evaluate the respective effectiveness of these two remedial approaches is difficult because of the methodological problems in all educational research. Ayres' approach, although it mentions cortical function, emphasizes subcortical structures and functions, the brainstem, thalamus, and vestibular mechanisms. All of these are functionally important to the integration of sensory and motor processes that subserve language and higher cognitive functions, but it is integration at the *cortical level* that provides the emergence of cognition, abstraction, and reasoning (Eccles, 1973; Luria, 1973). Ayres is fully aware of this, and throughout her book she cautions that her discussion of language disorders (the most common type of learning disabilities) includes only "the more elementary and fundamental aspects of auditory-language function" (Ayres, 1972a). As an occupational therapist she is suitably interested in manual dexterity, posture, and other behavioral signs of the status of sensorimotor integration, but as she makes clear, this dysfunction accounts only for "some aspects of learning disorders." Her goal is "sensory stimulation in order to strengthen neural integration, especially that neural integration that underlies learning and behavior"; it is not to supply remedial academic drills or the types of activities advised by most special educators.

Some studies have suggested that improving sensory integration improves academic scores (Ayres, 1972b) and that at kindergarten and first-grade level it is superior to academic remediation (Serwer, Shapiro, & Shapiro, 1973). An honors student of mine, comparing the relative effectiveness of the Distar II Program with a color-coding system (Scull, 1978) and a traditional phonics approach, found a combination of the Distar and the color coding superior either to the Distar alone or to an achromatic phonics program with second grade children (Wright, 1978). If color coding improves visual–language integration, as it seems to do, then all of these studies suggest real value in perceptual and sensorimotor training. Unfortunately, all three studies (i.e., Ayres, Serwer, and Wright) failed to control for the effects of different remedial teachers and therapists across groups.

My own clinical experience suggests that subcortical brain damage may not necessarily impair academic skills of adults with traumatic brain injuries. A woman with a benign and progressive brain tumor, seen in our laboratory, gradually developed double vision and difficulty in reading, arithmetic, and mental concentration. The tumor was located centrally just above the thalamus and as it grew it imposed pressure on the optic tracts. Although the woman was depressed and complained that she felt as though "a black cloud of fog" was on her mind, we found that she could read accurately, although slowly, and she could answer the arithmetic questions on the Wechsler (WAIS) if we encouraged her. This suggested that her perceptual and motor integrating functions were not defective and that she was not truly learning disabled. Within 24 hours of surgical removal of the tumor, which was about 2 in. in length and a half-inch thick, this lady could read, write, and do arithmetic perfectly normally, and her thinking was clear.

A 30-year-old man, seen in our laboratory, sustained a serious head injury in a traffic accident. His car was struck on the driver's side, the door was crushed in, and he was ejected through the front of the car. As a result, he suffered a fractured skull and severe cerebral concussion. He was unconscious for 6 days and then regained his faculties gradually over the next 5 days.

There were neurological and neuropsychological signs of brainstem damage with cortical sparing. There was no permanent interference with his oral speech or his reading and writing, all of which were normal, but he did develop marked emotional and personality changes in the form of depression and apathy. He lost his former enthusiasm for sports, boating, skiing, and even girls, all of which suggested thalamic damage. His scores on perception, sensorimotor integration, and abstract reasoning were all above average.

These two cases were studied in detail both neurologically and psychologically. Both cases sustained severe brainstem damage or dysfunction with no cortical damage, and both cases suffered no primary academic impairment. This evidence suggests that the cortical levels of integration are essential to academic learning, and that the subcortical levels (in these two cases, the thalamus and brainstem) can sustain rather severe injury or dysfunction without destroying academic ability, so long as the cortical integration is still functional.

It will probably be most useful for teachers to know that sensorimotor and perceptual training appear to improve the possibilities of successful academic learning *especially in young children,* but that remedial drills must also include language and academic content. Much more research is needed in this area to clarify the neuropsychological processes affected by indirect (sensorimotor training) and direct remediation (academic skill training). This question reduces itself to what is *relevant;* the evidence appears to indicate that both direct and indirect remediation are needed, the relative proportions being indicated by the age of the child and the severity of his or her learning problem.

Experimental Teaching

Once a program of remediation has been chosen on the basis of the neuropsychological and personal analysis of the child as well as a task analysis of the skills to be taught, its effectiveness should be checked periodically. If, after 2 or 3 weeks, the child is making little or no progress, a critical reexamination should be made of his measured potential and the teaching methods. If the teacher has exhausted all of his or her diagnostic hypotheses and has no further useful ideas, then help should be sought from the school psychologist, speech therapist, language specialist, or other professional who may possess better diagnostic skills. If that person is unable to offer any improvement to what is already being done and the child is still showing no progress, then a referral to a research center or university learning laboratory may be indicated. In fact, the best remedial teaching programs are research-based and experimentally monitored. This procedure demands a knowledgeable and imaginative psychologist, a back-up group of specialists, and a teacher willing to adapt and try new methods; and all of these people must be experimentally oriented. Leong (1982), drawing on Critchley, has recommended a number of requisites for effective teaching of reading disabilities, but these are applicable to any areas of learning and teaching problems: (1) early and efficient diagnosis; (2) study of speech and language development; (3) in-depth case studies and follow-ups; (4) studies of theory-based programs and remediation; (5) research on brain–behavior mechanisms in disabled readers; and (6) research on information processing in disabled readers.

The best program evaluation emerges from a multidisciplinary team approach. The teacher, if supplied with information from the child, the parents, the neurologist and other medical practitioners, the social worker or childcare worker (if involved), the school psychologist, and other teachers of the child, is better equipped to devise an effective remediation program. This may include remedial exercises that exploit the child's perceptual, motor, and cognitive strengths; that encourage an integration of his perceptual and motor functions; and that motivate him to learn through use of skilled behavior modification techniques.

Social Development

The study of children's social competence is a recent development in the experimental literature (Gresham, 1983). These studies have included proposed definitions of basic concepts, classifications of social skills and their measures, development of tests, and attempts to assess social validity. Experimental inquiries like these are important, but because they are still new and tentative, no attempt will be made here to discuss them. Instead, we will explore the LD child's social environment that includes the family, the school, the medical doctor or specialist, the school psychologist or educational diagnostician, the speech specialist, and the child's own perception of his disability.

The Role of the Parents

The parents of a chronically learning disabled child find themselves in a painfully conflicting situation. Living with their child on a daily basis, they are usually the first to become aware of his subtle and largely invisible disabilities. Because the child is usually of average or above-average intelligence level, but not always, the sensitive parent may hesitate to report the problem to anyone. If the parents (it is usually the mother) do consult the family doctor, they are usually told that the child is normally healthy (which he is) and will "grow out of" the symptoms reported by the parent. This may result in parental feelings of embarassment or frustration, and a belief by the doctor that he is dealing with an overanxious parent.

Parents of LD children during interviews provide an intriguingly similar type of information. They all report a disturbing suspicion that their child is different from their other children and a persistent assurance by all the professionals not to worry. Many family doctors have a pat response that "he will grow out of it," and many teachers deny there is anything wrong, other than inattention or laziness, until the problem becomes so complex that it can no longer be ignored. By this time, there are so many compounded problems of a perceptual, motor, cognitive, emotional, and social nature that the school staff members find they are not adequately equipped to deal with them. Let us listen to some of these parents.

Mrs. Wallace is an intelligent woman who was a successful nurse prior to her marriage. Mr. Wallace holds an honors degree in biology and chemistry and works in a government fisheries station. The Wallace's have three children, Donald, age 20, an honors science student at a university; Peter, age 17, who has always suffered with a specific language disability; and Mary, age 10, who has no learning problems. Her nurse's training alerted Mrs. Wallace to the possibility of a problem with Peter as early as his third year. Because he was slow to walk and talk, was clumsy, and had unusual feeding habits, she consulted their family doctor, who told her not to worry because there were lots of slow kids. "That was my first putdown," she said. In first grade the teacher was sarcastic and intolerant, and within a month Peter learned to hate school. By the time he was in Grade 3, the parents consulted the school principal, who refused to believe there was any real problem. Peter was quiet and amenable to control at school, so the visit to the principal made the Wallace's feel like mentally dull neurotics who were trying to fabricate a problem where one did not exist. What the principal and Peter's teacher did not know was that Peter frequently stormed into the house after a particularly frustrating day and smashed toys, dishes, and other things. One day, while telling his mother of a particularly unpleasant and unjust treatment at school, he picked up a cutting of material she was sewing and unconsciously pulled it to shreds as he talked.

Another mother, also a trained nurse, felt her son Carl was immature and not ready to enter first grade when he was 5 years 9 months old. Her family pediatrician reported he could find nothing wrong, but Carl's teacher, after 1 month of school, informed the parents, "He isn't seeing right." He was sent to an ophthalmologist, who reported that everything was O.K. However, everything was not O.K. so Carl was sent to see a child psychiatrist, who also could find nothing wrong. Because Carl was a healthy and cheery little boy, the psychiatrist advised the mother not to be overanxious. Carl had entered school with real enthusiasm, but by October 1st, he came home dejected and told his mother, "I know I'm not dumb, but I can't see what the teacher wants us to do. The other kids don't seem to have any difficulty doing it, but it makes no sense to me." A few months later he was referred to the university clinic, where a neuro-psychologist identified Carl's perceptual problems and communicated them to his parents. His auditory language skills were good but he had severe difficulties in the visual and tactile perceptual spheres. On tests of visual memory, figure–ground perception, tactile form recognition (ste-reognosis), finger localization, visual–motor skills, and right–left orienta-tion, Carl's scores were below average. These perceptual problems inter-fered seriously with his attempts to read, spell, and do arithmetic, because he was unable to remember and transcribe his auditory language into the correct visual–graphic symbols.

At the beginning of Grade 2, Carl's mother explained his problems to his new teacher, but because the teacher was not impressed with this important information, or did not understand it, or for some other reason, it was never recorded anywhere and not communicated to anyone else at the school. As a result, each succeeding September Carl's mother found herself faced with the same discouraging and repetitive task of explaining the details of Carl's perceptual and cognitive difficulties.

Not all LD children are as fortunate as Carl in having such a loyal, loving, responsible, and persistent mother, and those children are fre-quently neglected. All LD children need a persuasive advocate to protect them from the onslaughts of teachers, parents, physicians, and others with little or no knowledge of the subtleties of sensorimotor and neurolin-guistic functions in learning. Unfortunately, many of them possess no such protector.

Although teachers need training in understanding the LD child, so do parents. Mittler (1970) believes that "the involvement of parents in the treatment of the child is probably one of the most important developments of the future." This training includes knowledge of their child's strengths and weaknesses in learning. They should get this information from the school psychologist, the child's teachers, the family doctor, and anyone else involved in assessing and teaching him. Many intelligent parents, active in a local ACLD (Association for Children with Learning Disabili-ties) chapter, are better informed about the subtleties of learning disabili-ties than their child's teacher or school principal. One knowledgeable mother, while enrolling her LD son in a large junior high school, tried to explain his disabilities to the school principal and asked him if he were familiar with the term "learning disabilities." The principal answered yes, he thought so, he thought there might be one such student in the school.

To which the mother discerningly replied, "If you do, it is only because the others have quit." Obviously, her daily exposure to her LD child, her reading and study, and her active participation in the ACLD had provided her with a better knowledge of the prevalence of learning disabilities in the general school population.

So far, we have described cases of parents who were intelligent, responsible, and persistent advocates of their LD children. When told not to worry, they continued to look for answers and improved remedial programs for their disabled children. The frustrations and injustices that they and their children were constantly experiencing were infuriating, but they learned to curb their anger, knowing that to alienate anyone who might help is to threaten constructive action. Such behavior requires unusual courage, insight, and patience, and many parents have shown these admirable qualities.

However, a few parents are not as objective. They are angry and resentful that their child does not have an equal chance academically with other children and they project their anger to the school, physician, or psychologist. This is unfortunate not only for them but also for their child, because their negative attitudes may undermine much of the effectiveness of what a well-meaning teacher or psychologist is trying to do to help.

Only the parents of an LD child are aware of the family tensions generated by his presence. One mother described it as "living with a volcano." Marriage counsellors frequently report that breakdowns in the family unit usually occur following the advent of children. Children with no specific problems are likely to restrict the activities of their parents, to frustrate their ambitions, and to increase their anxieties. If both parents understand all this and are agreeable to tolerate these pressures for the advantages of having children, then the marriage is likely to survive or even strengthen. However, when one or more of their children is learning disabled, all of these parental pressures are intensified. The father or the mother may increase his or her knowledge and understand something of the child's genuine difficulties, while the other parent may refuse to read "all this modern nonsense" and deny the child is anything but incorrigible. Over time, violent arguments about the child may arise and drive him closer to one parent and away from the other, while both parents drift apart in a bitter quarrel. Likewise, both parents may have informed themselves of the child's problem but disagree about how to treat it. One parent wants the child seen by a child psychiatrist and the other refuses on the grounds that such a move is an admission of possible insanity and certain weakness. One parent favors a special school for the child and the other opposes this on the grounds that the child should be educated in a normal environment. Even if the parents are reasonably agreed on the child's treatment they are constantly faced with exposure to his emotional outbursts resulting from daily frustrations at school and the chance callous remarks of those around him. He is the helpless target of any child or teacher who wishes to exploit their hostility by drawing attention to his academic incompetence.

To summarize, the parents need to be informed regarding the nature of their child's learning disability. This information can come from professional consultations, reading, study, and active participation in the ACLD and other parents' groups.

The Role of the School

Not too many years ago it was not uncommon for the schools to expell a child for not conforming to their satisfaction. Most psychoeducational clinics have seen children subjected to such professional mishandling. Cruickshank has described the case of Jeff, who, by the age of 8, had been permanently excluded from the Boys' Club facilities in his city and expelled from the public school. Fortunately for Jeff, he was admitted to the university clinic–school where he made progress "through careful nurturing, a highly structured teaching program, parent involvement, and well-prepared teachers" (Cruickshank, 1977). Well-trained teachers for the neurologically handicapped child are in short supply, and until our schools are adequately staffed in this special area, many LD children are likely to be mistreated and their families to be frustrated and angry.

Interviews with parents repeatedly reveal a lack of confidence in the public school's ability to deal adequately with the education of children with subtle learning problems. A mother recently told me that after her LD son had been in a junior high school for 2 months, "It was evident that his teachers had no knowledge of his problems," even though she had explained them to the principal when enrolling him. The art teacher had put sarcastic remarks on the boy's report, and when his mother explained the visual-perceptual and visual–motor problems he had, the teacher replied naively, "Oh, I didn't know he wasn't normal." Parents are continually wounded by such cruel and insensitive remarks.

A high school teacher of a "modified English course" designed for the poorer students insisted that a dyslexic 16-year-old boy read five novels and write lengthy book reports on each. With help from his parents he composed and wrote out the first book report, which because of misspellings was returned for correction. On the fourth rewrite, the boy's mother, a past president of the local ACLD chapter, tried to explain to the teacher that it was impossible for this boy to read five novels and that because of his perceptual deficits it was highly likely he would continue to misspell some words no matter how many times he was asked to rewrite the report. The teacher refused to believe the boy had a problem; to her he was just lazy and careless.

In Chapters 3 and 8 we described the case of a girl who, at the age of 6, suffered a spontaneous hemorrhage in the left posterior part of her brain. To stop the bleeding, brain surgery was required. Following this trauma to her brain she experienced chronic visual–perceptual difficulties, although many of her high school teachers denied her disabilities. They thought her overprotective mother was making excuses for an academically mediocre student.

Such reports are meant not to put down teachers but to draw attention to the ignorance of some of them toward the nature of learning disabilities. Had the junior high school principal, in the first case, really understood what they boy's mother was telling him during the initial interview, he would have alerted his teachers and suggested an appropriate remedial program. Had the teachers been knowledgeable regarding perceptual deficits and learning disorders, they would have provided a suitable remedial teaching plan rather than resorting to sarcasm and stereotyping the boy as "abnormal."

The high school teacher, in the second case, had she understood the nature of dyslexia, would have provided the boy with suitable remedial drills and demanded realistic responses, instead of projecting her own prejudices by labeling him as lazy and careless.

Ignorance of the nature of learning disabilities usually leads to a denial and nonacceptance of the problem. Understanding leads to an acceptance and recognition of the problem, which is the first step to successful remediation.

When parents are asked their opinion of how to improve the prospects of their LD children, the most common answer is, "The teachers need more training in special education." Many government departments of education and universities, aware of this need, are planning improved training programs, not only for teachers, but also specially designed orientation courses in learning disabilities for school superintendents, principals, and other administrators. Many educators believe that postservice training in special education (after the teacher has had a year or two of successful classroom teaching) is more effective than preservice training (during a teacher training course prior to employment). Then only the most competent teachers should be selected for further training, which may be formal (a higher degree or diploma) or informal (an extra course or courses covering a topic the teacher needs and wants, workshops, conferences, visits to other classrooms or experimental clinics).

How the teacher may gain better training is a problem of professional education and is beyond the limits of this discussion other than to draw attention to its importance. There is a huge literature in this field that the interested reader may consult. Attempting to understand subtle learning problems in children, whether they are neurogenic or with no known cause, is stimulating and challenging for the teacher. Because of the gaps in our knowledge and also the rapid increase in new scientific insights, the successful teacher will need to continue to upgrade his or her knowledge and to maintain an experimental view of the child. Much more is to be gained by studying the child's types of perceptual errors and abnormal learning strategies than by berating him or her for hyperactive or restless behavior, which may very well be a secondary result of the primary nature of his disabilities. The child has the clues to his own remediation if the teacher is knowledgeable and sensitive enough to recognize them.

But academic understanding by itself is not enough. The teacher still needs a number of social and pedagogical skills that enable an easy communication with the student. "There is little reason to doubt that the dominant factor in successful teaching is and will always remain the teacher's skill in nourishing, and sometimes even arousing, the child's curiosity and interest and in providing a rich and challenging intellectual environment in which the child can find his own unique way toward understanding, knowledge, and skill" (N. Chomsky, 1970).

The Role of the Physician

The reader will have recognized from the discussions throughout this book that the contributions of the medical doctor are essential in the diagnosis of and decisions regarding remediation for the LD child. In making a neuropsychological study of such a child, a referral to a neurologist is the first step. Frequently referrals are made directly from a neurologist or neurosurgeon for neuropsychological assessment prior to brain surgery. Where testing is done following brain surgery, much information can be obtained regarding (1) the differences between pre- and post-surgery mental skills and (2) the new pattern of mental skills with which the patient may have to adapt, although testing about a year later will also be needed before any reliable predictions can be made about the permanence of any mental deficits.

Although diagnostic information usually comes from the pediatric neurologist, it also may include the neurosurgeon, the radiologist, the orthopedic surgeon, the internist, the ophthalmologist, the audiologist, the psychiatrist, the general practitioner, or any other medically trained person involved in the case.

An early diagnosis is desirable in cases of neurogenic learning problems because "research indicates that the earlier the diagnosis, the better the prognosis" (Tarnopol, 1971). However, sometimes the less experienced physician may obstruct such a move by assuring the mother she has nothing to worry about. If the request has been recommended to the mother by a psychologist, some general practitioners have been known to refuse it on the basis of its being a nonmedical referral. However, fortunately for the children who need this medically diagnostic help, the defensive medical doctor is in the minority, and most doctors are happy to cooperate on a diagnostic team that includes medical, psychological, and educational personnel.

Masland (1969) has drawn attention to the other extreme response by a medical doctor. With no neurological examination and no real knowledge of learning disabilities this doctor tells the parents that because the child is hyperactive he or she is brain damaged, and because he did not respond to the doctor's questions during the examination, the doctor may add another superficial diagnosis that the child is mentally dull or retarded. The implication is that the case is hopeless. Some years ago a medical doctor referred a boy to our laboratory because, he reported in his referral letter, the boy was incorrigible in school, was brain damaged (his diagnosis was made purely on observing the boy's restless behavior), and was mentally retarded (because the boy was reluctant to answer the doctor's questions). When the lad arrived at our laboratory, he was a bright-looking and alert boy who was cautious at first, but who was soon enjoying the variety of tests. He measured a WISC verbal IQ of 128 (superior), and on both a standard neurological examination and on our 5-hour battery of neuropsychological tests he showed no signs of brain damage or central nervous system dysfunction. His "incorrigible" behavior at school was his reaction to being told by the family doctor that he was brain damaged, to being expelled from school by the school principal, and from sensing his parents' feelings of panic regarding the whole situation. Careless medical examinations and superficial diagnostic reports are better ignored; the parent can be advised to consult a competent physician.

Many teachers and some psychologists insist, "Learning disabilities are an *educational* problem, *not* a *medical* one." It is certainly true that the definition and treatment of learning deficits is psychoeducational, but the diagnosis, if it is to be thorough and comprehensive, must include the findings of a medical examination. If the child suffers from a cerebral lesion or dysfunction, a biochemical imbalance, a nutritional problem, or a genetic defect, we need to know. If he is *free* of any or all of these, we will also need to know.

Those educators who insist that their responsibilities are exclusively educational should be reminded that some of the most valuable knowledge and practices in special education have come from medically trained scholars concerned about how children learn. Broca, Hughlings Jackson, Maria Montessori, and Alfred Binet all made significant contributions to our knowledge. Currently, Elena Boder, Macdonald Critchley, Marcel Kinsbourne, Orlando Schrager, Sylvia Richardson, and the late Julio de Quiros (all medically trained), to name just a few, are or have been in constant demand at conferences and through their writings by ACLD groups and others striving to improve their knowledge of learning disabilities.

Once the teacher or school psychologist is persuaded of the value of the medical input (and this is particularly important for the multihandicapped child) he or she will still need to establish some reliable channels of communication. How this is done will vary with the size of the school and/or the city and the skills of the people involved. Frequently, the psychologist is in a favored position to organize a meeting of the parents, the child's teacher(s), and the family doctor. The doctor may agree to have this meeting at his or her office to save time, and its essential value is to enhance the respect of each member for the other. The doctor may not be willing to provide time for more than one meeting, so matters of inter-disciplinary communication regarding medical findings and medication therapies should be discussed. Sometimes a one-paragraph summary of the child's medical problems is adequate and can be dictated by the doctor very quickly immediately following the conference. If the child's diet is radically altered or if he is put on large doses of vitamins or other medication designed to have behavioral effects, this should be reported to the school so that the child's teachers can provide observational feedback regarding his behavior.

One of the significant influences of the neuropsychological approach to learning disabilities in the last 20 years is its tendency to reduce the professional isolation of medical doctors and school personnel and to include important medical knowledge in the decisions regarding remedial treatment.

The Role of the Clinical or School Psychologist

The psychologist's chief function is to adopt and develop improved diagnostic and treatment facilities for the LD child, and he or she does this through research and careful therapeutic procedures. The role of the clinical neuropsychologist has emerged within the last 20 years, and because of its recency it is still taking shape. However, in most applied settings, to my knowledge, he or she is the "middleman" on the team between the neurologist or other medical person and the teacher and/or parent. This seems to be a spontaneous result of the psychologist's training in research methods and clinical procedures that leads to communication with medical personnel, teachers, and parents. Also, the pressures of practice are not as rigid as they are on the teacher or physician. The psychologist can reserve time to observe a child in depth, confer with the parents periodically, and be available to the child's teacher. The skillful psychologist will create experimental clinical tasks specifically to investigate the learning strategies of the child under consideration. The busy teacher and the active physician are not likely free or willing to devote as much time to one case. As well as developing unique testing activities to study a particular child, the school psychologist should have an ongoing group study to investigate the validity of some concept or test technique in the rapidly expanding field of neuropsychology.

The psychologist's relation with the LD child should be warm and nonthreatening and can be measured by the success of his or her skill in communicating with the child. Teachers are frequently put off by the psychologist's report which, they will tell you, indicates nothing that they did not already know about the child and may be couched in a smoke-screen of professional jargon. Parents can also be put off by abstruse language and what appears to them to be a preoccupation with a professional role quite remote from the needs of their child. Many excellent clinical researchers have failed to be very effective in a parent consultation because of their lack of "the common touch."

If the psychologist hopes that his or her findings are to be used in the remedial treatment of the child, then he or she must be careful not to pose as an "expert" advising the teacher, but as a colleague on a professional team on which the teacher enjoys equal input. Frequently some young Ph.D. psychologists can hardly wait to use their research knowledge to tell the teachers what to do. In my experience, remedial prescriptions made unilaterally by the clinical or school psychologist usually end up ignored in a filing cabinet. If the psychologist, in consultation with the teacher, shares his or her findings and listens to the teacher explain the types of remedial procedures that she could use based on these findings, they can then produce a joint prescription that will most likely be used since the teacher has been involved in producing it.

Because of the rapid advances and discoveries in neuropsychology and its impact on neurolinguistics and learning generally, the successful clinical psychologist will need to cultivate a program of ongoing professional development. Personal contact with an active group of referring neurologists and neurosurgeons and special educators can provide a constant source of stimulation, refinement, correction, and development of the psychologist's knowledge of neuropsychology and its relation to learning. The complexity of this relationship demands constant study if the clinical psychologist is to stay abreast of the emerging new knowledge and remain competent in understanding how to use it.

The Role of the Speech and Language Specialist[1]

Because most learning problems include some aspect of language impairment it is important that the professional team include someone with special knowledge and skills in the diagnosis and treatment of linguistic problems. The qualifications of this person may be quite variable in school systems where certification is not required. It may range from a research

[1] For assistance in preparing this section I am indebted to Brenda Costa, M.A., Speech Pathologist, and Sherri McIntyre, M.A., Director of Speech Pathology Programs at the Queen Alexandra Hospital–G. R. Pearkes Center.

speech pathologist, an audiologist or linguist, to a classroom teacher with no special training in language development or diagnostic skills. In many of the United States, speech and hearing specialists are required to have a Masters Degree and supervised clinical training to be certified by the American Speech–Hearing–Language Association. In Canada similar standards are required for membership in the Canadian Speech and Hearing Association, and professional licensing is required by some provincial governments.

The chief areas of expertise concern the use of audiological screening, diagnosis, and interpretation of the nature of hearing loss and/or auditory imperception; analysis and explanation of an aphasia or communication disorder; knowledge of normal language development and the hierarchical structure of language, psycholinguistics, diagnosis, and treatment of speech problems; and skills in interpreting all of this so that the teacher will want to make use of it. Only rarely would one person be professionally qualified to supply all of these services, so the speech or language specialist in different school systems will have greater strengths and/or professional qualifications in some of these skills and less in others.

Most school systems carry out group screening tests for hearing in kindergarten or first grade. These usually are administered by the school or public health nurse. Any severe or unusual hearing cases from this initial screening may be referred to an audiologist in a local hospital, clinic, or research center. If the child happens to live in a rural area where none of these facilities is available, then the child will have to travel some distance for professional assessment.

The professional team to deal with speech problems will vary in size and level of expertise in different school systems. In a large urban center, it may include, in addition to the child's teacher, an occupational therapist, a physiotherapist, the school psychologist, and the speech and hearing specialist. However in many remote rural areas, the teacher may have none of these disciplines for regular support and may have to depend on reading, summer courses, and intermittent professional advice. Between these extremes, only a psychologist or reading specialist may be available to aid the teacher, and in this situation it is hoped that he or she will develop many of the diagnostic competencies and remedial skills of the language specialist. No profession possesses "territorial rights" on language because it is central to all academic learning, so that the most successful use of professional expertise is to encourage all members of the team to assume an experimental approach and to broaden their knowledge and skills in treating language learning disorders.

Where school systems are fortunate enough to have professionally qualified speech and hearing specialists on their staffs, the teachers can seek continued help in knowing more about perceptual deficits, cognitive retardation, and the diagnostic rationale of particular cases. A continued interaction may be maintained between the teacher and the language specialist, so that the results of the speech therapy sessions may be included in the classroom teacher's teaching methods.

Like any successful applied scientist, the speech and hearing specialist will make experimental investigations of the language disabled child, assess his or her deficits in the light of normal language development, and delineate what seem to be the best remedial measures to aid the child. This information will be communicated not only to the child's teacher but to the other members of the professional team in their ongoing evaluation of the pedagogical efficacy of their remedial activities.

The Role of the Child

In a brief discussion of personality development, we can only refer to its importance in the growth of all children and the added obstacles that the LD child encounters. The development of the ego or self-concept is a longitudinal process that begins at birth and reaches maturity in late adolescence or young adulthood, although superficial changes in it no doubt continue all through life.

Many personality theorists have included the bodily sense of body image as basic to a sound personality structure (Allport, 1955; Maslow, 1955). Others have recognized it as basic to cognitive development (Piaget, 1952), and numerous special educators have accepted sensorimotor performance as essential to learning (Barsch, 1966; Kephart, 1966; Montessori, 1964). The child with no specific learning disabilities may still suffer problems in developing a poised and secure self-image because of a poor complexion, lack of feminine beauty in the girl, lack of adequate height or muscular development in the boy, etc. If we add to these common developmental frustrations poor sensorimotor coordination or clumsiness, perceptual deficits, defective directional sense, or some type of language impairment, we have an idea of the increased developmental problems of the LD child. It is particularly difficult for such a child to feel sure of his footing, his manual dexterity, his body image, and himself. It is also difficult for him to feel competent in relation to his environment; because his ego structure is frail, he is poorly equipped to identify strongly with things and people around him. His intellectual development is hindered by his learning disabilities, and all of these frustrations can be magnified by hostile or insensitive treatment by others.

To try to understand how such a child feels, let us look at the verbal account of a child who, at the age of 6 years, encountered brain surgery in the left posterior part of his brain just prior to entering first grade. His account is a recollection written at the age of 21.

> I remember the first week of school, better yet the first day. I remember being scared and not wanting to walk into the large strange classroom

with strange people. Everything was dark and dismal, at least that is what it seemed like to me. I walked around like a zombie, completely in my own world, and always a mad look on my face. No wonder most of my friends lost interest in me.

I remember my teacher's sarcastic ways. In my first week she wouldn't let me wear the knitted skull cap my mother had knitted to covered my shaved head. She made a fool of me in front of the class. I was scared of that teacher all year, and even today I shake at loud noises and being yelled at.

In grade 2 my teacher was young and attractive, but an old grouch like the first one. I was still up in the air (tense and anxious). I just wish I had been old enough to express my point of view instead of being pushed around by every one. No wonder I was so uptight, I was on tranquilizers. The worst part was that I took my yelling and screaming home to my family who didn't deserve it or want it. The trouble was that so much was ticking around in my head and I couldn't express myself logically so that others could understand what was wrong. I wish that I had had help.

This excerpt reveals many significant points that are important to the teacher of the brain-injured child. Traumatic brain damage in the initial stages pervades the patient's thinking. It is both frightening and depressing and tends to color the child's perceptions. The classroom was modern, bright, and colorful, but it seemed "dark and dismal" to this child. His first two teachers sould like ogres from his description, but again it is possible that he perceived them in a more frightening role than they appeared to the other children. It is interesting that he still remembers he had a "mad face." It is a common symptom for brain-damaged patients to have less tolerance to loud noises. For small children it is frightening. He remembers displacing his anger from school to home, and the unhappy confusion of a mild receptive aphasia.

While most learning disabled children may not have to endure as intense intellectual deficits as this traumatically damaged boy, their emotional frustrations from their inability to compete evenly are just as acute. Their disabilities, although "minimal," may be just enough to promote nasty name calling and social exclusion from a gang. Many LD children are made to suffer these personal attacks by other children, and they often report, as adults, that their elementary school teachers either were oblivious to these interpersonal occurrences or they made no attempt to stop them. Although it is important to encourage the independence of all children, the neurologically impaired child usually needs help in understanding his or her deficits and in adjusting successfully to them. Because some parents are unable to provide this help, it is desirable that special teachers recognize the common signs of language reduction, intolerance to noise, heightened anxiety, and difficult social adjustment.

Spreen (1983) studied 203 LD children who had been examined neuropsychologically and educationally in elementary school (all were between the ages of 8 and 12 years), again at age 18, and again at age 25. He found that LD children generally were handicapped in competing in school and as young adults in finding advanced education and vocational opportunities. Types of work and levels of income available to LD young adults tended to be simpler and lower. Spreen concluded that "personal adjustment is strained from childhood on."

Classifications for Therapy

The young or inexperienced teacher may feel confused or overwhelmed when faced with a child with a complex pattern of intellectual and emotional disabilities. A classification model may help to clarify one's thinking and direct one's knowledge systematically.

Any system of classifying learning disabled children is arbitrary, but the following scheme integrates the neurogenic LD child into the whole field.

1. Primary learning disabilities
   a. Traumatically brain damaged
   b. Congenital brain dysfunction
   c. Constitutionally hyperactive
   d. Congenital learning disability with no clear neurological or physiological signs (e.g., developmental dyslexia)
2. Secondary learning disabilities
   a. Sociogenic hyperactivity
   b. Emotional disturbance

Primary Learning Disabilities

Traumatically Brain Damaged

Throughout this book, detailed cases of traumatic brain damage in both adults and children have been presented. The reader will recognize that remediation may include both training the brain (Ayres, 1972a; de Quiros & Schrager, 1978) and training an academic skill (Engelmann & Bruner, 1975; Gillingham, 1965; Scull, 1978). Choice of drills may be selected to stress the child's perceptual strengths; the visually impaired child may have drills that emphasize auditory and tactile input (e.g., Gillingham or Distar) and the child with a phonetic imperception will do better with a system stressing visual and tactile–kinesthetic activities (e.g., color coding with a tactile alphabet and kinesthetic involvement). The language-impaired learner will likely respond best to remedial measures based on knowledge of aphasia and neurolinguistics.

Congenital Brain Dysfunction

At this point in our knowledge it is probable that remedial measures similar to those above will succeed with the child or adult learner with neurological "soft signs" because of the likelihood of neurological damage or dysfunction. In any event, an experimental approach with careful monitoring should indicate the best methods.

The Constitutionally Hyperactive Child

The child with a "subclinical epilepsy" (that is, one that is not intense enough to produce seizures but cerebrally disturbing enough to produce chronic hyperactivity) should be referred for a complete neurological examination. The neurologist may prescribe a medication program that may include anticonvulsive and/or stimulant drugs. As explained in Chapter 4 there has been a wide spectrum of disagreement among medical practitioners regarding the scientific efficacy of drug treatment of children, but studies by a number of careful researchers during the last decade have helped to clarify knowledge in this sphere and to discourage a promiscuous prescription of drugs for hyperactive children.

De Quiros and Schrager (1978) have discriminated (1) hyperactivity, (2) hypoactivity, and (3) restlessness, on a basis of different neurological functions. Hyperactivity results from inadequate motor disinhibition elicited by external stimuli and is strongly connected to minimal brain dysfunction. Restlessness includes poor postural disinhibition by weak internal or proprioceptive stimuli. It is mainly connected to vestibular–proprioceptive dissociation. This model suggests that treatment of hyperactivity, when it is organically caused, may profit from treatment including both drugs and psychotherapy. Although ritalin (methylphenidate) enjoys a wide medical approval as a choice in the treatment of hyperactivity, de Quiros and Schrager advise against its use. They propose the interesting and logical hypothesis that the brain has already attempted to compensate for its disability and that the use of drugs in these cases seems "to produce a greatly excited state in the patient" (p. 202) resulting from cortical excitation.

Because medical opinions on the possible risks of drug programs are mixed, there has been a growing interest in nondrug interventions (Prout, 1977). These may include parent training (B. Weiss, 1971; G. Weiss et al., 1971); operant procedures for shaping new behaviors and eliminating undesirable ones (Ross, 1974; Tymchuk, 1974); environmental manipulation, self-regulation, and cognitive training (Douglas, 1972, 1976, 1978; Meichenbaum, 1975, 1976); and possibly biofeedback (Prout, 1977). Douglas has modified the method of Meichenbaum in teaching hyperactive children to verbalize their actions during a learning situation, and she reports significant improvement in their attention and learning. For a detailed discussion of the prevention and management of hyperactivity see Ross and Ross (1982, especially Chapters 9 and 10).

Congenital Learning-Disabled Child with No Abnormal Physiological Signs

The developmental dyslexic child frequently is normally healthy and presents negative findings on a neurological examination. Nevertheless he or she is abnormally retarded in reading and writing and does not respond to normal teaching procedures.

A complete neuropsychological examination is still useful because it provides a more complete inventory of the child's perceptual, intellectual, and motor strengths. Frequently the child measures normally on all perceptual and motor skills singly but has difficulty integrating them. In such a case, remediation may include exercises to integrate two perceptual skills, then three, and then these three with the required motor response. If any perceptual or cognitive deficits are discovered, therapeutic treatment may be directed to exercise the weaknesses in company with the child's strengths.

Secondary Learning Disabilities

Sociogenic Hyperactivity

When there is no evidence of any organic cause of the child's hyperactivity, it seems reasonably safe to conclude that the problem is a purely psychological and social one. At our present level of knowledge, intervention programs based on a behavioral approach and/or a cognitive training model as described above (Douglas, 1978; Meichenbaum, 1976; Ross, 1974; Ross & Ross, 1982) seem to promise the best results.

Emotionally Disturbed Personality

Children with abnormal forms of behavior involving marked mood swings, poor social adaptability, or inappropriate social response may be primarily a psychiatric problem. Referral to a competent medical specialist might turn up an abnormal blood chemistry level, poor nutrition, or an unhealthy family environment. In such cases these children may be intellectually bright as measured by an intelligence test, but their learning problems are secondary to their emotional distress. Academic remediation normally will not be resumed until the medical problems of the child are reasonably resolved.

Summary

The choice of a particular remediation program should not be made on a basis of the teacher's prejudice or personal preference. It should follow an in-depth study of the child neurologically, psychologically, educationally, and socially and should be modified as indicated by the experimental findings from a progressive examination and evaluation.

11 Postscript

We find it a clinical and scientific advantage to acknowledge that there is both a neurology and psychology of learning . . . when we combine psychologic and neurologic constructs, we gain new insights into the differing types of learning disabilities.
Helmer R. Myklebust (1975a)

The following discussion attempts to clarify and summarize the thesis of this book by presenting the basic assumptions underlying the neuropsychological approach to understanding and treating learning disabilities.

Basic Assumptions

1. All behavior, including cognitive processes, which essentially are psychological, is mediated by the brain and central nervous system and their integrated and supporting physiological systems. All behavior has two aspects, the psychological and the physiological.

2. When all supporting and mediating organic subsystems are functioning normally, they usually can be ignored. The perception, understanding, and treatment of behavior, in this case, can deal successfully with behavior exclusively at the psychological or behavioral level.

3. When one or more of the physiological subsystems is dysfunctioning so as to impede normal perception, cognition, or motor response, then a consideration of behavior only at the psychological level is inadequate. In such cases both psychological and physiological processes and their interactions will need to be recognized for successful diagnosis and treatment.

4. The neuropsychological concept of behavior acknowledges all physiological subsystems (e.g., respiratory, circulatory, digestive) as essential to vegetative life, but the brain and central nervous system provide the most subtle, the most important, and the most remarkable aspects of human behavior. These are cortical function and creative mental life.

5. All behavior and neural function are perfectly correlated; one is caused by the other. "Each kind of mental activity has a distinct psychological structure and is effected through the joint activity of discrete cortical zones" (Luria, Simernitskaya, & Tubylevich, 1970). Clinical neuropsychological research, especially in the past 40 years, has revealed many brain–behavior relationships and is continuing to increase our knowledge of many areas not yet understood.

6. The physiologist, neurologist, neurosurgeon, and neuropsychologist frequently have direct access to data of genuine importance to the special educator, who will never be aware of this commanding information unless it is made available in a form relevant to educational theories and practices.

7. There is a systematic development and function of the human brain that reveals lawful relationships between its normal function and specific patterns of behavior; also systematic relationships exist between deficit functioning of the brain when it is damaged and specific behavior deficits. Clinical neurological studies of brain function and dysfunction have provided, and continue to provide, a large body of empirically established knowledge that can supply a useful level of predictive validity to the neurosurgeon, neurologist, and neuropsychologist. This knowledge can be invaluable to the special educator who will take the time to understand and use it.

8. Because of the unity of nature and its systematic and lawful functions, it is logical to conclude that brain functions among large samples or populations vary from perfect structural integrity and normal, healthy function to severe structural damage and inferior cerebral action. In the extreme cases of localized damage deficits in both the brain and behavior can frequently be identified unequivocally with the presence of hard neurological signs. In the borderline cases, the behavior deficit may be obvious, but the neurological dysfunction, when there is one, may have to be inferred through scientific speculation until more sensitive neurological test procedures are developed, or until neuropsychological knowledge is more complete.

9. Although there is no complete agreement on a definition, for practical reasons we accept that

Learning disabilities is a generic term that refers to a heterogeneous group of disorders due to identifiable or inferred central nervous system dysfunction. Such disorders may be manifested by delays in early development and/or difficulties in any of the following areas: attention, memory, reasoning, coordination, communicating, reading, writing, spelling, calculation, social competence, and emotional maturation. Learning disabilities are intrinsic to the individual and may affect learning and behavior in any individual, including those with potentially average, average, or above average intelligence. Learning disabilities are not due primarily to visual, hearing, or motor handicaps; to mental retardation, emotional disturbance, or environmental disadvantage; although they may occur concurrently with any of these.

Learning disabilities may arise from genetic variations, biochemical factors, events in the pre- to peri-natal period, or any other subsequent events resulting in neurological impairment. [Canadian Association for Children and Adults with Learning Disabilities, 1981]

10. Brain-damaged patients are not a homogeneous group and must be understood differentially in terms of the type of lesion (whether it is evolving, resolving, or static), of its locus, intensity, extent, and history. Similarly, learning disabled children or adults are not a homogeneous group and must be understood diagnostically in terms of the *nature* of their learning problems. A detailed neuropsychological battery of tests can provide information on perception (visual, auditory, and tactile–kinesthetic), both intramodally and intermodally; on language development (both understanding and expression); on mental imagery (both verbal and nonverbal); on reasoning (both inductive and deductive); on memory (both short-term and habitual); on sequencing (both verbal and nonverbal); on motor speed and accuracy; on cerebral dominance and handedness; on sensorimotor integration; and on academic achievement.

11. Chronic, localized lesions in critical parts of the language circuits, usually in the left hemisphere, or in critical parts of the cortex concerned with mediating spatial perception, usually in the right hemisphere, are permanent and have an established negative effect on perception and cognition. Research of others (Calanchini & Trout, 1971, especially pp. 215–219) and our own (e.g., cases of Sam and Will in Chapter 5) have shown a chronicity of learning deficit. The learning profiles of these children do not alter significantly over time; "the intact and deficient areas remain the same" (Calanchini & Trout, 1971). These same authors in describing one of these cases wrote, "His method of learning is unique for his brain." In such cases, a neuropsychological assessment provides a better basis for understanding and predicting the child's possible learning in the future.

12. Chronic brain lesions, while they mean that the cerebral deficit is permanent, do not mean that the child cannot improve in his or her learning achievement. While the child's learning profile may show the same "lows" and "highs" over time, he or she can be taught, through skilled remedial teaching, to make better use of intrinsic strengths. In brief, the child's intellectual "capacity" remains fixed but his learning strategies can improve.

13. Children with several neurological "soft signs" also are likely to retain most of them, and "many show additional and different signs in adulthood that were not seen in childhood" (Hern, 1984). Most of these children are learning impaired in school and tend to retain these disabilities in adulthood, although by then they may have learned compensatory strategies.

14. Minimal "soft signs" in children tend to present various cognitive and behavioral deficits in adulthood that restrict their training and vocational opportunities (Spreen, 1983). But again, they may learn compensatory strategies that can lead to occupational success and personal satisfaction. Many years ago, Somerset Maugham wrote a charming and amusing short story, "The Verger" (Maugham, 1953), about an adult dyslexic who amassed a fortune in business but who could neither read nor write. These types of cases are not uncommon but they seldom come to public notice because of the understandable desire of the successful dyslexic to conceal his disability.

Neuropsychological Principles

The clinical responsibility of neuropsychological assessment is a serious one, and to reach a level of clinical competence requires several years of training, preferably in a practicum under experienced supervision. Because it is beyond the scope of this book to explain this very complex subject, only some of the most reliable and tested principles are listed here. Each principle may stimulate a number of clinical investigating techniques, and a few examples of these are listed for purposes of illustration.

1. A left-hemisphere lesion or dysfunction, if in the area of the language circuits, may impede the understanding and expression of spoken and/ or written language, and/or result in an inability to repeat oral material on command. Such a dysfunction, if severe, results in some form of aphasia and, if minimal, in a specific language retardation. Such students will typically have poor achievement and difficulty in learning all verbal academic subjects, but they may be superior in mechanical design and invention, and all visual–spatial tasks such as geometry, cartography, and graphic and industrial arts.

   A few of the behavioral signs of left-hemisphere dysfunction include: a markedly lower verbal IQ relative to a performance IQ; the presence of language retardation (or aphasic symptoms) along with above-average or superior spatial–constructional skills; poor tactile form recognition in the right hand coupled with normal stereognosis in the left; poor finger localization in the right hand with normal awareness for the left; a right visual field defect with normal vision on the left; slow finger tapping in the right hand accompanying normal or fast tapping in the left hand; tactile suppression in the right hand when both hands are touched simultaneously, with habitual reporting of tactile stimulation in the left hand; tactile insensitivity in the right hand when stimulated with graded fine nylon hairs along with normal sensitivity in the left hand; and poor sequential perception and memory. Such symptoms are never used singly to indicate a neuropsychological diagnosis; they are evaluated in constellations (Reitan included a composite of 10 signs for his Impairment Index) and they are correlated with medical data (e.g., brain scan indications of abnormal functions in the left hemisphere with none in the right).

2. A right-hemisphere lesion or dysfunction, if in the medial and posterior cortical areas, typically impedes spatial perception and imagery and results in inferior achievement in arithmetic, geometry, map-drawing, graphic arts, and all types of mechanical and constructional skills. Such students may be competent in learning and achieving successfully in the language arts.

   Neuropsychological signs of right-hemisphere dysfunction appear on the opposite side to the signs listed above in item 1. Although an educator will not use these signs for a neuropsychological diagnosis, he or she can use them as invaluable information in understanding the nature of a child's learning problem, in terms of perception, cognition, motor response, and language competence.

3. Throughout this book we have attempted to observe the various behaviors that appear to be dominated by one cerebral hemisphere or the other. While knowledge of hemispheric functional asymmetry is a first step in our understanding of brain function, the essence of this understanding is how the two differentially functioning hemispheres *interact*. As Rourke (1982) has shown, during the past 30 years we have progressed through a "static" phase where behavioral deficits and localized brain lesions were related by performance on fixed batteries of psychological tests. Then followed a phase of cognitive neuropsychology in which attempts were made to identify the tasks that the tests were alleged to measure. The third, and present, phase is an attempt to escape the rigidity of the first two by examining the development of the human brain and its dynamic interactions in determining human behavior.

   The successful school neuropsychologist will need to be aware of the knowledge emanating from the first two phases and will need to follow the current and lively discussions of dynamic cerebral organization. If neuropsychological knowledge is to be used successfully in deciding on remediation programs, a complete and accurate model of brain function and behavior is a basic requisite. At present, such a model is not yet available nor is there general agreement on how the two cerebral hemispheres interact. While there is much segmental empirical evidence to enable us to use our knowledge of brain–behavior relationships, there is still much speculation on how these segments fit together in a functional model. Some theorists propose that the brain develops first from the left to the right side and that this left-right maturational gradient results in the leading side (usually the left) exerting an inhibitory influence on the lagging side (usually the right) (Corballis & Morgan, 1978). There are others who, using histological evidence of greater sensory and motor representation in the left hemisphere and greater areas of associative cortex in the right, have proposed a right-to-left shift in learning new material (Goldberg & Costa, 1981; Rourke, 1982). All of these theories at present, while enjoying much empirical support, still offer considerable speculation and have only a tentative status.

4. Intramodal analysis is profitable for analyzing learning problems, particularly when they involve a specific sense mode. For example, if visual–perceptual deficits seem to be related to a child's academic underachieving, the diagnostician will want to know about the level of functioning of the child's visual form recognition, letter and word form recognition, pictorial sequential memory, nonverbal visual sequential memory, verbal visual sequential memory, figure–ground perception, visual–manual reaction time, visual–motor accuracy and speed, and the relation of visual perception to cerebral dominance. A similar detailed analysis may need to be carried out in the auditory and tactile–kinesthetic sense modes if deficit functioning is detected in either of them.

5. Intermodal integration must be evaluated. Ayres (1976) has developed a detailed battery of tests suitable for measuring sensorimotor integration, and Geschwind, Luria, Myklebust, Reitan, Satz, Spreen and Benton, Aaron Smith, and many others have written regarding intermodal sensory, motor, and language integration at the cortical and subcortical levels.

It is sometimes found that a child is competent in perceptual–motor functions when the various sense modes are viewed separately. However, this child's inability to integrate visual, auditory, tactile, and motor expression may impede his or her learning to read, write, and spell.

Keogh (1982) has reminded us that "learning to move and moving to learn are two quite different ways to think about the role of movement in perceptual–motor training programs." He cautions against an un-

critical enthusiasm for endorsing the practice of moving to learn, because of the present lack of theory in movement development. Instead,
Keogh believes that we need to study movement learning disabilities,
that is, how the sensory–perceptual–cognitive systems determine
movement, and how the personal-social perceived environment influences movement indirectly.

6. The learning disabled child's cerebral dominance and handedness need
   to be known, and in the past this information has usually been unknown or ignored. Decisions to change a child's handedness should
   never be made without this information.

7. Learning disabilities, as we have seen, may be either verbal (largely
   left hemisphere) and/or nonverbal (largely right hemisphere). Myklebust (1975a,b), using a cognitive model, has shown that imagery may
   be weak because the original perceptual input may be distorted or
   partial. To develop a mental image of a chair, and this must precede
   the development of the concept of it, the child must recreate in his or
   her imagination the visual form and the tactile feel of sitting in a chair.
   The child whose nonverbal or spatial perceptions are accurate, vivid,
   and facile may be better equipped to produce a mental image, a symbol, and ultimately a concept of a class of objects known as "chair."
   Myklebust (1975b) thinks that nonverbal learning disturbances may be
   more debilitating than the verbal. They may include "deficiencies in
   ability to judge time, size, distance, and weight, to acquire spatial
   orientation, to learn right from left, and to learn directions" (p. 90).

The Knowledge of Brain Structure and Function

A study of brain structure and function has led most neuropsychologists
to "accept that at least the basic skills such as perception, movement and
language are separately organized within the cortex" (Warrington, 1970).
Luria (1973) has attributed attention to the brainstem; perception (including spatial interpretation) to the post-Rolandic cerebrum; and motor, sequential, planning, and temporal behavior to the frontal lobes. Whether it
is all as simplistically related as this is not certain, but it is true that a
detailed knowledge of brain functions will lead the school psychologist in
a systematic and thorough hunt for the possible attentional, perceptual,
linguistic, motor, or sequential deficits that an academically or socially
underachieving child may have. The teacher, with at least a gross or
practical understanding of the regional functions of the brain, will make a
better use of the knowledge supplied by the school psychologist and

should, because of this systematic functional knowledge of the brain, be able to produce more testable hypotheses in his or her choice of a successful plan of remediation. The child has the clues to the causes of his learning problems if the diagnostician has the understanding and knowledge to recognize them; and a knowledge of the structure and function of the child or adult's brain can help to direct the search for causes.

A Cautionary Note

A concentration on neuropsychological factors in behavior may cause a neglect of other equally important etiological variables. Since all human behavior results from a delicate and complex interaction between organic and psychosocial forces, any deviation in behavior or learning must be understood in this multicausal model. While we have examined only the neuropsychological causes in this book, there are, in addition to the psychosocial forces, a large number of other physiological determiners such as genetic defects, glandular dysfunctions, malnutrition, lead poisoning, etc. (Gaddes, 1978a).

To avoid a wrong diagnosis it will be useful to remember:

1. In examining the academically underachieving learner, the school psychologist or educational diagnostician (and this includes the teacher) must guard against searching for pathology and assuming that there must be something organically wrong with the referred child or adult. It is important to keep an open mind and assess the empirical evidence to decide how much of the learner's deficits are organically caused (if, in fact, they are), and how much they are sociogenically produced.

2. The diagnostic decision about the quality of underachievement may be carefully or superficially carried out. In the latter case it may be inaccurate and misleading. Ysseldyke and his colleagues (1983) have made a number of detailed studies of this process. Some of their findings have shown that:
   a. Team meetings of professionals to assess children's academic underachievement frequently include no input, or very little, from teachers.
   b. Sometimes decisions are made that ignore the collected data.
   c. Achievement and intelligence tend to be emphasized by educational team members, but most participants base their acceptance of a child's IQ on only *one* test. More than a third of them base their opinions of achievement on only *one* test, and frequently inadequate tests are used.

    d. In one study (Algozzine & Ysseldyke, 1981) about half of a group of decision makers ($N > 200$) identified *normal* students as needing special educational help.

    e. Depending on which current criteria are used to select underachievers, most *normal* students can be classified as LD.

Such studies show clearly that the decision-making process is too often inconsistent and unreliable, and to improve it, better trained professionals are needed on the team. To translate diagnostic test data into successful remedial treatment is probably the most difficult process in all of the professional demands of special education. Collecting large masses of test data is a waste of time unless the remedial measures suggested by them are monitored regularly, edited, and continually readjusted to provide successful results.

3. Even if it is obvious or highly probable that the person we are studying is suffering from a chronic brain dysfunction, this is not *the* single cause of his or her learning problems. Its effect on the learner's behavior (is he discouraged, indifferent, or hostile?) and relationships with his family and peers will still need to be considered.

4. If a neurological dysfunction is obvious or highly probable we must remember that, although there is a fairly large body of tested knowledge in neuropsychology, there are still many grey areas, ranging from partial or confused understanding to complete ignorance. Aaron Smith, in his presidential address to the International Neuropsychological Society (A. Smith, 1979) told a charming story which, in essence, indicated that at least half of what is taught in medical schools eventually turns out to be false. But the irony of the situation is that *we don't know which half!* This is likely true in clinical neuropsychology and special education as well, for both of these disciplines are applied studies, and in such cases practices and principles evolve unevenly, and frequently in situations of practical need.

5. To protect ourselves from serious mistakes that may have damaging effects on students, the diagnostician is wise to assume the view of the experimental scientist. He or she must not rely only on a favorite diagnosis or recommend a standard or simplistic remedial program but must study the child or adult systematically and in depth and look there for clues. A profile of standard scores is not enough; as well we need to know in detail the child's strengths, weaknesses, learning strategies, and relations with his or her social environment.

6. Pet theories, pet diagnoses, and pet remedial plans should be avoided. These are probably signs of a superficial knowledge of the whole field of learning disabilities and indications of a set of simplistic beliefs based on emotion and desire rather than on diagnostic understanding.

7. Special education includes many people with an "either–or" approach. Some support behavior modification or environmental causes

exclusively and deny that organic factors are either relevant or appropriate. Others refuse to have behavior modification practices in their schools because they are too mechanistic and impersonal. To view the learning disabled child or adult scientifically and objectively we cannot afford to exclude any area of tested knowledge or any form of remediation that promises possible help to the learner. No doubt the "either–or" approach could soon be erased if all school psychologists and LD specialists were required, in their graduate training, to spend an intensive supervised practicum stressing applied behavior analysis, and an equally intensive supervised practicum working with brain-injured learning disabled subjects, where neuropsychological assessment methods were used. Unfortunately, at present, only a small number of graduate training programs for school psychologists include neuropsychological assessment in their curricula (Hynd, Quackenbush, & Obrzut, 1979; Hynd & Obrzut, 1980).

As we have seen throughout this book, the impact of neuropsychology, first on experimental psychology in the 1940s and 1950s, then on clinical psychology in the 1960s, and finally on school psychology in the 1970s, has resulted in changes at an alarming speed. Such rapid growth has meant that practices have preceded theory, and molar hypotheses have come into use before they have been justified by all of the necessary microinvestigations. But "neurophysiological methods do not allow one to understand function instantly" (Barlow, 1980); it is a slow process of continuous experimental microinvestigations of exact or near-accurate understanding of small segments of knowledge. However, knowledge in this fractionated form is useless to the clinician unless it is integrated and related to the practical problems faced by the practitioner (in this case, the clinical psychologist, the school psychologist, or the special educator). Knowing all this, these professionals will understand that they are practicing a treatment procedure with limited knowledge and remedies yet to be fully related to theory. The 1980s have already seen important advances in behavioral neurology; it is hoped that this trend will continue so that by the 1990s our knowledge of the brain–behavior relationships will be significantly advanced and special education can boast of remedial measures more closely based on sound theory.

Appendix

Neuropsychological Tests

In Chapter 4, the use of neuropsychological tests is discussed as being useful for making a differential diagnosis of brain damage versus non-brain-damage in detecting cognitive deficits in brain-damaged and MBD subjects, and for assessing the pattern of behavioral and mental strengths, and weaknesses in both neurologically impaired and normal subjects. The trained clinical neuropsychologist may be competent to make all of these diagnoses, but in cases where an educational diagnostician has had no training in clinical neuropsychology, it is important that he or she avoid making neuropsychological statements and instead use the test results for understanding the child's pattern of cognitive competencies and deficits. This knowledge is essential for the preparation of an effective remedial program.

Following is a list of some of the tests used in the Victoria Neuropsychology Laboratory, but the choice will vary from clinic to clinic according to the training, experience, and personal preferences of each psychologist.

1. Victoria battery.
   a. Intelligence: Wechsler Test (WIPPSI, WISC-R, WAIS-R): Kaufman Assessment Battery for Children (K-ABC); Peabody Picture Vocabulary Test; Mattis Dementia Scale; Raven's Colored Progressive Matrices; Raven's Standard Progressive Matrices; Wisconsin Card Sorting Test; Halstead–Reitan Category Test (Booklet Form); French's Pictorial Test of Intelligence; Nonverbal Intelligence Test for Deaf and Hard of Hearing (Snijders and Snijders-Oomen. This test was developed by Professor J. Th. Snijders, Department of Psychology, University of Groningen, The Netherlands).
   b. Visual–Spatial–Constructional: Wechsler performance tests; Raven's Progressive Matrices; Halstead–Reitan Category Test; Benton Visual Retention Test; Embedded Figures Test; Dynamic Visual Retention Test; Three Dimensional Praxis Test; Rey–Osterrieth Complex Figure Test; Porteus Maze Test.
   c. Auditory: Dichotic Listening Test; Spreen–Benton Sound Recognition Test; Seashore Tonal Memory; Meikle Auditory Speech Perception; Spreen Sentence Repetition Test; Spreen–Benton Articulation Test.

d. Tactual: Benton Stereognosis Test; Halstead Tactual Performance Test; Esthesiometer; Benton Finger Localization Test; Spreen–Benton Tactile Naming Test.

e. Sensorimotor Integration: Reitan Trail-making Test; Finger Praxis; Purdue Pegboard; Visual–Manual Reaction Time; Auditory–Manual Reaction Time; Beery Test of Visual Motor Integration.

f. Body Image: Benton Right–Left Orientation Test; Lateral Dominance Test.

g. Motor Function: Reitan Finger Tapping; Hand-grip strength (Smedley Dynamometer).

h. Cerebral Dominance: Dichotic Listening Test; Lateral Preferences; and all tests of comparative lateral function.

i. Memory: Benton VRT: Rey Visual Design Learning Test; Wechsler Memory Scale; Memory for English Children's Stories; Sentence Repetition; Digit Span; Rey Auditory–Verbal Learning Test; Buschke's Restricted Reminding Procedure.

j. Language: Spreen–Benton Aphasia Battery (this includes 20 subtests of language function); Illinois Test of Psycholinguistic Abilities; Token Test; Boston Naming Test; Boston Diagnostic Aphasia Examination.

k. Educational Achievement: Wide Range Achievement Test; Peabody Individual Achievement; Gates–MacGinitie Reading Test (Grades 1–10); Gates–McKillop Diagnostic Reading Test; Stanford Diagnostic Reading Test (Blue, Grades 9–12 and community college level); Boder Test of Reading–Spelling Patterns.

l. Personality Tests.

2. Bannatyne has provided a detailed discussion of a large number of tests used for the assessment of learning disabled children (Bannatyne, 1971, Chap. XIV, p. 573ff).

3. Mattis has described a number of tests used at the Montefiore Hospital in the Bronx (Mattis, French, & Rapin, 1975).

4. The Halstead–Reitan Neuropsychological Test Battery for Adults (15 years and older), for older children (ages 9–14 years), and for younger children (ages 5–8 years) are available from Dr. R. M. Reitan, Neuropsychology Laboratory, 1338 E. Edison Street, Tucson, Arizona, 85719. These batteries, as well as being used for diagnosing learning disorders, are used by clinical neuropsychologists to assess brain functions and dysfunctions and adaptive abilities.

5. One of the most productive researchers and writers in the area of neuropsychology and learning disabilities is Dr. Byron P. Rourke at the University of Windsor. We list five of his representative publications (Rourke 1975, 1976a,b, 1978a,b; Rourke & Orr, 1977).

6. Early Detection. Several references may be useful (Eaves, Kendall, & Crichton, 1972; Jansky & de Hirsch, 1972; Satz, Taylor, Friel, & Fletcher 1978; Silver et al., 1976; Spreen, 1978).

7. Aphasia Testing.
   a. Goodglass, H., and Kaplan, E. *The assessment of aphasia and related disorders*. Philadelphia: Lea & Febiger, 1972.
   b. Spreen, O., and Benton, A. L. *Neurosensory center comprehensive examination for aphasia* [also known as the Spreen–Benton aphasia battery]. Produced and distributed by the Neuropsychology Laboratory, University of Victoria, Victoria, B.C., Canada, 1968 and 1977 (revised).

Description of the five nonverbal sequential tests used in the study of serial order (see Chapter 5, p. 162).

1. Visual Receptive Serial Order Test
   This is the Dynamic Visual Retention Test (DVRT; Gaddes, 1966a), which shows sequential patterns of lights on a display screen. The subject is asked to watch a standard pattern of lights and a test pattern in which one light is in a different position. The subject is asked to state which light in the sequence is different. This is a visual version of the Seashore Tonal Memory Test. The patterns of lights have recently been transferred to a disk for use on a microcomputer at two speeds.
   (a) Slow speed: Light exposure 1 second; interlight interval 1 second.
   (b) Fast speed: Light exposure 0.1 second; interlight interval 0.4 second.
   This test, on microcomputer disk, is available through the Neuropsychology Laboratory, University of Victoria, P.O. Box 1700, Victoria, B.C., Canada, V8W 2Y2

2. Visual Expressive Serial Order Test
   The apparatus for this test can be made in any technical shop. The device includes a telegrapher's key connected to a battery-powered 14-volt lamp. The experimenter taps out a serial pattern of lights while the subject watches. The subject is asked to remember the sequential pattern and to tap it out immediately.

3. Auditory Receptive Serial Order Test
   The subject listens to two serial patterns of taps presented on a tape recorder and is required to say whether the second pattern is the same or different from the first.

4. Auditory Expressive Serial Order Test
   Following the perception of a pattern of taps presented on a tape recorder, the subject is required to remember and imitate them with a drumstick on the edge of the table.

Glossary

A

Å. Also called Angstrom unit, the unit of electromagnetic wavelength equal to 10^{-7} mm.

Ablation. Cutting and removing a section of tissue. Cerebral ablation: surgical removal of a part of the brain.

Acalculia. An inability to carry out simple arithmetical calculations.

Agenesis. Failure of tissue or an organ to grow and develop normally.

Agnosia. A perceptual deficit; the inability to recognize the meaning of sensory stimuli.

Allergy. A specific and hypersensitive reaction to a particular substance to which most people show a normal reaction.

Aneurysm. The dilatation of the wall of an artery.

Angiogram. X-ray studies of the cerebral blood vessel system following injection of radiopaque material into the arterial system.

Angiography. The practice of studying the circulatory system with angiograms.

Angular Gyrus. A convolution located in the parietal cortices believed to be involved in cross-modal integration; a "tertiary" cortical zone in Luria's brain model.

Anomia. The inability to name an object that one recognizes and understands. A symptom of receptive aphasia.

Anoxia. A lack or reduction of oxygen in the body.

Aphasia. An inability, partial or complete, to understand or express language whether written or spoken, because of injury or disease of the language centers in the brain.

Aphasoid. A mild or moderate retardation in language development and competence; minimal aphasic symptoms.

Aplasia. Failure to grow and develop normally; agenesis.

Apraxia. A defective ability in the absence of severe sensory or motor loss for carrying out neuromuscular acts normally, even though the patient understands what is expected of him.

Arteriovenous Malformation. An abnormal space-occupying tangle of arteries and veins; a benign tumor of abnormally developed blood vessels; hemangioma.

Astereognosis. An impaired ability to recognize objects by touch alone.

Ataxia. Impaired neuromuscular coordination in voluntary muscular movements.

Athetoid. A reduced degree of athetosis.

Athetosis. Involuntary neuromuscular movements and facial grimaces as in cerebral palsy, caused by brain lesion(s).

414

Atrophy. Wasting away of live tissue.

Audiology. The study and treatment of hearing.

Auditory–Gnostic. The perception and understanding of auditory stimuli.

B

Babinski Reflex. Extension and fanning of the toes when the plantar surface of the foot is stroked.

Basal Ganglia (or Striatum). A cluster of nuclei located in the brainstem near the thalamus and concerned with various motor activities.

Behavioral Model. A concept of behavior stressing environmental influences.

Betz Cells. Large neurons in the deep layers of the motor cortex.

Bilateral. Pertaining to both sides of the body or both cerebral hemispheres.

Biochemistry. The chemical study of living tissue.

Biofeedback. A technique using operant conditioning to alter the brain waves of a patient. Clinically this may be used to reduce pulse rate, lower temperature, and alter other autonomic functions.

Brain Scan. A technique for detecting pathological brain tissue using radioactive material injected into the bloodstream. A radiation detector picks up the gamma rays emitted by the damaged tissue and produces a type of X-ray picture of the brain structure.

Brain Tumor. A swelling or abnormal enlargement of brain tissue; a space-occupying lesion; the abnormal tissue may be benign or malignant.

Brodmann's Cerebral Areas. The cortical areas numbered by Brodmann, a German neurologist; see Fig. 3.10.

C

Calcarine Fissure. A fissure on the mesial surface of the occipital lobe.

Callosal. Pertaining to the corpus callosum.

Carotid Artery. The large artery on each side of the neck that supplies blood to the brain.

Cathode Ray Oscilloscope. A vacuum tube; an electronic device that acts as an electron gun and serves as an instrument for detecting and measuring changes in a magnetic field; the basic design of a television picture tube.

Cerebellum. A division of the central nervous system situated on the posterior surface of the brain stem and involved in neuromuscular coordination.

Cervical. Pertaining to the neck. The cervical level of the spinal cord is at the level of the neck.

Choreiform. Mild, jerky, involuntary movements, frequently involving the hands; somewhat like chorea.

Clonic. Rapid alternate spasms of contraction and relaxation as in epileptic seizures.

CNS. Abbreviation for central nervous system.

Commissurotomy. A surgical procedure by which the commissures or neural fibers of the corpus callosum are severed. In some cases the complete corpus callosum may be cut and in others only part, frequently the anterior commissures. This procedure, frequently referred to as the "split-brain" technique, may be used for relief of intractible epilepsy. It incidentally provides split- and half-brain models with which to study various forms of human behavior and behavior change.

Concurrent Validity. Correlating a new test with the results of an established test known to be valid may provide a measure of concurrent validity for the new test if the measure correlating the two tests is high.

Construct Validity. If the correlation is positive and high between test scores and a particular type of hypothesized behavior in a theory (e.g., anxiety), the test is said to have construct validity.

Contra-Coup Effect. A sudden blow on one side of the head may produce damage to the opposite side of the brain.

Contralateral. Pertaining to the opposite side of the body or brain. Antonym for ipsilateral.

Convolution. An irregular convex formation in the brain; a gyrus.

Corpora Quadrigemina. Four rounded protuberances on the posterior surface of the midbrain. The two upper ones (the superior colliculi) are involved in vision; the two lower ones (the inferior colliculi) are involved in audition.

Corpus Callosum. Wide band of neural fibers interconnecting the two cerebral hemispheres.

Cortex. The convoluted outer layer of gray neural tissue that covers the brain. For convenience it is divided in frontal, parietal, temporal, and occipital lobes by the fissure of Rolando and the fissure of Sylvius. Both the left and right cerebral hemispheres are similarly divided.

Cortical Electrostimulation. During brain surgery a conscious patient may report specific experiences following electrostimulation of particular areas of the cerebral cortex. Stimulation of the motor strips may temporarily interfere with volitional motor activity or cause involuntary movements.

Cortices. Plural of cortex.

Craniotomy. Any operation on the cranium. In neurology it usually refers to brain surgery.

Cutaneous. The skin senses, usually thought to include touch, cold, warm, and pain.

Cyanosed. The skin takes on a blue color because of inadequate oxygen content in the blood.

Cyst. A liquid-filled sac; in abnormal form it shows as a swelling.

Cytology. The study of living cells.

D

Decussation. A crossing over from one side to the other. Neural decussation refers to the bodily sensory and motor tracts that cross over and connect to the contralateral cerebral hemisphere.

Dextral. Pertaining to the right side of the body.

Diaschisis. A localized brain lesion may impair the function of healthy tissue at some distance from it. These "distance effects" can be misleading if only behavioral signs are used for diagnosis.

Dichotic Listening. A technique for stimulating simultaneously both ears of a subject with different words, usually with similar initial sounds and lengths. This is used to investigate cerebral dominance for language.

Diplopia. Double vision.

Dorsal. Posterior, back part or surface.

Dynamometer. A device for measuring hand-grip strength.

Dysarthria. Defective articulation.

Dyscalculia. Faulty calculation ability; a mild or moderate aculculia.

Dysgraphia. Impaired ability to express ideas in writing.

Dysphasia. An impairment of speech; sometimes used as a synonym for aphasia.

Dysnomia. Faulty word-finding ability; a mild or moderate anomia.

Dysrhythmia. Abnormal rhythm of electrical changes in the brain; detected by the electroencephalogram.

E

Echoencephalogram. A device that directs high-frequency sound waves through the skull and brain tissue to detect brain tissue abnormalities. It is particularly used to detect shift of the midline in the brain resulting from a space-occupying lesion on one side.

EEG. Abbreviation for electroencephalogram.

Electrode Implantation in the Brain. Surgical insertion of metal electrodes to record the electrical changes in the cerebral locus of the electrode during specific behaviors.

Electroencephalogram. A tracing recorded on a moving graph showing the changes in electrical potential in various parts of the brain.

Empirical Validity. This refers to validating a test or a function by reference to real facts.

Encephalitis. Infection or inflammation of brain tissues.

Endocrine. Pertaining to the glands that secrete their hormones directly into the bloodstream.

Engram. The hypothesized neural trace; the concept that neural tissue manifests permanent change following learning.

Epilepsy. A seizure condition resulting from intense and abnormal electrical activity in the brain.

Epileptogenic Foci. Focal areas of pathological brain tissue that appear to be related to the occurrence of epileptic seizures.

Epithelial. Pertaining to the skin or outer covering.

Equipotentiality. The idea that within large areas of the cerebral cortex one part is equally as potent as another part for determining a particular type of behavior, e.g., Lashley's theory of mass action.

Esophagus. The membraneous tube connecting the throat with the stomach.

Euclidean. Two dimensional; spatial as in Euclidean geometry.

Evoked Potential. The measurement of electrical changes in the brain or central nervous system following environmental stimulation; e.g., light flashes in a subject's eyes will evoke sharp electrical changes in the posterior parts of the brain, and staccato sound patterns will evoke sequentially similar electrical changes in the temporal lobes.

Extremities. An arm, leg, hand, or foot; body parts distal from the brain.

F

Face Validity. A test that seems suitable for measuring a certain phenomenon purely on a logical basis but without any empirical testing is said to have face validity.

False Negatives. Those cases wrongly excluded from a category because of error in the selection instrument.

False Positives. Those cases wrongly included in a category because of error in the selection instrument.

Falx. A part of the brain deep in the longitudinal fissure that divides the cerebral hemispheres.

Familial. A family pattern; a syndrome that appears in several members of the same family (e.g., developmental dyslexia).

Foramen. An opening or passage.

G

Galvanic Skin Response. Electrical changes of the skin following certain stimuli; sometimes used as an indicator of emotion.

Ganglia. A group of nerve cells forming a sort of nerve center; usually located outside the brain and spinal cord.

Genetic Defects. Abnormal or subnormal physical or psychological symptoms resulting from a defective gene or chromosome pattern.

Gerstmann Syndrome. A configuration of behavioral symptoms stated by Gerstmann, a German neurologist, to result from a lesion of the parietal lobe on the dominant side. The syndrome includes finger agnosia, defective right–left orientation, agraphia, and acalculia.

Gestalt Psychology. A school of psychology that originated in Germany in 1912 and that stressed perception and a holistic view of behavior.

Granule Cells. In the cortex, the fourth layer contains many granular cells with short axons.

Gray Matter. The layman's term for the cortex made up largely of cell bodies that are gray in color.

Gyrus. A convolution or convex fold of tissue.

H

Haptic. Sense of touch; recognition of three-dimensional objects; stereognosis.

Hard Signs. These refer to unequivocal, medically documented signs of brain damage, such as brain surgery, cerebral bleeding, hemiplegia, brain tumor, or penetrating head injury.

Hemangioma. A tumor formed of a tangle of blood vessels.

Hematoma. A mass of effused blood following a hemorrhage.

Hemianopia. A half visual field defect; blindness or impaired vision in the left or right visual field.

Hemianopsia. Same as hemianopia.

Hemiasomatognosia. Being aware of only one half or one side of the body; the side contralateral to the brain lesion is neglected or ignored.

Hemiparesis. Partial paralysis of one side of the body.

Hemiplegia. Paralysis of one side of the body.

Heschl's Gyrus. Convolution on the floor of the fissure of Sylvius.

Histology. Microscopic study of the structure of bodily tissues.

Homeostasis. A principle of physiology describing the tendency of a dynamic energy system to seek a state of equilibrium or normality.

Hyperthyroidism. A condition in which the thyroid gland secretes too much thyroxin and the subject's behavior is marked by hyperactivity, irritability, and restlessness.

Hypothalamus. A portion of the thalamus contiguous to the optic chiasm; is related to the control of many visceral processes and emotional behavior.

Hypothyroidism. An underfunctioning of the thyroid gland often marked by apathy, overweight, and slow mentation.

I

Idiopathic. Of unknown cause.

Imperception. Impaired ability to understand environmental stimuli; agnosia.

Inferior colliculi. The two lower protuberances of the corpora quadrigemina; conduction centers in the auditory tracts.

Insult. In neurology, refers to a lesion or neurological tissue damage.

Internuncial neurons. Interconnecting neurons between sensory and motor neurons.

Intracerebral. Inside the brain or cerebrum.

Invaginated. An infolding of tissue.

Ipsilateral. On the same side; antonym for contralateral.

K

Kinesthesis. Awareness of the body and body parts in space; it includes awareness of balance and motion.

L

Lateral Geniculate Bodies. Two neural bodies, located in the thalamus, that are interconnecting centers for the visual tracts.

Lesion. Any tissue that is damaged or abnormal, e.g., by infection, trauma, or tumor.

Limbic System. A set of cerebral structures, inside the brain and above the brainstem, believed to be involved in emotional behavior and short-term memory. It may include the cingulate gyrus, isthmus, hippocampal gyrus, and uncus.

Loci. Plural of locus.

Locus. Place, site, or location; used in medicine to indicate a specific area or point in the body.

M

Mass Action. See equipotential.

MBD. Abbreviation of minimal brain dysfunction.

Medulla Oblongata. The part of the brainstem above the spinal cord and below the pons; a neural center for many vital functions.

Meningioma. A slowly growing tumor in the meninges or membranes covering the brain.

Mesial. Situated in the middle; at or near the middle line of the body.

Monaural Listening. Auditory stimulation of one ear alone, or one ear more strongly than the other.

Monotonic. Literal meaning, attracting in one direction. In statistics it is used to describe curvilinear relationships that are markedly skewed.

N

Neoplasm. New and abnormal growth of tissue; tumor.

Nucleus Centralis Lateralis. A neural center connecting the lateral surface of the thalamus and the parietal lobes.

Nystagmus. Involuntary oscillating movements of the eyeballs.

O

Obscuration. A phenomenon, during double or simultaneous stimulus (e.g., both hands or cheeks), in which a patient with a unilateral brain lesion reports that a stimulus is sensed weaker, but not completely extinguished, when applied to the side of the body contralateral to the lesion. It is a form of partial extinction.

Occlusion. The state of closure; e.g., blood flow through an artery might be obstructed or occluded.

Ontogenetic. Pertaining to the origin, growth, and development of a living organism.

Ophthalmology. Medical study and treatment of the eye.

Optic Chiasm. The point of decussation of the optic tracts.

Optic Chiasma. See optic chiasm.

P

Patellar Reflex. Knee jerk; response to sudden pressure on the tendon below the knee cap.

Perisylvian Region. The cortical areas contiguous to the fissure of Sylvius.

Phylogenetic. Pertaining to the origin and development of a phylum or species of living organism.

Planum Temporale. An area of differentiated nerve tissue on the floor of the Sylvian fissure. It is larger in the left temporal lobe in most people.

Pleasure Centers of the Brain. An area of the brain near the hypothalamus; when it is electrostimulated it produces sensations pleasurable to the animal or person.

Plethysmograph. Instrument for measuring changes in volume of parts of the body; usually involves changes in blood volume.

Pneumoencephalogram. X-ray study of the brain following injection of air into the lumbar subarachnoid space. The air passes into the ventricles or system of cavities in the brain and spinal column and appears black on the X-ray. It may enable the detection of ventricular abnormalities.

Pons. A connecting center of the brain stem for sensory and motor nerves.

Pontine. To do with the pons.

Positivistic View of Behavior. A model of behavior based on empirical evidence and avoiding untested speculation.

Post-Rolandic Area. The area just posterior to the fissure of Rolando; the sensory strips, parietal, occipital, and temporal lobes.

Primary Visual Cortex. Posterior area of the occipital lobes where the elements of vision are registered; Brodmann's Area 17.

Proactive Inhibition. Impaired memory for learned material because of recent learning of different material.

Prognosis. A prediction of the probable nature and course of a disease or impaired condition.

Proprioceptor. A sense organ in the tissues of the body providing information about body functions or kinesthesia.

Purkinje Cells. A large cell with numerous dendrites located in the cerebellum.

R

Receptive Aphasia. Impaired understanding of language, whether spoken or written.

Reticular System. A network of fibers in the brainstem that alerts the cortex to incoming stimuli.

Retroactive Inhibition. Impaired memory because of the disturbing effects of interpolated activity between original learning and recall.

Retrograde Amnesia. The inability to remember events for a fixed period prior to a traumatic event.

S

Sacral. Lower end of the backbone.

Scotoma. A blind spot or area of decreased vision in the visual fields.

Secondary Visual Cortex. Cortical area contiguous to Brodmann's Area 17; believed to be the visual association area; it provides "meaning" to visual sensation.

Sinistral. Pertaining to the left side of the body.

Soft Signs. Refer to minimal behavioral deviations in a child, reported by the neurologist, where the traditional neurological examination shows no clear signs of brain damage or dysfunction. These indications, such as neuromuscular clumsiness, involuntary twitching movements in the hands, and poor directional sense, are strongly suggestive of abnormal functioning of the central nervous system, but such a diagnosis is not supported by the usual neurological examination techniques. Consequently, these are suspected neurological signs.

Somatic Cells. Bodily cells, e.g., bone cells, blood cells, tissue cells, muscle cells.

Somesthesis. Bodily awareness.

Specific Learning Disability. A difficulty in learning despite normal intelligence and usual opportunities for academic instruction; it may result from a genetic defect or a subtle and localized brain dysfunction.

Stereognosis. Tactile form recognition.

Strabismus. A failure of normal convergence of the two eyes because of incoordination of the eye muscles (commonly called squint or cross-eyed).

Striate Cortex. Primary visual cortex in the occipital lobes, so named because of a white stripe formed by the connecting nerve fibers.

Striatum. See basal ganglia.

Striped Muscles. The skeletal muscles, so named because of striated cellular structure.

Subarachnoid Hemorrhage. The arachnoid is the middle layer of the meninges (thin sheets of tissue) that cover the brain and spinal cord. The space between it and one layer below it is filled with cerebrospinal fluid. In case of brain injuries, a hemorrhage occurring in this space is called a subarachnoid hemorrhage.

Subdural Hematoma. Bleeding in the membranes covering the brain; i.e., a collection of blood between the dura and the arachnoid.

Subliminal. Below a threshold of activation (*limen*, threshold).

Subthalamus. A division of the thalamus.

Sulcus. A fissure or depression.

Superior Colliculi. The two upper protuberances of the corpora quadrigemina; conduction centers in the visual tracts.

Suprasylvian. The area of the human cortex immediately above the fissure of Sylvius.

T

Topological. Refers to topology, a form of geometry that deals with spaces with flexible boundaries. Kurt Lewin in the 1930s proposed using topology to apply to psychology so that both time and space would be included.

Toxic. Pertaining to poison or a poisonous condition.

Tumor. A new growth or neoplasm, which may be malignant or benign. A mass of tissue that grows independently of its surrounding structures and that has no physiological use.

U

Unilateral Brain Damage. Damage in either the left or the right hemisphere.

V

Ventral. Toward the front; anterior.

Ventricles. Fluid-filled cavities in the brain.

Visual–Gnostic. The perception and understanding of visual stimuli.

W

Wada Carotid Amytal Test. Refers to the test of speech dominance first developed by Dr. Juhn Wada in 1949. When amytal is injected into the left carotid artery it is carried to the left cerebral hemisphere in a matter of seconds, where it has an anesthetizing effect. In most patients this produces temporary interference with all language processes. When injected into the right carotid artery amytal usually interferes with the patient's ability for pictorial interpretation and spatial perception.

Wernicke's Aphasia. Receptive aphasia.

Wernicke's Area. The cerebral cortical area, usually in the left temporal area, believed to be involved in the understanding of language. It is believed to include one-third of the left superior temporal gyrus and part of the middle temporal gyrus.

Within-Child Model. A concept of child behavior that includes internal psychological and physiological variables, as opposed to a purely behavioral model.

References

Ackerman, P. T., Dykman, R., & Peters, J. Teenage status of hyperactive and nonhyperactive learning disabled boys. *American Journal of Orthopsychiatry*, 1977, *47*, 577–596.

Adams, J. Clinical neuropsychology and the study of learning disorders. *Pediatric Clinics of North America*, 1973, *20*, 587–598.

Adams, J. Visual and tactile integration and cerebral dysfunction in children with learning disabilities. *Journal of Learning Disabilities*, 1978, *11*, 197–204.

Alavi, A., Reivich, M., Greenberg, J., Hand, P., Rosenquist, A., Rintelmann, W., Christman, D., Fowler, J., Goldman, A., MacGregor, R., & Wolf, A. Mapping of functional activity in brain with ^{18}F-Fluoro-Deoxyglucose. *Seminars in Nuclear Medicine*, 1981, XI, 1, 24–31.

Algozzine, B., & Ysseldyke, J. E. Special education services for normal students; better safe than sorry? *Exceptional Children*, 1981, *48*, 238–243.

Allport, G. W. *Becoming, basic considerations for a psychology of personality.* New Haven: Yale University Press, 1955.

Aman, N. G., & Sprague, R. L. The state dependent effect of methylphenidate and dextroamphetamine. *Journal of Nervous and Mental Diseases*, 1974, *158*, 268–279.

Annett, M. A model of the inheritance of handedness and cerebral dominance. *Nature* (London), 1964, *204*, 59–60.

Annett, M. The growth of manual preference and speed. *British Journal of Psychology*, 1970a, *61*, 545–558.

Annett, M. Handedness, cerebral dominance and the growth of intelligence. *In* Bakker, D. J., & Satz, P. (Eds.), *Specific reading disability, advances in theory and method*. Rotterdam: Rotterdam University Press, 1970b, 61–79.

Annett, M. The distribution of manual asymmetry. *British Journal of Psychology*, 1972, *63*, 343–358.

Annett, M. Handedness in the children of two left-handed parents. *British Journal of Psychology*, 1974, *65*, 129–131.

Ayers, D., & Downing, J. The development of linguistic concepts and reading achievement. Invited paper presented at the International Reading Research Seminar on Linguistic Awareness and Learning to Read, University of Victoria, Victoria, B.C., Canada, June 26–30, 1979.

Ayres, A. J. Sensory integrative processes and neuropsychological learning disabilities. *In* Hellmuth, J. (Ed.), *Learning disorders,* Vol. 3. Seattle: Special Child Publications, 1968, 41–58.

Ayres, A. J. *Sensory integration and learning disorders.* Los Angeles: Western Psychological Services, 1972a.

Ayres, A. J. Improving academic scores through sensory integration. *Journal of Learning Disabilities,* 1972b, *6,* 338–343.

Ayres, A. J. Sensorimotor foundations of academic ability. *In* Cruickshank, W. M., & Hallahan, D. P. (Eds.), *Perceptual and learning disabilities in children,* Vol. 2. Syracuse: Syracuse University Press, 1975, 300–358.

Ayres, A. J. *Interpreting the Southern California Sensory Integration Tests.* Los Angeles: Western Psychological Services, 1976.

Bakker, D. J. *Temporal order in disturbed reading.* Rotterdam: Rotterdam University Press, 1972.

Bakker, D. J. Perceptual asymmetries and reading proficiency. *In* Bortner, M. (Ed.), *Cognitive growth and development: Essays in memory of Herbert G. Birch.* New York: Brunner/Mazel, 1979, 134–152.

Bakker, D. J., & Satz, P. *Specific reading disability, advances in theory and method.* Rotterdam: Rotterdam University Press, 1970.

Bakker, D. J., Teunissen, J., & Bosch, J. Development of laterality-reading patterns. *In* Knights, R. M., & Bakker, D. J. (Eds.), *The neuropsychology of learning disorders.* Baltimore: University Park Press, 1976, 207–220.

Bakker, D. J., & Van Rijnsoever, R. Language proficiency and lateral position in the classroom. *Bulletin of the Orton Society,* 1977, XXVII, 37–53.

Balow, B., Rubin, R., & Rosen, J. J. Perinatal events as precursors of reading disability. *Reading Research Quarterly,* 1975–1976, 11(1), 36–71.

Bannatyne, A. *Language, reading, and learning disabilities, psychology, neuropsychology, diagnosis and remediation.* Springfield, IL: Charles C Thomas, 1971.

Barlow, H. B. Cortical function: A tentative theory and preliminary tests. *In* McFadden, D. (Ed.), *Neural mechanisms in behavior.* New York: Springer-Verlag, 1980, 143–171.

Barnsley, R. H., & Rabinovitch, M. S. Handedness: proficiency versus stated preference. *Perceptual and Motor Skills,* 1970, *30,* 343–362.

Barsch, R. H. Six factors in learning. *In* Hellmuth, J. (Ed.), *Learning disorders,* Vol. 1. Seattle: Special Child Publications, 1965, 328–343.

Barsch, R. H. Teacher needs—motor training. *In* Cruickshank, W. M. (Ed.), *The teacher of brain-injured children.* Syracuse: Syracuse University Press, 1966, 183–195.

Barsch, R. H. *Achieving perceptual-motor efficiency: A space-oriented approach to learning.* Seattle: Special Child Publications, 1967.

Bartel, N. R. Problems in mathematics achievement. *In* Hammill, D. D., & Bartel, N. R., *Teaching children with learning and behavior problems,* 2nd Ed. Boston: Allyn & Bacon, 1978, 99–146.

Bateman, B. Learning disabilities—yesterday, today, and tomorrow. *Exceptional Children,* 1964, *31*(4), 167–177.

Bay, E. Principles of classification and their influence on our concepts of aphasia. *In* de Reuck A. V. S., & O'Connor, M. (Eds.), *CIBA Foundation symposium: Disorders of language: Proceedings.* Boston: Little, Brown, 1964.

Beery, K. E. *Developmental test of visual-motor integration*. Chicago: Follett Educational Corporation, 1967.

Benson, D. F. Graphic orientation disorders of left handed children. *Journal of Learning Disabilities*, 1970, *3*, 126–131.

Benson, D. F. Aphasia. *In* Heilman, K. M., & Valenstein, E. (Eds.), *Clinical neuropsychology*. New York: Oxford University Press, 1979, 22–58.

Benson, D. F., & Geschwind, N. Cerebral dominance and its disturbances. *Pediatric Clinics of North America*, 1968, *15*(3), 759–769.

Benson, D. F., & Geschwind, N. The alexias. *In* Vinken, P. J., & Bruyn, B. W. (Eds.), *Handbook of clinical neurology*, Vol. 4. Amsterdam: North-Holland Publishing Co., 1969, 112–140.

Benson, D. F., & Greenberg, J. P. Visual form agnosia. *American Medical Association Archives of Neurology*, 1969, *2*, 82–89.

Benton, A. L. Significance of systematic reversal in right-left discrimination, *Acta Psychiatrica et Neurologica Scandinavica*, 1958, *33*(2), 129–137.

Benton, A. L. *Right-left discrimination and finger localization*. New York: Hoeber-Harper, 1959.

Benton, A. L. The fiction of the Gerstmann syndrome. *Journal of Neurology, Neurosurgery, and Psychiatry*, 1961, *24*, 176–181.

Benton, A. L. The visual retention test as a constructional praxis task. *Confinia Neurologica*, 1962a, *22*, 141–155.

Benton, A. L. Behavioral indices of brain injury in school children. *Child Development*, 1962b, *33*, 199–208.

Benton, A. L. Developmental aphasia and brain damage. *In* Kirk, S. A., & Becker, W. (Eds.), *Conference on children with minimal brain impairment*. Urbana, IL: University of Illinois, 1963a, 71–91.

Benton, A. L. *The revised visual retention test*. 3rd Ed. New York: The Psychological Corporation, 1963b.

Benton, A. L. Developmental aphasia and brain damage. *Cortex*, 1964, *1*, 40–52.

Benton, A. L. The problem of cerebral dominance. *The Canadian Psychologist*, 1965, *6a*(4), 332–346.

Benton, A. L. Problems of test construction in the field of aphasia. *Cortex*, 1967, *3*, 42–46.

Benton, A. L. Differential behavioral effects in frontal lobe disease. *Neuropsychologia*, 1968, *6*, 53–60.

Benton, A. L. Disorders of spatial orientation. *In* Vinken, P. J., & Bruyn, G. W. (Eds.), *Handbook of clinical neurology*, Vol. 3. Amsterdam: North-Holland Publishing Co., 1969a.

Benton, A. L. *The three dimensional praxis test: Manual of instructions*. Victoria: Neuropsychology Laboratory, University of Victoria, Victoria, B.C., Canada, 1969b.

Benton, A. L. *Stereognosis test*. Victoria: Department of Psychology, University of Victoria, Victoria, B.C., Canada, 1969c.

Benton, A. L. *Der Benton-Test, Handbuch* (Multiple Choice Form). Bern: Hans Huber, 1972.

Benton, A. L. Developmental dyslexia: Neurological aspects. *In* Friedlander, W. J. (ed.), *Advances in Neurology*. New York: Raven Press, 1975, 1–47.

Benton, A. L. Reflections on the Gerstmann Syndrome. *Brain and Language*, 1977, *4*, 45–62.

Benton, A. L., & Blackburn, H. L. Practice effects in reaction time tasks in brain-injured patients. *Journal of Abnormal and Social Psychology*, 1957, *54*(1), 109–113.

Benton, A. L., Hamsher, K. deS., Varney, N. R., & Spreen, O. *Contributions to neuropsychological assessment, a clinical manual*. New York: Oxford University Press, 1983.

Benton, A. L., Levin, H. S., & Varney, N. R. Tactile perception of direction in normal subjects. *Neurology*, 1973, *23*, 1248–1250.

Bereiter, C. Development in writing. *In* Gregg, L. W., & Steinberg, E. R. (Eds.), *Cognitive processes in writing*. Hillsdale, NJ: L. Erlbaum, 1980, 73–93.

Berlin, C. I., Lowe-Bell, S. S., Cullen, J. K., Thompson, C. L., & Stafford, M. R. Is speech "special"? Perhaps the temporal lobectomy patient can tell us. *Journal of the Acoustical Society of America*, 1972, *52*(2), 702–705.

Berlin, C. I., Lowe-Bell, S. S., Janetta, P. J., & Kline, D. G. Central auditory deficits after temporal lobectomy. *Archives of Otolaryngology*, 1972, *96*, 4–10.

Berlucchi, G., & Buchtel, H. A. Some trends in the neurological study of learning. *In* Gazzaniga, M. S., & Blakemore, C. (Eds.), *Handbook of psychobiology*. New York: Academic Press, 1975, 481–498.

The Bible. King James version, 1605.

Binet, A., & Simon, T. Language et Pensée. *Année Psychologie*, 1908, *14*, 284–339. [Quoted in Myklebust, H. R. Childhood aphasia: an evolving concept. *In* Travis, L. E. (Ed.), *Handbook of speech pathology and audiology*. New York: Appleton-Century-Crofts, 1971, 1181–1202.]

Birch, H. G. (Ed.). *Brain damage in children, the biological and social aspects*. Baltimore: Williams & Wilkins, 1964.

Birch, H. G. Nutritional factors in mental retardation. Paper presented at Fifth Annual Neuropsychology Workshop, University of Victoria, Victoria, B.C., Canada, 1970.

Black, F. W. Neurological dysfunction and reading disorders. *Journal of Learning Disabilities*, 1973, *6*, 313–316.

Blackburn, H. L. Effects of motivating instructions on reaction time in cerebral disease. *Journal of Abnormal and Social Psychology*, 1958, *56*(3), 359–366.

Blackburn, H. L., & Benton, A. L. Simple and choice reaction time in cerebral disease. *Confinia Neurologica*, 1955, *15*(6), 327–338.

Blakemore, C., & Cooper, G. F. Development of the brain depends on the visual environment. *Nature*, 1970, *228*, 477–478.

Blakemore, C., & Mitchell, D. E. Environmental modification of the visual cortex and the neural basis of learning and memory. *Nature,* 1973, *241,* 467–468.

Blau, T. H. Unusual measures for the spelling invalid. *In* Arena, J. I. (Ed.), *Building spelling skills in dyslexic children.* San Rafael: Academic Therapy Publications, 1968, 1–3.

Boder, E. Developmental dyslexia: prevailing diagnostic concepts and a new diagnostic approach. *In* Myklebust, H. R. (Ed.), *Progress in learning disabilities,* Vol. II. New York: Grune & Stratton, 1971, 293–321.

Bogen, J. E. Some educational aspects of hemispheric specialization. *U.C.L.A. Educator,* 1975, *17,* 24–32.

Boll, T. J. Behavioral correlates of cerebral damage in children aged 9 through 14. *In* Reitan, R. M., & Davison, L. A. (Eds.), *Clinical neuropsychology: Current status and applications.* Washington, DC: Winston & Sons, 1974, 91–120.

Boring, E. G. *A history of experimental psychology.* 2nd Ed., New York: Appleton-Century-Crofts, 1957.

Bradshaw, J. L. Peripherally presented and unreported words may bias the perceived meaning of a centrally-fixated homograph. *Journal of Experimental Psychology,* 1974, *103,* 1200–1202.

Bradshaw, J. L., & Nettleton, N. C. *Human cerebral asymmetry.* Englewood Cliffs, NJ: Prentice-Hall, 1983.

Brady, J. V. Ulcers in "executive" monkeys. *Scientific American,* October 1958, 3–6.

Brain, Sir Russell. *Clinical neurology.* London: Oxford University Press, 1960.

Brain, W. R. *Speech disorders: Aphasia, apraxia and Agnosia.* London: Butterworths, 1961.

Brenner, M. W., Gillman, S., Zangwill, O. L., & Farrell, M. Visuo-motor disability in school children. *British Medical Journal,* 1967, *4,* 259–262.

Briggs, G. G., Nebes, R. D., & Kinsbourne, M. Intellectual differences in relation to personal and family handedness. *Quarterly Journal of Experimental Psychology,* 1976, *28,* 591–601.

Broadbent, D. E. The role of auditory localization in attention and memory span. *Journal of Experimental Psychology,* 1954, *47,* 191–196.

Brodmann, K. Verleichende Lokalisationslehre der Grosshirnrinde in ihren Prinzipien dergestellt auf Grund des Zellenbanes. Leipzig: Barth, 1909.

Brown, B., Haegerstrom-Portnoy, G., Adams, A. J., Yingling, C. D., Galin, D., Herron, J., & Marcus, M. Predictive eye movements do not discriminate between dyslexic and control children. *Neuropsychologia,* 1983, *21*(2), 121–123.

Brown, E. R. Neuropsychological interference mechanisms in aphasia and dyslexia. *In* Rieber, R. W. (Ed.), *The neuropsychology of language.* New York: Plenum Press, 1976, 25–43.

Bryden, M. P. "Tachistoscopic perception and serial order." Unpublished Ph.D. thesis, McGill University, 1960a.

Bryden, M. P. Tachistoscopic recognition of non-alphabetical material. *Canadian Journal of Psychology,* 1960b, *14,* 78–86.

Bryden, M. P. Order of report in dichotic listening. *Canadian Journal of Psychology,* 1962, *16,* 291–299.

Bryden, M. P. Left-right differences in tachistoscopic recognition. *Journal of Experimental Psychology,* 1963, *66*(6), 568–571.

Bryden, M. P. The manipulation of strategies of report in dichotic listening. *Canadian Journal of Psychology,* 1964, *18,* 126–138.

Bryden, M. P. Accuracy and order of report in tachistoscopic recognition. *Canadian Journal of Psychology,* 1966, *20,* 262–272.

Bryden, M. P. A model for the sequential organization of behavior. *Canadian Journal of Psychology, Revue Canadienne de Psychologie,* 1967, *21*(1), 37–56.

Bryden, M. P. Laterality effects in dichotic listening; relations with handedness and reading ability in children. *Neuropsychologia,* 1970, *8,* 443–450.

Bryden, M. P. *Laterality, functional asymmetry in the intact brain.* New York: Academic Press, 1982.

Bryden, M. P. Perceptual asymmetry in vision: Relation to handedness, eyedness, and speech lateralization. *Cortex,* 1973 *9,* 418–435.

Bryden, M. P. Measuring handedness with questionnaires. *Neuropsychologia,* 1977, *15,* 617–624.

Bryden, M. P., & Allard, F. A. Do auditory perceptual asymmetries develop? *Cortex,* 1981, *17,* 313–318.

Bryden, M. P., Hécaen, H., & DeAgostini, M. Patterns of cerebral organization. *Brain and Language,* 1983, *20,* 249–262.

Buffery, A. W. H. Sex differences in the neuropsychological development of verbal and spatial skills. *In* Knights, R. M., & Bakker, D. J. (Eds.), *The neuropsychology of learning disorders, theoretical approaches.* Baltimore: University Park Press, 1976, 187–205.

Buffery, A. W. H., & Gray, J. A. Sex differences in the development of spatial and linguistic skills. *In* Ounsted, C., & Taylor, D. C. (Eds.), *Gender differences: Their ontogeny and significance.* Edinburgh: Churchill Livingstone, 1972, 123–157.

Butters, N., Barton, M., & Brody, B. A. Role of the right parietal lobe in the mediation of crossmodal associations and reversible operations in space. *Cortex,* 1970, *6,* 174–190.

Butters, N., & Brody, B. A. The role of the left parietal lobe in the mediation of the intra- and cross-modal associations. *Cortex,* 1968, *4,* 328–343.

Calanchini, P. R., & Trout, S. S. The neurology of learning disabilities. *In* Tarnopol, L. (Ed.), *Learning disorders in children, diagnosis, medication, education.* Boston: Little, Brown, 1971, 207–251.

Calvin, W. H. *The throwing madonna, essays on the brain.* New York: McGraw-Hill, 1983.

Calvin, W. H., & Ojemann, G. A. *Inside the brain*. New York: Mentor Books, 1980.

Canadian Association for Children and Adults with Learning Disabilities, Kildare House, 323 Chapel Street, Ottawa, Ontario, Canada K1N 7Z2.

Cawley, J. F. Commentary on whole issue devoted to mathematics. *Topics in Learning and Learning Disabilities*, 1981, *1*(3), 89–93.

Carmon, A., & Benton, A. L. Tactile perception of direction and number in patients with unilateral cerebral disease. *Neurology* (Minneapolis), 1969, *19*, 525–532.

CELDIC Report. "One Million Children." A national study of Canadian children with emotional and learning disorders. Toronto: Leonard Crainford, 1970.

Chalfant, J. C., & Scheffelin, M. A. *Central processing dysfunctions in children: A review of research*. NINDS Monograph No. 9. Bethesda, MD: U.S. Department of Health, Education, and Welfare, 1969.

Chall, J. S., & Mirsky, A. F. *Education and the brain* (The Seventy-seventh Yearbook of the National Society for the Study of Education, Part II). Chicago: The University of Chicago Press, 1978.

Chapman, R. M., & Bragdon, H. R. Evoked responses to numerical and nonnumerical visual stimuli while problem solving. *Nature,* September 12, 1964, 1155–1157.

Chomsky, C. "Consciousness *is* relevant to linguistic awareness." Invited paper presented at the International Reading Research Seminar on Linguistic Awareness and Learning to Read, University of Victoria, Victoria, B.C., Canada, June 26–30, 1979.

Chomsky, N. Phonology and reading. *In* Levin, H., & Williams, J. P. (Eds.), *Basic studies on reading*. New York: Basic Books, 1970, 3–18.

Clark, C. "The reliability of ear advantage and attentional capacity in dichotic listening." Unpublished Ph.D. dissertation, University of Victoria, B.C., Canada, 1981.

Clarke, E., & Dewhurst, K. *An illustrated history of brain function*. Oxford: Sandford, 1972.

Clark, R. W. *Einstein: The life and times*. New York: The World Publishing Co., 1971.

Clements, S. D. *Minimal brain dysfunction in children*. NINDB Monograph No. 3. Washington, DC: U.S. Depart. of Health, Education, and Welfare, 1966.

Cohn, R. Developmental dyscalculia. *Pediatric Clinics of North America,* 1968, *15*(3), 651–668.

Cohn, R. Arithmetic and learning disabilities. *In* Myklebust, H. R. (Ed.), *Progress in learning disabilities,* Vol. II. New York: Grune & Stratton, 1971, 322–389.

Colbourn, C. J. Can laterality be measured? *Neuropsychologia,* 1978, *16*, 283–289.

Coleman, J. C. *Abnormal psychology and modern life,* 2nd Ed. Chicago: Scott, Foresman, 1956.

Coles, G. S. The learning-disabilities test battery: empirical and social issues. *Harvard Educational Review*, 1978, *48*(3), 313–340.

Collins, A., & Gentner, D. A framework for a cognitive theory of writing. *In* Gregg, L. W., & Steinberg, E. R. (Eds.), *Cognitive processes in writing*. Hillsdale, NJ: L. Erlbaum, 1980, 51–72.

Coltheart, M., Patterson, K., & Marshall, J. C. (Eds.). *Deep dyslexia*. London: Routledge & Kegan Paul, 1980.

Conel, J. L. *Postnatal development of the human cerebral cortex*. Vols. I–VI. Cambridge: Harvard University Press, 1939–1963. [Quoted in Pribram, K. H. *Languages of the brain*. Englewood Cliffs, NJ: Prentice-Hall, 1971, p. 27.]

Conners, C. K. The syndrome of minimal brain dysfunction: Psychological aspects. *Pediatric Clinics of North America*, 1967, *14*, 749–766.

Conners, C. K. A teacher rating scale for use in drug studies with children. *American Journal of Psychiatry*, 1969, *126*, 884–888.

Conners, C. K. Learning disabilities and stimulant drugs in children: theoretical implications. *In* Knights, R. M., & Bakker, D. J. (Eds.), *The neuropsychology of learning disorders*. Baltimore: University Park Press, 1976, 389–401.

Conners, C. K., Eisenberg, L., & Sharpe, L. Effects of methylphenidate (ritalin) on paired-associate learning and porteus maze performance in emotionally disturbed children. *Journal of Consulting Psychology*, 1964, *28*, 14–22.

Corballis, M. C., & Morgan, M. J. On the biological basis of human laterality: I. Evidence for a maturational left-right gradient. *The Behavioral and Brain Sciences*, 1978, *2*, 261–336.

Coren, S., & Porac, C. Fifty centuries of right-handedness: The historical record. *Science*, November 1977, *198*, 631–632.

Coulter, D. L. *Hypoconnection syndromes in learning-disabled children*. Paper presented at Child Neurology Society Meeting, Minneapolis, 1981.

Cratty, B. J. *Developmental sequences of perceptual-motor tasks*. Baldwin, NY: Educational Activities, 1967.

Cratty, B. J. Movement and the intellect. *In* Hellmuth, J. (Ed.), *Learning disorders*, Vol. 3. Seattle: Special Child Publications, 1968, 524–536.

Cratty, B. J., & Martin, M. M. *Perceptual-motor efficiency in children*. Philadelphia: Lea & Febiger, 1969.

Cravioto, J., De Licardie, E. R., & Birch, H. G. Nutrition, growth and neurointegrative development: An experimental and ecologic study. *Pediatrics*, 1966, *38*(Suppl. 2), 319–372.

Critchley, M. *The dyslexic child*. London: William Heinemann, 1970.

Critchley, M., & Critchley, E. A. *Dyslexia defined*. London: William Heinemann Medical Books Ltd., 1978.

Cruickshank, W. M. *A teaching method for brain-injured and hyperactive children*. Syracuse: Syracuse University Press, 1961.

Cruickshank, W. M. (Ed.). *The teacher of brain-injured children*. Syracuse: Syracuse University Press, 1966.

Cruickshank, W. M. The psychoeducational match. *In* Cruickshank, W. M., & Hallahan, D. P. (Eds.), *Perceptual and learning disabilities in children,* Vol. 1. Syracuse: Syracuse University Press, 1975, 71–112.

Cruickshank, W. M. *Learning disabilities in home, school, and community.* Syracuse: Syracuse University Press, 1977.

Cruickshank, W. M. Learning disabilities: a definitional statement. *In* Polak, E. (Ed.), *Issues and initiatives in learning disabilities: Selected papers from the First National Conference on Learning Disabilities.* Ottawa: Canadian Association for Children with Learning Disabilities, 1979.

Cruickshank, W. M. Straight is the bamboo tree. *Journal of Learning Disabilities,* 1983, *16*(4), 191–197.

Cruickshank, W. M., Bice, H. V., Wallen, N. E., & Lynch, K. S. *Perception and cerebral palsy: Studies in figure-background relationship.* Syracuse: Syracuse University Press, 1957.

Cummings, J. L., Benson, D. F., Walsh, M. J., & Levine, H. L. Left-to-right transfer of language dominance: A case study. *Neurology,* 1979, *29,* 1547–1550.

Dabbs, J. M., & Choo, G. Left-right carotid blood flow predicts specialized mental ability. *Neuropsychologia,* 1980, *18,* 711–713.

Das, J. P., Kirby, J. R., & Jarman, R. F. *Simultaneous and successive cognitive processes.* New York: Academic Press, 1979.

Davis, H. Enhancement of evoked cortical potentials in humans related to a task requiring a decision. *Science,* 1964, *145,* 182–183.

Davis, J., & Reitan, R. M. A methodological note on the relationship between ability to copy a simple configuration and Wechsler verbal and performance I.Q.'s. *Perceptual and Motor Skills,* 1966, *22,* 381–382.

Davis, A. E., & Wada, J. A. Hemispheric asymmetries of visual and auditory information processing. *Neuropsychologia,* 1977, *15,* 799–806.

De Ajuriaguerra, J., & Tissot, R. The apraxias. *In* Vinken, P. J., & Bruyn, G. W. (Eds.), *Handbook of clinical neurology,* Vol. 4. Amsterdam: North-Holland Publishing Co., 1969, 48–66.

de Hirsch, K. Prediction in reading disability: A review of the literature. *In* Hayes, A., & Silver, A. (Eds.), *Report of the interdisciplinary committee on reading disability.* Washington, DC: Center for Applied Linguistics, 1971.

de Hirsch, K., Jansky, J. J., & Langford, W. S. *Predicting reading failure.* New York: Harper & Row, 1966.

Déjerine, J. 1892. His famous case is described and discussed by Norman Geschwind, in "The anatomy of acquired disorders of reading." *In* Money, J. (Ed.), *reading disability.* Baltimore: The Johns Hopkins Press, 1962, 115–129.

Delacato, C. *The diagnosis and treatment of speech and reading problems,* 6th Ed. Springfield, IL: Charles C Thomas, 1963.

De La Cruz, F. F., Fox, B. H., & Roberts, R. H. (Eds.) "Minimal Brain Dysfunction." *Annals of the New York Academy of Sciences,* 1973, *205* (whole volume).

Delgado, J. M. R. *Physical control of the mind*. New York: Harper-Colophon Books, 1971.

Delgado, J. M. R., Roberts, W. W., & Miller, N. E. Learning motivated by electrical stimulation of the brain. *American Journal of Physiology,* 1954, *179,* 587–593.

Denckla, M. B. Minimal brain dysfunction and dyslexia: Beyond diagnosis by exclusion. *In* Blaw, M. E., Rapin, I., & Kinsbourne, M. (Eds.), *Child neurology.* New York: Spectrum Publications, 1977.

Denckla, M. B. Minimal brain dysfunction. *In* Chall, J. S., & Mirsky, A. F. (Eds.), *Education and the brain* (The Seventy-Seventh Yearbook of the National Society for the Study of Education). Chicago: The University of Chicago Press, 1978, 223–268.

Denckla, M. B. Childhood learning disabilities. *In* Heilman, K. M., & Valenstein, E. (Eds.), *Clinical neuropsychology.* New York: Oxford University Press, 1979, 535–573.

Denckla, M. B. Learning for language and language for learning. *In* Kirk, U. (Ed.) *Neuropsychology of language, reading, and spelling.* New York: Academic Press, 1983, 33–43.

de Quiros, J. B., & Schrager, O. L. *Neuropsychological fundamentals in learning disabilities.* San Rafael: Academic Therapy Publications, 1978.

DeRenzi, E., Pieczuro, A., & Vignolo, L. A. Ideational apraxia: A quantitative study. *Neuropsychologia,* 1968, *6,* 41–52.

DeRenzi, E., & Vignolo, L. A. The Token Test: a sensitive test to detect receptive disturbances in aphasics. *Brain,* 1962, *85,* 665–678.

Dimond, S. J., & Beaumont, J. G. (Eds.). *Hemisphere functions of the human brain.* London: Elek Science, 1974.

Doake, D. B. "Reading: a language learning activity." Invited paper presented at the International Reading Research Seminar on Linguistic Awareness and Learning to Read, University of Victoria, Victoria, B.C., Canada, June 26–30, 1979.

Dodwell, P. Some factors affecting the hearing of words presented dichotically. *Canadian Journal of Psychology,* 1964, *18,* 72–79.

Doehring, D. G. *Patterns of impairment in specific reading disability.* Bloomington: Indiana University Press, 1968.

Doehring, D. G., Backman, J., & Waters, G. Theoretical models of reading disabilities, past, present, and future. *Topics in Learning & Learning Disabilities,* 1983, *3*(1), 84–95.

Dolch, E. W. *A manual for remedial reading.* New Canaan: Garrard Publishing Co., 1945.

Douglas, V. I. Stop, look and listen: The problem of sustained attention and impulse control in hyperactive and normal children. *Canadian Journal of Behavioral Science,* 1972, *4,* 259–282.

Douglas, V. I. Perceptual and cognitive factors as determinants of learning disabilities: A review chapter with special emphasis on attentional factors. *In*

Knights, R. M., & Bakker, D. J. (Eds.), *The neuropsychology of learning disorders*. Baltimore: University Park Press, 1976, 413–421.

Douglas, V. I. "Hyperactivity, theory and treatment." Paper presented at Thirteenth Annual Neuropsychology Workshop, University of Victoria, Victoria, B.C., Canada, 1978.

Dowling, J. E. Elements of retinal function. *In* Schmitt, F. O., & Worden, F. G. (Eds.), *The neurosciences, fourth study program*. Cambridge: The M.I.T. Press, 1979, 161–181.

Downing, J. A. *The initial teaching alphabet reading experiment*. Chicago: Scott, Foresman, 1964.

Drake, W. E. Clinical and pathological findings in a child with a developmental learning disability. *Journal of Learning Disabilities*, 1968, *1*(9), 486–502.

Drew, A. L. A neurological appraisal of familial congenital word blindness. *Brain*, 1956, *79*, 440.

Drewe, E. A. An experimental investigation of Luria's theory on the effects of frontal lobe lesions in man. *Neuropsychologia*, 1975, *13*, 421–429.

Duffy, F. H. Topographic display of evoked potentials: clinical applications of brain electrical activity mapping (BEAM). *Annals of the New York Academy of Sciences*, 1982, *388*, 183–196.

Duffy, F. H., Burchfiel, J. L., & Lombroso, C. T. Brain electrical activity mapping (BEAM): a method for extending the clinical utility of EEG and evoked potential data. *Annals of Neurology*, April 1979, *5*(4), 309–321.

Durbrow, H. C. Children who cannot write. *Bulletin of the Orton Society*, 1963, XIII, 115–118.

Dunn, L. M. *Expanded manual for the Peabody Picture Vocabulary Test*. Circle Pines, MN: American Guidance Service, 1965.

Dykman, R. A., & Gantt, H. A case of experimental neurosis and recovery in relation to the orienting response. *Journal of Psychology*, 1960, *50*, 105–110.

Eaves, L. C., Kendall, D. C., & Crichton, J. U. The early detection of minimal brain dysfunction. *Journal of Learning Disabilities*, 1972, *5*(8), 454–462.

Eccles, J. C. *The Understanding of the Brain*. New York: McGraw-Hill, 1973.

Efron, R. Temporal perception, aphasia and déjà vu. *Brain*, 1963, *86*, 403–424.

Eisenberg, L. Reading retardation. I Psychiatric and sociologic aspects. *Pediatrics*, 1966, *37*(2), 352–365.

Emmerich, D., Goldenbaum, D., Hayden, D., Hoffman, L., & Treffets, J. Meaningfulness as a variable in dichotic hearing. *Journal of Experimental Psychology*, 1965, *69*, 433–436.

Engelmann, S. Relationship between psychological theories and the act of teaching. *Journal of School Psychology*, 1967, *5*, 93–100.

Engelmann, S., & Bruner, E. C. *Distar reading II, Teacher's guide*. Chicago: Science Research Associates, 1975.

Epstein, W. Temporal schemata in syntactically structured material. *Journal of Genetic Psychology*, 1963, *68*, 157–164.

Fantz, R. L. The origin of form perception. *Scientific American,* 1961, *204,* 66–72.

Fedio, P., & Mirsky, A. F. Selective intellectual deficits in children with temporal lobe or centrencephalic epilepsy. *Neuropsychologia,* 1969, *7,* 287–300.

Fedio, P., & Van Buren, J. M. Memory deficits during electrical stimulation of the speech cortex in conscious man. *Brain and Language,* 1974, *1,* 29–42.

Ferguson, J. H., & Boller, F. A different form of agraphia: Syntactic writing errors in patients with motor speech and movement disorders. *Brain and Language,* 1977, *4,* 382–389.

Fernald, G. M. *Remedial techniques in basic school subjects.* New York: McGraw-Hill, 1943.

Finucci, J. M., Isaacs, S. D., Whitehouse, C. C., & Childs, B. Classification of spelling errors and their relationship to reading ability, sex, grade placement, and intelligence. *Brain and Language,* 1983, *20,* 340–355.

Flechsig, P. Meine myelogenetische Hirnlehre mit biographischer Einleitung, 1927. Described in Nash, *Journal of Developmental Psychology.* Englewood Cliffs, NJ: Prentice-Hall, 1970, p. 98.

Folsom, A. T. The epilepsies. *In* Haywood, H. C. (Ed.). *Brain damage in school age children.* Washington, DC: The Council for Exceptional Children, 1968, 62–86.

Fontenot, D. J., & Benton, A. L. Tactile perception of direction in relation to hemispheric locus of lesion. *Neuropsychologia,* 1971, *9,* 83–88.

Frauenheim, J. G., & Heckerl, J. R. A longitudinal study of psychological and achievement test performance in severe dyslexic adults. *Journal of Learning Disabilities,* 1983, *16*(5), 339–347.

Frederiks, J. A. M. The agnosias. *In* Vinken, P. J., & Bruyn, G. W. (Eds.), *Handbook of clinical neurology,* Vol. 4. Amsterdam: North-Holland Publishing Co., 1969a, 13–47.

Frederiks, J. A. M. Disorders of the body schema. *In* Vinken, P. J., & Bruyn, G. W. (Eds.), *Handbook of clinical neurology,* Vol. 4. Amsterdam: North-Holland Publishing Co., 1969b, 207–240.

Freidus, E. Methodology for the classroom teacher. *In* Hellmuth, J. (Ed.), *The special child in Century 21.* Seattle: Special Child Publications, 1964, 303–321.

Freidus, E. The needs of teachers for specialized information on number concepts. *In* Cruickshank, W. M. (Ed.), *The teacher of brain-injured children.* Syracuse: Syracuse University Press, 1966, 111–128.

Friederici, A. D., Schoenle, P. W., & Goodglass, H. Mechanisms underlying writing and speech in aphasia. *Brain and Language,* 1981, *13,* 212–222.

Frostig, M. The role of perception in the integration of psychological functions. *In* Cruickshank, W. M., & Hallahan, D. P. (Eds.), *Perceptual and learning disabilities in children,* Vol. 1. Syracuse: Syracuse University Press, 1975, 115–146.

Frostig, M., & Maslow, P. *Movement education: Theory and practice.* Chicago: Follett, 1970.

Fry, D. B. The development of the phonological system in the normal and the deaf child. *In* Smith, F., & Miller, G. A. (Eds.), *The genesis of language*. Cambridge: The M.I.T. Press, 1966, 187–206.

Gaddes, W. H. The mental effects of pellagra. Unpublished Master's Thesis, University of British Columbia, 1946.

Gaddes, W. H. The performance of normal and brain-damaged subjects on a new dynamic visual retention test. *The Canadian Psychologist*, 1966a, *7a*, Inst. Suppl., 313–323.

Gaddes, W. H. The needs of teachers for specialized information on handedness, finger localization, and cerebral dominance. *In* Cruickshank, W. M. (Ed.), *The teacher of brain-injured children*. Syracuse: Syracuse University Press, 1966b, 207–221.

Gaddes, W. H. Neuropsychological approach to learning disorders. *Journal of Learning Disabilities*, 1968, *1*(9), 523–534.

Gaddes, W. H. Can educational psychology be neurologized? *Canadian Journal of Behavioral Science*, 1969a, *1*(1), 38–49.

Gaddes, W. H. *Dynamic visual retention test, manual of instructions and norms*. Victoria: Neuropsychology Laboratory, University of Victoria, Victoria, B.C., Canada, 1969b.

Gaddes, W. H. Learning disorders in the neurologically handicapped. *British Columbia Medical Journal*, 1972, Vol. *14*(1), 13–16.

Gaddes, W. H. Neurological implications for learning. *In* Cruickshank, W. H. & Hallahan, D. P. (Eds.), *Perceptual and learning disabilities in children*, Vol. 1. Syracuse: Syracuse University Press, 1975, 148–194.

Gaddes, W. H. Prevalence estimates and the need for definition of learning disabilities. *In* Knights, R. M., & Bakker, D. J. (Eds.), *The neuropsychology of learning disorders*. Baltimore: University Park Press, 1976, 3–24.

Gaddes, W. H. Learning disabilities: The search for causes. *In Bell Canada Monograph on Learning Disabilities*, Canadian Association for Children with Learning Disabilities, 4820 Van Horne Avenue, Montreal, Quebec, Canada, 1978.

Gaddes, W. H. An examination of the validity of neuropsychological knowledge in educational diagnosis and remediation. *In* Hynd, G. W., & Obrzut, J. E. (Eds.), *Neuropsychological assessment and the school-age child; issues and procedures*. New York: Grune & Stratton, 1981a, 27–85.

Gaddes, W. H. Neuropsychology, fact or mythology, educational help or hindrance? *School Psychology Review*, 1981b, X (3), 322–330.

Gaddes, W. H. Serial order behavior: to understand it, a scientific challenge, an educational necessity. *In* Cruickshank, W. M., & Lerner, J. W. (Eds.), *Coming of Age, Vol. 3, The best of ACLD*. Syracuse: Syracuse University Press, 1982, 87–107.

Gaddes, W. H. Applied educational neuropsychology: Theories and problems. *Journal of Learning Disabilities*, 1983, *16*(9), 511–514.

Gaddes, W. H., & Crockett, D. J. *The Spreen-Benton Aphasia tests, normative data as a measure of normal language development*, Research Monograph

No. 25. Department of Psychology, University of Victoria, Victoria, B.C., Canada, 1973.

Gaddes, W. H., & Crockett, D. J. The Spreen-Benton Aphasia tests, normative data as a measure of normal language development. *Brain and Language,* 1975, *2,* 257–280. [This is a shorter version of the departmental monograph of the same name, 1973. The Monograph contains a complete set of all the graphs and tables. The text is essentially similar.]

Gaddes, W. H., & Spellacy, F. J. *Serial order perceptual and motor performances in children and their relation to academic achievement.* Research Monograph No. 35. Victoria, B.C., Canada: Department of Psychology, University of Victoria, 1977.

Gaddes, W. H., & Tymchuk, A. J. *A validation study of the dynamic visual retention test in functional localization of cerebral damage and dysfunction.* Research Monograph No. 38, Victoria, B.C., Canada: Department of Psychology, University of Victoria, 1967.

Galaburda, A. Developmental dyslexia: current anatomical research. *Annals of Dyslexia,* 1983, XXXIII, 41–53.

Galaburda, A. M., & Eidelberg, D. Symmetry and asymmetry in the human posterior thalamus. II. Thalamic lesions in a case of developmental dyslexia. *Archives of Neurology,* 1982, *39,* 333–336.

Galaburda, A. M., & Kemper, T. L. Cytoarchitectonic abnormalities in developmental dyslexia: A case study. *Annals of Neurology,* 1979, *6*(2), 94–100.

Gallagher, J. J. A comparison of brain-injured and non-brain-injured mentally retarded children on several psychological variables. *Monographs of the Society for Research in Child Development,* 1957, *22*(2, Serial 65).

Gallagher, J. J. Children with developmental imbalances: A psychoeducational definition. *In* Cruickshank, W. M. (Ed.), *The teacher of brain-injured children.* Syracuse: Syracuse University Press, 1966, 23–33.

Galton, F. *Inquiries into human faculty and its development.* London: J. M. Dent & Sons, 1907.

Gardner, E. *Fundamentals of neurology.* Philadelphia: W. B. Saunders, 1968 (5th Ed.)/1975 (6th Ed.).

Gazzaniga, M. S., Bogen, J. E., & Sperry, R. W. Observations on visual perception after disconnection of the cerebral hemispheres in man. *Brain,* 1965, *88,* 221–236.

Gazzaniga, M. S., & Hillyard, S. A. Language and speech capacity of the right hemisphere. *Neuropsychologia,* 1971, *9,* 273–280.

Geffen, G., Traub, E., & Stierman, I. Language laterality assessed by unilateral ECT and dichotic monitoring. *Journal of Neurology, Neurosurgery & Psychiatry,* 1978, *41,* 354–359.

Geldard, F. A. *The human senses,* 2nd Ed. New York: John Wiley, 1972.

Gellner, L. *A neurophysiological concept of mental retardation and its educational implications.* Chicago: The Dr. Julian D. Levinson Research Foundation, 519 South Wolcott Street, 1959.

Geschwind, N. The anatomy of acquired disorders of reading. *In* Money, J. (Ed.), *Reading disability*. Baltimore: The Johns Hopkins Press, 1962, 115–129.

Geschwind, N. Disconnexion syndromes in animals and man. *Brain, 1965, 88,* Part II, 237–294, and Part III, 585–644.

Geschwind, N. Language and the brain. *Scientific American, 1972, 226*(4), 76–83.

Geschwind, N. The apraxias: Neural mechanisms of disorders of learned movement. *American Scientist, 1975, 63,* 188–195.

Geschwind, N. Asymmetries of the brain—New developments. *Bulletin of the Orton Society, 1979a, 29,* 67–73.

Geschwind, N. Anatomical foundations of language and dominance. *In The neurological bases of language disorders in children: Methods and directions for research.* NINCDS Monograph #22, 1979b, 145–157.

Geschwind, N. Why Orton was right. *Annals of Dyslexia*. Baltimore: The Orton Dyslexia Society, 1982, XXXII, 13–30.

Geschwind, N. Biological associations of left-handedness. *Annals of Dyslexia,* 1983, XXXIII, 29–40.

Geschwind, N., & Levitzky, W. Human brain: Left-right asymmetries in temporal speech region. *Science, 1968, 161,* 186–187.

Geschwind, N., Quadfasel, F. A., & Segarra, J. M. Isolation of the speech area. *Neuropsychologia, 1968, 6,* 327–340.

Getman, G. N. The needs of teachers for specialized information on the development of visuomotor skills in relation to academic performance. *In* Cruickshank, W. M. (Ed.), *The teacher of brain-injured children.* Syracuse: Syracuse University Press, 1966, 153–168.

Gibson, E. E. Learning to read. *Science, 1965, 148,* 1066–1072.

Gillingham, A. *Remedial training for children with specific disability in reading, spelling, and penmanship,* 7th Ed. Cambridge, MA: Educators Publishing Service, 1965

Gillingham, A., & Stillman, B. *Remedial work for reading, spelling, and penmanship.* New York: Hackett & Wilhelms, 1936.

Glasser, W. *Schools without failure.* New York: Harper & Row, 1969.

Goldberg, E., & Costa, L. D. Hemisphere differences in the acquisition and use of descriptive systems. *Brain and Language, 1981, 14,* 144–173.

Golden, C. J. The Luria-Nebraska children's battery: Theory and formulation. *In* Hynd, G. W., Obrzut, J. E. (Eds.), *Neuropsychological assessment and the school-age child: Issues and procedures.* New York: Grune & Stratton, 1981, 277–302.

Goldscheider, A. Unrersuchungen uber den Muskelsinn. II. Ueber die Empfindung der Schwere und des Widerstandes. *In Gesammelte Abhandlungen von A. Goldscheider, Vol. II.* Leipzig: Barth, 1898. Cited by Geldard, F. A. *The Human Senses, 2nd Ed.* New York: John Wiley, 1972.

Goldstein, K. *The organism.* New York: American Book Co., 1939.

Goldstein, K. *Human nature in the light of psychopathology.* New York: Schocken Books, 1940.

Goldstein, K. *Aftereffects of brain-injuries in war.* New York: Grune & Stratton, 1942.

Goodglass, H. & Kaplan, E. *The assessment of aphasia and related disorders.* Philadelphia: Lea and Febiger, 1972.

Gordon, H. Left-handedness and mirror writing especially among defective children. *Brain,* 1920, *43,* 313–368.

Gottlieb, G. Ontogenesis of sensory function in birds and mammals. *In* Tobach, E., Aronson, L. R., & Shaw, E. (Eds.), *The biopsychology of development.* New York: Academic Press, 1971, 67–128.

Gottschalk, J. A. Temporal order in the organization of children's behavior. Unpublished M. A. Thesis, McGill University, 1962.

Gottschalk, J. A. Spatiotemporal organization in children. Unpublished Ph.D. Thesis, McGill University, 1965.

Gray, J., & Wedderburn, A. Grouping strategies with simultaneous stimuli. *Quarterly Journal of Experimental Psychology,* 1960, *12,* 180–184.

Gregg, L. W., and Steinberg, E. R. (Eds.). *Cognitive processes in writing.* Hillsdale, NJ: L. Erlbaum, 1980.

Gregory, R. L. *Eye and brain: The psychology of seeing.* New York: McGraw-Hill (World University Library), 1966.

Gresham, F. M. Social validity in the assessment of children's social skills: Establishing standards for social competency. *Journal of Psychoeducational Assessment,* 1983, *1,* 299–307.

Grossman, S. P. The biology of motivation. *In* Chall, J. S., & Mirsky, A. F. (Eds.), *Education and the brain* (The Seventy-seventh Yearbook of the National Society for the Study of Education, Part II). Chicago: The University of Chicago Press, 1978, 103–142.

Guetzkow, H. S., & Bowman, P. H. *Men and hunger.* Elgin, IL: Brethren Publishing House, 1946.

Gur, R. C., Gur, R. E., Rosen, A. D., Warach, S., Alavi, A., Greenberg, J., & Reivich, M. A cognitive-motor network demonstrated by positron emission tomography. *Neuropsychologia,* 1983, *21*(6), 601–606.

Guthrie, E. R. *The psychology of learning.* New York: Harper, 1935.

Guthrie, E. R. The status of systematic psychology. *The American Psychologist,* 1950, *5*(4), 97–101.

Hallahan, D. P., & Cruickshank, W. M. *Psychoeducational foundations of learning disabilities.* Englewood Cliffs, NJ: Prentice-Hall, 1973.

Hallgren, B. Specific dyslexia: A clinical and genetic study. *Acta Psychiatrica et Neurologica,* Suppl., 1950, *65,* 1.

Halstead, W. C. *Brain and intelligence.* Chicago: University of Chicago Press, 1947.

Harris, A. J. *Harris tests of lateral dominance: Manual of directions for administration and interpretation,* 3rd Ed. New York: Psychological Corporation, 1958.

Harris, L. J. Left-handedness: Early theories, facts, and fancies. *In* Herron, J. (Ed.), *Neuropsychology of left-handedness*. New York: Academic Press, 1980, 3–78.

Hartlage, L. C., & Hartlage, P. L. Application of neuropsychological principles in the diagnosis of learning disabilities. *In* Tarnopol, L., & Tarnopol, M. (Eds.), *Brain function and reading disabilities*. Baltimore: University Park Press, 1977, 111–146.

Hartlage, L. C., & Reynolds, C. R. Neuropsychological assessment and the individualization of instruction. *In* Hynd, G. W., Obrzut, J. E. (Eds.), *Neuropsychological assessment and the school-age child: Issues and procedures*. New York: Grune & Stratton, 1981, 355–378.

Harvey, J. E. The effects of permanent and temporary occlusion of the middle cerebral artery in the monkey. Unpublished Ph.D. Dissertation, Department of Surgery, The University of Chicago, 1950.

Harvey, J. E., & Rasmussen, T. Occlusion of the middle cerebral artery. *American Medical Association Archives of Neurology and Psychiatry*, 1951, *66*, 20–29.

Haslam, R. H. A. Teacher awareness of some common pediatric neurologic disorders. *In* Haslam, R. H. A., & Valletutti, P. J. (Eds.), *Medical problems in the classroom*. Baltimore: University Park Press, 1975, 51–74.

Haywood, H. C. (Ed.). *Brain damage in school age children*. Washington, DC: The Council for Exceptional Children, 1968.

Head, H., & Holmes, G. Sensory disturbances from cerebral lesions. *Brain*, 1911, *34*, 102–254. [Described by J. A. M. Frederiks *In* Vinken, P. J., & Bruyn, G. W. (Eds.), *Handbook of clinical neurology*, Vol. 4. Amsterdam: North-Holland Publishing Co., 1969, 208.]

Hebb, D. O. The effect of early and late brain injury upon test scores, and the nature of normal adult intelligence. *Proceedings of the American Philosophical Society*, 1942a, *85*, 275–292.

Hebb, D. O. Verbal test material independent of special vocabulary difficulty. *Journal of Educational Psychology*, 1942b, *33*, 691–696.

Hebb, D. O. *Organization of behavior*. New York: Wiley, 1949.

Hebb, D. O. *A textbook of psychology*. Philadelphia: Saunders, 1958 (1st Ed)/ 1966 (2nd Ed)/1972 (3rd Ed).

Hebb, D. O., & Morton, N. W. The McGill Adult Comprehension Examination: "Verbal situation" and "picture anomaly" series. *Journal of Educational Psychology*, 1943, *34*, 16–25.

Hebb, D. O., & Penfield, W. Human behavior after extensive bilateral removal from the frontal lobes. *Archives of Neurology and Psychiatry*, 1940, *44*, 421–438.

Hebb, D. O., & Thompson, W. R. The social significance of animal studies. *In* Lindzey, G. (Ed.), *Handbook of social psychology*. Cambridge, MA: Addison-Wesley, 1954, 532–561.

Hécaen, H. Acalculia. *In* Mountcastle, V. B. (Ed.), *Interhemispheric relations and cerebral dominance*. Baltimore: The Johns Hopkins University Press, 1962, 235–237.

Hécaen, H. Aphasic, apraxic and agnosic syndromes in right and left hemisphere lesions. *In* Vinken, P. J., & Bruyn, G. W. (Eds.), *Handbook of clinical neurology*, Vol. 4. Amsterdam: North-Holland Publishing Co., 1969, 291–311.

Hécaen, H., & de Ajuriaguerra, J. *Left-handedness, manual superiority and cerebral dominance*. New York: Grune & Stratton, 1964.

Hécaen, H., & Sauget, J. Cerebral dominance in left-handed subjects. *Cortex*, 1971, *7*, 19–48.

Heilman, K. M., & Valenstein, E. (Eds.), *Clinical neuropsychology*. New York: Oxford University Press, 1979.

Hermann, K. *Reading disability*. Springfield, IL: Charles C Thomas, 1959.

Hern, A. Neurological signs in learning disabled children: persistence over time, and incidence in adulthood compared to normal learners. Unpublished Ph.D. Dissertation, University of Victoria, 1984.

Hernández-Peón, R., Scherrer, H., & Jouvet, M. Modification of electric activity in cochlear nucleus during "attention" in unanesthetized cats. *Science*, 1956, *123*, 331–332.

Hernández-Peón, R., & Sterman, M. B. Brain functions. *Annual Review of Psychology*, 1966, *17*, 363–395.

Heron, W. Perception as a function of retinal locus and attention. *American Journal of Psychology*, 1957, *70*, 38–48.

Herrick, C. J. *Brains of rats and men*. Chicago: University of Chicago Press, 1926.

Herrick, C. J. Apparatus of optic and visceral correlation in the brain of amblystoma. *The Journal of Comparative Psychology*, 1944, *37*(2), 97–105.

Herron, J. Two hands, two brains, two sexes. *In* Herron, J. (Ed.), *Neuropsychology of left-handedness*. New York: Academic Press, 1980, 233–260.

Hertzig, M. Stability and change in nonfocal neurologic signs. *Journal of the American Academy of Child Psychiatry*, 1982, *21*, 231–236.

Hess, R. *EEG handbook, Sandoz monographs*. Zurich: Sandoz, 1966.

Hicks, R. E., & Kinsbourne, M. Human handedness: A partial cross-fostering study. *Science*, 1976a, *192*, 908–910.

Hicks, R. E., & Kinsbourne, M. On the genesis of human handedness: A review. *Journal of Motor Behavior*, 1976b, *8*, 257–266.

Hicks, R. E., & Kinsbourne, M. Human handedness. *In* M. Kinsbourne (Ed.), *Asymmetrical function of the brain*. New York: Cambridge University Press, 1977.

Higenbottam, J. A. An investigation of lateral and perceptual preference relationships. Unpublished Ph.D. Dissertation, University of Victoria, 1971.

Hilgard, E. R. *Theories of learning*. New York: Appleton-Century-Crofts, 1948.

Hirsch, H. V. B., & Jacobson, M. The perfectible brain: Principles of neuronal development. *In* Gazzaniga, M. S., & Blakemore, C. (Eds.), *Handbook of psychobiology*. New York: Academic Press, 1975, 107–137.

Hiscock, M. Language lateralization in children: Dichotic listening studies. Paper presented at the Symposium on Hemispheric Specialization in the Developing Brain, International Neuropsychological Society, New York, January 31–February 3, 1979.

Hobson, J. Sex-differences in primary mental abilities. *Journal of Educational Psychology*, 1947, *41*, 126–132.

Hordijk, W. Épilepsie en links-handigheid. *Nederlands Tijdschrift voor Geneeskunde*, 1952, 96(5), 263–269. Cited in Hécaen, H. & de Ajuriaguerra, J. *Left-handedness*. New York: Grune & Stratton, 1964.

Horton, A. M. Behavioral neuropsychology in the schools. *School Psychology Review*, 1981, *10*(3), 367–372.

Hounsfield, G. N. Computerized axial scanning (tomography): Part 1: Description of system. *British Journal of Radiology*, 1973, *46*, 1016–1022.

Hubel, D. H. The visual cortex of the brain. *Scientific American*, 1963, *209*(5), 54–62.

Hubel, D. H., & Wiesel, T. N. Receptive fields of single neurones in the cat's striate cortex. *Journal of Physiology*, 1959, *148*, 574–591.

Huheey, J. E. Concerning the origin of handedness in humans. *Behavior Genetics*, 1977, *7*(1), 29–32.

Hundleby, G. D. Effectiveness of the Benton Right-Left discrimination test in identifying children with reading disabilities. Unpublished Master's Thesis, Faculty of Education, University of Victoria, 1969.

Hunter, J., & Jasper, H. H. Effects of thalamic stimulation in unanesthetised animals. *Electroencephalography and Clinical Neurophysiology*, 1949, *1*, 305–324.

Hynd, G. W. Training the school psychologist in neuropsychology; perspectives, issues, and models. *In* Hynd, G. W., & Obrzut, J. E. (Eds.), *Neuropsychological assessment and the school-age child: Issues and procedures*. New York: Grune & Stratton, 1981, 379–404.

Hynd, G. W., Hayes, F., & Snow, J. Neuropsychological screening with school-age children: Rationale and conceptualization. *Psychology in the Schools*, 1982, *19*, 446–451.

Hynd, G. W., & Obrzut, J. E. Neuropsychological assessment and consultation in the public schools. Paper presented at the annual convention of the National Association of School Psychologists, Washington, DC, April, 1980.

Hynd, G. W., & Obrzut, J. E. (Eds.). *Neuropsychological assessment and the school-age child: Issues and procedures*. New York: Grune & Stratton, 1981.

Hynd, G. W., Quackenbush, R., & Obrzut, J. E. Training school psychologists in neuropsychological assessment: Current practices and trends. Paper presented at the Annual Convention of the National Association of School Psychologists, San Diego, CA, March 1979.

Ingvar, D. H., & Risberg, J. Increase of regional cerebral blood flow during mental effort in normals and in patients with focal brain disorders. *Experimental Brain Research*, 1967, *3*, 195–211.

Ingvar, D. H., & Schwartz, M. S. Blood flow patterns induced in the dominant hemisphere by speech and reading. *Brain,* 1974, *97*(II), 273–288.

Inhelder, B. *The diagnosis of reasoning in the mentally retarded,* 2nd Ed. New York: Chandler Publishing, 1968.

Jackson, J. H. *Selected writings of John Hughlings Jackson,* Vol. II. London: Staples Press, 1958.

Jacobsen, C. F. Functions of frontal association area in primates. *American Medical Association Archives of Neurology and Psychiatry,* 1935, *33,* 558–569.

Jacobson, M. Development, specification and diversification of neuronal circuits. *In* Schmidt, F. O. (Ed.), *The neurosciences: Second study program.* New York: Rockefeller University Press, 1970, 116–129.

James, W. *The principles of psychology.* New York: Henry Holt & Co., 1890.

Jansky, J., & de Hirsch, K. *Preventing reading failure.* New York: Harper & Row, 1972.

Jastak, J. F., & Jastak, S. R. *The Wide Range Achievement Test.* Wilmington, DE: Guidance Associates, 1965.

John, E. R. Switchboard versus statistical theories of learning and memory. *Science,* 1972, *177,* 850–864.

Johnson, D. J., & Myklebust, H. R. Dyslexia in childhood. *In* Hellmuth, J. (Ed.), *Learning disorders,* Vol. 1. Seattle: Special Child Publications, 1965, 259–292.

Johnson, D. J., & Mylkebust, H. R. *Learning disabilities: Educational principles and practices.* New York: Grune & Stratton, 1967.

Johnson, S. W., & Morasky, R. L. *Learning disabilities.* Boston: Allyn & Bacon, 1977.

Kabat, H., & Dennis, C. Decerebration in the dog by complete temporary anemia. *Proceedings of the Society for Experimental Biology and Medicine,* 1938, *38,* 864.

Kabat, H., Dennis, C., & Baker, A. B. Recovery of function following arrest of the brain circulation. *American Journal of Physiology,* 1941, *132,* 737.

Kalverboer, A. F. Neurobehavioral relationships in young children: Some remarks on concepts and methods. *In* Knights, R. M., & Bakker, D. J. (Eds.), *The neuropsychology of learning disorders.* Baltimore: University Park Press, 1976, 173–183.

Karpov, B. A., Luria, A. R., & Yarbuss, A. L. Disturbances of the structure of active perception in lesions of the posterior and anterior regions of the brain. *Neuropsychologia,* 1968, *6,* 157–166.

Kaufman, A. S., & Kaufman, N. L. *K-ABC interpretive manual.* Circle Pines, MN: American Guidance Service, 1983.

Kee, D. W., Bathurst, K., & Hellige, J. B. Lateralized interference of repetitive finger tapping: Influence of familial handedness, cognitive load and verbal production. *Neuropsychologia,* 1983, *21*(6), 617–624.

Keogh, J. The study of movement learning disabilities. *In* Das, J. P., Mulcahy, R. F., & Wall, A. E. (Eds.), *Theory and research in learning disabilities.* New York: Plenum Press, 1982, 237–251.

Kephart, N. C. *The slow learner in the classroom*. Columbus, OH: Merrill, 1960 (1st Ed)/1971 (2nd Ed).

Kephart, N. C. Perceptual-motor aspects of learning disabilities. *Exceptional Children*, 1964, *31*, 201–216.

Kephart, N. C. The needs for teachers for specialized information on perception. *In* Cruickshank, W. M. (Ed.), *The teacher of brain-injured children*. Syracuse: Syracuse University Press, 1966, 169–180.

Kephart, N. C. The perceptual-motor match. *In* Cruickshank, W. M., & Hallahan, D. P. (Eds.), *Perceptual and learning disabilities in children*, Vol. 1. Syracuse: Syracuse University Press, 1975, 63–69.

Kertesz, A., Lesk, D., & McCabe, P., Isotope localization of infarcts in aphasia. *Archives of Neurology*, 1977, *34*, 590–601.

Kertesz, A., & McCabe, P. Recovery patterns and prognosis in aphasia. *Brain*, 1977, *100*, 1–18.

Kimble, D. P., & Pribram, K. H. Hippocampectomy and behavior sequences. *Science*, 1963, *139*, 824–825.

Kimura, D. The effect of letter position on recognition. *Canadian Journal of Psychology*, 1959, *13*(1), 1–10.

Kimura, D. Some effects of temporal-lobe damage on auditory perception. *Canadian Journal of Psychology*, 1961a, *15*(3), 156–165.

Kimura, D. Cerebral dominance and the perception of verbal stimuli. *Canadian Journal of Psychology*, 1961b, *15*(3), 166–171.

Kimura, D. Left-right differences in the perception of melodies. *Quarterly Journal of Experimental Psychology*, 1964, *16*, 355–358.

Kimura, D. Dual functional asymmetry of the brain in visual perception. *Neuropsychologia*, 1966, *4*, 275–285.

Kimura, D. Functional asymmetry of the brain in dichotic listening. *Cortex*, 1967, *3*, 163–178.

Kimura, D. Spatial localization in left and right visual fields. *Canadian Journal of Psychology*, 1969, *28*(6), 445–458.

Kimura, D. The asymmetry of the human brain. *Scientific American*, 1973a, *228*(3), 70–78.

Kimura, D. Manual activity during speaking—I. Right-handers. *Neuropsychologia*, 1973b, *11*, 45–50.

Kimura, D. Manual activity during speaking—II. Left-handers. *Neuropsychologia*, 1973c, *11*, 51–55.

Kimura, D. The neural basis of language qua gesture. *In* Avakian-Whitaker, H., & Whitaker, H. A. (Eds.), *Studies in neurolinguistics*, Vol. 2. New York: Academic Press, 1976.

Kimura, D., & Durnford, M. Normal studies on the function of the right hemisphere in vision. *In* Dimond, S. J., & Beaumont, J. G. (Eds.), *Hemisphere function in the human brain*. London: Elek Science, 1974, 25–47.

Kinsbourne, M. The neuropsychology of learning disabilities. Paper presented at *Seventh Annual Neuropsychology Workshop*, University of Victoria, Victoria, B.C., Canada, 1972.

Kinsbourne, M. Mechanisms of hemispheric interaction in man. *In* Kinsbourne,

M., & Smith, W. L. (Eds.), *Hemispheric disconnection and cerebral function.* Springfield, IL: Charles C Thomas, 1974.

Kinsbourne, M. Minor hemisphere language and cerebral maturation. *In* Lenneberg, E. H., & Lenneberg, E. (Eds.), *Foundations of Language Development,* Vol. 2. New York: Academic Press, 1975a, 107–116.

Kinsbourne, M. The ontogeny of cerebral dominance. *Annals of the New York Academy of Sciences,* 1975b, *263,* 244–250.

Kinsbourne, M. The mechanism of hemispheric control of the lateral gradient of attention. *In* Rabbitt, P. M. A., & Dornic, S. (Eds.), *Attention and performance V.* London: Academic Press, 1975c.

Kinsbourne, M., & Cook, J. Generalized and lateralized effects of concurrent verbalization on a unimanual skill. *Quarterly Journal of Experimental Psychology,* 1971, *23,* 341–345.

Kinsbourne, M., & Hiscock, M. Cerebral lateralization and cognitive development. *In* Chall, J., & Mirsky, A. F. (Eds.), *Education and the brain* (Seventy-seventh Yearbook of the National Society for the Study of Education). Chicago: The University of Chicago Press, 1978, 169–222.

Kinsbourne, M., & McMurray, J. The effect of cerebral dominance on time sharing between speaking and tapping by preschool children. *Child Development,* 1975, *46,* 240–242.

Kinsbourne, M., & Smith, W. L. (Eds.) *Hemispheric disconnection and cerebral function.* Springfield, IL: Charles C. Thomas, 1974.

Kinsbourne, M., & Warrington, E. K. Disorders of spelling. *Journal of Neurology, Neurosurgery and Psychiatry,* 1964, *27,* 224–228.

Kirby, J. R., & Ashman, A. F. Planning skills and mathematics achievement: Implications regarding learning disability. *Journal of Psychoeducational Assessment,* 1984, *2,* 9–22.

Kirk, S. A. *The diagnosis and remediation of psycholinguistic disabilities.* Urbana: University of Illinois Press, 1966.

Kirk, S. A., & Bateman, B. Diagnosis and remediation of learning disabilities. *Exceptional Children,* 1962, *29,* 73–78.

Kirk, S. A., & Becker, W., (Eds.), *Conference on Children with Minimal Brain Impairment.* Urbana: University of Illinois, 1963. (mimeo.)

Kirk, S. A., McCarthy, J., & Kirk, W. *The Illinois test of psycholinguistic abilities (revised edition).* Urbana: Illinois University Press, 1968.

Kirk, U. Introduction: Toward the understanding of the neuropsychology of language, reading and spelling. *In* Kirk, U. (Ed.), *Neuropsychology of language, reading, and spelling.* New York: Academic Press, 1983a, 3–31.

Kirk, U. (Ed.). *Neuropsychology of language, reading, and spelling.* New York: Academic Press, 1983b.

Klonoff, H. Factor analysis of a neuropsychological battery for children aged 9 to 15. *Perceptual and Motor Skills,* 1971, *32,* 603–616.

Kløve, H. The relationship of differential electroencephalographic patterns to the distribution of Wechsler-Bellevue scores. *Neurology,* 1959, *9,* 871–876.

Kløve, H. Clinical neuropsychology. *Medical Clinics of North America*, 1963, *11*, 1647–1658.

Kløve, H., & Matthews, C. G. Psychometric and adaptive abilities in epilepsy with differential etiology. *Epilepsia*, 1966, *7*, 330–338.

Kløve, H., & Reitan, R. M. The effect of dysphasia and spatial distortion on Wechsler-Bellevue results. *American Medical Association Archives of Neurology and Psychiatry*, 1958, *80*, 708–713.

Knights, R. M. *Normative data on tests for evaluating brain damage in children from 5 to 14 years of age*. London, Ontario: Department of Psychology, The University of Western Ontario, Research Bulletin #20, June, 1966.

Knights, R. M. A review of the neuropsychological research program. *Special Education*, 1970 (Nov.), 9–27.

Knights, R. M. Battery of neuropsychological tests. Department of Psychology, Carleton University, Ottawa, Ontario, Canada, 1971. (mimeo.)

Knights, R. M. The effects of cerebral lesions on the psychological test performance of children. Final Report, March, 1973, Carleton University, Ottawa, Ontario, Canada.

Knights, R. M., & Bakker, D. J. (Eds.). *The neuropsychology of learning disorders, theoretical approaches*. Baltimore: University Park Press, 1976.

Knights, R. M., & Ogilvie, R. M. Comparison of Test Results from Normal and Brain Damaged Children. *Research Bulletin* No. 53, Department of Psychology, University of Western Ontario, London, Ontario, Canada, July, 1967.

Knopman, D. S., Rubens, A. B., Klassen, A. C., Meyer, M. W., & Niccum, N. Regional cerebral blood flow patterns during verbal and nonverbal auditory activation. *Brain and Language*, 1980, *9*, 93–112.

Kolb, B., & Whishaw, I. Q. *Fundamentals of human neuropsychology*. San Francisco: W. H. Freeman & Co., 1980, 2nd Ed., 1984.

Krashen, S. D. Lateralization, language learning, and the critical period: Some new evidence. *Language and Learning*, 1973, *23*, 63–74.

Krech, D. The chemistry of learning. *Saturday Review*, January 20, 1968, 48ff.

Landau, W. M., Goldstein, R., & Kleffner, F. R. Congenital aphasia, a clinico-pathologic study. *Neurology*, 1960, 915–921.

Landis, D. A scan for mental illness. *Discover*, October 1980, 26–28.

Landis, T., Regard, M., Graves, R., & Goodglass, H. Semantic paralexia: A release of right hemispheric function from left hemispheric control? *Neuropsychologia*, 1983, *21*(4), 359–364.

Lansdell, H. A sex difference in effect of temporal-lobe neurosurgery on design preference. *Nature*, 1962, *194*, 852–854.

Lashley, K. S. Studies in cerebral function in learning. *Psychobiology*, 1920, *2*, 55–136.

Lashley, K. S. *Brain mechanisms and intelligence: A quantitative study of injuries to the brain*. Chicago: University of Chicago Press, 1929.

Lashley, K. S. In search of the engram. In *Society of Experimental Biology*

Symposium No. 4: Physiological Mechanisms in Animal Behavior. Cambridge, England: Cambridge University Press, 1950, 478–505.

Lashley, K. S. The problem of serial order in behavior. *In* Jeffress, L. A. (Ed.), *Cerebral mechanisms in behavior, the Hixon symposium.* New York: Wiley, 1951.

Lenneberg, E. H. Speech as a motor skill with special reference to nonaphasic disorders. *In* Beelugi, U., & Brown, R. (Eds.), *Acquisition of Language.* Monograph of the Society for Research in Child Development. Ser. No. 92, Vol. 29, No. 1, 1964.

Lenneberg, E. H. The natural history of language. *In* Smith, F., & Miller, G. A. (Eds.), *The genesis of language, a psycholinguistic approach.* Cambridge, MA: The M.I.T. Press, 1966, 219–252.

Lenneberg, E. H. *Biological foundations of language.* New York: Wiley, 1967.

Lenneberg, E. H. The effect of age on the outcome of central nervous system disease in children. *In* Isaacson, R. L. (Ed.), *The neuropsychology of development, a symposium.* New York: Wiley, 1968, 147–170.

Lenneberg, E., Pogash, K., Cohlan, A. & Doolittle, J. Comprehension deficits in acquired aphasia. *Proceedings of the Academy of Aphasia,* 1976. Discussed by E. R. Brown in Rieber, R. W. (Ed.) *The neuropsychology of language.* New York: Plenum Press, 1976, 25–43.

Leong, C. K. Dichotic listening with related tasks for dyslexics—Differential use of strategies. *Bulletin of the Orton Society,* 1975, XXV, 111–126.

Leong, C. K. Lateralization in severely disabled readers in relation to functional cerebral development and synthesis of information. *In* Knights, R. M., & Bakker, D. J. (Eds.), *The neuropsychology of learning disorders.* Baltimore: University Park Press, 1976, 221–231.

Leong, C. K. Laterality and reading proficiency in children. *Reading Research Quarterly,* 1980, *15*(2), 185–202.

Leong, C. K. Promising areas of research into learning disabilities with emphasis on reading disabilities. *In* Das, J. P., Mulcahy, R. F., & Wall, A. E. (Eds.), *Theory and research in learning disabilities.* New York: Plenum Press, 1982, 3–26.

Levin, H. S. Evaluation of the tactile component in a proprioceptive feedback task. *Cortex,* 1973, *9,* 197–203.

Levine, D. Prosopagnosia and visual object agnosia: A behavioral study. *Brain and Language,* 1978, *5,* 341–365.

Levy, J. Possible basis for the evolution of lateral specialization of the human brain. *Nature,* 1969, *224,* 614–615.

Levy, J. Psychobiological implications of bilateral asymmetry. *In* Dimond, S. J., Beaumont, J. G. (Eds.), *Hemisphere function in the human brain.* London: Elek Science, 1974, 121–183.

Levy, J., & Nagylaki, T. A model for the genetics of handedness. *Genetics,* 1972, *72,* 117–128.

Lezak, M. D. *Neuropsychological assessment.* New York: Oxford University Press, 1976/1983.

Lhermitte, F., & Gautier, J.-C. Aphasia. *In* Vinken, P. J., & Bruyn, B. W. (Eds.), *Handbook of clinical neurology,* Vol. 4. Amsterdam: North-Holland Publishing Co., 1969, 84–104.

Liberman, A. M., Cooper, F. S., Shankweiler, D. P., & Studdert-Kennedy, M. Perception of the speech code. *Psychological Review,* 1967, *74*(6), 431–461.

Lowe, A. D., & Campbell, R. A. Temporal discrimination in aphasoid and normal children. *Journal of Speech and Hearing Research,* 1965, *8,* 313–314.

Luria, A. R. Neuropsychology in the local diagnosis of brain damage. *Cortex,* 1964, *1,* 3–18.

Luria, A. R. *Higher cortical functions in man.* New York: Basic Books, 1966.

Luria, A. R. *Traumatic aphasia, its syndromes, psychology and treatment.* The Hague: Mouton, 1970.

Luria, A. R. *The working brain.* Harmondsworth: Penguin Books, 1973.

Luria, A. R., Simernitskaya, E. G., & Tubylevich, B. The structure of psychological processes in relation to cerebral organization. *Neuropsychologia,* 1970, *8,* 13–19.

Maccoby, E. E., & Jacklin, C. N. *The psychology of sex differences.* Stanford: Stanford University Press, 1974.

MacLean, P. D. The limbic system with respect to two basic life principles. *In* Brazier, M. A. B. (Ed.), *The central nervous system and behavior.* Washington, DC: National Science Foundation, 1959.

Mahl, G. F., Rothenberg, A., Delgado, J. M. R., & Hamlin, H. Psychological responses in the human to intracerebral electrical stimulation. *Psychosomatic Medicine,* 1964, *26*(4), 337–368.

Malatesha, R. N., & Aaron, P. G. (Eds.), *Reading disorders; Varieties and treatments.* New York: Academic Press, 1982.

Malatesha, R. N., & Dougan, D. R. Clinical subtypes of developmental dyslexia: Resolution of an irresolute problem. *In* Malatesha, R. N., & Aaron, P. G. *Reading disorders: Varieties and treatments.* New York: Academic Press, 1982, 69–92.

Manter, J. T., & Gatz, A. J. *Essentials of clinical neuroanatomy and neurophysiology,* 2nd Ed. Philadelphia: F. A. Davis Co., 1961.

Maria, K., & MacGinitie, W. H. Reading comprehension disabilities: Knowledge structures and nonaccommodating text processing strategies. *Annals of Dyslexia,* 1982, XXXII, 33–59.

Mark, V. H., & Ervin, F. R. *Violence and the brain.* New York: Harper & Row, 1970.

Marshall, J. C., & Newcombe, F. The conceptual status of deep dyslexia: An historical perspective. *In* Coltheart, M., Patterson, K., & Marshall, J. C. (Eds.), *Deep dyslexia.* London: Routledge & Kegan Paul, 1980, 1–21.

Masland, R. L. Children with minimal brain dysfunction; a national problem. *In* Tarnopol, L. (Ed.), *Learning disabilities: Introduction to educational and medical management.* Springfield, IL: Charles C. Thomas, 1969.

Maslow, A. H. Deficiency motivation and growth motivation. *In* Jones, M. R.

(Ed.), *Nebraska symposium on motivation*. Lincoln, NE: University of Nebraska Press, 1955.

Maspes, P. E. Le syndrome expérimental chez l'homme de la section du splénium du corps calleux alexie visuelle pure hemianopsique. *Revue Neurologique (Paris)*, 1948, *80*(2), 100–112.

Masserman, J. H. Is the hypothalamus a center of emotion? *Psychosomatic Medicine*, 1941, *3*, 3–25.

Masserman, J. H. Experimental neuroses. *Scientific American*, 1950, *182*(3), 38–43.

Mateer, C., & Kimura, D. Impairment of nonverbal oral movements in aphasia. *Brain and Language*, 1976, *4*, 262–276.

Mateer, F. *Child behavior: A critical and experimental study of young children by the method of conditioned reflexes*. Boston: R. G. Badger, 1918.

Mateer, F. *Glands and efficient behavior*. New York: Appleton-Century-Crofts, 1935.

Matthews, C. G., & Folk, E. D. Finger localization, intelligence, and arithmetic in mentally retarded subjects. *American Journal of Mental Deficiency*, 1964, *69*(1), 107–113.

Matthews, C. G., & Kløve, H. Differential psychological performances in major motor, psychomotor, and mixed seizure classifications of known and unknown etiology, *Epilepsia*, 1967, *8*, 117–128.

Mattingly, I. G. Reading, linguistic awareness and language acquisition. Invited position paper presented at the International Reading Research Seminar on Linguistic Awareness and Learning to Read, University of Victoria, Victoria, B.C., Canada, June 26–30, 1979.

Mattis, S. Dyslexia syndromes: A working hypothesis that works. *In* Benton, A. L., & Pearl, D. (Eds.), *Dyslexia, an appraisal of current knowledge*. New York: Oxford University Press, 1978, 45–58.

Mattis, S., French, J. H., & Rapin, I. Dyslexia in children and young adults: three independent neuropsychological syndromes. *Developmental Medicine and Child Neurology*, 1975, *17*, 150–163.

Maugham, W. S. The verger. *In The complete short stories of W. Somerset Maugham, Vol. II*. New York: Doubleday & Co., 1953, 572–578.

McCulloch, W. S., & Brodey, W. M. The biological sciences. *In* Hutchins, R. M., & Adler, M. J. (Eds.), *The Great Ideas Today 1966*. Chicago: Encyclopaedia Britannica, Inc., 1966, 288–334.

McGeer, P. L., McGeer, E. G., & Innanen, V. T. Dendro axonic transmission. I. Evidence from receptor binding of dopaminergic and cholinergic agents. *Brain Research*, 1979, *169*, 433–441.

McGinnis, M. A. *Aphasic children: Identification and education by the association method*. Washington, DC: Volta, 1963.

McGlone, J., & Davidson, W. The relation between cerebral speech laterality and spatial ability with special reference to sex and hand preference. *Neuropsychologia*, 1973, *11*, 105–113.

McGlone, J., & Kertesz, A. Sex differences in cerebral processing of visuospatial tasks. *Cortex,* 1973, *9,* 313–320.

McGuire, W. J. Attitudes and opinions. *Annual Review of Psychology,* 1966, *17,* 474–514.

McLaughlin, J. P., Dean, P., & Stanley, P. Aesthetic preference in dextrals and sinistrals. *Neuropsychologia,* 1983, *21*(2), 147–153.

McLeod, J. *Psychometric identification of children with learning disabilities.* Saskatoon: University of Saskatchewan, 1978.

McMahon, S. A., & Greenberg, L. M. Serial neurologic examination of hyperactive children. *Pediatrics,* 1977, *59,* 585–587.

McRae, D. L., Branch, C. L., & Milner, B. The occipital horns and cerebral dominance. *Neurology,* 1968, *18,* 95–98.

Meichenbaum, D. Self-instructional methods. *In* Kanfer, F. H., & Goldstein, A. P. (Eds.), *Helping people change: A textbook of methods.* New York: Pergamon Press, 1975, 357–391.

Meichenbaum, D. Toward a cognitive theory of self-control. *In* Schwartz, G. E., & Shapiro, D. (Eds.), *Consciousness and self-regulation,* Vol. 1. New York: Plenum Press, 1976, 223–260.

Meyer, A. The frontal lobe syndrome, the aphasias and related conditions, a contribution to the history of cortical localization. *Brain,* 1974, *97,* 565–600.

Meyer, D. E., & Schvaneveldt, R. W. Facilitation in recognizing pairs of words: Evidence of a dependence between retrieval operations. *Journal of Experimental Psychology,* 1971, *90,* 227–234.

Meyer, V., & Yates, H. J. Intellectual changes following temporal lobectomy for psychomotor epilepsy. *Journal of Neurosurgery and Psychiatry,* 1955, *18,* 44–52.

Miller, E. Handedness and the pattern of human ability. *British Journal of Psychology,* 1971, *62,* 111–112.

Miller, G. A., & Lenneberg, E. *Psychology and biology of language and thought.* New York: Academic Press, 1978.

Milner, B. Intellectual function of the temporal lobes. *Psychological Bulletin,* 1954, *51,* 42–62.

Milner, B. Psychological defects produced by temporal lobe excision. In *The brain and human behavior,* Vol. 36, Proceedings of the Association for Research in Nervous and Mental Disease. Baltimore: Williams & Wilkins, 1958, *36,* 244–257.

Milner, B. Laterality effects in audition. *In* Mountcastle, V. B. (Ed.), *Interhemispheric relations and cerebral dominance.* Baltimore: The Johns Hopkins University Press, 1962, 177–195.

Milner, B. Effects of different brain lesions on card sorting. *Archives of Neurology,* 1963, *9,* 90–100.

Milner, B. Some effects of frontal lobectomy in man. *In* Warren, J. M., & Akert, K. A. (Eds.), *The frontal granular cortex and behavior.* New York: McGraw-Hill, 1964, 313–334.

Milner, B., Amnesia following operation on the temporal lobes. *In* Whitty, C. W. M., & Zangwill, O. L. (Eds.), *Amnesia*. London: Butterworth & Co., 1966, 109–133.

Milner, B. Brain mechanisms suggested by studies of temporal lobes. *In* Darley, F. L. (Ed.), *Brain mechanisms underlying speech and language*. New York: Grune & Stratton, 1967, 122–145.

Milner, B. Visual recognition and recall after right temporal-lobe excision in man. *Neuropsychologia*, 1968, *6*, 191–209.

Milner, B. Evidence of bilateral speech. Paper presented at Tenth Annual Neuropsychology Workshop, University of Victoria, Victoria, B.C., 1975.

Milner, B., Branch, C., & Rasmussen, T. Observations on cerebral dominance. *In* de Reuck, A. V. S., & O'Connor, M. (Eds.), *Ciba Foundation symposium on disorders of language*. London: J. & A. Churchill, 1964, 200–214.

Milner, B., Branch, C., & Rasmussen, T. Evidence for bilateral speech representation in some non-right handers. *Transactions of the American Neurological Association*, 1966, *91*, 306–308.

Milner, P. M. A neural mechanism for the immediate recall of sequences. *Kybernetick*, 1961, *1*, 76–81.

Milner, P. M. *Physiological psychology*. New York: Holt, Rinehart and Winston, 1970.

Minskoff, J. G. Differential approaches to prevalence estimates of learning disabilities, *Annals of the New York Academy of Sciences*, 1973, *205*, 139–145.

Mishkin, M., & Forgays, D. G. Word recognition as a function of retinal locus. *Journal of Experimental Psychology*, 1952, *43*, 43–48.

Mittler, P. (Ed.) *The psychological assessment of mental and physical handicaps*. London: Methuen, 1970.

Molfese, D. L. Cerebral asymmetry in infants, children and adults: auditory evoked responses to speech and musical stimuli. *Journal of the Acoustical Society of America*, 1973, *53*, 363–373.

Money, J. Dyslexia: A postconference review. *In* Money, J. (Ed.), *Reading disability, progress, and research needs in dyslexia*. Baltimore: The Johns Hopkins University Press, 1962, 9–33.

Montessori, M. *The Montessori method: Scientific pedagogy as applied to child education in the "children's houses."* (Translated by Anne E. George.) New York: F. A. Stokes, 1912.

Montessori, M. *The Montessori method*. New York: Schocken Books, 1964.

Montessori, M. *Spontaneous activity in education*. New York: Schocken Books, 1965.

Montgomery, P., & Richter, E. *Sensorimotor integration for developmentally disabled children: A handbook*. Los Angeles: Western Psychological Services, 1977.

Morrell, F. Electrophysiological contributions to the neural basis of learning. *Physiological Reviews*, 1961, *41*(3), 443–494.

Morrell, F. Colloquium presentation, Massachusetts Institute of Technology, Cambridge, MA, 1967.

Moruzzi, G., & Magoun, H. W. Brain stem reticular formation and activation of the EEG. *Electroencephalography and clinical neurophysiology,* 1949, *1,* 455–473.

Moscovitch, M. Information processing and the cerebral hemispheres. *In* Gazzaniga, M. S. (Ed.), *Handbook of behavioral neurobiology, Vol. 2, Neuropsychology.* New York: Plenum Press, 1979.

Moscovitch, M. A model of hemispheric organization based on studies of hemispheric specialization in normal and brain-damaged people. Invited paper presented at Fifteenth Annual Neuropsychology Workshop, University of Victoria, Victoria, B.C., Canada, 1980.

Moss, J. W. Neuropsychology: One way to go. *The Journal of Special Education,* 1979, *13*(1), 45–49.

Mountcastle, V. B. (Ed.) *Interhemispheric relations and cerebral dominance.* Baltimore: The Johns Hopkins University Press, 1962.

Muehl, S., & Forell, E. R. A follow-up study of disabled readers: variables related to high school reading performance. *Reading Research Quarterly,* 1973, *9,* 110–123.

Myers, P. I., & Hammill, D. D. *Methods for learning disorders.* New York: Wiley, 1969.

Myklebust, H. R. *Auditory disorders in children: A manual for differential diagnosis.* New York: Grune & Stratton, 1954.

Myklebust, H. R. Psychoneurological learning disorders in children. *In* Kirk, S. A., & Becker, W. (Eds.), *Conference on children with minimal brain impairment.* Urbana: University of Illinois, 1963.

Myklebust, H. R. *The psychology of deafness.* New York: Grune & Stratton, 1964.

Myklebust, H. R. *Development and disorders of written language,* Vol. I. New York: Grune & Stratton, 1965.

Myklebust, H. R. Learning disabilities: Definition and overview. *In* Myklebust, H. R. (Ed.), *Progress in learning disabilities,* Vol. I. New York: Grune & Stratton, 1967a, 1–15.

Myklebust, H. R. (Ed.) *Progress in learning disabilities,* Vol. I. New York: Grune & Stratton, 1967b.

Myklebust, H. R. (Ed.) *Progress in learning disabilities,* Vol. II. New York: Grune & Stratton, 1971a.

Myklebust, H. R. Childhood aphasia: An evolving concept; and Childhood aphasia: Identification, diagnosis, remediation. Chapters 46 and 47 *in* Travis, L. E. (Ed.), *Handbook of speech pathology and audiology.* New York: Appleton-Century-Crofts, 1971b, 1181–1217.

Myklebust, H. R. *Development and disorders of written language,* Vol. II. New York: Grune & Stratton, 1973a.

Myklebust, H. R. Identification and diagnosis of children with learning disabilities: An interdisciplinary study of criteria. *In* Walzer, S., & Wolff, P. H. (Eds.), *Minimal cerebral dysfunction in children.* New York: Grune & Stratton, 1973b.

Myklebust, H. R. (Ed.) *Progress in learning disabilities.* Vol. III. New York: Grune & Stratton, 1975a.

Myklebust, H. R. Nonverbal learning disabilities: assessment and intervention. *In* Myklebust, H. R. (Ed.), *Progress in learning disabilities,* Vol. III. New York: Grune & Stratton, 1975b, 85–121.

Myklebust, H. R. Preface in Myklebust, H. R. (Ed.), *Progress in learning disabilities, Vol. V.* New York: Grune & Stratton, 1983.

Myklebust, H. R., & Boshes, B. *Final report, minimal brain damage in children.* Washington, DC: U.S. Department of Health, Education, and Welfare, 1969.

Myklebust, H. R., & Brutten, M. A study of the visual perception of deaf children. *Acta Oto-laryngolica,* 1953, Supplementum 105. Whole Monograph, 126 pp.

Näätänen, R. Evoked potential, EEG, and slow potential correlates of selective attention. *Acta Psychologica,* 1970, *33,* 178–192.

Naidoo, S. *Specific dyslexia.* London: Pitman, 1972.

National Advisory Committee on Handicapped Children, *Special Education for Handicapped Children,* First Annual Report. Washington, DC: U.S. Dept. of Health, Education, and Welfare, Office of Education, 1968.

Nelson, H. E., & Warrington, E. K. Developmental spelling retardation. *In* Knights, R. M., & Bakker, D. J. (Eds.) *The neuropsychology of learning disorders.* Baltimore: University Park Press, 1976, 325–332.

Netter, F. H. *The CIBA Collection of Medical Illustrations,* Vol. I, *Nervous System.* New York: CIBA, 1962.

Nolan, K. A., & Caramazza, A. An analysis of writing in a case of deep dyslexia. *Brain and Language,* 1983, *20,* 305–328.

Obrzut, J. E. Neuropsychological procedures with school-age children. *In* Hynd, G. W., & Obrzut, J. E. (Eds.), *Neuropsychological assessment and the school-age child: Issues and procedures.* New York: Grune & Stratton, 1981, 237–275.

Ojemann, G. A. Mental arithmetic during human thalamic stimulation. *Neuropsychologia,* 1974, *12,* 1–10.

Ojemann, G. A. Language and the thalamus: Object naming and recall during and after thalamic stimulation. *Brain and Language,* 1975, *2,* 101–120.

Ojemann, G. A. Individual variability in cortical localization of language. *Journal of Neurosurgery,* 1979, *50,* 164–169.

Ojemann, G. A. Interrelationships in the brain organization of language-related behaviors: Evidence from electrical stimulation mapping. *In* Kirk, U. (Ed.), *Neuropsychology of language, reading, and spelling.* New York: Academic Press, 1983, 129–152.

Ojemann, G. A., & Mateer, C. Human language cortex: Localization of memory, syntax, and sequential motor-phoneme identification systems. *Science,* 1979, *205,* 1401–1403.

Ojemann, G. A., & Whitaker, H. A. Language localization and variability. *Brain and Language,* 1978, *6,* 239–260.

Oldfield, R. C. The assessment and analysis of handedness: The Edinburgh inventory. *Neuropsychologia,* 1971, *9,* 97–113.

Olds, J. Pleasure centres in the brain. *Scientific American,* 1956, *195*(4), 105–116.

Orton, S. T. "Word-blindness" in school children. *Archives of Neurology and Psychiatry,* 1925, *14,* 581–615.

Orton, S. T. Reading disability. *Genetic Psychology Monographs,* 1926, *14,* 335–453.

Orton, S. T. Specific reading disability—Strephosymbolia. *Journal of the American Medical Association,* 1928, *90,* 1095–1099.

Orton, S. T. *Reading, writing and speech problems in children.* New York: W. W. Norton, 1937.

Ott, J. N. *Health and light.* New York: Pocket Books, 1976.

Ounsted, C., & Taylor, D. C. (Eds.) *Gender differences: Their ontogeny and significance.* Edinburgh: Churchill Livingstone, 1972.

Owen, W. A. Effects of motivating instructions on reaction time in grade school children. *Child Development,* 1959, *30,* 261–267.

Paine, R. S. Minimal chronic brain syndromes in children. *Developmental Medicine and Child Neurology,* 1962, *4,* 21–27.

Paine, R. S. Organic neurological factors related to learning disorders. *In* Hellmuth, J. (Ed.), *Learning disorders,* Vol. 1. Seattle: Special Child Publications, 1965, 1–29.

Paivio, A., & te Linde, J. Imagery, memory, and the brain. *Canadian Journal of Psychology,* 1982, *36*(2), 243–272.

Partain, C. L., James, A. E., Rollo, F. D. & Price, R. R. (Eds). *Nuclear magnetic resonance (NMR) imaging.* Philadelphia: W. B. Saunders, 1983.

Pavlidis, G. Th. How can dyslexia be objectively diagnosed? *Reading,* 1979, *13*(3), 3–15.

Pavlidis, G. Th. Erratic sequential eye movements in dyslexics: Comments and reply to Stanley *et al. British Journal of Psychology,* 1983, *74,* 189–193.

Pavlov, I. P. *Lectures on conditioned reflexes.* New York: International Publishers, 1928.

Penfield, W. *No man alone, a neurosurgeon's life.* Boston: Little, Brown, 1977.

Penfield, W., & Roberts, L. *Speech and brain mechanisms.* Princeton: Princeton University Press, 1959.

Pennington, H., Galliani, C. A., & Voegele, G. E. Unilateral electroencephalographic dysrhythmia and children's intelligence. *Child Development,* 1965, *36,* 539–546.

Pettit, J. M., & Noll, J. D. Cerebral dominance in aphasia recovery. *Brain and Language,* 1979, *7,* 191–200.

Phillips, J. L. *The Origins of Intellect: Piaget's Theory.* San Francisco: W. H. Freeman, 1969 (1st Ed.)/1975 (2nd Ed.).

Piaget, J. *The child's conception of number.* London: Routledge & Kegan Paul, 1941.

Piaget, J. *The origins of intelligence in children.* New York: International Universities Press, 1952.

Piaget, J. *The language and thought of the child.* New York: Humanities Press, 1965.

Piaget, J., & Inhelder B. *The child's conception of space.* London: Routledge & Kegan Paul, 1956.

Piaget, J., & Inhelder, B. *Mental imagery in the child.* London: Routledge & Kegan Paul, 1971.

Pierson, J. M., Bradshaw, J. L., & Nettleton, N. C. Head and body space to left and right, front and rear—I. Unidirectional competitive auditory stimulation. *Neuropsychologia,* 1983, *21*(5), 463–473.

Pihl, R. O. Learning disabilities: programs in the schools. *In* Myklebust, H. R. (Ed.), *Progress in learning disabilities,* Vol. III. New York: Grune & Stratton, 1975, 19–48.

Pirozzolo, F. J. *The neuropsychology of developmental reading disorders.* New York: Praeger Publishers, 1979.

Plato, *The Republic.* Great Books of the Western World, Vol. 7. Toronto: Encyclopaedia Britannica, 1952, 295–441.

Poeck, K., & Orgass, B. The concept of the body schema: A critical review and some experimental results. *Cortex,* 1971, *7*(3), 254–277.

Pollack, C. Neuropsychological aspects of reading and writing. *Bulletin of the Orton Society,* 1976, XXVI, 19–33.

Population 1921–1971, Revised Annual Estimates. Statistics Canada, Ottawa, Canada. Catalogue 91-512, 55.

Pribram, K. H. Neurological notes on the art of educating. *In* Hilgard, E. R. (Ed.), *Sixty-third Yearbook, National Society for the Study of Education.* Chicago: University of Chicago Press, Part I, 1964, 78–110.

Pribram, K. H. *Languages of the brain.* Englewood Cliffs, NJ: Prentice-Hall, 1971.

Prout, H. T. Behavioral intervention with hyperactive children: A review. *Journal of Learning Disabilities,* 1977, *10*(3), 141–146.

Provins, K. A. Motor skills, handedness, and behaviour. *Australian Journal of Psychology,* 1967, *19,* 137–150.

Quadfasel, F. A., & Goodglass, H. Specific reading disability and other specific disabilities. *Journal of Learning Disabilities,* 1968, *1*(10), 590–600.

Rabinovitch, R. D. Reading and learning disabilities. *In* Arieti, S. (Ed.), *American handbook of psychiatry.* New York: Basic Books, 1959, 857–859.

Ratcliff, G., Dila, C., Taylor, L., & Milner, B. The morphological asymmetry of the hemispheres and cerebral dominance for speech: A possible relationship. *Brain and Language,* 1980, *11,* 87–98.

Raven, J. C. *The Coloured Progressive Matrices Test.* London: Lewis, 1965.

Reed, D. W. A theory of language, speech, and writing. *In* Singer, H., & Ruddell, R. B. (Eds.), *Theoretical models and processes of reading.* Newark, DE: International Reading Association, 1970, 219–238.

Reed, H. B. C. Some relationships between neurological dysfunction and behavioral deficits in children. *In* Kirk, S. A., & Becker, W. (Eds.), *Conference on Children with Minimal Brain Impairment.* Urbana: University of Illinois, 1963, 54–70.

Reed, J. C., & Reitan, R. M. Verbal and performance differences among brain-injured children with lateralized motor deficits. *Perceptual and Motor Skills,* 1969, *29,* 747–752.

Reitan, R. M. Certain differential effects of left and right cerebral lesions in human adults. *Journal of Comparative and Physiological Psychology,* 1955a, *48,* 474–477.

Reitan, R. M. Investigation of the validity of Halstead's measures of biological intelligence. *American Medical Association Archives of Neurology and Psychiatry,* 1955b, *73,* 28–35.

Reitan, R. M. Investigation of relationships between "psychometric" and "biological" intelligence. *Journal of Nervous and Mental Disease,* 1956, *123,* 536–541.

Reitan, R. M. The validity of the Trail Making Test as an indicator of organic brain damage. *Perceptual and Motor Skills,* 1958, *8,* 271–276.

Reitan, R. M. *The effects of brain lesions on adaptive abilities in human beings.* Indianapolis: Indiana University Medical Center, 1959. (mimeo.)

Reitan, R. M. *Manual for administering and scoring the Reitan–Indiana Neuropsychological Battery for Children (aged 5 through 8).* Indianapolis: University of Indiana Medical Center, 1964a.

Reitan, R. M. Psychological deficits resulting from cerebral lesions in man. *In* Warren, J. M., & Akert, K. A. (Eds.), *The frontal granular cortex and behavior.* New York: McGraw-Hill, 1964b, 301.

Reitan, R. M. The needs of teachers for specialized information in the area of neuropsychology. *In* Cruickshank, W. M. (Ed.), *The teacher of brain-injured children.* Syracuse: Syracuse University Press, 1966a, 225–243.

Reitan, R. M. Diagnostic inferences of brain lesions based on psychological test results. *The Canadian Psychologist,* 1966b, *7a*(4), Inst. Suppl., 368–388.

Reitan, R. M. Psychological effects of cerebral lesions in children of early school age. *In* Reitan, R. M., & Davison, L. A. (Eds.), *Clinical neuropsychology: Current status and applications.* Washington, DC: Winston, 1974, 53–89.

Reitan, R. M., & Boll, T. J. Neuropsychological correlates of minimal brain dysfunction. *Annals of the New York Academy of Sciences,* 1973, *205,* 65–88.

Reitan, R. M., & Davison, L. A. *Clinical neuropsychology: Current status and applications.* Washington, D.C.: Winston, 1974.

Reitan, R. M., & Heineman, C. E. Interactions of neurological deficits and emotional disturbances in children with learning disorders: methods for differential assessment. *In* Hellmuth, J. (Ed.), *Learning disorders,* Vol. 3. Seattle: Special Child Publications, 1968, 93–135.

Riese, W. Kurt Goldstein—The Man and His Work. *In* Simmel, M. L. (Ed.), *The reach of mind, essays in memory of Kurt Goldstein.* New York: Springer Publishing Co., 1968.

Risberg, J., Halsey, J. H., Wills, E. L., & Wilson, E. M. Hemispheric specialization in normal man studied by bilateral measurements of the regional cerebral blood flow—a study with the 133-Xe inhalation technique. *Brain,* 1975, *98,* Pt. III, 511–524.

Risberg, J., & Ingvar, D. H. Patterns of activation in the grey matter of the dominant hemisphere during memorizing and reasoning—A study of regional cerebral blood flow changes during psychological testing in a group of neurologically normal patients. *Brain,* 1973, *96*(4), 737–756.

Robb, P. *Epilepsy, a manual for health workers.* Bethesda, MD: NIH Publication, No. 82-2350, September 1981.

Roberts, L. Childhood aphasia and handedness. *In* West, R. (Ed.), *Childhood aphasia.* San Francisco: California Society for Crippled Children and Adults, 1962, 45–46.

Robinson, N. M., & Robinson, H. B. *The mentally retarded child, a psychological approach,* 2nd Ed. New York: McGraw-Hill, 1976, 255.

Rockel, A. J., Hiorns, R. W., & Powell, T. P. S. Numbers of neurons through full depth of neocortex. *Proceedings of the Anatomy Society of Britain and Ireland,* 1974, *118,* 371.

Rosen, B. R., & Brady, T. J. Principles of nuclear magnetic resonance for medical application, *Seminars in Nuclear Medicine,* 1983, XIII (4), 308–318.

Rosenzweig, M. R. Auditory localization. *Scientific American,* 1961, *205,* 132–142.

Rosenzweig, M. R. Environmental complexity, cerebral change, and behavior. *American Psychologist,* 1966, *21*(4), 321–332.

Rosenzweig, M. R., Krech, D., Bennett, E. L., & Diamond, M. C. Modifying brain chemistry and anatomy by enrichment or impoverishment of experience. *In* Newton, G., & Levine, S. (Eds.), *Early experience and behaviour.* Springfield, IL: Charles C. Thomas, 1968.

Rosner, J. *Helping children overcome learning difficulties,* 2nd Ed. New York: Walker & Co., 1979.

Ross, A. D. *Psychological disorders of children, a behavioral approach to theory, research and therapy.* New York: McGraw-Hill, 1974.

Ross, D. M., & Ross, S. A. *Hyperactivity, research, theory, action.* New York: Wiley, 1976.

Ross, D. M., & Ross, S. A. *Hyperactivity: Current issues, research, and theory, 2nd Edition.* New York: Wiley, 1982.

Rourke, B. P. Brain-behavior relationships in children with learning disabilities: A research program. *American Psychologist,* 1975, *30,* 911–920.

Rourke, B. P. Issues in the neuropsychological assessment of children with learning disabilities. *Canadian Psychological Review,* 1976a, *17,* 89–102.

Rourke, B. P. Reading retardation in children: Developmental lag or deficit? *In* Knights, R. M., & Bakker, D. J. (Eds.), *The neuropsychology of learning disorders*. Baltimore: University Park Press, 1976b, 125–137.

Rourke, B. P. Neuropsychological research in reading retardation: A review. *In* Benton, A. L., & Pearl, D. (Eds.), *Dyslexia: An appraisal of current knowledge*. London: Oxford University Press, 1978a, 141–171.

Rourke, B. P. Reading, spelling and arithmetic disabilities: A neuropsychological perspective. *In* Myklebust, H. R. (Ed.), *Progress in learning disabilities*, Vol. 4. New York: Grune & Stratton, 1978b, 97–120.

Rourke, B. P. Neuropsychological assessment of children with learning disabilities. *In* Filskov, S. B., & Boll, T. J. (Eds.), *Handbook of clinical neuropsychology*. New York: Wiley-Interscience, 1981.

Rourke, B. P. Central processing deficiencies in children: Toward a developmental neuropsychological model. *Journal of Clinical Neuropsychology*, 1982, *4*(1), 1–18.

Rourke, B. P., Bakker, D. J., Fisk, J. L., & Strang, J. D. *Child neuropsychology, an introduction to theory, research, and clinical practice*. New York: Guilford, 1983.

Rourke, B. P., & Finlayson, M. A. J. Neuropsychological significance of variations in patterns of academic performance: verbal and visual-spatial abilities. *Journal of Abnormal Child Psychology*, 1978, *6*, 121–133.

Rourke, B. P., & Gates, R. D. Neuropsychological research and school psychology. *In* Hynd, G. W., & Obrzut, J. E. (Eds.), *Neuropsychological assessment and the school-age child*. New York: Grune & Stratton, 1981, 3–25.

Rourke, B. P., & Orr, R. R. Prediction of the reading and spelling performances of normal and retarded readers: a four year follow-up. *Journal of Abnormal Child Psychology*, 1977, *5*(1), 9–20.

Russell, E. W., Neuringer, C., & Goldstein, G. *Assessment of brain damage*. New York: Wiley-Interscience, 1970.

Russell, W. R., & Espir, M. L. E. *Traumatic aphasia, a study of aphasia in war wounds of the brain*. London: Oxford University Press, 1961.

Rutter, M., Graham, P., & Yule, W. *A Neuropsychiatric Study in Childhood*. Philadelphia: Lippincott, 1970.

Rutter, M., Tizard, J., & Whitmore, K. (Eds.), *Education, health and behaviour*. London: Longmans, 1970.

Salk, L. The role of the heart beat in the relations between mother and infant. *Scientific American*, 1973, *228*(5), 24–29.

Sandström, C. Sex differences in localization and orientation. *Acta Psychologica*, 1953, *9*, 82–96.

Sanides, F. Comparative neurology of the temporal lobe in primates including man with reference to speech. *Brain and Language*, 1975, *2*, 396–419.

Satz, P. Pathological left-handedness: An explanatory model. *Cortex*, 1972, *8*, 121–135.

Satz, P. Left-handedness and early brain insult: An explanation. *Neuropsychologia*, 1973, *11*, 115–117.

Satz, P. Laterality tests: An inferential problem. *Cortex,* 1977, *13,* 208–212.

Satz, P., Achenbach, K., & Fennell, E. Correlations between assessed manual laterality and predicted speech laterality in a normal population. *Neuropsychologia,* 1967, *5,* 295–310.

Satz, P., & Fletcher, J. M. Early screening tests: Some uses and abuses. *Journal of Learning Disabilities,* 1979, *12,* 43–50.

Satz, P., & Sparrow, S. S. Specific developmental dyslexia: A theoretical formulation. *In* Bakker, D. J., & Satz, P. (Eds.), *Specific reading disability: Advances in theory and method.* Rotterdam: Rotterdam University Press, 1970, 17–40.

Satz, P., Taylor, H. G., Friel, J., & Fletcher, J. M. Some developmental and predictive precursors of reading disabilities: A six year follow-up. *In* Benton, A. L., & Pearl, D. (Eds.), *Dyslexia: An appraisal of current knowledge.* New York: Oxford University Press, 1978.

Sauerwein, H., & Lassonde, M. C. Intra- and interhemispheric processing of visual information in callosal agenesis. *Neuropsychologia,* 1983, *21*(2), 167–171.

Sawrey, W. L., & Sawrey, J. M. Conditioned fear and restraint in ulceration. *Journal of Comparative and Physiological Psychology,* 1964, *57*(1), 150–151.

Sawrey, W. L., & Sawrey, J. M. UCS effects on ulceration following fear conditioning. *Psychonomic Science,* 1968, *10*(3), 85–86.

Sawrey, W. L., & Wiesz, J. D. An experimental method of producing gastric ulcers. *Journal of Comparative and Physiological Psychology,* 1956, *49,* 269–270.

Schain, R. J. *Neurology of childhood learning disorders.* Baltimore: Williams & Wilkins, 1972.

Schmidt, R. F. (Ed.) *Fundamentals of sensory physiology.* New York: Springer-Verlag, 1978a.

Schmidt, R. F. (Ed.) *Fundamentals of neurophysiology,* 2nd Ed. New York: Springer-Verlag, 1978b.

Schmitt, B. D. The minimal brain dysfunction myth. *American Journal of Diseases of Children,* 1975, *129,* 1313–1318.

Schmitt, F. O., & Worden, F. G. (Eds.) *The neurosciences, fourth study program.* Cambridge, MA: The M.I.T. Press, 1979.

Schulman, J. L., Kaspar, J. C., & Throne, G. M. *Brain damage and behavior.* Springfield, IL: Charles C. Thomas, 1965.

Scoville, W. B., & Milner, B. Loss of recent memory after bilateral hippocampal lesions. *Journal of Neurology, Neurosurgery, and Psychiatry,* 1957, *20*(11), 11–19.

Scrimshaw, N. S., & Gordon, J. E. (Eds.) *Malnutrition, learning and behavior.* Cambridge, MA: The M.I.T. Press, 1968.

Scull, J. W. *The Cedar Lodge colour reading project.* Cobble Hill, B. C., Canada: Cedar Lodge Centre, 1978.

Scull, J., & McNie, G. Residential treatment for children with severe learning disabilities. *Special Education in Canada,* 1980, *55*(1), 25–29.

Seashore, C. E., Lewis, D., & Saetveit, J. G. *Seashore measures of musical talents, manual, revised 1960.* New York: The Psychological Corporation, 1960.

Segalowitz, S. J. (Ed.). *Language functions and brain organization.* New York: Academic Press, 1983.

Segalowitz, S. J., & Bryden, M. P. Individual differences in hemispheric representation of language. *In* Segalowitz, S. J. (Ed.), *Language functions and brain organization.* New York: Academic Press, 1983, 341–372.

Segalowitz, S. J., & Gruber, F. A. (Eds.). *Language development and neurological theory.* New York: Academic Press, 1977.

Seino, M., & Wada, J. A. Chronic focal cortical epileptogenic lesion and behavior. *Epilepsia,* 1964, *5,* 321–333.

Selz, M. Halstead–Reitan neuropsychological test batteries for children. *In* Hynd, G. W., & Obrzut, J. E. (Eds.), *Neuropsychological assessment and the school-age child: Issues and procedures.* New York: Grune & Stratton, 1981, 195–235.

Semmes, J. A non-tactual factor in astereognosis. *Neuropsychologia,* 1965, *3,* 295–315.

Senden, M.v. Raum- und Gestaltauffasung bei operierten Blindgeborenen vor und nach der Operation. Leipzig: Barth, 1932. Described in D. O. Hebb, *Organization of Behavior,* 1949.

Senf, G. M. Development of immediate memory for bisensory stimuli in normal children and children with learning disorders. *Developmental Psychology Monograph,* 1969, *6,* 1–29.

Senf, G. M. Can neuropsychology really change the face of special education? *The Journal of Special Education,* 1979, *13*(1), 51–56.

Serwer, B. L., Shapiro, B. J., & Shapiro, P. P. The comparative effectiveness of four methods of instruction on the achievement of children with specific learning disabilities. *Journal of Special Education,* 1973, *7*(3), 241–249.

Shankweiler, D. P. Effects of success and failure instructions on reaction time in patients with brain damage. *Journal of Comparative and Physiological Psychology,* 1959, *52*(5), 546–549.

Shankweiler, D., & Studdert-Kennedy, M. A continuum of lateralization for speech perception. *Brain and Language,* 1975, *2*(2), 212–225.

Sherrington, C. S. *The integrative action of the nervous system.* New Haven: Yale University Press, 1906.

Sherrington, C. S. *Man on his nature,* 2nd Ed. Cambridge: Cambridge University Press, 1951.

Shure, G. H., & Halstead, W. C. Cerebral localization of intellectual processes. *Psychological Monographs: General and Applied,* 1958, *72*(12), Whole No. 465.

Sidtis, J. J. On the nature of the cortical function underlying right hemisphere auditory perception. *Neuropsychologia, 1980, 18,* 321–330.

Sidtis, J. J., & Bryden, M. P. Asymmetrical perception of language and music: Evidence for independent processing strategies. *Neuropsychologia, 1978, 16,* 627–632.

Silver, A. A. Prevention. *In* Benton, A. L., & Pearl, D. (Eds.), *Dyslexia, an appraisal of current knowledge.* New York: Oxford University Press, 1978, 351–376.

Silver, A. A., & Hagin, R. A. *Search.* New York: Bellevue Medical Center, 1975.

Silver, A. A., Hagin, R. A., Devito, E., Kreeser, H., & Scully, E. A search battery for scanning kindergarten children for potential learning disability. *Journal of the American Academy of Child Psychiatry, 1976, 15,* 224–239.

Silverman, L. J., & Metz, A. S. Number of pupils with specific learning disabilities in local public schools in the United States: Spring 1970. *Annals of the New York Academy of Sciences, 1973, 205,* 146–157.

Skinner, B. F. *The behavior of organisms.* New York: Appleton-Century, 1938.

Skinner, B. F. *Verbal behavior.* New York: Appleton-Century-Crofts, 1957.

Skinner, H. A. *The origin of medical terms,* 2nd Ed. Baltimore: Williams & Wilkins, 1961.

Sladen, B. K. Inheritance of dyslexia. *Bulletin of the Orton Society,* 1970, XX, 30–40.

Smart, R. G. Conflict and conditioned aversive stimuli in the development of experimental neuroses. *Canadian Journal of Psychology,* 1965, *19*(3), 208–223.

Smith, A. Neuropsychological testing in neurological disorders. *In* Friedlander, W. J. (Ed.), *Advances in neurology,* Vol. 7. New York: Raven Press, 1975, 49–110.

Smith, A. Focusing on the hole rather than the doughnut. Presidential Address, International Neuropsychological Society, 1979. *The INS Bulletin,* March 1979.

Smith, M. E. *In* Thompson, G. G., *Child Psychology,* 2nd Ed. Boston: Houghton Mifflin Co., 1962, 368.

Smith, S. D., Kimberling, W. J., Pennington, B. F., & Lubs, H. A. Specific reading disability: Identification of an inherited form through linkage analysis. *Science,* 1983, *219,* 1345–1347.

Spellacy, F. J. Ear preference in the dichotic presentation of patterned nonverbal stimuli. Unpublished Ph.D. Dissertation, University of Victoria, Victoria, B.C., Canada, 1969.

Spellacy, F. J. Lateral preferences in the identification of patterned stimuli. *Journal of the Acoustical Society of America,* 1970, *47*[2(2)], 574–578.

Spellacy, F. J. Neuropsychological differences between violent and nonviolent adolescents. *Journal of Clinical Psychology,* 1977, *33*(4), 966–969.

Spellacy, F. J. Neuropsychological discrimination between violent and nonviolent men. *Journal of Clinical Psychology,* 1978, *34*(1), 49–52.

Spellacy, F. J., & Blumstein, S. Ear preference for language and non-language sounds: A unilateral brain function. *Journal of Auditory Research*, 1970, *10*, 349–355.

Spellacy, F. J., & Spreen, O. A short form of the Token Test. *Cortex*, 1969, *5*, 390–397.

Sperry, R. W. The great cerebral commissure. *Scientific American*, 1964, *210*, 240–250.

Sperry, R. W. Lateral specialization of cerebral function in the surgically separated hemispheres. *In* McGuigan, F. J. (Ed.), *The psychophysiology of thinking*. New York: Academic Press, 1973.

Sperry, R. W. Lateral specialization in the surgically separated hemispheres. *In* Schmitt, F. O., & Worden, F. G. (Eds.), *The neurosciences, third study program*. Cambridge, MA: The M.I.T. Press, 1974, 5–19.

Sprague, R. L., & Sleator, E. K. Drugs and dosages: Implications for learning disabilities. *In* Knights, R. M., & Bakker, D. J. (Eds.), *The neuropsychology of learning disorders*. Baltimore: University Park Press, 1976, 351–366.

Spreen, O. *Sound recognition test*. Victoria, B. C., Canada: Department of Psychology, University of Victoria, 1969.

Spreen, O. Neuropsychology of learning disorders: Post-conference review. *In* Knights, R. M., & Bakker, D. J. (Eds.), *The neuropsychology of learning disorders, theoretical approaches*. Baltimore: University Park Press, 1976, 445–467.

Spreen, O. Prediction of school achievement from kindergarten to grade five: Review and report of a follow-up study. *Research Monograph No. 33*. Victoria, B. C., Canada: Department of Psychology, University of Victoria, 1978.

Spreen, O. Learning disabled children growing up: A follow-up into adulthood. Victoria, B.C.: Department of Psychology, University of Victoria, 1983.

Spreen, O., & Benton, A. L. *Neurosensory Center Comprehensive Examination for Aphasia*. Victoria, B. C., Canada: Department of Psychology, University of Victoria, 1969 and 1977 (Revised Edition).

Spreen, O., Benton, A. L., & Fincham, R. W. Auditory agnosia without aphasia. *Archives of Neurology*, 1965, *13*, 84–92.

Spreen, O., & Gaddes, W. H. Developmental norms for 15 neuropsychological tests age 6 to 15. *Cortex*, 1969, *5*, 171–191.

Spreen, O., Tupper, D., Risser, A., Tuokko, H., & Edgell, D. *Human developmental neuropsychology*. New York: Oxford University Press, 1984.

Staller, J., Buchanan, D., Singer, M., Lappin, J., & Webb, W. Alexia without agraphia: An experimental case study. *Brain and Language*, 1978, *5*, 378–387.

Standing, E. M. *Maria Montessori, her life and work*. New York: Mentor Books, 1962.

Statistics of Special Education for Exceptional Children. Dominion Bureau of Statistics (Canada), Catalogue 81-537, Table 5, pp. 60–61, 1966.

Stevenson, J., & Richman, N. The prevalence of language delay in a population of three-year-old children and its association with general retardation. *Developmental Medicine and Child Neurology*, 1976, *18*, 431–441.

Stewart, R. J. C., & Platt, B. S. Nervous system damage in experimental protein-calorie deficiency. *In* Scrimshaw, N. S., & Gordon, J. E. (Eds.), *Malnutrition, learning and behavior*. Cambridge, MA: The M.I.T. Press, 1968, 168–180.

Stoch, M. B., & Smythe, P. M. Undernutrition during infancy, and subsequent brain growth and intellectual development. *In* Scrimshaw, N. S., & Gordon, J. E. (Eds.), *Malnutrition, learning and behavior*. Cambridge, MA: The M.I.T. Press, 1968, 278–289.

Stominger, A. Z., & Bashir, A. S. A nine-year follow-up of 50 language delayed children. Paper presented at the annual meeting of the American Speech and Hearing Association, 1977, Chicago. (Quoted by D. B. Tower in NINCDS Monograph No. 22, p. vii.)

Stott, D. H. *Programmed reading kits 1 and 2, manual*. Toronto: Gage, 1970.

Strang, J. D., & Rourke, B. P. Concept formation/non-verbal reasoning abilities of children who exhibit specific academic problems with arithmetic. *Journal of Clinical Child Psychology*, 1983, *12*(1), 33–39.

Stratton, G. M. Vision without inversion of the retinal image. *Psychological Review*, 1897, *4*, 341–360; 463–481.

Strauss, A. A., & Kephart, N. C. *Psychopathology and education of the brain-injured child*, Vol. II. New York: Grune & Stratton, 1955.

Strauss, A. A., & Lehtinen, L. E. *Psychopathology and education of the brain-injured child*. New York: Grune & Stratton, 1947.

Strauss, A. A., & Werner, H. Deficiency in the finger schema in relation to arithmetic disability (finger agnosia and acalculia). *American Journal of Orthopsychiatry*, 1938, *8*, 719–725.

Strauss, E., & Wada, J. Lateral preferences and cerebral speech dominance. *Cortex*, 1983, *19*, 165–177.

Strother, F. C. Minimal cerebral dysfunction: A historical overview. *Annals of the New York Academy of Sciences*, 1973, *205*, 6–17.

Subirana, A. The prognosis in aphasia in relation to cerebral dominance and handedness. *Brain*, 1958, *81*, 415–425.

Subirana, A. The relationship between handedness and cerebral dominance. *International Journal of Neurology*, 1964, *4*, 215–235.

Subirana, A. Handedness and cerebral dominance. *In* Vinken, P. J., & Bruyn, G. W. (Eds.), *Handbook of clinical neurology*, Vol. 4. Amsterdam: North-Holland Publishing Co., 1969, 248–272.

Tallal, P. Auditory perceptual factors in language and learning disabilities. *In* Knights, R. M., & Bakker, D. J. (Eds.), *The neuropsychology of learning disorders*. Baltimore: University Park Press, 1976, 315–323.

Tallal, P., & Piercy, M. Developmental aphasia: Impaired rate of non-verbal processing as a function of sensory modality. *Neuropsychologia*, 1973a, *11*, 389–398.

Tallal, P., & Piercy, M. Defects of non-verbal auditory perception in children with developmental aphasia. *Nature,* 1973b, *241*(5390), 468–469.

Tallal, P., & Piercy, M. Developmental aphasia: Rate of auditory processing and selective impairment of consonant perception. *Neuropsychologia,* 1974, *12*(1), 83–94.

Tallal, P., & Stark, R. Perceptual prerequisites for language development. *In* Kirk, U. (Ed.), *Neuropsychology of language, reading, and spelling.* New York: Academic Press, 1983, 97–106.

Tarnopol, L. Introduction to neurogenic learning disorders. *In* Tarnopol, L. (Ed.), *Learning disorders in children, diagnosis, medication, education.* Boston: Little, Brown, 1971.

Teuber, H.-L. Some alterations in behavior after cerebral lesions in man. *In Evolution of Nervous Control.* Washington, DC: American Association for the Advancement of Science, 1959, 157–194.

Teuber, H.-L. The riddle of frontal lobe function in man. *In* Warren, J. M., & Akert, K. A. (Eds.), *The frontal granular cortex and behavior.* New York: McGraw-Hill, 1964, 410–444.

Teuber, H.-L. Somatosensory disorders due to cortical lesions. Preface: Disorders of higher tactile and visual functions. *Neuropsychologia,* 1965, *3,* 287–294.

Teuber, H.-L. Evidence of neural plasticity. Major invited speaker, Tenth Annual Neuropsychology Workshop, University of Victoria, Victoria, B. C., Canada, March 1975.

Teuber, H.-L., Battersby, W., & Bender, M. *Visual field defects after penetrating missile wounds of the brain.* Cambridge, MA: Harvard University Press, 1960.

Teuber, H.-L., & Mishkin, M. Judgment of visual and postural vertical after brain injury. *Journal of Psychology,* 1954, *38,* 161–175.

Teuber, H.-L., & Weinstein, S. Ability to discover hidden figures after cerebral lesions. *American Medical Association Archives of Neurology and Psychiatry,* 1956, *76,* 369–379.

Teyler, T. J. The brain sciences: An introduction. *In* Chall, J. S., & Mirsky, A. F. (Eds.), *Education and the brain* (The Seventy-seventh Yearbook of the National Society for the Study of Education, Part II). Chicago: The University of Chicago Press, 1978, 1–32.

Thompson, G. G. *Child Psychology,* 2nd Ed. Boston: Houghton Mifflin, 1962.

Thompson, R. F., Berger, T. W., & Berry, S. D. An introduction to the anatomy, physiology, and chemistry of the brain. *In* Wittrock, M. C. (Ed.), *The brain and psychology.* New York: Academic Press, 1980, 3–32.

Thorndike, E. L. *The original nature of man,* Vol. I. New York: Teachers College, Columbia University, 1913.

Tizard, B. Theories of brain localization from Flourens to Lashley. *Medical History,* 1959, *3,* 132–145.

Torgesen, J. K. The role of nonspecific factors in the task performance of learning disabled children: A theoretical assignment. *Journal of Learning Disabilities,* 1977, *10*(1), 33–40.

Townes, B. D., Trupin, E. W., Martin, D. C., & Goldstein, D. Neuropsychological correlates of academic success among elementary school children. *Journal of Consulting and Clinical Psychology,* 1980, *48*(6), 675–684.

Trites, R. L. *Neuropsychological test manual.* Montreal: Ronalds Federated, 1977.

Trites, R. L., & Fiedorowicz, C. Follow-up study of children with specific (or primary) reading disability. *In* Knights, R. M., & Bakker, D. J. (eds.), *The neuropsychology of learning disorders.* Baltimore: University Park Press, 1976, 41–50.

Tymchuk, A. J. *Behavior modification with children, a clinical training manual.* Springfield, IL: Charles C. Thomas, 1974.

Umilta, C., Bagnara, S., & Simion, F. Laterality effects for simple and complex geometrical figures, and nonsense patterns. *Neuropsychologia,* 1978, *16*, 43–49.

Valett, R. E. *Learning disabilities, diagnostic-prescriptive instruments.* Belmont, CA: Lear Siegler-Fearon, 1973.

Valk, J. Neuroradiology and learning disabilities. *Tÿdschrift voor Orthopedagogiek,* 1974 (Nov.), *NR 11*, 303–323.

Van Bergeijk, W. A., & David, E. E. Delayed handwriting. *Perceptual and Motor Skills,* 1959, *9*, 347–357.

Van Duyne, H. J., Bakker, D., & de Jong, W. Development of ear-asymmetry related to coding processes in memory in children. *Brain and Language,* 1977, *4*(2), 322–334.

Vellutino, F. R. Toward an understanding of dyslexia: Psychological factors in specific reading disability. *In* Benton, A. L., & Pearl, D. (Eds.), *Dyslexia, an appraisal of current knowledge.* New York: Oxford University Press, 1978, 63–111.

Von Bonin, G. Anatomical asymmetries of the cerebral hemispheres. *In* Mountcastle, V. B. (Ed.), *Interhemispheric relations and cerebral dominance.* Baltimore: The Johns Hopkins University Press, 1962, 1–6.

Wada, J. A., Clarke, R., & Hamm, A. Cerebral hemispheric asymmetry in humans. *Archives of Neurology,* 1975, *32*, 239–246.

Wada, J. A., & Rasmussen, T. Intracarotid injection of sodium amytal for the lateralization of cerebral speech dominance. *Journal of Neurosurgery,* 1960, *17*, 266–282.

Walker, D. R. Biofeedback: A potentially useful adjunct to conventional medical treatment. Unpublished paper, Department of Psychology, University of Victoria, Victoria, B.C., Canada, 1976.

Walsh, K. W. *Neuropsychology, a clinical approach.* Edinburgh: Churchill Livingstone, 1978.

Walzer, S., & Richmond, J. B. The epidemiology of learning disorders. *Pediatric Clinics of North America,* 1973, *20*(3), 549–565.

Warrington, E. K. Neurological deficits. *In* Mittler, P. (Ed.), *The psychological assessment of mental and physical handicaps.* London: Methuen & Co., 1970, 261–288.

Warrington, E. K., James, M., & Kinsbourne, M. Drawing disability in relation to laterality of cerebral lesion. *Brain,* 1966, *89,* 53–82.

Warrington, E. K., & Taylor, A. M. The contribution of the right parietal lobe to object recognition. *Cortex,* 1973, *60,* 152–164.

Watson, J. B. *Psychology from the standpoint of a behaviorist.* Philadelphia: J. B. Lippincott, 1919 (1st Ed)/1924 (2nd Ed).

Watson, J. B. *Behaviorism.* New York: W. W. Norton, 1924.

Webb, T. E., & Berman, P. H. Stereoscopic form disappearance in temporal lobe dysfunction. *Cortex,* 1973, *9,* 239–245.

Webster's New Twentieth Century Dictionary, 2nd Ed. New York: The World Publishing Company, 1968.

Wechsler, D. *Wechsler Intelligence Scale for Children.* New York: Psychological Corporation, 1949.

Wechsler, D. *Measurement and appraisal of adult intelligence,* 4th Ed. Baltimore: Williams & Wilkins, 1958.

Wechsler, D., & Hagin, R. A. The problem of axial rotation in reading disability. *Perceptual and Motor Skills,* 1964, *19,* 319–326.

Weinberg, W., Walter, W. G., & Crow, H. J. Intracerebral events in humans related to real and imaginary stimuli. *Electroencephalography and Clinical Neurophysiology,* 1970, *29*(1), 1–9.

Weinberger, L. M., Gibbon, M. H., & Gibbon, J. H., Jr. Temporary arrest of the circulation to the central nervous system. *Archives of Neurology and Psychiatry,* 1940, *43,* 961.

Weinstein, S., & Teuber, H.-L. Effects of penetrating brain injury on intelligence test scores. *Science,* 1957, *125,* 1036–1037.

Weisenburg, T., & McBride, K. E. *Aphasia, a clinical and psychological study.* New York: The Commonwealth Fund, 1935; reprinted by Hafner, New York, 1964.

Weiss, B. Treatment of hyperactivity in children. *Current Psychiatric Therapy,* 1971, *10,* 26–29.

Weiss, G., Minde, K., Werry, J. S., Douglas, V., & Nemeth, E. Studies on the hyperactive child, VIII: Five-year follow-up. *Archives of General Psychiatry,* 1971, *24,* 409–414.

Weiss, P. Autonomous versus reflexogenous activity of the central nervous system. *Proceedings of the American Philosophical Society,* 1941, 84, 53–64.

Wender, P. H. *Minimal brain dysfunction in children.* New York: Wiley, 1971.

Wender, P. H. Minimal brain dysfunction in children: Diagnosis and management, *Pediatric Clinics of North America,* 1973, *20*(1), 187–202.

Wender, P. H. Hypothesis for a possible biochemical basis of minimal brain dysfunction. *In* Knights, R. M., & Bakker, D. J. (Eds.), *The neuropsychol-*

ogy of learning disorders, theoretical approaches. Baltimore: University Park Press, 1976, 111–122.

Wepman, J. M. Auditory perception and imperception. *In* Cruickshank, W. M., & Hallahan, D. P. (Eds.), *Perceptual and learning disabilities in children,* Vol. 2. Syracuse: Syracuse University Press, 1975, 259–298.

Werner, H., & Strauss, A. A. Pathology of figure-background relation in the child. *Journal of Abnormal and Social Psychology,* 1941, *36,* 236–248.

Werry, J. S. Developmental hyperactivity. *The Pediatric Clinics of North America,* 1968, *15*(3), 581–599.

Wertheim, N. The amusias. *In* Vinken, P. J., & Bruyn, G. W. (Eds.), *Handbook of Clinical Neurology,* Vol. 4. Amsterdam: North-Holland Publishing Co., 1969, 195–206.

West, R. (Ed.) *Childhood Aphasia.* San Francisco: California Society for Crippled Children and Adults, 1962.

Wexler, B. E., Halwes, T., & Heninger, G. R. Use of a statistical significance criterion in drawing inferences about hemispheric dominance for language function from dichotic listening data. *Brain and Language,* 1981, *13,* 13–18.

White, R. W. Motivation reconsidered: The concept of competence. *Psychological Review,* 1959, *66*(5), 297–333.

White, K., & Ashton, R. Handedness assessment inventory. *Neuropsychologia,* 1976, *14,* 261–264.

Wiener, J., Barnsley, R. H., & Rabinovitch, M. S. Serial order ability in good and poor readers. *Canadian Journal of Behavioural Science,* 1970, *2*(2), 116–123.

Wikler, A. W., Dixon, J. F., & Parker, J. B. Brain function in problem children and controls: Psychometric, neurological and electroencephalographic comparison. *American Journal of Psychiatry,* 1970, *127,* 634–645.

Wilson, L. F. Assessment of congenital aphasia. *In* Rappaport, S. R. (Ed.), *Childhood aphasia and brain damage:* Vol. II. Narberth, PA: Livingston Publishing Co., 1965, 7–52.

Witelson, S. F. Early hemisphere specialization and interhemisphere plasticity: An empirical and theoretical review. *In* Segalowitz, S. J., & Gruber, F. A. (Eds.), *Language development and neurological theory.* New York: Academic Press, 1977, 213–287.

Witelson, S. F. Bumps on the brain: Right-left anatomic asymmetry as a key to functional lateralization. *In* Segalowitz, S. J. (Ed.), *Language functions and brain organization.* New York: Academic Press, 1983, 117–144.

Witelson, S. F., & Pallie, W. Left hemisphere specialization for language in the newborn. *Brain,* 1973, *96,* 641–646.

Witkin, H. Sex differences in perception. *Transactions of the New York Academy of Science,* 1949, *12,* 22–26.

Wittrock, M. C. (Ed.). *The brain and psychology.* New York: Academic Press, 1980a.

Wittrock, M. C. Learning and the brain. *In* Wittrock, M. C. (Ed.), *The brain and psychology.* New York: Academic Press, 1980b, 371–403.

Wolf, S., & Wolff, H. G. Evidence on the genesis of peptic ulcer in man. *Journal of the American Medical Association*, 1942, *120*, 670–675.

Wolpe, J. *Psychotherapy by reciprocal inhibition*. Stanford, CA: Stanford University Press, 1958.

Wooldridge, D. E. *The machinery of the brain*. New York: McGraw-Hill, 1963.

Wright, K. L. The relative values of three reading programs in facilitation of reading acquisition amongst Grade Two students. Undergraduate Honors Thesis, Departmental Monograph, Department of Psychology, University of Victoria, Victoria, B. C., Canada, 1978.

Ysseldyke, J. E., & Algozzine, B. On making psychoeducational decisions. *Journal of Psychoeducational Assessment*, 1983, *1*(2), 187–195.

Yule, W., & Rutter, M. Epidemiology and social implications of specific reading retardation. *In* Knights, R. M., & Bakker, D. J. (Eds.), *The neuropsychology of learning disorders*. Baltimore: University Park Press, 1976, 25–39.

Yule, W., Rutter, M., Berger, M., & Thompson, J. Over- and underachievement in reading: Distribution in the general population. *British Journal of Educational Psychology*, 1974, *44*, 1–12.

Zaidel, D., & Sperry, R. W. Lateralized tests for temporal sequential order in the left and right hemispheres of man. *Biology Annual Report* (California Institute of Technology), 1973, p. 54.

Zaidel, E. Linguistic competence and related functions in the right cerebral hemisphere of man following commissurotomy and hemispherectomy. Unpublished Ph.D. Dissertation, California Institute of Technology, 1973.

Zaidel, E. The split and half brains as models of congenital language disability. *In The neurological bases of language disorders in children: Methods and directions for research. NINCDS Monograph No. 22.* Bethesda, MD: U.S. Department of Health, Education, and Welfare, August 1979, 55–89.

Zangwill, O. L. *Cerebral dominance and its relation to psychological functions*. London: Oliver & Boyd, 1960.

Zangwill, O. L. Thought and the brain. *British Journal of Psychology*, 1976, *67*, 301–314.

Zurif, E. B., & Bryden, M. P. Familial handedness and left-right differences in auditory and visual perception. *Neuropsychologia*, 1969, *7*, 179–188.

Index of Names

Subject Index

A

X